The Constitution of Phenomenal Consciousness

Advances in Consciousness Research (AiCR)

ISSN 1381-589X

Provides a forum for scholars from different scientific disciplines and fields of knowledge who study consciousness in its multifaceted aspects. Thus the Series includes (but is not limited to) the various areas of cognitive science, including cognitive psychology, brain science, philosophy and linguistics. The orientation of the series is toward developing new interdisciplinary and integrative approaches for the investigation, description and theory of consciousness, as well as the practical consequences of this research for the individual in society.
From 1999 the Series consists of two subseries that cover the most important types of contributions to consciousness studies:
Series A: Theory and Method. Contributions to the development of theory and method in the study of consciousness; Series B: Research in Progress. Experimental, descriptive and clinical research in consciousness.
This book is a contribution to Series A.

For an overview of all books published in this series, please see
http://benjamins.com/catalog/aicr

Volume 92

The Constitution of Phenomenal Consciousness. Toward a science and theory
Edited by Steven M. Miller

The Constitution of Phenomenal Consciousness

Toward a science and theory

Edited by

Steven M. Miller

Monash University

John Benjamins Publishing Company

Amsterdam / Philadelphia

The paper used in this publication meets the minimum requirements of the American National Standard for Information Sciences – Permanence of Paper for Printed Library Materials, ANSI Z39.48-1984.

DOI 10.1075/aicr.92

Cataloging-in-Publication Data available from Library of Congress:
LCCN 2014046964 (PRINT) / 2014049343 (E-BOOK)

ISBN 978 90 272 1359 4 (HB)
ISBN 978 90 272 6878 5 (E-BOOK)

John Benjamins Publishing Co. · P.O. Box 36224 · 1020 ME Amsterdam · The Netherlands
John Benjamins North America · P.O. Box 27519 · Philadelphia PA 19118-0519 · USA

Table of contents

Section II. Philosophy of mind

Acknowledgments

In 1996, three years after graduating from medicine, I resolved to study the brain. I had been reading Edward Hundert's book *Philosophy, Psychiatry and Neuroscience: Three Approaches to the Mind*. For many years I had read books on philosophy of mind, psychology and consciousness, and had been exposed to undergraduate neuroscience, psychology and psychiatry. My medical studies, grounded as they were in science, led me to believe that understanding the brain was critical to understanding the mind. However, I was equally aware that neuroscience and psychology could not do all the work. Philosophy was essential too, particularly on the issue of brain/mind relations. Hundert's interdisciplinary approach opened my eyes to the possibility of meaningfully exploring the nexus between science and philosophy in this context. The next book I read was Francis Crick's *The Astonishing Hypothesis*, which consolidated my decision to begin by focusing on the brain.

With no specific research plans, I approached John ('Jack') Pettigrew, an eminent Australian neuroscientist who had given lectures during my undergraduate years at the University of Queensland. Jack graciously offered to supervise me on one of two projects: neurochemistry-based studies on oxidative stress, or looking for a physiological switch between the two cerebral hemispheres. My plan at the time was to learn more about the brain in general, and to allow that study to inform my interest in the philosophy of mind and consciousness, so I promptly chose the hemisphere-switching project. Fortunately, Jack's plans for this work were not yet crystallized, thus providing an ideal environment for the bug of scientific hypothesis and discovery to bite me and take hold.

Within a few months, a conjunction of factors drove me to propose that binocular rivalry – the involuntary perceptual switching that occurs when the left and right eye each view a different image – might be a hemisphere-switching phenomenon. Though initially unconvinced, Jack capitulated to my enthusiasm for this idea. We thus had built, a crude headset with mirrors attached in front of each eye to induce rivalry. On the first day of experimenting with this headset, we found exactly what we were looking for, and more. I am especially grateful to Jack for the stimulating and accommodating environment provided by him, under his Directorship of the Vision, Touch and Hearing Research Centre. I am also grateful to Guang Bin Liu for the technical assistance he provided as this work developed.

In 2000, just prior to my departure from Jack's lab, I was writing a paper for a special issue on binocular rivalry for the now defunct journal, *Brain and Mind*. It was then that the idea underlying the present volume, and its predecessor, emerged. Whilst detailing the various perception-dependent neural activities that had been

DOI 10.1075/aicr.92.001ack

identified during binocular rivalry, I realized that no matter how precise and detailed such understanding became, there would remain a problem for the scientific study of consciousness – that of distinguishing which of these neural correlates had anything to do with visual consciousness during rivalry, or in other words, which neural activities were actually constitutive of the visually conscious state.

Six years later, Matthew Kirkcaldie and Perminder Sachdev invited me to participate in a workshop on Neurophilosophy at the International Neuropsychiatry Association World Congress in Sydney. Several presentations from that workshop became papers for a special issue of *Acta Neuropsychiatrica*, edited by Gin Malhi. There I developed the correlation/constitution distinction problem and addressed some of the philosophical issues it entails. I was therefore, as I had originally hoped to do, exploring the nexus between the science and philosophy of consciousness (the result of which is this book and its companion). I am grateful to Matthew, Perminder and Gin, for the impetus to develop my interdisciplinary interests.

I am indebted to several people who helped bring to life and to completion, the project of this book and its companion. Trung Ngo, who joined Jack's lab shortly after I did, and with whom I have worked closely now for over a decade, was an endless source of assistance and helpful discussion during development of the project and preparation of the book manuscripts. He also cast his keen editorial eye over all of the contributions. Jakob Hohwy, in addition to writing for the present volume, has been a great sounding board for me since the project's inception. It was of course, invaluable for a neuroscientist who has a strong interest in philosophy to be able to discuss this project with a philosopher who has a strong interest in neuroscience.

I am grateful also to Maxim Stamenov, Chief Editor of *Advances in Consciousness Research*, who invited me to contribute to this series after attending my presentation at the 2010 annual meeting of the Association for the Scientific Study of Consciousness in Toronto. My dealings with Maxim since, and with staff at John Benjamins, have been a pleasure. I am of course, also particularly grateful to the contributing authors in this and the companion volume for their stimulating papers, willingness to review other authors' contributions and patience whilst the project was completed.

In August 2014, as this volume was nearing completion, I sustained a serious, though fortunately non-permanent, sporting injury. The care and concern I received whilst recovering from this was a reminder to me of the importance of human connectedness. I am grateful to all those who wished me well and offered to help.

Finally, I thank my family for their support and encouragement over many years, and for enabling me to follow my own path. Both books are dedicated to them.

Steven Miller
Melbourne
October, 2014

The constitution of visual and phenomenal consciousness

An introduction

Steven M. Miller
Monash University, Melbourne

This book is the second of two companion volumes. As noted in the introduction to the first volume – *The Constitution of Visual Consciousness: Lessons from Binocular Rivalry* (Advances in Consciousness Research Vol. 90) – human vision is rich in content and experience. We perceive contours, colors, contrast, brightness, shapes, textures, objects, relations, depth, and motion. Upon all this we construct meaning, we involuntarily or voluntarily focus or deflect attention, and we can be either conscious, or unconscious, of presented visual information. For content of which we *are* visually conscious, there is a qualitative or experiential aspect. It is like something for us to perceive the color blue, for example, and on this basis, we are said to be phenomenally conscious of the color blue, or of blueness.

Visual consciousness is not usually an isolated perceptual experience. Blueness is experienced in conjunction with blue objects or scenes. The form, context, motion and meaning of these objects or scenes contribute to the overall phenomenal state. Along with the visual experience, a wide range of non-visual content is experienced in domains such as audition (the sound of waves lapping), olfaction (the smell of salt in the air), somatosensation (the touch of cool water), interoception (the sense of bodily relaxation), and affect (the feeling of happiness). Phenomenal consciousness is thus complex, multimodal and dynamic, and it readies us for action (or in the case of a blue seascape, for inaction).

Something in our brains constitutes the experience of blueness, and indeed the experience of all the phenomenal riches of a blue seascape. This book, and its predecessor, is about exactly *what* constitutes phenomenal consciousness, and exactly *how* the science and philosophy of consciousness can approach this constitution question. The strategy of the two books is specific. The first was written by scientists and laid groundwork by focusing on one domain – vision. Moreover, within that domain, it focused on one particular visual phenomenon – binocular rivalry – a detailed analysis of which speaks directly to the methodological problem of identifying the constitution of visual consciousness. The present volume turns from visual consciousness

DOI 10.1075/aicr.92.01mil

to phenomenal consciousness more generally, and is written by both scientists and philosophers.

Together, the two books address the nature of phenomenal consciousness and its study. Philosophers have long been interested in such questions. Indeed, these issues are fundamental concerns in the philosophy of mind. However, it has been only in recent decades that scientists have been able to openly tackle the study of consciousness. Progress has been rapid and the scientific study of consciousness has flourished into a healthy, vibrant, interdisciplinary field of research (a fact attested to by the existence of this book series). Despite such progress, it is debatable to what degree scientists and philosophers meaningfully interact in this pursuit, as opposed to merely tolerating each other's presence, or merely straying into each other's field. It is my view that meaningful interdisciplinary interaction between scientists and philosophers is not only possible, but desirable. It is my hope that the present volume in particular is evidence of this.

Before engaging in interdisciplinary discourse on the science and philosophy of consciousness, there was, as I have mentioned, groundwork to be done. Indeed, I requested the reader's patience throughout the first volume, for it contained less explicit discussion of the study of consciousness than might have been expected from its title. Its contents were nonetheless critical to understanding the question of the constitution of consciousness, and to understanding at least part of an answer.

I concluded the introductory chapter of the first book by noting to the reader that upon reaching the end of the volume, they would have traversed the landscape of existing knowledge on the human brain's constituents, organization and processes, on the visual system in even more detail, on common investigative techniques used in modern human neuroscience, and on the phenomenon of binocular rivalry in exquisite detail. I noted that at that point, they may have wondered what had been learned of the constitution of visual consciousness and the correlation/constitution distinction problem. I suggested that to properly understand such issues, examination would be required of just what is meant by 'consciousness', 'correlation', and 'constitution'.[1] It is in the current volume that these notions, and the nature of explanation in consciousness science, are addressed explicitly and that the lessons learned from the previous volume can be utilized.

1. It should be noted from the outset that the sense of 'constitution' referred to throughout this and the previous volume is *not* that associated with the continental phenomenologist, Edmund Husserl. Indeed, neither book addresses the constitution of consciousness in phenomenological terms.

Lessons from binocular rivalry

In any project addressing the constitution of phenomenal consciousness, it is of course critical to look at the brain and its constituents. Thus the chapter following my introduction in the preceding volume focused on such constituents, at both fine and coarse scales: genes, molecules, cells (including neurons), neural circuits, and neural systems. Constituents alone however, are meaningless in the absence of context. Hence, also examined was the organization of the brain's constituents, the processes in which such constituents engage, and their functional role in giving rise to human perception, cognition and behavior. Armed with this overview, the next chapter then explored the visual system in even greater detail, providing a firm basis for the subsequent focus on visual consciousness and binocular rivalry. It outlined the breathtaking depth, breadth and complexity of understanding of the human visual system's constituents, structure and function, and highlighted in what domains knowledge is likely to progress.

Thereafter, chapters in the preceding volume all dealt explicitly with binocular rivalry. This is a curious visual phenomenon that involves alternating perception of two different images when each image is presented separately, one to each eye, at the same time and in the same retinal location. This was chosen as the target phenomenon for several reasons: (1) the ability of binocular rivalry to enable simple tracking of a dynamically changing visual scene; (2) the visual system being the best characterized of all brain systems; (3) the ability of binocular rivalry to be studied with a wide variety of modern neuroscientific investigative tools and manipulated in a wide variety of ways; (4) the dissociation that binocular rivalry provides, between neural activity that correlates with stable stimulus presentation and neural activity that correlates with alternating visual perception; and (5) the clear illustration that binocular rivalry provides of the correlation/constitution distinction problem. Thus, the first volume aimed to disentangle binocular rivalry in great detail, by examining multiple methodological approaches to it, from multiple perspectives, so that analysis could be subsequently applied, in the present volume, to the question of the constitution of consciousness. The preceding volume also provided a timely update on the state of the field of binocular rivalry research.

The reader was therefore introduced to binocular rivalry by examining historical approaches to investigation of the phenomenon (rooted in the study of binocular vision), and early attempts to link the study of rivalry to notions of attention and consciousness. Thereafter, in several papers, a detailed overview of contemporary binocular rivalry psychophysics was presented, thus demonstrating the extraordinary degree of detail now possessed by rivalry researchers on the phenomenon's spatial and temporal dynamics, stimulus and observer factors relevant to selection, dominance and suppression, the relationship between rivalry and other cognitive phenomena such as attention, memory, emotion and decision-making, the genetic, molecular and comparative aspects of rivalry, and the modulation of rivalry by pharmacological agents and clinical conditions.

Psychophysical investigation of binocular rivalry has been carried out not only to try to fully characterize the phenomenon, but also to understand brain mechanisms underlying rivalry and its modulation. Indeed, rivalry mechanisms and models have been the focus of intensive psychophysical, cognitive, computational, and neurophysiological investigation in the last two decades (these approaches are outlined in various chapters of the first volume). Thus, the classical psychophysical study of rivalry has now been complemented by application of a wide range of modern neuroscientific investigative techniques in both animals and humans. Methods such as single-unit and local field potential electrophysiology, electroencephalography and magnetoencephalography, various brain-imaging techniques, and various brain stimulation techniques such as transcranial magnetic stimulation (TMS) and caloric vestibular stimulation can be, and have all been, applied to study rivalry, to further knowledge of its underlying neural mechanisms. Chapters in the first volume dealt with principles of these methodologies, advantages and disadvantages of each method, current and outstanding knowledge regarding the signals of various recording methods and the effects of various stimulation methods, application of these methods in the study of rivalry, results of such investigations and controversies therein, and the prospects for future rivalry research with emerging technologies and combined techniques.

The result of all of the above approaches to the study of binocular rivalry is a large body of knowledge on various aspects of the phenomenon, but as yet no definitive neurophysiological mechanistic understanding. Just what in the brain is happening during perceptual selection, perceptual alternation (including dominance and suppression mechanisms) and during rivalry modulation remains obscure and there is yet to be proven, an agreed-upon mechanistic explanation of binocular rivalry. Despite this lack of definitive understanding, there is much that *is* known about the neurophysiology of rivalry. As this nascent understanding develops, the enormous body of psychophysical and other evidence concerning rivalry and its modulation will gradually come to be understood mechanistically, at all levels from molecular to large-scale neural systems.

How does all this knowledge of rivalry – classical, recent and emerging – inform the scientific study of consciousness? The unique ability of binocular rivalry to enable identification of neural correlates of consciousness has justified the many claims of its utility in consciousness research. However, the purpose of the present volume and its predecessor is to delve even further into the implications for consciousness science of all this correlate-finding. It is possible that no amount of correlate-finding alone will lead to an understanding of the constitution (or basis, mechanism or substrate) of visual consciousness, and that this correlation/constitution distinction problem presents a very real challenge for the science of consciousness. The problem also carries the potential for new approaches in the philosophy of mind (much of which is concerned with the philosophy of phenomenal consciousness), thus enabling a two-way interdisciplinary discourse: science informs the philosophy of consciousness and philosophy informs the science of consciousness. These books seek to improve understanding of the correlation/constitution distinction problem, to present it as exemplified by findings from binocular rivalry research, to detail the empirical and conceptual territory within which it is situated and to address its philosophical and theoretical implications.

Section I papers: The scientific study of consciousness

In the first three papers, additional groundwork is laid to contextualize the correlation/constitution distinction problem before turning to it explicitly. Thus Chris Klink, Matthew Self, Victor Lamme and Pieter Roelfsema provide a detailed overview of prominent theories in the literature on the scientific study of consciousness, including important early frameworks, the phenomenal/access distinction, global neuronal workspace theory, recurrent processing, essential nodes of microconsciousness, re-entrant dynamic core theory, information integration theory, duplex vision theory and the attention/consciousness distinction. In addition, they provide an overview of common methodological strategies in this field, thus building on chapters in the previous volume that dealt with current neuroscientific measurement techniques. Strategies ('paradigms') covered, beyond binocular rivalry, include forced-choice discrimination and detection tasks, flash suppression, motion-induced blindness, masking and a range of attention- and memory-based approaches. As well as providing the reader with a primer of the field, the authors show how the scientific study of consciousness is advancing through the intermingling of theoretical and empirical approaches.

Most of the papers in the present volume focus on the notion of phenomenal consciousness. It is therefore important to also include some examination of the sense of consciousness informed by contrasting the conscious (aware, aroused) state with unconscious and altered states of consciousness. Vanessa Charland-Verville, Audrey Vanhaudenhuyse, Steven Laureys and Olivia Gosseries do just that, detailing current clinical and neuroscientific understanding of coma and various disorders of consciousness, as well as anesthesia and sleep, at the systems level. The disorders of consciousness they address include unresponsive wakefulness syndrome, the minimally conscious state, akinetic mutism and the locked-in syndrome. The authors discuss brain-imaging findings that highlight the importance for consciousness of functional connectivity between brain regions, including rapid causal interactions between midline and lateral fronto-parietal networks (as well as cortico-cortical, cortico-thalamo-cortical and brainstem connections). Also discussed are brain-imaging data relevant to a range of spontaneous brain networks, including the default mode, as well as brain-imaging, electrophysiological and brain stimulation studies of passive and active responses to external stimulation in disorders of consciousness. The range of cases covered by the authors illustrates the mechanistic parallels between pathological, pharmacological and physiological alterations of consciousness.

In addition to addressing the distinction between the conscious state and various states of altered consciousness and unconsciousness, consideration is required of the close relationship between (content) phenomenal consciousness and attention, report and memory. This topic is taken up by Jeroen van Boxtel and Nao Tsuchiya who draw on the distinction between phenomenal and access consciousness. They begin by outlining studies that have conceptually and empirically dissociated phenomenal consciousness from (access-based) attention, report and memory. The authors then address the debate in the literature concerning whether attention and consciousness can be dissociated. They also point out how examination of bistable stimuli like rivalry, including the search to identify the neural constitution of consciousness, needs to take account of the potentially confounding element of report, both in terms of the act of report affecting neural responses and reports failing to accurately depict what a subject has experienced. Next, van Boxtel and Tsuchiya address the potential confounds related to iconic and fragile memory utilizing studies of inattentional and change blindness and the classic work of Sperling. Finally, they examine the sufficiency and necessity of report and memory for phenomenal consciousness (thus complementing their earlier examination of such with respect to attention and consciousness). The authors conclude that reports are neither necessary nor sufficient for consciousness, that the issue for iconic and fragile memory is not yet settled and that this requires further study.

The focus then turns explicitly to the correlation/constitution distinction problem. I provide context for the problem with respect to other hard problems in consciousness science and philosophy of mind, as well as historical context and an overview of the problem's explication with reference to binocular rivalry. I next set out to examine the problem in the context of widely accepted foundations of consciousness science. Particular attention is paid to the notion of the minimally sufficient neural correlates of consciousness, and the empirical approaches entailed by this terminology. I focus on inhibition, stimulation and combined inhibition/stimulation strategies for distinguishing constitutive neural activity from correlated but non-constitutive upstream and downstream neural activity. The failures of inhibition and stimulation approaches are detailed, and I propose the Jenga analogy to illustrate my arguments. I then however, claim that combined inhibition/stimulation approaches – dubbed 'isolated stimulation' – could perhaps identify at least some constitutive neural activity. However, it is also argued that this empirical approach fails to identify the whole constitution of consciousness, particularly due to the possibility of redundancy, and hence there remains a correlation/constitution distinction problem for consciousness science. After discussing a range of clarifications, potential objections and related scientific and philosophical issues, I conclude by proposing, on the basis of the analyses undertaken, new foundational claims for the science of consciousness.

Jakob Hohwy and Tim Bayne then further examine the notion of the neural correlates of consciousness and associated challenges for science, identifying horizontal (causal and consequential) and vertical (mechanistic) dimensions. They consider the former to be confounds, while the latter the target, in the science of consciousness. Also examined are the terms 'minimally' and 'sufficient' in the definition of the minimally sufficient neural correlates of consciousness. Here the authors discuss redundancy in relation to the minimality requirement and differentiating neural correlates in relation to the sufficiency requirement. Next, Hohwy and Bayne examine what the payoffs for science will be in distinguishing the actual neural basis of consciousness from merely correlated upstream and downstream processes. Their analysis in this regard deals with notions of explanation, prediction and manipulation in consciousness science and they caution that in all three domains, the payoffs may be less than expected. Thereafter, the authors consider various strategies (with a focus on rivalry) to screen off upstream and downstream correlates from the 'real' correlates or basis of consciousness. Examining a range of methodological approaches in this regard, they outline the substantial empirical and conceptual challenges facing such screening off processes for both upstream and downstream cases. An additional challenge posed is that of distinguishing neural correlates of action-dependent and action-independent conscious states, and determining what would be the implications of such a distinction for consciousness science. Finally, Hohwy and Bayne take up analysis of the vertical correlate challenge, assessing whether one level of description ought to be privileged in the search for neural correlates of consciousness.

In the next two papers, Tom de Graaf and Alexander Sack, and Jaan Aru, Talis Bachman, Wolf Singer and Lucia Melloni, address the correlation/constitution distinction problem using their preferred terminology. They divide neural correlates of consciousness into precursors or prerequisites and consequences (equivalent to upstream and downstream correlates, respectively, in my preferred terminology and that of Hohwy and Bayne), and the key target – the neural substrate or basis of consciousness, or the 'real' or 'proper' or 'true' neural correlates of consciousness. Both groups focus on the contrast between experimental trials with consciousness and those without – the so-called contrastive method – and emphasize the failure of this method in disentangling (or 'distilling') the various neural correlates of consciousness. The authors outline their respective rationales for dividing neural correlates and address a range of phenomena (including rivalry), most of which involve contrasting visibility and invisibility of a stimulus. They describe each category of neural correlate and present cases from the scientific literature – focusing on electrophysiology, brain-imaging and TMS – regarding likely candidates for each, with an outline also of the logic underlying such studies (such as attempting to manipulate precursor or consequence processes while holding the substrate constant, or vice versa). Both groups also discuss the issue of timing in the brain and the prospects and difficulties this factor poses for identifying the neural substrate or basis of consciousness. Additional strategies discussed by de Graaf and Sack include cross-literature integration, brain interference generally, unconscious perception paradigms (in which brain regions are active despite a stimulus not being perceived) and experimental manipulations focusing on attention and performance. Additional strategies discussed by Aru et al. include a similar suggestion to revisit existing literature, and refining experimental manipulations to more closely take account of gradual variation in the quality of consciousness across trials, changes in the perceptual quality of a stimulus over time within trials, variation in perception of complex stimuli across trials, and perceptual learning effects.

Thereafter, Jaak Panksepp presents a wide range of cross-species evolutionary evidence from affective (as opposed to sensory–perceptual) neuroscience regarding the subcortical constitution of phenomenal consciousness. He sets out the case that primordial affective conscious states were the first types of experience to emerge in vertebrate evolution and that this was due to the survival value conferred by brains with valence-encoding and closely linked emotional response systems. Panksepp describes the primary-process emotional construct nomenclature he has developed and brain stimulation experiments (inducing reward and punishment) that support inference regarding cross-species homology-based affective-emotional experiences. He notes that such a focus has been overlooked, if not actively neglected, in consciousness science despite the potential for comparative neuroscientific and neuroethological approaches. Next, the author examines the historical context for such neglect, and the role of behaviorism and a subsequent focus on tertiary-level cognitive (cortical-based) consciousness in excluding the affective-emotional domain. He then outlines a five-point empirical strategy for decoding the neural constitution of phenomenal-affective consciousness. Finally, Panksepp provides some ontological reflections stemming from his proposals and speculates on the potential grounding of tertiary-process cognitive consciousness in primary-process affective consciousness. On this view, the potential for higher-order conscious states such as self-awareness, reflective and ruminatory capacities are seen to be evolutionarily built not only upon, but actually from, primary and ancestrally older affective consciousness.

In the last paper of the section, Antti Revonsuo explores the notion of explanation in consciousness science, drawing on the explanatory framework generally applied within the biological sciences and within cognitive neuroscience in particular. He outlines how in future consciousness science will employ a multilevel framework of explanation, thus incorporating different dimensions of the causal-mechanical network of consciousness. It is argued that a detailed description of the phenomenon itself is first required, and Revonsuo describes his model system – the dreaming brain. Thereafter, the explanatory dimensions of the causal-mechanical network are outlined: downward-looking (constitutive) explanation, backward-looking (etiological) explanation and upward-looking (contextual) explanation. The author notes: (1) within the downward-looking dimension, there must be an intelligible structural or part-whole relation between the lower constitutive mechanisms and the higher phenomenal level, not just an inexplicable correlation or covariance between empirical data and mental occurrence; (2) the backward-looking dimension tracks the causal antecedents of consciousness, at three temporal scales – immediate external and internal causes, developmental causes and evolutionary causes; and (3) the upward-looking dimension concerns the phenomenal level interacting with even higher levels of organization including neural, behavioral and organism-environment interactions. Revonsuo concludes by showing how the multilevel explanatory framework can be put to work, shedding light on the convergence of top-down and bottom-up constraints, on neuroimaging the right (phenomenal) level of organization in the brain, and on distinguishing the correlates, causes and constituents of consciousness. On the latter, he outlines how his research group has approached this problem empirically, utilizing timing of electrophysiological signals and behavioral responses, and TMS.

Section II papers: Philosophy of mind

To introduce this section, Zoe Drayson provides an overview of phenomenal consciousness and related philosophical territory, including what makes it a unique phenomenon and why it has proven so difficult to study and explain empirically and theoretically. Thus Drayson discusses the subjective and private nature of phenomenal states and properties, and the special knowledge of them possessed by the subject. Direct first-person knowledge of our conscious states is contrasted with the objective, measurable third-person data with which science deals. Next, the author examines the perennial issue in philosophy of mind concerning whether consciousness is part of the physical world (i.e., whether physicalism is true). Type and token identity theory is introduced as is the functionalist response based on the notion of multiple realizability, and the minimal form of physicalism based on the supervenience relation. Thereafter, non-physicalist positions are presented including challenges from thought experiments like the neuroscientist Mary knowledge argument and the zombie conceivability argument, with their implications for property dualism contrasted with the stronger claim (due to Descartes) of substance dualism. Drayson then takes up issues of mental causation, representationalist approaches to consciousness, why consciousness exists and what it is for, and top-down versus bottom-up theories. Finally, she addresses the notion of explanation in the science and philosophy of consciousness, with a focus on the explanatory gap between physical states and subjective experiences, and physicalist and non-physicalist responses to such a gap.

Next, Martin Mahner introduces the reader to fundamental concepts in metaphysics and ontology, drawing on the highly developed, detailed and integrated work of Mario Bunge. Mahner argues that despite philosophy of mind commonly employing metaphysical notions such as objects (things), properties, states, events and processes, and relations such as identity, supervenience, causation and emergence, there is no fully fledged metaphysical theory adopted or agreed-upon by philosophers of mind. Bunge's materialist (substance, emergentist) ontology is presented as a way forward for philosophy of mind in this respect, and for addressing perennial problems in this domain. Mahner outlines different types of properties and thereafter examines notions of states, events/processes and causes. He discusses how each notion relates to the others and what relevance these notions have to mind and brain, with a focus on nomological (lawful) properties. Next, Mahner discusses systems and mechanisms, noting that the four important aspects of a system are its composition (natural parts), its (immediate) environment, its structure (the set of relations amongst components, with the specific level of organization also important for any analysis of a system), and its mechanisms (the characteristic processes or changes of systems of a given kind). He concludes by applying the lessons from Bunge's ontology to examination of: (1) why other ontologies in philosophy of mind fall short, (2) the zombie argument, and (3) machine consciousness.

Andrew Melnyk then brings scientific evidence to bear on the brain–mind problem, utilising a phenomenon widely discussed in philosophy of mind – pain. He sets out to show why the scientific evidence, with purely philosophical considerations set to one side, justifies considering pain to be material (materialism) rather than immaterial (dualism). Melnyk acknowledges that he is not the first to argue that scientific evidence favors materialism about pain (or sensations in general), but claims that his account of how it does so is superior to previous such accounts. He starts by providing an overview of what materialism and dualism amount to, and thereafter discusses several empirical studies reporting correspondences between pain states (and their felt properties) and brain states. Melnyk suggests that the reviewed evidence supports an empirical supervenience claim in which introspectible changes or variations in pains always occur with simultaneous empirically observable changes or variations in neural states. He asks how this claim can be accommodated by the materialist and dualist positions, and brings to bear evidential principles (including super-empirical criteria such as parsimony and fit with background knowledge) to argue that the empirical supervenience claim supports materialist over (relevant) dualist positions. Melnyk concludes, modestly, that even if humans favor dualism because they introspect their own pains, an Alien – whose own introspections would be irrelevant – should be led by the scientific evidence to conclude that pain is material.

Picking up issues raised in Drayson's introduction to phenomenal consciousness, Berit Brogaard points out that philosophers can hold: (1) that there is no explanatory gap or ontological gap for phenomenal consciousness (e.g., a priori physicalism); (2) that there is an explanatory gap but that consciousness is nonetheless fully determined by the physical facts, and hence there is no ontological gap (e.g., a posteriori physicalism); or (3) that the explanatory gap does indeed entail an ontological gap (e.g., property dualism). Brogaard, however, aims to explore yet another position – that there is in fact an ontological gap, but no explanatory gap. She starts by asserting a non-physicalist position on consciousness but considers that such a position should not exclude the possibility that science could explain consciousness. Next, a priori and a posteriori physicalism are outlined, including detailed discussion of the (Mary) knowledge argument against physicalism. Brogaard distinguishes a first-person explanatory gap, about which she considers physics will not likely ever have much to say, and a third-person explanatory gap which arises if not all third-person (scientific) mental facts follow a priori from the physical facts. Thereafter, she discusses the phenomenal concept strategy and the zombie conceivability argument (with the latter claimed to support the existence of an ontological gap between the physical and the mental). The author then returns to her aim, arguing that an ontological gap could exist with no (third-person) explanatory gap if there exist microphenomenal elementary forces which can explain macroscopic conscious experiences. On this variant of panpsychism, it is claimed that consciousness and physical phenomena arise from different types of fundamental entities that do not reduce to one another (an ontological gap) but that science can nonetheless give a full third-person account of how macroscopic phenomenal experiences arise (no explanatory gap). Brogaard concludes by arguing why neuroscience and the search for neural correlates of consciousness can be considered nonreductive.

The focus thereafter turns more explicitly to relational issues in philosophy, with Benjamin Curtis and Harold Noonan first providing an overview of the constitution relation as it has been applied to objects and persons. Taking a classic example, they ask that if a statue and its constituent clay are identical, how is it that only the former fails to survive reshaping the clay into a ball? The authors outline various responses to such questions, with a focus on the notion of generic constitutionalism – the view that non-identical things can stand in the relation of being composed of the same matter at the same time. Although providing an overview of aspects of the material constitution literature, Curtis and Noonan indicate that theirs is nonetheless a novel formulation of such issues. They discuss the notion of sortal concepts – concepts associated with identity conditions under which persisting things fall – and explain that questions about personal identity can be asked in terms of the necessary (passing away and preservation) conditions of membership of sortal kinds (such as 'statue' or 'person'). They note that puzzles of constitution challenge what would seem otherwise plausible answers to such questions. Thereafter, arguments for and against generic constitutionalism are discussed, other more specific constitution views are surveyed, and other constitution puzzles are examined (such as The Ship of Theseus). Finally, Curtis and Noonan compare puzzles of object constitution with those for persons.

Turning then to relational issues in philosophy of mind, Douglas Keaton starts by briefly summarising the mind–body (mind–brain) problem and notes that answers like 'conscious states are brain states' under-specify the relational options. After consideration of what metaphysics actually is, and composition and determination relations, Keaton then addresses three metaphysical mind–brain relations in detail – constitution, realization and identity. He considers these to be species of explanatory necessitation relations (i.e., relations which explain the fact that brain or neural states *necessitate* conscious or phenomenal states). Having assessed and contrasted these three relations, Keaton next turns to their application in the context of the science of consciousness. He puts forward the proposal that each relation makes a specific prediction about what sort of neural activity (or brain facts) would occupy the 'minimal surround' (defined as non-constitutive or non-core neural activity that is nonetheless part of the minimally sufficient neural correlate of consciousness). Thus the author argues that realization requires the minimal surround to include the obtaining of certain counterfactual facts about the brain, constitution requires it to include the obtaining of certain facts about the brain but not counterfactual facts, and identity requires that the minimal surround includes nothing.

Benjamin Kozuch and Uriah Kriegel then address why there is a need for a philosophy of consciousness to accompany the science of consciousness. They consider that it is philosophy's mandate to: (1) address confusions in the methodological, conceptual and philosophical foundations of consciousness science, particularly with respect to the search for neural correlates of consciousness; and (2) pick up where the science leaves off by interpreting what correlate-finding implies regarding deeper metaphysical relations. The authors critically examine the so-called content-matching paradigm in the search for neural correlates of consciousness, arguing this is a poor strategy because neural representation of particular conscious content may not be the actual neural basis of that content. Taking binocular rivalry as an example, they consider mismatches between experiential content and neural representation to be more informative for consciousness science and argue that the associated eliminative inference process helps identify the neural basis of experienced content. In turning to the metaphysical relation between neural and phenomenal properties, Kozuch and Kriegel discuss: (1) identity theory and reductive materialism; (2) metaphysical supervenience, phenomenal-neural constitution and non-reductive materialism; (3) nomological supervenience, neural-phenomenal causation and naturalistic dualism; and (4) contingent supervenience and non-naturalistic dualism. They argue that the three candidate relations for explaining identified neural-phenomenal correlations are identity, constitution and causation. Because these hypotheses may be empirically equivalent however, each is subjected to an initial appraisal according to super-empirical virtues. The authors conclude that if such virtues do not convey good reasons to believe one hypothesis over another, there may be no way to choose among them.

Next, Derk Pereboom outlines his nonreductive physicalist approach to the mental, arguing that the relation between the phenomenal and the microphysical is one of material constitution rather than identity. Starting with analysis of the (Mary) knowledge argument in terms of truths about the qualitative nature that introspective modes of presentation represent phenomenal properties as having, Pereboom argues that it is an open possibility whether phenomenal properties are in fact accurately represented by such modes (i.e., that a qualitative inaccuracy hypothesis might be true). On this account Mary might in fact already know all truths derivable from microphysical facts prior to leaving the room precisely because her introspections upon leaving the room are not truthful representations, even if she learns a new mode of presentation outside of the room. Thus, it is argued, the open possibility of the qualitative inaccuracy hypothesis reduces the force of the knowledge argument. Pereboom also considers whether introspective evidence alone should count in weighing up physicalist versus antiphysicalist positions, noting instead that wider considerations are required (such as appeal to the success of physical explanations in the history of science). He then applies the qualitative inaccuracy hypothesis to the conceivability argument and considers the hypothesis supports one of two options to maintain a physicalist view of the phenomenal (that the phenomenal is not what it seems) while the other option (that the physical is not what it seems) is supported by Russellian monism. On the latter view, as yet unidentified absolutely intrinsic physical properties provide categorical bases for known microphysical properties and account for phenomenal consciousness (with the notion of absolutely intrinsic property resting upon that of constitution without identity). Pereboom then turns specifically to material constitution, setting out a formal characterization of the relation and arguing that it applies at the microphysical and intervening levels but that the mental is also grounded in the physical by identity with abstract compositional properties.

Benjamin Curtis thereafter draws on his earlier paper with Noonan, addressing what the issues they discussed entail for the neuroscience of consciousness. Starting with examination of the notion of constitution as it is applied in consciousness science, and the metaphysical dependency entailment therein, Curtis points out that on either a constitution or correlation approach, the related entities are events (neural and phenomenal) rather than objects. He notes that claiming a material constitution relation applies to consciousness suggests that brain states (events) and phenomenal states (events) will need to have applied to them, synchronic and diachronic conditions (thus determining the spatial extent of the event at any time it is occurring and its start and end times). Examples of applying such conditions to other event-types are provided and thereafter Curtis points out some problems. Brain states being physical events will have physical synchronic extents but phenomenal states, being mental events, will have mental synchronic extents and it is hard to therefore see how brain states and phenomenal states synchronically coincide. But he leaves open the possibility that the relation in question is simply occurral constitution as opposed to material constitution and hence that the synchronic problem might not be such a problem. However, Curtis notes that the diachronic extent problem is an important one. He thus argues that: (1) neuroscience needs to have genuine sortal kinds that can answer questions concerning the diachronic extent of brain states (events); and (2) there is not yet an obvious way to determine the diachronic extents of phenomenal states (events), particularly for rich streams of phenomenal consciousness.

Lastly, Jonathan Opie and Gerard O'Brien argue that because the special sciences have abandoned (strongly) reductionist and functionalist explanations, preferring instead mechanistic explanations, the science of consciousness will follow suit. They start by proposing that the success of mechanistic explanation justifies the introduction into ontology of a new category of essence (the essence of a thing being that which makes it the kind of thing it is). Hence rather than microphysical or functional essences, phenomena produced by mechanisms have structural essences. The focus of the latter is on constituent organization rather than (microphysical) composition or (functional) causal analysis. After reviewing the notion of mechanistic explanation, and its deductive nomological-based strong reductionist and multiple-realizability-based functionalist predecessors, Opie and O'Brien turn to the ontological entailments of the mechanistic approach to explanation. They point out that because mechanistic and microphysical (strong reductionistic) explanation are not compatible, it is often considered that mechanistic explanation accords better with functionalism, however, that this is at odds with its emphasis on material structure. The authors then argue why structural as opposed to functional properties are preferable and indeed more fundamental, noting that structure explains functional characteristics and not the converse and thus that any ontology of natural kinds should privilege structural essences.

Further, they employ the notion of multiple composability (of a set of parts which can be organized such that they form more than one higher-level kind) to support their contention. Finally, Opie and O'Brien return to phenomenal consciousness, applying their analyses from philosophy of science and ontology to philosophy of mind. They do so by: (1) looking at the neuroscience of consciousness (and at the connectionist approach in particular); (2) rejecting microphysicalist and functionalist ontologies of consciousness; and (3) suggesting instead that consciousness is a certain kind of material structure. On this view, it is in virtue of possessing structural properties that neural activity constitutes consciousness.

Toward a science and theory

As mentioned early in this introduction, by the end of the first volume of the companion set, the reader would have traversed the landscape of existing knowledge on the human brain's constituents, organization and processes, on the visual system in even more detail, on common investigative techniques used in modern human neuroscience, and on the phenomenon of binocular rivalry in exquisite detail. At the end of the present volume, the reader will have built upon this groundwork and examined what is meant by 'consciousness', 'correlation' and 'constitution', the methodological correlation/constitution distinction problem, notions of explanation in consciousness science, and relational, epistemological and ontological issues that surround phenomenal consciousness. The disciplines contributing to the discussion include neuroscience, cognitive neuroscience, vision science and neurology on the one hand, and metaphysics, philosophy of mind and philosophy of science on the other. The papers include focused reviews and original works within each discipline as well as contributions that make important connections between them. If the aim of the companion volumes has been achieved, the interdisciplinary engagement evident within them, particularly in the present volume, will have demonstrated that the study of consciousness cannot involve science or theory alone. Indeed, empirical and theoretical investigators should not merely tolerate each other's presence or stray into each other's field, but rather must meaningfully engage if substantive progress is to be made.

SECTION I

The scientific study of consciousness

Theories and methods in the scientific study of consciousness

P. Christiaan Klink[i,ii], Matthew W. Self[i], Victor A. F. Lamme[ii] and Pieter R. Roelfsema[i,ii,iii]
[i]Netherlands Institute for Neuroscience / [ii]University of Amsterdam / [iii]Vrije Universiteit, Amsterdam

The scientific study of consciousness has gained much interest over the past several decades. Here, we provide a primer on the topic by introducing the most commonly used concepts, the most prominent scientific theories, and an overview of broadly used methods of studying consciousness. With a focus on visual perception, we discuss the distinction between phenomenology and cognitive accessibility in the context of the different consciousness theories and highlight elements in which these theories are either complementary or more or less in agreement.

1. Introduction

Studying consciousness is not a straightforward endeavor. Even when the broad phenomenon of consciousness is narrowed down to visual or perceptual awareness and we assume that it must somehow arise from the brain, there is still a lot of room left to argue. Much of the ongoing debate may however be stemming from the fact that consciousness is a rather poorly defined phenomenon. Most researchers will agree that consciousness is a (neuro)biological phenomenon and that the mechanisms which give rise to consciousness will have to be located in the brain. However, while there are numerous ideas of what constitutes these mechanisms available in the literature there is currently no generally accepted theory of consciousness. In this chapter we will briefly introduce the most influential scientific theories of consciousness, the main points of discussion between them, and the most common experimental paradigms used in the scientific study of consciousness. With a focus on visual perception, this chapter does not aim to provide a complete account of the current state of affairs in the scientific study of consciousness, nor does it aim to resolve any ongoing discussions about the use of specific terminology in consciousness research. Due to space

DOI 10.1075/aicr.92.02kli

limitations, we will also not be able to give a very detailed philosophical account of the conceptual differences between theories of consciousness, nor an advanced overview of the experimental data that supports or opposes the different ideas. Instead, this chapter should rather be regarded as a primer, constructed with the purpose to equip the reader with basic knowledge on the topic and provide a firm starting point for further deliberation and investigation.

2. Phenomenal and access consciousness

The scientific problem of consciousness can either be framed in purely biological, in broader cognitive, or in altogether more theoretical philosophical terms. These different approaches are not necessarily mutually exclusive, as they conceptualize aspects of consciousness on fundamentally different levels. A distinction between phenomenal consciousness and access consciousness, for instance, was first introduced in philosophy (Block, 1995, 1996). In this theoretical construct, phenomenal consciousness is equated to raw experiences, or qualia (Chalmers, 1996), i.e., what *it is like* to experience something (Nagel, 1974). Access consciousness on the other hand relates to the subset of information that is more broadly available to cognitive functions such as giving a verbal report, reasoning, or performing motor actions. This distinction also roughly maps upon the philosophically defined 'hard' and 'easy' problems of consciousness (Chalmers, 1995). Here, the hard problem deals with explaining *how* phenomenal consciousness or the nature of conscious experience arises from a physical system such as the brain. This is also referred to as 'the explanatory gap' (Levine, 1983). The (relatively) easy problems of consciousness are concerned with explaining cognitive functions commonly ascribed to access consciousness. The contrast between a hard/phenomenal side of consciousness on the one hand, and an easy/access side of consciousness on the other hand, is either explicitly or implicitly central to most prevailing scientific theories of consciousness. From a biological point of view this has mainly led to a search for either the neural substrates that give rise to consciousness or neural substrates that are specifically involved in some element of conscious processing. Introduced as the search for neural correlates of consciousness (NCC) (Crick & Koch, 1990, 1998, 2003), this latter approach in particular seems to avoid the hard problem of consciousness altogether. While the term "neural correlate of consciousness" is broadly encountered in the scientific study of consciousness, it is important to realize that there is probably not a single NCC, but multiple ones that depend on the type or the content of consciousness. This becomes clear in the formal definition of NCC, introduced as *the minimal set of neuronal events and mechanisms jointly sufficient for a specific conscious percept* (Koch, 2004) (Figure 1). Some researchers believe that the accumulation of knowledge about the NCCs related to the easy problem of consciousness may eventually resolve the hard problem (Crick & Koch, 2003), while others limit the applicability of the search for NCCs to access

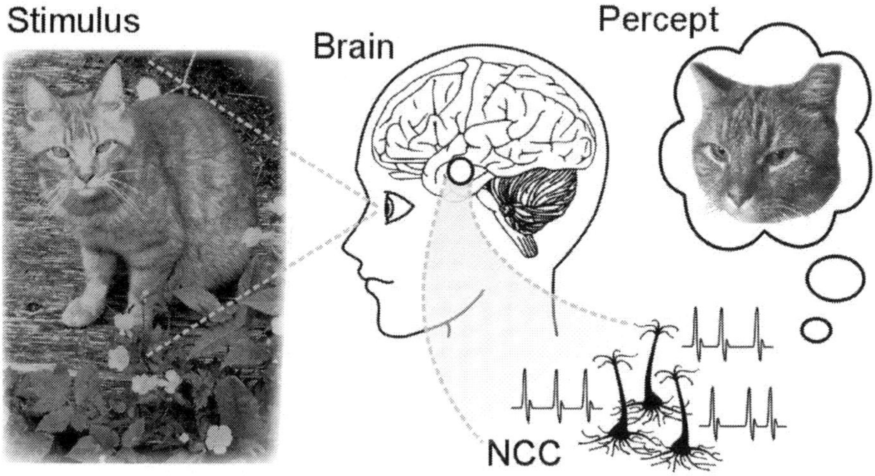

Figure 1. The neural correlates of consciousness (NCC) are the minimal set of neural substrates that are jointly sufficient for a particular conscious percept. In this example, an observer looks at a scene that includes a cat. The neural activity that uniquely corresponds to the conscious percept (here, spiking activity in the inferotemporal cortex) of that cat is the NCC of its perceptual experience. Adapted with permission from Koch (2004).

consciousness (Gaillard et al., 2009), or ignore the distinction altogether for now (Rees, Kreiman, & Koch, 2002). In addition, as correlations do not necessarily imply causality, NCCs cannot directly tell us anything about the cause, or even more, the constitution of consciousness (Miller, 2007, this volume). This concern has also been articulated as the necessity to look for mechanisms or 'explanatory correlates' of consciousness (Seth, 2009, 2010). It may be possible to partially get around this issue by assigning different NCCs to phenomenal and access consciousness (Block, 2005a; Gaillard et al., 2009; Miller, 2007). Within this subdivision, different phenomenal experiences yield different phenomenal NCCs while access NCCs comprises the neural mechanisms by which experience is made available for further cognitive processing (Block, 2005a). This distinction does however not solve the problem that among the many neural processes that constitute the 'grand neural correlate of consciousness' there may be many that are not directly concerned with creating the content of consciousness but that are either merely facilitative or even a consequence of consciousness. This problem has been recognized and in order to account for it, a distinction has been proposed between neural constituents (i.e., composing elements) of consciousness and neural correlates of consciousness (Miller, 2001, 2007, this volume; Revonsuo, 2001, this volume). This issue of *constituents* vs. *correlates* of consciousness is discussed at length on scientific and philosophical grounds throughout this volume.

Importantly, while a distinction between phenomenal and access consciousness (and their corresponding NCCs) is central to many theories of consciousness, it is not directly clear how this distinction could be investigated. It has indeed been argued that it is impossible to distinguish the raw conscious experience of phenomenal consciousness from the functional availability of access consciousness, simply because the empirical investigation of consciousness by definition requires the product of some sort of cognitive function (Cohen & Dennett, 2011). This limitation would then restrict the scope of scientific investigation to access consciousness, rendering the concept of phenomenal consciousness useless for any theory of consciousness. Others disagree with this point of view (Lamme, 2010) and stress that a proper theory of consciousness should not only address the subjective experience of a conscious percept, but also and perhaps foremost the constitution of the content of this experience (Fahrenfort & Lamme, 2012). These opposing viewpoints do however agree that there should at least be two stages of processing involved in the constitution of conscious experience, namely the creation of perceptual content and the conscious experience of this same content. What they disagree on is which of these stages is most interesting in studying the mechanisms of consciousness (Block, 2005b; Cohen & Dennett, 2011; Fahrenfort & Lamme, 2012).

2.1 Consciousness consensus?

This lack of consensus on what it is precisely that should be studied may be the biggest hurdle in the scientific study of consciousness. The absence of a precise, generally accepted definition of consciousness may confound discussions about the experimental investigation of its neural basis before it has even started. Describing mechanisms of consciousness in neural terms may offer a solution here (Lamme, 2006). On a coarse mechanistic level, for instance, there already seems to be somewhat of a consensus on the sort of neural processing stages that are important for the constitution of conscious visual experience. The flow of visual information through the brain is rather well described by decades of visual neuroscience (Felleman & Van Essen, 1991; Maunsell & Newsome, 1987; Price, 2013). In brief, when light patterns hit photoreceptor cells in the mammalian retina they instigate a chain of neural processing that starts within the retina and then moves to the primary visual cortex in the occipital lobe of the brain where it is split into two pathways for further processing. One pathway takes a ventral route into the temporal lobes while the other follows a dorsal route through parietal cortex (Goodale & Milner, 1992; Merigan & Maunsell, 1993; Mishkin & Ungerleider, 1982). Both pathways are connected to frontal lobe regions and motor areas where the visual information arrives in less than 200 ms (Lamme & Roelfsema, 2000; Tovee, 1994). In addition to this fast forward direction of processing there are also backward projections of information processing. Whenever information reaches a particular functional area it is processed in a specific way and not only fed through to the next area along the forward path but also back to previous areas to establish a complex network of recurrent processing (Lamme, Supèr, & Spekreijse, 1998). Most consciousness researchers will agree with this rough description of visual processing, and most will also subscribe to the idea that whereas all visual information is essentially already present at the level of the retina, additional neural processing is required for conscious experiences to arise. Opinions however start to deviate when you ask where or when along the chain of processing unconscious sensory information becomes a conscious experience. Some theories make an even more subtle subdivision into unconscious/subliminal, pre-conscious and conscious stages (Dehaene, Changeux, Naccache, Sackur, & Sergent, 2006; Kouider & Dehaene, 2007) or, as mentioned before, into unconscious, phenomenally conscious and access conscious states (Block, 1995, 1996, 2005a; Lamme, 2003, 2006, 2010). Is this merely a matter of terminology (Block, 2005b)? Unfortunately not. While the differences between consciousness theories on what is conscious and what is not are derived mostly from philosophical considerations, neural arguments also play a role (Lamme, 2006). Together these differences have strong implications for the practical aspects of the scientific study of consciousness. The brain is an immensely complex organ with processing algorithms that crucially depend on space, time and the type of neural code. Without theoretical focus it will be virtually impossible to study a poorly defined phenomenon such as consciousness in an organ as complex as the brain. Scientific theories of consciousness, guided by dialogues between philosophers and neuroscientists, are therefore crucial in providing the starting points for experimental investigation into the neural nature of consciousness. However, without experimental data to constrain the many theories of consciousness, these dialogues run the danger of turning into mutual monologues where arguments are perpetually repeated and no real progress is made. Fortunately for the field, the required approach of intermingled theoretical and experimental efforts is exactly the road that is currently taken.

3. From framework to theories

The renewal of scientific interest in the biological nature of consciousness can to a large extent be attributed to an influential series of publications in the 1990s in which a general framework was proposed to study consciousness experimentally (Crick & Koch, 1990, 1995, 1998, 2003). While far from being a full-blown theory, this framework introduced a number of concepts and ideas that are now ubiquitous in many theories of consciousness. As an important starting point, the framework suggests to aim our efforts at the visual system, both because of its experimental accessibility and the rich tradition of vision research in neuroscience. The framework further suggests to stay away from the hard problem of consciousness and focus on NCCs, with the hope that an eventual increased understanding of the NCCs will pave the way for a sensible approach to investigate the nature of qualia (Crick & Koch, 2003). Other notable elements of the 'framework for consciousness' are the idea that much of what the brain does happens unconsciously, that the content of conscious experience is determined by competitive interactions between dynamic coalitions of neurons that encode explicit representations of stimulus features, that attention may act as a biasing force in this dynamic competition and gate the content of visual awareness, and that the frontal regions of the brain are somehow essential in establishing conscious experience (Crick & Koch, 2003; Koch, 2004). Further emphasis is given to the characteristics of connectivity and interneuronal communication, with a distinction between the roles of feedforward and feedback connections as well as different functional roles for different types of neurons or neural coding schemes (e.g., spiking and oscillations). These elements are recurring themes in many of today's most prominent scientific theories of consciousness that we will introduce in the following sections. We will emphasize the potential implementations of these theories in terms of neural processing and their relation with the phenomenal/access consciousness distinction. With this approach we limit our review to scientific theories that have their roots in the known physiology and anatomy of the brain. There are also theories of consciousness that go beyond the brain, for instance by looking for mechanisms of consciousness in large electromagnetic fields surrounding the brain (McFadden, 2002a, 2002b) or by proposing quantum mechanisms in microtubules of the neuronal cytoskeleton as a driving force behind conscious experience (Hameroff, 2006a, 2006b). However, as these theories currently lack convincing evidence or testable predictions (Koch & Hepp, 2006) they will not be discussed here any further. After introducing the main biologically inspired scientific theories of consciousness, we will go over a number of experimental paradigms that have been instrumental in clarifying neural aspects of consciousness in the past and will likely keep doing so in the future.

3.1 Global (neuronal) workspace theory

The global workspace theory (GWT) (Baars, 1993, 1997) is a simple qualitative cognitive theory of consciousness that strongly resembles the mechanism of working memory. It is a contrastive theory that focuses on the distinction between conscious and unconscious processing. Conceptually, unconscious processing is represented by a number of distinct distributed local processes that compete for conscious access. Conscious experience takes shape when widespread activity in these nodes is broadcasted into a global workspace. GWT does not directly map onto the phenomenal/access consciousness division. In the original interpretation, the information in the ongoing activity of the distributed local nodes is thought to be unconscious, while the content that is broadcasted into the global workspace would correspond directly to access consciousness. This strict interpretation leaves no substrate for phenomenal consciousness and restricts GWT to access consciousness. It is however also possible to interpret GWT in a way that allows for an access/phenomenal consciousness distinction. To this end, one has to assume that among the distributed local nodes of unconscious processing there are processes that can potentially be broadcasted into the global workspace and processes that cannot. In this construct, the nodes that cannot broadcast into the workspace remain unconscious, the conglomerate of potential broadcasters constitute phenomenal consciousness, and the few nodes that are broadcasting into the global workspace represent access consciousness (Raffone & Pantani, 2010). Related to such an interpretation it has been suggested that phenomenal consciousness 'overflows' access consciousness with more information than can be cognitively accessed at any time (Block, 2011). Attention could play a crucial role here as a selection mechanism that picks a specific group of potential broadcasters from the phenomenal-subset of nodes and allows them to give rise to access consciousness.

A neuronal interpretation of GWT (Dehaene, Kerszberg, & Changeux, 1998; Dehaene & Naccache, 2001), aptly dubbed global neuronal workspace theory (GNWT), assumes a critical distinction between two classes of functional elements. The first class is formed by a broadly distributed network of more or less specialized local processing nodes of neurons. The activity of these nodes is triggered automatically and their internal computations are performed in isolation from each other, largely outside the scope of consciousness. Such characteristics fit well with the organization of early sensory cortex, where different features are processed in specialized cortical regions (Felleman & Van Essen, 1991; Grill-Spector & Malach, 2004; Mesulam, 1998). Visual motion processing, for instance, primarily occurs in a small region of cortex called MT (middle temporal) or V5. Cells in this specific cortical area are however relatively insensitive to color (Born & Bradley, 2005), whereas neurons in another region known as V4 show the opposite characteristic of being highly sensitive to color, but not so much to motion (Roe et al., 2012). It must however be noted that these functional distinctions are not absolute. In fact, MT-cells are still somewhat modulated by color signals (Seidemann, Poirson, Wandell, & Newsome, 1999), whereas the activity of V4-cells is also slightly influenced by visual motion (Ferrera, Rudolph, & Maunsell, 1994). The second class of functional elements in GNWT is formed by the workspace units that are characterized by their extensive connectivity with distant brain areas and mostly located in parietal, cingulate and prefrontal cortex. The broad network of workspace neurons essentially represents access consciousness. In a more recent version of GNWT, the local processing nodes that are not communicating with the workspace nodes are divided into two classes. Nodes that are not activated strongly enough to broadcast their content to the workspace are labeled 'subliminal' and their information will never reach (access) consciousness (Figure 2a). On the other hand, the nodes that are in principle active enough to communicate with the workspace neurons (the potential broadcasters) are called 'preconscious'. They are thought to require an attentional boost to become part of the network that involves the workspace neurons and constitutes (access) consciousness

(Dehaene, Changeux, Naccache, Sackur, & Sergent, 2006; Kouider & Dehaene, 2007). As such, the preconscious nodes can perhaps be thought of as constituting phenomenal consciousness. However, current theories disagree on this interpretation. While the phenomenal/access theory claims phenomenal consciousness as a kind of consciousness (Lamme, 2010), GNWT places the preconscious nodes outside the scope of consciousness by labeling it preconscious (Dehaene et al., 2006).

3.2 Recurrent processing

The recurrent processing theory is perhaps the most extensive neurobiological explanation for (visual) consciousness that is explicitly centered on the phenomenal/access separation. First conceived as a potential explanation for the neuronal correlates of figure-ground segregation (Lamme, 1995; Zipser, Lamme, & Schiller, 1996), the idea of assigning different roles to feedforward, feedback and recurrent processing of visual information has now evolved into a general theory of conscious visual perception (Lamme, 2006, 2010). The basic idea of the theory is that visual information follows a sequential processing path from its entrance into the nervous system at the retina towards output systems such as the motor and prefrontal areas of the brain (Lamme & Roelfsema, 2000). Within approximately 200 ms, information flows from primary visual cortex to output areas in what is called a fast feedforward sweep (FFS). As the FFS travels up the visual cortical hierarchy, the different cortical regions extract features of the encoded image, filling in an increasing amount of detail and allowing rapid categorization of the visual information. As soon as the feedforward train of information passes a cortical processing station there are additional projections evoked that communicate in opposite and tangential directions through feedback and lateral connections respectively (Figure 2b). Together these non-feedforward connections are called "recurrent" and in the absence of a rapidly following second FFS that acts as a mask they are an automatic consequence of the FFS. Crucial elements in the recurrent processing theory of visual consciousness are the type of processing, feedforward versus recurrent, and the depth of processing.

Not all stimuli will evoke a FFS that goes all the way up to output areas to influence behavior. Due to competition, many features or stimuli that are represented in the earlier processing areas will not be represented in later stages. The role of attention and its relation to consciousness is debated, but in one view of recurrent processing theory, attention is thought to play a crucial role in the competition between these features by gating stimulus information, either by boosting the strength of their representation (Carrasco, Ling, & Read, 2004; Treue, 2003), or by active gating of the feedforward processing stream (Bosman et al., 2012; Hopfinger, Buonocore, & Mangun, 2000). With such an interpretation, attention is distinct from consciousness and analogous to the depth of processing. Combining the proposed role of attention with the feedforward-recurrent dichotomy, four distinct stages of processing have been identified (Lamme, 2003, 2006). First, superficial feedforward processing involves activity that remains in earlier cortical stages due to a lack of attention and active masking. Second, deep feedforward processing is used as a term to denote feedforward processing that goes all the way up the cortical hierarchy to prefrontal and motor areas because the corresponding stimulus is attended. Crucially however it does not evoke recurrent processing, for instance because of a mask, and therefore remains invisible/unconscious. Third, superficial recurrent processing can be evoked by an unattended stimulus that is not masked. Recurrent processing for these stimuli remains limited to early processing stages. Finally, deep or wide recurrent processing is caused by unmasked, attended stimuli that are processed all the way up to output and evoke a wide pattern of recurrent activity along the way. The central idea is that recurrent processing is a prerequisite for any type of consciousness, but that the depth of recurrent processing distinguishes phenomenal from access consciousness with superficial recurrent processing in early areas corresponding to phenomenal consciousness and deep recurrent processing including frontoparietal brain regions denoting access consciousness (Lamme, 2006, 2010). This is precisely where this interpretation of recurrent processing theory deviates from global neuronal workspace theory: it asserts that even without the inclusion of frontoparietal access networks, there can exist consciousness in the form of a phenomenal visual experience but observers are simply not able to report it. In GNWT this state corresponds to the activation of preconscious nodes, yet these are labeled unconscious. Again, it all depends on the interpretation of the term 'conscious'. GNWT takes an introspective approach and claims that visual information is only conscious when it is accessed and reported, whereas the recurrent processing theory takes a neurobiological point of view and states that if the information is present in the brain and it could *in principle* be accessed for report, it is already conscious. A detailed philosophical account of the nature of phenomenal consciousness can be found elsewhere in this volume (see Drayson, this volume).

The distinction between attention and consciousness is not undisputed (see also Section 3.6 in this chapter), and other theories of recurrent processing propose that recurrent processes correspond to what psychologists call "top-down" or "task-driven" attention (Lamme & Roelfsema, 2000; Roelfsema, 2006). In this view, consciousness and attention refer to the same phenomenon because they both depend on recurrent processing. In addition to the debate about the precise relation between attention and consciousness, the strict identification of recurrent processing with consciousness is also not universally supported. Crucially, because any stimulus that is represented in sensory cortex, even those that remain unconscious, will undergo some 'local' recurrent processing by the reciprocal connections between the cortical layers, it remains to be specified how much recurrent processing is required for a stimulus to reach awareness.

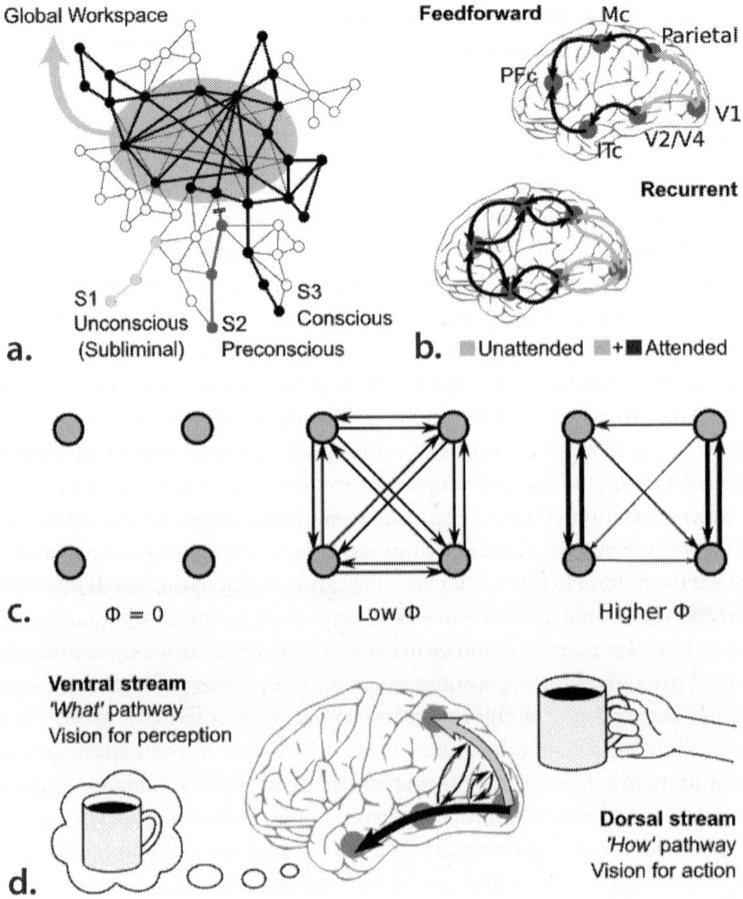

Figure 2. Theories of consciousness. **(a)** In global workspace theory, stimuli are consciously perceived if the sensory neurons that encode their features become part of a broad network of interconnected neural assemblies (the global workspace). For this to occur the neural representation of a stimulus should be both strong enough and attended (S3). Stimulus representations that are too weak (S1) cannot connect to the workspace regardless of the attentional state. They remain unconscious/subliminal. Preconscious representations are strong enough yet unattended (S2). They can in principle connect to the workspace if attention is shifted towards them. Adapted with permission from Dehaene et al. (2006). **(b)** In the latest rendition of the recurrent processing theory, the 'quality of consciousness' depends on the type of neural processing and the attentional state. Stimuli that are only processed in a feedforward manner (e.g., because they are masked) remain invisible. If they are attended they may however still evoke neural processing in 'higher' cortical areas. Consciousness crucially depends on the presence of recurrent processing. Unattended stimuli will only evoke local recurrent processing and give rise to phenomenal consciousness whereas attended stimuli ignite a broad network of recurrent processing leading to access consciousness. (PFc, prefrontal cortex;

3.3 Essential nodes of microconsciousness

Both the recurrent processing theory and the GNWT make a distinction between unconscious processing in local neuronal nodes and engagement of a broader neural network as a requirement for consciousness. The theory of micro-consciousnesses (Zeki, 2001, 2008; Zeki & Bartels, 1998a, 1998b) takes a radically different approach. It proposes that there is no such thing as a single unified visual consciousness, but that the total of conscious experience is instead made up from a larger number of feature-selective so-called essential nodes that are distributed in time and space and that are by themselves sufficient to cause awareness of the feature they are selective for if their activity levels are high enough to pass a certain consciousness-threshold. The information from the essential nodes is then thought to 'postconsciously' bind together into a coherent single perceptual experience called macroconsciousness. Finally, the microconsciousness theory postulates a third level of consciousness dubbed unified consciousness where the content of macroconsciousness becomes available to linguistic and communication systems. The basic idea of spatially separated essential nodes representing not only the processing but also the perceptual site of a visual feature is, similarly to the processing nodes in GWT, inspired by the known architecture of the visual cortex. As we noted before, different visual features are indeed selectively encoded in different regions of the visual cortex, e.g., color in V4 and motion in MT/V5. Experiments have furthermore shown that humans are generally a few tens of milliseconds earlier aware of color than they are of visual motion (Arnold, Clifford, & Wenderoth, 2001; Moutoussis & Zeki, 1997a, 1997b), favoring a temporal distinction between microconsciousnesses. Within the microconsciousness theory, phenomenal consciousness can be assigned both to each essential node separately (feature awareness) and to macroconsciousness as a whole (perception of objects and scenes). Access consciousness on the other hand would then be restricted to the executive output systems at the third level of unified consciousness.

Mc, motor cortex; ITc, inferotemporal cortex). **(c)** The information integration theory equates consciousness with information integration in complex systems and quantifies it with phi (Φ). A neural system of unconnected nodes (top) has a Φ of zero because it cannot integrate the information of the individual units. A system in which every unit is equally strongly connected to every other unit (middle) will have a low Φ because there is little or no specialization possible. Highest Φ-values are obtained with systems that are highly connected in a heterogeneous way (bottom). Such systems allow the existence of specialized, strongly connected subsystems (the left and right pairs in this example) while maintaining the potential for broader information integration. **(d)** The duplex vision theory assumes different roles for the dorsal and ventral processing pathways. While the two pathways do exchange information, activity in the ventral ('what') stream is thought to promote conscious perception (e.g., seeing a coffee mug) while activity in the dorsal ('how') stream is used for motor planning (e.g., grasping the mug).

3.4 The reentrant dynamic core and information integration theory

The theory of microconsciousness is perhaps the most localist account among the neurobiological theories of consciousness. On the other end of the spectrum, the reentrant dynamic core theory (RDCT) takes an extreme globalist stand by assigning consciousness to a wide range of dynamic interactions between groups of neurons within the network that connects nuclei in the thalamus with regions of cortex (Edelman, 1993; Edelman & Tononi, 2000; Tononi & Edelman, 1998). The hypothesis follows from a more general framework of brain functioning called 'neural darwinism' or 'neuronal group selection theory' (Edelman, 1987; Edelman & Mountcastle, 1978). In this framework, brain functioning depends on three stages of selection. The first stage is the genetic and epigenetic establishment of basic heterogeneous connectivity patterns during early development. As life progresses, these primary connections are in continuous competition, allowing synaptic reinforcement through experience and behavior. In the final stage called 'reentry', massive parallel networks of reciprocally connected thalamocortical neuronal ensembles (the dynamic core) allow spatiotemporal coordination of neural activity and give rise to coordinated brain function. RDCT does not say much about unconscious brain processes, but it does propose that the integration of information from different brain regions through reentrant coupling of neuronal ensembles is necessary for consciousness to arise. The idea of a dynamic core is reminiscent of the earlier discussed global workspace. It has indeed been argued that the two theories may complement each other in such a way that the dynamic core essentially provides the neuronal substrate for the global workspace (Edelman, Gally, & Baars, 2011). Like GWT, the RDCT does not directly map upon the phenomenal/access distinction. However, the momentary perceptual experiences arising from integrated reentrant activity in the dynamic core that are labeled primary (sensorimotor) consciousness or 'the remembered present' are akin to the idea of phenomenal consciousness. Primary consciousness is furthermore contrasted with a higher-order consciousness that requires language, allows verbal reports, and thus somewhat resembles access consciousness.

The concept of information integration that is central to the dynamic core hypothesis is further formalized in the information integration theory (IIT) of consciousness (Tononi, 2004). This theory is built around the notion that consciousness is both differentiated and integrated. Differentiation means that any specific momentary conscious state is different from the many other potential states. The integrated aspect on the other hand, refers to the large amount of information about different features that comprises such a conscious state (e.g., the shape and color of an object) and in which the information of one feature cannot be experienced separately from that of another. The analogy of a digital camera may clarify this idea (Tononi, 2008). The sensor chip of such a camera consists of numerous small photodetectors that each carries a binary signal. With one million of such detectors, the camera as a whole has an information encoding capacity of $2^{1,000,000}$ bits, which allows the construction of a huge number of unique images. The camera is however not considered conscious because the individual detectors are completely independent of one another preventing the integration of all this information. Humans on the other hand do integrate the different features that make up a visual scene, allowing us to become aware of it. IIT uses this principle to quantify consciousness based on a system's information integration capacity (Tononi, 2008; Tononi & Koch, 2008). This measure, labeled Φ (phi) and measured in bits, uses information theory to calculate the capacity for information integration based on the complexity and entropy of the system. With IIT it is thus theoretically possible to calculate the amount of consciousness of a complex system. In practice, this turns out to be a task of inconceivable proportion for a large biological system like the brain. To illustrate the basic idea, imagine a hypothetical organism with a brain consisting of only a few neurons. If these neurons are not connected to each other, there will be no integration of the information carried by individual cells and Φ will be zero. Connecting each neuron to all other neurons does allow information integration, but as everything that happens in such a network is interconnected there is no differentiation and Φ is not raised very much. The highest possible Φ for such an extremely simple system will be obtained with an intermediate solution where units are clustered in specialized assemblies of strongly interconnected cells while the assemblies themselves are more sparsely connected (Figure 2c). In the end, Φ depends on the number of individual units, assemblies and their connectivity patterns (Tononi & Sporns, 2003). For the human brain, sporting billions of neurons, trillions of connections and an unidentified number of functional assemblies, Φ cannot be calculated with today's technology but the basic computational principles already lead to some interesting ideas when they are applied to smaller, simplified systems (Oizumi, Albantakis, & Tononi, 2014). Recurrent processing between functionally specialized nodes for instance would significantly increase Φ compared to a system where the same nodes are operating in isolation from each other. Furthermore, within IIT there could be many parallel functional networks with a relatively low Φ that constitute broad phenomenal consciousness while a smaller number of networks with higher Φ represent access consciousness. It could perhaps even be the case that the reason why these access networks have higher Φ is because they are (recurrently) connected to an additional output system. This is of course all very speculative, but it illustrates the potential of the IIT perspective to capture the phenomenology of consciousness in a firm computational framework (Oizumi et al., 2014) and unify other, more biologically inspired, theories of consciousness.

3.5 Duplex vision theory: Action and perception

The existence of two major brain pathways along which visual information is processed has given rise to the duplex vision theory (DVT) (Goodale, 2004; Goodale & Milner, 1992; Goodale, Milner, Jakobson, & Carey, 1991; Milner & Goodale, 1993). Beyond the primary visual cortex feedforward processing of visual information occurs either in an inferotemporal direction (ventral pathway) or a posterior parietal direction (dorsal pathway). The best known functional separation that maps onto these processing pathways is that of specific 'what' and 'where' pathways (Mishkin & Ungerleider, 1982). This division is based on the features that are processed in areas along the two pathways. Areas that make up the ventral pathway are predominantly concerned with the processing of object features such as shape and color, whereas areas along the dorsal pathway are primarily involved in the representation of spatial aspects such as motion direction and speed. The DVT takes a different approach and classifies the pathways not on input characteristics, but on the type of output system with which they are linked. Information that is processed along the ventral stream is thought to be used by perceptual output systems and give rise to conscious experience whereas information in the dorsal stream is used for automatic visuomotor acts (Goodale & Milner, 1992). This distinction led to the nomenclature in which the ventral pathway is labeled the 'what', or 'vision for perception' stream and the dorsal pathway the 'how' or 'vision for action' stream (Figure 2d). Under normal circumstances the what and how pathways work together in establishing adaptive behavior but patient studies reveal that they can also work in isolation, i.e., objects may be perceived without observers being able to coordinate motor actions in response to them (Pöppel, Held, & Frost, 1973; Weiskrantz, Warrington, Sanders, & Marshall, 1974), and similarly observers may not be able to recognize an object while their corresponding motor actions remain adequate (Goodale et al., 1991; James, Culham, Humphrey, Milner, & Goodale, 2003).

3.6 Attention and consciousness

The relation between attention and consciousness is an ongoing topic of discussion (Dehaene et al., 2006; Koch & Tsuchiya, 2007, 2012; Lamme, 2004; Marchetti, 2012; Posner, 1994; van Boxtel, Tsuchiya, & Koch, 2010a). Attention plays a role in many theories of consciousness, sometimes as a biasing or gating factor that influences the content of conscious experience and sometimes as a prerequisite for consciousness to occur altogether. While there seems to be consensus about the fact that consciousness and attention are closely related, some scholars go a step further and propose that attention is a fundamental requirement for consciousness or even the exact same thing (Cohen, Cavanagh, Chun, & Nakayama, 2012; Jackendoff, 1996; Merikle, Smilek, & Eastwood, 2001; Posner, 1994, 2012). The potential conflation of consciousness and attention is not helped by the fact that even though both concepts may be intuitively accessible, they both lack a universally accepted definition. From a theoretical point of view, one may argue that attention is a *mechanism* and consciousness a *state*, which would make the two concepts of a fundamentally different nature ruling out the possibility that they are the same. This does however not mean that they can easily be distinguished experimentally. Multiple studies in the past few years have specifically been designed to dissociate attention and consciousness and resolve this issue (Cohen et al., 2012; van Boxtel, Tsuchiya, & Koch, 2010b; Watanabe et al., 2011), but they have not managed to silence the discussion completely. In order to truly disentangle the biological bases of attention and consciousness, if this is even possible, we may need to return to more neurobiological approaches of the issue instead of relying on the many existing behavioral paradigms alone. An in depth discussion of the relation between attention and consciousness can be found elsewhere in this volume (see van Boxtel & Tsuchiya, this volume).

4. Paradigms used to study consciousness

There are numerous paradigms available to study consciousness. Here we will focus on studies of visual awareness that have addressed the key question: "What are the differences between neural activities that lead to awareness of a visual stimulus and those that do not?" It is clear from this question that the awareness of the stimulus needs to be varied whilst simultaneously measuring some aspect of its neural representation. The most obvious approach to achieve this aim would be to vary the intensity (e.g., luminance, contrast, duration etc.) of a stimulus and to have observers report their awareness. The measure of neural activity, be it single-unit activity, blood level oxygen dependent signal, or event-related potential could then be sorted according to whether the observer was aware of the stimulus. This simple approach suffers from two key problems: firstly it is unclear how awareness should be measured and secondly it is difficult to dissociate changes in neural activity that were due to changes in the physical properties of the stimulus from changes that were due to the difference between the aware and non-aware states.

Historically, awareness of a stimulus has been measured using approaches ranging from subjective verbal reports to forced-choice approaches where performance is objectively assessed. Subjective approaches suffer from the problem that observers are free to set their own criteria as to when they report being aware of a stimulus. Different observers may choose very different criteria making assessment of the aware/non-aware state difficult. Forced-choice paradigms on the other hand suffer from the problem that the observer is forced to categorize their phenomenal experience into one of two (or more) categories, which may not reflect their underlying experience. Forced-choice paradigms also suffer from the less obvious problem that participants can perform better than chance for stimuli of which they claim not to be aware. Most famously, patients who display 'blindsight' are able to perform well on certain visual tasks while claiming to be unaware of the stimulus (Pöppel et al., 1973; Pöppel, Brinkmann, Von Cramon, & Singer, 1978; Stoerig & Cowey, 2007; although see Zeki & ffytche, 1998).

This result raises an interesting issue; how can we know whether a blindsight patient is truly unaware of the visual stimulus? For example, patient GY, who is clinically blind in his right hemifield, is able to correctly discriminate the direction of motion of fast-moving stimuli presented in his blind hemi-field, while claiming that he had no awareness of these stimuli (Weiskrantz, Barbur, & Sahraie, 1995). If we use the objective criteria of his performance on the motion discrimination task then we would classify GY as being aware. On the other-hand, if we trust the verbal report then we would classify him as unaware. To provide stricter measures of awareness, studies have moved from using forced-choice discrimination questions (e.g., was it moving left-or-right?) to detection tasks (e.g., was the stimulus present or not?). The disadvantage of discrimination tasks is that even very weak forms of neural activity, which may not normally lead to awareness of the stimulus, may be sufficient to discriminate between two forced-choice alternatives. Using detection tasks with high numbers of catch-trials in which the stimulus is absent, and presenting the stimuli in random orders with random timings can provide a measure of awareness, which matches more closely the ability of the patient to subjectively report awareness of a visual stimulus. However, the disadvantage of detection tasks is that the patient is free to set their own criterion level at which to respond that they have seen the stimulus. A patient that is biased or reluctant to report a weak sensation as being aware may show poor performance on detection tasks and good performance on discrimination tasks. A possible solution to this conundrum is to use signal detection theory. Using signal-detection theory it is possible to derive a measure of sensitivity (*d'*) that is independent of the patient's response bias and decision criterion (Macmillan & Creelman, 1991). Such an analysis was carried out by Azzopardi and Cowey (1997) who determined that GY shows higher sensitivity on discrimination tasks compared to detection tasks.

Other studies have taken a different approach in which the report of a participant is accompanied by a confidence rating or wager on the correctness of the response (Galvin, Podd, Drga, & Whitmore, 2003; Kolb & Braun, 1995; Kornbrot, 2006; Kunimoto, Miller, & Pashler, 2001; Maniscalco & Lau, 2012; Persaud, McLeod, & Cowey, 2007). These studies have utilized the logic that if subjects are aware of a stimulus then there should be a good correlation between their objective performance and their (trial-by-trial) confidence in whether their decision was correct. Conversely if blindsight patients are truly unaware of the visual stimulus then they should show little correlation between their performance on a detection/discrimination task and their confidence about their decision. Applications of signal detection theory to confidence judgments have allowed researchers to generate separate sensitivity measures for the primary task (Type-I sensitivity) and the ability of subjects to judge the correctness of their responses (Type-II sensitivity) (Galvin et al., 2003; Maniscalco & Lau, 2012). This measure of sensitivity has been suggested to capture the 'meta-cognitive' abilities of subjects, that is, the ability to make a judgment about one's own awareness. High meta-cognitive ability has been proposed as a hallmark of a conscious process and dissociations between perceptual abilities and meta-cognitive abilities could signal evidence for perception without awareness (Ko & Lau, 2012; Persaud et al., 2007).

Despite the advances discussed here it remains difficult to assess whether someone was aware of a visual stimulus based purely on behavioral reports. The approaches we discuss below typically avoid this problem by using stimulus configurations for which observers are both subjectively and objectively unaware of aspects of the stimulus.

4.1 Paradigms to study the NCC

A key approach to studying visual awareness that was outlined by Crick and Koch (2003) is to dissociate patterns of neural activity that are the result of changes in the visual stimulus from those that are due to changes in awareness. To achieve this goal it is important that the physical stimulation of the retina is held constant across different awareness conditions (Kim & Blake, 2005). The companion to this volume (Miller, 2013) extensively describes what is perhaps the most well-known example of such a paradigm – binocular rivalry (Blake & Logothetis, 2002). In binocular rivalry the retinal input is held constant and the observer's awareness spontaneously fluctuates between different states. Changes in neural activity observed between these different states can therefore not be attributed to the stimulus itself but should be assigned to some aspect of the change in awareness. Such paradigms have perhaps provided the most revealing insights so far concerning the NCC.

4.1.1 *(Continuous) Flash suppression and motion-induced blindness*

While binocular rivalry provides a clear and dramatic switch in awareness it suffers from the problem that the timing of these switches are unpredictable (though they follow a well-described probability distribution). An alternative paradigm, flash suppression (Wilke, Logothetis, & Leopold, 2003; Wolfe, 1984) and its close relative, continuous flash suppression (Tsuchiya & Koch, 2005), provide the ability to present a stimulus to one retina and render it entirely invisible by simultaneously presenting a different, salient stimulus to the other retina. In the original description of this paradigm (Wilke et al., 2003; Wolfe, 1984) the stimulus that will become invisible (the 'unaware' stimulus) is first presented for several seconds to one eye while a neutral background is presented to the other eye. This leads to adaptation of the neural representation of the target stimulus. The target stimulus is then rendered invisible by the sudden presentation of a high-intensity stimulus to the other eye. This stimulus normally consists of high-contrast colored squares ('Mondrians') or a field of moving dots. This paradigm yields a very reliable and complete disappearance of the target stimulus for several seconds until a rivalrous state resumes. This paradigm was developed further into 'continuous flash suppression' (Tsuchiya & Koch, 2005). In this version a stream of continuously changing Mondrians is presented to one-eye. A low-intensity stimulus is then presented to the other eye for a brief period and remains entirely invisible. In this way a stream of stimuli can be presented to one eye without the observer ever being aware of them. This allows researchers to determine the fate of the neural representation of the unaware stimulus using electrophysiological or imaging techniques.

One factor that complicates the interpretation of binocular rivalry and flash suppression studies is the requirement for monocular presentation of the stimulus and the presence of the competing stimulus in the other eye. This problem is avoided in the motion-induced blindness (MIB) paradigm. In MIB studies large, binocularly presented, high-contrast shapes (bright yellow circles in the original description) spontaneously disappear from view when they are surrounded by a field of coherently moving dots (Bonneh, Cooperman, & Sagi, 2001). The dots are also presented binocularly and never overlap with the circle and yet observers report the spontaneous disappearance of one, or more, of the circles, sometimes for seconds at a time. Several studies have used this paradigm to address the question of how the neural representations of the circles change when observers report their disappearance from awareness.

4.1.2 *Masking*

Another class of paradigms renders stimuli invisible by limiting the duration of processing of the stimulus or by exploiting the strong inhibitory connections that exist between the representations of nearby objects. Collectively known as masking paradigms, these approaches vary substantially in their implementation, i.e., whether the mask was presented before or after the stimulus (or both) and whether the mask spatially overlaps the stimulus, shares borders with it or simply surrounds it. These different forms of masking are likely to render the masked stimulus invisible through different mechanisms. For example backwards masking, in which a high-contrast pattern is presented shortly after the stimulus offset, has been suggested to work through preventing recurrent processing of the masked stimulus (Fahrenfort, Scholte, & Lamme, 2007; Lamme, Zipser, & Spekreijse, 2002). On the other hand, simultaneous contrast masking, in which a pattern is presented at the same time as the target stimulus but does not overlap spatially, likely works through suppressive connections between the mask and the unaware stimulus (Macknik, 2006). For foveal vision, contrast masking is highly similar to a phenomenon called visual crowding in which the conscious perception of an object is impaired by presenting it with accompanying flanker stimuli (Levi, 2008; Pelli & Tillman, 2008; Whitney & Levi, 2011). In peripheral vision however, the spatial characteristics of crowding and masking are rather different suggesting that crowding is in fact a distinct mechanism (Levi, 2008). Furthermore, while contrast masking appears to erase a stimulus from awareness by preventing feature detection, the presence of a crowded object can generally be detected. Its specific characteristics however are not recognized, presumably as a result of excessive feature integration between the target stimulus and the flankers (Pelli, Palomares, & Majaj, 2004), a process that seems to occur after the flankers are consciously perceived (Wallis & Bex, 2011).

Masking studies are particularly interesting for two reasons. Firstly many studies have varied the parameters of the mask to attempt to infer what aspect(s) of the neural representation of the masked stimulus is (are) necessary for awareness. Secondly masking studies have been used to study the neural networks that can be activated by a masked (and unconscious) stimulus. These latter studies have revealed that the masked stimulus can activate areas throughout the visual hierarchy up to and including motor output areas (Dehaene et al., 1998; Moutoussis & Zeki, 2002) (albeit at lower intensities than an unmasked stimulus). The depth of processing of the masked stimulus can also be inferred by subsequent priming effects. For example a masked word can prime observers on a sentence completion task, meaning that some semantic processing of the mask has occurred, even though the observer remains completely unaware of the masked prime (Dehaene et al., 1998, 2001; Greenwald, Draine, & Abrams, 1996; Marcel, 1983; Nakamura, Dehaene, Jobert, Le Bihan, & Kouider, 2007).

4.1.3 *Attentional paradigms*

Patients with damage to the right parietal and temporoparietal cortex often suffer from hemispatial neglect. This condition is characterized by an inability to orient attention towards the contralateral (usually left) visual field. Patients with such a condition are often capable of perceiving stimuli presented to the neglected hemifield if they are presented in isolation, however in the presence of a competing stimulus in the normal hemifield patients often fail to report stimuli in the neglected field (Driver & Mattingley, 1998; Rees et al., 2000; Rees, Wojciulik, et al., 2002). These findings were the original impetus behind arguments that attention is a necessary requirement for visual awareness. This argumentation was leant further support through the development of the change-blindness paradigm (Intraub, 1997; O'Regan, Rensink, & Clark, 1999; Rensink, O'Regan, & Clark, 1997; Simons & Levin, 1997; Simons & Rensink, 2005). In the original version of this paradigm observers view two sequentially presented visual scenes separated briefly by a blank screen. In one of the two scenes a change is introduced such as the removal of an object, or a change in color of a region of the scene. Surprisingly, observers fail to report the change, even after many repeated viewings of the scenes. The intervening blank period is critical, as it masks the onset transients, which would otherwise immediately reveal the location of the change. Initially this paradigm was argued to constitute evidence that we are only aware of stimuli that we attend to. When presented with the alternating visual scenes we randomly move our attention around the scene and we only become aware of the change if we happen to attend to the changing object. However an alternative interpretation would be that we are aware of much more of the content of the visual scene than just the region/object we are attending to (as would be our subjective experience), and that we are only able to encode attended items into working memory, allowing us to complete the task. Perhaps a more direct demonstration of the importance of attention for awareness comes from inattentional blindness paradigms (Mack, 2003; Mack & Rock, 1998). Observers can miss a very salient item in a visual scene if their attention is directed to other features in the scene. This was dramatically demonstrated by the now famous 'Gorillas in our midst' paradigm in which observers often miss the presence of a man in a Gorilla suit that walks through two teams playing basketball if they are instructed to attend to the team playing in white (Simons & Chabris, 1999). Such a paradigm gets to the heart of the role of attention in awareness. Are observers phenomenally aware of the Gorilla, but unable to report its presence? Or does diverting attention away from a stimulus render observers completely unaware of its presence?

The final paradigm that we will consider that manipulates awareness through manipulating attention is the attentional blink paradigm (Broadbent & Broadbent, 1987; Raymond, Shapiro, & Arnell, 1992). In a typical attentional blink task observers view a stream of rapidly (6–20 Hz) presented items, typically letters or numbers. The observer must perform two tasks, for example to press a button immediately as soon as the letter 'X' appears, and to report whether a presented number was odd or even at the end of the trial. The critical manipulation is the time delay between the appearance of the 'X' and the appearance of the number, the stimulus onset asynchrony (SOA). If the number is presented at a long SOA then observers have no trouble reporting the number. If however the number was presented at a short SOA then performance on the number task can fall to chance levels. Notably this does not occur if the number is presented immediately after the 'X', a phenomenon known as 'lag 1 sparing' (Potter, Chun, Banks, & Muckenhoupt, 1998). The attentional blink has mostly been used as a behavioral paradigm with the aim being to understand the mechanisms that lead to the reduced performance at short SOAs. A few studies have also used the attentional blink paradigm as a form of masking to render stimuli unaware and study the representation of the 'blinked' stimulus (Martens & Wyble, 2010).

4.1.4 *Memory paradigms*

In experiments that require observers to report perceptual experience, the report is often given after the experience. This means that some form of memory about the preceding perceptual experience is involved in the probing process. This memory element can be investigated by extending the interval between the experience and the report and by adding additional stimuli or tasks in this interval period. Interestingly, the perceptual characteristics of visual short-term memory (Figure 3) may reveal important aspects of the mechanisms that give rise to conscious visual experiences (Crick & Koch, 1990; Lamme, 2004). Distinct phases of visual short term memory can be distinguished. A brief (< 0.5 s) iconic memory contains a rich representation of recent visual experience (Sperling, 1960), while a much longer (seconds to minutes) visual working memory only maintains a very limited subset of about four representations (Luck & Vogel, 1997). The transition from iconic to working memory depends on attention and subsequent visual stimulation. In the absence of subsequent stimulation, the rich information in iconic memory transfers to a fragile but rich form of longer lasting (seconds) memory from which attention can select a number of objects and features that far surpasses the classic capacity of working memory (Landman, Spekreijse, & Lamme, 2003; Sligte, Scholte, & Lamme, 2008; Sligte, Wokke, Tesselaar, Scholte, & Lamme, 2010; Vandenbroucke, Sligte, & Lamme, 2011). This fragile short-term memory is however erased by new visual stimulation (Pinto, Sligte, Shapiro, & Lamme, 2013; Sligte, Scholte, & Lamme, 2009), leaving an observer with only the content of working memory from which to report. The attention-gated promotion of elements of a weak but rich visual representation to cognitive report systems strongly resembles the theoretical construct of the attention-gated transition from phenomenal to access consciousness making these memory paradigms an interesting approach to sample the mechanisms of visual consciousness (Crick & Koch, 1990; Kouider, de Gardelle, Sackur, & Dupoux, 2010; Lamme, 2010).

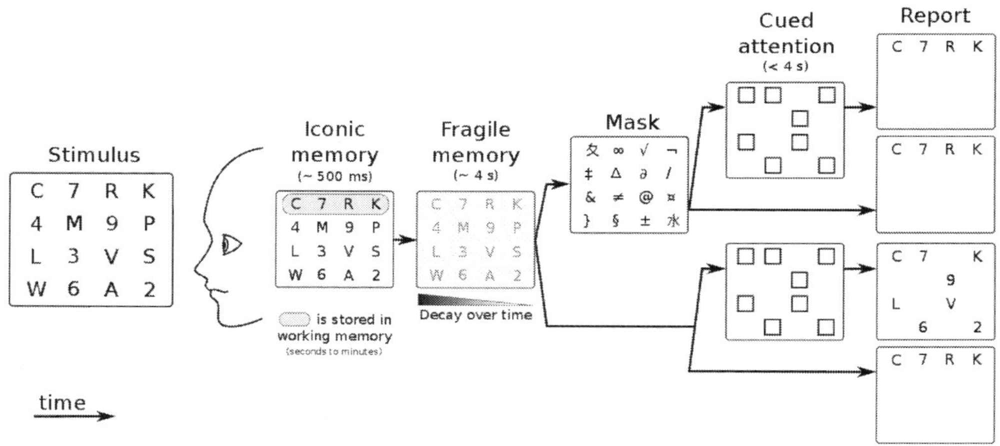

Figure 3. The structure of visual short-term memory. A rich representation of a stimulus is kept in iconic memory for about 500 ms, after which a more fragile but still high capacity form of memory slowly decays over a period of up to four seconds. This fragile memory is erased by subsequent stimulation (mask), but in the absence of masking stimulation, attentional cues at particular spatial locations (indicated by squares) can recover more details from this memory than can be kept in the limited capacity of working memory that persists for seconds to minutes. Note that the cue-squares indicated potentially cued locations and the Report column the potential reports. In reality only one location will be cued at each time and only one report will be given.

4.1.5 *Other paradigms*

Here we have focused on visual studies which have searched for the NCC by keeping the stimulation of the retina as similar as possible while varying the contents of the observers' visual consciousness (Kim & Blake, 2005). There are many other approaches available to study consciousness for which we do not have space to cover in detail here but which we will briefly address. An alternative approach to studying awareness is to make changes to the global state of consciousness of the subject. An obvious example is anesthesia, which completely removes awareness of the environment. However as anesthesia globally alters brain activity it may be difficult to identify the critical neural processes that lead to awareness. Similar arguments can be made for studies that have examined the brain-activity patterns of subjects in a persistent vegetative state (PVS). Recent studies have demonstrated that some patients in PVS, though apparently completely unresponsive to external stimuli, are able to perform visual imagery experiments as assessed by the patterns of brain activity they produce in functional magnetic resonance imaging studies (Owen & Coleman, 2008; Owen et al., 2006). These results have of course great consequences for the treatment of patients in PVS, but also for our understanding of awareness (see Charland-Verville, Vanhaudenhuyse, Laureys, & Gosseries, this volume). These apparently unresponsive patients can follow complex instructions and change their brain activity in a manner similar to normal subjects. This result suggests a dissociation between the neural systems that enable motor-output and those that result in awareness of the environment. Similar dissociations also occur in rapid eye movement (REM) sleep states, where some form of visual awareness (which may be more akin to visual imagery) may be present yet motor output is inhibited (except eye movements) (Braun et al., 1998). Studying these states is of course extremely difficult because, even though significant progress is being made (Horikawa, Tamaki, Miyawaki, & Kamitani, 2013), we still lack a method to reliably assess the contents of awareness in these cases. Similar problems exist for studies of visual imagery itself: the experimenter has little control over the exact contents of the participant's awareness making it difficult to assess the underlying neural mechanisms which lead to the formation of mental images. Nevertheless imaging studies have provided evidence that visual imagery reactivates similar areas of cortex that are activated by physical stimulation of the retina (Klein, Paradis, Poline, Kosslyn, & Le Bihan, 2000; Knauff, Kassubek, Mulack, & Greenlee, 2000; Kosslyn, Thompson, Kim, & Alpert, 1995).

5. Conclusion

This overview of the most prominent current theories and methods in the scientific study of consciousness illustrates the large interest in the neurobiological basis of consciousness. Even though the presented theories differ on numerous aspects, there appears to be some consensus on the type of neural mechanisms that are important for the establishment of conscious experience. Notwithstanding the ongoing discussion as to when a neuronal representation of a visual scene transfers from being unconscious to conscious, the general scheme of broad and rich neuronal representations that require integration to become accessible for other cognitive systems is a recurrent feature of many theories. In addition to ongoing theoretical discussions, the field may benefit from continuing the recent neuroscientific approach to consciousness based on experimentation and data. By centering the scientific study of consciousness on its measurable underlying neural mechanisms we may be able to avoid misinterpretations of theoretical terminology and exploit the functional overlap between existing theories. Theoretical insights on the nature of consciousness will still be very useful in guiding the proposed experimental efforts, but constraining future (iterations of) theories with the growing body of data seems to be the most promising way to come to a true understanding of the neurobiology of consciousness (Lamme, 2006, 2010).

References

Arnold, D.H., Clifford, C.W., & Wenderoth, P. (2001). Asynchronous processing in vision: Color leads motion. *Current Biology*, 11(8), 596–600. DOI: 10.1016/S0960-9822(01)00156-7

Azzopardi, P., & Cowey, A. (1997). Is blindsight like normal, near-threshold vision? *Proceedings of the National Academy of Sciences USA*, 94(25), 14190–14194. DOI: 10.1073/pnas.94.25.14190

Baars, B.J. (1993). *A cognitive theory of consciousness*. New York, NY: Cambridge University Press.

Baars, B.J. (1997). *In the theater of consciousness: The workspace of the mind*. New York, NY: Oxford University Press. DOI: 10.1093/acprof:oso/9780195102659.001.1

Blake, R., & Logothetis, N.K. (2002). Visual competition. *Nature Reviews Neuroscience*, 3(1), 13–21. DOI: 10.1038/nrn701

Block, N. (1995). On a confusion about a function of consciousness. *Behavioral and Brain Sciences*, 18(2), 227–287. DOI: 10.1017/S0140525X00038188

Block, N. (1996). How can we find the neural correlate of consciousness? *Trends in Neurosciences*, 19(11), 456–459. DOI: 10.1016/S0166-2236(96)20049-9

Block, N. (2005a). Two neural correlates of consciousness. *Trends in Cognitive Sciences*, 9(2), 46–52. DOI: 10.1016/j.tics.2004.12.006

Block, N. (2005b). The merely verbal problem of consciousness. *Trends in Cognitive Sciences*, 9(6), 270. DOI: 10.1016/j.tics.2005.04.009

Block, N. (2011). Perceptual consciousness overflows cognitive access. *Trends in Cognitive Sciences*, 15(12), 567–575. DOI: 10.1016/j.tics.2011.11.001

Bonneh, Y.S., Cooperman, A., & Sagi, D. (2001). Motion-induced blindness in normal observers. *Nature*, 411(6839), 798–801. DOI: 10.1038/35081073

Born, R.T., & Bradley, D.C. (2005). Structure and function of visual area MT. *Annual Review of Neuroscience*, 28, 157–189. DOI: 10.1146/annurev.neuro.26.041002.131052

Bosman, C. A., Schoffelen, J.-M., Brunet, N., Oostenveld, R., Bastos, A. M., Womelsdorf, T., Rubehn, B., Stieglitz, T., De Weerd, P., & Fries, P. (2012). Attentional stimulus selection through selective synchronization between monkey visual areas. *Neuron*, 75(5), 875–888. DOI: 10.1016/j.neuron.2012.06.037
Braun, A. R., Balkin, T. J., Wesensten, N. J., Gwadry, F., Carson, R. E., Varga, M., Baldwin, P., Belenky, G., & Herscovitch, P. (1998). Dissociated pattern of activity in visual cortices and their projections during human rapid eye movement sleep. *Science*, 279(5347), 91–95. DOI: 10.1126/science.279.5347.91
Broadbent, D. E., & Broadbent, M. H. (1987). From detection to identification: Response to multiple targets in rapid serial visual presentation. *Perception & Psychophysics*, 42(2), 105–113. DOI: 10.3758/BF03210498
Carrasco, M., Ling, S., & Read, S. (2004). Attention alters appearance. *Nature Neuroscience*, 7(3), 308–313. DOI: 10.1038/nn1194
Chalmers, D. J. (1995). Facing up to the problem of consciousness. *Journal of Consciousness Studies*, 2(3), 200–219.
Chalmers, D. J. (1996). *The conscious mind: In search of a fundamental theory*. New York, NY: Oxford University Press.
Cohen, M. A., Cavanagh, P., Chun, M. M., & Nakayama, K. (2012). The attentional requirements of consciousness. *Trends in Cognitive Sciences*, 16(8), 411–417. DOI: 10.1016/j.tics.2012.06.013
Cohen, M. A., & Dennett, D. C. (2011). Consciousness cannot be separated from function. *Trends in Cognitive Sciences*, 15(8), 358–364. DOI: 10.1016/j.tics.2011.06.008
Crick, F., & Koch, C. (1990). Towards a neurobiological theory of consciousness. *Seminars in the Neurosciences*, 2, 263–275. DOI: 10.1016/B978-0-12-185254-2.50021-8
Crick, F., & Koch, C. (1995). Are we aware of neural activity in primary visual cortex? *Nature*, 375(6527), 121–123. DOI: 10.1038/375121a0
Crick, F., & Koch, C. (1998). Consciousness and neuroscience. *Cerebral Cortex*, 8(2), 97–107. DOI: 10.1093/cercor/8.2.97
Crick, F., & Koch, C. (2003). A framework for consciousness. *Nature Neuroscience*, 6(2), 119–126. DOI: 10.1038/nn0203-119
Dehaene, S., Changeux, J.-P., Naccache, L., Sackur, J., & Sergent, C. (2006). Conscious, preconscious, and subliminal processing: A testable taxonomy. *Trends in Cognitive Sciences*, 10(5), 204–211. DOI: 10.1016/j.tics.2006.03.007
Dehaene, S., Kerszberg, M., & Changeux, J.-P. (1998). A neuronal model of a global workspace in effortful cognitive tasks. *Proceedings of the National Academy of Sciences USA*, 95(24), 14529–14534. DOI: 10.1073/pnas.95.24.14529
Dehaene, S., & Naccache, L. (2001). Towards a cognitive neuroscience of consciousness: Basic evidence and a workspace framework. *Cognition*, 79(1–2), 1–37. DOI: 10.1016/S0010-0277(00)00123-2
Dehaene, S., Naccache, L., Cohen, L., Bihan, D. L., Mangin, J. F., Poline, J. B., & Rivière, D. (2001). Cerebral mechanisms of word masking and unconscious repetition priming. *Nature Neuroscience*, 4(7), 752–758. DOI: 10.1038/89551
Dehaene, S., Naccache, L., Le Clec'H, G., Koechlin, E., Mueller, M., Dehaene-Lambertz, G., van de Moortele, P. F., & Le Bihan, D. (1998). Imaging unconscious semantic priming. *Nature*, 395(6702), 597–600. DOI: 10.1038/26967
Driver, J., & Mattingley, J. B. (1998). Parietal neglect and visual awareness. *Nature Neuroscience*, 1(1), 17–22. DOI: 10.1038/217

Edelman, G. M. (1987). *Neural darwinism: The theory of neuronal group selection.* New York, NY: Basic Books.

Edelman, G. M. (1993). Neural darwinism: Selection and reentrant signaling in higher brain function. *Neuron*, 10(2), 115–125. DOI: 10.1016/0896-6273(93)90304-A

Edelman, G. M., Gally, J. A., & Baars, B. J. (2011). Biology of consciousness. *Frontiers in Psychology*, 2, 4. DOI: 10.3389/fpsyg.2011.00004

Edelman, G. M., & Mountcastle, V. B. (1978). *The mindful brain: Cortical organization and the group-selective theory of higher brain function.* Cambridge, MA: MIT Press.

Edelman, G. M., & Tononi, G. (2000). *A universe of consciousness: How matter becomes imagination.* New York, NY: Basic Books.

Fahrenfort, J. J., & Lamme, V. A. F. (2012). A true science of consciousness explains phenomenology: Comment on Cohen and Dennett. *Trends in Cognitive Sciences*, 16(3), 138–139. DOI: 10.1016/j.tics.2012.01.004

Fahrenfort, J. J., Scholte, H. S., & Lamme, V. A. F. (2007). Masking disrupts reentrant processing in human visual cortex. *Journal of Cognitive Neuroscience*, 19(9), 1488–1497. DOI: 10.1162/jocn.2007.19.9.1488

Felleman, D., & Van Essen, D. C. (1991). Distributed hierarchical processing in the primate cerebral cortex. *Cerebral Cortex*, 1(1), 1–47. DOI: 10.1093/cercor/1.1.1

Ferrera, V. P., Rudolph, K. K., & Maunsell, J. H. (1994). Responses of neurons in the parietal and temporal visual pathways during a motion task. *Journal of Neuroscience*, 14(10), 6171–6186.

Gaillard, R., Dehaene, S., Adam, C., Clémenceau, S., Hasboun, D., Baulac, M., Cohen, L., & Nacchache, L. (2009). Converging intracranial markers of conscious access. *PLoS Biology*, 7(3), e61. DOI: 10.1371/journal.pbio.1000061

Galvin, S. J., Podd, J. V, Drga, V., & Whitmore, J. (2003). Type 2 tasks in the theory of signal detectability: Discrimination between correct and incorrect decisions. *Psychonomic Bulletin & Review*, 10(4), 843–876. DOI: 10.3758/BF03196546

Goodale, M. A. (2004). An evolving view of duplex vision: Separate but interacting cortical pathways for perception and action. *Current Opinion in Neurobiology*, 14(2), 203–211. DOI: 10.1016/j.conb.2004.03.002

Goodale, M. A., & Milner, A. (1992). Separate visual pathways for perception and action. *Trends in Neurosciences*, 15(1), 20–25. DOI: 10.1016/0166-2236(92)90344-8

Goodale, M. A., Milner, A. D., Jakobson, L. S., & Carey, D. P. (1991). A neurological dissociation between perceiving objects and grasping them. *Nature*, 349(6305), 154–156. DOI: 10.1038/349154a0

Greenwald, A. G., Draine, S. C., & Abrams, R. L. (1996). Three cognitive markers of unconscious semantic activation. *Science*, 273(5282), 1699–1702. DOI: 10.1126/science.273.5282.1699

Grill-Spector, K., & Malach, R. (2004). The human visual cortex. *Annual Review of Neuroscience*, 27, 649–677. DOI: 10.1146/annurev.neuro.27.070203.144220

Hameroff, S. (2006a). The entwined mysteries of anesthesia and consciousness: Is there a common underlying mechanism? *Anesthesiology*, 105(2), 400–412. DOI: 10.1097/00000542-200608000-00024

Hameroff, S. (2006b). Consciousness, neurobiology and quantum mechanics: The case for a connection. In J. A. Tuszynski (Ed.), *The emerging physics of consciousness* (pp. 193–253). Berlin: Springer-Verlag. DOI: 10.1007/3-540-36723-3_6

Hopfinger, J. B., Buonocore, M. H., & Mangun, G. R. (2000). The neural mechanisms of top-down attentional control. *Nature Neuroscience*, 3(3), 284–291. DOI: 10.1038/72999

Horikawa, T., Tamaki, M., Miyawaki, Y., & Kamitani, Y. (2013). Neural decoding of visual imagery during sleep. *Science*, 340(6132), 639–642. DOI: 10.1126/science.1234330

Intraub, H. (1997). The representation of visual scenes. *Trends in Cognitive Sciences*, 1(6), 217–222. DOI: 10.1016/S1364-6613(97)01067-X

Jackendoff, R. (1996). How language helps us think. *Pragmatics & Cognition*, 4(1), 1–34. DOI: 10.1075/pc.4.1.03jac

James, T.W., Culham, J., Humphrey, G.K., Milner, A.D., & Goodale, M.A. (2003). Ventral occipital lesions impair object recognition but not object-directed grasping: An fMRI study. *Brain*, 126(11), 2463–2475. DOI: 10.1093/brain/awg248

Kim, C., & Blake, R. (2005). Psychophysical magic: Rendering the visible "invisible". *Trends in Cognitive Sciences*, 9(8), 381–388. DOI: 10.1016/j.tics.2005.06.012

Klein, I., Paradis, A.-L., Poline, J.B., Kosslyn, S.M., & Le Bihan, D. (2000). Transient activity in the human calcarine cortex during visual-mental imagery: An event-related fMRI study. *Journal of Cognitive Neuroscience*, 12(Suppl. 2), 15–23. DOI: 10.1162/089892900564037

Knauff, M., Kassubek, J., Mulack, T., & Greenlee, M.W. (2000). Cortical activation evoked by visual mental imagery as measured by fMRI. *Neuroreport*, 11(18), 3957–3962. DOI: 10.1097/00001756-200012180-00011

Ko, Y., & Lau, H. (2012). A detection theoretic explanation of blindsight suggests a link between conscious perception and metacognition. *Philosophical Transactions of the Royal Society of London B: Biological Sciences*, 367(1594), 1401–1411. DOI: 10.1098/rstb.2011.0380

Koch, C. (2004). *The quest for consciousness: A neurobiological approach*. Englewood, CO: Roberts & Company.

Koch, C., & Hepp, K. (2006). Quantum mechanics in the brain. *Nature*, 440(7084), 611. DOI: 10.1038/440611a

Koch, C., & Tsuchiya, N. (2007). Attention and consciousness: Two distinct brain processes. *Trends in Cognitive Sciences*, 11(1), 16–22. DOI: 10.1016/j.tics.2006.10.012

Koch, C., & Tsuchiya, N. (2012). Attention and consciousness: Related yet different. *Trends in Cognitive Sciences*, 16(2), 103–104. DOI: 10.1016/j.tics.2011.11.012

Kolb, F.C., & Braun, J. (1995). Blindsight in normal observers. *Nature*, 377(6547), 336–338. DOI: 10.1038/377336a0

Kornbrot, D.E. (2006). Signal detection theory, the approach of choice: Model-based and distribution-free measures and evaluation. *Perception & Psychophysics*, 68(3), 393–414. DOI: 10.3758/BF03193685

Kosslyn, S.M., Thompson, W.L., Kim, I.J., & Alpert, N.M. (1995). Topographical representations of mental images in primary visual cortex. *Nature*, 378(6556), 496–498. DOI: 10.1038/378496a0

Kouider, S., De Gardelle, V., Sackur, J., & Dupoux, E. (2010). How rich is consciousness? The partial awareness hypothesis. *Trends in Cognitive Sciences*, 14(7), 301–307. DOI: 10.1016/j.tics.2010.04.006

Kouider, S., & Dehaene, S. (2007). Levels of processing during non-conscious perception: A critical review of visual masking. *Philosophical Transactions of the Royal Society of London B: Biological Sciences*, 362(1481), 857–875. DOI: 10.1098/rstb.2007.2093

Kunimoto, C., Miller, J., & Pashler, H. (2001). Confidence and accuracy of near-threshold discrimination responses. *Consciousness and Cognition*, 10(3), 294–340. DOI: 10.1006/ccog.2000.0494

Lamme, V.A.F. (1995). The neurophysiology of figure-ground segregation in primary visual cortex. *Journal of Neuroscience*, 15(2), 1605–1615.

Lamme, V. A. F. (2003). Why visual attention and awareness are different. *Trends in Cognitive Sciences*, 7(1), 12–18. DOI: 10.1016/S1364-6613(02)00013-X

Lamme, V. A. F. (2004). Separate neural definitions of visual consciousness and visual attention: A case for phenomenal awareness. *Neural Networks*, 17(5–6), 861–872. DOI: 10.1016/j.neunet.2004.02.005

Lamme, V. A. F. (2006). Towards a true neural stance on consciousness. *Trends in Cognitive Sciences*, 10(11), 494–501. DOI: 10.1016/j.tics.2006.09.001

Lamme, V. A. F. (2010). How neuroscience will change our view on consciousness. *Cognitive Neuroscience*, 1(3), 204–220. DOI: 10.1080/17588921003731586

Lamme, V. A. F., & Roelfsema, P. R. (2000). The distinct modes of vision offered by feedforward and recurrent processing. *Trends in Neurosciences*, 23(11), 571–579. DOI: 10.1016/S0166-2236(00)01657-X

Lamme, V. A. F., Supèr, H., & Spekreijse, H. (1998). Feedforward, horizontal, and feedback processing in the visual cortex. *Current Opinion in Neurobiology*, 8(4), 529–535. DOI: 10.1016/S0959-4388(98)80042-1

Lamme, V. A. F., Zipser, K., & Spekreijse, H. (2002). Masking interrupts figure-ground signals in V1. *Journal of Cognitive Neuroscience*, 14(7), 1044–1053. DOI: 10.1162/089892902320474490

Landman, R., Spekreijse, H., & Lamme, V. A. F. (2003). Large capacity storage of integrated objects before change blindness. *Vision Research*, 43(2), 149–164. DOI: 10.1016/S0042-6989(02)00402-9

Levi, D. M. (2008). Crowding – An essential bottleneck for object recognition: A mini-review. *Vision Research*, 48(5), 635–654. DOI: 10.1016/j.visres.2007.12.009

Levine, J. (1983). Materialism and qualia: The explanatory gap. *Pacific Philosophical Quarterly*, 64(4), 354–361.

Luck, S. J., & Vogel, E. K. (1997). The capacity of visual working memory for features and conjunctions. *Nature*, 390(6657), 279–281. DOI: 10.1038/36846

Mack, A. (2003). Inattentional blindness: Looking without seeing. *Current Directions in Psychological Science*, 12(5), 180–184. DOI: 10.1111/1467-8721.01256

Mack, A., & Rock, I. (1998). *Inattentional blindness*. Cambridge, MA: MIT Press.

Macknik, S. L. (2006). Visual masking approaches to visual awareness. *Progress in Brain Research*, 155, 177–215. DOI: 10.1016/S0079-6123(06)55011-3

Macmillan, N. A., & Creelman, D. C. (1991). *Detection theory: A user's guide*. Cambridge, MA: Cambridge University Press.

Maniscalco, B., & Lau, H. (2012). A signal detection theoretic approach for estimating metacognitive sensitivity from confidence ratings. *Consciousness and Cognition*, 21(1), 422–430. DOI: 10.1016/j.concog.2011.09.021

Marcel, A. J. (1983). Conscious and unconscious perception: Experiments on visual masking and word recognition. *Cognitive Psychology*, 15(2), 197–237. DOI: 10.1016/0010-0285(83)90009-9

Marchetti, G. (2012). Against the view that consciousness and attention are fully dissociable. *Frontiers in Psychology*, 3, 36. DOI: 10.3389/fpsyg.2012.00036

Martens, S., & Wyble, B. (2010). The attentional blink: Past, present, and future of a blind spot in perceptual awareness. *Neuroscience and Biobehavioral Reviews*, 34(6), 947–957. DOI: 10.1016/j.neubiorev.2009.12.005

Maunsell, J. H. R., & Newsome, W. T. (1987). Visual processing in monkey extrastriate cortex. *Annual Review of Neuroscience*, 10, 363–401. DOI: 10.1146/annurev.ne.10.030187.002051

McFadden, J. (2002a). Synchronous firing and its influence on the brains electromagnetic field. *Journal of Consciousness Studies*, 9(4), 23–50.
McFadden, J. (2002b). The conscious electromagnetic information (Cemi) field theory: The hard problem made easy? *Journal of Consciousness Studies*, 9(8), 45–60.
Merigan, W. H., & Maunsell, J. H. (1993). How parallel are the primate visual pathways? *Annual Review of Neuroscience*, 16, 369–402. DOI: 10.1146/annurev.ne.16.030193.002101
Merikle, P., Smilek, D., & Eastwood, J. (2001). Perception without awareness: Perspectives from cognitive psychology. *Cognition*, 79(1–2), 115–134. DOI: 10.1016/S0010-0277(00)00126-8
Mesulam, M. M. (1998). From sensation to cognition. *Brain*, 121(6), 1013–1052. DOI: 10.1093/brain/121.6.1013
Miller, S. M. (2001). Binocular rivalry and the cerebral hemispheres: With a note on the correlates and constitution of visual consciousness. *Brain and Mind*, 2(1), 119–149. DOI: 10.1023/A:1017981619014
Miller, S. M. (2007). On the correlation/constitution distinction problem (and other hard problems) in the scientific study of consciousness. *Acta Neuropsychiatrica*, 19(3), 159–176. DOI: 10.1111/j.1601-5215.2007.00207.x
Miller, S. M. (Ed.). (2013). *The constitution of visual consciousness: Lessons from binocular rivalry*. Advances in Consciousness Research (Vol. 90). Amsterdam, The Netherlands: John Benjamins Publishing Company. DOI: 10.1075/aicr.90
Milner, A., & Goodale, M. A. (1993). Separate visual pathways for perception and action. *Progress in Brain Research*, 95, 317–337. DOI: 10.1016/S0079-6123(08)60379-9
Mishkin, M., & Ungerleider, L. G. (1982). Contribution of striate inputs to the visuospatial functions of parieto-preoccipital cortex in monkeys. *Behavioural Brain Research*, 6(1), 57–77. DOI: 10.1016/0166-4328(82)90081-X
Moutoussis, K., & Zeki, S. (1997a). A direct demonstration of perceptual asynchrony in vision. *Proceedings of the Royal Society of London B: Biological Sciences*, 264(1380), 393–399. DOI: 10.1098/rspb.1997.0056
Moutoussis, K., & Zeki, S. (1997b). Functional segregation and temporal hierarchy of the visual perceptive systems. *Proceedings of the Royal Society of London B: Biological Sciences*, 264(1387), 1407–1414. DOI: 10.1098/rspb.1997.0196
Moutoussis, K., & Zeki, S. (2002). The relationship between cortical activation and perception investigated with invisible stimuli. *Proceedings of the National Academy of Sciences USA*, 99(14), 9527–9532. DOI: 10.1073/pnas.142305699
Nagel, T. (1974). What is it like to be a bat? *Philosophical Review*, 83(4), 435–450. DOI: 10.2307/2183914
Nakamura, K., Dehaene, S., Jobert, A., Le Bihan, D., & Kouider, S. (2007). Task-specific change of unconscious neural priming in the cerebral language network. *Proceedings of the National Academy of Sciences USA*, 104(49), 19643–19648. DOI: 10.1073/pnas.0704487104
Oizumi, M., Albantakis, L., & Tononi, G. (2014). From the phenomenology to the mechanisms of consciousness: Integrated Information Theory 3.*0*. *PLoS Computational Biology*, 10(5), e1003588. DOI: 10.1371/journal.pcbi.1003588
O'Regan, J. K., Rensink, R. A., & Clark, J. J. (1999). Change-blindness as a result of "mudsplashes". *Nature*, 398(6722), 34. DOI: 10.1038/17953
Owen, A. M., & Coleman, M. R. (2008). Detecting awareness in the vegetative state. *Annals of the New York Academy of Sciences*, 1129, 130–138. DOI: 10.1196/annals.1417.018

Owen, A. M., Coleman, M. R., Boly, M., Davis, M. H., Laureys, S., & Pickard, J. D. (2006). Detecting awareness in the vegetative state. *Science*, 313(5792), 1402. DOI: 10.1126/science.1130197

Pelli, D. G., Palomares, M., & Majaj, N. J. (2004). Crowding is unlike ordinary masking: Distinguishing feature integration from detection. *Journal of Vision*, 4(12), 12. DOI: 10.1167/4.12.12

Pelli, D. G., & Tillman, K. A. (2008). The uncrowded window of object recognition. *Nature Neuroscience*, 11(10), 1129–1135. DOI: 10.1038/nn.2187

Persaud, N., McLeod, P., & Cowey, A. (2007). Post-decision wagering objectively measures awareness. *Nature Neuroscience*, 10(2), 257–261. DOI: 10.1038/nn1840

Pinto, Y., Sligte, I. G., Shapiro, K. L., & Lamme, V. A. F. (2013). Fragile visual short-term memory is an object-based and location-specific store. *Psychonomic Bulletin & Review*, 20(4), 732–739. DOI: 10.3758/s13423-013-0393-4

Pöppel, E., Brinkmann, R., Von Cramon, D., & Singer, W. (1978). Association and dissociation of visual functions in a case of bilateral occipital lobe infarction. *Archiv für Psychiatrie und Nervenkrankheiten*, 225(1), 1–21. DOI: 10.1007/BF00367348

Pöppel, E., Held, R., & Frost, D. (1973). Residual visual function after brain wounds involving the central visual pathways in man. *Nature*, 243(5405), 295–296. DOI: 10.1038/243295a0

Posner, M. I. (1994). Attention: The mechanisms of consciousness. *Proceedings of the National Academy of Sciences USA*, 91(16), 7398–7403. DOI: 10.1073/pnas.91.16.7398

Posner, M. I. (2012). Attentional networks and consciousness. *Frontiers in Psychology*, 3, 64. DOI: 10.3389/fpsyg.2012.00064

Potter, M. C., Chun, M. M., Banks, B. S., & Muckenhoupt, M. (1998). Two attentional deficits in serial target search: The visual attentional blink and an amodal task-switch deficit. *Journal of Experimental Psychology: Learning, Memory, and Cognition*, 24(4), 979–992. DOI: 10.1037/0278-7393.24.4.979

Price, N. S. C. (2013). Overview of visual system structure and function. In S. M. Miller (Ed.), *The constitution of visual consciousness: Lessons from binocular rivalry* (pp. 37–76). Advances in Consciousness Research (Vol. 90). Amsterdam, The Netherlands: John Benjamins Publishing Company. DOI: 10.1075/aicr.90.03pri

Raffone, A., & Pantani, M. (2010). A global workspace model for phenomenal and access consciousness. *Consciousness and Cognition*, 19(2), 580–596. DOI: 10.1016/j.concog.2010.03.013

Raymond, J. E., Shapiro, K. L., & Arnell, K. M. (1992). Temporary suppression of visual processing in an RSVP task: An attentional blink? *Journal of Experimental Psychology: Human Perception and Performance*, 18(3), 849–860. DOI: 10.1037/0096-1523.18.3.849

Rees, G., Kreiman, G., & Koch, C. (2002). Neural correlates of consciousness in humans. *Nature Reviews Neuroscience*, 3(4), 261–270. DOI: 10.1038/nrn783

Rees, G., Wojciulik, E., Clarke, K., Husain, M., Frith, C., & Driver, J. (2000). Unconscious activation of visual cortex in the damaged right hemisphere of a parietal patient with extinction. *Brain*, 123(8), 1624–1633. DOI: 10.1093/brain/123.8.1624

Rees, G., Wojciulik, E., Clarke, K., Husain, M., Frith, C., & Driver, J. (2002). Neural correlates of conscious and unconscious vision in parietal extinction. *Neurocase*, 8(5), 387–393. DOI: 10.1093/neucas/8.5.387

Rensink, R. A., O'Regan, J. K., & Clark, J. J. (1997). To see or not to see: The need for attention to perceive changes in scenes. *Psychological Science*, 8(5), 368–373. DOI: 10.1111/j.1467-9280.1997.tb00427.x

Revonsuo, A. (2001). Can functional brain imaging discover consciousness in the brain? *Journal of Consciousness Studies*, 8(3), 3–23.

Roe, A. W., Chelazzi, L., Connor, C. E., Conway, B. R., Fujita, I., Gallant, J. L., Lu, H., & Vanduffel, W. (2012). Toward a unified theory of visual area V4. *Neuron*, 74(1), 12–29. DOI: 10.1016/j.neuron.2012.03.011

Roelfsema, P. R. (2006). Cortical algorithms for perceptual grouping. *Annual Review of Neuroscience*, 29, 203–227. DOI: 10.1146/annurev.neuro.29.051605.112939

Seidemann, E., Poirson, A. B., Wandell, B. A., & Newsome, W. T. (1999). Color signals in area MT of the macaque monkey. *Neuron*, 24(4), 911–917. DOI: 10.1016/S0896-6273(00)81038-7

Seth, A. K. (2009). Explanatory correlates of consciousness: Theoretical and computational challenges. *Cognitive Computation*, 1(1), 50–63. DOI: 10.1007/s12559-009-9007-x

Seth, A. K. (2010). The grand challenge of consciousness. *Frontiers in Psychology*, 1, 5. DOI: 10.3389/fpsyg.2010.00005

Simons, D. J., & Chabris, C. F. (1999). Gorillas in our midst: Sustained inattentional blindness for dynamic events. *Perception*, 28(9), 1059–1074. DOI: 10.1068/p2952

Simons, D. J., & Levin, D. T. (1997). Change blindness. *Trends in Cognitive Sciences*, 1(7), 261–267. DOI: 10.1016/S1364-6613(97)01080-2

Simons, D. J., & Rensink, R. A. (2005). Change blindness: Past, present, and future. *Trends in Cognitive Sciences*, 9(1), 16–20. DOI: 10.1016/j.tics.2004.11.006

Sligte, I. G., Scholte, H. S., & Lamme, V. A. F. (2008). Are there multiple visual short-term memory stores? *PLoS ONE*, 3(2), e1699. DOI: 10.1371/journal.pone.0001699

Sligte, I. G., Scholte, H. S., & Lamme, V. A. F. (2009). V4 activity predicts the strength of visual short-term memory representations. *Journal of Neuroscience*, 29(23), 7432–7438. DOI: 10.1523/JNEUROSCI.0784-09.2009

Sligte, I. G., Wokke, M. E., Tesselaar, J. P., Scholte, H. S., & Lamme, V. A. F. (2010). Magnetic stimulation of the dorsolateral prefrontal cortex dissociates fragile visual short-term memory from visual working memory. *Neuropsychologia*, 49(6), 1578–1588. DOI: 10.1016/j.neuropsychologia.2010.12.010

Sperling, G. (1960). Negative afterimage without prior positive image. *Science*, 131(3413), 1613–1614. DOI: 10.1126/science.131.3413.1613

Stoerig, P., & Cowey, A. (2007). Blindsight. *Current Biology*, 17(19), R822–R824. DOI: 10.1016/j.cub.2007.07.016

Tononi, G. (2004). An information integration theory of consciousness. *BMC Neuroscience*, 5, 42. DOI: 10.1186/1471-2202-5-42

Tononi, G. (2008). Consciousness as integrated information: A provisional manifesto. *Biological Bulletin*, 215(3), 216–242. DOI: 10.2307/25470707

Tononi, G., & Edelman, G. M. (1998). Consciousness and complexity. *Science*, 282(5395), 1846–1851. DOI: 10.1126/science.282.5395.1846

Tononi, G., & Koch, C. (2008). The neural correlates of consciousness: An update. *Annals of the New York Academy of Sciences*, 1124, 239–261. DOI: 10.1196/annals.1440.004

Tononi, G., & Sporns, O. (2003). Measuring information integration. *BMC Neuroscience*, 4, 31. DOI: 10.1186/1471-2202-4-31

Tovee, M. J. (1994). How fast is the speed of thought? *Current Biology*, 4(12), 1125–1127. DOI: 10.1016/S0960-9822(00)00253-0

Treue, S. (2003). Visual attention: The where, what, how and why of saliency. *Current Opinion in Neurobiology*, 13(4), 428–432. DOI: 10.1016/S0959-4388(03)00105-3

Tsuchiya, N., & Koch, C. (2005). Continuous flash suppression reduces negative afterimages. *Nature Neuroscience*, 8(8), 1096–1101. DOI: 10.1038/nn1500

van Boxtel, J. J. A., Tsuchiya, N., & Koch, C. (2010a). Consciousness and attention: On sufficiency and necessity. *Frontiers in Psychology*, 1, 217. DOI: 10.3389/fpsyg.2010.00217

van Boxtel, J. J. A., Tsuchiya, N., & Koch, C. (2010b). Opposing effects of attention and consciousness on afterimages. *Proceedings of the National Academy of Sciences USA*, 107(19), 8883–8888. DOI: 10.1073/pnas.0913292107

Vandenbroucke, A. R., Sligte, I. G., & Lamme, V. A. F. (2011). Manipulations of attention dissociate fragile visual short-term memory from visual working memory. *Neuropsychologia*, 49(6), 1559–1568. DOI: 10.1016/j.neuropsychologia.2010.12.044

Wallis, T. S. A., & Bex, P. J. (2011). Visual crowding is correlated with awareness. *Current Biology*, 21(3), 254–258. DOI: 10.1016/j.cub.2011.01.011

Watanabe, M., Cheng, K., Murayama, Y., Ueno, K., Asamizuya, T., Tanaka, K., & Logothetis, N. (2011). Attention but not awareness modulates the BOLD signal in the human V1 during binocular suppression. *Science*, 334(6057), 829–831. DOI: 10.1126/science.1203161

Weiskrantz, L., Barbur, J. L., & Sahraie, A. (1995). Parameters affecting conscious versus unconscious visual discrimination with damage to the visual cortex (V1). *Proceedings of the National Academy of Sciences USA*, 92(13), 6122–6126. DOI: 10.1073/pnas.92.13.6122

Weiskrantz, L., Warrington, E. K., Sanders, M. D., & Marshall, J. (1974). Visual capacity in the hemianopic field following a restricted occipital ablation. *Brain*, 97(4), 709–728. DOI: 10.1093/brain/97.1.709

Whitney, D., & Levi, D. M. (2011). Visual crowding: A fundamental limit on conscious perception and object recognition. *Trends in Cognitive Sciences*, 15(4), 160–168. DOI: 10.1016/j.tics.2011.02.005

Wilke, M., Logothetis, N. K., & Leopold, D. A. (2003). Generalized flash suppression of salient visual targets. *Neuron*, 39(6), 1043–1052. DOI: 10.1016/j.neuron.2003.08.003

Wolfe, J. M. (1984). Reversing ocular dominance and suppression in a single flash. *Vision Research*, 24(5), 471–478. DOI: 10.1016/0042-6989(84)90044-0

Zeki, S. (2001). Localization and globalization in conscious vision. *Annual Review of Neuroscience*, 24, 57–86. DOI: 10.1146/annurev.neuro.24.1.57

Zeki, S. (2008). The disunity of consciousness. *Progress in Brain Research*, 168, 11–18. DOI: 10.1016/S0079-6123(07)68002-9

Zeki, S., & Bartels, A. (1998a). The autonomy of the visual systems and the modularity of conscious vision. *Philosophical Transactions of the Royal Society of London B: Biological Sciences*, 353(1377), 1911–1914. DOI: 10.1098/rstb.1998.0343

Zeki, S., & Bartels, A. (1998b). The asynchrony of consciousness. *Proceedings of the Royal Society of London B: Biological Sciences*, 265(1405), 1583–1585. DOI: 10.1098/rspb.1998.0475

Zeki, S., & ffytche, D. H. (1998). The Riddoch syndrome: Insights into the neurobiology of conscious vision. *Brain*, 121(1), 25–45. DOI: 10.1093/brain/121.1.25

Zipser, K., Lamme, V. A. F., & Schiller, P. H. (1996). Contextual modulation in primary visual cortex. *Journal of Neuroscience*, 16(22), 7376–7389.

The scientific study of coma and related states

Vanessa Charland-Verville, Audrey Vanhaudenhuyse,
Steven Laureys and Olivia Gosseries*
Coma Science Group, Cyclotron Research Centre and Neurology Department, University Hospital of Liège and University of Liège, Liège

The past 15 years have provided an unprecedented collection of discoveries that bear upon our scientific understanding of consciousness. Taken together, recent studies show that awareness is an emergent property of the collective behavior of frontoparietal top-down connectivity. Within this network, external (sensory) awareness depends on lateral prefrontal/parietal cortices while internal (self) awareness correlates with precuneal/mesiofrontal midline activity. An improved assessment of brain function in coma and related states is not only changing nosology and medical care but also offers a better-documented diagnosis and prognosis and helps to further identify the neural correlates of human consciousness. This chapter provides an overview of the scientific study of coma and related states at the macroscopic systems level.

1. The concept of consciousness

Several questions arise when we consider the concept of consciousness: how is it that we are aware? What are the properties that allow such consciousness? A broad definition of consciousness would be that it corresponds to a state of awareness of the self and surroundings allowing a subject to develop interactions with different stimuli. According to Searle (2000), conscious experience is characterized by three interdependent and essential properties: the qualitative aspect (sensations related to an experience), the subjective aspect (experience in the first person) and appearance of unity

---

* We thank Erik Ziegler and Pasquale Charland for their help in finalizing the manuscript. This work was funded by the Belgian National Funds for Scientific Research (FNRS), Fonds Léon Fredericq, James S. McDonnell Foundation; Mind Science Foundation; European Commission (Mindbridge, DISCOS, DECODER & COST); Public Utility Foundation "Université Européenne du Travail" and "Fondazione Europea di Ricerca Biomedica". VCV is Research Fellow, AV and OG are PostDoctoral Researchers, and SL is Research Director at FNRS. AV is also in Department of Algology and Palliative Care.

DOI 10.1075/aicr.92.03cha

(unified and integrated framework). Other factors specific to the subject may also play a role in conscious experience, such as intentionality, mood, personality, genetic properties, etc. (Baars, 2002, 2005).

From a neuroanatomical point of view, it appears that consciousness is an emergent property of functional connectivity between particular cortical regions within the global neuronal workspace or the fronto-parietal network (Baars, 2005; Dehaene & Changeux, 2011) (see Figures 2 and 4). Neuroimaging studies have also highlighted the importance of thalamo-cortical functional connectivity, especially thalamo-cortical loops, in the emergence of awareness (Edelman & Tononi, 2000). Since the last decade, consciousness theories have emerged from experimental and clinical approaches with healthy subjects and patients with disorders of consciousness (DOC). Of particular interest, the integrated information theory of consciousness (Tononi, 2008, 2012) suggests that awareness depends on the brain's capacity to sustain complex patterns of internal communication between specific regions; to interact as a single network (integration), as well as to choose from a large amount of available responses (information).

For clinicians and neuroscientists, consciousness can be reduced into two key components: wakefulness (i.e., the level of arousal) and awareness (i.e., the level of conscious experience) (Zeman, 2001). Arousal (or wakefulness) is determined by the presence of eye opening, muscle tone and of an electroencephalogram trace characterized by rapid frequency (for a review see (Damasio & Meyer, 2009). Arousal is seen as a prerequisite for higher-level brain functioning. The modulation of wakefulness depends on the integrity of the brainstem and thalamus as well as their cortical projections (Steriade, 1996; Vogt & Laureys, 2005). In turn, the level of awareness is assessed with the patient's active participation in the manifestation of directed behaviors in response to different stimuli or commands (Majerus, Gill-Thwaites, Andrews, & Laureys, 2005). From a neurochemical point of view, arousal or wakefulness is mediated by a complex network encompassing cholinergic reticulothalamic projections, glutaminergic thalamocortical projections, and reticulocortical projections (a network of dopaminergic, noradrenergic, serotonergic, and cholinergic projections) (Jones, 2003; Schwartz & Roth, 2008). Awareness, on the other hand, involves the activity of a widespread thalamo-cortical and fronto-parietal network. Behaviorally, awareness can be inferred from following commands or non-reflex behaviors (Laureys, Faymonville, Goldman, et al., 2000). In general, these two components are positively correlated: the more you are awake, the more you are conscious. For example, patients in a coma or general anesthesia are neither awake nor aware. However, other clinical conditions such as the unresponsive wakefulness syndrome (UWS/VS; previously referred to as vegetative state), minimally conscious state (MCS), akinetic mutism, grand mal seizures and sleepwalking show a dissociation between wakefulness and awareness. In these states, patients show either a normal level of arousal while being totally unaware or present a fluctuating level of both conditions (i.e., MCS and akinetic mutism state) (Laureys, 2005). It is also possible to observe the opposite dissociation in rapid eye movement (REM) sleep (Laureys, 2005) where the subjects report conscious experience in the absence of responsiveness (see Figure 1).

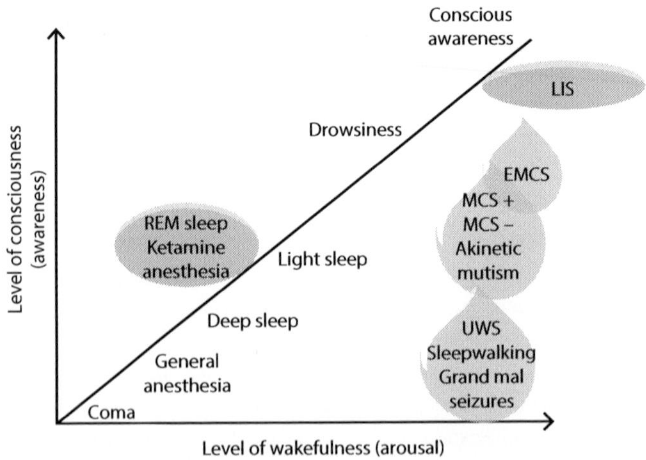

Figure 1. The two main components of consciousness: wakefulness (the level of arousal) and awareness (the level of consciousness).

UWS = unresponsive wakefulness syndrome
MCS– = minimally conscious minus
MCS+ = minimally conscious plus
EMCS = emergence from minimally conscious state
LIS = locked-in syndrome (Adapted from S. Laureys, 2005, *Trends Cogn Sci*, 9:556–559.)

Awareness can further be divided into two anti-correlated brain networks, namely the external conscious content, resulting from our experience of the outside world, and the internal conscious content, referring to introspection and self-consciousness states. Internal content also includes the sum of all cognitive and affective responses sustained by the cerebral cortex (James, 1890; Posner, Saper, Schiff, & Plum, 2007) (see Figure 2). External awareness is associated with the activation of dorsolateral prefrontal cortices and posterior parietal cortices while the internal awareness network is associated with activity related to midline posterior cingulate cortices/precuneus and anterior cingulate/medial prefrontal cortices. Conscious patients show signs of arousal and purposeful contextual behaviors reflecting the presence of social and emotional feelings and the ability to orient their attention to environmental stimuli (Damasio & Meyer, 2009). The inner content of consciousness is, however, more difficult to identify in DOC patients as they cannot communicate. To address this issue, researchers work with healthy controls that are able to give a feedback and thus allows direct reportability of the conscious experience's content (Dehaene & Naccache, 2001).

Neuroimaging and electrophysiological studies of coma, sleep and anesthesia have highlighted the relationships between awareness and: (1) global brain function; (2) regional brain function; (3) changes in functional connectivity; (4) primary versus associative cortical activation in response to external stimuli (Laureys & Schiff, 2012). Of clinical importance, this knowledge now allows improving diagnosis of patients with DOC, which remains very challenging at the bedside. The purposes of

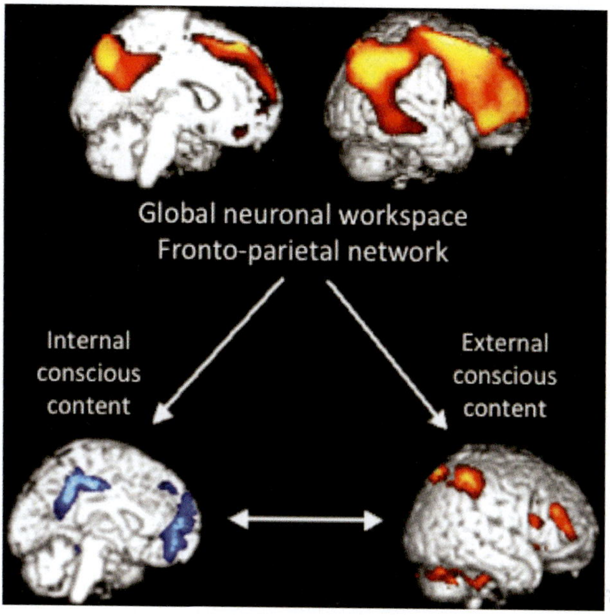

Figure 2. The fronto-parietal network encompassing midline (i.e., anterior cingulate/mesiofrontal and precuneus/posterior cingulate cortices) and lateral (i.e., prefrontal and posterior parietal) associative cortices whose activity is linked with conscious awareness. Within this widespread network, two separate awareness systems can be identified: internal and external. Internal network encompasses the midline precuneus/posterior cingulate and mesiofrontal/anterior cingulate cortices and is linked to stimulus-independent and self-related thoughts. External awareness network encompasses lateral parietal and dorsolateral prefrontal cortices and is linked with stimulus-dependent or perceptual awareness of the environment. (Adapted from Boly et al., 2008, *Hum Brain Mapp*, 29:868–874.)

this chapter are to review brain function in DOC from both a clinical and a neuroscience perspective at a macroscopic level, and to discuss parallel findings from other states of altered consciousness such as sleep and anesthesia.

2. Pathological, pharmacological and physiological states of altered consciousness

2.1 Disorders of consciousness

2.1.1 *Clinical entities*

When surviving a severe brain insult, patients are usually plunged in a period of unconsciousness referred to as "coma" where they are totally unarousable and unconscious (Posner et al., 2007). This period is transient and after some days or weeks, patients may evolve to brain death or show a more favorable outcome. When physicians observe the return of arousal without the presence of awareness, patients are diagnosed as being in an UWS/VS (Laureys et al., 2010). UWS/VS is considered irreversible 12 months after a traumatic etiology and 3 months after an anoxic etiology. After that temporal window, the chances of recovering signs of consciousness are close to zero (Multi-Society Task Force on PVS, 1994). The perplexity that arises from such a paradoxical condition – a person completely aroused but totally unaware – yields a lot of ethical debates and raises important questions about ending a patient's life (Demertzi et al., 2012). In our quest for a better understanding of DOC and to provide better decision-making capabilities for physicians and families, the UWS/VS condition offers a unique opportunity to study the neural correlates of (un)consciousness. Indeed, as mentioned previously, these patients represent a dissociation between the two main components of consciousness (i.e., arousal and awareness) (Jennett & Plum, 1972).

Patients who do recover from UWS/VS classically evolve to an MCS, which is characterized by the presence of inconsistent but reproducible purposeful behaviors (e.g., response to verbal commands, visual pursuit) (Giacino et al., 2002). Although they demonstrate signs of consciousness, they still cannot reliably communicate their thoughts or wishes preventing them from expressing themselves (Giacino et al., 2009). This state has recently been divided into two independent clinical categories based on bedside and neuroimaging evaluations. When patients show responses to command, they receive the diagnosis of MCS *plus* (+), whereas MCS *minus* (–) patients only show non-reflexive signs of consciousness that are not related to language processing (e.g., visual pursuit or localization to pain) (Bruno, Vanhaudenhuyse, Thibaut, Moonen, & Laureys, 2011). Compared to MCS+ patients, MCS– patients may suffer from a significant general brain metabolism decrease in the left hemisphere, particularly in regions that are functionally linked to speech comprehension and production, as well as in premotor and sensorimotor cortices (Bruno, Majerus, et al., 2012). Differential diagnosis of MCS patients is therefore mainly due to the functional recovery (or not) of speech processing areas. The clinical category of MCS patients also include another condition known as *akinetic mutism* (Cairns, Oldfield, Pennybacker, & Whitteridge, 1941). Akinetic mute patients show significantly less behavioral and speech initiation due to brain lesions in mesiofrontal cortices (Giacino, 1997; Laureys, Berré, & Goldman, 2001). Like UWS/VS, MCS may be a chronic or transient state. Acute UWS/VS patients who rapidly evolve to an MCS after their brain insult tend to show a higher rate of functional recovery (Bruno, Gosseries, Vanhaudenhuyse, Chatelle, & Laureys, 2010; Luauté et al., 2010). Patients who emerge or *exit* from an MCS (EMCS) are diagnosed based on the observation of functional communication and/or functional use of objects (Giacino et al., 2002). Although EMCS patients recover a normal level of consciousness, their cognitive abilities (e.g., speech and attentive capacities) may remain impaired due to the primary insult (Giacino et al., 2002). Thus, the differentiation between MCS+ and EMCS is still controversial because significant cognitive impairments make it difficult for the patients to reliably and consistently demonstrate functional behaviors that are required for attributing the diagnosis (Bernat, 2002).

Finally, locked-in syndrome (LIS) or *pseudocoma* patients are often misdiagnosed as being unconscious (Bruno, Bernheim, Schnakers, & Laureys, 2008). After a transient period of coma, they regain normal levels of arousal and awareness, while remaining paralyzed and voiceless due to a ventral pontine lesion producing supranuclear motor de-efferentation (Plum & Posner, 1983). The anatomy of the responsible lesion is such that most of LIS patients are left with a primary method of communication through vertical eye movements (Gosseries, Bruno, Vanhaudenhuyse, Laureys, & Schnakers, 2009). At the bedside, LIS patients can superficially resemble UWS/VS patients or akinetic mutism (Bruno et al., 2009). LIS includes three kinds of clinical entities according to the motor and verbal handicap severity (Bauer, Gerstenbrand, & Rumpl, 1979): the complete LIS is characterized by a complete paralysis including all eye movements; the classical LIS is characterized by a total paralysis with the exception of vertical eye movements and blinking; and the incomplete LIS is characterized by the return of some voluntary movements.

More recently, the term *functional LIS* has been introduced to account for patients who show non-behavioral evidence of consciousness and/or communication only when measured via neuroimaging testing (Bruno, Vanhaudenhuyse, et al., 2011; Laureys & Schiff, 2012). Similarly, the terms functional MCS or *non-behavioral* MCS (abbreviated MCS*) have been proposed to account for when bedside examination shows no evidence of consciousness but neurodiagnostic work-up does (Gosseries, Zasler, & Laureys, 2014; Vogel et al., 2013).

2.1.2 *Clinical evaluation of consciousness*

The differential diagnosis in DOC is of major importance for medical, ethical and legal reasons, and it is therefore particularly important to avoid misdiagnosis between conscious and unconscious patients. Indeed, care management and treatment plans will differ significantly for UWS/VS and MCS as the latter are known to show a better recovery rate (Bruno, Ledoux, et al., 2012; Luauté et al., 2010). Misdiagnosis can also lead to critical consequences regarding end-of-life decision-making (Andrews, 2004).

Previous clinical investigations showed an important misdiagnosis rate that can reach up to 40% (Schnakers, Vanhaudenhuyse, et al., 2009). This rate can be attributed to the highly subjective aspect of the assessments and/or of the patients' level of handicap (i.e., spasticity, tracheotomy, impaired cognitive capacities and fluctuating arousal) (Schnakers, 2012). In an effort to provide a more accurate diagnosis, standardized assessment tools have been developed. The first standardized scale that was introduced to evaluate the level of consciousness was the Glasgow Coma Scale (GCS) developed in the 1970s by Teasdale and Jennett (1974). However, despite its international success, clinicians were quickly confronted with the scale's limits. For instance, the verbal component is very difficult or impossible to assess in intubated patients. The scale also does not consider the evaluation of brainstem reflexes, resulting in a significant loss of information for the patients' diagnosis and prognosis (Rowley & Fielding, 1991). This gap was then filled by the Glasgow-Liège Scale (GLS) (Born, 1988). The GLS uses the information of the GCS while adding the evaluation of brainstem reflexes. Recently, the Full Outline of UnResponsiveness (FOUR) scale (Wijdicks, Bamlet, Maramattom, Manno, & McClelland, 2005) was validated and proposed to replace the GCS in acute settings. The FOUR is specifically developed to detect patients with UWS/VS, MCS, LIS, and may also contribute to a brain death diagnosis (Bruno, Ledoux, et al., 2011; Wijdicks et al., 2005). It assesses eye and motor responses, as well as brainstem reflexes and respiration patterns. Visual tracking is also assessed as it is one of the first signs of consciousness reappearing in MCS patients (Giacino et al., 2002). Compared to the GCS/GLS, the FOUR does not include an evaluation of verbal functions. The advantage of the FOUR scale is that it is short to perform and can be easily used in intensive care units (Schnakers et al., 2006).

Among available neurobehavioral scales to assess consciousness, the Coma Recovery Scale-Revised (CRS-R) is considered the most sensitive in detecting UWS/VS and MCS. Because of its high reliability, the use of this scale is recommended in chronic settings (Seel et al., 2010). The CRS-R consists of six subscales (auditory, visual, motor, oro-motor functions as well as communication and arousal) hierarchically organized. The total score is between 0 (coma) and 23 (EMCS). Although standarized scales can increase the accuracy of bedside diagnosis, clinical assessments can still be highly compromised when a patient lacks behavioral responsiveness. Indeed, in some cases, the absence of purposeful behaviors does not necessarily guarantee the absence of awareness (Sanders, Tononi, Laureys, & Sleigh, 2012). Therefore, in order to complement the clinical gold standard, clinicians now turn to neuroimaging technology. In measuring the brain's spontaneous and stimuli-dependent neuronal activity, functional neuroimaging tools offer a straightforward and objective way to measure residual brain functioning in DOC patients, as we will see in Section 3 (Laureys, 2004; Laureys & Schiff, 2012; Schiff, 2006).

2.2 Anesthesia

In surgical settings, it is possible to induce a state of pharmacological coma or reversible altered awareness. Pharmacologically induced states of unconsciousness are commonly referred to as deep sedation or general anesthesia. Sedatives include the classic anesthetic agents (e.g., benzodiazepine, barbiturates, propofol, and halogenated compounds such as desflurane or sevoflurane), the dissociative anesthetic agents (e.g., ketamine, nitrous oxide), and the minimally sedative agents (e.g., alpha 2-adrenergic agonists such as clonidine or dexmedetomidine) (Boly, Sanders, Mashour, & Laureys, 2013; Boveroux et al., 2008). First, classic anesthetic agents are used to induce graded states of sedation and combine alterations of wakefulness and awareness. Second, dissociative anesthetic agents are able to abolish external conscious processes while maintaining internal conscious processes (e.g., dreaming under ketamine). Finally, minimally sedative agents induce graded variations in arousal levels with the possibility of relatively preserved cognitive functions at lower sedation levels (Boveroux et al., 2008). Among the mentioned list above, intravenous propofol is one of the most widely used anesthetic agent in surgical settings to induce a short and reversible state of unconsciousness similar to what is observed in non-REM sleep (Shafer, 1995).

2.3 Sleep

In the study of human consciousness, sleep represents a natural manifestation of arousal and awareness modulations in contrast to what can be observed in DOC or anesthesia (Laureys, 2005). A normal physiological state of unconsciousness (i.e., sleep) refers to a transient loss of arousal and awareness leading to diminished responses to external stimuli, reflected by the closed eyes and muscle inactivity, accompanied by well-defined electroencephalography patterns (e.g., slow waves, spindles) (Riedner et al., 2007). Subjects who are awakened from slow wave sleep (the deepest stage of sleep) tend not to report any conscious experience during that stage, suggesting they were unconscious (Stickgold, Malia, Fosse, Propper, & Hobson, 2001). When subjects are awakened from REM sleep, they usually report conscious experience inferred by the description of vivid narrative dreams (Tononi & Laureys, 2009). Narratives of a conscious experience are reported in approximately 80% of subjects when awakened from the REM sleep stage but also in 23 to 74% of non-REM sleep awakenings, though vivid dreams are more common during REM sleep (Nir & Tononi, 2010; Rechtshaffen, 1973; Siclari, Larocque, Postle, & Tononi, 2013).

In the next section, the neuroimaging studies that have provided insight into brain function in both normal and altered states of consciousness will be discussed (see Figure 3).

3. Functional neuroimaging and neurophysiological markers in altered states of consciousness

3.1 Brain metabolism at rest

3.1.1 *Global brain activity*

[^{18}F]-fluorodeoxyglucose positron emission tomography (FDG-PET) imaging studies in DOC patients have shown a decrease in global metabolic activity of about 25 to 72% of normal levels regardless of the etiology (Gosseries, Bruno, et al., 2011; Laureys, Owen, & Schiff, 2004) while LIS patients tend to show similar metabolic activity when compared to healthy awake controls (Laureys et al., 2005).

Global brain metabolism decrease is however not specific to DOC. Indeed, during slow wave sleep, healthy individuals can show up to 60% of diminished activity while recovering nearly normal waking values during REM sleep (Maquet et al., 1990). Moreover, healthy volunteers under general anesthesia can show a massive decrease that closely resembles UWS/VS and the deep sleep state (Alkire et al., 1999), returning

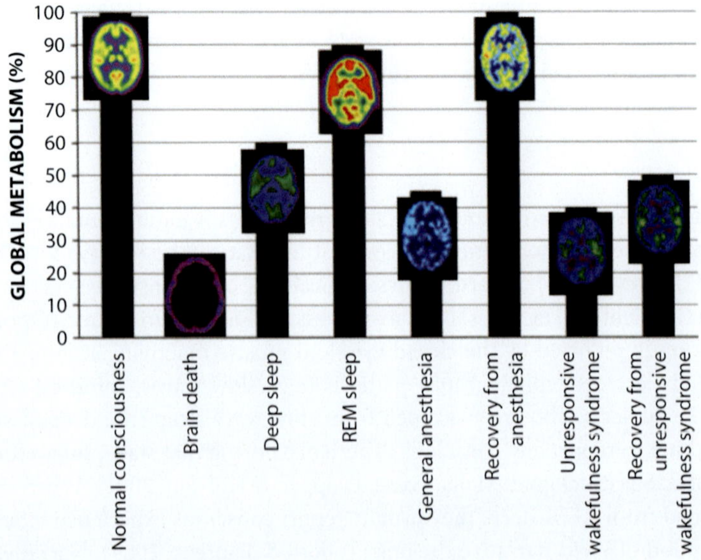

Figure 3. Global cerebral metabolism values in healthy volunteers and in various altered states of consciousness. (Adapted from Laureys et al., 2004, *Lancet Neurol*, 3: 537–546.)

to normal activity when recovering consciousness. However, not all anesthetic agents have the same effect on global metabolism. For example, halothane or isoflurane anesthetics are accompanied by a global diminution of cerebral metabolism from 40% to 50% of normal values, whereas a decrease of only 28% is reported under propofol anesthesia (Boveroux et al., 2008).

Global brain activity measurements using FDG-PET showed that the presence of awareness is not associated with the level of overall brain activity. In fact, in some patients recovering from UWS/VS, no noticeable changes have been observed when looking at global values of brain metabolism (Laureys, Lemaire, Maquet, Phillips, & Franck, 1999), and some awake healthy volunteers may have global brain metabolism values comparable to those observed in UWS/VS patients (Laureys, 2005). Based on these findings, it seems that consciousness is not an emerging property of global brain function but rather arises from the functional connectivity of specific brain regions (Laureys, Faymonville, Goldman, et al., 2000; Laureys, Lemaire, et al., 1999).

3.1.2 *Regional brain activity*

Advanced statistical analyses have allowed for the identification of selective and systematic impairment in UWS/VS patients in a widespread fronto-parietal network encompassing midline (i.e., anterior cingulate/mesiofrontal and precuneus/posterior cingulate cortices) and lateral (i.e., prefrontal and posterior parietal) associative cortices (Laureys, Goldman, et al., 1999; Laureys, Lemaire, et al., 1999; Lull et al., 2010) (see Figure 4). Within this network, of particular interest is the precuneus/posterior

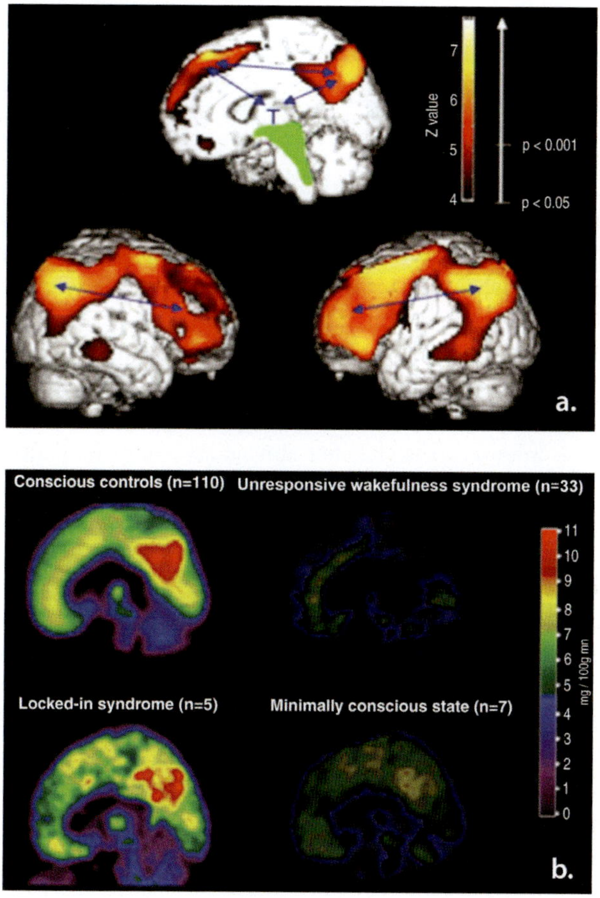

Figure 4. The fronto-parietal network and precuneus/posterior cingulate cortex. (**a**) Functional connectivity between the fronto-parietal network and the thalamus (T). These regions are known to be hypometabolic in unconsciousness and in altered states of consciousness. (Adapted with permission from Laureys et al., 1999, *Neuroimage*, 9: 377–382.) (**b**) The precuneus/posterior cingulate cortex region activation in normal consciousness, locked-in syndrome and disorders of consciousness. This region is thought to be the best indicator of conscious processing as illustrated with the level of glucose metabolism. (Adapted from Laureys et al., 2004, *Lancet Neurol*, 3: 537–546.)

cingulate cortex, which shows the highest energy consumption in awake healthy volunteers and LIS patients, and may therefore represent a key area for identifying conscious processing (Laureys, Owen, & Schiff, 2004). The lack of awareness in UWS/VS would be characterized by a "disconnection syndrome" of cortico-cortical and thalamo-cortical pathways encompassing fronto-parietal cortices (Giacino, Hirsch, Schiff, & Laureys, 2006). These findings led to the hypotheses that consciousness emerges from fronto-parietal connectivity (Baars, Ramsoy, & Laureys, 2003; Laureys, 2005) and that a basic requirement for a conscious experience would be that the specialized brain areas can engage in rapid causal interactions (Dehaene, Changeux, Naccache, Sackur, & Sergent, 2006; Del Cul, Baillet, & Dehaene, 2007; Laureys, 2005; Tononi, 2004).

Recovery from DOC seems to be dependent on functional restoration of this fronto-parietal network and part of its cortico-thalamo-cortical and brainstem connections (Laureys, Faymonville, Luxen, et al., 2000). This was illustrated in a post-traumatic MCS patient where arousal and cognitive functions were enhanced after the application of deep brain stimulation in the intralaminar nuclei of the thalami (Schiff et al., 2007). Recent work has also highlighted the importance of functional connectivity between fronto-parietal cortices and the brainstem (Silva et al., 2010). Based on the latter neuroimaging observations, development of "consciousness classifiers" for clinical use has followed. The classifier aims at assessing automatically the functional integrity of the fronto-parietal network as well as calculating the probability of being either UWS/VS or LIS based on objective FDG-PET data (Phillips et al., 2011). However, the classifier does not yet allow distinguishing between UWS/VS and MCS conditions with high certainty.

Loss of consciousness under anesthesia is also closely linked to the loss of functional integrity of the fronto-parietal network. During pharmacological coma, higher-order associative areas are more likely to be affected by the hypnotic agent than lower-order cortical regions such as the primary sensory cortices (Guldenmund, Vanhaudenhuyse, Boly, Laureys, & Soddu, 2012). Indeed, the fronto-parietal network decreases in activity during general anesthesia using propofol while primary cortices are often spared (Fiset et al., 1999; Kaisti et al., 2003). The precuneus/posterior cingulate cortex is also shown to be highly sensitive to several anesthetic agents such as the inhalational agent sevoflurane and propofol (Fiset et al., 1999; Kaisti et al., 2003). FDG-PET images obtained in healthy volunteers receiving intravenous propofol showed a correlation between the decrease in precuneal/posterior cingulate metabolism level and the deepening of sedation (Bonhomme et al., 2001). Similar effects have been observed with the use of the inert noble gas xenon at doses maintaining loss of consciousness (Rex et al., 2008).

In addition to the effect of anesthetic drugs on the functional activity of the fronto-parietal network and its precuneus/posterior cingulate cortex hub, some researchers have argued that the most consistent effect produced by most anesthetic agents involve thalamic metabolism and cortico-thalamo-cortical connectivity, suggesting that the thalamus may serve as a consciousness switch (Alkire, Haier, & Fallon, 2000; White & Alkire, 2003). This argument is in line with further neuroimaging studies on DOC highlighting the importance of thalamic projections with the fronto-parietal network, and more importantly cortico-thalamic loops, in the emergence of consciousness (Edelman & Tononi, 2000; Laureys, Owen, Schiff, 2004; Tononi, 2004). On the other hand, some authors argue that cortical deactivation seems more important than thalamic deactivation for a pharmacological loss of consciousness (Velly et al., 2007). In line with that hypothesis, thalamic activity was recorded using deep brain stimulation electrodes in patients anesthetized with either propofol or sevoflurane. While the cortical electrical activity changed dramatically during the deepening of the sedation, very little change was recorded in the thalamus (Velly et al., 2007). Similarly, another study showed that loss of consciousness under propofol was accompanied by a decrease in backward cortico-cortical connectivity from frontal to parietal cortices, while thalamo-cortical connectivity remained unchanged (Boly et al., 2012). These results emphasize the importance of cortico-cortical connectivity and communication for maintaining an awareness state and suggest a direct effect of propofol anesthesia on cortical activity.

Data obtained during physiological loss of consciousness are similar to what is observed in pathological and pharmacological states in terms of regional brain function changes (see Figure 5). Indeed, the fronto-parietal network, and more specifically the precuneus/posterior cingulate cortex, also progressively decrease their activity during non-REM sleep (Vogt & Laureys, 2005). Moreover, in some cases of parasomnia like somnambulism (sleepwalking), large areas of frontal and parietal association cortices remain deactivated (Bassetti, Vella, Donati, Wielepp, & Weder, 2000).

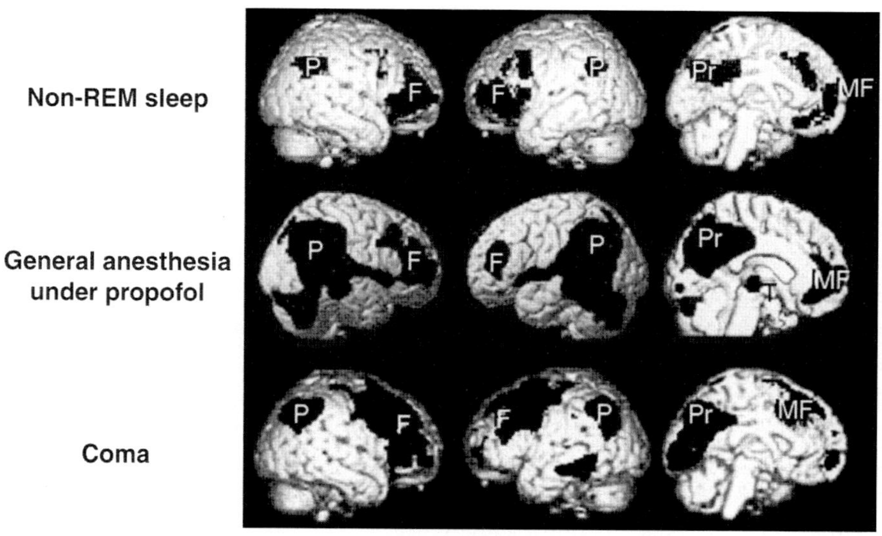

Figure 5. Regional brain metabolism decreases in various states of unconsciousness. F, prefrontal; MF, mesiofrontal; P, posterior parietal cortex; Pr, precuneus/posterior cingulate cortex; T, thalamus. (Adapted from Boveroux et al., 2008, *Int Anesthesiol Clin*, 46: 131–146.)

3.2 Spontaneous brain function

Recently, there has been growing interest in spontaneous brain activity and its relation to cognition and behavior. Pioneering work using functional magnetic resonance imaging (fMRI) has allowed identification of spontaneous brain activity in specific brain regions arranged in particular networks. Among these, the default mode is the most widely studied resting state network and is thought to reflect internal awareness and self-related processes (i.e., spontaneous thoughts, inner speech and mind wandering) (Fox et al., 2005; Heine et al., 2012; Vanhaudenhuyse et al., 2011). It encompasses the precuneus/posterior cingulate cortex, the parieto-temporal junction and the prefrontal cortex (Raichle et al., 2001). The term "default mode" was proposed to account for the consistent brain activity decrease in this particular set of areas during cognitive processes when compared with the passive resting condition (Raichle et al., 2001). In DOC patients, the strength of functional connectivity integrity of most regions of the default mode network (DMN) has been found to linearly correlate with the level of consciousness (Boly et al., 2009; Vanhaudenhuyse et al., 2010) (see Figure 6). More particularly, it was highlighted that the connectivity strength of the precuneus could most reliably differentiate conscious from unconscious patients (Vanhaudenhuyse et al., 2010). The correlation between the level of consciousness and the connectivity strength within the DMN has also been demonstrated in anesthesia (Greicius et al., 2008) and in deep sleep (but not during light sleep) (Horovitz et al., 2009; Larson-Prior et al., 2009).

Additionally, other spontaneous networks have been identified in healthy volunteers during rest. These include "large-scale higher-order" (i.e., bilateral executive control and salience networks) and "lower-level" sensorimotor-sensory (auditory and visual networks) (for a review see Heine et al., 2012). The executive control network (encompassing the bilateral middle, inferior and superior frontal cortices, bilateral inferior parietal lobes, anterior cingulate cortex/supplementary motor area, and bilateral insular cortices) is involved in cognitive functions such as language processing but also in perceptual, somesthetic, and nociception processing (Laird et al., 2011; Smith et al., 2009). This network is also known as the extrinsic system and is modulated via external sensory stimulation and linked to goal-directed behaviors. The executive network is anti-correlated to the DMN's activity (i.e., intrinsic system; see Figure 2). The salience network (encompassing fronto-insular and anterior cingulate cortex with connections to subcortical and limbic structures) is involved in the orientation towards salient emotional stimuli (Seeley et al., 2007), conflict monitoring, information integration, and response selection (Cole & Schneider, 2007; Roberts & Hall, 2008). The salience network has been hypothesized to act like a switch between the internal attention (or DMN activity) and external output (Menon & Uddin, 2010). Moreover, neuroimaging studies on pain in healthy individuals highlighted this network's activation when subjects are confronted to stimulus-induced painful stimulation and during anticipation of pain (Menon & Uddin, 2010; Ploner, Lee, Wiech, Bingel, & Tracey, 2010; Wiech et al., 2010). In line with this observation, it has been suggested that measuring the functional preservation of the salience network

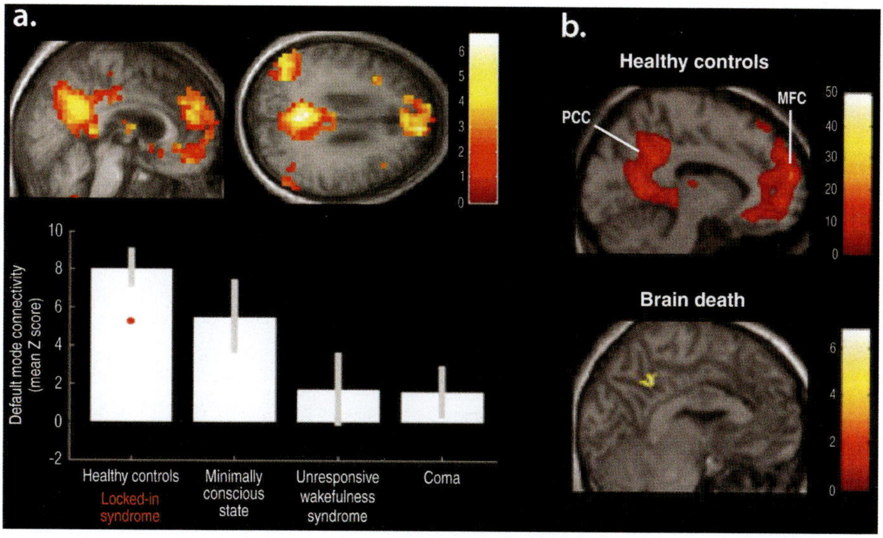

Figure 6. The default mode network encompassing midline fronto-parietal brain regions. **(a)** The default mode network's functional connectivity seems to be correlated with the patient consciousness level as assessed by the Coma Recovery Scale-Revised (adapted from Vanhaudenhuyse et al., 2010, *Brain*, 133: 161–171.) **(b)** Absence of the network's functional connectivity in a brain death patient. PCC, posterior cingulate cortex; MFC, medial frontal cortex. (Adapted from Boly et al., 2009, *Hum Brain Mapp*, 30: 2393–2400.)

could help clinicians to assess the level of discomfort in non-communicative patients (Chatelle et al., 2014). The sensorimotor network (encompassing the supplementary motor area/midcingulate cortex, bilateral primary motor cortex, and bilateral middle frontal gyri) is involved in motor tasks (Biswal, Yetkin, Haughton, & Hyde, 1995). Finally, the auditory network encompasses primary and secondary auditory cortices, including Heschl's gyrus, bilateral superior temporal gyri and posterior insular cortex while the visual network encompasses the primary visual cortices, the middle temporal visual association area and the temporo-occipital junction.

The correlation between the loss of consciousness and decreased connectivity in most areas of the DMN and executive-control networks was objectified during deep sleep (Samann et al., 2011) and general anesthesia (Boveroux et al., 2010). Moreover, negative correlations between DMN and lateral fronto-parietal cortex activity were found to be present during wakefulness but decreased proportionally with loss of consciousness in anesthesia (see Figure 7) (Boveroux et al., 2010). In contrast, the auditory and visual networks functional connectivity does not appear to change during deep sleep or general anesthesia, suggesting that the resting state activity in these areas is present without the need for conscious awareness. These results highlight that unconsciousness could be associated with a breakdown of cerebral temporal architecture

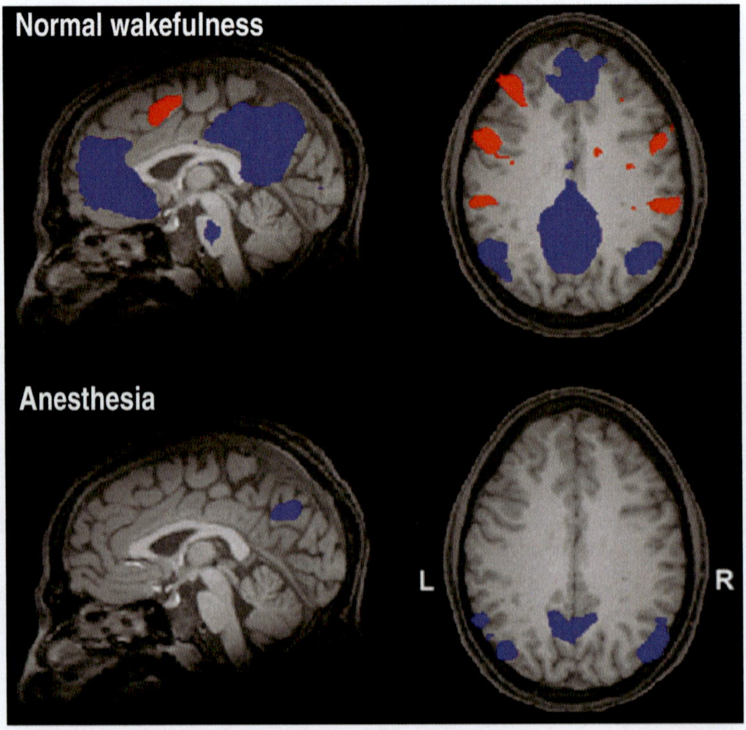

Figure 7. The spontaneous fMRI BOLD activity in the default mode network (regions in blue; reflect self-related thoughts) that anti-correlates with the activity of a lateral fronto-parietal extrinsic system (in red; considered to be linked with conscious perception of the external world). Here, this anti-correlated activity is shown for normal wakefulness and during deep anesthesia. Of note is the absence of the extrinsic fronto-parietal system activity in the condition of altered awareness (anesthesia). (Adapted from Heine et al., 2012, *Front Psychol*, 23: 295.)

modifying networks connectivity and preventing communication between lower-level sensory and higher-order fronto-parietal cortices (Boveroux et al., 2010).

Electroencephalography (EEG) has also been used for the differentiation between UWS/VS and MCS patients. For instance, quantitative EEG, such as EEG-entropy and bispectral measurements, are strongly correlated with the clinical diagnosis obtained with repeated CRS-R assessments at the bedside (Gosseries, Schnakers, et al., 2011; Schnakers, Ledoux, et al., 2008). A recent resting EEG study using coherence measures (i.e., measure of connectivity between two electrodes sites) showed that MCS patients have a better connected network in the theta and alpha bands compared to UWS/VS patients, who show an increase of delta power and a decrease of alpha power when compared with healthy controls (Lehembre, Bruno, et al., 2012).

3.3 Passive brain function during external stimulation

In addition to measuring resting brain function and connectivity, neuroimaging studies have identified brain areas that remain active to external stimulation in unconsciousness. Studies using external (noxious or auditory) stimulation showed robust activation in subcortical and primary sensory cortices in unconscious patients (Laureys & Schiff, 2012). In fact, FDG-PET data obtained in UWS/VS patients, general anesthesia and deep sleep show that external stimulation may still activate primary low-level cortices, but fail to reach higher-order associative areas (Boly et al., 2004, 2008; Boveroux et al., 2008; Laureys, Faymonville, Degueldre, et al., 2000; Maquet, 2010). Further work on pain perception in DOC showed that MCS patients still activate higher-order cortical regions in response to nociceptive stimulation while UWS/VS patients only activate primary sensory cortices, the thalamus and the brainstem (Boly et al., 2008). The similarities between MCS patients and healthy subjects' brain activity stress the importance of pain management in non-communicative patients.

Recent studies using fMRI with passive stimulation paradigms in UWS/VS patients confirm the above FDG-PET results showing functionally disconnected primary sensory cortices from higher-order associative areas regardless of stimulus modality (Coleman et al., 2007; Rodriguez-Moreno, Schiff, Giacino, Kalmar, & Hirsch, 2010). In contrast with what is observed in UWS/VS patients, MCS patients show a more intense and widespread cortical activation (i.e., going from primary sensory cortices to associative cortices and to higher-level frontal areas) during passive stimulation, suggesting more efficient information integration and processing (Bruno, Gosseries, Ledoux, Hustinx, & Laureys, 2011; Di et al., 2007). Studies using stimuli with emotional content, such as babies' cries or the patient's own name, also produce more intense and widespread brain activity in MCS patients than neutral stimuli like 'beeps' (Boly et al., 2004; Laureys, Perrin, et al., 2004). Particularly, the amygdala, which is known to be involved in the recognition and assessment of sensory stimuli with emotional valence, shows more extensive activity when patients hear the voice of a loved one than when hearing a stranger's voice (Bekinschtein et al., 2004). In addition, speech areas are also activated when the narration contains personal information or when a family member reads the text rather than someone unrelated (Schiff et al., 2005). These studies suggest that in MCS patients higher-order auditory processes are involved when hearing stimuli, and that the context and the emotional value influence the intensity of brain activation. Aside from this, it has also been shown that some UWS/VS patients can have atypical brain activity to auditory stimulation. That is, they will show similar patterns of activity as those of MCS patients and controls. This activity has been considered to have a potential prognostic value (Di et al., 2007).

Recordings of cognitive event-related potentials (ERPs) are also used to measure brain activity in response to passive stimulation. ERPs assess electrical brain responses to stimulations across time and can be performed at the patient's bedside. ERPs can either be considered as exogenous or endogenous. Short-latency ERPs (starting between 0 and 100ms) are linked to primary cortices ascending processes and are not necessarily the result of conscious processing, while cognitive or late latency ERPs (starting after 100ms) are thought to reflect cortical and sub-cortical activity including associative areas (Lehembre, Gosseries, et al., 2012). Thus, late latency ERPs are linked to cognitive processing and may be less present, or present but delayed in patients with DOC (Vanhaudenhuyse, Laureys, & Perrin, 2008) and some studies have shown that their presence can be correlated with the recovery of consciousness (for a review see Lehembre, Gosseries, et al., 2012).

In numerous studies, ERPs responses to the subject's own name have been recorded in order to assess integrity of linguistic and self-recognition processes. For instance, the P300 wave (i.e., occurring about 300ms after the presentation of a given stimulus) can be observed in LIS patients (Perrin et al., 2006). In DOC, as expected, the results are less straightforward. It has been shown that MCS patients still elicited P300 responses (although delayed compared to controls) when hearing salient (i.e., own name) or deviant words in a spoken list. Interestingly, 60% of the UWS/VS patients in this study cohort could also produce a P300 response similar to MCS patients when hearing their own name (Perrin et al., 2006). Based on these findings, the authors suggest that the P300 can be informative regarding residual cognitive linguistic processing in non-communicative severely brain damaged patients. However, they emphasize that the passive brain responses elicited in patients cannot yet be distinguished, thus preventing the diagnostic utility of the P300.

As in pathological states, when simple auditory stimuli are presented to the anesthetized subjects under propofol or sevoflurane, extensive decrease of activation in intensity and extent can be observed. Temporal lobes can however still be activated without recruiting higher-level associative cortical regions during unresponsiveness (Heinke et al., 2004; Plourde et al., 2006; Veselis, Feshchenko, Reinsel, Beattie, & Akhurst, 2005). When assessing more complex cognitive functions like language comprehension and semantics, primary brain activation of perceptual processing may remain present during deep sedation but activation in brain areas related to higher-level analysis of the stimuli is again impaired, even at relatively low levels of sedation (Davis et al., 2007; Plourde et al., 2006).

Finally, to complement these approaches, transcranial magnetic stimulation (TMS), together with high-density EEG, has been employed recently to evaluate effective connectivity (i.e., the influence one neural system exerts over another) at the bedside. TMS/EEG measures report that, in UWS/VS patients, a simple and local electrical response is obtained after stimulating the cortical site, indicating a breakdown of effective connectivity like that previously observed in unconscious sleeping or anesthetized subjects (Ferrarelli et al., 2010; Massimini et al., 2005; Rosanova et al., 2012). In MCS patients, TMS/EEG triggers much more complex activations in the brain that involve sequentially distant cortical areas ipsilateral and contralateral to the site of stimulation (see Figure 8), similar to activations recorded in LIS patients (Rosanova et al., 2012). Moreover, a recent TMS-EEG metric has been proposed to differentiate conscious from unconscious states at the individual level (Casali et al., 2013).

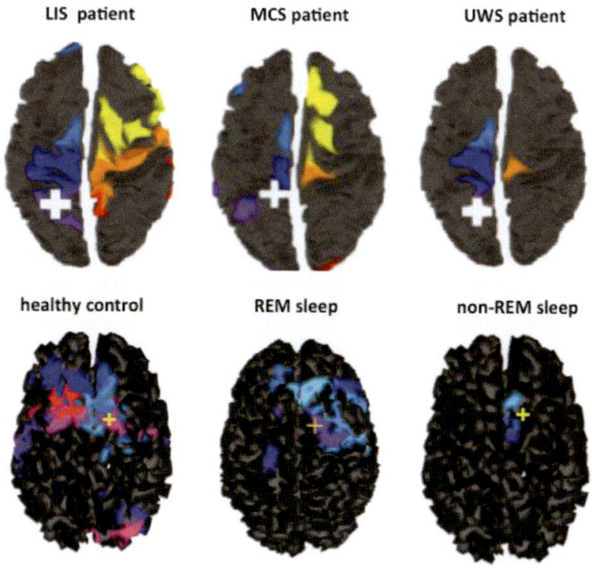

Figure 8. Effective connectivity experiment with the use of TMS/EEG in normal healthy volunteers during wakefulness, in an LIS patient as well as in pathological and physiological altered states of consciousness (LIS, locked-in syndrome; MCS, minimally conscious state; UWS/VS, unresponsive wakefulness syndrome; REM sleep, rapid eye movement sleep; non-REM sleep, non-rapid eye movement sleep). The white and yellow crosses indicate the sites of stimulation. In parallel with the bedside evaluation of consciousness, it can be observed that the TMS-evoked cortical responses are much more widespread in conscious states (LIS, MCS, EMCS) than in unconscious states (UWS/VS). (Adapted from Rosanova et al., 2012, *Brain*, 135: 1308–1320.)

3.4 Active brain function during external stimulation

Contrary to passive paradigms mentioned above, studies using active paradigms allow identifying voluntary or goal-directed responses to specific commands. In some cases, these active procedures can even permit non-communicative and LIS patients to interact more efficiently with their surroundings without requiring any motor or language functions. Some years ago, researchers used an original fMRI active paradigm in a patient diagnosed as UWS/VS. When lying in the scanner, the patient was asked to perform two mental imagery tasks, which were previously validated in a healthy control population (Boly et al., 2007). The patient had to imagine herself playing tennis and wandering around her house when hearing the specific verbal command (Owen et al., 2006). During the scanning session, the patient was able to reliably perform the tasks by voluntarily modulating her brain activity, that is, she could accurately activate the same brain regions as the healthy control group (i.e., supplementary motor areas for the motor task and parahippocampal gyri for the visuo-spatial task). The same active paradigm was then performed in 54 DOC patients, which enabled measurement of voluntary signs of consciousness in another UWS/VS and 3 MCS patients (Monti et al., 2010). However, it is important to note that in the whole group of MCS patients included in the study, only these 3 MCS patients out of 31 could accurately perform the tasks. This ratio suggests a quite low sensitivity of the technique (Bruno, Gosseries, et al., 2011). This fMRI paradigm has been adapted to allow an MCS patient to functionally communicate. Indeed, the patient correctly answered 5 out of 6 autobiographical questions when the investigators asked him to perform the motor imagery task to answer "yes" and to perform the visuo-spatial task to answer "no" (Monti et al., 2010).

Active fMRI paradigms are not easily accessible for most patients and this technique can be expensive and sometimes invasive with long scanning sessions. Therefore, active ERPs represent a complementary approach to record voluntary brain processes with the advantage of being transportable to the bedside. Using an auditory paradigm presenting a list of spoken names including the subject's own name, DOC patients were first asked to passively listen to this list (as reported in the study of Perrin et al., 2006, in Section 3.3) and second to count the number of times they heard their own name or an unfamiliar name. The results showed that the P300 wave was of greater amplitude when MCS patients had to count, especially when counting their own name as compared to the passive condition (Schnakers, Perrin, et al., 2008). This active paradigm also allowed identifying signs of conscious information processing in a patient diagnosed as being in a coma but who was actually a case of complete LIS (Schnakers, Perrin, et al., 2009) (see Figure 9). Similarly, conscious cognitive processes

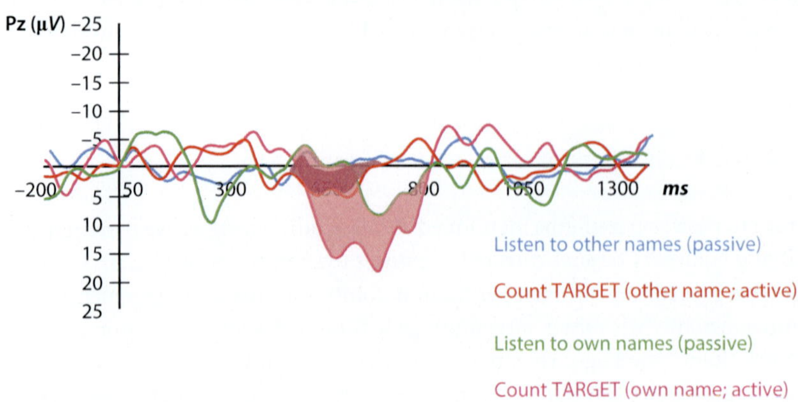

Figure 9. Cognitive event-related potentials (P300) after listening to the subject's own name or another name (passive condition) and after counting the subject's own name or another name (active condition) in an LIS patient who was mistakenly diagnosed as being in a coma. The active version of the paradigm elicits a greater brain response than when only listening to the stimuli. (Adapted from Schnakers et al., 2008, *Neurology*, 71:1614–1620.)

were detected in a comparable EEG study in 3 out of 16 UWS/VS patients where they were asked to imagine movements of their right hand and toes (Cruse et al., 2011). fMRI and EEG active paradigms can therefore detect signs of consciousness in several UWS/VS patients (Naci, Cusack, Jia, & Owen, 2013).

4. Pharmacological vs. physiological altered states of consciousness

It has been suggested that anesthesia is comparable to sleep and that common mechanisms could be involved in the loss of consciousness (Alkire, Hudetz, & Tononi, 2008). Indeed, sleep states and general anesthesia do share electroencephalographic and behavioral features. For instance, as in DOC, sensory input and pain perception are attenuated and there is an inhibition of motor output in both conditions (Campagna, Miller, & Forman, 2003). EEG recordings in deep sleep and under propofol show an increase of activity in low-frequency bands in median frontal areas compared to waking state (Clement et al., 2008; Sleigh, Andrzejowski, Steyn-Ross, & Steyn-Ross, 1999).

TMS/EEG studies have shown that the loss of consciousness during anesthesia and deep sleep could be linked to a decrease in effective connectivity (Ferrarelli et al., 2010; Massimini, Boly, Casali, Rosanova, & Tononi, 2009; Massimini et al., 2005, 2010). Decrease in effective connectivity during deep sleep and anesthesia reflects an alteration in the brain's ability to integrate information that could therefore reduce the level of consciousness (Tononi, 2008). In contrast, during REM sleep, effective connectivity is similar to what is observed in wakefulness (Massimini et al., 2010). In fact, in normal awake and in REM sleep conditions, the application of TMS produced a complex, long-range activation between cortical areas, as observed in MCS and LIS patients. In both non-REM sleep and anesthesia, TMS triggered local and stereotypical positive-negative slow wave responses (Massimini et al., 2010).

Sleep studies results have also been paralleled with anesthesia. For instance, it has been previously shown that propofol's effect would interact with numerous brain regions that are implicated in the initiation and maintenance of sleep state (Lydic & Baghdoyan, 2005). In parallel with cortical activity, subcortical neuronal networks involved in the generation of sleep (i.e., pontine cholinergic, brainstem noradrenergic, hypothalamic ventrolateral preoptic nucleus, and tuberomammilar nucleus) may also mediate some anesthetic effects (Campagna et al., 2003; Goodman & Mann, 1967; Keifer, Baghdoyan, & Lydic, 1996). During anesthesia, dreaming can be experienced by the subject and it occurs in at least 27% of patients anesthetized with propofol and in 28% of patients undergoing desflurane anesthesia (Leslie et al., 2009). Given the amnesic effects of anesthetic agents, these data likely underestimate the true prevalence of dreaming because the reports required the recall of dreams. In a recent study of dreaming under anesthesia experience of surgery was not described by any patient who reported dreams (Leslie et al., 2009). This can be explained by the fact that anesthesia is a state of disconnected consciousness, similar to REM sleep, where experience is insulated from the environment.

Despite some similarities in brain mechanisms, anesthesia and sleep are clearly not identical conditions and differ in their underlying biological background and neural correlates. On the one hand, as opposed to natural sleep, anesthesia induces dramatic changes in airway muscle control, decreasing both ventilatory and upper airway dilator muscle activity (Eikermann et al., 2009). On the other hand, while the loss of consciousness in non-REM sleep and anesthesia is characterized by an increase in signal intensity within the frontal cortex in the delta frequency band, anesthesia induces an increase in signal intensity in the gamma frequency band which is not observed during sleep (Gugino et al., 2001; John & Prichep, 2005). Furthermore, EEG data show that the slow waves recorded from subjects under propofol anesthesia are spatially scattered compared to slow waves recorded during sleep (Ferrarelli et al., 2010). In addition, slow waves recorded during anesthesia tend to include significantly more voxels than cortical slow waves recorded during non-REM sleep (Murphy et al., 2011). Propofol slow waves are also more diffuse and can originate in occipital and temporal cortex, which is usually not the case during sleep (Murphy et al., 2011). Another difference that can be observed is hemispheric lateralization (left>right) during anesthesia, which is less prominent in sleep (Murphy, Riedner, Huber, Massimini, & Ferrarelli, 2009).

The differences observed between the slow waves recorded during sleep and under propofol anesthesia can be explained by the fact that propofol interacts with GABA receptors and it seems unlikely that these receptors reproduce accurately the heterogeneous topography of neuromodulation in the brain during sleep (Veselis et al., 2004).

5. Conclusion

This paper aimed to illustrate parallel findings between pathological, pharmacological and physiological altered states of consciousness with a particular focus on DOC. DOC represent a daily challenge from clinical, ethical and legal perspectives. The misdiagnosis rate in this population is still quite high and occurs most often as the result of failure to detect purposeful movements. Therefore, new solutions, like standardized behavioral scales and neuroimaging testing, have been proposed to achieve better diagnosis. In addition, functional neuroimaging and electrophysiological resting state, passive and active paradigms aim at detecting residual brain function and signs of consciousness. Nevertheless, clinical improvements cannot be achieved without a better comprehension of conscious processing and consciousness recovery mechanisms.

Thus, parallel research on other altered states of consciousness has brought important insights to our understanding of consciousness and validation of findings in DOC. Even though the mechanisms of such altered consciousness are not directly comparable, results obtained in sleep and anesthesia share much in common in terms of brain functional connectivity. For instance, the lack of external and internal awareness is observed not only in UWS/VS patients but also in slow-wave sleep

(Maquet et al., 2005) and in general anesthesia (Kaisti et al., 2003). FDG-PET studies have allowed identifying a systematic regional metabolism decrease in a widespread set of fronto-parietal associative areas in all states of unconsciousness. In line with studies in awake volunteers (Dehaene & Changeux, 2011), these findings emphasize the potential role of fronto-parietal association cortices in the genesis of awareness. fMRI resting state studies show that connectivity in the DMN is reduced under altered states of consciousness, such as sleep, sedation/anesthesia, hypnotic state, and clinical states of DOC (UWS/VS, MCS, coma, and brain death). EEG studies with active paradigms have allowed identifying conscious cognitive processing in non-communicative patients. Because some patients may not be able to accurately process sensory stimuli, complementary TMS/EEG studies show that it is possible to differentiate consciousness from unconsciousness at the individual level through the measure of cortical effective connectivity.

In conclusion, this chapter has summarized and shed light on neural correlates of awareness with the comparison of three principal altered states of consciousness. However, further studies are needed to confirm the similarity of some results and to link anesthesia, slow-wave sleep and unconscious/minimally conscious states. As understanding progresses, clinicians will be aided in terms of diagnosis, prognosis and treatment options (including drug development). Along with the acquisition of new knowledge on consciousness and its disorders, there remains a challenge to translate research from the lab to the bedside, together with an evolving well-defined ethical framework (Fins, 2009; Fins & Schiff, 2010).

References

Alkire, M. T., Haier, R. J., & Fallon, J. H. (2000). Toward a unified theory of narcosis: Brain imaging evidence for a thalamocortical switch as the neurophysiologic basis of anesthetic-induced unconsciousness. *Consciousness and Cognition*, 9(3), 370–386. DOI: 10.1006/ccog.1999.0423

Alkire, M. T., Hudetz, A. G., & Tononi, G. (2008). Consciousness and anesthesia. *Science*, 322(5903), 876–880. DOI: 10.1126/science.1149213

Alkire, M. T., Pomfrett, C. J., Haier, R. J., Gianzero, M. V., Chan, C. M., Jacobsen, B. P., & Fallon, J. H. (1999). Functional brain imaging during anesthesia in humans: Effects of halothane on global and regional cerebral glucose metabolism. *Anesthesiology*, 90(3), 701–709. DOI: 10.1097/00000542-199903000-00011

Andrews, K. (2004). Medical decision making in the vegetative state: Withdrawal of nutrition and hydration. *Neurorehabilitation*, 19(4), 299–304.

Baars, B. J. (2002). The conscious access hypothesis: Origins and recent evidence. *Trends in Cognitive Sciences*, 6(1), 47–52. DOI: 10.1016/S1364-6613(00)01819-2

Baars, B. J. (2005). Global workspace theory of consciousness: Toward a cognitive neuroscience of human experience. *Progress in Brain Research*, 150, 45–53. DOI: 10.1016/S0079-6123(05)50004-9

Baars, B. J., Ramsoy, T. Z., & Laureys, S. (2003). Brain, conscious experience and the observing self. *Trends in Neurosciences*, 26(12), 671–675. DOI: 10.1016/j.tins.2003.09.015

Bassetti, C., Vella, S., Donati, F., Wielepp, P., & Weder, B. (2000). SPECT during sleepwalking. *Lancet*, 356(9228), 484–485. DOI: 10.1016/S0140-6736(00)02561-7

Bauer, G., Gerstenbrand, F., & Rumpl, E. (1979). Varieties of the locked-in syndrome. *Journal of Neurology*, 221(2), 77–91. DOI: 10.1007/BF00313105

Bekinschtein, T., Leiguarda, R., Armony, J., Owen, A., Carpintiero, S., Niklison, J., Sigman, L., Olmos, L., & Manes, F. (2004). Emotion processing in the minimally conscious state. *Journal of Neurology, Neurosurgery and Psychiatry*, 75(5), 788. DOI: 10.1136/jnnp.2003.034876

Bernat, J. L. (2002). Questions remaining about the minimally conscious state. *Neurology*, 58(3), 337–338. DOI: 10.1212/WNL.58.3.337

Biswal, B., Yetkin, F. Z., Haughton, V. M., & Hyde, J. S. (1995). Functional connectivity in the motor cortex of resting human brain using echo-planar MRI. *Magnetic Resonance in Medicine*, 34(4), 537–541. DOI: 10.1002/mrm.1910340409

Boly, M., Coleman, M. R., Davis, M. H., Hampshire, A., Bor, D., Moonen, G., Maquet, P. A., Pickard, J. D., Laureys, S., & Owen, A. M. (2007). When thoughts become action: An fMRI paradigm to study volitional brain activity in non-communicative brain injured patients. *Neuroimage*, 36(3), 979–992. DOI: 10.1016/j.neuroimage.2007.02.047

Boly, M., Faymonville, M.-E., Peigneux, P., Lambermont, B., Damas, P., Del Fiore, G., Degueldre, C., Franck, G., Luxen, A., Lamy, M., Moonen, G., Maquet, P., & Laureys, S. (2004). Auditory processing in severely brain injured patients: Differences between the minimally conscious state and the persistent vegetative state. *Archives of Neurology*, 61(2), 233–238. DOI: 10.1001/archneur.61.2.233

Boly, M., Faymonville, M.-E., Schnakers, C., Peigneux, P., Lambermont, B., Phillips, C., Lancellotti, P., Luxen, A., Lamy, M., Moonen, G., Maquet, P., & Laureys, S. (2008). Perception of pain in the minimally conscious state with PET activation: An observational study. *Lancet Neurology*, 7(11), 1013–1020. DOI: 10.1016/S1474-4422(08)70219-9

Boly, M., Moran, R., Murphy, M., Boveroux, P., Bruno, M.-A., Noirhomme, Q., Ledoux, D., Bonhomme, V., Brichant, J. F., Tononi, G., Laureys, S., & Friston, K. (2012). Connectivity changes underlying spectral EEG changes during propofol-induced loss of consciousness. *Journal of Neuroscience*, 32(20), 7082–7090. DOI: 10.1523/JNEUROSCI.3769-11.2012

Boly, M., Phillips, C., Balteau, E., Schnakers, C., Degueldre, C., Moonen, G., Luxen, A., Peigneux, P., Faymonville, M. E., Maquet, P., & Laureys, S. (2008). Consciousness and cerebral baseline activity fluctuations. *Human Brain Mapping*, 29(7), 868–874. DOI: 10.1002/hbm.20602

Boly, M., Sanders, R. D., Mashour, G. A., & Laureys, S. (2013). Consciousness and responsiveness: Lessons from anaesthesia and the vegetative state. *Current Opinion in Anesthesiology*, 26(4), 444–449. DOI: 10.1097/ACO.0b013e3283628b5d

Boly, M., Tshibanda, L., Vanhaudenhuyse, A., Noirhomme, Q., Schnakers, C., Ledoux, D., Boveroux, P., Garweg, C., Lambermont, B., Phillips, C., Luxen, A., Moonen, G., Bassetti, C., Maquet, P., & Laureys, S. (2009). Functional connectivity in the default network during resting state is preserved in a vegetative but not in a brain dead patient. *Human Brain Mapping*, 30(8), 2393–2400. DOI: 10.1002/hbm.20672

Bonhomme, V., Fiset, P., Meuret, P., Backman, S., Plourde, G., Paus, T., Bushnell, M. C., & Evans, A. C. (2001). Propofol anesthesia and cerebral blood flow changes elicited by vibrotactile stimulation: A positron emission tomography study. *Journal of Neurophysiology*, 85(3), 1299–1308.

Born, J. D. (1988). The Glasgow-Liege Scale. Prognostic value and evolution of motor response and brain stem reflexes after severe head injury. *Acta Neurochirurgica*, 91(1–2), 1–11. DOI: 10.1007/BF01400520

Boveroux, P., Bonhomme, V., Boly, M., Vanhaudenhuyse, A., Maquet, P., & Laureys, S. (2008). Brain function in physiologically, pharmacologically, and pathologically altered states of consciousness. *International Anesthesiology Clinics*, 46(3), 131–146. DOI: 10.1097/AIA.0b013e318181a8b3

Boveroux, P., Vanhaudenhuyse, A., Bruno, M.-A., Noirhomme, Q., Lauwick, S., Luxen, A., Degueldre, C., Plenevaux, A., Schnakers, C., Phillips, C., Brichant, J. F., Bonhomme, V., Maquet, P., Greicius, M. D., Laureys, S., & Boly, M. (2010). Breakdown of within- and between-network resting state functional magnetic resonance imaging connectivity during propofol-induced loss of consciousness. *Anesthesiology*, 113(5), 1038–1053. DOI: 10.1097/ALN.0b013e3181f697f5

Bruno, M., Bernheim, J. L., Schnakers, C., & Laureys, S. (2008). Locked-in: Don't judge a book by its cover. *Journal of Neurology, Neurosurgery and Psychiatry*, 79(1), 2. DOI: 10.1136/jnnp.2007.125294

Bruno, M.-A., Gosseries, O., Ledoux, D., Hustinx, R., & Laureys, S. (2011). Assessment of consciousness with electrophysiological and neurological imaging techniques. *Current Opinion in Critical Care*, 17(2), 146–151. DOI: 10.1097/MCC.0b013e328343476d

Bruno, M.-A., Gosseries, O., Vanhaudenhuyse, A., Chatelle, C., & Laureys, S. (2010). Etat végétatif et état de conscience minimale: Un devenir pire que la mort. In L. Puybasset (Ed.), *Enjeux éthiques en réanimation* (pp. 119–127). Paris: Springer. DOI: 10.1007/978-2-287-99072-4_13

Bruno, M.-A., Ledoux, D., Lambermont, B., Damas, F., Schnakers, C., Vanhaudenhuyse, A., Gosseries, O., & Laureys, S. (2011). Comparison of the Full Outline of UnResponsiveness and Glasgow Liege Scale/Glasgow Coma Scale in an intensive care unit population. *Neurocritical Care*, 15(3), 447–453. DOI: 10.1007/s12028-011-9547-2

Bruno, M.-A., Ledoux, D., Vanhaudenhuyse, A., Gosseries, O., Thibaut, A., & Laureys, S. (2012). Prognosis of patients with altered state of consciousness. In C. Schnakers & S. Laureys (Eds.), *Coma and disorders of consciousness* (pp. 11–23). Paris: Springer-Verlag. DOI: 10.1007/978-1-4471-2440-5_2

Bruno, M.-A., Majerus, S., Boly, M., Vanhaudenhuyse, A., Schnakers, C., Gosseries, O., Boveroux, P., Kirsch, M., Demertzi, A., Bernard, C., Hustinx, R., Moonen, G., & Laureys, S. (2012). Functional neuroanatomy underlying the clinical subcategorization of minimally conscious state patients. *Journal of Neurology*, 259(6), 1087–1098. DOI: 10.1007/s00415-011-6303-7

Bruno, M.-A., Schnakers, C., Damas, F., Pellas, F., Lutte, I., Bernheim, J., Majerus, S., Moonen, G., Goldman, S., & Laureys, S. (2009). Locked-in syndrome in children: Report of five cases and review of the literature. *Pediatric Neurology*, 41(4), 237–246. DOI: 10.1016/j.pediatrneurol.2009.05.001

Bruno, M.-A., Vanhaudenhuyse, A., Thibaut, A., Moonen, G., & Laureys, S. (2011). From unresponsive wakefulness to minimally conscious PLUS and functional locked-in syndromes: Recent advances in our understanding of disorders of consciousness. *Journal of Neurology*, 258(7), 1373–1384. DOI: 10.1007/s00415-011-6114-x

Cairns, H., Oldfield, R. C., Pennybacker, J. B., & Whitteridge, D. (1941). Akinetic mutism with an epidermoid cyst of the third ventricle. *Brain*, 64(4), 273–290. DOI: 10.1093/brain/64.4.273

Campagna, J. A., Miller, K. W., & Forman, S. A. (2003). Mechanisms of actions of inhaled anesthetics. *New England Journal of Medicine*, 348(21), 2110–2124. DOI: 10.1056/NEJMra021261

Casali, A. G., Gosseries, O., Rosanova, M., Boly, M., Sarasso, S., Casali, K. R., Casarotto, S., Bruno, M. A., Laureys, S., Tononi, G., & Massimini, M. (2013). A theoretically based index of consciousness independent of sensory processing and behavior. *Science Translational Medicine*, 5(198), 198ra105. DOI: 10.1126/scitranslmed.3006294

Chatelle, C., Thibaut, A., Bruno, M.-A., Boly, M., Bernard, C., Hustinx, R., Schnakers, C., & Laureys, S. (2014). Nociception coma scale-revised scores correlate with metabolism in the anterior cingulate cortex. *Neurorehabilitation and Neural Repair*, 28(2), 149–152. DOI: 10.1177/1545968313503220

Clement, E. A., Richard, A., Thwaites, M., Ailon, J., Peters, S., & Dickson, C. T. (2008). Cyclic and sleep-like spontaneous alternations of brain state under urethane anaesthesia. *PLoS One*, 3(4), e2004. DOI: 10.1371/journal.pone.0002004

Cole, M. W., & Schneider, W. (2007). The cognitive control network: Integrated cortical regions with dissociable functions. *Neuroimage*, 37(1), 343–360. DOI: 10.1016/j.neuroimage.2007.03.071

Coleman, M. R., Rodd, J. M., Davis, M. H., Johnsrude, I. S., Menon, D. K., Pickard, J. D., & Owen, A. M. (2007). Do vegetative patients retain aspects of language comprehension? Evidence from fMRI. *Brain*, 130(10), 2494–2507. DOI: 10.1093/brain/awm170

Cruse, D., Chennu, S., Chatelle, C., Bekinschtein, T. A., Fernandez-Espejo, D., Pickard, J. D., Laureys, S., & Owen, A. M. (2011). Bedside detection of awareness in the vegetative state: A cohort study. *Lancet*, 378(9809), 2088–2094. DOI: 10.1016/S0140-6736(11)61224-5

Damasio, A., & Meyer, K. (2009). Consciousness: An overview of the phenomenon and of its possible neural basis. In S. Laureys & G. Tononi (Eds.), *The neurology of consciousness: Cogntive neuroscience and neuropathology* (pp. 3–14). Oxford, UK: Elsevier Ltd.

Davis, M. H., Coleman, M. R., Absalom, A. R., Rodd, J. M., Johnsrude, I. S., Matta, B. F., Owen, A. M., & Menon, D. K. (2007). Dissociating speech perception and comprehension at reduced levels of awareness. *Proceedings of the National Academy of Sciences USA*, 104(41), 16032–16037. DOI: 10.1073/pnas.0701309104

Dehaene, S., & Changeux, J.-P. (2011). Experimental and theoretical approaches to conscious processing. *Neuron*, 70(2), 200–227. DOI: 10.1016/j.neuron.2011.03.018

Dehaene, S., Changeux, J.-P., Naccache, L., Sackur, J., & Sergent, C. (2006). Conscious, preconscious, and subliminal processing: A testable taxonomy. *Trends in Cognitive Sciences*, 10(5), 204–211. DOI: 10.1016/j.tics.2006.03.007

Dehaene, S., & Naccache, L. (2001). Towards a cognitive neuroscience of consciousness: Basic evidence and a workspace framework. *Cognition*, 79(1–2), 1–37. DOI: 10.1016/S0010-0277(00)00123-2

Del Cul, A., Baillet, S., & Dehaene, S. (2007). Brain dynamics underlying the nonlinear threshold for access to consciousness. *PLoS Biology*, 5(10), e260. DOI: 10.1371/journal.pbio.0050260

Demertzi, A., Gosseries, O., Bruno, M.-A., Schnakers, C., Vanhaudenhuyse, A., Chatelle, C., Charland-Verville, V., Thibaut, A., Thonnard, M., & Laureys, S. (2012). The ethics of managing disorders of consciousness. In C. Schnakers & S. Laureys (Eds.), *Coma and disorders of consciousness* (pp. 147–154). Paris: Springer-Verlag. DOI: 10.1007/978-1-4471-2440-5_14

Di, H. B., Yu, S. M., Weng, X. C., Laureys, S., Yu, D., Li, J. Q., Qin, P. M., Zhu, Y. H., Zhang, S. Z., & Chen, Y. Z. (2007). Cerebral response to patient's own name in the vegetative and minimally conscious states. *Neurology*, 68(12), 895–899. DOI: 10.1212/01.wnl.0000258544.79024.d0

Edelman, G.M., & Tononi, G. (2000). *A universe of consciousness: How matter becomes imagination*. New York, NY: Basic Books.

Eikermann, M., Fassbender, P., Zaremba, S., Jordan, A.S., Rosow, C., Malhotra, A., & Chamberlin, N.L. (2009). Pentobarbital dose-dependently increases respiratory genioglossus muscle activity while impairing diaphragmatic function in anesthetized rats. *Anesthesiology*, 110(6), 1327–1334. DOI: 10.1097/ALN.0b013e3181a16337

Ferrarelli, F., Massimini, M., Sarasso, S., Casali, A., Riedner, B.A., Angelini, G., Tononi, G., & Pearce, R.A. (2010). Breakdown in cortical effective connectivity during midazolam-induced loss of consciousness. *Proceedings of the National Academy of Sciences USA*, 107(6), 2681–2686. DOI: 10.1073/pnas.0913008107

Fins, J.J. (2009). The ethics of measuring and modulating consciousness: The imperative of minding time. *Progress in Brain Research*, 177, 371–382. DOI: 10.1016/S0079-6123(09)17726-9

Fins, J.J., & Schiff, N.D. (2010). In the blink of the mind's eye. *Hastings Center Report*, 40(3), 21–23. DOI: 10.1353/hcr.0.0257

Fiset, P., Paus, T., Daloze, T., Plourde, G., Meuret, P., Bonhomme, V., Hajj-Ali, N., Backman, S.B., & Evans, A.C. (1999). Brain mechanisms of propofol-induced loss of consciousness in humans: A positron emission tomographic study. *Journal of Neuroscience*, 19(13), 5506–5513.

Fox, M.D., Snyder, A.Z., Vincent, J.L., Corbetta, M., Van Essen, D.C., & Raichle, M.E. (2005). The human brain is intrinsically organized into dynamic, anticorrelated functional networks. *Proceedings of the National Academy of Sciences USA*, 102(27), 9673–9678. DOI: 10.1073/pnas.0504136102

Giacino, J.T. (1997). Disorders of consciousness: Differential diagnosis and neuropathologic features. *Seminars in Neurology*, 17(2), 105–111. DOI: 10.1055/s-2008-1040919

Giacino, J.T., Ashwal, S., Childs, N., Cranford, R., Jennett, B., Katz, D.I., Kelly, J.P., Rosenberg, J.H., Whyte, J., Zafonte, R.D., & Zasler, N.D. (2002). The minimally conscious state: Definition and diagnostic criteria. *Neurology*, 58(3), 349–353. DOI: 10.1212/WNL.58.3.349

Giacino, J.T., Hirsch, J., Schiff, N., & Laureys, S. (2006). Functional neuroimaging applications for assessment and rehabilitation planning in patients with disorders of consciousness. *Archives of Physical Medicine and Rehabilitation*, 87(12 Suppl. 2), S67–S76. DOI: 10.1016/j.apmr.2006.07.272

Giacino, J.T., Schnakers, C., Rodriguez-Moreno, D., Kalmar, K., Schiff, N., & Hirsch, J. (2009). Behavioral assessment in patients with disorders of consciousness: Gold standard or fool's gold? *Progress in Brain Research*, 177, 33–48. DOI: 10.1016/S0079-6123(09)17704-X

Goodman, S.J., & Mann, P.E. (1967). Reticular and thalamic multiple unit activity during wakefulness, sleep and anesthesia. *Experimental Neurology*, 19(1), 11–24. DOI: 10.1016/0014-4886(67)90003-9

Gosseries, O., Bruno, M.-A., Chatelle, C., Vanhaudenhuyse, A., Schnakers, C., Soddu, A., & Laureys, S. (2011). Disorders of consciousness: What's in a name? *Neurorehabilitation*, 28(1), 3–14.

Gosseries, O., Bruno, M.-A., Vanhaudenhuyse, A., Laureys, S., & Schnakers, C. (2009). Consciousness in the locked-in syndrome. In S. Laureys & G. Tononi (Eds.), *The neurology of consciousness: Cognitive neuroscience and neuropathology* (pp. 191–203). Oxford, UK: Elsevier Ltd.

Gosseries, O., Schnakers, C., Ledoux, D., Vanhaudenhuyse, A., Bruno, M.-A., Demertzi, A., Noirhomme, Q., Lehembre, R., Damas, P., Goldman, S., Peeters, E., Moonen, G., & Laureys, S. (2011). Automated EEG entropy measurements in coma, vegetative state/unresponsive wakefulness syndrome and minimally conscious state. *Functional Neurology*, 26(1), 25–30.

Gosseries, O., Zasler, N. D., & Laureys, S. (2014). Recent advances in disorders of consciousness: Focus on the diagnosis. *Brain Injury*, 28(9), 1141–1150. DOI: 10.3109/02699052.2014.920522

Greicius, M. D., Kiviniemi, V., Tervonen, O., Vainionpää, V., Alahuhta, S., Reiss, A. L., & Menon, V. (2008). Persistent default-mode network connectivity during light sedation. *Human Brain Mapping*, 29(7), 839–847. DOI: 10.1002/hbm.20537

Gugino, L. D., Chabot, R. J., Prichep, L. S., John, E. R., Formanek, V., & Aglio, L. S. (2001). Quantitative EEG changes associated with loss and return of consciousness in healthy adult volunteers anaesthetized with propofol or sevoflurane. *British Journal of Anaesthesia*, 87(3), 421–428. DOI: 10.1093/bja/87.3.421

Guldenmund, P., Vanhaudenhuyse, A., Boly, M., Laureys, S., & Soddu, A. (2012). A default mode of brain function in altered states of consciousness. *Archives Italiennes de Biologie*, 150(2–3), 107–121.

Heine, L., Soddu, A., Gomez, F., Vanhaudenhuyse, A., Tshibanda, L., Thonnard, M., Charland-Verville, V., Kirsch, M., Laureys, S., & Demertzi, A. (2012). Resting state networks and consciousness: Alterations of multiple resting state network connectivity in physiological, pharmacological, and pathological consciousness states. *Frontiers in Psychology*, 3, 295. DOI: 10.3389/fpsyg.2012.00295

Heinke, W., Fiebach, C. J., Schwarzbauer, C., Meyer, M., Olthoff, D., & Alter, K. (2004). Sequential effects of propofol on functional brain activation induced by auditory language processing: An event-related functional magnetic resonance imaging study. *British Journal of Anaesthesia*, 92(5), 641–650. DOI: 10.1093/bja/aeh133

Horovitz, S. G., Braun, A. R., Carr, W. S., Picchioni, D., Balkin, T. J., Fukunaga, M., & Duyn, J. H. (2009). Decoupling of the brain's default mode network during deep sleep. *Proceedings of the National Academy of Sciences USA*, 106(27), 11376–11381. DOI: 10.1073/pnas.0901435106

James, W. (1890). *Principles of psychology*. London, UK: Macmillan. DOI: 10.1037/11059-000

Jennett, B., & Plum, F. (1972). Persistent vegetative state after brain damage. A syndrome in search of a name. *Lancet*, 1(7753), 734–737. DOI: 10.1016/S0140-6736(72)90242-5

John, E. R., & Prichep, L. S. (2005). The anesthetic cascade: A theory of how anesthesia suppresses consciousness. *Anesthesiology*, 102(2), 447–471. DOI: 10.1097/00000542-200502000-00030

Jones, B. E. (2003). Arousal systems. *Frontiers in Bioscience*, 8, s438–s451. DOI: 10.2741/1074

Kaisti, K. K., Langsjo, J. W., Aalto, S., Oikonen, V., Sipila, H., Teras, M., Hinkka, S., Metsähonkala, L., & Scheinin, H. (2003). Effects of sevoflurane, propofol, and adjunct nitrous oxide on regional cerebral blood flow, oxygen consumption, and blood volume in humans. *Anesthesiology*, 99(3), 603–613. DOI: 10.1097/00000542-200309000-00015

Keifer, J. C., Baghdoyan, H. A., & Lydic, R. (1996). Pontine cholinergic mechanisms modulate the cortical electroencephalographic spindles of halothane anesthesia. *Anesthesiology*, 84(4), 945–954. DOI: 10.1097/00000542-199604000-00023

Laird, A. R., Fox, P. M., Eickhoff, S. B., Turner, J. A., Ray, K. L., Mckay, D. R., Glahn, D. C., Beckmann, C. F., Smith, S. M., & Fox, P. T. (2011). Behavioral interpretations of intrinsic connectivity networks. *Journal of Cognitive Neuroscience*, 23(12), 4022–4037. DOI: 10.1162/jocn_a_00077

Larson-Prior, L. J., Zempel, J. M., Nolan, T. S., Prior, F. W., Snyder, A. Z., & Raichle, M. E. (2009). Cortical network functional connectivity in the descent to sleep. *Proceedings of the National Academy of Sciences USA*, 106(11), 4489–4494. DOI: 10.1073/pnas.0900924106

Laureys, S. (2004). Functional neuroimaging in the vegetative state. *Neurorehabilitation*, 19(4), 335–341.

Laureys, S. (2005). The neural correlate of (un)awareness: Lessons from the vegetative state. *Trends in Cognitive Sciences*, 9(12), 556–559. DOI: 10.1016/j.tics.2005.10.010

Laureys, S., Berré, J., & Goldman, S. (2001). Cerebral function in coma, vegetative state, minimally conscious state, locked-in syndrome and brain death. In J. L. Vincent (Ed.), *Yearbook of intensive care and emergency medicine* (pp. 386–396). Berlin: Springer-Verlag.

Laureys, S., Celesia, G. G., Cohadon, F., Lavrijsen, J., León-Carrión, J., Sannita, W. G., Sazbon, L., Schmutzhard, E., von Wild, K. R., Zeman, A., & Dolce, G. (2010). Unresponsive wakefulness syndrome: A new name for the vegetative state or apallic syndrome. *BMC Medicine*, 8, 68. DOI: 10.1186/1741-7015-8-68

Laureys, S., Faymonville, M.-E., Degueldre, C., Fiore, G. D., Damas, P., Lambermont, B., Janssens, N., Aerts, J., Franck, G., Luxen, A., Moonen, G., Lamy, M., & Maquet, P. (2000). Auditory processing in the vegetative state. *Brain*, 123(8), 1589–1601. DOI: 10.1093/brain/123.8.1589

Laureys, S., Faymonville, M.-E., Goldman, S., Degueldre, C., Phillips, C., Lambermont, B., Aerts, J., Lamy, M., Luxen, A., Franck, G., & Maquet, P. (2000). Impaired cerebral connectivity in vegetative state. In A. Gjedde, S. B. Hansen, G. M. Knudsen, & O. B. Paulson (Eds.), *Physiological imaging of the brain with PET* (pp. 329–334). San Diego, CA: Academic Press.

Laureys, S., Faymonville, M.-E., Luxen, A., Lamy, M., Franck, G., & Maquet, P. (2000). Restoration of thalamocortical connectivity after recovery from persistent vegetative state. *Lancet*, 355(9217), 1790–1791. DOI: 10.1016/S0140-6736(00)02271-6

Laureys, S., Goldman, S., Phillips, C., Van Bogaert, P., Aerts, J., Luxen, A., Franck, G., & Maquet, P. (1999). Impaired effective cortical connectivity in vegetative state: Preliminary investigation using PET. *Neuroimage*, 9(4), 377–382. DOI: 10.1006/nimg.1998.0414

Laureys, S., Lemaire, C., Maquet, P., Phillips, C., & Franck, G. (1999). Cerebral metabolism during vegetative state and after recovery to consciousness. *Journal of Neurology, Neurosurgery & Psychiatry*, 67(1), 121–122. DOI: 10.1136/jnnp.67.1.121

Laureys, S., Owen, A. M., & Schiff, N. D. (2004). Brain function in coma, vegetative state, and related disorders. *Lancet Neurology*, 3(9), 537–546. DOI: 10.1016/S1474-4422(04)00852-X

Laureys, S., Pellas, F., Van Eeckhout, P., Ghorbel, S., Schnakers, C., Perrin, F., Berré, J., Faymonville, M. E., Pantke, K. H., Damas, F., Lamy, M., Moonen, G., & Goldman, S. (2005). The locked-in syndrome: What is it like to be conscious but paralyzed and voiceless? *Progress in Brain Research*, 150, 495–511. DOI: 10.1016/S0079-6123(05)50034-7

Laureys, S., Perrin, F., Faymonville, M.-E., Schnakers, C., Boly, M., Bartsch, V., Majerus, S., Moonen, G., & Maquet, P. (2004). Cerebral processing in the minimally conscious state. *Neurology*, 63(5), 916–918. DOI: 10.1212/01.WNL.0000137421.30792.9B

Laureys, S., & Schiff, N. D. (2012). Coma and consciousness: Paradigms (re)framed by neuroimaging. *Neuroimage*, 61(2), 478–491. DOI: 10.1016/j.neuroimage.2011.12.041

Lehembre, R., Bruno, M.-A., Vanhaudenhuyse, A., Chatelle, C., Cologan, V., Leclercq, Y., Soddu, A., Macq, B., Laureys, S., & Noirhomme, Q. (2012). Resting-state EEG study of comatose patients: A connectivity and frequency analysis to find differences between vegetative and minimally conscious states. *Functional Neurology*, 27(1), 41–47.

Lehembre, R., Gosseries, O., Lugo, Z., Jedidi, Z., Chatelle, C., Sadzot, B., Laureys, S., & Noirhomme, Q. (2012). Electrophysiological investigations of brain function in coma, vegetative and minimally conscious patients. *Archives Italiennes de Biologie*, 150(2–3), 122–139.

Leslie, K., Sleigh, J., Paech, M.J., Voss, L., Lim, C.W., & Sleigh, C. (2009). Dreaming and electroencephalographic changes during anesthesia maintained with propofol or desflurane. *Anesthesiology*, 111(3), 547–555. DOI: 10.1097/ALN.0b013e3181adf768

Luauté, J., Maucort-Boulch, D., Tell, L., Quelard, F., Sarraf, T., Iwaz, J., Boisson, D., & Fischer, C. (2010). Long-term outcomes of chronic minimally conscious and vegetative states. *Neurology*, 75(3), 246–252. DOI: 10.1212/WNL.0b013e3181e8e8df

Lull, N., Noe, E., Lull, J.J., Garcia-Panach, J., Chirivella, J., Ferri, J., López-Aznar, D., Sopena, P., & Robles, M. (2010). Voxel-based statistical analysis of thalamic glucose metabolism in traumatic brain injury: Relationship with consciousness and cognition. *Brain Injury*, 24(9), 1098–1107. DOI: 10.3109/02699052.2010.494592

Lydic, R., & Baghdoyan, H.A. (2005). Sleep, anesthesiology, and the neurobiology of arousal state control. *Anesthesiology*, 103(6), 1268–1295. DOI: 10.1097/00000542-200512000-00024

Majerus, S., Gill-Thwaites, H., Andrews, K., & Laureys, S. (2005). Behavioral evaluation of consciousness in severe brain damage. *Progress in Brain Research*, 150, 397–413. DOI: 10.1016/S0079-6123(05)50028-1

Maquet, P. (2010). Understanding non rapid eye movement sleep through neuroimaging. *World Journal of Biological Psychiatry*, 11(Suppl. 1), 9–15. DOI: 10.3109/15622971003637736

Maquet, P., Dive, D., Salmon, E., Sadzot, B., Franco, G., Poirrier, R., von Frenckell, R., & Franck, G. (1990). Cerebral glucose utilization during sleep-wake cycle in man determined by positron emission tomography and [18F]2-fluoro-2-deoxy-d-glucose method. *Brain Research*, 513(1), 136–143. DOI: 10.1016/0006-8993(90)91099-3

Maquet, P., Ruby, P., Maudoux, A., Albouy, G., Sterpenich, V., Dang-Vu, T., Desseilles, M., Boly, M., Perrin, F., Peigneux, P., & Laureys, S. (2005). Human cognition during REM sleep and the activity profile within frontal and parietal cortices: A reappraisal of functional neuroimaging data. *Progress in Brain Research*, 150, 219–227. DOI: 10.1016/S0079-6123(05)50016-5

Massimini, M., Boly, M., Casali, A., Rosanova, M., & Tononi, G. (2009). A perturbational approach for evaluating the brain's capacity for consciousness. *Progress in Brain Research*, 177, 201–214. DOI: 10.1016/S0079-6123(09)17714-2

Massimini, M., Ferrarelli, F., Huber, R., Esser, S.K., Singh, H., & Tononi, G. (2005). Breakdown of cortical effective connectivity during sleep. *Science*, 309(5744), 2228–2232. DOI: 10.1126/science.1117256

Massimini, M., Ferrarelli, F., Murphy, M., Huber, R., Riedner, B., Casarotto, S., & Tononi, G. (2010). Cortical reactivity and effective connectivity during REM sleep in humans. *Cognitive Neuroscience*, 1(3), 176–183. DOI: 10.1080/17588921003731578

Menon, V., & Uddin, L.Q. (2010). Saliency, switching, attention and control: A network model of insula function. *Brain Structure & Function*, 214(5–6), 655–667. DOI: 10.1007/s00429-010-0262-0

Monti, M.M., Vanhaudenhuyse, A., Coleman, M.R., Boly, M., Pickard, J.D., Tshibanda, L., Owen, A.M., & Laureys, S. (2010). Willful modulation of brain activity in disorders of consciousness. *New England Journal of Medicine*, 362(7), 579–589. DOI: 10.1056/NEJMoa0905370

Murphy, M., Bruno, M.-A., Riedner, B.A., Boveroux, P., Noirhomme, Q., Landsness, E.C., Brichant, J.F., Phillips, C., Massimini, M., Laureys, S., Tononi, G., & Boly, M. (2011). Propofol anesthesia and sleep: A high-density EEG study. *Sleep*, 34(3), 283–291.

Murphy, M., Riedner, B.A., Huber, R., Massimini, M., Ferrarelli, F., & Tononi, G. (2009). Source modeling sleep slow waves. *Proceedings of the National Academy of Sciences USA*, 106(5), 1608–1613. DOI: 10.1073/pnas.0807933106

Naci, L., Cusack, R., Jia, V. Z., & Owen, A. M. (2013). The brain's silent messenger: Using selective attention to decode human thought for brain-based communication. *Journal of Neuroscience*, 33(22), 9385–9393. DOI: 10.1523/JNEUROSCI.5577-12.2013

Nir, Y., & Tononi, G. (2010). Dreaming and the brain: From phenomenology to neurophysiology. *Trends in Cognitive Sciences*, 14(2), 88–100. DOI: 10.1016/j.tics.2009.12.001

Owen, A. M., Coleman, M. R., Boly, M., Davis, M. H., Laureys, S., & Pickard, J. D. (2006). Detecting awareness in the vegetative state. *Science*, 313(5792), 1402. DOI: 10.1126/science.1130197

Perrin, F., Schnakers, C., Schabus, M., Degueldre, C., Goldman, S., Bredart, S., Faymonville, M. E., Lamy, M., Moonen, G., Luxen, A., Maquet, P., & Laureys, S. (2006). Brain response to one's own name in vegetative state, minimally conscious state, and locked-in syndrome. *Archives of Neurology*, 63(4), 562–569. DOI: 10.1001/archneur.63.4.562

Phillips, C. L., Bruno, M.-A., Maquet, P., Boly, M., Noirhomme, Q., Schnakers, C., Vanhaudenhuyse, A., Bonjean, M., Hustinx, R., Moonen, G., Luxen, A., & Laureys, S. (2011). "Relevance vector machine" consciousness classifier applied to cerebral metabolism of vegetative and locked-in patients. *Neuroimage*, 56(2), 797–808. DOI: 10.1016/j.neuroimage.2010.05.083

Ploner, M., Lee, M. C., Wiech, K., Bingel, U., & Tracey, I. (2010). Prestimulus functional connectivity determines pain perception in humans. *Proceedings of the National Academy of Sciences USA*, 107(1), 355–360. DOI: 10.1073/pnas.0906186106

Plourde, G., Belin, P., Chartrand, D., Fiset, P., Backman, S. B., Xie, G., & Zatorre, R. J. (2006). Cortical processing of complex auditory stimuli during alterations of consciousness with the general anesthetic propofol. *Anesthesiology*, 104(3), 448–457. DOI: 10.1097/00000542-200603000-00011

Plum, F., & Posner, J. B. (1983). *The diagnosis of stupor and coma*. Philadelphia, PA: FA Davis.

Posner, J. B., Saper, C. B., Schiff, N. D., & Plum, F. (2007). *Plum and Posner's diagnosis of stupor and coma*. New York, NY: Oxford University Press.

Raichle, M. E., MacLeod, A. M., Snyder, A. Z., Powers, W. J., Gusnard, D. A., & Shulman, G. L. (2001). A default mode of brain function. *Proceedings of the National Academy of Sciences USA*, 98(2), 676–682. DOI: 10.1073/pnas.98.2.676

Rechtshaffen, A. (1973). The psychophysiology of mental activity during sleep. In F. McGuigan & R. Schoonover (Eds.), *The psychophysiology of thinking: Studies of covert processes* (pp. 153–205). Ann Arbor, MI: Academic Press. DOI: 10.1016/B978-0-12-484050-8.50011-X

Rex, S., Meyer, P. T., Baumert, J. H., Rossaint, R., Fries, M., Bull, U., & Schaefer, W. M. (2008). Positron emission tomography study of regional cerebral blood flow and flow-metabolism coupling during general anaesthesia with xenon in humans. *British Journal of Anaesthesia*, 100(5), 667–675. DOI: 10.1093/bja/aen036

Riedner, B. A., Vyazovskiy, V. V., Huber, R., Massimini, M., Esser, S., Murphy, M., & Tononi, G. (2007). Sleep homeostasis and cortical synchronization: III. A high-density EEG study of sleep slow waves in humans. *Sleep*, 30(12), 1643–1657.

Roberts, K. L., & Hall, D. A. (2008). Examining a supramodal network for conflict processing: A systematic review and novel functional magnetic resonance imaging data for related visual and auditory stroop tasks. *Journal of Cognitive Neuroscience*, 20(6), 1063–1078. DOI: 10.1162/jocn.2008.20074

Rodriguez-Moreno, D., Schiff, N. D., Giacino, J., Kalmar, K., & Hirsch, J. (2010). A network approach to assessing cognition in disorders of consciousness. *Neurology*, 75(21), 1871–1878. DOI: 10.1212/WNL.0b013e3181feb259

Rosanova, M., Gosseries, O., Casarotto, S., Boly, M., Casali, A. G., Bruno, M.-A., Mariotti, M., Boveroux, P., Tononi, G., Laureys, S., & Massimini, M. (2012). Recovery of cortical effective connectivity and recovery of consciousness in vegetative patients. *Brain*, 135(4), 1308–1320. DOI: 10.1093/brain/awr340

Rowley, G., & Fielding, K. (1991). Reliability and accuracy of the Glasgow Coma Scale with experienced and inexperienced users. *Lancet*, 337(8740), 535–538. DOI: 10.1016/0140-6736(91)91309-I

Samann, P. G., Wehrle, R., Hoehn, D., Spoormaker, V. I., Peters, H., Tully, C., Holsboer, F., & Czisch, M. (2011). Development of the brain's default mode network from wakefulness to slow wave sleep. *Cerebral Cortex*, 21(9), 2082–2093. DOI: 10.1093/cercor/bhq295

Sanders, R. D., Tononi, G., Laureys, S., & Sleigh, J. W. (2012). Unresponsiveness not equal unconsciousness. *Anesthesiology*, 116(4), 946–959. DOI: 10.1097/ALN.0b013e318249d0a7

Schiff, N. D. (2006). Multimodal neuroimaging approaches to disorders of consciousness. *Jouranl of Head Trauma Rehabilitation*, 21(5), 388–397. DOI: 10.1097/00001199-200609000-00003

Schiff, N. D., Giacino, J. T., Kalmar, K., Victor, J. D., Baker, K., Gerber, M., Fritz, B., Eisenberg, B., Biondi, T., O'Connor, J., Kobylarz, E. J., Farris, S., Machado, A., McCagg, C., Plum, F., Fins, J. J., & Rezai, A. R. (2007). Behavioural improvements with thalamic stimulation after severe traumatic brain injury. *Nature*, 448(7153), 600–603. DOI: 10.1038/nature06041

Schiff, N. D., Rodriguez-Moreno, D., Kamal, A., Kim, K. H., Giacino, J. T., Plum, F., & Hirsch, J. (2005). fMRI reveals large-scale network activation in minimally conscious patients. *Neurology*, 64(3), 514–523. DOI: 10.1212/01.WNL.0000150883.10285.44

Schnakers, C. (2012). Clinical assessment of patients with disorders of consciousness. *Archives Italiennes de Biologie*, 150(2–3), 36–43.

Schnakers, C., Giacino, J., Kalmar, K., Piret, S., Lopez, E., Boly, M., Malone, R., & Laureys, S. (2006). Does the FOUR score correctly diagnose the vegetative and minimally conscious states? *Annals of Neurology*, 60(6), 744–745. DOI: 10.1002/ana.20919

Schnakers, C., Ledoux, D., Majerus, S., Damas, P., Damas, F., Lambermont, B., Lamy, M., Boly, M., Vanhaudenhuyse, A., Moonen, G., & Laureys, S. (2008). Diagnostic and prognostic use of bispectral index in coma, vegetative state and related disorders. *Brain Injury*, 22(12), 926–931. DOI: 10.1080/02699050802530565

Schnakers, C., Perrin, F., Schabus, M., Hustinx, R., Majerus, S., Moonen, G., Boly, M., Vanhaudenhuyse, A., Bruno, M. A., & Laureys, S. (2009). Detecting consciousness in a total locked-in syndrome: An active event-related paradigm. *Neurocase*, 15(4), 271–277. DOI: 10.1080/13554790902724904

Schnakers, C., Perrin, F., Schabus, M., Majerus, S., Ledoux, D., Damas, P., Boly, M., Vanhaudenhuyse, A., Bruno, M. A., Moonen, G., & Laureys, S. (2008). Voluntary brain processing in disorders of consciousness. *Neurology*, 71(20), 1614–1620. DOI: 10.1212/01.wnl.0000334754.15330.69

Schnakers, C., Vanhaudenhuyse, A., Giacino, J., Ventura, M., Boly, M., Majerus, S., Moonen, G., & Laureys, S. (2009). Diagnostic accuracy of the vegetative and minimally conscious state: Clinical consensus versus standardized neurobehavioral assessment. *BMC Neurology*, 9, 35. DOI: 10.1186/1471-2377-9-35

Schwartz, J., & Roth, T. (2008). Neurophysiology of sleep and wakefulness: Basic science and clinical implications. *Current Neuropharmacology*, 6(4), 367–378. DOI: 10.2174/157015908787386050

Searle, J. R. (2000). Consciousness. *Annual Review of Neuroscience*, 23, 557–578. DOI: 10.1146/annurev.neuro.23.1.557

Seel, R. T., Sherer, M., Whyte, J., Katz, D. I., Giacino, J. T., Rosenbaum, A. M., Hammond, F. M., Kalmar, K., Pape, T. L., Zafonte, R., Biester, R. C., Kaelin, D., Kean, J., & Zasler, N. (2010). Assessment scales for disorders of consciousness: Evidence-based recommendations for clinical practice and research. *Archives of Physical Medecine and Rehabilitation*, 91(12), 1795–1813. DOI: 10.1016/j.apmr.2010.07.218

Seeley, W. W., Menon, V., Schatzberg, A. F., Keller, J., Glover, G. H., Kenna, H., Reiss, A. L., & Greicius, M. D. (2007). Dissociable intrinsic connectivity networks for salience processing and executive control. *Journal of Neuroscience*, 27(9), 2349–2356. DOI: 10.1523/JNEUROSCI.5587-06.2007

Shafer, A. (1995). Metaphor and anesthesia. *Anesthesiology*, 83(6), 1331–1342. DOI: 10.1097/00000542-199512000-00024

Siclari, F., Larocque, J. J., Postle, B. R., & Tononi, G. (2013). Assessing sleep consciousness within subjects using a serial awakening paradigm. *Frontiers in Psychology*, 4, 542. DOI: 10.3389/fpsyg.2013.00542

Silva, S., Alacoque, X., Fourcade, O., Samii, K., Marque, P., Woods, R., Mazziotta, J., Chollet F., & Loubinoux, I. (2010). Wakefulness and loss of awareness: Brain and brainstem interaction in the vegetative state. *Neurology*, 74(4), 313–320. DOI: 10.1212/WNL.0b013e3181cbcd96

Sleigh, J. W., Andrzejowski, J., Steyn-Ross, A., & Steyn-Ross, M. (1999). The bispectral index: A measure of depth of sleep? *Anesthesia and Analgesia*, 88(3), 659–661.

Smith, S. M., Fox, P. T., Miller, K. L., Glahn, D. C., Fox, M. P., Mackay, C. E., Filippini, N., Watkins, K. E., Toro, R., Laird, A. R., & Beckmann, C. F. (2009). Correspondence of the brain's functional architecture during activation and rest. *Proceedings of the National Academy of Sciences USA*, 106(31), 13040–13045. DOI: 10.1073/pnas.0905267106

Steriade, M. (1996). Arousal: Revisiting the reticular activating system. *Science*, 272(5259), 225–226. DOI: 10.1126/science.272.5259.225

Stickgold, R., Malia, A., Fosse, R., Propper, R., & Hobson, J. A. (2001). Brain-mind states: I. Longitudinal field study of sleep/wake factors influencing mentation report length. *Sleep*, 24(2), 171–179.

Teasdale, G., & Jennett, B. (1974). Assessment of coma and impaired consciousness. A practical scale. *Lancet*, 2(7872), 81–84. DOI: 10.1016/S0140-6736(74)91639-0

The Multi-Society Task Force on PVS. (1994). *New England Journal of Medicine*, 330(22), 1572–1579. DOI: 10.1056/NEJM199406023302206

Tononi, G. (2004). An information integration theory of consciousness. *BMC Neuroscience*, 5, 42. DOI: 10.1186/1471-2202-5-42

Tononi, G. (2008). Consciousness as integrated information: A provisional manifesto. *Biological Bulletin*, 215(3), 216–242. DOI: 10.2307/25470707

Tononi, G. (2012). Integrated information theory of consciousness: An updated account. *Archives Italiennes de Biologie*, 150(4), 293–329.

Tononi, G., & Laureys, S. (2009). The neurology of consciousness: An overview. In S. Laureys & G. Tononi (Eds.), *The neurology of consciousness: Cogntive neuroscience and neuropathology* (pp. 375–412). Oxford, UK: Elsevier Ltd. DOI: 10.1016/B978-0-12-374168-4.00028-9

Vanhaudenhuyse, A., Demertzi, A., Schabus, M., Noirhomme, Q., Bredart, S., Boly, M., Phillips, C., Soddu, A., Luxen, A., Moonen, G., & Laureys, S. (2011). Two distinct neuronal networks mediate the awareness of environment and of self. *Journal of Cognitive Neuroscience*, 23(3), 570–578. DOI: 10.1162/jocn.2010.21488

Vanhaudenhuyse, A., Laureys, S., & Perrin, F. (2008). Cognitive event-related potentials in comatose and post-comatose states. *Neurocritical Care*, 8(2), 262–270. DOI: 10.1007/s12028-007-9016-0

Vanhaudenhuyse, A., Noirhomme, Q., Tshibanda, L. J., Bruno, M.-A., Boveroux, P., Schnakers, C., Soddu, A., Perlbarg, V., Ledoux, D., Brichant, J. F., Moonen, G., Maquet, P., Greicius, M. D., Laureys, S., & Boly, M. (2010). Default network connectivity reflects the level of consciousness in non-communicative brain-damaged patients. *Brain*, 133(1), 161–171. DOI: 10.1093/brain/awp313

Velly, L. J., Rey, M. F., Bruder, N. J., Gouvitsos, F. A., Witjas, T., Regis, J. M., Peragut, J. C., & Gouin, F. M. (2007). Differential dynamic of action on cortical and subcortical structures of anesthetic agents during induction of anesthesia. *Anesthesiology*, 107(2), 202–212. DOI: 10.1097/01.anes.0000270734.99298.b4

Veselis, R. A., Feshchenko, V. A., Reinsel, R. A., Beattie, B., & Akhurst, T. J. (2005). Propofol and thiopental do not interfere with regional cerebral blood flow response at sedative concentrations. *Anesthesiology*, 102(1), 26–34. DOI: 10.1097/00000542-200501000-00008

Veselis, R. A., Feshchenko, V. A., Reinsel, R. A., Dnistrian, A. M., Beattie, B., & Akhurst, T. J. (2004). Thiopental and propofol affect different regions of the brain at similar pharmacologic effects. *Anesthesia and Analgesia*, 99(2), 399–408.

Vogel, D., Markl, A., Yu, T., Kotchoubey, B., Lang, S., & Müller, F. (2013). Can mental imagery functional magnetic resonance imaging predict recovery in patients with disorders of consciousness? *Archives of Physical Medicine and Rehabilitation*, 94(10), 1891–1898. DOI: 10.1016/j.apmr.2012.11.053

Vogt, B. A., & Laureys, S. (2005). Posterior cingulate, precuneal and retrosplenial cortices: Cytology and components of the neural network correlates of consciousness. *Progress in Brain Research*, 150, 205–217. DOI: 10.1016/S0079-6123(05)50015-3

White, N. S., & Alkire, M. T. (2003). Impaired thalamocortical connectivity in humans during general-anesthetic-induced unconsciousness. *Neuroimage*, 19(2), 402–411. DOI: 10.1016/S1053-8119(03)00103-4

Wiech, K., Lin, C. S., Brodersen, K. H., Bingel, U., Ploner, M., & Tracey, I. (2010). Anterior insula integrates information about salience into perceptual decisions about pain. *Journal of Neuroscience*, 30(48), 16324–16331. DOI: 10.1523/JNEUROSCI.2087-10.2010

Wijdicks, E. F. M., Bamlet, W. R., Maramattom, B. V., Manno, E. M., & McClelland, R. L. (2005). Validation of a new coma scale: The FOUR score. *Annals of Neurology*, 58(4), 585–593. DOI: 10.1002/ana.20611

Zeman, A. (2001). Consciousness. *Brain*, 124(7), 1263–1289. DOI: 10.1093/brain/124.7.1263

De-confounding the neural constitution of phenomenal consciousness from attention, report and memory*

Jeroen J. A. van Boxtel and Naotsugu Tsuchiya
Monash University, Melbourne

In this chapter, we discuss possible confounds that need to be carefully controlled for when the neural constitution of phenomenal conscious perception is studied. First, we discuss previous psychological or neural studies that clearly dissociated confounding factors (in particular, attention, report and memory) from phenomenal consciousness. We discuss several important phenomena and experimental methods (e.g., aftereffects, change blindness and inattentional blindness, and brain-imaging results) whose implications for the theory of consciousness might be contaminated by the influence of attention, report and memory. Finally, we discuss necessity and sufficiency of report and memory for phenomenal consciousness.

1. Introduction

In this chapter, we will use the word 'consciousness' to refer to the 'contents' of consciousness, rather than the state or level of consciousness (e.g., as opposed to coma, dreamless sleep or anesthesia) (Laureys, 2005; Charland-Verville, Vanhaudenhuyse, Laureys, & Gosseries, this volume). Further, we assume that the ultimate goal of the study of consciousness is to reveal how objective, physical neural activity gives rise to subjective, phenomenal conscious experience (Block, 2005) (sometimes called the 'hard problem'; Chalmers, 1996), rather than revealing how we can make sense of the functional and externally observable aspects of consciousness (sometimes called access consciousness; Block, 2005). We mainly discuss the relationship between phenomenal consciousness and some psychological concepts, namely, attention, report and memory, which are intimately related to the concept of access consciousness.

---

* NT was funded by a PRESTO award from the Japan Science and Technology Agency (JSTA), and is also affiliated with Decoding and Controlling Brain Information, JSTA, Chiyoda-ku, Tokyo, Japan, 102-8266.

DOI 10.1075/aicr.92.04box

Much of the early work on consciousness has depended on introspection. Indeed, introspection remains a crucial starting point for those of us who take subjective phenomenal consciousness as a serious target of scientific studies (Lamme, 2010). Introspection involves three psychological mechanisms: to attend to subjective experiences, to hold them in memory and to report on them later. The relationship between these mechanisms that allow access to the contents of consciousness – attention, report and memory – and phenomenal consciousness remains unclear. While they interact intimately, it is not known to what extent they depend on each other and to what degree neural mechanisms are shared among them.

For each of these access mechanisms, we first showcase past studies that clearly dissociated them from phenomenal consciousness, in terms of conceptual framework or neural correlates. We also consider the roles these processes might play in some of the important phenomena in consciousness research, such as aftereffects, change blindness (Rensink, O'Regan, & Clark, 1997) and inattentional blindness (Mack & Rock, 1998).

Finally, to better understand the relationship between phenomenal and access consciousness, we consider sufficiency and necessity of each of these access mechanisms for phenomenal consciousness.

2. De-confounding access consciousness from phenomenal consciousness

2.1 Minimizing top-down attention with a demanding concurrent task

The relationship between attention and consciousness has been extensively debated. While some scholars argue for their tight relationship (Chun & Wolfe, 2000; De Brigard & Prinz, 2010; Jackendoff, 1996; Mack & Rock, 1998; Marchetti, 2012; Merikle & Joordens, 1997; Mole, 2008; O'Regan & Noë, 2001; Posner, 1994; Prinz, 2010; Srinivasan, Srivastava, Lohani, & Baijal, 2009), others argue that these are separable processes (Baars, 2005; Bachmann, 2006; Block, 2005; Dehaene, Changeux, Naccache, Sackur, & Sergent, 2006; Hardcastle, 1997; Iwasaki, 1993; Kentridge, Heywood, & Weiskrantz, 2004; Koch, 2004; Koch & Tsuchiya, 2007; Lamme, 2003; Naccache, Blandin, & Dehaene, 2002; Tsuchiya & Koch, 2008a, 2008b; Velmans, 1996; Woodman & Luck, 2003; Wundt, 1874; for a review see van Boxtel, Tsuchiya, & Koch, 2010a).

We have previously argued that top-down attention and consciousness can be dissociated (Koch & Tsuchiya, 2007). We also showed that opposing effects of attention and consciousness can be observed in some cases (van Boxtel, Tsuchiya, & Koch, 2010b). Building upon these empirical findings, we have argued that top-down attention and phenomenal consciousness may have different biological, functional purposes (van Boxtel et al., 2010a); attention allows the brain to "analyze" a selected location, feature and/or object by allocating resources to it, while consciousness allows it to "synthesize" a unified experience from past and present information with future planning. This synthesis happens by binding information across different sensory modalities represented in distant brain regions into a globally accessible workspace-like structure (Baars, 2005; Dehaene et al., 2006) to achieve maximally integrated information (Oizumi, Albantakis, & Tononi, 2014; Tononi, 2010).

One of the successful examples of de-confounding attentional effects from conscious perception comes from the study of motion aftereffects (MAEs) using functional magnetic resonance imaging (fMRI). Initially neural activity in human middle temporal/V5 complex (MT+), a motion-sensitive area, was shown to be correlated with the perception of the MAE (Tootell et al., 1995). Later, however, this correlation was demonstrated to be primarily due to the increase in attention when the MAE was perceived. When attention was diverted, MT did not show a differential activation due to the MAEs (Huk, Ress, & Heeger, 2001; but see Castelo-Branco et al., 2009).

Other recent neuroimaging studies that aimed to dissociate the neural correlates of consciousness from those of top-down attention include approaches such as backward masking (Tse, Martinez-Conde, Schlegel, & Macknik, 2005) and interocular suppression (Lee, Blake, & Heeger, 2007; Watanabe et al., 2011). Indeed, while previous fMRI studies reported putative neural correlates of consciousness in V1 (Polonsky, Blake, Braun, & Heeger, 2000; Tong & Engel, 2001), it has recently been argued by Watanabe and colleagues (Watanabe et al., 2011) that these findings are mainly due to confounding attentional effects, much like the previous example of motion aftereffects. These studies require the previous findings on the neural correlates of consciousness to be revisited with a tighter control on attentional effects (Koch & Tsuchiya, 2012). Future studies of the neural correlates (or neural constituents; Miller, 2007; see Miller, this volume; Revonsuo, this volume) of phenomenal consciousness would need to rule out the confounding effects of top-down attention, for example, by independently manipulating the (1) amount of top-down attention via a concurrent demanding attentional task and (2) visibility of the stimulus, in a 2 × 2 design (Figure 1) (Kanai, Tsuchiya, & Verstraten, 2006; van Boxtel et al., 2010b; Watanabe et al., 2011).

2.2 Neural effects of reports

Ambiguous bistable stimuli have been used extensively in consciousness research because they allow researchers to present subjects with physically unchanging stimuli that induce multi-stable subjective percepts (Blake & Logothetis, 2002; Sterzer, Kleinschmidt, & Rees, 2009; Tong, Meng, & Blake, 2006; recently reviewed in Miller, 2013). In these studies, the researchers typically classify trials according to the subjects' perceptual reports and try to find the neural activities that correlate with the changes in phenomenal percepts but not with the changes in the physical stimuli.

Such an approach, however, has two potential confounds. The first is introduced by the act of report, which activates an array of neural mechanisms potentially unrelated to phenomenological consciousness. The second is a gap between what subjects actually experience and what experimenters assume the subjects experience based

Full factorial comparison

		Attention manipulation	
		Attention distracted	**Attention** focussed
Visibility Manipulation	Show mask	Low Attention Invisible	High Attention Invisible
	No mask	Low Attention Invisible	High Attention Invisible

Figure 1. The 2 × 2 design for independent manipulation of top-down attention and conscious visibility of the stimulus (Kanai et al., 2006; van Boxtel et al., 2010b; Watanabe et al., 2011). Subjects are asked to carry out one of two attention tasks while viewing either a visible or invisible target stimulus. At the same time, dependent variables such as aftereffects (Kanai et al., 2006), afterimages (van Boxtel et al., 2010b) or hemodynamic responses in the brain (Watanabe et al., 2011) are measured.

on the report. For example, during binocular rivalry the subject is often asked to report which of two competing stimuli is perceived, without the option to report intermediate, mixed percepts. We consider two recent experiments to make these points clearer.

2.2.1 *Effects of reports on local field potentials and firing rate*

The first case comes from neural recording studies in monkeys. Wilke and colleagues (Wilke, Mueller, & Leopold, 2009) used depth electrodes to record neural activity from a pulvinar nucleus in the thalamus, which has widespread connectivity with various visual and other cortical areas. They analyzed single neuron spiking activity as well as local population activity, called the local field potential (LFP). Currently, spiking activities are considered to reflect mainly the output from a brain area while LFPs, especially at the low frequency bands such as alpha (9–14 Hz) to beta (15–30 Hz) range, are considered to reflect mainly the input into the brain area (Logothetis, 2002). Using a form of ambiguous stimuli, called generalized flash suppression, Wilke and colleagues (Wilke, Logothetis, & Leopold, 2003) found that both single neuron activities and LFPs correlated with monkeys' perceptual reports, but not the physical stimulus characteristics (Figure 2).

One of the most intriguing findings is that when the trained monkeys were passively viewing the stimuli (instead of actively tracking the visibility by holding and releasing a lever), the power in the low frequency range of LFPs no longer followed the percept, but the single neuron spike activities continued to be correlated with the conscious percept. Thus, the low-frequency LFPs in the pulvinar were likely to

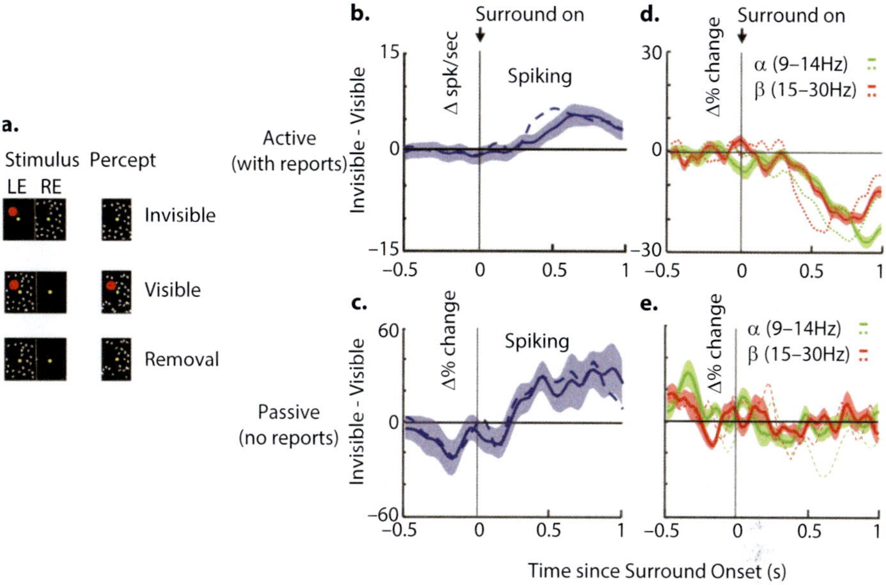

Figure 2. Neural correlates of consciousness (NCC), access (NCA) and phenomenal consciousness or qualia (NCQ). **(a)** Wilke and colleagues used a generalized flash suppression paradigm (Wilke et al., 2003) to render a red circular stimulus in the left eye invisible by presenting randomly moving dots surrounding the red stimulus presented to the right eye. When both stimuli are presented to the left eye, the red stimulus remained visible. In a control condition, they did not present the red stimulus. **(b, c)** While recording spiking activity in the pulvinar, some neurons signaled the visibility of the stimulus independent of the presence **(b)** or absence **(c)** of report, suggesting that these spiking activities are a possible NCQ. Solid lines indicate the difference in firing rate between visible vs. (perceptually) invisible trials, while dotted lines indicate the difference in firing rate between visible vs. physical removal trials. **(d, e)** The alpha (9–14 Hz) and beta (15–30 Hz) band power of LFPs in the pulvinar reflected the visibility of the red stimulus only when the monkeys reported the visibility **(d)**, but not when they did not report the visibility of the stimulus **(e)**, indicating that these are likely to be NCA, but not NCQ. Figure modified from Wilke et al. (2009).

be produced by the act of report itself and unlikely to be a neural constituent of phenomenal consciousness, while neural firing in the pulvinar may be a constituent of phenomenal consciousness. In humans, analogous findings have been documented: some brain activities can be modulated depending on the task requirement without altering percepts (Jack, Shulman, Snyder, McAvoy, & Corbetta, 2006).

Given these findings, it will be important for future studies to check if the proposed neural correlates or neural constituents continue to be observed even if subjects do not overtly report the percept. Of course, care must be taken such that some indirect measure (e.g., eye movements: (Enoksson, 1968; Fox, Todd, & Bettinger, 1975; Fries, Roelfsema, Engel, Konig, & Singer, 1997; Hayashi & Tanifuji, 2012; stabilization: Leopold, Wilke, Maier, & Logothetis, 2002; or stimulus manipulations: e.g., Wilke et al., 2009) allows the gauging of the subjects' conscious percepts even in the absence of the report. Recently, this approach has indeed been pursued, and binocular rivalry perception was tracked by analyzing involuntary eye-moments and pupil dilations (Frässle, Sommer, Jansen, Naber, & Einhäuser, 2014).

2.2.2 *Reports fail to capture what subjects really experience*

Even when care is taken to control for the possible neural effects of the mechanism behind the report, there is still a potential confound related to the fact that the report often only marginally captures the true subjective experience. As an example we will focus on brain imaging studies of perception of ambiguous stimuli, or visual rivalry. Several studies reported that the activity in two frontal areas, namely, dorsolateral prefrontal cortex (DLPFC) and right inferior frontal gyrus (IFG), increased at the time of transition from one percept to the other during the viewing of ambiguous stimuli (e.g., Lumer, Friston, & Rees, 1998; Sterzer & Kleinschmidt, 2007). This increase was obtained by contrasting the perceptual transition-related activities between genuine rivalry and a replay condition that mimicked the percept during the genuine rivalry (Figure 3a). The transient activity in DLPFC and IFG was much stronger when the transitions were induced internally in a genuine rivalry condition, than when they were induced externally in a replay condition (Figure 3b). This finding was interpreted as showing the critical function of the frontal regions in conscious perceptual switches during rivalry.

A recent study by Knapen and colleagues casts doubt on the assumption of the above contrastive method (Knapen, Brascamp, Pearson, van Ee, & Blake, 2011). While the previous studies used a replay movie with abrupt transitions between the alternative percepts, Knapen et al. created a replay in which they tried to faithfully reproduce the phenomenology by introducing variable duration and smoothness for each transition (Figure 3a). With this more realistic replay, they no longer found increased activity specific to the genuine rivalry in the frontal areas (Figure 3c).

Then, what does the transition-related activity in the frontal regions reflect? Knapen and colleagues suggest that frontal activity is related to the intermediate percepts that belong to neither of the two response options. The frontal areas DLPFC and IFG have been known to be activated in a variety of tasks and stimuli other than ambiguous stimuli, many of them involve conflict situations (not necessarily perceptual in nature) and response inhibition (Hampshire, Chamberlain, Monti, Duncan, & Owen, 2010; Ricci & Blundo, 1990; Swick, Ashley, & Turken, 2008). Response inhibition in particular may be key to understanding the nature of the transition-related activity, because during a perceptual transition subjects have to inhibit the response for the upcoming percept until it becomes totally dominant. The response inhibition might become stronger when the duration of transition becomes longer. This is one possible explanation why duration-matched replay produced as strong a fronto-parietal activation as genuine rivalry (Figure 3c).

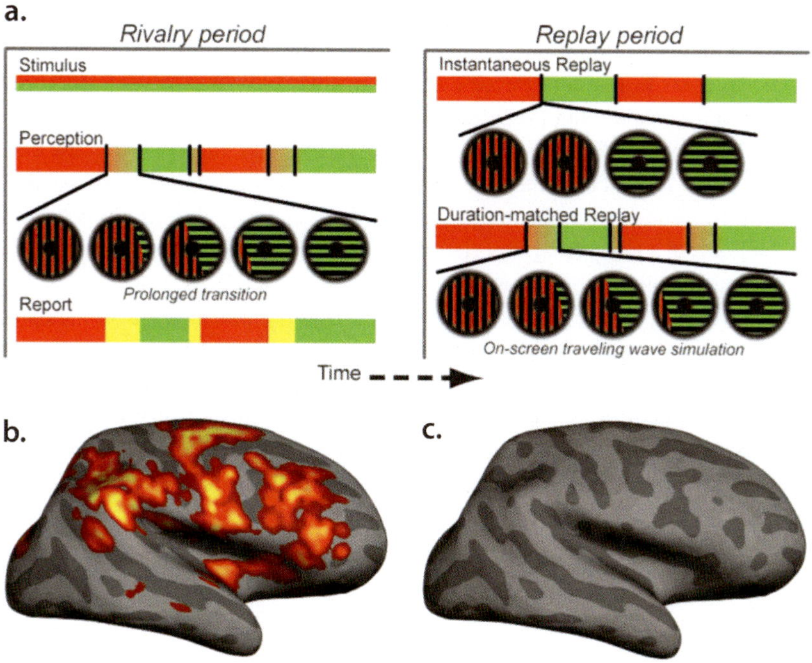

Figure 3. Report related confound introduced by a less faithful replay of what subjects really experience. (**a**) An exemplar time course of genuine rivalry. One eye received a red grating, while the other eye received a green grating (top). Actual subjective experience shows highly complex dynamics, involving various durations of intermediate percepts (rows 2 and 3). As a control condition, a perceptually matched replay movie can be presented to both eyes without interocular conflict. However, if the replay is reproduced from binary responses, the variable nature of each perceptual transition cannot be captured (e.g., Instantaneous replay; top right of panel **a**). With a third response option of accurately reporting the transitional states (yellow in row 4 in left column of panel **a**), a more faithful replay can be reproduced (e.g., duration-matched replay; bottom right of panel **a**). (**b**) Brain activity contrasted at the perceptual transition between genuine rivalry and instantaneous replay (without faithfully reproduced transitions), indicating a widespread right-lateralized front-parietal activity including DLPFC and IFG, replicating previous studies. (**c**) No difference in the brain activity between genuine rivalry and duration-matched replay. Figure modified from Knapen et al. (2011).

Furthermore, recent work has shown passive observation of visual rivalry is not affected by disruption of DLPFC or IFG through transcranial magnetic stimulation (TMS) (de Graaf, de Jong, Goebel, van Ee, & Sack, 2011). It has also been shown that the cortical thickness of DLPFC and IFG were not correlated with individual differences in the rate of rivalry transitions, while parietal areas were (Kanai, Carmel, Bahrami, & Rees, 2011; Kanai & Rees, 2011). (Note that these authors used bistable structure-from-motion stimuli that generally have instantaneous perceptual switches.) Furthermore, the aforementioned study by Frässle and colleagues (2014) found that frontal brain areas were not involved during perceptual switches in binocular rivalry when explicit reports were not requested from observers, by tracking perceptual transitions via eye movements or pupil dilations. Taken together, the activity in the frontal areas may not be critical in perceptual transitions. These studies underline the importance of de-confounding co-occurring processes (such as response inhibition during discrete reports of a perceptual experience that is more gradual) from the neural constitution of phenomenal consciousness.

To summarize, the first case (Frässle et al., 2014; Wilke et al., 2009) showed a possibility that even within a given area, different neural measures may or may not be sensitive to the phenomenology itself or influenced by the act of report itself. The second case (Knapen et al., 2011) reminds us of the importance of taking subjective reports seriously, and providing report options (and replay conditions) that more closely resemble the perceptual experience.

2.3 Memory confound: Amnesia or blindness?

With memory we will here refer to the processes involved in encoding and retrieving mnemonic representation, and not the representation itself.

Memory is traditionally divided into different types: iconic memory, short-term (or working) memory, and long-term memory. Recently, Lamme and colleagues (Vandenbroucke, Sligte, & Lamme, 2011) suggested there is yet another category of memory, which they term 'fragile' short-term memory, which sits between iconic and short-term memory. Because currently the debate on the link between conscious perception and memory is mainly focused on iconic and fragile memory, we will focus mostly on the issues related to iconic and fragile memory.

2.3.1 *Possible memory confounds in inattentional and change blindness*

Memory confounds in consciousness research may be found in inattentional and change blindness. In inattentional blindness (Mack & Rock, 1998; Wolfe, Horowitz, & Kenner, 2005), subjects are initially asked to perform a demanding task (e.g., length judgment on a horizontal versus a vertical bar of a cross). After a couple of trials, a salient object is presented at fixation. Sixty to eighty percent of subjects do not notice the presence of this unexpected target and claim they did not see anything but the task relevant stimulus (i.e., the cross). Similarly, in change blindness (Rensink et al., 1997; Tse, 2004; Wolfe, Reinecke, & Brawn, 2006), a stimulus is flashed on a display for a while, and then replaced by a uniform gray screen for a fraction of a second, after which a second stimulus is presented that contains a major change from its original, followed by another gray screen. When this sequence is repeated until subjects detect the major change, it can take them a surprisingly long time to notice a big change. Both studies are often interpreted as showing the importance of attention for consciousness.

However, other interpretations for these phenomena are also possible. Subjects may in fact have perceived the unexpected stimulus or the change, but they rapidly forgot all those that were unattended and not stored in visual short term memory (Lamme, 2010). This interpretation puts more emphasis on the need for memory to *report* a percept, rather than the need for attention to *perceive* a stimulus. This possibility is called 'inattentional amnesia' (Wolfe, 1999). Another possibility is that subjects do perceive the gist of the image correctly, masking the accurate detection of a less meaningful change in the scene (Sampanes, Tseng, & Bridgeman, 2008). Yet another possibility is that this blindness is caused by the failure of expectation, which is supported by a neural mechanism that is distinct from those for attention and memory (Braun, 2001; Kok, Rahnev, Jehee, Lau, & de Lange, 2012; Summerfield & Egner, 2009).

In sum, it is still debated whether inattentional and change blindness are really cases of loss of phenomenal consciousness (but see Cartwright-Finch & Lavie, 2007). They might rather reflect loss of memory. Also, it is still unclear how these phenomena are related to gist perception, which seems to be largely immune to attentional distraction. Again, future studies are required to better understand the nature of phenomenal consciousness in these "blindness" situations. Overall, this brief overview shows that there is a need to consider the possible confound of memory in the study of consciousness.

2.3.2 *Iconic memory and phenomenal consciousness: Sperling's experiment*

Memory confounds have actually been noticed rather early and have been addressed in a classic work by George Sperling (Sperling, 1960). In one experiment, he confronted subjects with a briefly presented array of 12 letters. Although subjects spontaneously reported that they vividly saw 12 letters in an array, they could correctly identify only about four to five letters of the array when asked to report as many letters as possible (i.e., in the full report condition). Based just on this observation, it might have been erroneously concluded that subjects actually experienced only four or five letters at the time of stimulus presentation and that seeing the whole array was an illusion.

With the invention of a partial report paradigm, however, Sperling de-confounded a memory bottleneck from lack of perception at the time of the array presentation. In the partial report paradigm, subjects were shown the same array as in the full-report condition, but now cued to report the letters in a randomly chosen row after the array disappeared from the display. In this case, subjects' responses were correct in about three out of the maximum of four, independent of the cued location. These findings suggested that subjects somehow stored at least nine letters (three letters times three rows) in the partial report condition, while they were able to report only four of them in the full report condition because of interference that operated when they reported the whole array from memory.

The result of Sperling's experiment has been taken to imply that a large capacity iconic memory system exists with a limited capacity to read out from it. That is, sometime after the stimulus disappeared and when the subject was asked to report on it, information in iconic memory was lost.

As Sperling's experiment exemplifies, there are some problems related to memory in consciousness research. First, memory is fragile. Even if the question regarding the stimulus array is asked right after the array disappeared, iconic memory can be overridden by new visual information (Coltheart, 1980a, 1980b; Lamme, 2010). Second, an observer's ability to retrieve information from memory is limited. However, we may not notice this limitation in everyday situations, because we can revisit focused objects by making eye movements when the need arises for a more detailed analysis. In that respect, the world can be considered as our memory device that resides outside of our brain (O'Regan, 1992; O'Regan & Noë, 2001).

These limitations are not a problem if observers are simply asked to report on limited aspects of a stimulus at a time he/she perceives it. However, as Sperling's paradigm has shown, when we use more complicated stimuli and ask about many items at one time, memory will form a bottleneck for the amount of items we can report. Accordingly, memory limits what can be concluded about the underlying conscious experiences.

2.3.3 *Iconic memory and phenomenal consciousness: The contents of iconic memory*

Two recent studies investigated the nature of iconic memory in more detail. First, de Gardelle, Sackur and Kouider (2009) used the partial report paradigm combined with occasional free recall trials (Figure 4a). After an array of letters was presented, subjects reported items in a row that was cued by an auditory tone. In a departure from Sperling's original study, on some trials subjects had to recall the items from the uncued rows. Their recall was assisted by a list of letters, pseudo-letters (rotated or flipped real letters) or wingdings (e.g., smiley faces), which may or may not have been present in the uncued rows. Interestingly, when the uncued row included a pseudo-letter, subjects reported seeing the associated real (unflipped) letter more often than the pseudo-letter. Subjects maintained however they saw those real letters and not the flipped version. The authors proposed that the feeling of seeing the entire array emerges from the interplay between partially accessible information and expectations, and that the conscious experience is not as rich as usually assumed.

Importantly, this study does also show that subjects were certainly not answering randomly. When tested on pseudo-letters, they often selected the associated real letters, suggesting that some gist of the letter was correctly perceived. Moreover, when the gist of the non-attended stimuli differed completely from that of letters (e.g., smiley faces), subjects were just as good as with attended items. Thus, this study indicates that some aspects of iconic memory (i.e., the gist) are very rich indeed and that there are some aspects of the letter array that are consciously perceived even without attention being directed there by a cue.

The second line of studies investigated the nature of the contents of iconic memory using a change blindness paradigm (Landman, Spekreijse, & Lamme, 2003; Phillips, 2011; Sligte, Scholte, & Lamme, 2008; Vandenbroucke, Barrett, Seth, Fahrenfort, & Lamme, 2014; Vandenbroucke et al., 2011). Subjects were briefly shown a set of 4–32 stimuli, which was followed by a blank period of up to several seconds, and a second

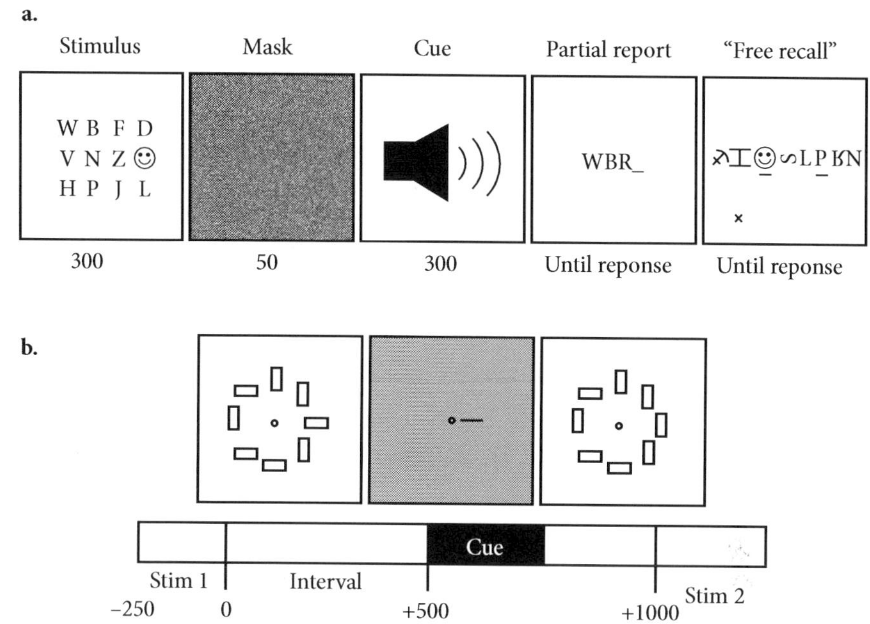

Figure 4. Partial report paradigms in iconic memory research. **(a)** In a study by de Gardelle et al. (2009), subjects were shown a 4 × 3 array of letters. On some trials, pseudo-letters (e.g., mirrored letters) or catch items (e.g. smiley faces) were also included. After a brief mask, an auditory cue was presented to indicate which row needed to be reported. The subject tried to recall as many letters as possible in the cued row. On some trials a "free recall" followed in which 3–8 items were shown to subjects, and they indicated which ones they remembered seeing in the uncued rows. **(b)** In a study by Sligte et al. (2008), subjects were shown an array of 4–32 items, followed by a blank period, and then a second array of items. Subjects reported if a cued item had changed between the two presentations. The cue could occur during the initial array (stim1), during the interval (as shown in this figure) or during the second array (stim2). Panel **(a)** is modified from de Gardelle et al. (2009), panel **(b)** is modified from Sligte et al. (2008).

set of stimuli (Figure 4b). Subjects had to report if a cued item had changed. Subjects were relatively poor at this task when they relied on working memory via a cue presented after the onset of the second stimulus (which erased the fragile memory trace of the previous stimulus), and they were of course very good when the item was cued at the moment the first set of items was shown. However, subjects were also remarkably good when the item was cued in between the two sets of stimuli, even when retinal afterimages were erased, which presumably forces subjects to rely on fragile memory. Based on this and other findings, Lamme and colleagues (Vandenbroucke et al., 2011) proposed that phenomenal consciousness is closely related to the contents of a fragile memory system that lasts longer than iconic memory but has a larger capacity than short-term (or working) memory. Fragile memory is more stable than iconic memory, in that it is only erased by a new visual input when that input is at the same location (Pinto, Sligte, Shapiro, & Lamme, 2013). It is also notable that the representation in fragile memory is introspectively accessible to the same degree as working memory, as measured via the accuracy of metacognition (Vandenbroucke et al., 2014).

By employing the partial report paradigm, the nature of iconic and fragile memory has been investigated in the hope of gaining insights into conscious experiences (but see Phillips, 2011). Further studies are needed to understand the exact relation between iconic and fragile memory and consciousness.

3. On sufficiency and necessity

In the preceding section, we showcased several studies that were successful in de-confounding the effects of attention, report, or memory from phenomenal consciousness. However, there are many more aspects of access consciousness that are awaiting further disentanglement. This knowledge can help determine which aspects are necessary and sufficient for consciousness. In a previous review (van Boxtel et al., 2010a), we focused on the issue of sufficiency and necessity of top-down attention for the contents of consciousness. In this chapter, we now ask the same question about reports and memories.

3.1 Report

Here, we consider necessity and sufficiency of reports – or more precisely, the access to reportable information – for phenomenal conscious perception. Currently, this is a topic under intense discussion (Block, 2007). We believe that reports are neither necessary nor sufficient to experience most forms of phenomenal consciousness.

3.1.1 *Is a report sufficient to cause conscious experience?*

Is a report sufficient for phenomenal consciousness? Does the presence of report guarantee the presence of phenomenal consciousness?

Clearly, when employing a strict approach the answer is no. Not every report will guarantee a conscious experience of the reported percept, for example when someone is lying. However, there are some cases that suggest that the act of reporting itself might cause one to truly consciously see something that was not physically present.

In the case of false memories, people are absolutely certain to have seen something even though they have not seen the event. Thus, internal processes can generate brain activity that is consistent with (but not caused by) certain external stimuli. Other research employed detection tasks and categorized trials as "false alarms" (i.e., the subject reported seeing the to-be-detected stimulus, but it was not physically present) and "hits" (i.e., the subject reported seeing the to-be-detected stimulus, and it was physically present). These trials have very similar phenomenal content, even though the physical input content is very different. It was found that brain activity as measured by fMRI in false alarms trials was also very similar to hit trials in both early visual cortex (Ress & Heeger, 2003) and frontal cortex (Pessoa & Padmala, 2005), and both conditions caused higher activity than misses (i.e., the physical stimulus presented but subjects reported not seeing it) and correct rejections (i.e., no stimulus presented, no percept reported). Again, this suggests that certain brain patterns can be evoked in detection paradigms that can cause the subject to actually perceive a stimulus that is not there.

Other than false memory and false alarm trials in detection paradigms, there exist situations where certain neural activities are invoked to give rise to clear conscious perception, such as visual imagery, dreams and pathological hallucinations.

Taken together, these phenomena suggest that top-down processes, including the processes associated with the report, can produce phenomenal consciousness, provided that the evidence provided from the external input is weak or absent. As to reports, the act of report itself is known to cause neural activation in motor and pre-motor areas, which is connected with percept-related areas. It is plausible that this report-related neural activity in turn injects neural noise into perception-related brain areas, pushing a subthreshold signal above threshold. In this case, the report could cause a percept that would not have occurred without the report task. Report therefore may be sufficient to cause (or be conducive to) consciousness under certain limited circumstances.

Having said that, it is not straightforward to interpret these data as strong evidence for sufficiency of reports for conscious perception. In fact, the cause and effect relationship could be reversed: noise in the visual system causes a suprathreshold activation, which in turn evokes a percept and a false-alarm report. At the moment, it is unclear whether the act of report alone can induce vivid phenomenal consciousness.

3.1.2 *Is a report necessary for conscious experience?*

Are reports or even the ability to make reports necessary to have a conscious experience? From an evolutionary point of view, it is extremely unlikely that phenomenal consciousness evolved after (or at the same time as the) acquisition of verbal or motor reports. We humans have conscious experience all the time from the moment we get up in the morning until we fall asleep at night as well as during vivid dreaming in sleep (Siclari, Larocque, Postle, & Tononi, 2013). However, we rarely report what we experience to other people, except during psychophysical experiments and limited other occasions. Reports are almost always inadequate to capture and convey the richness of phenomenal consciousness to others. Furthermore, non-speaking animals such as human babies (Kouider et al., 2013), other higher apes, and monkeys, are likely to have some form of phenomenal experience without verbal reportability, even though what kind of experience they have is unknown at this point. It is possible, however, that language allows one to elaborate on an experience, which might facilitate categorization ability and endow the observer with a finer phenomenal conscious experience. Thus, we do not deny a possibility that some forms of phenomenal consciousness might rely on reportability. Having said that, once the ability to experience elaborated categorical phenomenal consciousness is gained through experience and learning, the volitional ability to report seems no longer necessary for a phenomenal experience to occur. For example, vivid consciousness seems to be experienced by locked-in syndrome patients (Bauby, 1997) and by some vegetative or minimally conscious patients (Monti et al., 2010; Owen et al., 2006), both of whom have lost almost all motor modalities to report. However, again, it is unclear exactly what kind of conscious phenomenology they are experiencing. In the future, it might be possible to communicate with these patients directly via advanced mind-reading and brain-machine interfaces and ask what they are really experiencing (Fernández-Espejo & Owen, 2013). In sum, we believe reports are not necessary to experience at least some form of phenomenal consciousness.

If reports are not necessary for consciousness, we need to try to de-confound them when we try to study the neural mechanisms of phenomenal consciousness. In the past, the effects of report have been largely ignored. However, recent evidence suggests its critical role in the interpretation of the neural correlates of consciousness, as we reviewed in Section 2.2 (Frässle et al., 2014; Knapen et al., 2011; Wilke et al., 2009). Future studies need to refine the concept of the neural correlates of consciousness (NCC) into the neural correlates of phenomenal consciousness or qualia (NCQ) and access (NCA) (see Kanai & Tsuchiya, 2012). It would also be important to compare the results of experiments by varying the modality of reports and verify if the conclusion holds regardless of the modality of reports. Some initial efforts have been made to separate stimulus, decision, and report-related brain activity (Hulme, Friston, & Zeki, 2009; Imamoglu, Kahnt, Koch, & Haynes, 2012; Wilke et al., 2009).

3.2 Iconic and/or fragile memory

Here, we consider necessity and sufficiency of iconic and/or fragile memory for phenomenal conscious perception. As the notion of fragile memory is a recent one, most of the traditional debates have concerned iconic memory. In the rest of the section, by "iconic" memory, we always mean "iconic and/or fragile" memory. Future studies are needed to clarify how much of the discussion here applies to iconic and/or fragile memory.

3.2.1 *Sufficiency of iconic memory for consciousness*

Some researchers claim that we are conscious of all the contents of iconic memory, making it a de facto carrier of consciousness (Lamme, 2010). Others believe that only those objects in iconic memory that are attended to are stored in short-term (or working) memory and are consciously perceived (Rensink, 2002). This latter framework assumes that attention and the memory system are tightly coupled, which has been supported by both empirical and modeling work (Deco & Rolls, 2005; Henderson & Hollingworth, 1999; Jonides et al., 2008; Oberauer, 2002).

In Section 2.3.3 we discussed studies that investigated the contents of iconic memory. The overall data supports the idea that iconic memory can contain a large amount of visual data, but is perhaps not limitless. Interestingly, iconic memory seems to capture the gist of an unattended scene as well as the specific information in an attended stimulus (see Section 2.3.3; de Gardelle et al., 2009). Does the fact that one has an iconic memory of stimulus S, guarantee that he or she consciously perceives that stimulus S? We do not know the answer to this question, and the sufficiency of iconic memory for phenomenal consciousness is currently hotly debated (Block, 2011; Brown, 2011; Lamme, 2010; Phillips, 2011; Vandenbroucke et al., 2014).

3.2.2 *Necessity of iconic memory for consciousness*

Most studies so far do not directly address the question of whether iconic memory is necessary to experience conscious phenomenology. Would a person with a lesion that prevents him/her from having an iconic memory be unable to have phenomenal consciousness? Can we knock down iconic memory with TMS without interfering with phenomenal consciousness?

Iconic memory, induced by external stimulation, is clearly not necessary for consciousness, as is exemplified by vivid phenomenal consciousness experienced in visual imagery and dreaming. These types of conscious experiences may rely on episodic memory system and top-down attentional access to mnemonic representations, but they do not necessarily rely on the iconic memory mechanisms (Keogh & Pearson, 2011). While the relationship between visual imagery and short-term memory (e.g., Cattaneo, Vecchi, Pascual-Leone, & Silvanto, 2009) or visual imagery and working memory (e.g., Keogh & Pearson, 2011) has been studied, the interaction between visual imagery and iconic memory seems difficult to study. We believe such a study could shed light on the necessity of iconic memory for phenomenal consciousness.

4. Conclusion

There are widespread changes in the brain associated with changes in conscious visual perception, involving early and late visual areas and beyond, such as fronto-parietal areas. However, it is difficult to single out the neural constituents (or even the neural correlates) of phenomenal consciousness excluding confounds due to attention, report and memory.

While attention, memory and report do represent an integral part of our everyday conscious perception, whether they are necessary and sufficient for phenomenal consciousness is a different question. This question needs to be scrutinized for each of these processes individually in future studies.

What will the future bring? Attention research has a long history, and it may provide useful pointers as to how we could proceed with research on consciousness.

Attention research has shown us that there are different types of attention: focal/spatial attention, feature-based attention and object-based attention. Are there any such subdivisions we could make for consciousness?

In this chapter we have employed one of the possible divisions, namely the division of consciousness in phenomenal and access consciousness. This division is relatively well supported, but not universally accepted (Dehaene et al., 2006; Lau & Rosenthal, 2011).

Other subdivisions may be uncovered. For example, even though it may sound foreign to us now to talk about feature-based consciousness, it is possible that one has the clear impression of having seen something in a briefly presented stimulus (say the color red), but that otherwise the scene is beyond description to the subject (Ramsøy & Overgaard, 2004).

A potentially stronger case can be made for a distinction between gist consciousness and attention-driven consciousness. As previously mentioned, when briefly presented with a stimulus, we have the impression of seeing everything. Even though observers may incorrectly claim to have seen a certain stimulus in an unattended region, they are often correct about the gist of that stimulus (de Gardelle et al., 2009). Indeed, it seems that we need very little, if any, attention to perceive the gist of a scene (Fei-Fei, VanRullen, Koch, & Perona, 2002; but also see Cohen, Alvarez, & Nakayama, 2011). Consistent with these findings, psychophysical studies suggest we may be aware of simple stimulus features without attention (gist consciousness), but that they may be misbound, and that recurrent attention-related activation is necessary for binding of features (Koivisto & Silvanto, 2011; Treisman & Schmidt, 1982) – i.e., attention-driven consciousness. Future research has the potential to reveal which of these, or other subdivisions, can be maintained. It is likely however that consciousness will not survive as a monolithic concept.

We believe that future tasks should try to decouple consciousness from its potential confounds. Recent studies (van Boxtel et al., 2010b; Watanabe et al., 2011) have started to manipulate attention and consciousness independently. The results of these studies urge us to re-think the relationship between attention and consciousness. We expect similar thought-provoking findings would emerge by de-confounding the effects of report and memory as well.

The development of well-controlled tasks (see Box 1) may one day be able to reveal the neural constituents of phenomenological consciousness.

BOX 1. *Experimental approach to investigating consciousness*

In this chapter we have discussed the problems that consciousness research is facing, and specifically highlighted problems related to confounds due to attention, report and memory. Here we briefly describe the characteristics of an ideal experiment that addresses these problems.

Attention

— Use a 2 × 2 design for manipulating top-down attention (high versus low) and conscious awareness of a stimulus (visible versus invisible). Ideally, the visual input to the subjects should be identical in all conditions and each trial should be randomly chosen from each condition to avoid unwanted attention-related effects (e.g., expectation of a condition).

Memory

— A well-controlled 2 × 2 design with memory (present vs. absent) and conscious awareness of a stimulus seems impossible. Therefore we suggest using an experimental paradigm in which the subject reports his/her perception at the moment it is perceived, to prevent unwanted confounds such as "inattentional amnesia".

Report

— Use a paradigm that is not dependent on the subject's explicit report, and therefore not sensitive to criterion shifts or the act of report itself. Apart from using indirect measures of perception such as involuntary eye-movements, one could employ a paradigm that independently manipulates the report and consciousness in a 2 × 2 design (e.g., report vs. no report × visible vs. invisible). Another approach would be to use a different modality of report for manipulation of report (e.g., report by an eye movement vs. report by a lever). In the latter design, we could exclude any neural activation that is correlated to a specific response modality from the neural correlates of phenomenal consciousness or qualia (NCQ).

A successful exemplar method is the afterimage/aftereffect procedure. This procedure allows the experimenter to manipulate attentional states, and conscious visibility during the presentation of the inducer, while measuring the effects of the manipulations on the aftereffect, thus separating the experimental manipulations from the measurement phase (Bachmann & Murd, 2010; Murd & Bachmann, 2011; van Boxtel et al., 2010b). Aftereffects also allow for an immediate report of what is perceived, thus limiting memory influences. Eye-movement measurements (Frässle et al., 2014; Fries et al., 1997) and clever use of nulling-paradigms (Brascamp, van Boxtel, Knapen, & Blake, 2010) may allow for a response bias free report.

References

Baars, B. J. (2005). Global workspace theory of consciousness: Toward a cognitive neuroscience of human experience. *Progress in Brain Research*, 150, 45–53. DOI: 10.1016/S0079-6123(05)50004-9

Bachmann, T. (2006). A single metatheoretical framework for a number of conscious-vision phenomena. In Q. Jing, M. R. Rosenzweig, G. d'Ydewalle, H. Zhang, H.-C. Chen, & K. Zhang (Eds.), *Progress in psychological science around the world. Volume 1 Neural, cognitive and developmental issues* (pp. 229–242). Hove, UK: Psychology Press.

Bachmann, T., & Murd, C. (2010). Covert spatial attention in search for the location of a color-afterimage patch speeds up its decay from awareness: Introducing a method useful for the study of neural correlates of visual awareness. *Vision Research*, 50(11), 1048–1053. DOI: 10.1016/j.visres.2010.03.013

Bauby, J.-B. (1997). *The diving bell and the butterfly* (J. Leggatt, Trans.). New York, NY: Alfred A. Knopf.

Blake, R., & Logothetis, N. K. (2002). Visual competition. *Nature Reviews Neuroscience*, 3(1), 13–21. DOI: 10.1038/nrn701

Block, N. (2005). Two neural correlates of consciousness. *Trends in Cognitive Sciences*, 9(2), 46–52. DOI: 10.1016/j.tics.2004.12.006

Block, N. (2007). Consciousness, accessibility, and the mesh between psychology and neuroscience. *Behavioral and Brain Sciences*, 30(5–6), 481–499.

Block, N. (2011). Perceptual consciousness overflows cognitive access. *Trends in Cognitive Sciences*, 15(12), 567–575. DOI: 10.1016/j.tics.2011.11.001

Brascamp, J. W., van Boxtel, J. J. A., Knapen, T. H. J., & Blake, R. (2010). A dissociation of attention and awareness in phase-sensitive but not phase-insensitive visual channels. *Journal of Cognitive Neuroscience*, 22(10), 2326–2344. DOI: 10.1162/jocn.2009.21397

Braun, J. (2001). It's great but not necessarily about attention. *Psyche*, 7(6). Retrieved from http://www.theassc.org/files/assc/2500.pdf

Brown, R. (2011). The myth of phenomenological overflow. *Consciousness and Cognition*, 21(2), 599–604. DOI: 10.1016/j.concog.2011.06.005

Cartwright-Finch, U., & Lavie, N. (2007). The role of perceptual load in inattentional blindness. *Cognition*, 102(3), 321–340. DOI: 10.1016/j.cognition.2006.01.002

Castelo-Branco M., Kozak L. R., Formisano E., Teixeira J., Xavier J., & Goebel R. (2009). Type of featural attention differentially modulates hMT + responses to illusory motion aftereffects. *Journal of Neurophysiology*, 102(5), 3016–3025. DOI: 10.1152/jn.90812.2008

Cattaneo, Z., Vecchi, T., Pascual-Leone, A., & Silvanto, J. (2009). Contrasting early visual cortical activation states causally involved in visual imagery and short-term memory. *European Journal of Neuroscience*, 30(7), 1393–1400. DOI: 10.1111/j.1460-9568.2009.06911.x

Chalmers, D. J. (1996). *The conscious mind: In search of a fundamental theory*. New York, NY: Oxford University Press.

Chun, M. M., & Wolfe, J. M. (2001). Visual attention. In E. B. Goldstein (Ed.), *Blackwell handbook of perception* (pp. 272–310). Oxford, UK: Blackwell.

Cohen, M. A., Alvarez, G. A., & Nakayama, K. (2011). Natural-scene perception requires attention. *Psychological Science*, 22(9), 1165–1172. DOI: 10.1177/0956797611419168

Coltheart, M. (1980a). Iconic memory and visible persistence. *Perception & Psychophysics*, 27(3), 183–228. DOI: 10.3758/BF03204258

Coltheart, M. (1980b). The persistences of vision. *Philosophical Transactions of the Royal Society of London B: Biological Sciences*, 290(1038), 57–69. DOI: 10.1098/rstb.1980.0082

De Brigard, F., & Prinz, J. (2010). Attention and consciousness. *Wiley Interdisciplinary Reviews: Cognitive Science*, 1(1), 51–59. DOI: 10.1002/wcs.27

de Gardelle, V., Sackur, J., & Kouider, S. (2009). Perceptual illusions in brief visual presentations. *Consciousness and Cognition*, 18(3), 569–577. DOI: 10.1016/j.concog.2009.03.002

de Graaf, T. A., de Jong, M. C., Goebel, R., van Ee, R., & Sack, A. T. (2011). On the functional relevance of frontal cortex for passive and voluntarily controlled bistable vision. *Cerebral Cortex*, 21(10), 2322–2331. DOI: 10.1093/cercor/bhr015

Deco, G., & Rolls, E. T. (2005). Attention, short-term memory, and action selection: A unifying theory. *Progress in Neurobiology*, 76(4), 236–256. DOI: 10.1016/j.pneurobio.2005.08.004

Dehaene, S., Changeux, J.-P., Naccache, L., Sackur, J., & Sergent, C. (2006). Conscious, preconscious, and subliminal processing: A testable taxonomy. *Trends in Cognitive Sciences*, 10(5), 204–211. DOI: 10.1016/j.tics.2006.03.007

Enoksson, P. (1968). Studies in optokinetic binocular rivalry with a new device. *Acta Ophthalmologica*, 46(1), 71–74. DOI: 10.1111/j.1755-3768.1968.tb02496.x

Fei-Fei, L., VanRullen, R., Koch, C., & Perona, P. (2002). Rapid natural scene categorization in the near absence of attention. *Proceedings of the National Academy of Sciences USA*, 99(14), 9596–9601. DOI: 10.1073/pnas.092277599

Fernández-Espejo, D., & Owen, A.M. (2013). Detecting awareness after severe brain injury. *Nature Reviews Neuroscience*, 14(11), 801–809. DOI: 10.1038/nrn3608

Fox, R., Todd, S., & Bettinger, L.A. (1975). Optokinetic nystagmus as an objective indicator of binocular rivalry. *Vision Research*, 15(7), 849–853. DOI: 10.1016/0042-6989(75)90265-5

Frässle, S., Sommer, J., Jansen, A., Naber, M., & Einhäuser, W. (2014). Binocular rivalry: Frontal activity relates to introspection and action but not to perception. *Journal of Neuroscience*, 34(5), 1738–1747. DOI: 10.1523/JNEUROSCI.4403-13.2014

Fries, P., Roelfsema, P.R., Engel, A.K., König, P., & Singer, W. (1997). Synchronization of oscillatory responses in visual cortex correlates with perception in interocular rivalry. *Proceedings of the National Academy of Sciences USA*, 94(23), 12699–12704. DOI: 10.1073/pnas.94.23.12699

Hampshire, A., Chamberlain, S.R., Monti, M.M., Duncan, J., & Owen, A.M. (2010). The role of the right inferior frontal gyrus: Inhibition and attentional control. *Neuroimage*, 50(3), 1313–1319. DOI: 10.1016/j.neuroimage.2009.12.109

Hardcastle, V.G. (1997). Attention versus consciousness: A distinction with a difference. *Cognitive Studies*, 4(3), 56–66.

Hayashi, R., & Tanifuji, M. (2012). Which image is in awareness during binocular rivalry? Reading perceptual status from eye movements. *Journal of Vision*, 12(3), 5. DOI: 10.1167/12.3.5

Henderson, J.M., & Hollingworth, A. (1999). High-level scene perception. *Annual Review of Psychology*, 50, 243–271. DOI: 10.1146/annurev.psych.50.1.243

Huk, A.C., Ress, D., & Heeger, D.J. (2001). Neuronal basis of the motion aftereffect reconsidered. *Neuron*, 32(1), 161–172. DOI: 10.1016/S0896-6273(01)00452-4

Hulme, O.J., Friston, K.F., & Zeki, S. (2009). Neural correlates of stimulus reportability. *Journal of Cognitive Neuroscience*, 21(8), 1602–1610. DOI: 10.1162/jocn.2009.21119

Imamoglu, F., Kahnt, T., Koch, C., & Haynes, J.-D. (2012). Changes in functional connectivity support conscious object recognition. *Neuroimage*, 63(4), 1909–1917. DOI: 10.1016/j.neuroimage.2012.07.056

Iwasaki, S. (1993). Spatial attention and two modes of visual consciousness. *Cognition*, 49(3), 211–233. DOI: 10.1016/0010-0277(93)90005-G

Jack, A.I., Shulman, G.L., Snyder, A.Z., McAvoy, M., & Corbetta, M. (2006). Separate modulations of human V1 associated with spatial attention and task structure. *Neuron*, 51(1), 135–147. DOI: 10.1016/j.neuron.2006.06.003

Jackendoff, R. (1996). How language helps us think. *Pragmatics and Cognition*, 4(1), 1–34. DOI: 10.1075/pc.4.1.03jac

Jonides, J., Lewis, R.L., Nee, D.E., Lustig, C.A., Berman, M.G., & Moore, K.S. (2008). The mind and brain of short-term memory. *Annual Review of Psychology*, 59, 193–224. DOI: 10.1146/annurev.psych.59.103006.093615

Kanai, R., Carmel, D., Bahrami, B., & Rees, G. (2011). Structural and functional fractionation of right superior parietal cortex in bistable perception. *Current Biology*, 21(3), R106–R107. DOI: 10.1016/j.cub.2010.12.009

Kanai, R., & Rees, G. (2011). The structural basis of inter-individual differences in human behaviour and cognition. *Nature Reviews Neuroscience*, 12(4), 231–242. DOI: 10.1038/nrn3000

Kanai, R., & Tsuchiya, N. (2012). Qualia. *Current Biology*, 22(10), R392–6. DOI: 10.1016/j.cub.2012.03.033.

Kanai, R., Tsuchiya, N., & Verstraten, F. A. (2006). The scope and limits of top-down attention in unconscious visual processing. *Current Biology*, 16(23), 2332–2336. DOI: 10.1016/j.cub.2006.10.001

Kentridge, R. W., Heywood, C. A., & Weiskrantz, L. (2004). Spatial attention speeds discrimination without awareness in blindsight. *Neuropsychologia*, 42(6), 831–835. DOI: 10.1016/j.neuropsychologia.2003.11.001

Keogh, R., & Pearson, J. (2011). Mental imagery and visual working memory. *PLoS ONE*, 6(12), e29221. DOI: 10.1371/journal.pone.0029221

Knapen, T., Brascamp, J., Pearson, J., van Ee, R., & Blake, R. (2011). The role of frontal and parietal brain areas in bistable perception. *Journal of Neuroscience*, 31(28), 10293–10301. DOI: 10.1523/JNEUROSCI.1727-11.2011

Koch, C. (2004). *The quest for consciousness: A neurobiological approach*. Englewood, CO: Roberts & Company.

Koch, C., & Tsuchiya, N. (2007). Attention and consciousness: Two distinct brain processes. *Trends in Cognitive Sciences*, 11(1), 16–22. DOI: 10.1016/j.tics.2006.10.012

Koch, C., & Tsuchiya, N. (2012). Attention and consciousness: Related yet different. *Trends in Cognitive Sciences*, 16(2), 103–105. DOI: 10.1016/j.tics.2011.11.012

Koivisto, M., & Silvanto, J. (2011). Relationship between visual binding, reentry and awareness. *Consciousness and Cognition*, 20(4), 1293–1303. DOI: 10.1016/j.concog.2011.02.008

Kok, P., Rahnev, D., Jehee, J. F. M., Lau, H. C., & de Lange, F. P. (2012). Attention reverses the effect of prediction in silencing sensory signals. *Cerebral Cortex*, 22(9), 2197–2206. DOI: 10.1093/cercor/bhr310

Kouider, S., Stahlhut, C., Gelskov, S. V., Barbosa, L. S., Dutat, M., de Gardelle, V., Christophe, A., Dehaene, S., & Dehaene-Lambertz, G. (2013). A neural marker of perceptual consciousness in infants. *Science*, 340(6130), 376–380. DOI: 10.1126/science.1232509

Lamme, V. A. F. (2003). Why visual attention and awareness are different. *Trends in Cognitive Sciences*, 7(1), 12–18. DOI: 10.1016/S1364-6613(02)00013-X

Lamme, V. A. F. (2010). How neuroscience will change our view on consciousness. *Cognitive Neuroscience*, 1(3), 204–220. DOI: 10.1080/17588921003731586

Landman, R., Spekreijse, H., & Lamme, V. A. F. (2003). Large capacity storage of integrated objects before change blindness. *Vision Research*, 43(2), 149–164. DOI: 10.1016/S0042-6989(02)00402-9

Lau, H., & Rosenthal, D. (2011). Empirical support for higher-order theories of conscious awareness. *Trends in Cognitive Sciences*, 15(8), 365–373. DOI: 10.1016/j.tics.2011.05.009

Laureys, S. (2005). The neural correlate of (un)awareness: Lessons from the vegetative state. *Trends in Cognitive Sciences*, 9(12), 556–559. DOI: 10.1016/j.tics.2005.10.010

Lee, S.-H., Blake, R., & Heeger, D. J. (2007). Hierarchy of cortical responses underlying binocular rivalry. *Nature Neuroscience*, 10(8), 1048–1054. DOI: 10.1038/nn1939

Leopold, D. A., Wilke, M., Maier, A., & Logothetis, N. K. (2002). Stable perception of visually ambiguous patterns. *Nature Neuroscience*, 5(6), 605–609. DOI: 10.1038/nn0602-851

Logothetis, N. K. (2002). The neural basis of the blood-oxygen-level-dependent functional magnetic resonance imaging signal. *Philosophical Transactions of the Royal Society of London B: Biological Sciences*, 357(1424), 1003–1037. DOI: 10.1098/rstb.2002.1114

Lumer, E. D., Friston, K. J., & Rees, G. (1998). Neural correlates of perceptual rivalry in the human brain. *Science*, 280(5371), 1930–1934. DOI: 10.1126/science.280.5371.1930

Mack, A., & Rock, I. (1998). *Inattentional blindness*. Cambridge, MA: MIT Press.
Marchetti, G. (2012). Against the view that consciousness and attention are fully dissociable. *Frontiers in Psychology*, 3, 36. DOI: 10.3389/fpsyg.2012.00036
Merikle, P. M., & Joordens, S. (1997). Parallels between perception without attention and perception without awareness. *Consciousness and Cognition*, 6(2–3), 219–236. DOI: 10.1006/ccog.1997.0310
Miller, S. M. (2007). On the correlation/constitution distinction problem (and other hard problems) in the scientific study of consciousness. *Acta Neuropsychiatrica*, 19(3), 159–176. DOI: 10.1111/j.1601-5215.2007.00207.x
Miller, S. M. (Ed.). (2013). *The constitution of visual consciousness: Lessons from binocular rivalry*. Advances in Consciousness Research (Vol. 90). Amsterdam, The Netherlands: John Benjamins Publishing Company. DOI: 10.1075/aicr.90
Mole, C. (2008). Attention and consciousness. *Journal of Consciousness Studies*, 15(4), 86–104.
Monti, M. M., Vanhaudenhuyse, A., Coleman, M. R., Boly, M., Pickard, J. D., Tshibanda, L., Owen, A. M., & Laureys, S. (2010). Willful modulation of brain activity in disorders of consciousness. *New England Journal of Medicine*, 362(7), 579–589. DOI: 10.1056/NEJMoa0905370
Murd, C., & Bachmann, T. (2011). Spatially localized motion aftereffect disappears faster from awareness when selectively attended to according to its direction. *Vision Research*, 51(10), 1157–1162. DOI: 10.1016/j.visres.2011.03.008
Naccache, L., Blandin, E., & Dehaene, S. (2002). Unconscious masked priming depends on temporal attention. *Psychological Science*, 13(5), 416–424. DOI: 10.1111/1467-9280.00474
Oberauer, K. (2002). Access to information in working memory: Exploring the focus of attention. *Journal of Experimental Psychology: Learning, Memory, and Cognition*, 28(3), 411–421. DOI: 10.1037/0278-7393.28.3.411
Oizumi, M., Albantakis, L., & Tononi, G. (2014). From the phenomenology to the mechanisms of consciousness: Integrated Information Theory 3.*0. PLoS Computational Biology*, 10(5), e1003588. DOI: 10.1371/journal.pcbi.1003588
O'Regan, J. K. (1992). Solving the "real" mysteries of visual perception: The world as an outside memory. *Canadian Journal of Psychology*, 46(3), 461–488. DOI: 10.1037/h0084327
O'Regan, J. K., & Noë, A. (2001). A sensorimotor account of vision and visual consciousness. *Behavioral and Brain Sciences*, 24(5), 939–973. DOI: 10.1017/S0140525X01000115
Owen, A. M., Coleman, M. R., Boly, M., Davis, M. H., Laureys, S., & Pickard, J. D. (2006). Detecting awareness in the vegetative state. *Science*, 313(5792), 1402. DOI: 10.1126/science.1130197
Pessoa, L., & Padmala, S. (2005). Quantitative prediction of perceptual decisions during near-threshold fear detection. *Proceedings of the National Academy of Sciences USA*, 102(15), 5612–5617. DOI: 10.1073/pnas.0500566102
Phillips, I. B. (2011). Perception and iconic memory: What Sperling doesn't show. *Mind & Language*, 26(4), 381–411. DOI: 10.1111/j.1468-0017.2011.01422.x
Pinto, Y., Sligte, I. G., Shapiro, K. L., & Lamme, V. A. F. (2013). Fragile visual short-term memory is an object-based and location-specific store. *Psychonomic Bulletin & Review*, 20(4), 732–739. DOI: 10.3758/s13423-013-0393-4
Polonsky, A., Blake, R., Braun, J., & Heeger, D. J. (2000). Neuronal activity in human primary visual cortex correlates with perception during binocular rivalry. *Nature Neuroscience*, 3(11), 1153–1159. DOI: 10.1038/80676

Posner, M. I. (1994). Attention: The mechanisms of consciousness. *Proceedings of the National Academy of Sciences USA*, 91(16), 7398–7403.
Prinz, J. (2010). When is perception conscious? In B. Nanay (Ed.), *Perceiving the world: New essays on perception* (pp. 310–332). New York, NY: Oxford University Press. DOI: 10.1093/acprof:oso/9780195386196.003.0011
Ramsøy, T. Z., & Overgaard, M. (2004). Introspection and subliminal perception. *Phenomenology and the Cognitive Sciences*, 3(1), 1–23. DOI: 10.1023/B:PHEN.0000041900.30172.e8
Rensink, R. A. (2002). Change detection. *Annual Review of Psychology*, 53, 245–277. DOI: 10.1146/annurev.psych.53.100901.135125
Rensink, R. A., O'Regan, J. K., & Clark, J. J. (1997). To see or not to see: The need for attention to perceive changes in scenes. *Psychological Science*, 8(5), 368–373. DOI: 10.1111/j.1467-9280.1997.tb00427.x
Ress, D., & Heeger, D. J. (2003). Neuronal correlates of perception in early visual cortex. *Nature Neuroscience*, 6(4), 414–420. DOI: 10.1038/nn1024
Ricci, C., & Blundo, C. (1990). Perception of ambiguous figures after focal brain lesions. *Neuropsychologia*, 28(11), 1163–1173. DOI: 10.1016/0028-3932(90)90052-P
Sampanes, A. C., Tseng, P., & Bridgeman, B. (2008). The role of gist in scene recognition. *Vision Research*, 48(21), 2275–2283. DOI: 10.1016/j.visres.2008.07.011
Siclari, F., Larocque, J. J., Postle, B. R., & Tononi, G. (2013). Assessing sleep consciousness within subjects using a serial awakening paradigm. *Frontiers in Psychology*, 4, 542. DOI: 10.3389/fpsyg.2013.00542
Sligte, I. G., Scholte, H. S., & Lamme, V. A. F. (2008). Are there multiple visual short-term memory stores? *PLoS ONE*, 3(2), e1699. DOI: 10.1371/journal.pone.0001699
Sperling, G. (1960). The information available in brief visual presentations. *Psychological Monographs: General and Applied*, 74(11), 1–29. DOI: 10.1037/h0093759
Srinivasan, N., Srivastava, P., Lohani, M., & Baijal, S. (2009). Focused and distributed attention. *Progress in Brain Research*, 176, 87–100. DOI: 10.1016/S0079-6123(09)17606-9
Sterzer, P., & Kleinschmidt, A. (2007). A neural basis for inference in perceptual ambiguity. *Proceedings of the National Academy of Sciences USA*, 104(1), 323–328. DOI: 10.1073/pnas.0609006104
Sterzer, P., Kleinschmidt, A., & Rees, G. (2009). The neural bases of multistable perception. *Trends in Cognitive Sciences*, 13(7), 310–318. DOI: 10.1016/j.tics.2009.04.006
Summerfield, C., & Egner, T. (2009). Expectation (and attention) in visual cognition. *Trends in Cognitive Sciences*, 13(9), 403–409. DOI: 10.1016/j.tics.2009.06.003
Swick, D., Ashley, V., & Turken, A. U. (2008). Left inferior frontal gyrus is critical for response inhibition. *BMC Neuroscience*, 9, 102. DOI: 10.1186/1471-2202-9-102
Tong, F., & Engel, S. A. (2001). Interocular rivalry revealed in the human cortical blind-spot representation. *Nature*, 411(6834), 195–199. DOI: 10.1038/35075583
Tong, F., Meng, M., & Blake, R. (2006). Neural bases of binocular rivalry. *Trends in Cognitive Sciences*, 10(11), 502–511. DOI: 10.1016/j.tics.2006.09.003
Tononi, G. (2010). Information integration: Its relevance to brain function and consciousness. *Archives Italiennes de Biologie*, 148(3), 299–322.
Tootell, R. B. H., Reppas, J. B., Dale, A. M., Look, R. B., Sereno, M. I., Malach, R., Brady, T. J., & Rosen, B. R. (1995). Visual motion aftereffects in human cortical area MT revealed by functional magnetic resonance imaging. *Nature*, 375(6527), 139–141. DOI: 10.1038/375139a0
Treisman, A., & Schmidt, H. (1982). Illusory conjunctions in the perception of objects. *Cognitive Psychology*, 14(1), 107–141. DOI: 10.1016/0010-0285(82)90006-8

Tse, P. U. (2004). Mapping visual attention with change blindness: New directions for a new method. *Cognitive Science*, 28(2), 241–258. DOI: 10.1207/s15516709cog2802_6

Tse, P. U., Martinez-Conde, S., Schlegel, A. A., & Macknik, S. L. (2005). Visibility, visual awareness, and visual masking of simple unattended targets are confined to areas in the occipital cortex beyond human V1/V2. *Proceedings of the National Academy of Sciences USA*, 102(47), 17178–17183. DOI: 10.1073/pnas.0508010102

Tsuchiya, N., & Koch, C. (2008a). Attention and consciousness. *Scholarpedia*, 3(5), 4173. DOI: 10.4249/scholarpedia.4173

Tsuchiya, N., & Koch, C. (2008b). The relationship between consciousness and attention. In S. Laureys & G. Tononi (Eds.), *The neurology of consciousness: Cognitive neuroscience and neuropathology* (pp. 63–77). London, UK: Academic Press.

van Boxtel, J. J. A., Tsuchiya, N., & Koch, C. (2010a). Consciousness and attention: On sufficiency and necessity. *Frontiers in Consciousness Research*, 1, 217. DOI: 10.3389/fpsyg.2010.00217

van Boxtel, J. J. A., Tsuchiya, N., & Koch, C. (2010b). Opposing effects of attention and consciousness on afterimages. *Proceedings of the National Academy of Sciences USA*, 107(19), 8883–8888. DOI: 10.1073/pnas.0913292107

Vandenbroucke, A. R. E., Sligte, I. G., Barrett, A. B., Seth, A. K., Fahrenfort, J. J., & Lamme, V. A. F. (2014). Accurate metacognition for visual sensory memory representations. *Psychological Science*, 25(4), 861–873. DOI: 10.1177/0956797613516146

Vandenbroucke, A. R. E., Sligte, I. G., & Lamme, V. A. F. (2011). Manipulations of attention dissociate fragile visual short-term memory from visual working memory. *Neuropsychologia*, 49(6), 1559–1568. DOI: 10.1016/j.neuropsychologia.2010.12.044

Velmans, M. (Ed.). (1996). *The science of consciousness: Psychological, neuropsychological and clinical reviews*. London, UK: Routledge. DOI: 10.4324/9780203360019

Watanabe, M., Cheng, K., Murayama, Y., Ueno, K., Asamizuya, T., Tanaka, K., & Logothetis, N. (2011). Attention but not awareness modulates the BOLD signal in the human V1 during binocular suppression. *Science*, 334(6057), 829–831. DOI: 10.1126/science.1203161

Wilke, M., Logothetis, N. K., & Leopold, D. A. (2003). Generalized flash suppression of salient visual targets. *Neuron*, 39(6), 1043–1052. DOI: 10.1016/j.neuron.2003.08.003

Wilke, M., Mueller, K. M., & Leopold, D. A. (2009). Neural activity in the visual thalamus reflects perceptual suppression. *Proceedings of the National Academy of Sciences USA*, 106(23), 9465–9470. DOI: 10.1073/pnas.0900714106

Wolfe, J. M. (1999). Inattentional amnesia. In V. Coltheart (Ed.), *Fleeting memories: Cognition of brief visual stimuli* (pp. 71–94). Cambridge, MA: MIT Press.

Wolfe, J. M., Horowitz, T. S., & Kenner, N. M. (2005). Cognitive psychology: Rare items often missed in visual searches. *Nature*, 435(7041), 439–440. DOI: 10.1038/435439a

Wolfe, J. M., Reinecke, A., & Brawn, P. (2006). Why don't we see changes?: The role of attentional bottlenecks and limited visual memory. *Visual Cognition*, 14(4–8), 749–780. DOI: 10.1080/13506280500195292

Woodman, G. F., & Luck, S. J. (2003). Dissociations among attention, perception, and awareness during object-substitution masking. *Psychological Science*, 14(6), 605–611. DOI: 10.1046/j.0956-7976.2003.psci_1472.x

Wundt, W. (1874). *Grundzüge der physiologischen Psychologie*. Leipzig: Engelmann.

The correlation/constitution distinction problem

Foundations, limits and explanation in consciousness science*

Steven M. Miller
Monash University, Melbourne

The science of consciousness is founded on identifying the minimally sufficient neural correlates of consciousness. However, I have argued that science really seeks identification of the neural *constitution* of consciousness, and that there are no empirical strategies for distinguishing the correlates and constitution of consciousness. Here I review this correlation/constitution distinction problem, drawing on recording, inhibition, stimulation and combined inhibition/stimulation approaches. I propose the Jenga analogy to explain why the minimally sufficient neural correlates of consciousness should not be considered the ultimate target of consciousness science. I then show how combined inhibition/stimulation strategies might identify some constitutive neural activities but not the whole constitution of consciousness. Clarifications, objections and related issues are also discussed and I propose new foundational claims for consciousness science.

1. Introduction

It is now beyond question that consciousness can be studied scientifically. Despite this burgeoning field however, consciousness is a unique phenomenon and its study poses challenges that do not arise in other sciences. This is especially so when considering *phenomenal* consciousness (subjective experience, qualia, or the 'what-it-is-like'

* A shorter version of this paper was published in a special issue of *Frontiers in Psychology* (Miller, 2014). I am grateful to Jakob Hohwy, Trung Ngo, Anthony Hannan, Nao Tsuchiya, Jeroen van Boxtel, Tom de Graaf, Talis Bachmann, Giulio Tononi and the two reviewers of the shorter version (Alexander Maier and Jaan Aru) for helpful comments and discussions regarding this work. The paper has also benefited from my interactions with many other authors in the present volume. Thanks also to Phillip Law for assistance with the figures.

DOI 10.1075/aicr.92.05mil

aspect of our conscious states; Nagel, 1974; see Drayson, this volume). The notion of phenomenal consciousness continues to elicit vigorous debate with many of the issues having roots in the classical other minds problem in philosophy, which concerns the privacy of mental states – in phenomenal consciousness terms, knowing what it is like to be another subject (or what I term, the problem of direct intersubjective exchange; Miller, 1999, 2007). Phenomenal consciousness also raises scientific problems, such as identifying where in human development it commences and in which species of biological organism it exists. I have claimed that there are no evident scientific strategies to settle such issues other than appealing to indirect and inferential evidence (Miller, 2007). These are hard problems of consciousness indeed but different again is *the* hard problem (Chalmers, 1996), one formulation of which asks: if all the relationships between certain brain states and certain phenomenal states could be known, why should *those* relationships exist and not others, and why indeed should there be any phenomenal consciousness at all?

In light of such philosophical and scientific problems, philosophers have asked whether purely physical facts could entail all there is to know about phenomenal consciousness or whether we meet an unavoidable *explanatory gap* (Levine, 1983; Jackson, 1986). As discussed by Drayson (this volume), substance dualists – who believe that physical brains and mental states are composed of fundamentally different substances – consider the existence of an explanatory gap provides support for their position. On the other hand, physicalists – who believe that physical brains and mental states are fundamentally composed of the same substance, but who vary in their stance on the relation between the physical and the mental – respond to the notion of an explanatory gap by either: (1) denying that such a gap (or phenomenal consciousness itself) exists; (2) holding that the gap exists only due to the limitations of *current* science; or (3) holding that the gap exists because we are limited in our cognitive capacity to fully understand phenomenal consciousness.

The various problems of phenomenal consciousness mentioned above appear hard, indeed so hard as to raise doubts about their tractability, though they arguably vary in their scientific and philosophical relevance. In the context of these problems, I have sought to name and analyse a further problem of phenomenal consciousness. It is a problem with important implications for philosophy of mind and very direct implications for consciousness *science* (Miller, 2001, 2007).

2. Two paths to the problem

The science of consciousness is founded on searching for the neural correlates of consciousness (Crick, 1994; Crick & Koch, 1990, 1998; usually referred to as 'NCC' but here as 'NCrC', unless quoting directly). Specifically, consciousness science seeks to identify the *minimally sufficient* NCrC. Chalmers (2000) provided a foundational work concerning this notion, in a paper entitled, 'What is a neural correlate of consciousness?' His paper is widely cited, as is his definition of the NCrC (p. 31):

> An NCC is a minimal neural system N such that there is a mapping from states of N to states of consciousness, where a given state of N is sufficient, under conditions C, for the corresponding state of consciousness.

Also widely cited is the shorter definition by Koch (2004, p. 16) in which the NCrC is considered to be the 'minimal set of neuronal events and mechanisms jointly sufficient for a specific conscious percept'. Although there has been some discussion of Chalmers' definitions and claims, and the methodological assumptions on which they are based (e.g., Bayne, 2007; Bayne & Hohwy, 2013; Hohwy, 2007, 2009; Neisser, 2012; Noë & Thompson, 2004), there has been less scrutiny than might be expected for a foundational work in a nascent scientific discipline.

A few years ago, two groups of scientists (Aru, Bachmann, Singer, & Melloni, 2012; de Graaf, Hsieh, & Sack, 2012; see also the chapters from both groups, this volume) independently parsed NCrCs into 'NCrC substrate' or 'NCrC proper' on the one hand (the construct of interest for consciousness science) and 'NCrC precursors/prerequisites' and 'NCrC consequences' on the other (constructs of lesser interest). Their partition was aimed at developing strategies to distinguish these various NCrCs.[1] In proposing this terminology however, these authors were unaware that the problem of identifying which, from among many, NCrCs are most directly relevant to consciousness had been appreciated, named and analyzed a decade prior.

Both Antti Revonsuo (2000, 2001, 2006, this volume) and myself (Miller, 2001, 2007, 2013a, 2014) have been explicitly concerned with just how science will distinguish the neural *correlates* and the neural *constitution* of consciousness (NCnC). Our paths to this problem were however, different. Revonsuo's (2000, 2001) concern was that current scientific methodologies – brain recording techniques in particular – are not capable of targeting the right level of organization in the brain (which he termed, 'the phenomenal level'). Revonsuo (2006, this volume) also developed a highly detailed level-based biological framework for a consciousness research program that seeks to discover the *constitutive mechanisms* of consciousness.

Although I have a great deal of affinity with Revonsuo's concerns and his framework, my development of the issue occurred as follows. Working on the phenomenon of binocular rivalry in the late 1990's, I too favored biologically-based explanatory principles for phenomenal consciousness (Miller, 1998, 1999). I was also concerned with limitations to the scientific study of neural systems with subjectivity (Miller, 1999). In 2000, whilst writing about electrophysiological, brain-imaging and brain stimulation studies of binocular rivalry for a special issue of *Brain and Mind*, it occurred to me that no amount of recording, disablement (inhibition) and stimulation correlational data could inform the question of which neural activities actually

1. Note that the plural 'NCrCs' indicates the many individual neural activities that correlate with a specific state of consciousness. This is different to 'the NCrC' which is a collective term commonly used to denote the set of all NCrCs for such a state. More points of clarification and definition are detailed below.

constituted the rivaling conscious states. This struck me as a major problem because *it is the neural constitution of consciousness that the scientific study of consciousness ultimately seeks to understand* (Miller, 2001). I noted (Miller, 2001) that although the problem of identifying the constitution of consciousness had been *alluded to* by investigators in the science of consciousness, such as Francis Crick, Christof Koch and Nikos Logothetis (Crick, 1994; Crick & Koch, 1998; Logothetis, 1998), it required much more than such passing reference.[2] I therefore sought to name and examine the *correlation/constitution distinction problem* (herewith, Cr/Cn distinction problem) so that it might be addressed *explicitly*, with a view to its solution or dissolution, or indeed to its acceptance as an ultimate epistemic limit.

Explicating the Cr/Cn distinction problem utilizing binocular rivalry data, my initial analysis, unlike Revonsuo's, led me to be concerned that perhaps even future scientific methodologies, including those targeting the right level of organization in the brain, might fail to solve the problem (Miller, 2001). I suggested there were no obvious corollaries regarding the NCnC from studies of the NCrC. I therefore proposed that consciousness science might require entirely new scientific strategies if it is to move from mere correlation to actual constitution. My initial concerns were restated and developed in a subsequent paper (Miller, 2007), in which I noted (p. 161, italics in original):

> If we imagine that through the employment of all current and future neuroscientific methods (in all contexts, under all conditions and with all methodological constraints overcome), we were able to obtain a complete, real-time and multimodal description of all the NCC and all observable properties of such, would we be satisfied that we had obtained a comprehensive understanding of the neuroscience of consciousness? I assert not, because *not every neural correlate of a conscious state is necessarily constitutive of that state.*

In both my 2001 and 2007 papers, I discussed how NCrC recording, inhibition (disablement) and stimulation techniques – either alone or in combination – failed to distinguish correlated but non-constitutive neural activities that are *upstream* or *downstream* from correlated constitutive neural activities. (This upstream/downstream terminology is equivalent to precursors/consequences terminology and is also used by others; e.g., Chalmers, 2000; Hohwy & Bayne, this volume.[3]) I considered therefore, that these empirical approaches failed to yield conclusions regarding the NCnC, and that entirely new approaches might be needed. In Miller (2007), as well as extending my discussion of the inadequacy of inhibition and stimulation approaches to

2. I expect the problem to have been alluded to by many other authors as well, as I continue to discover (e.g., Bachmann, 2000, p. 125; Frith, Perry, & Lumer, 1999, p. 109).

3. It should also be noted that in addition to correlated non-constitutive activities upstream and downstream from correlated constitutive activities, there can be correlated non-constitutive activities that are *parallel* to correlated constitutive activities. For simplicity, in the arguments that follow I do not consider the parallel category further.

identifying the NCnC, I also situated the Cr/Cn distinction problem in the context of other hard problems of consciousness (see Section 1 of the present paper) and briefly discussed philosophical implications of using 'constitution' terminology in explicating the problem, (see Section 9.1 and 9.2 of the present paper). I noted that the Cr/Cn distinction problem should not be proclaimed intractable until every effort has been made to solve or dissolve it and that even if it turns out to be intractable, this would not threaten physicalist (or materialist) ontologies (see Section 9.3 of the present paper).

On this background, the present work (see also Miller, 2014) substantially extends analysis of the Cr/Cn distinction problem, particularly with respect to empirical neuroscientific strategies. By way of a roadmap for what follows, Section 3 provides an overview of Chalmers' (2000) foundational paper regarding what a neural correlate of consciousness ought to be. In Sections 4 and 5, I then discuss in detail, neural inhibition approaches that challenge those foundational issues, and I propose the Jenga analogy to support my arguments. Thereafter, in Section 6, neural stimulation and combined inhibition/stimulation approaches are discussed, and I suggest that although the latter may provide the best evidence for identifying at least some constitutive neural activities, they fail to fully solve the Cr/Cn distinction problem. Section 7 then outlines various points of clarification, while Section 8 presents and defends against six potential objections to the arguments made. In Section 9, I discuss a range of related scientific and philosophic issues while in Section 10, I conclude by proposing new foundational claims for consciousness science.

3. Another look at the foundations of consciousness science

As mentioned above, the Cr/Cn distinction problem is neatly exposed when considering NCrCs during binocular rivalry. This visual phenomenon – in which *dynamic* perceptual alternations are induced by *static* presentation of a different image to each eye – provides several advantages for the scientific study of consciousness (reviewed in Miller, 2013b). In particular, binocular rivalry allows for dissociation between neural activity correlated with a subject's perceptual alternations and neural activity correlated with image presentation. Thus, *perception-dependent* neural activity is rightly considered a neural correlate of visual consciousness during rivalry. However, the perception-dependent data for rivalry from electrophysiological and brain-imaging *recording* studies (reviewed in many chapters in Miller, 2013a, and depicted in Figure 2a further below) yield a wide array of such NCrCs. This *makes evident* the Cr/Cn distinction problem. That is, because not every NCrC is necessarily constitutive of that conscious state, we can ask *which* NCrCs from this array are actually constitutive. Moreover, we can ask what methodologies science might employ to experimentally examine various hypotheses in this regard.

Thus, on a literal interpretation, the term 'NCrC' means neural activities (e.g., neural spiking, local field potentials, and the large-scale electrophysiological activity that generates EEG and other brain-imaging signals) that are perception-dependent and thus that correlate with a subject's momentary and changing conscious state. On this sense of the NCrC term, and as mentioned above, it is clear that the study of binocular rivalry has been a spectacular success in identifying NCrCs, at least for visual consciousness. But Chalmers' (2000) analysis of NCrC terminology shows the term to encompass a much more complex conceptual entity.

Chalmers (2000) considers an NCrC to be a system whose state correlates *directly* with a state of consciousness. He asks whether an NCC is required to be necessary and sufficient for the corresponding state of consciousness, but notes that the possibility of there being more than one NCrC for a given conscious state makes the necessity criterion too strong. He states therefore that only sufficiency is required, but that not any sufficiency will do. Mere sufficiency allows irrelevant processes into an NCrC and hence an NCrC must be a *minimally* sufficient system for the corresponding conscious state. Chalmers notes (p. 25; square brackets added):

> By this definition, [a neural system] N will be an NCC when (1) the states of N suffice for the corresponding states of consciousness, and (2) no proper part M of N is such that the states of M suffice for the corresponding states of consciousness. In this way, we pare down any potential NCC to its core: Any irrelevant material will be whittled away, and an NCC will be required to contain only the core processes that suffice for the conscious state in question.

Chalmers next distinguishes the 'total NCC' from the 'core NCC', pointing out (p. 26; square brackets added):

> A total NCC builds in everything [the totality of physical processes] and thus automatically suffices for the corresponding conscious states. A core NCC, on the other hand, contains only the "core" processes that correlate with consciousness. The rest of the total NCC will be relegated to some sort of background conditions required for the correct functioning of the core.

Chalmers goes on to note (pp. 26–27, italics in original):

> In the normal visual environment, we can expect that the contents of visual systems from V1 through IT will all correlate with the contents of visual consciousness, and that even the contents of the retina will do so to some extent. The reason is that in normal cases all these will be linked in a straightforward causal chain, and the systems in question will not be dissociated. But it seems wrong to say that merely because of this, all the systems (perhaps even the retina) should count as an NCC.
>
> The moral of this is that we need a finer-grained criterion to dissociate these systems and to distinguish the core NCC from processes that are merely causally linked to it. To do this, we have to require correlation across a range of *unusual cases*, as well as across normal cases, since it is these cases that yield interesting dissociations.

Chalmers then discusses a range of unusual cases such as unusual input (including binocular rivalry), brain stimulation and lesion studies and arrives at the following general definition of an NCrC (in which the unusual cases are relevant to the phrase, 'under conditions C'; p. 31):

> An NCC is a minimal neural system N such that there is a mapping from states of N to states of consciousness, where a given state of N is sufficient, under conditions C, for the corresponding state of consciousness.

Chalmers' analysis is predominantly conceptual rather than a detailed methodological approach to identifying the NCrC, but he does discuss the lesion case in some depth. He notes (p. 28), "if we find an abnormal case in which neural system N is damaged but a previously corresponding conscious state C is preserved, then N is not a neural correlate of C", and he goes on to say that (pp. 28–29), "the mere fact that correlation can be destroyed by this sort of lesion does not obviously imply that N is not an NCC in a normal brain." Importantly, he states (p. 29):

> It may be that even smaller lesions can destroy a correlation in this way. For example, it is not implausible that for any candidate NCC N, there is some other local system in the brain (perhaps a downstream area) whose proper functioning is required for activity in N to yield the usual effects that go with consciousness, and for N to yield consciousness itself. This second system might not itself be an NCC in any intuitive sense; it might merely play an enabling role, in the way that proper functioning of the heart plays an enabling role for functioning of the brain. If that is so, then if one lesions this single area downstream, activity in N will no longer correlate with consciousness. In this way, any potential NCC might be ruled out by a localized lesion elsewhere.

However, despite passages such as this, Chalmers' ensuing discussion of lesion cases does not lead him to a Cr/Cn distinction problem (to which I am led), but rather to concern about the fact that lesion cases cause altered architecture of the brain, such that (p. 29) "changes to brain architecture can change the location of an NCC, so that a physical state which was an NCC in a normal brain will not be an NCC in the altered brain". He goes on to therefore note that an NCrC should be architecture-dependent not architecture-independent. Chalmers' discussion of the lesion case, including 'even smaller lesions', is certainly methodologically troubling for him (see his ensuing discussion; pp. 29–31), and he concludes that lesion studies are methodologically dangerous, that we should be very cautious in using them to draw conclusions about NCrC location and that they may even need to be left out of NCrC identification altogether.[4] He does note, however, that (p. 30, italics in original):

4. Although Chalmers expresses caution over the lesion analysis case, no one would deny that modern understanding of the brain and its functional specialization owes a great debt to such neuropsychological analysis. Phenomenological dysfunction following destruction of certain brain regions by cerebrovascular insult, brain tumors, traumatic brain injury or surgery

> Even if correlation across abnormal cases is not *required* for system N to be an NCC, it may be that correlation across abnormal cases can provide good *evidence* that N is an NCC, and that failure of such correlation in some cases provides good evidence that N is not an NCC.

Chalmers discusses in far less detail, the methodological NCrC approach to the normal brain, unusual input and brain stimulation. He notes nonetheless that there are interpretive complexities with unusual input and brain stimulation too, but he considers these cases and the normal brain case to be those over which an NCrC should be required to hold (with perhaps some 'good' lesion approaches also being admitted). The present analyses aim to address in detail, inhibition and stimulation empirical strategies – and their interpretive complexities – that surround the notion of the minimally sufficient NCrC.

Chalmers' analysis of what an NCrC should be considered to be is also frank in its intentions (p. 31):

> It makes sense to have a definition of NCC that fits the way the notion is generally used in the field, and that can make sense of empirical research in the area. At the same time we want a definition of NCC to be coherent and well-motivated in its own right, such that an NCC is something worth looking for, and such that the definition can itself be used to assess various hypotheses about the identity of an NCC.

His intentions for the definitions are made additionally clear in the following passage (p. 37):

> Defining an NCC solely in terms of correlation seems to capture standard usage best, and it also makes the search more clearly defined and the methodology clearer. Correlations are easy for science to study. It also means that the search for an NCC can be to a large extent theoretically neutral rather than theoretically loaded. Once we have found an NCC, one might hope that it will turn out to be a system dedicated to consciousness, or that it will turn out to yield an explanation of consciousness, but these are further questions. In the meantime the search for an NCC as defined poses a tractable empirical question with relatively clear parameters, one that researchers of widely different theoretical persuasions can engage in.

He also notes (p. 37, italics in original):

> An NCC is defined to be a *correlate* of consciousness. From this, it does not automatically follow that an NCC will be a system solely or mainly dedicated to consciousness, or even that an NCC will be the brain system most responsible for the generation of consciousness. It certainly does not follow that an NCC will yield

has informed mechanistic understanding of normal brain function enormously (Damasio & Damasio, 1989; Howieson, Bigler, & Tranel, 2012), as has direct electrical stimulation of the brain (Borchers, Himmelbach, Logothetis, & Karnath, 2012; see Section 6).

> an explanation of consciousness, and it is not even guaranteed that identifying an NCC will be the key to understanding processes underlying consciousness. If one were to define an NCC in these stronger terms, it would be far from obvious that there must be an NCC, and it would also be much less clear how to search for an NCC.

Thus, Chalmers' intentions for his foundational analysis are to constrain the discussion to 'correlation' terminology, so as to be theoretically neutral rather than theoretically loaded, and to provide a tractable methodology for NCrC identification, and thus a way forward for consciousness science. He nonetheless accepts that even if the thus-defined NCrC was identified, this wouldn't necessarily *explain* consciousness and may not even be the key to understanding processes underlying consciousness. Despite this acknowledgement, he does not *explicitly* consider the potential for a Cr/Cn distinction problem, perhaps because of his reluctance to shift the discussion beyond notions of correlation. He does however acknowledge that the degree of difficulty in the search for an NCrC is dependent on how the notion is defined. While Chalmers' formulation of the minimally sufficient NCrC construct acknowledges the empirical potential it provides, it does not adequately examine the empirical entailment of the 'minimally sufficient' qualifier or the methodological details of such entailment.

Despite the valuable contribution provided by Chalmers' conceptual proposals, there are several problems with accepting his formulation as unchallenged foundations for consciousness science. Indeed, Chalmers himself considered his work to be 'conceptual spadework' that would require refinement. If my contention above is accurate – that consciousness science wishes to ultimately identify the NCnC – then it is noteworthy that this construct is nowhere to be seen in Chalmers' analysis. It is a construct that can be conveyed using a wide range of terms such as the neural 'basis', 'mechanism', or 'substrate' of consciousness (see Miller, 2007, for more terms), so concerns over the entailed philosophical commitments of 'constitution' terminology should not be reason to avoid such a construct, or something like it.[5] Moreover, once we admit talk of such notions, questions arise regarding: (1) whether by minimally

5. There are differences between the terms 'basis', 'mechanism', 'substrate' and 'constitution', however in most of what follows, I use these terms synonymously. Hence, by 'NCnC' I mean to equally imply the neural 'basis', 'mechanism' or 'substrate' of consciousness. At times I will state these terms in full to remind the reader of this point and indeed, on this broad construal, one could even 'define' the NCnC as the neural basis, mechanism or substrate of consciousness. However, although the Cr/Cn distinction problem is able to be appreciated and analyzed using any of these broadly synonymous terms, use of 'constitution' terminology becomes relevant and informative later, as a specific relation within philosophy of mind (with additional implications for science thereafter). It is because of the relational complexities in the philosophical domain that I resist any further simple definition of the NCnC. For example, a definition could be proposed that states the NCnC is the neural activity that simply *is* the conscious state in question, but any such definition then invites debate about contrasting the 'is of identity' with the 'is of constitution' (see Miller, 2007, and various papers in section II of this volume).

sufficient NCrC, we mean the very same thing as the neural basis, mechanism, substrate or constitution of consciousness; (2) whether these constructs pick out the same or different neural activity sets; and (3) if they could pick out *different* neural activity sets, which should be considered the ultimate empirical target for consciousness science.

4. Stepwise inhibition

As discussed above, the notion of the minimally sufficient NCrC was created to distinguish it from the *merely* sufficient NCrC. However, the distinction between the merely and minimally sufficient NCrC *entails* an empirical strategy. If we are to arrive at identification of the minimally sufficient NCrC, we will presumably need to *remove* NCrCs one by one to assess whether each has minimally sufficient status. It is critical here to note that when I refer to an NCrC being minimally sufficient, or having minimally sufficient status, I mean to say that it is a *part* of the whole minimally sufficient neural activity set. Similarly, when I refer to an NCrC being constitutive, or having constitutive status, I mean to say that it is a *part* of the whole NCnC. Returning to the empirical approach to reducing the merely sufficient NCrC to the minimally sufficient NCrC, the most obvious means of doing this is by *stepwise inhibition* (disablement) of neurons, neuron types, local or distributed neural circuits, specific brain regions or sets of NCrCs.[6]

Chalmers' (2000) definitions would seem to imply something like a stepwise inhibition empirical strategy when he states (p. 25), as noted above, "In this way, we pare down any potential NCC to its core: Any irrelevant material will be whittled away, and an NCC will be required to contain only the core processes that suffice for the

6. On the issue of neuron types, Koch (2004, p. 282) refers to perception-dependent neural activity high in the visual processing pathway (inferior temporal cortex, IT; superior temporal sulcus, STS) during binocular rivalry as follows:

> It is implausible that all of the storied IT and STS neurons that follow the percept express its phenomenological attributes directly. Some must be involved in the underlying winner-take-all operations; others must relay the winner's identity to the motor centres to initiate behavior or to short term memory for future recall; some must carry a transient signal indicative of a perceptual switch; and still others might represent the same information but in a delayed manner.
>
> When considering the temporal profile of cellular responses in these areas, I am struck by their extreme heterogeneity. An entire menagerie of distinct patterns can be observed. Some cells fire in a transient manner whereas others respond in a more sustained fashion. Some fire in bursts, some show a pronounced, rhythmic discharge in the 4 to 6 Hz range, while others peak early before settling down to a more sedate and sustained pace of firing. Do these reflect discrete cell types with discrete functions and connectivity patterns? This will be important to know.

conscious state in question." There is some conflict in Chalmers' view here, given his willingness to whittle away but not to lesion. We therefore need to qualify the *type* of inhibition to be employed in identifying the minimally sufficient NCrC, and select methods that do not induce gross lesions and consequent architectural disruption (such as that induced by stroke, tumor, injury or surgery). Although current methods such as inhibitory transcranial magnetic stimulation could be employed – and indeed this method provides striking and immediate perceptual disruption during binocular rivalry (Miller et al., 2000; see also Ngo, Barsdell, Law, & Miller, 2013) – for conceptual clarity we might postulate future highly specific molecular knockout techniques in which this or that NCrC can be selectively and reversibly inhibited. Such techniques were predicted by Crick and Koch (1998; see also the quote further below from Fenno, Yizhar, & Deisseroth, 2011) and are *currently* being developed and refined, with stunning progress, in the field of optogenetics (as detailed further below; Fenno et al., 2011; see also Klink, van Wezel, & van Ee, 2013). Although harmless application of such techniques in humans remains a very long way off, we can nonetheless begin to think through how such highly selective inhibitory techniques could, *in principle*, assist with identification of the NCnC.

As I have previously noted (Miller, 2001, 2007), if we inhibit an NCrC and consciousness disappears (or degrades), this might suggest the inhibited NCrC *is* constitutive in the normal case but does not actually prove its constitutive status. This is because such an NCrC might simply be *necessary and supportive* for consciousness without being constitutive of it. Conversely, if we inhibit an NCrC and consciousness does not disappear (or degrade), this might suggest the inhibited NCrC is *non*-constitutive in the normal case but does not prove such non-constitutive status. This is because such an NCrC might simply be *redundantly* constitutive. Because of these uncertainties, I have claimed that stepwise inhibition does not lead to conclusions regarding the NCnC. However, it certainly *does* lead to conclusions regarding the minimally sufficient NCrC.

5. The Jenga analogy

To illustrate how the minimally sufficient NCrC and the NCnC are constructs that can pick out different neural activity sets, and to schematize the stepwise inhibition approach described above, I here propose the Jenga analogy. This analogy is from the popular game in which blocks are removed from a tower structure, one by one, until eventually a *critical point* is reached and the tower falls. An upright tower in this analogy (see Figure 1 further below) represents a *specific* conscious state or content being present while the fallen tower represents the absence (or degradation) of that conscious state or content. Each block in the tower represents an NCrC that correlates with that specific conscious state or content. This follows the distinction by Koch (2004) between 'specific factors' and 'enabling factors', with the former dealing with particular conscious states or content and the latter with the overall state of being conscious. Although this distinction is itself the subject of considerable conceptual and methodological controversy (see Bayne, 2007; Bayne & Hohwy, 2013; Hohwy, 2007, 2009; Hohwy & Bayne, this volume; Neisser, 2012; Noë & Thompson, 2004), I sidestep this debate and constrain the ensuing discussion to just specific factors.[7]

As the case of binocular rivalry illustrates (Figure 2a; see also Miller, 2013a), there are many (specific factor) NCrCs for a given conscious state and these can include specific brain regions or specific neural populations within brain regions. In the Jenga analogy, each NCrC block can thus be considered representative of a specific factor NCrC at either local, distributed or regional levels.[8] The first step in the stepwise inhibition strategy is to use recording techniques to create an NCrC specific factor map for a specific (target) conscious state. Several further stipulations for the Jenga analogy are required. First, the entire tower is considered to be the outcome of previous strategies to 'screen off' irrelevant *neural* activities (Hohwy, 2009; Hohwy & Bayne, this volume). Hence, on this analogy, already screened off would be (1) neural activities that do *not* correlate with specific conscious states or content; (2) neural activities that correlate with specific conscious states or content, but do so only in a *loose* fashion, in which the correlation can be broken one way or another;[9] (3) neural activities that correlate with specific conscious states or content but whose precise *timing* provides clear ascription of either upstream or downstream, rather than constitutive, status (see also Aru et al., this volume; de Graaf & Sack, this volume; Hohwy & Bayne, this volume; Revonsuo,

7. Bayne and Hohwy (2013; see also Hohwy & Bayne, this volume) refer to *differentiating* NCrCs, which are considered neural states that are selectively implicated in particular kinds of conscious states in an already conscious creature.

8. As neurophysiological understanding develops, so too will the notion of what an NCrC block could be taken to be in this analogy – that is, what appropriate 'units' of neurophysiological signalling will turn out to be. For now however, each block represents individual NCrCs such as those being identified at various levels of constituents, organization and processes in studies of binocular rivalry.

9. In my view, and without wishing to undermine or dismiss these important conceptual and methodological efforts, I consider the strategies so far proposed to distinguish NCrC precursors/prerequisites, NCrC proper/substrate, and NCrC consequences by de Graaf and Sack (this volume), and Aru, Bachmann, Singer and Melloni (this volume), generally fall into this category, appealing to ever more refined means of identifying loosely from tightly correlated neural activities. Thus, for example, it is suggested by Aru et al. (this volume) that we refine experimental manipulations to more closely take account of gradual variation in the quality of consciousness across trials, changes in the perceptual quality of a stimulus over time within trials, and variation in perception of complex stimuli across trials. This refinement certainly helps to close in on the constitution of consciousness but the Jenga analogy begins only *after* application of such strategies.

this volume);[10] and (4) neural activities that correlate with specific conscious states or content but whose known mechanistic functions provide grounds for clear ascription as non-constitutive.[11] What remains after such a screening off process therefore, is a tower of neural activities that *tightly* correlate with a specific conscious state or content and whose precise timing or known mechanistic functions cannot be used to accurately ascribe upstream, downstream or constitutive status.[12]

Second, NCrC blocks in the lower third of the tower (colored yellow) represent tightly correlated non-constitutive upstream activities (tightly correlated NCrC precursors or NCrC prerequisites), those in the upper third (colored blue) represent tightly correlated non-constitutive downstream activities (tightly correlated NCrC consequences) and those in the middle third (colored red) represent tightly correlated *constitutive* NCrCs (the NCnC). Third, the upright tower at the critical point beyond which any further block removal will result in its collapse and the disappearance (or degradation) of the target conscious state represents the minimally sufficient NCrC.

Consider now that each of the thus-defined tightly correlated neural activity blocks in the Jenga tower can be described by only *one* of the following conjunctions:

(1) non-constitutive and non-minimally sufficient
(2) non-constitutive and minimally sufficient
(3) constitutive and non-minimally sufficient
(4) constitutive and minimally sufficient

10. That is, neural activities could be tightly correlated with specific conscious states or content but the correlation might nonetheless be slightly phase-shifted, either ahead of, or following, the state. The case of rivalry is illustrative here, when focusing on clean, abrupt rivalling states (thus setting aside mixed percepts and wave-like transitions between states). Thus, neural activity correlations with sufficient temporal resolution (such as single-unit electrophysiology) could yield fine timing discriminations that might permit of clear partition of upstream NCrCs and downstream NCrCs on such a timing basis alone. It is just as possible however, that fine phase-shifts in various NCrCs may not provide the clarity we seek regarding the neural basis, mechanism, substrate or constitution of consciousness because the threshold for where such phase-shifting should signal constitutive irrelevance is itself problematic. The importance and complexity of timing in the brain is likely to be a source of interpretive difficulty and this fact underscores the problems being discussed in the present paper. Nonetheless, in cases for which clear ascription appears possible, timing can be used to screen off candidates for constitutive neural activity. For a detailed source on the issue of timing and phenomenal consciousness, see Bachmann (2000) and for a more recent example of timing studies, see Liu, Agam, Madsen and Kreiman (2009).

11. I provided an example of this fourth category in my first explication of the Cr/Cn distinction problem (Miller, 2001) in terms of the expected correlated neural activity that would be found in subcortical nuclei controlling eye-movement tracking (optokinetic nystagmus) during rivalry with drifting gratings. Despite being correlated with consciousness during such rivalry, the known mechanistic function of eye movement nuclei suggests a non-constitutive role for this individual NCrC.

12. Herewith, I combine points (2), (3) and (4) such that when I refer to *tightly* correlated NCrCs, I mean to also include the precise timing and mechanistic function issues.

Consider further, the following two possibilities (P), each of which is to be considered in isolation (because complexities arise when they are considered together):

> Possibility 1 (P1): Considering all individual NCrCs that have survived the screening off process, the possibility of non-constitutive minimally sufficient NCrCs means that the minimally sufficient NCrC could be a *larger* set of neural activities than the neural basis, mechanism, substrate or constitution of consciousness.
>
> Possibility 2 (P2): Imagining just the neural basis, mechanism, substrate or constitution of consciousness, the possibility of redundancy (the possibility of constitutive non-minimally sufficient NCrCs) means that the minimally sufficient NCrC could be a *smaller* set of neural activities than the neural basis, mechanism, substrate or constitution of consciousness.

Suppose now, that the first five correlated non-constitutive upstream activity blocks are removed but the conscious state remains and the tower stays upright. Those NCrCs are therefore *non*-minimally sufficient. Further suppose however, that removal of the sixth correlated non-constitutive upstream activity block does lead to the disappearance (or degradation) of the conscious state and to falling of the tower. That sixth NCrC *is* minimally sufficient. But the Jenga analogy shows that an NCrC can be minimally sufficient *without* necessarily being constitutive. In this way, the minimally sufficient NCrC could be a larger set of neural activities than the NCnC (see Figure 1 below). The downstream case is a little more complex (see Aru et al., this volume; de Graaf & Sack, this volume; Hohwy & Bayne, this volume; van Boxtel & Tsuchiya, this volume), and it is not always clear what should be regarded as an upstream activity and what a downstream activity, particularly given the unclear neurophysiological role of feedback. However, the difference between upstream and downstream cases isn't particularly important for the point I am making and P1 is illustrated clearly with reference to just the upstream case.

Next imagine the set of neural activities that is the NCnC and consider that due to the possibility of redundancy in this neural activity set, five NCrC blocks could be removed without the disappearance (or degradation) of the conscious state and with the tower remaining upright. Those five neural activities are therefore *non*-minimally sufficient despite being actually constitutive. Removal of the sixth correlated constitutive neural activity block however, takes the tower passed its critical point and the conscious state disappears (or degrades) and the tower falls. This sixth NCrC block then is *both* constitutive and minimally sufficient. In this way, the minimally sufficient NCrC within this (imagined) constitutive neural activity set could be a smaller set of neural activities than the NCnC (Figure 1).

The issue of claiming larger versus smaller sets is complicated when conceiving of P1 and P2 *together*, but the key message here is not about the overall size of the different neural activity sets, but rather that the minimally sufficient NCrC and the NCnC *can be different sets of neural activities*. Other important complexities include combinatorial and order complexities (i.e., whether the critical block removal would be critical *whenever* it is removed, or only when removed *after* removal of the previous five blocks, or only after removal of the previous five blocks in *that* specific order).

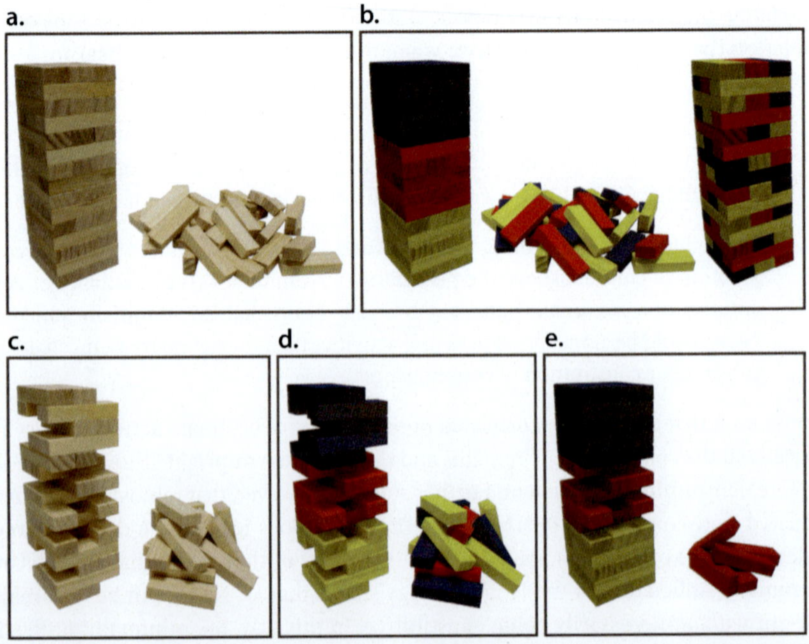

Figure 1. The Jenga analogy schematizes the stepwise inhibition strategy inherent in distinguishing the merely sufficient from the minimally sufficient NCrC and shows how the minimally sufficient NCrC can differ from the NCnC. In all panels, the upright tower represents the presence of a specific conscious state (or content) while in (a) and (b) the fallen tower (rubble) represents the loss (or degradation) of that state. Each block represents a perception-dependent NCrC that correlates with the specific conscious state (i.e., a specific factor NCrC). The whole tower is what remains after a process of screening off non-correlated neural activities and NCrCs that are only loosely correlated with consciousness or whose precise timing or known mechanistic function indicates they are not candidates for the NCnC. **(a)** and **(c)** depict real-world situations, while **(b)**, **(d)** and **(e)** depict colored subdivisions that could only be identified if the Cr/Cn distinction problem is solvable. In **(b)**, **(d)** and **(e)**, yellow blocks represent tightly correlated non-constitutive upstream activities (NCrC precursors/prerequisites), blue blocks represent tightly correlated non-constitutive downstream activities (NCrC consequences) and red blocks represent correlated constitutive activities (the NCnC). The right tower in **(b)** represents a more distributed depiction of the colored subdivisions than the left tower in **(b)**. In **(c)** and **(d)**, the upright tower with NCrC blocks removed is at the critical point beyond which any further block removal will result in the disappearance (or degradation) of the conscious state and collapse of the tower. The upright tower in **(c)** and **(d)** thus represents the minimally sufficient NCrC. Blocks in this critical point tower have minimally sufficient status, while those removed from it do not. In P1 (see main text), the possibility of non-constitutive minimally sufficient NCrCs (remaining yellow and blue blocks in **d**) means that the minimally sufficient NCrC could be a larger set of neural activities than the neural basis, mechanism, substrate or constitution of consciousness

(i.e., the tower in (**d**) is a larger set of blocks than the red middle third of the left tower in **b**). In P2 (see main text), the possibility of redundancy in the NCnC (i.e., the possibility of constitutive non-minimally sufficient NCrCs; removed red blocks in **e**) means that the minimally sufficient NCrC could be a smaller set of neural activities than the neural basis, mechanism, substrate or constitution of consciousness (i.e., the red remaining blocks in the tower in (**e**) is a smaller set of blocks than the red middle third of the left tower in (**b**); note P1 and P2 are not meant to be considered together – see main text). The stepwise inhibition strategy can therefore be used to assign minimally sufficient status to each block in the Jenga tower in (**a**) (thus the real-world situation of getting from **a** to **c**). However, the Cr/Cn distinction problem claims that there are no evident strategies to readily assign color status (constitutive red versus non-constitutive yellow/blue) to each of the NCrC blocks (thus it is not clear how to get from **a** to **b**). The analogy shows that although we might get from (**a**) to (**c**) using the stepwise inhibition approach, this will not satisfy consciousness science because we still cannot assign color status to either the remaining or removed blocks in (**c**) (we cannot get from **c** to **d**). Through this analogy it is claimed that the ultimate target of consciousness science is not to identify the minimally sufficient NCrC, but rather to distinguish constitutive (red) NCrCs from non-constitutive (yellow/blue) NCrCs. That is, it is ultimately the neural basis, mechanism, substrate or constitution of consciousness that we seek to understand and this construct can pick out a different neural activity set from that of the minimally sufficient NCrC.

Despite these complexities, what is important here is that while the empirical strategy of stepwise inhibition can identify an NCrC's minimally sufficient status, it cannot identify its constitutive status. As the Jenga analogy shows, and as depicted in Figure 2 using the case of binocular rivalry, while stepwise inhibition achieves identification of the minimally sufficient NCrC, it cannot identify (1) which of the *remaining* blocks are constitutive of the conscious state and which are not, or (2) which of the *removed* blocks are constitutive of the conscious state and which are not.[13]

This is not to say that identifying the minimally sufficient NCrC through stepwise inhibition would be an insignificant achievement for consciousness science. On the

13. It is important to note that the Jenga analogy is just that – an analogy. It *schematizes* the stepwise inhibition approach to illustrate the points I am making. There is certainly no implied direct equivalence between removing a block from a tower of mechanically related blocks on the one hand, and inhibiting a neuron, neural circuit or set of neural circuits within an exquisitely complex, dynamic and inter-related neural system with the capacity for functional and structural reorganization, on the other. Aside from differences in complexity between a Jenga tower and a neural system, there are further points of difference such as the effect that inhibiting a neuron has on the neuron's milieu and on non-neural structures like nearby glia and vasculature (Logothetis, 2010). Because of these issues, problems of interpretation can arise with respect to whether it is the neural inhibition that is (or is not) changing consciousness or it is the secondary physiological effects of that inhibition. The same interpretive problems arise regarding neural stimulation (discussed in the next section, where further caveats are raised).

contrary, it would be a *major* achievement. However, the problem remains of just how science will experimentally distinguish the neural activity sets of the minimally sufficient NCrC and the NCnC (or if these are in fact the very same sets, how this can be shown to be the case). In my view then, the minimally sufficient NCrC construct should not be considered the ultimate empirical target for consciousness science because it could *include* neural activities that are *not* part of the neural basis, mechanism, substrate or constitution of consciousness (P1) and it could *exclude* neural activities that *are* (P2). The minimally sufficient NCrC notion, for all its worth, subtly shifts the target of consciousness science to an empirically tractable one, while the real target remains elusive due to the Cr/Cn distinction problem.

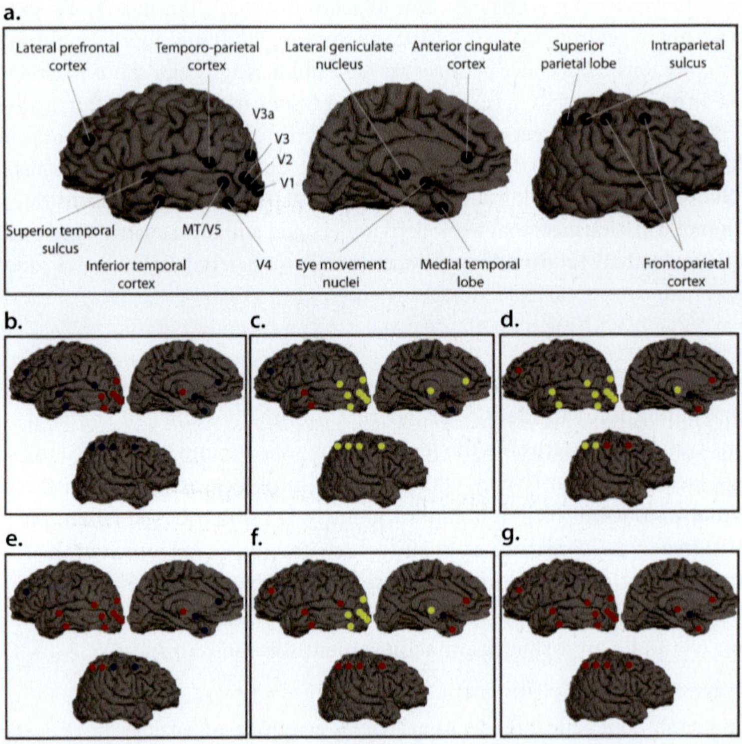

Figure 2. The Cr/Cn distinction problem is clearly illustrated with reference to the phenomenon of binocular rivalry. (**a**) Research using electrophysiological (single-unit and local field potential), brain-imaging and brain stimulation (and inhibition) approaches has identified a wide array of NCrCs during binocular rivalry and related phenomena such as flash suppression (for details, see Miller, 2013a; for even further electrophysiological NCrCs during rivalry and related phenomena, see Figure 6 in Boly et al., 2013). As I have noted previously (Miller, 2001, 2007), binocular rivalry is not normal vision and hence brings with it a range of neurophysiological features that

may have more to do with rivalry itself than with visual consciousness (see also Blake, Brascamp, & Heeger, 2014). Nonetheless, binocular rivalry does offer a multitude of advantages for the scientific study of visual consciousness and these have been outlined elsewhere (see Editorial Introduction of this volume and Miller, 2013b). For present purposes, the existence of multiple NCrCs during rivalry raises the issue of which activities can be said to constitute a specific conscious state rather than being merely correlated with it. There are multiple hypotheses possible for which NCrCs are upstream from (i.e., precursors or prerequisites), which are downstream from (i.e., consequences), and which are constitutive of, consciousness. These competing hypotheses are indicated by the color-coding alternatives in the smaller panels (which follows the color coding of the Jenga analogy in Figure 1). Hence constitutive NCrCs could be: **(b)** just lower-level visual processing correlates (with high-level visual and non-visual correlates reflecting stimulus feature selection and high level processing, but not actually constituting experience of the stimulus); **(c)** just high-level visual processing correlates (with lower-level correlates representing stimulus features and initiating the rivalry process, and non-visual regions both selecting for such features and being readouts of such selection, but not actually constituting experience of the stimulus); **(d)** just anterior non-visual correlates (with lower-level and high-level visual processing correlates providing required stimulus processing, and posterior non-visual regions selecting stimulus features, but not actually constituting experience of the stimulus); **(e)** the combination of low-level and high-level visual processing correlates and selection-related posterior non-visual regions (with anterior non-visual correlates being the readout of the visual state, but not actually constituting experience of the stimulus); **(f)** the combination of anterior and posterior non-visual processing correlates and high-level visual processing correlates (with lower-level correlates representing stimulus features and initiating the rivalry process, but not actually constituting experience of the stimulus); or **(g)** the whole combination of low-level and high-level visual processing correlates, and anterior and posterior non-visual correlates. While this NCrC array could be subjected to the stepwise inhibition strategy underlying the notion of the minimally sufficient NCrC, the problem of assigning the appropriate color-coding to each NCrC cannot be solved with the same strategy because of the Cr/Cn distinction problem. There are several caveats to interpreting this figure including issues such as: not all neurons in each area will exhibit perception-dependent firing (e.g., V1/V2, V4, middle temporal area, MT); even when perception-dependent in V4 and MT, this includes a proportion of neurons with the opposite expected firing pattern (i.e., lower firing rates when their preferred stimulus is perceived and higher firing rates when their preferred stimulus is suppressed); some of the regions correlate with transitions between rivaling states (or with reporting of such states) rather than with the visual states themselves; some regions are targets of rivalry temporal parameter modulation rather than consciousness modulation per se; regions engaged in attentional selection and top-down modulation could be considered either upstream or downstream activities; and there may be important binding mechanisms that physiologically link individual NCrCs (see main text).

6. Stepwise stimulation and combined inhibition/stimulation

If recording strategies make evident the Cr/Cn distinction problem and stepwise inhibition can identify an NCrC's minimally sufficient but not constitutive status, what might the strategy of neural stimulation achieve? And indeed, exactly how would such a strategy be applied in the context of studying consciousness? Perhaps the first distinction required here is that between stimulation of currently *inactive* NCrCs and those *already active*. On the one hand, stimulation of already active correlated neurons, neuron types, local or distributed neural circuits, brain regions or sets of NCrCs, would generally not be expected to change a conscious state (irrespective of whether these stimulated NCrCs are constitutive or not). On the other hand, when stimulating currently *inactive* correlated neurons, neuron types, local or distributed neural circuits, brain regions or sets of NCrCs, a changed conscious state might suggest a constitutive role for such NCrCs but such a role is not proven by this strategy. This is because the stimulated NCrC might in fact be *non*-constitutive with its stimulation simply activating downstream NCrCs that *are* constitutive. In this case there may be conclusions possible regarding the *causal chain* of neural processing for that state, but there are no corollaries regarding the NCnC.[14]

What about *combinations* of inhibition and stimulation? I have previously asserted (Miller, 2007, p. 165) that, "by recording from, disabling and stimulating various NCrCs, there do not seem to be any obvious corollaries regarding the NCnC." However, development of the Jenga analogy now leads me to reassess this assertion. Consider the following experimental scenario – the *reverse* Jenga strategy – which might at least *in principle*, and *partially*, address issues of constitution. This strategy again requires a highly specific and powerful inhibitory, and now also stimulatory, technical capacity, i.e., the ability to selectively inhibit, disinhibit and stimulate

14. This is not the place to discuss in detail the difference between the causation and constitution relation. Suffice to say, I believe the causation relation should be restricted to usage in which one neural activity causes another (hence in the context of causal chain processing) or in the context of mechanistic explanation in which a mechanism or operational part has causal influence on other mechanisms or operational parts (see Craver, 2007, for more on the distinction between causal/etiological and constitutive mechanisms). I do not think the causation relation should be used in the context of the brain–mind relation. That is, brain states constitute mental states, or are identical with them, or realize them, or the relation is one of supervenience, but brain states do not cause mental states. These matters are taken up in much greater detail in Keaton (this volume) and Kozuch and Kriegel (this volume). For the view that causation *is* in fact the relevant brain–mind relation, see Neisser (2012). On the issue of mental causation (i.e., whether mental states could cause brain states and behavior), I do not address this at all, but a constitution, identity, realization or supervenience relation would not preclude mental states causing *other* brain states and consequent behavior – these relations would just preclude mental states causing their *own* brain states.

specifically tagged neurons, neuron-types, local or distributed neural circuits, specific brain regions and sets of NCrCs. Note here also that stimulation is a *further* physiological step beyond mere disinhibition to resting state activity. It is also to be noted that the arguments above and below concern inhibition and stimulation of *excitatory* rather than inhibitory neurons, though it is acknowledged that (1) physiological inhibitory neural activity is a fundamental feature of cortical microcircuits and is "electrically inseparable from excitation" (Borchers et al., 2012, p. 66); (2) neurons that correlate with a specific conscious state by *decreasing* their firing rate are not addressed by these arguments; and (3) *modulation* of neural activity is not addressed by these arguments. All of these issues (and those in footnote 13) make the arguments I wish to present more complex than is required at this stage, but I do not discount their relevance.

Again optogenetics comes to mind when positing a highly specific and powerful inhibitory and stimulatory technique and it is worth quoting in full, the first two paragraphs of a recent review of this technique (Fenno et al., 2011, p. 390, square brackets in original):

> In describing unrealized prerequisites for assembling a general theory of mind, Francis Crick observed that the ability to manipulate individual components of the brain would be needed, requiring "a method by which all neurons of just one type could be inactivated, leaving the others more or less unaltered" (Crick, 1979, p. 222). Extracellular electrical manipulation does not readily achieve true inactivation, and even electrical excitation, while allowing for temporal precision in stimulating within a given volume, lacks specificity for cell type. However, pharmacological and genetic manipulations can be specific to cells with certain expression profiles (in the best case) but lack temporal precision on the timescale of neural coding and signaling.
>
> Because no prior technique has achieved both high-temporal and cellular precision within intact mammalian neural tissue, there has been strong pressure to develop a new class of technology. As a result of these efforts, neurons now may be controlled with optogenetics for fast, specific excitation or inhibition within systems as complex as freely moving mammals [for example, with microbial opsin methods, light-induced inward cation currents may be used to depolarize the neuronal membrane and positively modulate firing of action potentials, while optical pumping of chloride ions can induce outwards currents and membrane hyperpolarization, thereby inhibiting spiking (Figure 1)]. These optogenetic tools of microbial origin (Figure 1) may be readily targeted to subpopulations of neurons within heterogeneous tissue and function on a temporal scale commensurate with physiological rates of spiking or critical moments in behavioral tests, with fast deactivation upon cessation of light. With these properties, microbe-derived optogenetic tools fulfil the criterion set forth by Crick in 1979.
>
> (Deisseroth, 2010, 2011)

Others have commented on the prospects for consciousness science offered by optogenetics (e.g., Tononi & Koch, 2008).[15] The technique has recently been applied in mice to examine top-down modulation of visual processing (Zhang et al., 2014) and can be applied in *Drosophila* in the context of visual rivalry (Miller, Ngo, & van Swinderen, 2012). For examples of brain stimulation techniques currently applicable in humans, including those already applied or capable of being applied to binocular rivalry, such as transcranial magnetic stimulation, vestibular stimulation techniques, transcranial direct current stimulation, and electrical microstimulation, see Been, Ngo, Miller and Fitzgerald (2007), Borchers et al. (2012), Cohen and Newsome (2004), Histed, Ni and Maunsell (2013), Klink et al. (2013), Law et al. (2013), Ngo et al. (2013), Reppas and Newsome (2007), Sengpiel (2013), Sterzer (2013), and Thomson and Fitzgerald (2013). Despite the value of such techniques for stimulating (and in some cases inhibiting) neural activity, they entail various disadvantages and interpretive complexities such as: (1) whether they in fact cause stimulation or inhibition; (2) their spatial imprecision and hence unintended effects on other local and regional neural targets; (3) individual variation, regional variation and neuronal morphological variation in stimulatory and inhibitory thresholds (and consequent perceptual and behavioral effects); and (4) the ability of such techniques to be detected by the subject. The in principle 'pure' inhibition/stimulation methodology on which the arguments in the present paper are grounded would avoid these problems, as far as is physiologically possible. And of course, knowing just how far this is physiologically possible will require a great deal of further neurophysiological understanding (see for example, the interpretive cautions outlined by Logothetis, 2010, regarding emerging optogenetic studies).

Nonetheless, with an optogenetics-style technique as an example of the type of in principle methodology to which I am referring, consider that the first step in the reverse Jenga scenario is to use recording techniques to create a tightly correlated NCrC specific factor map for a specific (target) conscious state.[16] Next, leaving

---

15. Indeed, Tononi and Koch (2008, p. 257) note in their update of the NCrC program:

> The growing ability of neuroscientists to manipulate in a reversible, transient, deliberate, and delicate manner identified populations of neurons using methods from molecular biology combined with optical stimulation enables the intrepid neuroengineer to move from correlation – observing that a particular conscious state is associated with some neural or hemodynamic activity – to causation.

While agreeing with such a sentiment, I would argue that the intrepid neuroengineer should wish to go beyond not just the correlates of consciousness, but also beyond causation (see footnote 14), to ultimately reach the constitution of consciousness.

16. The reverse Jenga strategy could theoretically be applied without a specific factor NCrC map first being identified with recording techniques (though the consequent trial and error task would be far more onerous). Such a scenario might be envisaged if developments in highly precise combined inhibition and stimulation technologies occur more rapidly than developments in highly precise recording technologies. However, this is perhaps unlikely given optogenetics, for example, is not just an inhibition and stimulation technique but is also itself

enabling factor NCrCs untouched, *all* previously mapped specific factor NCrCs are inhibited.[17] In addition, all non-correlated causal chain components, and all loosely correlated NCrCs, are inhibited. The crucial final intervention then is to stepwise dis-inhibit *and* activate (stimulate) each previously mapped, tightly correlated specific factor NCrC. Under these circumstances, if the target conscious state is reported then this would seem to provide the strongest evidence possible that the disinhibited and stimulated NCrC is actually constitutive (and thus has constitutive status).[18]

Note that in the case of P1 with the stepwise inhibition strategy, the reason a non-constitutive but minimally sufficient NCrC is minimally sufficient is because of its *input* to the NCnC (i.e., its role in causal chain processing, albeit in this case, a correlated rather than non-correlated causal chain role). Without such minimally sufficient non-constitutive NCrC activity, there could not be the required activity in the NCnC and there could not thus be the conscious state. However, in the reverse Jenga case just described, the NCnC is *directly* activated (stimulated) and thus, unlike the stepwise inhibition case, there is no dependency on minimally sufficient non-constitutive NCrCs. So in the reverse Jenga case, with this dependency condition removed, if the target conscious state appears with particular NCrC stimulation – and with other NCrCs inhibited, given the strategy is a *stepwise* combined inhibition/stimulation process – this reasonably implies constitutive status of the stimulated NCrC.

With the reverse Jenga strategy, we are thus able to *build* the middle third of the tower to its critical point of minimal sufficiency. Indeed, by identifying the tower at this critical point of just its middle third, it can be stated that what has in fact been identified is the *minimally sufficient NCnC*.[19] The reverse Jenga approach thus, arguably (see later), provides *partial* solution to the Cr/Cn distinction problem because it overcomes the obstacle of P1 and identifies *some* constitutive neural activities. However, to fully solve the Cr/Cn distinction problem, we need to achieve identification of *the whole set*

---

a recording technique. Hence developments in its (safe) recording capacity are likely to occur more or less concurrently with developments in its (safe) inhibitory and stimulatory capacity.

17. It is not clear what it would be like for a subject to be in a state in which all specific factor NCrCs were inhibited but all enabling factor NCrCs remained active, but this is an issue I have side-stepped and is debated elsewhere (Hohwy, 2009; Hohwy & Bayne, this volume; Neisser, 2012; Noë & Thompson, 2004). Confusion could also arise if one were to describe non-constitutive causal chain specific factor processes as themselves enabling factors, so this should be avoided. Enabling factors should be restricted to those neural activities present for *all* conscious states in a conscious creature.

18. Neural activity for reporting will thus also need to remain untouched; this of course raises issues of access versus phenomenal consciousness (Block, 1995, 1996; discussed in Klink, Self, Lamme, & Roelfsema, this volume) but again this is not my point here. For more on reporting and downstream NCrCs, see Aru et al. (this volume), de Graaf and Sack (this volume), Hohwy and Bayne (this volume), and van Boxtel and Tsuchiya (this volume).

19. In the case of combined inhibition/stimulation (and indeed, only in this case), the minimally sufficient NCrC and the minimally sufficient NCnC can be considered equivalent constructs.

of constitutive neural activities. To do that would require also overcoming the obstacle of P2 which would involve identifying not just the middle third of the tower at its critical point of minimal sufficiency, but the exact *boundaries* of that (whole) middle third (i.e., the exact boundaries of the NCnC; Figure 3).

To show why the reverse Jenga approach fails to fully solve the Cr/Cn distinction problem, consider the following further specific combined inhibition/stimulation scenarios (herewith I refer to the combined inhibition/stimulation approach as '*isolated* stimulation'). First, isolated stimulation of non-constitutive NCrCs in the bottom or top third of the tower – whether they are minimally sufficient NCrCs or not – would *not* induce the target conscious state. Consequently, these NCrCs can be reasonably excluded as constitutive neural activities. Second, after the conscious state first appears due to isolated stimulation of the minimally sufficient NCnC, and then as redundantly constitutive NCrCs are *additionally* disinhibited and stimulated, the conscious state will *not* change, so this will not allow a distinction to be made between redundantly constitutive NCrCs and non-constitutive NCrCs. Hence the whole set of constitutive neural activities cannot be identified.

The next isolated stimulation scenario is also informative. Thus, we can ask what would occur with isolated stimulation of redundantly constitutive NCrCs when the minimally sufficient NCnC is not also stimulated (i.e., whether that would induce the conscious state). Here the issue depends on the nature of the redundancy and the notion of *neural multiple realizability* (see Miller, 2007). That is, it may be that the minimally sufficient NCnC is a *fixed* set of neural activities for a particular conscious state, without activation of which there will never be that conscious state. In such a scenario – which invokes the notion of *necessity* rather than sufficiency – the usual case would involve a conscious state being constituted by activation of that fixed minimally sufficient neural set *and* by any additional redundantly constitutive neural activities. But another alternative is that the minimally sufficient NCnC may be a *variable* set of neural activities for a particular conscious state, such that *separate* isolated stimulation of two or more different sets of neural activities could induce (and constitute) the target conscious state, even though in the normal case *both* or *all* of these sets are constitutive. This would be a case of neural multiple realizability, whereby two or more different neural states could nonetheless constitute the same phenomenal state.[20] Note

20. Note that in philosophy, multiple realizability refers to functional roles, including consciousness, being realized by *any* substrate, not just neural activity, with such roles thus being substrate-independent. My interest in multiple realizability however, concerns just *neural* multiple realizability. In Miller (2007), I argued that within the bounds of the problem of direct intersubjective exchange and the Cr/Cn distinction problem, the science of consciousness could nonetheless make progress on issues of neural multiple realizability. As it turns out, such progress was already underway, utilizing the phenomenon of rivalry (Maier, Logothetis, & Leopold, 2007). These investigators examined the perception-dependency of single-unit responses to a variety of bistable stimuli and showed, amongst other findings, that the same perceptual state can be correlated with different neural activity patterns in macaque middle temporal (MT) area.

that this notion of neural multiple realizability however, is still one in which redundancy is involved.

There is yet another, perhaps extreme, alternative in which neural multiple realizability could occur without any involvement of redundancy. That is, it could be that the whole scenario of isolated stimulation radically changes the NCnC, such that neural activities that are never constitutive in the normal case (perhaps tightly-correlated upstream or downstream NCrCs) *become constitutive* in the case of isolated stimulation. We might describe this as *radical* neural multiple realizability, in which isolated stimulation of non-constitutive NCrCs in the bottom or top third of the tower – whether they are minimally sufficient or not – *could* conceivably induce (and constitute) the target conscious state. If this extreme scenario were to hold, it would mean that constitutive neural activities would still be identified by the isolated stimulation strategy but that such constitutive activity would bear no relationship to constitutive activity in the normal case. Achieving that identification would be far less relevant to consciousness science than achieving identification of constitutive activity in the normal case.

While radical neural multiple realizability can't be totally excluded as a possibility, its likelihood can be questioned. That is, while the brain exhibits remarkable capacity for rapid and substantial plastic change – such as reorganization of somatosensory maps following deafferentation (Merzenich et al., 1983; Ramachandran, Stewart, & Rogers-Ramachandran, 1992; Weiss et al., 2000) – such changes nonetheless take days to weeks to occur. While radical neural multiple realizability for a specific conscious state may be highly probable after days to weeks, for it to confound the isolated stimulation strategy, it would need to involve more or less instantaneous reorganization of the NCnC. Instantaneous reorganization of the NCnC in this way would seem highly *im*probable.

Non-radical neural multiple realizability (Figure 3), however, is a far more likely possibility, as is redundancy in the NCnC, certainly in the case of within-region neural activity (see next section and footnote 20). Both non-radical neural multiple realizability and redundancy, given their higher probability, challenge consciousness science and account for the isolated stimulation strategy's failure to identify the exact boundaries of the NCnC. To reiterate what each possibility involves, recall P2 above in the case of redundancy, and in the case of non-radical neural multiple realizability, we can state:

> Possibility 3 (P3): Non-radical neural multiple realizability involves the possibility that more than one *subset* of constitutive neural activity can be minimally sufficient for a conscious state when separately subjected to isolated stimulation.

In summary then, with the isolated stimulation empirical strategy, while the obstacle of P1 is overcome (arguably, see later), the obstacles of P2 and P3 are not. And while minimally sufficient constitutive neural activities might be identified by isolated stimulation, redundantly constitutive neural activities cannot be distinguished from non-constitutive neural activities (P2) and hence the whole NCnC cannot be identified. Moreover, initially identified minimally sufficient constitutive neural activities may turn out to not be the *only* minimally sufficient constitutive neural activities (P3). Nonetheless, the reverse Jenga scenario may enable identification of some constitutive neural activities (indeed, minimally sufficient constitutive neural activities) and such identification would represent very significant progress in consciousness science. However, because this strategy fails to identify the exact boundaries of the NCnC, the Cr/Cn distinction problem is not solved and we may therefore only *close in* on the constitution of consciousness.[21,22]

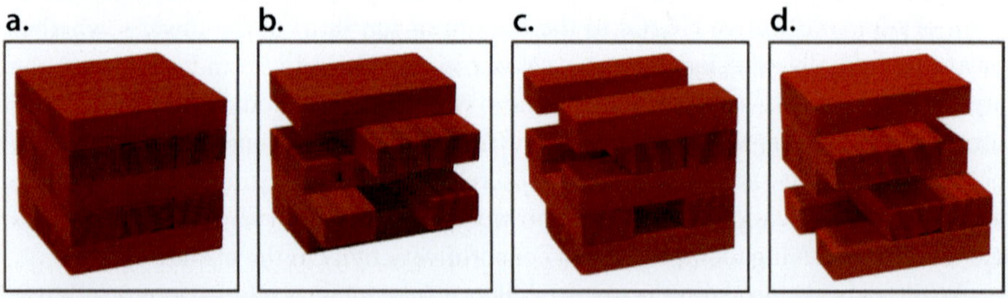

Figure 3. The Jenga analogy illustrates notions of redundancy in the NCnC and non-radical neural multiple realizability. The isolated stimulation strategy is (arguably) able to identify at least some constitutive neural activities (red colored blocks), specifically the minimally sufficient NCnC (**b**), though it is not able to identify the boundaries of the whole NCnC (**a**). Hence while (**b**) may be identified using isolated stimulation, we are not able to get from (**b**) to (**a**) with this method. Moreover, the isolated stimulation strategy could demonstrate that more than one subset of constitutive neural activities is minimally sufficient constitutive neural activity (e.g., **c** and **d**) and if so, (**b**), (**c**) and (**d**) would be non-radical neural multiple realizations of a specific conscious state.

7. Clarifications

At this stage, some points of clarification are required before proceeding to discussing potential objections to the presented arguments and to proposing new foundational claims for consciousness science.

21. Given the redundancy problem (P2), the 'closing in' notion may be misleading because isolated stimulation would actually overshoot such closing in, through its exclusion of redundantly constitutive neural activities. Nonetheless, identification of at least some constitutive neural activity is what is meant by 'closing in' on the problem.

22. For a detailed analysis of many of the principles I have been discussing from the perspective of philosophy of science, see Craver (2007). Craver's analysis includes discussion (with specific scientific examples) of notions of mere correlates, interference and stimulation interventions, redundancy, and constitutive relevance (on the latter, see Section 9.1). He provides examples of scientific approaches to dealing with redundancy, but not in the context of consciousness.

7.1 Between- and within-region cases

When considering the notions of redundancy in the NCnC (P2) and non-radical neural multiple realizability (P3), it should be noted that these possibilities apply both *between* and *within* specific brain regions. In Figure 2, the stepwise inhibition strategy and the obstacles of P1 and P2 were illustrated for the case of binocular rivalry. This phenomenon also serves to illustrate P2 and P3 in the between- and within-region cases. Thus, constraining our analysis to perception-dependent neural activities (which the Jenga and reverse Jenga analogies require), and setting aside the fact that rivalry is not normal vision, consider the following.

In the between-region case, a visual state (during rivalry, with motion, color and complex images) is constituted say, by IT/STS (inferior temporal/superior temporal sulcus) neural activity *and* V4/MT (middle temporal) neural activity (this being the whole specific factor NCnC for each rivaling state), but (1) the visual state would not be affected by inhibition of V4/MT activity because V4/MT activity is redundantly constitutive; *and* (2) isolated stimulation of IT/STS neurons induces the visual state and is thus minimally sufficient constitutive neural activity for it, but isolated stimulation of V4/MT activity does not induce the visual state and thus is not minimally sufficient constitutive neural activity for it; *or* (3) separate isolated stimulation of either IT/STS or V4/MT induces the visual state and thus both can be considered minimally sufficient constitutive neural activity for it (and non-radical multiple realizations of it).

In the within-region case, a visual state during rivalry is constituted say, by IT/STS neural activity (this being the whole specific factor NCnC for each rivaling state), but (1) the visual state would not be affected by inhibition of *some* IT/STS neural activity because that inhibited activity is redundantly constitutive; *and* (2) isolated stimulation of some IT/STS activity induces the visual state and is thus minimally sufficient constitutive neural activity for it, but isolated stimulation of the remaining (or some other) IT/STS activity does not induce the visual state and is thus not minimally sufficient constitutive neural activity for it; *or* (3) separate isolated stimulation of either some IT/STS activity or of remaining (or some other) IT/STS activity induces the visual state and thus both can be considered minimally sufficient constitutive neural activity for it (and non-radical multiple realizations of it).

While the between-region case above is certainly conceivable, the within-region case, especially for the redundancy possibility (P2), must be considered *highly probable*. That is, it is highly probable that thousands, tens of thousands, hundreds of thousands or millions of neurons are specific factor constituents for a conscious state, and it is highly improbable that every one of them would need to be active to constitute that state. Hence it is highly improbable that every one of them would need to be stimulated in the isolated stimulation case, to induce (and constitute) the target state. Within-region redundancy also raises further issues of importance for consciousness science and I address these in Section 8.2 when considering an objection to the redundancy argument.

It is important to also be mindful in this context however, of existing data from electrical microstimulation studies. It is a remarkable fact from such studies that stimulation of relatively few MT neurons (perhaps just hundreds) can *bias* a monkey's perceptual decision regarding motion direction (Britten, Shadlen, Newsome, & Movshon, 1992; Cohen & Newsome, 2004, 2009; Ditterich, Mazurek, & Shadlen, 2003; Salzman & Newsome, 1994; Shadlen & Kiani, 2013; see Sengpiel, 2013, for discussion of this data in the context of binocular rivalry and for the point that microstimulation has never been applied to rivalry). One cannot necessarily extrapolate from those studies however, in which stimulation of relatively few neurons can influence discrimination under difficult decision-making conditions, to the notion that there will be similarly few neurons constitutive for a specific conscious state. That is, it does not follow that the number of neurons it takes to bias competition within pools of active neurons, and to thus influence a subject's difficult decision, is equivalent to the number of specific factor neurons constituting a conscious state. There may be similarly few neurons determining competition between conscious states (such as during rivalry) but this is a different matter to the number of specific factor neurons constituting each state.

Nonetheless, it may turn out that the activity of fewer neurons than we expect is the (specific factor) neural basis, mechanism, substrate or constitution of a conscious state. This will, at the end of the day, be an empirical matter that strategies like isolated stimulation, should they come to pass, will determine. It is also noteworthy that Newsome himself is not afraid to examine the issue of just what his and his contemporaries' microstimulation work means for the issue of the neural basis, mechanism, substrate or constitution of subjective experience (Cohen & Newsome, 2004; Reppas & Newsome, 2007). He concludes (Reppas & Newsome, 2007, p. 7) that, "The development of a non-invasive technique to modify precisely and locally neural activity in humans will probably be necessary to address such questions satisfactorily."

7.2 Linking, binding or index processes

The next point of clarification concerns my previous acknowledgement (Miller, 2007) that searching for this or that NCrC or set of NCrCs might be misguided and that it is instead a neurophysiological process *linking* or *binding* multiple NCrCs, such as, for example, recurrent processing (Klink et al., this volume; Lamme, 2006, 2010) or oscillatory activity and temporal synchrony (Fries, 2005; Fries, Castelo-Branco, Engel, & Singer, 2005; Singer, 2001; though see Shadlen & Movshon, 1999; see also Sengpiel, 2013), that *indexes* the neural basis, mechanism, substrate or constitution of consciousness. It is certainly possible that physiological processes between, or that bind, individual NCrCs could index phenomenally conscious neural activity over and above the tight correlations observed in each of those individual NCrCs. But if so, there will likely be various sets of recurrently, temporally or otherwise bound NCrCs for a conscious state, and we can ask which set should be assigned constitutive status and how will various hypotheses in this regard be tested.

Perhaps each bound neural set could be considered an 'individual' NCrC and the same obstacles of P1–P3 would apply.

Alternatively, even if there are not various sets of indexed or bound neural activities – because all such sets should rather be considered just one larger set – there can still be various hypotheses proposed regarding whether all individual NCrC components of that one larger set are constitutive, or just some. In other words, it can be claimed that a neurophysiological process linking or binding various individual NCrCs, indexes the neural basis, mechanism, substrate or constitution of consciousness, but it is a *further claim* to hold that all neurons or all brain regions participating in such a process are constitutive. That further claim is itself a hypothesis, with rival hypotheses being based on the notion that only some neurons, neuron types, local or distributed neural circuits, specific brain regions or sets of NCrCs participating in the index/binding process are constitutive.

To test hypotheses in this regard would require intervening through stepwise inhibition and stepwise isolated stimulation to prevent and reintroduce, respectively, the relevant index or binding process, and observing what happens to the conscious state in each case. In such experiments, it may turn out that in the absence of the index or binding process there is *never* the conscious state and this would certainly inform consciousness science. But it may also turn out that inhibition of one component of an indexed/bound neural set does not lead to the absence of the index/binding process in remaining components of the set and does not lead to a change in the target conscious state. Would that inhibited component therefore be considered non-constitutive or redundantly constitutive? And could isolated stimulation of various subsets of indexed/bound NCrCs be minimally sufficient constitutive neural activity? The index/binding process case does not seem to enable us to avoid the obstacles of P1 and P2 for stepwise inhibition and P2 and P3 for stepwise isolated stimulation.

7.3 A caveat on isolated stimulation

A further point of clarification relates to earlier reference to isolated stimulation only *arguably* enabling identification of at least some constitutive neural activities. That is, the above discussion of possible index processes that link or bind different neural activities raises an important potential complication for the isolated stimulation strategy. A scenario could be postulated whereby isolated stimulation of the (putative) minimally sufficient NCnC could fail to induce the target conscious state if that neural activity set required for its correct functioning, intact connections to other (disinhibited and active) neural activity sets (such as non-correlated causal chain components, loosely correlated NCrCs or tightly correlated non-constitutive NCrCs). Such a scenario would potentially then lead to an inability to distinguish the minimally sufficient NCnC and non-constitutive minimally sufficient NCrCs (and even non-correlated causal chain components) and this is precisely the obstacle of P1. In such a scenario therefore, it could be claimed that isolated stimulation does *not* in fact overcome the obstacle of P1. This is a concern addressed further in Section 8.4, where I discuss a potential objection based on a postulated requirement for intact connection even to disinhibited and *inactive* neural sets.

7.4 The Cr/Cn distinction problem for enabling factors

The final point of clarification concerns what the Cr/Cn distinction problem looks like for *enabling* as opposed to specific factors. Recall that enabling factors are the "tonic conditions and systems" (Koch, 2004, p. 88) required for a subject to be conscious at all, while specific factors deal with specific conscious states or content. The arguments presented above, it was explicitly stated, are to be applied to specific factors only. I also explicitly side-stepped the complexities of separating and distinguishing the enabling from specific factors (see Section 5 and footnote 17) and I again wish to side-step that debate (acknowledging nonetheless, that elements of the debate may be of relevance here). Despite this, some brief comments can be made regarding how the presented arguments might apply to enabling factors. I do not provide details of the actual conditions and systems required for a subject to be conscious at all, as these can be found in the chapter by Charland-Verville, Vanhaudenhuyse, Laureys and Gosseries (this volume).

First, the Cr/Cn distinction problem for enabling factors is similar in many respects to that for specific factors. Thus upon examining an array of neural systems whose activity tightly correlates with the presence of *any* conscious state (i.e., the state of being conscious at all, irrespective of the content of that state), it is readily conceivable that only some might be constitutive of that state while others might merely correlate with it, without being constitutive of it. Hence there is equally a Cr/Cn distinction problem for enabling factors and each enabling factor can, like each specific factor, be considered to match just one of the following conjunctions: (1) non-constitutive and non-minimally sufficient, (2) non-constitutive and minimally sufficient, (3) constitutive and non-minimally sufficient, or (4) constitutive and minimally sufficient. Second, recording strategies make evident the Cr/Cn distinction problem for enabling factors rather than help to solve it. Third, although the strategy of stepwise inhibition can identify the minimally sufficient status of an enabling factor, it cannot identify its constitutive status (because of P1 and P2; with the same rationale as applies for specific factors). Fourth, isolated stimulation of enabling factors can (arguably) identify at least some constitutive (enabling factor) neural activity but cannot identify the whole (enabling factor) NCnC, due to P2.

While these principles do not fundamentally differ whether applied to specific or enabling factors, not all aspects of the Cr/Cn distinction problem will necessarily be the same for both factor types. Thus, for example, notions of non-radical multiple realizability (P3) would seem substantially *less* likely in the case of enabling factors. Other differences may lie in the screening off process required just to arrive at the tightly correlated enabling factor array. Thus for enabling factors, the process of excluding a constitutive role to a reasonable degree of certainty on the basis of correlations being loose rather than tight, on specific timing of the correlations or on the known mechanistic functions of the neural activities in question, may be substantially different from the screening off process for specific factors. Despite these and other potential differences, the central problems posed by P1 and P2 seem just as applicable to enabling factors as they are to specific factors.

8. Objections

There are at least six potential objections to the arguments presented thus far.

8.1 Definition objections

It could be argued that Chalmers' (2000) definition of the minimally sufficient NCrC would exclude the sorts of scenarios I have discussed. Chalmers' reluctance to make reference to notions of the neural basis, mechanism, substrate or constitution of consciousness makes it somewhat difficult to interpret his original definitions and qualifications. Here I attempt this in a manner that does not avoid reference to the NCnC, but rather draws in this notion. For example, recall that Chalmers distinguishes the 'total NCC' from the 'core NCC', pointing out (p. 26; square brackets added):

> A total NCC builds in everything [the totality of physical processes] and thus automatically suffices for the corresponding conscious states. A core NCC, on the other hand, contains only the "core" processes that correlate with consciousness. The rest of the total NCC will be relegated to some sort of background conditions required for the correct functioning of the core.

The above passage might be seen to be distinguishing specific and enabling factors. Indeed Chalmers (2000, p. 33) implies exactly this when referring to distinguishing the NCrC for background states from the NCrC for specific contents of consciousness, but his total/core distinction also means to even more broadly incorporate "some sort of wide-ranging although skeletal brain state, involving aspects of processes from a number of regions of the brain" (p. 26).

If we wished to push the argument that Chalmers' definitions define away scenarios P1 and P2, the total/core NCrC quote above could be widened in such a way that the total NCrC is defined to *include* non-constitutive but nonetheless minimally sufficient upstream and downstream NCrCs, while the core NCrC is defined to exclude these NCrCs, with the core NCrC notion then supposed to be the crucial sense of 'minimally sufficient NCrC'. But if this move is made, we would just run into the Cr/Cn distinction problem by a different name. It would become the total correlate/core correlate distinction problem and the scenarios I have discussed would change little due to the name change. So appeal to definitions here, rather than undermining the Cr/Cn distinction problem, instead underscores it.

A definition objection might also be mounted if we look closely again at the following (p. 25; square brackets added):

> By this definition, [a neural system] N will be an NCC when (1) the states of N suffice for the corresponding states of consciousness, and (2) no proper part M of N is such that the states of M suffice for the corresponding states of consciousness. In this way, we pare down any potential NCC to its core: Any irrelevant material will be whittled away, and an NCC will be required to contain only the core processes that suffice for the conscious state in question.

However, this passage – in the terminology of the present paper – also serves to underscore rather than object to P1 and P2. In the case of P1, can N be seen to be the neural basis, mechanism, substrate or constitution of consciousness and to be the remaining set after having whittled away from a larger set L (of which N is a proper part) any irrelevant material (hence any correlated non-constitutive neural activity)? The problem here is that the whittling away process to get from L to N, if it is to be via stepwise inhibition, doesn't whittle out correlated non-constitutive neural activity at all. It rather can only whittle out non-minimally sufficient NCrCs to arrive at the set of minimally sufficient NCrCs. In doing so, we do indeed distinguish the minimally sufficient NCrC from the merely sufficient NCrC but we have not whittled out non-constitutive NCrCs to arrive at constitutive ones. Isolated stimulation, on the other hand, can (arguably) identify the minimal set N (the minimally sufficient NCrC or the minimally sufficient NCnC) of which there is no proper part M such that states of M would suffice for the corresponding states of consciousness.

In the case of P2, if we take L to be the (imagined) NCnC and we whittle away any redundancy (we whittle away any constitutive non-minimally sufficient neural activities using stepwise inhibition, or again we invoke isolated stimulation) we could indeed be left with N (a proper part of L) whose states suffice for the corresponding states of consciousness, but of which no proper part M exists whose states also suffice for the corresponding states of consciousness. Thus redundancy (P2) is not dealt with by Chalmers' definition and neither does the definition contain any clue as to how we could identify L (the whole NCnC) in this case.

Here though, it could be argued that my introduction of the new set L is problematic and instead if one viewed P2 only in terms of sets N and M, the redundancy case would indeed be dealt with. Hence, in the case of P2, if we take N to be the (imagined) NCnC and we whittle away any redundancy (we whittle away any constitutive non-minimally sufficient neural activities using stepwise inhibition, or again we invoke isolated stimulation) we could in fact be left with M (a proper part of N) whose states *do* in fact suffice for the corresponding states of consciousness. Chalmers may well have this scenario in mind when he notes (p. 25):

> There is a technical problem for the minimality requirement. It may turn out that there is significant redundancy in a neural correlate of consciousness, such that, for example, a given conscious visual content is represented redundantly in many cells in a given area. If this is so, then that visual area as a whole might not qualify as a minimal sufficient system, since various smaller components of it might themselves correlate with the conscious state. In this case the definition above would imply that various such small components would each be an NCC. One could deal with this sort of case by noting that the problem arises only when the states of the various smaller systems are themselves wholly correlated with each other. (If their mutual correlation can be broken, so can their correlation with consciousness, so that the overall system or some key subsystem will again emerge as the true NCC). Given this, one could stipulate that where states of minimal sufficient systems are wholly correlated with each other, it is the union of the system that should be regarded as an NCC, rather than the individual systems. So an NCC would be a minimal system whose state is sufficient for a given conscious state and is not wholly correlated with the state of any other system.

Chalmers is thus suggesting that the relevant target for consciousness science should be taken to be the union of redundant and non-redundant wholly-correlated neural activities, rather than just the non-redundant wholly-correlated neural activities. But in the absence of any reference to constitutive neural activity, this definition *stipulation*, rather than defining away the redundancy notion and the problem for science therein, actually underscores the very point of P2 (and for that matter P1) because it does not indicate how to distinguish redundantly constitutive NCrCs from non-constitutive but tightly-correlated (wholly-correlated) NCrCs. There is not, in my view, a *technical* problem for the minimality requirement, but rather a *fundamental* problem for it, as I have been arguing.

8.2 Triviality objection

It could be claimed that redundancy (P2) and non-radical neural multiple realizability (P3) are but *trivial* possibilities. This objection would hold that if we had identified the minimally sufficient NCnC using the isolated stimulation strategy, we need not be concerned about failing to go on to achieve identification of the whole NCnC because any differences between these two neural activity sets is trivial. There are two responses to this objection and both draw on the notion of *explanation* in consciousness science (a notion discussed more fully in Bayne, 2007; Chalmers, 1996; Drayson, this volume; Hohwy, 2007, 2009; Hohwy & Bayne, this volume; Hohwy & Frith, 2004; Keaton, this volume; Neisser, 2012; Opie & O'Brien, this volume; Revonsuo, 2000, 2001, 2006, this volume; and Seth, 2009).

Explanation is a somewhat vexed issue in consciousness science because of 'the hard problem' discussed by Chalmers (1996) in which even identification of the whole NCnC could still leave unanswered questions such as *how* it is that *that* particular set of neural activities constitutes consciousness and *why* it is that there should be any consciousness at all. Despite the possibility of explanatory gaps in the study of consciousness (Levine, 1983), some degree of explanation *can* still be sought and achieved in the scientific study of consciousness, in particular with respect to the notion of *mechanistic explanation* in the biological sciences (Bechtel, 1994; Craver, 2007; Hohwy & Bayne, this volume; Horst, 2007; Machamer, Darden, & Craver, 2000; Mahner, this volume; Neisser, 2012; Oizumi, Albantakis, & Tononi, 2014; Opie & O'Brien, this volume; Revonsuo, 2000, 2001, 2006, this volume; cf. Irvine, 2013, who appeals to mechanistic explanation to argue why there cannot even be a science of consciousness).[23]

It could be argued, as Jakob Hohwy has pointed out to me, that we need not worry about identifying redundantly constitutive neural activities because if a conscious state does not disappear (or degrade) when a redundantly constitutive NCrC is inhibited, then the difference between the minimally sufficient NCnC and the whole NCnC is a *difference-without-a-difference* (and any such difference is therefore trivial). As such, the argument would hold that, being redundant, the unidentified constitutive NCrCs could do no *explanatory work* even if they were identifiable. My reply however, is that a difference-without-a-difference for consciousness does not amount to a difference-without-a-difference for consciousness *science*.

That is, we can reasonably wish to answer the following questions: (1) is there in fact any redundancy in the NCnC? (2) if so, why should there be such redundancy? (3) is such redundancy based on a critical *size* of neural activities (a critical number of involved neurons, neuron types and neural circuits)? (4) is such redundancy based on a critical *location* of neural activities? (5) is such redundancy based on a critical *combination* of stepwise inhibition when applying that empirical strategy? (6) is such redundancy based on a critical *order* of stepwise inhibition when applying that empirical strategy? (7) is there non-radical neural multiple realizability within the NCnC (which draws on the notion of redundancy) when applying the isolated stimulation empirical strategy? (8) and how does such redundancy relate to index or binding processes? Answers to such questions would seem, in my view, far from devoid of explanatory power (just as understanding many such issues would help to *mechanistically explain* when and why a Jenga tower might fall).

The second response to the triviality objection rests on the fact that *the* major element of the scientific study of consciousness, at least currently, is the search not for explanations as such, but rather for identification of *which* neural activities are the basis, mechanism, substrate or constitution of consciousness. This is fundamentally a process of identifying the relevant neural activities, not of explaining how and why *those* activities do the constituting. That is, the issue with which I have been concerned in this paper (and with which consciousness science appears most concerned) is one of determining

23. The arguments I have presented thus far have considered the terms neural 'basis', 'mechanism', 'substrate' and 'constitution' of consciousness as synonymous, but in the context of mechanistic explanation, the term 'mechanism' has its own implications (just as the 'constitution' term has its own implications also; see Sections 9.1 and 9.2).

inclusion and exclusion into the constitutive neural activity set. Understanding explanatory mechanisms may of course help with this identification process, but consciousness science could conceivably identify the NCnC even without understanding some explanatory mechanistic principles relevant to that neural activity set.

Hence in summary, appeals to the absence of explanatory power in redundantly constitutive NCrCs do not support their identification as trivial, because (1) issues regarding redundantly constitutive NCrCs can in fact do explanatory work, and (2) despite their redundancy, redundantly constitutive NCrCs are nonetheless constitutive activities and are thus legitimately part of the neural basis, mechanism, substrate or constitution of consciousness. As such, we should seek their identification and we should consider what scientific strategies might achieve this goal.

8.3 Wait-and-see objection

Another potential objection concerns Crick and Koch's (1998) suggestion that hard problems of consciousness be set aside until science makes more progress. It is not clear if such a caution should include the Cr/Cn distinction problem given its clear scientific relevance, but obviously in my view, it should not. That said, there is certainly an important message in the wait-and-see approach and indeed I have previously noted (Miller, 2007, p. 165) that, "future scientific work may show that the notion of the Cr/Cn distinction is somehow fundamentally misguided (in a way that cannot yet be appreciated because the science is not yet done)." Similarly, Revonsuo (2006, p. 292) rightly cautions us over imaginary neuroscience scenarios when he says: "In the absence of the relevant empirical facts, we simply cannot imagine or foresee the perfect future science regarding *any* phenomenon."

I am entirely accepting of the fact that as neuroscience progresses, particularly with respect to dynamic mechanistic multilevel explanation of neural processing within *and* outside of consciousness science, any or all of the scenarios and claims made in this paper may require refinement, revision or indeed rejection. For example, the technique of optogenetics as applied in the context of the current paper would also be capable of being applied in many other neuroscientific contexts (e.g., sensory coding, voluntary movement and various executive functions). As such application advances understanding of neural coding, signaling, dynamics and function, and understanding of the relationship between neural processing and the phenomena being studied, so too such understanding will have flow-on implications for consciousness science. In addition to optogenetics, developments will occur (as discussed in several papers in Miller, 2013a) with other recording, inhibition and stimulation methods, and signal analysis approaches therein, to improve the spatial and temporal resolution of each technique, to enable combined methodological approaches, to accurately map structural and functional neural connections, to improve neural spike detection and sorting and neural population, source and network modeling, to facilitate integration of knowledge across the various levels targeted by each technique, and in general to develop a more detailed understanding of subcellular, neural, neural circuit and large-scale/regional/systems processing.

Conversely, as neuroscientific understanding progresses, the presented scenarios and claims may rather become strengthened (for example, the claim that the isolated stimulation strategy identifies some constitutive neural activities may not be questionable after all). Moreover, the presented scenarios and claims may go beyond the realm of 'in principle' and instead become *directly testable.* Until there is development of a safe, reversible and 'pure' recording, inhibitory and stimulatory technique, it would be unwise to not accept likely revision to the presented scenarios and claims. Just as this and other neuroscientific progress will help to disentangle the complexities of the microstimulation and decision-making literature, and the broader neural coding and processing issues within which those complexities lie (see references in Section 7.1; reviewed in Shadlen & Kiani, 2013; see also Sengpiel, 2013), so too it will help to disentangle the complexities of recording, inhibition and stimulation scenarios within consciousness science. We may wish to wait and see on such issues before getting too conceptually entangled, but in my view it would be unwise to hold that the conceptual analyses and proposals presented here should not be further discussed and debated, or should not even have been embarked upon.

8.4 Integrated Information Theory objection

A further potential objection is that stemming from Integrated Information Theory (IIT; Oizumi et al., 2014; see also Klink et al., this volume). IIT is a highly complex and developed theory of consciousness, with its own detailed conceptual definitions and tools, that starts with phenomenological axioms and proceeds to formalize these into, "postulates that prescribe how physical mechanisms, such as neurons or logic gates, must be configured to generate experience (phenomenology)" (Oizumi et al., 2014, p. 1). IIT is based heavily on mechanistic causal roles – though specifically in IIT, and importantly in the present context, only differences that make a difference – and involves perturbation (again important in the present context) of the elements of candidate sets into all possible states, and identification of maximally irreducible cause-effect repertoires and structure. IIT does not permit for P1, P2 or P3 because it takes the *inactive* elements in maximally irreducible cause-effect structure to be just as critical as the active elements. Additionally, through an exclusion postulate, among overlapping candidate sets of mechanistic elements, only one forms a complex – that with the maximum quantity of integrated conceptual information – and hence no subsets or supersets of those mechanistic elements can form a complex.

It will take someone better versed than myself in IIT to properly set out the detailed objections to P1, P2 and P3 that stem from the theory, but from the brief description above, some clues to the objections should be visible. The arguments presented in this paper are based on an excitation approach to constitutive neural activity, albeit with an acknowledgement of the physiological inseparability of excitatory and inhibitory processes (and other caveats). However, IIT considers inactive (i.e., resting state, or disinhibited and not stimulated) neural states to be just as critical to the constitution (structure) of a conscious state as stimulated neurons, and on this construal, the isolated stimulation scenario I have been discussing would be considered inaccurate. Note though, that this way of thinking would also lead to objecting to the notion of the minimally sufficient NCrC, insofar as that construct also relies on excitatory correlates rather than the set of relevant active *and* inactive neural elements.

Instead, IIT would argue that the constitution of consciousness is identifiable by identifying the (neural) complex with the maximum quantity of integrated conceptual information and that once this complex has been identified, adding anything to it or subtracting anything from it must change the conscious state, however minimal that change may be. On this construal and on the axioms and postulates of IIT, P1, P2 and P3 are not possibilities at all. This IIT objection to the present arguments is testable, in principle, and if the identified complex with the maximum quantity of integrated conceptual information can in fact be added to or subtracted from without a concomitant change in the conscious state, it will then be IIT that is found wanting.

8.5 Specificity objection

This objection would hold that there may be a Cr/Cn distinction problem in consciousness science but that it is not *specific* to consciousness science. Rather, such a problem applies in many scientific domains and hence there is nothing special about phenomenal consciousness in virtue of its presenting this epistemic problem. Horst (2007, p. 4, italics in original), for example, argues that, "in some sense, in the sciences it is *explanatory gaps all the way down*." Horst here is referring to the attempted reduction of biology to chemistry, and chemistry to physics, and so on. His analysis also specifically concerns whether consciousness, or indeed any object of scientific enquiry, can be reduced to its constituents, but not reduced in just any way. That is, the reductionist debate in philosophy of mind is one that intimately involves part-whole relations (discussed in more detail in Section 9.1), however rather than being primarily concerned with the specific relation between parts and wholes, the important issue in this debate is whether the reduced phenomena are, in so doing, explained *without remainder*.

There are substantial metaphysical issues bound up in answering this question and I do not intend to address these. Indeed, a specificity objection in the current context is not in itself concerned primarily with such metaphysical matters. Rather, the objection mounted by analogy with the explanatory gap and the reduction debate would hold that if reduction without remainder has proven largely elusive in all sciences – as Horst (2007) argues is the case – the failure of reduction in consciousness science should come as no great surprise. Consequently, the explanatory gap presented by phenomenal consciousness is not particularly important, being but one amongst ubiquitous epistemic gaps, and so too for the Cr/Cn distinction problem.

As discussed in Section 1, the explanatory gap or hard problem of consciousness is a different issue to the Cr/Cn distinction problem, but it can readily be asked whether there also exists a Cr/Cn distinction problem for non-conscious objects of scientific enquiry, and thus whether there are *Cr/Cn distinction problems all the way down*. Restricting ourselves to the biological sciences (as opposed to say chemistry or physics), outside of the neuroscience domain we might ask whether complex biological processes, such as say digestion, at some point in their mechanistic explanation also face the problem of distinguishing constituents from among mere correlates. And within the cognitive neuroscience domain, we might ask whether a Cr/Cn distinction problem exists in describing say memory or attention (notwithstanding close relationships between these cognitive processes and consciousness; see van Boxtel & Tsuchiya, this volume). Similarly outside the cognitive neuroscience domain, we might ask whether a Cr/Cn distinction problem exists in describing neural functions with no relationship to conscious states, such as say brainstem control of respiratory drive.

There are three potential responses to such issues. First, it may be the case that there is not in fact a substantive Cr/Cn distinction problem for non-conscious objects of scientific enquiry. Second, it may be that there is indeed a substantive Cr/Cn distinction problem in all the non-conscious cases just described, and in general, and hence that it is in fact Cr/Cn distinction problems all the way down. Third, it may be that there are Cr/Cn distinction problems all the way down but that the particular Cr/Cn distinction problem for consciousness is unique in an important way.[24]

To examine whether there may be Cr/Cn distinction problems all the way down, one approach would be to apply the types of analyses presented in this paper to processes such as digestion and neural respiratory drive (for simplicity, I leave aside the cognitive neuroscience phenomena that are more intimately related to consciousness). Hence we may start by collating the array of correlates (physiological and neural, respectively) of each process and subject such an array to a screening off method based on loose correlations, timing or known mechanistic functions. With such methods we might exclude, with a reasonable degree of certainty, particular correlates as having constitutive status. Thereafter we would need to ask whether the remaining array of correlates of digestion or neural respiratory drive could include at least some which are *not* in fact constitutive of these phenomena, irrespective of whether they may be minimally sufficient for such processes (with their stepwise inhibition causing the absence, or degradation, of such processes). Conversely, perhaps constitutive elements of such processes can be inhibited without subsequent absence (or degradation) of the processes, hence implying redundancy in these phenomena too. And perhaps even further scenarios could include non-radical multiple realizability for such processes.

The question in need of answering is whether these scenarios are impossible or unlikely for cases such as digestion or neural respiratory drive, or possible and likely,

24. Horst (2007) similarly asks whether the explanatory gap for consciousness (and intentionality) might be different from all other explanatory gaps in the sciences. He expresses an intuition that it is indeed different, but he resists this intuition.

or rather possible and likely but in an importantly different way to such scenarios for consciousness. In answering this, one issue to consider is how phenomenal consciousness is defined relative to how digestion or neural respiratory drive is defined. Thus it could be argued that phenomenal consciousness is defined, fundamentally, by our direct experiences. We know what we mean when we refer to the various phenomenal elements of a blue seascape because of having had direct experience of such phenomenal states. We don't have direct experience of digestion or neural respiratory drive in a similar way. Rather, we may start with vague notions such as what happens to food in the body after it is eaten, or what makes us breathe, but to arrive at clearer notions of digestion and neural respiratory drive is to already understand, at least to some extent, the mechanistic elements involved.

Hence digestion and neural respiratory drive are defined in ways much more intimately connected to their mechanistic basis, than is phenomenal consciousness. Because of this, it could be argued that to understand mechanisms of digestion and neural respiratory drive is to fully understand digestion and neural respiratory drive. On this construal, non-constitutive correlates of processes like digestion and neural respiratory drive might be impossible or at least unlikely because full mechanistic understanding would have excluded such correlates. That said, perhaps a detailed mechanistic analysis of processes like digestion and neural respiratory drive – which I am not providing here and which would require considerable discussion – should occur before one commits to admission or denial of possibilities like P1, P2 and P3 for non-conscious processes.[25]

However, the third possibility is worth discussing further here. That is, that even if there are in fact Cr/Cn distinction problems all the way down, the particular problem for consciousness is unique in an important way. I have previously indicated (Miller, 2007) that, intuitively, the Cr/Cn distinction problem seems different for phenomenal consciousness than for other targets within cognitive neuroscience precisely because of the problems that phenomenal consciousness has famously caused in philosophy (see Drayson, this volume; note also in this regard that there does not appear to be an equally hard problem of identifying digestion or neural respiratory drive, or even memory or attention, in phylogeny and ontogeny as there does for identifying phenomenal consciousness in phylogeny and ontogeny). It seems, in my view, difficult to deny that what escapes scientific enquiry in the case of the Cr/Cn distinction problem for consciousness is different to, and less trivial than, what escapes scientific enquiry in the case of the problem for non-conscious targets (if indeed one admits the latter type of Cr/Cn distinction problem at all). There are not two perspectives – a first- and third-person perspective – of digestion or of neural respiratory drive, and hence the Cr/Cn distinction problem for these non-conscious phenomena has nothing to do

25. Such detailed mechanistic analyses are common in the mechanistic explanation literature. Hence Craver (2007), for example, as mentioned in footnote 22, addresses interference strategies and redundancy issues in mechanistic explanation within neuroscience, with specific examples, though not specifically in relation to consciousness.

with failing to identify the physical boundaries of the first-person perspective. Yet this is precisely what fails in the case of the Cr/Cn distinction problem for consciousness.

Still, one might argue that the Cr/Cn distinction problem for non-conscious targets and that for conscious targets are both examples of how scientific enquiry fails to identify the physical boundaries of the target phenomenon and hence that there is no special difference between these cases. But it appears equally arguable that the problem for conscious targets causes scientific enquiry to fail in a unique way, because by failing to identify the physical boundaries of conscious targets, description of *both* the third- and the first-person perspectives is incomplete (see also Section 9.1, footnote 32).[26] It can also be asked whether scientific method itself differs in the case of conscious versus non-conscious targets.

8.6 Theoretical loading objection

Finally, it might be argued that the Cr/Cn distinction problem need not be addressed, or could be set aside, because the very notion of constitution is a theoretically loaded one, in a manner that might be seen to commit one to a particular view on the relation between mind and brain. Thus, as mentioned above, Chalmers (2000) states (p. 37), "the search for an NCC as defined poses a tractable empirical question with relatively clear parameters, one that researchers of widely different theoretical persuasions can engage in." There are several responses to the charge that the notion of the Cr/Cn distinction problem brings with it unwanted theoretical baggage.

First, it should by now be clear that the Cr/Cn distinction problem is able to be posed every bit as clearly with reference to the neural basis, mechanism or substrate of consciousness, without any mention of 'constitution' if one objected to relational commitments therein. As such the problem is no more theoretically loaded than would be a Cr/neural basis problem or a Cr/neural mechanism problem or a Cr/neural substrate problem. So the theoretical loading objection, thus construed, would mean that the only permissible talk should be that of correlates, with no mention permissible of constructs such as the neural basis, mechanism, substrate or constitution of consciousness. This seems an unnecessary restriction. Scientists in particular are quite capable of dealing with methodological problems and leaving to one side any metaphysical implications of the terminology they use.

Second, the claim that only 'correlate' talk should be allowed is even less defensible when considering that such terminology is itself not entirely free from theoretical loading (or in some cases, from tautology). Thus as I have noted (Miller, 2001, footnote 36, p. 140):

26. This bears on well-known knowledge arguments against physicalism (see Brogaard, this volume; Drayson, this volume; Pereboom, this volume) which I discuss in more detail in Miller (2007). There, I also discuss the implications of epistemic limits for ontological matters (see also Section 9.3 of the present paper).

> Objections to the 'neural correlates' terminology have also been raised on philosophical grounds. Smart's (1959) concern was that you cannot correlate something with itself and given that consciousness and (the relevant) brain processes refer to the same thing, you cannot have neural correlates of consciousness. For a related objection, see Mahner and Bunge (1997). Place (1990) on the other hand, draws on Boring (1933), holding that a perfect correlation is identity.

I don't wish to here explore issues concerning relations such as correlation, constitution and identity (such issues are taken up briefly in Section 9.2 and Miller, 2007, and at length in subsequent papers in this volume). I merely point out that if an identity theorist like Smart would object on purely theoretical grounds to the possibility of such a thing as an NCrC, then NCrC terminology may not be as theory-neutral as it is claimed to be. Others too have pointed out that Chalmers' (2000) definitions are not as theory-neutral as claimed. Hence Revonsuo (2006) notes the representationalism loading inherent in Chalmers' constructs. In addition, as I have pointed out previously (Miller, 2007), NCrC terminology is tautological when distinctions are made between 'correlates' and 'true correlates' (Crick, 1994; Crick & Koch, 1998; Chalmers, 2000, also refers at times to a 'true NCC'), because by definition, if a correlate correlates it is a true correlate. So whilst in my view, Crick and Koch mean NCrC when they refer to 'correlates', and the neural basis, mechanism, substrate or constitution of consciousness when they refer to 'true correlates', there should be avoidance of tautological terminology like the latter.

Third, far from restricting the discussion to NCrC terminology so as to remain (supposedly) theory-neutral, actually addressing the theory-laden aspect of chosen terminology is, in my view, useful work for philosophers to do. It is in this arena that relational issues should be addressed. Indeed, the science of consciousness ought to be a fundamentally interdisciplinary endeavor, in which scientists and philosophers meaningfully engage (see Editorial Introduction, this volume). Restricting foundational issues in the scientific study of consciousness to correlation terms only, just so scientists need not be dragged into relational discussions, is not in the spirit of consciousness science being a truly interdisciplinary endeavor. Moreover, not only is there interesting philosophical work to be done in applying the constitution relation to brains and minds (to which it is seldom applied), there are also important issues for science that emerge from such application.

9. Related scientific and philosophic issues

There are many additional issues associated with the notion of constitution and the Cr/Cn distinction problem, with both explanatory and other theoretical implications.

9.1 A mereology of phenomenal consciousness

An important scientific issue concerns at what *level* of neural processing consciousness is constituted (Hohwy & Bayne, this volume; Miller, 2007; Opie & O'Brien, this volume; Revonsuo, 2000, 2001, 2006, this volume)? This is another constitution problem that both the science *and* philosophy of consciousness will need to address. Thus, should the NCnC be considered most relevant at the level only of constitutive action potentials? Or perhaps at the level only of the electrophysiological processes of distributed constitutive neural circuits and networks (bound as they may or may not be)? Or perhaps both levels are constitutively relevant? And what is the relation of NCnC *micro*constituents (subcellular molecular constituents)[27] to consciousness? Should the NCnC be considered to include all microconstituent processes, or only some? And if just some, which, and how will we test hypotheses in this regard? In this context, the term 'constitution' takes on additional relevance over and above 'basis', 'mechanism' and 'substrate' and specifically, different *grains* of constitution can be appreciated – i.e., at coarse (systems), fine (individual neurons and microcircuits) and very fine (subcellular) scales.

The issue of various grains of constitution suggests, in my view, a *mereology of phenomenal consciousness*. Mereology is the branch of philosophy that deals with the relationship between parts and wholes. It has mostly concerned itself with analysis of part-whole relations for static objects. Two famous examples include analysis of part-whole relations and personal identity implications of a statue and its constituent clay and a wooden ship and its constituent planks (see Curtis, this volume; Curtis & Noonan, this volume; Keaton, this volume; and Pereboom, this volume). By contrast, there has been little mereological analysis directed at *process*-based physiological systems. Also, and somewhat remarkably, the constitution relation is seldom explicitly applied in philosophy of mind (though with a few notable exceptions, as discussed in Miller, 2007). That is not to say that the issue of part-whole relations is never discussed in philosophy of mind. Indeed, it is a critical aspect of both mechanistic explanation with respect to consciousness (see Revonsuo, this volume) and the reductionism debate (see Section 8.5; in the reductionism debate though, as mentioned above, the issue is less about the relation *per se* between parts and wholes, and more about whether explanation of the parts *fully* explains the whole).

27. Microconstituents should not to be confused with *microphysical* (subatomic) constituents, as referred to in the reductionism literature.

It is my contention that the philosophy of consciousness needs to (1) engage in mereological analysis of processes to better understand part-whole relations of physiological and specifically neural systems, and (2) thereafter, focus on what additionally may be relevant in considering a mereology of the NCnC.[28] A mereology of phenomenal consciousness will require concerted interdisciplinary interaction amongst philosophers and scientists, with updating of the analyses as neuroscientific knowledge itself progresses. It is important to note that extension of the classical mereological focus on objects to (neurophysiological) processes should be undertaken to *complement* mechanistic explanation approaches (which also deal with component parts, and specifically their causal operations, activities and organization) – particularly *dynamic* mechanistic explanation (see Bechtel & Abrahamsen, 2010, 2013) – rather than as an alternative to it.

The notion of a mereology of processes differs from the mechanistic approach to activities in a subtle but potentially important way. Craver (2007, p. 136) notes, "There are no mechanisms without active organization, and no mechanistic explanation is complete or correct if it does not capture correctly the mechanism's active organization." Craver's notion of activities (Craver, 2007; Machamer et al., 2000) is one with a decidedly mechanistic flavor. In addition, Craver (2007) outlines the importance of attending to the notion of *constitutive relevance* in mechanistic explanation (i.e., identifying relevant components and their interactions and excluding irrelevant components and their interactions). While this is no doubt indeed important for mechanistic explanation – and for finding constitutive mechanisms of consciousness (as sought by Revonsuo, 2006) – understanding the constitution of consciousness may need to take more than just a mechanistic explanation form.[29] Although the mechanistic explanation form may turn out to actually be the best way by which to understand the constitution of consciousness, mereological approaches, in my view, also need developing.

This will not however, be easy territory. Craver's (2007) use of the notion of 'constitutive explanation' (used in the mechanistic context) is not intended to have metaphysical relational implications. Thus he notes, (p. 20), "Metaphysicians reserve the term 'constitutive' for a specific relation that has more entanglements than I intend." A metaphysical mereological notion of 'constitutive' may well, I suggest, have different implications for the notion of constitutive relevance than the mechanistic notion of 'constitutive'. Mereological analysis in the context of phenomenal consciousness will need to address: (1) whether a detailed account of the constitutive mechanisms of consciousness is equivalent to a detailed account of the constitution of consciousness;

28. See Mahner (this volume) and Mahner and Bunge (1997) for ontological fundamentals regarding processes and events, and Curtis (this volume) who applies principles from the material constitution literature to brain states (and events) and phenomenal states (and events).

29. Indeed, this is why the title of Miller (2014) – 'Closing in on the Constitution of Consciousness' – stands in contrast to the title of a chapter in Revonsuo (2006) – 'Closing in on the Mechanisms of Consciousness'.

(2) whether identification of the causal operations, activities and organization of component parts of the constitutive mechanisms of consciousness fully answers all the questions posed in the first paragraph of this subsection; and (3) questions (1) and (2) posed in the next subsection.[30,31,32]

9.2 The relation between brain and mind

The mereological constitution relation discussed above deals with another central and perennial issue in philosophy of mind: the relation between brain and mind. Indeed, all of the papers in Section II of this volume address this issue in one way or another.

30. In answering how we might test hypotheses regarding which microconstituents can be considered part of the NCnC and which not (hence which are constitutively relevant), microconstituent stepwise inhibition could be applied, with assessment of whether a conscious state changes or does not change accordingly. However, drawing conclusions from such interventions, and determining whether a Cr/Cn distinction problem also exists at this level, would seem to require the combination of mereological and mechanistic analyses that I am advocating.

31. It is important to distinguish microconstituents that might be constitutively relevant to the *form* of a conscious phenomenon from those relevant to the *feel* of the phenomenon. Hence as Ngo et al. (2013) discussed, individual variation in the rate of binocular rivalry is known to be around 50% genetically determined. Thus some, as yet unknown, molecular factor(s) influences rivalry rate. While this molecular factor(s) can be considered constitutively relevant to the form of rivalry, there is no indication that the same factor(s) also influences what each rivaling state feels like to the observer. This type of form-determining genetic/molecular constituent can be contrasted with one that directly affects phenomenal consciousness. In this regard, as Ngo et al. (2013) also discuss, the rate of binocular rivalry is known to be slower in subjects with the heritable psychiatric condition, bipolar disorder (manic depression). However, there is nothing to suggest that visual phenomenal consciousness during rivalry in a clinically well bipolar subject is any different to that of someone without the disorder, even though the switch rate is slower. But the same genetic/molecular factor(s) determining slow rivalry rate in bipolar disorder does become a feel-determining constituent when a bipolar subject becomes clinically unwell. This is clearly the case in the affective domain with respect to episodes of mania and depression but also in the perceptual domain, because such episodes can be associated with heightening and diminishing, respectively, of various perceptual experiences (e.g., color perception).

32. Related to this mereology discussion, an additional point to make regarding the specificity objection is that one could argue that there is no, or perhaps far less, need for a mereology of non-conscious processes over and above mechanistic explanation of the constituent parts, operations and organization of such processes. This is in contrast to a mereology of conscious processes, the results of which may well inform understanding of consciousness and its constitution. Thus it seems that once the mechanisms of non-conscious processes are fully described, there is less need to ask questions concerning the metaphysical relation between such parts and their wholes than is the case for conscious processes.

Thus it can be asked what similarities and differences there are between the constitution relation and others that purport to describe the brain–mind relation, such as identity, supervenience, realization, emergence and causation? In addition, questions that I consider require addressing by philosophers include (1) whether the constitution relation in the case of phenomenal consciousness is a unique constitution relation, and if so, in what way is it unique? (2) if indeed unique, does it simply look nothing like a constitution relation in the usual parts-whole sense, even for processes? (3) does the uniqueness of the constitution relation in this particular case tell us something about the uniqueness of consciousness and the place of consciousness in nature?

9.3 Epistemic limits and ontology

Finally, another central and perennial issue in philosophy of mind – the ontological issue of whether consciousness and mind are entirely physically (materially) composed – is also relevant in the context of the Cr/Cn distinction problem. If with the Cr/Cn distinction problem, science meets an epistemic limit, what does such a limit mean for these ontological matters? Elsewhere (Miller, 2007), I have outlined in detail my views concerning what epistemic issues do and do not imply for the ontology of consciousness. In summary, I do not believe that consciousness having unique epistemic properties and presenting unique epistemic limits threatens its substance monist (physicalist, materialist) ontological status. Rather, such epistemic properties – tied as they are to specific *organizational* properties of the brain (see Opie & O'Brien, this volume) – have ontological implications only insofar as ontology is concerned with what types of things exist. Specifically, consciousness may be an organizationally and epistemically unique thing but it is not somehow non-physical or non-material because of these unique organizational and epistemic properties.

That said, as a scientist myself, I am hesitant to contemplate potential boundaries to scientific knowledge, particularly when so much, especially in the brain sciences, remains to be discovered (see Section 8.3). Consequently, I make no proclamation in Miller (2007), or in the present paper, regarding limits to the scientific study of phenomenal consciousness due to the Cr/Cn distinction problem. Rather, I have pointed out where the limits appear to be and argued that if we are to move beyond these, we may need new scientific strategic proposals. Indeed, addressing specific empirical strategies in this context has been the point of the analyses in this paper, with an underlying contention that explicitly addressing the Cr/Cn distinction problem cannot but further our understanding of it. And if our best conceptual and empirical efforts fail (suggesting that with phenomenal consciousness, science does in fact meet a limit) then we will have indeed learned something about consciousness and its place in nature.

We will have discovered that in addition to the perennial and widely-appreciated philosophical issues surrounding phenomenal consciousness, epistemic limits in this arena need not be due to phenomenal consciousness not existing, or to current scientific methods not being advanced enough as yet, or to human cognitive capacities not being able to fully grasp what phenomenal consciousness is (see Section 1). Rather, phenomenal consciousness may be unique in the order of things by virtue of the Cr/Cn distinction problem it poses for science (or if such Cr/Cn distinction problems exist all the way down, then by virtue of the type of Cr/Cn distinction problem phenomenal consciousness poses for science). This would be a different limit condition to those of the hard phylogeny and ontogeny problems, the impossibility of direct intersubjective exchange and questions about how and why phenomenal consciousness is constituted in the way that it is.[33]

10. New foundations for the science of consciousness

In this paper (and Miller, 2014), we have seen through the Jenga analogy that the minimally sufficient NCrC construct can pick out a different neural activity set to that of the NCnC. We have also seen that while application of the stepwise inhibition empirical strategy can distinguish the merely sufficient from the minimally sufficient NCrC, it fails to make any progress on identifying constitutive neural activities (due to P1 and P2). In addition, while application of the isolated stimulation empirical strategy can (arguably) identify some constitutive neural activities, it fails to make any progress on identifying the whole NCnC (due to P2 and P3).

Although the Cr/Cn distinction problem remains unsolved, as are other (mereological) consciousness constitution problems, the analyses I have presented suggest new conceptual foundations for consciousness science, depicted by the following claims (C). These claims are proposed for further discussion and notably, they include reference to specific empirical strategies and to possibilities P1–P3. There are many aspects of consciousness science not dealt with by these claims, so this is not intended to be an exhaustive list. It is merely a list of claims arising from the main analyses I have undertaken. The proposed claims are:

C1: Setting aside notions of the hard problem of consciousness, the explanatory gap, hard phylogeny and ontogeny problems of consciousness, and the problem of direct intersubjective exchange, the ultimate aim of consciousness science is not to identify the minimally sufficient neural correlates of consciousness, but rather to identify the (whole) neural basis, mechanism, substrate or constitution of consciousness.

C2: The current foundational construct of consciousness – the minimally sufficient neural correlates of consciousness – can pick out a different neural activity set to that picked out by the neural basis, mechanism, substrate or constitution of consciousness.

33. Although phenomenal consciousness may be unique in the order of things, Mahner (this volume) reminds us that mental properties are just yet another example of qualitative novelty in this world.

C3: If by 'under conditions C' in Chalmers' (2000) definition of the minimally sufficient neural correlates of consciousness, we mean stepwise inhibition – the most obvious empirical approach to distinguishing the merely sufficient from the minimally sufficient neural correlates of consciousness – then the minimally sufficient neural correlates of consciousness construct is limited by its inclusion of neural activities that are not in fact part of the neural basis, mechanism, substrate or constitution of consciousness, and by its exclusion of neural activities that are. Consciousness science can nonetheless continue to work toward identifying the minimally sufficient neural correlates of consciousness using recording strategies and the stepwise inhibition strategy.

C4: If by 'under conditions C' in the definition of the minimally sufficient neural correlates of consciousness we mean isolated stimulation, then the minimally sufficient neural correlates of consciousness construct is equivalent to the minimally sufficient neural constitution of consciousness construct and at least some constitutive neural activities will (arguably) be identifiable. Whichever term is preferred, this neural activity set can be different to that of the *whole* neural basis, mechanism, substrate or constitution of consciousness and hence neither construct with the minimally sufficient qualifier should be considered the ultimate target of consciousness science.

C5: Because of the possibilities of redundancy in the neural constitution of consciousness (i.e., of constitutive non-minimally sufficient neural correlates of consciousness) and of non-radical neural multiple realizability, there is not yet evident an empirical strategy to identify the whole neural constitution of consciousness. Empirical approaches to this problem need to be developed, and may require entirely new scientific strategies.[34]

The science of consciousness is young and thriving. There is a great deal of empirical and conceptual work to be done in this field and the foundational map charted by Chalmers (2000) needs to be reassessed and built upon, with a focus on empirical

34. An abbreviated, conjoined and simpler set of claims, without specific reference to empirical strategies and to P1–P3, would be:

C1: The ultimate aim of consciousness science is not to identify the minimally sufficient neural correlates of consciousness, but rather to identify the (whole) neural basis, mechanism, substrate or constitution of consciousness.

C2: The current foundational construct of consciousness – the minimally sufficient neural correlates of consciousness – can pick out a different neural activity set to that picked out by the neural basis, mechanism, substrate or constitution of consciousness. Consciousness science can nonetheless continue to work toward identifying the minimally sufficient neural correlates of consciousness.

C3: Although there may be empirical strategies to identify some constitutive neural activity, there is not yet evident a strategy to identify the whole neural constitution of consciousness. Empirical approaches to this problem need to be developed, and may require entirely new scientific strategies.

strategies. The analyses and new foundational claims presented here are an attempt in this direction. Consciousness remains, as ever, an intriguing subject of intellectual discourse. It is today also rightly situated at the frontier of scientific endeavor.

References

Aru, J., Bachmann, T., Singer, W., & Melloni, L. (2012). Distilling the neural correlates of consciousness. *Neuroscience & Biobehavioral Reviews*, 36(2), 737–746. DOI: 10.1016/j.neubiorev.2011.12.003

Bachmann, T. (2000). *Microgenetic approaches to the conscious mind.* Advances in Consciousness Research (Vol. 25). Amsterdam, The Netherlands: John Benjamins Publishing Company. DOI: 10.1075/aicr.25

Bayne, T. (2007). Conscious states and conscious creatures: Explanation in the scientific study of consciousness. *Philosophical Perspectives*, 21(1), 1–22. DOI: 10.1111/j.1520-8583.2007.00118.x

Bayne, T., & Hohwy, J. (2013). Consciousness: Theoretical approaches. In A.E. Cavanna, A. Nani, H. Blumenfeld, & S. Laureys (Eds.), *Neuroimaging of consciousness* (pp. 23–35). Berlin: Springer-Verlag. DOI: 10.1007/978-3-642-37580-4_2

Bechtel, W. (1994). Levels of description and explanation in cognitive science. *Minds and Machines*, 4(1), 1–25. DOI: 10.1007/BF00974201

Bechtel, W., & Abrahamsen, A. (2010). Dynamic mechanistic explanation: Computational modeling of circadian rhythms as an exemplar for cognitive science. *Studies in History and Philosophy of Science Part A*, 41(3), 321–333. DOI: 10.1016/j.shpsa.2010.07.003

Bechtel, W., & Abrahamsen, A.A. (2013). Thinking dynamically about biological mechanisms: Networks of coupled oscillators. *Foundations of Science*, 18(4), 707–723. DOI: 10.1007/s10699-012-9301-z

Been, G., Ngo, T.T., Miller, S.M., & Fitzgerald, P.B. (2007). The use of tDCS and CVS as methods of non-invasive brain stimulation. *Brain Research Reviews*, 56(2), 346–361. DOI: 10.1016/j.brainresrev.2007.08.001

Blake, R., Brascamp, J., & Heeger, D.J. (2014). Can binocular rivalry reveal neural correlates of consciousness? *Philosophical Transactions of the Royal Society of London B: Biological Sciences*, 369(1641), 20130211. DOI: 10.1098/rstb.2013.0211

Block, N. (1995). On a confusion about a function of consciousness. *Behavioral and Brain Sciences*, 18(2), 227–287. DOI: 10.1017/S0140525X00038188

Block, N. (1996). How can we find the neural correlate of consciousness? *Trends in Neurosciences*, 19(11), 456–459. DOI: 10.1016/S0166-2236(96)20049-9

Boly, M., Seth, A.K., Wilke, M., Ingmundson, P., Baars, B., Laureys, S., Edelman, D.B., & Tsuchiya, N. (2013). Consciousness in humans and non-human animals: Recent advances and future directions. *Frontiers in Psychology*, 4, 625. DOI: 10.3389/fpsyg.2013.00625

Borchers, S., Himmelbach, M., Logothetis, N., & Karnath, H.-O. (2012). Direct electrical stimulation of human cortex – the gold standard for mapping brain functions? *Nature Reviews Neuroscience*, 13(1), 63–70.

Britten, K.H., Shadlen, M.N., Newsome, W.T., & Movshon, J.A. (1992). The analysis of visual motion: A comparison of neuronal and psychophysical performance. *Journal of Neuroscience*, 12(12), 4745–4765.

Chalmers, D. J. (1996). *The conscious mind: In search of a fundamental theory.* New York, NY: Oxford University Press.

Chalmers, D. J. (2000). What is a neural correlate of consciousness? In T. Metzinger (Ed.), *Neural correlates of consciousness: Empirical and conceptual questions* (pp. 17–39). Cambridge, MA: MIT Press.

Cohen, M. R., & Newsome, W. T. (2004). What electrical microstimulation has revealed about the neural basis of cognition. *Current Opinion in Neurobiology*, 14(2), 169–177. DOI: 10.1016/j.conb.2004.03.016

Cohen, M. R., & Newsome, W. T. (2009). Estimates of the contribution of single neurons to perception depend on timescale and noise correlation. *Journal of Neuroscience*, 29(20), 6635–6648. DOI: 10.1523/JNEUROSCI.5179-08.2009

Craver, C. F. (2007). *Explaining the brain: Mechanisms and the mosaic unity of neuroscience.* Oxford, UK: Oxford University Press. DOI: 10.1093/acprof:oso/9780199299317.001.0001

Crick, F. (1994). *The astonishing hypothesis: The scientific search for the soul.* New York, NY: Touchstone.

Crick, F., & Koch, C. (1990). Towards a neurobiological theory of consciousness. *Seminars in the Neurosciences*, 2, 263–275. DOI: 10.1016/B978-0-12-185254-2.50021-8

Crick, F., & Koch, C. (1998). Consciousness and neuroscience. *Cerebral Cortex*, 8(2), 97–107. DOI: 10.1093/cercor/8.2.97

Damasio, H., & Damasio, A. R. (1989). *Lesion analysis in neuropsychology.* New York, NY: Oxford University Press.

de Graaf, T. A., Hsieh, P.-J., & Sack, A. T. (2012). The 'correlates' in neural correlates of consciousness. *Neuroscience & Biobehavioral Reviews*, 36(1), 191–197. DOI: 10.1016/j.neubiorev.2011.05.012

Ditterich, J., Mazurek, M. E., & Shadlen, M. N. (2003). Microstimulation of visual cortex affects the speed of perceptual decisions. *Nature Neuroscience*, 6(8), 891–898. DOI: 10.1038/nn1094

Fenno, L., Yizhar, O., & Deisseroth, K. (2011). The development and application of optogenetics. *Annual Review of Neuroscience*, 34, 389–412. DOI: 10.1146/annurev-neuro-061010-113817

Fries, P. (2005). A mechanism for cognitive dynamics: Neuronal communication through neuronal coherence. *Trends in Cognitive Sciences*, 9(10), 474–480. DOI: 10.1016/j.tics.2005.08.011

Fries, P., Castelo-Branco, M., Engel, A. K., & Singer, W. (2005). The functional role of oscillatory neuronal synchronization for perceptual organization and selection. In D. Alais & R. Blake (Eds.), *Binocular rivalry* (pp. 259–281). Cambridge, MA: MIT Press.

Frith, C., Perry, R., & Lumer, E. (1999). The neural correlates of conscious experience: An experimental framework. *Trends in Cognitive Sciences*, 3(3), 105–114. DOI: 10.1016/S1364-6613(99)01281-4

Histed, M. H., Ni, A. M., & Maunsell, J. H. R. (2013). Insights into cortical mechanisms of behaviour from microstimulation experiments. *Progress in Neurobiology*, 103, 115–130. DOI: 10.1016/j.pneurobio.2012.01.006

Hohwy, J. (2007). The search for neural correlates of consciousness. *Philosophy Compass*, 2(3), 461–474. DOI: 10.1111/j.1747-9991.2007.00086.x

Hohwy, J. (2009). The neural correlates of consciousness: New experimental approaches needed? *Consciousness and Cognition*, 18(2), 428–438. DOI: 10.1016/j.concog.2009.02.006

Hohwy, J., & Frith, C. (2004). Can neuroscience explain consciousness? *Journal of Consciousness Studies*, 11(7–8), 180–198.

Horst, S. (2007). *Beyond reduction: Philosophy of mind and post-reductionist philosophy of science*. New York, NY: Oxford University Press.

Howieson, D. B., Bigler, E. D., & Tranel, D. (2012). *Neuropsychological assessment* (5th ed.). New York, NY: Oxford University Press.

Irvine, E. (2013). *Consciousness as a scientific concept: A philosophy of science perspective*. Studies in Brain and Mind (Vol. 5). Dordrecht, The Netherlands: Springer. DOI: 10.1007/978-94-007-5173-6

Jackson, F. (1986). What Mary didn't know. *Journal of Philosophy*, 83(5), 291–295. DOI: 10.2307/2026143

Klink, P.C., van Wezel, R.J.A., & van Ee, R. (2013). The future of binocular rivalry research: Reaching through a window on consciousness. In S.M. Miller (Ed.), *The constitution of visual consciousness: Lessons from binocular rivalry* (pp. 305–332). Advances in Consciousness Research (Vol. 90). Amsterdam, The Netherlands: John Benjamins Publishing Company. DOI: 10.1075/aicr.90.12kli

Koch, C. (2004). *The quest for consciousness: A neurobiological approach*. Englewood, CO: Roberts & Company.

Lamme, V.A.F. (2006). Towards a true neural stance on consciousness. *Trends in Cognitive Sciences*, 10(11), 494–501. DOI: 10.1016/j.tics.2006.09.001

Lamme, V.A.F. (2010). How neuroscience will change our view on consciousness. *Cognitive Neuroscience*, 1(3), 204–220. DOI: 10.1080/17588921003731586

Law, P.C.F., Paton, B.K., Thomson, R.H., Liu, G.B., Miller, S.M., & Ngo, T.T. (2013). Dichoptic viewing methods for binocular rivalry research: Prospects for large-scale clinical and genetic studies. *Twin Research and Human Genetics*, 16(6), 1033–1078. DOI: 10.1017/thg.2013.76

Levine, J. (1983). Materialism and qualia: The explanatory gap. *Pacific Philosophical Quarterly*, 64(4), 354–361.

Liu, H., Agam, Y., Madsen, J.R., & Kreiman, G. (2009). Timing, timing, timing: Fast decoding of object information from intracranial field potentials in human visual cortex. *Neuron*, 62(2), 281–290. DOI: 10.1016/j.neuron.2009.02.025

Logothetis, N. (1998). Object vision and visual awareness. *Current Opinion in Neurobiology*, 8(4), 536–544. DOI: 10.1016/S0959-4388(98)80043-3

Logothetis, N.K. (2010). Bold claims for optogenetics. *Nature*, 468(7323), E3–E4. DOI: 10.1038/nature09532

Machamer, P., Darden, L., & Craver, C.F. (2000). Thinking about mechanisms. *Philosophy of Science*, 67(1), 1–25. DOI: 10.1086/392759

Mahner, M., & Bunge, M. (1997). *Foundations of biophilosophy*. Berlin: Springer-Verlag. DOI: 10.1007/978-3-662-03368-5

Maier, A., Logothetis, N.K., & Leopold, D.A. (2007). Context-dependent perceptual modulation of single neurons in primate visual cortex. *Proceedings of National Academy of Sciences USA*, 104(13), 5620–5625. DOI: 10.1073/pnas.0608489104

Merzenich, M.M., Kaas, J.H., Wall, J.T., Sur, M., Nelson, R.J., & Felleman, D.J. (1983). Progression of change following median nerve section in the cortical representation of the hand in areas 3b and 1 in adult owl and squirrel monkeys. *Neuroscience*, 10(3), 639–665. DOI: 10.1016/0306-4522(83)90208-7

Miller, S.M. (1998). *Biology and consciousness: Further extending the phenotype*. Poster presented at the *2nd Annual Meeting of the Association for the Scientific Study of Consciousness*, Bremen, Germany. Retrieved from http://www.theassc.org/files/assc/ASSC2_Program3.pdf

Miller, S.M. (1999). *The phenomenal phenotype: Evolution and ontology*. Paper presented at the *3rd Annual Meeting of the Association for the Scientific Study of Consciousness*, Ontario, Canada. Retrieved from http://www.theassc.org/files/assc/ASSC3_abstr.pdf

Miller, S.M. (2001). Binocular rivalry and the cerebral hemispheres: With a note on the correlates and constitution of visual consciousness. *Brain and Mind*, 2(1), 119–149. DOI: 10.1023/A:1017981619014

Miller, S.M. (2007). On the correlation/constitution distinction problem (and other hard problems) in the scientific study of consciousness. *Acta Neuropsychiatrica*, 19(3), 159–176. DOI: 10.1111/j.1601-5215.2007.00207.x

Miller, S.M. (Ed.). (2013a). *The constitution of visual consciousness: Lessons from binocular rivalry*. Advances in Consciousness Research (Vol. 90). Amsterdam, The Netherlands: John Benjamins Publishing Company. DOI: 10.1075/aicr.90

Miller, S.M. (2013b). Visual consciousness and binocular rivalry: An introduction. In S.M. Miller (Ed.), *The constitution of visual consciousness: Lessons from binocular rivalry* (pp. 1–13). Advances in Consciousness Research (Vol. 90). Amsterdam, The Netherlands: John Benjamins Publishing Company. DOI: 10.1075/aicr.90.01mil

Miller, S.M. (2014). Closing in on the constitution of consciousness. *Frontiers in Psychology*, 5, 1293. DOI: 10.3389/fpsyg.2014.01293

Miller, S.M., Liu, G.B., Ngo, T.T., Hooper, G., Riek, S., Carson, R.G., & Pettigrew, J.D. (2000). Interhemispheric switching mediates perceptual rivalry. *Current Biology*, 10(7), 383–392. DOI: 10.1016/S0960-9822(00)00416-4

Miller, S.M., Ngo, T.T., & van Swinderen, B. (2012). Attentional switching in humans and flies: Rivalry in large and miniature brains. *Frontiers in Human Neuroscience*, 5, 188. DOI: 10.3389/fnhum.2011.00188

Nagel, T. (1974). What is it like to be a bat? *Philosophical Review*, 83(4), 435–450. DOI: 10.2307/2183914

Neisser, J. (2012). Neural correlates of consciousness reconsidered. *Consciousness and Cognition*, 21(2), 681–690. DOI: 10.1016/j.concog.2011.03.012

Ngo, T.T., Barsdell, W.N., Law, P.C.F., & Miller, S.M. (2013). Binocular rivalry, brain stimulation and bipolar disorder. In S.M. Miller (Ed.), *The constitution of visual consciousness: Lessons from binocular rivalry* (pp. 211–252). Advances in Consciousness Research (Vol. 90). Amsterdam, The Netherlands: John Benjamins Publishing Company. DOI: 10.1075/aicr.90.09ngo

Noë, A., & Thompson, E. (2004). Are there neural correlates of consciousness? *Journal of Consciousness Studies*, 11(1), 3–28.

Oizumi, M., Albantakis, L., & Tononi, G. (2014). From the phenomenology to the mechanisms of consciousness: Integrated Information Theory 3.0. *PLoS Computational Biology*, 10(5), e1003588. DOI: 10.1371/journal.pcbi.1003588

Ramachandran, V.S., Stewart, M., & Rogers-Ramachandran, D.C. (1992). Perceptual correlates of massive cortical reorganization. *Neuroreport*, 3(7), 583–586. DOI: 10.1097/00001756-199207000-00009

Reppas, J.B., & Newsome, W.T. (2007). Brain stimulation: Feeling the buzz. *Current Biology*, 17(10), R358–R360. DOI: 10.1016/j.cub.2007.03.038

Revonsuo, A. (2000). Prospects for a scientific research program on consciousness. In T. Metzinger (Ed.), *Neural correlates of consciousness: Empirical and conceptual questions* (pp. 57–75). Cambridge, MA: MIT Press.

Revonsuo, A. (2001). Can functional brain imaging discover consciousness in the brain? *Journal of Consciousness Studies*, 8(3), 3–23.

Revonsuo, A. (2006). *Inner presence: Consciousness as a biological phenomenon*. Cambridge, MA: MIT Press.

Salzman, C. D., & Newsome, W. T. (1994). Neural mechanisms for forming a perceptual decision. *Science*, 264(5156), 231–237. DOI: 10.1126/science.8146653

Sengpiel, F. (2013). The neuron doctrine of binocular rivalry. In S. M. Miller (Ed.), *The constitution of visual consciousness: Lessons from binocular rivalry* (pp. 167–186). Advances in Consciousness Research (Vol. 90). Amsterdam, The Netherlands: John Benjamins Publishing Company. DOI: 10.1075/aicr.90.07sen

Seth, A. (2009). Explanatory correlates of consciousness: Theoretical and computational challenges. *Cognitive Computation*, 1(1), 50–63. DOI: 10.1007/s12559-009-9007-x

Shadlen, M. N., & Kiani, R. (2013). Decision making as a window on cognition. *Neuron*, 80(3), 791–806. DOI: 10.1016/j.neuron.2013.10.047

Shadlen, M. N., & Movshon, J. A. (1999). Synchrony unbound: A critical evaluation of the temporal binding hypothesis. *Neuron*, 24(1), 67–77. DOI: 10.1016/S0896-6273(00)80822-3

Singer, W. (2001). Consciousness and the binding problem. *Annals of the New York Academy of Sciences*, 929, 123–146. DOI: 10.1111/j.1749-6632.2001.tb05712.x

Sterzer, P. (2013). Functional neuroimaging of binocular rivalry. In S. M. Miller (Ed.), *The constitution of visual consciousness: Lessons from binocular rivalry* (pp. 187–210). Advances in Consciousness Research (Vol. 90). Amsterdam, The Netherlands: John Benjamins Publishing Company. DOI: 10.1075/aicr.90.08ste

Thomson, R. H., & Fitzgerald, P. B. (2013). Investigating the structure and function of the brain: A methodological overview. In S. M. Miller (Ed.), *The constitution of visual consciousness: Lessons from binocular rivalry* (pp. 141–165). Advances in Consciousness Research (Vol. 90). Amsterdam, The Netherlands: John Benjamins Publishing Company. DOI: 10.1075/aicr.90.06tho

Tononi, G., & Koch, C. (2008). The neural correlates of consciousness: An update. *Annals of the New York Academy of Sciences*, 1124, 239–261. DOI: 10.1196/annals.1440.004

Weiss, T., Miltner, W. H. R., Huonker, R., Friedel, R., Schmidt, I., & Taub, E. (2000). Rapid functional plasticity of the somatosensory cortex after finger amputation. *Experimental Brain Research*, 134(2), 199–203. DOI: 10.1007/s002210000456

Zhang, S., Xu, M., Kamigaki, T., Do, J. P. H., Chang, W.-C., Jenvay, S., Miyamichi, K., Luo, L., & Dan, Y. (2014). Long-range and local circuits for top-down modulation of visual cortex processing. *Science*, 345(6197), 660–665. DOI: 10.1126/science.1254126

The neural correlates of consciousness

Causes, confounds and constituents*

Jakob Hohwy and Tim Bayne
Monash University / University of Manchester

This chapter develops a framework for addressing the neural correlates of consciousness. We begin by distinguishing the kinds of neural correlates that are of central interest to the science of consciousness (what we call 'NCCs') from the kinds of neural correlates that are more peripheral to consciousness science and which are typically regarded as confounds from the perspective of consciousness research. We also examine various aspects of the NCCs, arguing that the notion involves complexities that have often been overlooked in the literature. We then consider a number of reasons for placing NCCs at the center of consciousness research, before considering a number of methodological challenges faced by consciousness science in attempting to distinguish the NCCs from neural correlates of other types.

1. Introduction

The search for the neural correlates of consciousness is now some three decades old, and progress has been made on a number of fronts. Developments in neuroimaging, the use of single cell recordings, and various forms of neural intervention (e.g., deep brain stimulation and transcranial magnetic stimulation) have generated new forms of data for consciousness science. But despite this progress, questions remain concerning what precisely a neural correlate of consciousness is, what roles the neural correlates of consciousness should have in the science of consciousness, and how the neural correlates of consciousness can be identified. The central aim of this chapter is to develop a framework in which these issues can be addressed.[1]

* This paper has been written with the support of European Research Council grant 313552 *The Architecture of Consciousness*, as well as Australian Research Council Future Fellowship (FT100100322) and Discovery (DP0984572) grants, for which we are very grateful.

1. For other overviews of the notion of an NCC see Chalmers (2000) and several chapters in the present volume.

DOI 10.1075/aicr.92.06hoh

In the most generic sense of the notion, a neural correlate of consciousness is a neural state or process that correlates with some conscious state or process. Appeals to correlation are involved in two kinds of scientific projects. The first kind of project is *horizontal*, and aims to determine whether or not correlated variables are related as cause and effect. The second kind of project is *vertical*, and aims to determine whether or not correlated variables are related in a non-causal manner, as might occur when a mechanism at one level of analysis realizes a phenomenon of interest at another level. For example, one might use data regarding a correlation between memory and long-term potentiation in order to argue that long-term potentiation is the mechanism underlying memory.

We can distinguish three kinds of neural correlates of consciousness; two of these correlates are 'horizontal' whereas the third is 'vertical' (Figure 1). Firstly, there are what we will call *upstream* neural correlates of consciousness, such as activity in early visual cortex which is the immediate causal precursor of the visual experience of an apple. Secondly, there are *downstream* correlates of consciousness, such as the neural activity implicated in using the visual experience of an apple for decision-making or belief-formation.

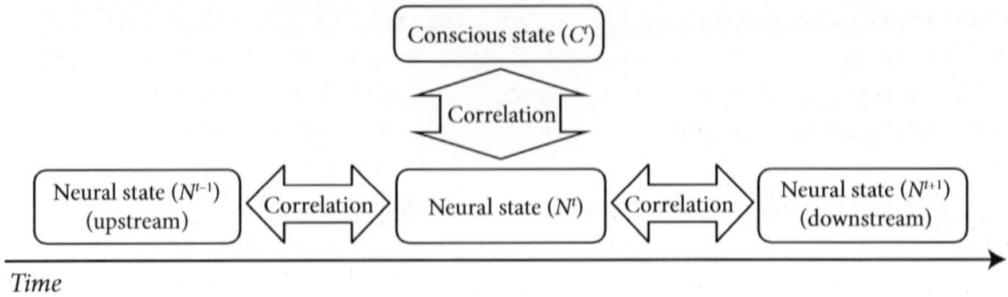

Figure 1. Horizontal and vertical NCCs. C^t is the conscious state of interest, occurring at time t; N^t is the NCC for C^t whereas the upstream and downstream correlates are not part of the NCC for C^t. See main text for further discussion.

Although an account of these 'horizontal' correlates would be a valuable thing to have, both are typically regarded as *confounds* from the perspective of the science of consciousness. The science of consciousness is not primarily interested in the neural processes that are causally upstream or downstream of consciousness, but is instead, interested in the vertical correlates of consciousness. More specifically, the focus of scientific interest is on the physical *basis* or *substrate* of consciousness.[2] We will call such states the 'NCCs' and will reserve the lower case 'nccs' for the generic notion of a neural correlate of consciousness. (Thus, all NCCs are nccs, but only some nccs are NCCs.)

2. For other discussions of these distinctions (albeit not under these labels) see: Aru, Bachmann, Singer, and Melloni (2012, this volume); de Graaf, Hsieh, and Sack (2012); de Graaf and Sack (this volume); Miller (2001, 2007, this volume); and Revonsuo (2000, 2001, 2006, this volume).

The precise nature of the relationship between conscious states and their NCCs is of course a matter of some dispute. Some theorists take conscious states to be *identical* to brain states, others regard conscious states as in some sense *constituted* by brain states, and still others hold that although conscious states are neither identical to nor constituted by brain states they do *supervene* on them such that any two subjects in the same brain states will be in the same conscious states (at least if we hold the laws of nature fixed).[3] However, the disagreement about the metaphysics of consciousness has little direct bearing on the NCC project, for all that the project requires is that certain neural states 'underlie' consciousness, either by way of identity, constitution, or mere supervenience.[4]

In light of the foregoing it is clear that referring to the NCC project as the "NCC project" is potentially misleading, for the project is concerned only with neural correlates of a certain type – to a first approximation, what we have referred to as the 'vertical correlates'. (See Section 6 for discussion as to why this is only a first approximation.) In many ways it would be preferable to describe this project in terms of the search for the neural *substrates* or *basis* of consciousness, but in our view the "NCC" terminology is now so deeply entrenched that any attempt to displace it is bound to fail.

The notion of an NCC is often characterized in terms of *minimal sufficiency* (e.g., Chalmers, 2000). The rough idea is that a neural state *N* is an NCC of conscious state *C* if and only if the existence of *N* is – given the laws of nature – minimally sufficient for the existence of *C*. In other words, the existence of *N* suffices for the existence of *C*, and there is no proper part of this neural state that would itself suffice for the presence of the corresponding conscious state. There are two crucial terms in this definition – 'minimal' and 'sufficiency' – and both are worthy of close examination.

The motivation for characterizing NCCs in terms of *minimal* sufficiency is clear: one wants to isolate only those neural features that are directly implicated in consciousness. Obviously a great many neural states and processes will be causally necessary for any particular conscious state, but the NCC project is interested in a relationship that is not merely causal. However, what precisely counts as minimal sufficiency on any particular occasion may not be entirely clear, and developing an analysis of this notion that is fit for its purpose is far from straightforward (Miller, 2001, 2007, this volume).

One challenge derives from the possibility of *redundancy*. Suppose that neural activity generates conscious states in something akin to the way in which the activity of individuals generates social facts. Imagine that the William James Appreciation

3. To say that conscious states supervene on brain states allows that two subjects can be in the same type of conscious states without being in the same type of brain states. Unlike identity, supervenience is an asymmetric relation.

4. These themes are not novel, and in fact can be found in the work of the turn-of-the-Century writer William Mitchell (1907), who discussed the neural correlates of consciousness in very sophisticated terms, devoting his neuroscientifically informed last chapter of *Structure and Growth of the Mind* "to the indirect explanation of experience and the mind, that is to say, to their immediate physical correlates" (1907, p. 450).

Society of Bundoora is meeting on a particular occasion, and 10 members of the Society are present. Because the quorum for an official meeting of the Society is set at nine members the gathering qualifies as an official meeting of the Society. Intuitively, each of the 10 members that is present plays a direct role in making it the case that this is an official meeting of the Society, even though no single individual was required for meeting the quorum.

Similarly, it is possible that the activity of a particular neuronal population qualifies as a part of the NCC for a conscious state *C* even though *C* would still have existed even if that neuronal population had not been active. Using a simplified example, one might imagine conscious state *C* for which 10 neurons appear to be the NCC; this NCC might be thought to exemplify redundancy in one of two ways. It might be that *C* occurs only when neurons 1 to 10 fire but further intervention might reveal that neuron number 10 is redundant; *C* will occur even when neuron number 10 is inactivated. This type of redundancy does not however seem problematic; given this new knowledge, neuron number 10 should not have been considered part of the NCC in the first place. As we see it, for this type of redundancy, the standard approach of the NCC project will suffice.

A second type of redundancy would occur if it was found that *C* only occurs when neurons 1 to 10 fire and in addition that *any one* of the 10 neurons could fail to fire and *C* would still occur as long as the other nine fire. Now it seems any individual part of the NCC is redundant: even though *C* will occur when only nine neurons fire, none of those nine is indispensable for *C*. If 'minimal' in the notion of the NCC implies that any NCC is non-redundant, then in this case the conscious state *C* would have no NCC. It may be that the brain is endowed with this type of redundancy in order to ensure a kind of robustness against dropout of individual units. Indeed, it's plausible to suppose that such a situation might be common: many conscious states might involve both right- and left-hemisphere processes, even though activity in a single hemisphere would have sufficed for the conscious state. How should science respond when faced with this type of redundancy problem?

One option is to stick with the NCC approach, but to change the "resolution" of the enquiry: instead of describing the NCC in terms of individual units it should instead be described in terms of groups of units (in this case how *C* depends systematically on groups of nine neurons). A further option is to make the redundancy itself a target of contrastive explanation: here one would seek to identify the NCC for a state *C* that is made robust by this type of redundancy, rather than for a state *C** which does not exemplify this kind of robustness (contrastive analysis of this sort is central to the NCC project, see Hohwy & Frith, 2004). These applications of the NCC approach speak to the challenge of screening off levels in the vertical dimension, after having successfully screened off upstream and downstream correlates; we discuss this further in Section 6.

Overall, the notion of 'minimal' thus seems open to refinement. Whereas we have argued that there is some scope for applying the standard NCC approach to redundancy scenarios, there is debate about how much of a challenge to the NCC approach redundancy may be (Miller, this volume).

What about the notion of *sufficiency*? The idea here is that activation of the relevant neural state 'generates' the relevant conscious state all by itself – no other neural activity is required. Suppose that *N* functions as the NCC of *C*. Other neural activity might be needed in order for the creature to be in state *N*, but if *N* is really an NCC of *C* then no neural activity over and above *N* is needed in order to bring *C* into existence. (Of course, it might often be difficult to know whether *N* itself suffices for the existence of *C* – we return to this issue below.)[5]

The notion of an NCC that we have just identified differs in one important way from that which is actually employed in the science of consciousness. In a typical example of NCC research, experimenters look for the neural states that are correlated with changes in fine-grained conscious states. For example, in binocular rivalry studies researchers look for the neural activity that correlates with the changes in the creature's perceptual experiences (see e.g., Logothetis, Leopold, & Sheinberg, 2003; Logothetis & Schall, 1989; Sheinberg & Logothetis, 1997). Research of this kind is not able to identify the minimally sufficient basis of the conscious states in question, for it doesn't control for the fact that the creature is conscious in both conditions. At most, such research can uncover the neural states that are minimally sufficient for a certain kind of conscious content *in a creature that is already conscious*, but to say that activity in a neural system *N* suffices for a certain conscious state in a conscious creature is not to say that that activity is itself minimally sufficient for consciousness.

These reflections indicate that the science of consciousness is not primarily concerned with NCCs as characterized above, but with what we might call *differentiating* NCCs, where a differentiating NCC is that component of a state's overall NCC which is implicated in conscious states of that particular type (Bayne, 2007; Hohwy, 2009).[6] In scientific contexts, the non-differentiating components of a state's NCC – that is, the neural activity which is an element of a state's minimally sufficient neural basis but which is not uniquely associated with conscious states of that particular type – is often ignored. In effect, an NCC for a conscious state of type *C* is often equated with the neural state that is minimally sufficient of type *C* states in creatures that are already conscious. This approach is not in itself objectionable, but it should not be forgotten that an account of the differentiating NCCs falls well short of an account of the NCCs as such.

5. There are other complications concerning the notion of minimal sufficiency that also deserve attention. For example, there may be conscious state kinds K^1 such that tokens of K^1 can occur only in the context of tokens of conscious states of kind K^2. The NCCs of K^1-type states will, intuitively, 'include' more than just the conscious state in question, but will also include conscious states of other kinds.

6. Block (2005) and Chalmers (2000) refer to differentiating correlates as *core correlates*, drawing on Shoemaker's (1981) distinction between *core* and *total* realizers. We prefer to avoid this label as it suggests that differentiating correlates reflect a more important part of the overall NCCs than do non-differentiating correlates.

It is possible to distinguish NCCs for different types of conscious states (Chalmers, 2000). For the most part the NCC project has focused on fine-grained conscious states, such as the conscious states associated with the taste of coffee, sharp pain, or the perception of color. Specific conscious states are often referred to as conscious contents, for they are typically individuated in terms of their intentional contents (roughly speaking, the property in the world that the conscious state in question represents).[7] Non-specific conscious states, such as those states associated with alert wakefulness, rapid eye movement-dreaming, light anesthesia, and delirium (for example), will also have distinctive neural correlates. Such states are sometimes referred to as 'background states' (Chalmers, 2000) or 'levels' (Laureys, 2005) of consciousness, but we prefer to call them 'modes of consciousness' (Bayne & Hohwy, 2015). Although less effort has been directed towards identifying the NCCs of conscious modes, they have not been entirely neglected, and we are beginning to get a grip on the kinds of neural systems implicated in this aspect of consciousness (Alkire & Miller, 2005; Boly, Sanders, Mashour, & Laureys, 2013; Brown, Lydic, & Schiff, 2010; Charland-Verville, Vanhaudenhuyse, Laureys, & Gosseries, this volume; Giacino, Fins, Laureys, & Schiff, 2014; Goldfine & Schiff, 2011). A third type of conscious state that falls within the scope of the NCC project is the state of being conscious – what is sometimes called 'creature consciousness'. It is plausible that there won't be a distinctive neural correlate for the property of being conscious as such, but that a neural state will be sufficient for consciousness only in virtue of being sufficient for a specific type of conscious state.

With the foregoing in hand, we can identify three sets of questions that need to be addressed. The first set of questions concerns the aims and ambitions of NCC research: what might an account of the NCCs provide us with, which could not be provided by an account of either the upstream or downstream nccs? A second set of questions concerns the relationship between the analysis of an NCC provided above and the science of consciousness: to what extent does the notion of an NCC that we have just characterized map on to the notion as it is employed in consciousness research? A third set of questions concerns the methodological challenges that we face in identifying the NCCs: how might we screen off the upstream- and downstream nccs from the NCCs?

7. We are ignoring here two questions that have loomed very large in the recent philosophical discussion of consciousness: (1) Can differences in phenomenal character be reduced to differences in intentional content? (2) Are intentional contents to be identified with properties?

2. Explanation, prediction and manipulation

The search for the NCCs is often regarded as the primary aim of the (neuro)science of consciousness. Those who place the search for the NCCs at the center of their research typically assume both that identifying the NCCs will have a significant pay-off, and that that pay-off can be obtained only by identifying the NCCs. Are either of these assumptions justified?

One motivation for focusing on the NCCs is *explanatory*. Many hope that an account of the NCCs will enable us to explain consciousness, and in particular to provide better explanations of consciousness than those that are provided by the upstream- or downstream-nccs. But despite the widespread endorsement of this aim, there are good reasons to wonder what kind of explanatory pay-off the NCC project might provide even if successful.

The central problem here is posed by the infamous 'explanatory gap' between neural state and processes on the one hand and conscious states and processes on the other (Chalmers, 1996; Levine, 1983). Neural activity seems capable of explaining only structure and function, but consciousness appears to have qualitative properties that are not purely structural or functional. In other words, neurally based explanations appear doomed to leave the 'what it's likeness' of conscious experience unexplained.[8]

The force of this worry is much disputed, for some theorists argue that the properties of consciousness are purely structural and functional, and that any appearance to the contrary is to be explained away. We will not take a position in this debate here, but will note that even if there are good reasons for thinking that certain aspects of consciousness are purely qualitative (and thus beyond the reach of neurally based explanation), there may be other, interesting aspects of consciousness that are structural and functional.

One dimension of consciousness that is plausibly regarded as primarily structural and functional involves modes of consciousness. Such states are largely – perhaps even fully – individuated by appeal to their structural and functional features, and thus are prime candidates for being explained by appeal to neural mechanisms. Indeed, it is clear that the contents of consciousness have structural and functional aspects, even if their phenomenal character is not exhausted by those aspects. In sum, although explanatory gap worries might undermine the hope that identifying the NCCs will provide an *exhaustive* explanation of consciousness, they do not threaten the claim

8. Note that moving from either nomological or functional conceptions of explanation to mechanistic conceptions – as Opie and O'Brien (this volume) recommend – leaves explanatory gap worries unaddressed, for such worries are independent of any particular model of explanation. The fundamental issue is that a full explanation of a phenomenon will represent it as being necessitated by its explanans, but insofar as neural explanations appeal only to structural and functional features they won't necessitate the purely qualitative features of consciousness.

that the NCC project will have *some* explanatory pay-off, nor do they undermine the assumption that that pay-off will require identifying the NCCs as such, as opposed to merely the upstream- or downstream-nccs.

But there are other challenges to the assumption that the NCC project will have an explanatory pay-off. A second challenge focuses on the fact that NCC research is typically concerned with differentiating NCCs rather than total NCCs (as we noted above). Even if identifying a state's total NCC sheds some explanatory light on it, it is surely a further question whether identifying its differentiating-NCC will shed any explanatory light on it. After all, an account of the differentiating-NCCs is silent on the issue of what makes the creature conscious in the first place.

Although there is something to this worry, its force is somewhat ameliorated by recognizing that explanation is typically contrastive. Rather than asking why *x* is the case, we often want to know why *x* rather than *y* is the case (Lipton, 2004). In the case of consciousness, one of our central interests is to explain why a conscious creature is in one kind of conscious state rather than another, and that is precisely the kind of question which an account of the differentiating NCCs is designed to answer (Hohwy & Frith, 2004). So, the science of consciousness may still have some explanatory pay-off even if the experimental design that it employs restricts it to identifying only the differentiating NCCs.

A third challenge to the explanatory potential of the NCC project derives from the possibility of multiple realization. Just as money is realized by physical objects of various kinds (e.g., coins, notes, seashells), so too it might be the case that conscious states are realized by neural states of various kinds (Block & Fodor, 1972). And although classical formulations of the type identity theory (Smart, 1959) imply that if *N* is a correlate of *C* in one creature then it must be a correlate of *C* in any creature, other formulations of the type identity theory (e.g., Kim, 1972; Lewis, 1972) do relativize the identities in question to particular species. Such accounts allow that *N* might function as the NCC of *C* in the members of one population but not another. Although it seems likely that the same kinds of (perhaps coarse-grained) neural states will form the neural basis of particular conscious states in neurotypical members of a single species, it is an open question whether conscious states of a certain kind have a single neural base across all species or indeed across all the members of a single species. Discovering that N_1 is *a* neural correlate of *C* might go some way towards explaining *C*, but it is very likely that this explanation will be at best only partial if it remains an open question whether N_1 is the *only* neural correlate of *C*. A full neurobiological explanation of *C* surely needs to be informed not only by an account of what neural states are *sufficient* for *C* but what neural states are *necessary* for *C*.

A second motivation for the NCC project focuses on the idea of *prediction*. The idea here is that identifying the NCCs will have a predictive payoff which goes beyond that provided by identifying the creature's upstream and downstream nccs.

But here too there are challenges that may not be obvious. For one thing, the possibility of multiple realization needs to be taken into account. If the neural basis of consciousness differs from one population to another, then one could use information about a person's neural states to predict their conscious states only by knowing which population to assign them to, and such a task may not always be entirely straightforward. As we have just noted, whether it is likely (or even possible) that NCCs are relativized to particular populations depends on the fundamental nature of the relationship between neural states and conscious states, but there is certainly some reason to take this possibility seriously. Note also that in many contexts an account of the upstream nccs may be almost as useful as an account of the NCCs when it comes to prediction. Suppose that the correlation between C^t and an upstream correlate (N^{t-1}) is almost as strong as the correlation between C^t and its NCC (N^t). In such a case, knowing that a creature is in state N^{t-1} will be almost as informative as knowing that it is in state N^t.

A third motivation for the NCC project involves an appeal to *manipulation*. The hope is that by identifying the NCCs we might be in a position to selectively manipulate the contents of a person's consciousness, ensuring that they are – or, as the case may be, are not – in conscious states of a certain kind. Such a capacity would have obvious clinical and therapeutic benefits. Is there any reason to think that identifying the NCCs will be uniquely helpful in enabling us to manipulate consciousness?

Not as far as we can see. Although identifying the NCCs of a state would certainly enable us to manipulate it, so too would identifying the state's upstream nccs. In fact, many of the points that we just made concerning prediction apply also to manipulation, for successful manipulation requires the ability to predict the consequences of one's manipulation. Our capacity to manipulate the relevant upstream correlates would simply be an extension of our current capacity to control a creature's conscious states by manipulating the relevant features of their environment (such as the stimuli to which they are exposed). Insofar as manipulation is one of the central aims of the neuroscience of consciousness, the contrast between upstream nccs and NCCs might be relatively unimportant.

This section has examined three ways in which one might justify the claim that the search for the NCCs ought to lie at the heart of the neuroscience of consciousness. We have suggested that none of these three lines of motivation is entirely straightforward: identifying the NCCs may not have the explanatory pay-off that many theorists assume, and from a predictive and manipulative point of view identifying the up-stream nccs might be (almost) as good as identifying the NCCs themselves. But although these points undermine the assumption that an account of the NCCs should be the 'holy grail' of consciousness research, they don't undermine the assumption that it should be a central concern of consciousness research.

3. Screening off: The upstream challenge

In order to identify the underlying NCCs of a particular conscious state, we will need to screen off both the upstream and downstream nccs (Figure 2).

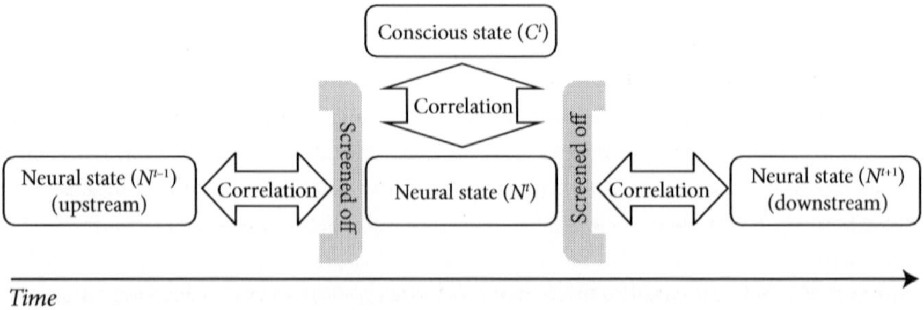

Figure 2. Neural correlates of conscious state *C* upstream and downstream from the NCC should be screened off.

A state's upstream correlates will typically feature among its causal antecedents. As such, upstream correlates are in principle dissociable from the relevant conscious state (assuming that causes are distinct existences from their effects). For example, even though activity at the retina is causally implicated in consciously perceiving a face, retinal activity can occur in the absence of conscious experience, as when (for example) the eyes are stimulated while sleeping or anesthetized. More generally, an upstream correlate of *C* cannot be minimally sufficient for the existence of *C* given that a subject could go out of existence in the interval between the occurrence of the upstream correlate and the occurrence of *C*. A state's downstream correlates will typically feature among its causal effects, and are thus also in principle dissociable from it (see next section).

Screening off can be extremely challenging. One method is to keep the subject's conscious states stable and vary up- and downstream states, N^{t-1} and N^{t+1}. This would indicate whether or not N^{t-1} and N^{t+1} are components of the minimally sufficient states for consciousness. In this vein, one can use masking, where the upstream processes are changed but the conscious state remains the same: one is unaware that a stimulus has been presented even though it is processed to some degree by the brain's early sensory systems (Kouider & Dehaene, 2007). Another method is to keep N^{t-1} and N^{t+1} stable and to vary the conscious state, which would show that N^{t-1} and N^{t+1} are not part of the minimally sufficient conditions for C^t. The neural state, N^t, which does vary with C^t would be part of the NCC. This method is used in binocular rivalry experiments, in which the input to the two eyes is kept stable (which should stabilize N^{t-1}) while the contents of the subject's conscious perception change. In this manner, activity that at first may have seemed to correlate most tightly with the conscious state is found to in fact correlate more tightly with presentation of the physical stimulus. As these considerations show, it takes considerable ingenuity to determine whether certain kinds of neural activity underpin a conscious state or merely feature among its causal antecedents or consequents.

Another screening off method that is employed in consciousness science involves direct neural stimulation or inhibition. Interventions of this kind are now carried out on patients about to undergo surgery for the treatment of epilepsy, and in non-brain damaged subjects, by using transcranial magnetic stimulation, anesthesia, and certain kinds of psychotropic drugs. These procedures can screen off neural activity that is upstream of the site of intervention from that which is causally downstream of it. However, because these interventions typically involve conscious organisms, they provide evidence concerning differentiating NCCs only, and leave unaddressed questions about total NCCs.

Of course, a further question in such cases will be whether the efforts to screen off have succeeded in identifying the truly *minimally* sufficient conditions for *C*, or whether there are interventions which would reveal states which are even better candidates for being regarded as the minimally sufficient conditions for *C*. Questions of this kind are part-and-parcel of normal scientific practice. For example, even if some intervention has given us reason to believe that a type of vegetable is the cause of a particular cancer, it may be reasonable to ask whether the vegetable is contaminated with a certain chemical, such that the 'real' cause of the cancer is the chemical rather than the vegetable. Whether such further questions should be asked will often depend on background knowledge about the causal net in question, for example, how its parameters are normally individuated and which causes typically have which effects. Identifying such background knowledge can of course be very difficult for an embryonic field like the science of consciousness.

Another paradigm for investigating the NCCs looks to the results of neurological damage (which can be conceived as a kind of accidental intervention). For example, some theorists have argued that V1 is not part of the neural correlate of visual experience on the grounds that patients with bilateral V1 damage still can have visual experiences (Crick & Koch, 1995a). Research in this vein does have a bearing on the search for the NCCs, but it must be interpreted carefully (Crick & Koch, 1995b; Pollen, 1995). Showing that patients who lack some V1 activity can still have experiences of type *C* at best shows that V1 is not *necessary* for *C*, it doesn't show that it is not an element of a neural state that is *sufficient* for *C*. In order to argue that V1 is an element of a state that is sufficient for *C* one would need to argue that conscious states are not multiply realized – in other words, that there aren't two distinct kinds of neural bases of *C* in neurotypical human beings. And even if that claim can be defended, it is a further question whether the neural basis of *C* type experiences in neurotypical individuals is identical to the neural basis of *C* type experiences in individuals who have suffered brain damage. Clearly, any search for the neural basis of consciousness must reckon with neural plasticity (see Chalmers, 2000).

Yet another method for screening off upstream nccs from the underlying NCCs involves an appeal to binocular rivalry. The aim here is to contrast conscious processing of a stimulus with unconscious processing of the same stimulus, and thus screen off neural activity that correlates with the contents of consciousness from that which correlates with the presentation of the physical stimulus itself. However, as we noted above, this paradigm does not control for consciousness as such. Thus, part of what it is to consciously experience, say, a face might involve activity that is independent of the experimental intervention. Because of this, additional data will be needed in order to distinguish neural processing that is upstream of the relevant conscious states from that which is involved in upstream *selection* of a stimulus for presentation into consciousness from the NCC of that state (Hohwy, 2009; Searle, 2000). Certain activity – such as that which occurs at the retina – is intuitively upstream of consciousness, but this intuition is not based on evidence delivered by the rivalry paradigm.

We have here used an aspect of the rivalry paradigm to generate a challenge to screening off upstream neural correlates. The aspect was noted upon in the previous section, as a problem concerning what explanatory contrast is relevant for the NCC: we said that at best this approach may deliver differentiating but not total neural correlates. Here that problem is deepened: we are suggesting that paradigms such as binocular rivalry may deliver only upstream correlates rather than differentiating NCCs as such.

4. Screening off: The downstream challenge

Let us turn now to the challenge of screening off mere downstream nccs from the NCCs. Put in its most abstract form, the central task here is that of finding ways of determining whether or not neural activity correlated with a conscious state *C* is a component of its NCC or whether it is merely causally downstream from it.

The most vivid form of this challenge is posed by what we might call the report problem (see also van Boxtel & Tsuchiya, this volume). In many contexts we rely on a subject's reports in order to determine what conscious states they are in; indeed, it is often assumed that introspective reports function as the gold standard of consciousness science (see e.g., Frith, Perry, & Lumer, 1999; Naccache, 2006). However, reporting one's conscious states requires not only that the contents of consciousness are *accessible* to various 'consuming systems' (i.e., those systems responsible for using conscious content in thought and action), but are in fact accessed by those consuming systems. Because of this, the very methodology of consciousness studies seems to demand that the neural states implicated in cognitive access will be implicated in any potential candidate for the NCC, even if those states are not actually minimally sufficient for the conscious states in question. To put the problem in terms of the idiom of screening off, the challenge centers on the question of whether it is possible to screen off the neural activity implicated in report given that our only scientific access to consciousness appears to demand report (Block, 2007).

One response to the report problem is to set it aside on the grounds that the mechanisms involved in report – or at least of 'cognitive access' – are not *downstream* of consciousness, but are part and parcel of consciousness (Cohen & Dennett, 2011; Kanwisher, 2001; Kouider, de Gardelle, Sackur, & Dupoux, 2010). In our view, although this position must be taken seriously, it ought to be an open question whether certain forms of consciousness might be independent of cognitive access. And even if *certain* forms of cognitive access are constitutive of consciousness, it is unclear precisely which forms of cognitive access are constitutive of consciousness and which forms are merely causally downstream of – and thus in principle separable from – it. Thus, a version of the challenge outlined above remains even if certain forms of cognitive access are implicated in consciousness itself.

In order to address this challenge it would be useful to identify which 'consuming systems' are implicated in producing reports and which are not. In the vast majority of cases, report requires the activation of certain elements of the sensorimotor system. (A possible exception to this rule is the use of neuroimaging to identify a person's reports.) Although the reports elicited in consciousness science are typically verbal, reports can involve button presses or indeed any other movement that goes proxy for a judgment. But whether or not the report in question involves speech, the neural activity associated with the report of a conscious state will reflect not merely that conscious state but also the mechanisms of cognitive access involved in generating that report.

One technique for addressing the report problem involves varying the kinds of reports that subjects are required to give (Marcel, 1993). For example, one can ask subjects to report their experiences verbally on some trials and via button presses on others. Neural activity that is seen on one set of trials (say, the verbal ones) but not the other set of trials is presumably not part of the NCC for the relevant conscious states but is instead merely downstream activity implicated in a particular type of reporting behavior. By contrast, activity that obtains in both types of response (and which has already been screened off from upstream activity) will be a candidate for being (part of) the relevant NCC.

Although far from trivial, it is clear how one might screen off the sensorimotor aspects of report in this way. However, other aspects of report are much more challenging to screen off. Consider the intuitively plausible idea that in order to report one's conscious states one must form an introspective judgment about them. Arguably, the formation of introspective judgments involves metacognitive processes that may not be implicit in the neural correlates of the first-order conscious states themselves.

In response to this worry, one might argue that the kinds of reports required by – and indeed typically seen in – consciousness science are environmental rather than introspective. Although subjects may indeed be asked to say what conscious states they are in, they typically comply with this instruction by describing the state of their environment. In response to the question, 'Did you have a red experience or a blue experience?' one need only report whether the stimulus was red or blue. (Indeed, in most studies subjects are not in fact asked what conscious states they are in but are simply asked to categorize the presented stimulus.) But if consciousness science doesn't require introspective report does it follow that the report problem can be avoided?

Perhaps not. Although reporting whether or not a stimulus was presented in a certain trial does not require forming an explicit introspective belief about one's own state of mind, it does presumably implicate higher, metacognitive order processes of various kinds, such as those implicated in determining whether to report the presence of a stimulus (see Lau, 2008). It is an open question whether metacognitive processes of this kind are essentially implicated in consciousness itself, or whether they are downstream of consciousness. Hence even without explicit introspection, a version of the report problem seems to persist.

One way in which one might attempt to at least mitigate the seriousness of the report problem would be to develop tools that enable us to determine a subject's conscious states without requiring reports of any kind. In this regard, one might be tempted to use *intentional agency* as a marker of consciousness (Bayne, 2013; Bayne & Hohwy, 2014; Shea & Bayne, 2010). Not only is it plausible to think that consciousness is correlated with intentional agency at a creature-based level, it is also plausible to suppose that a creature's intentional actions might provide some guidance to the particular conscious states that it is in, and that we might consult a creature's patterns of intentional agency in order to ascribe conscious states to it.

Of course, there are questions about the degree to which intentional agency requires consciousness, for cognitive science suggests that many behaviors involve the activity of 'zombie systems' (Crick & Koch, 2001). But this worry should not be overplayed, for although certain types of behavior are indeed under unconscious control, the vast majority of intentional activity is guided by the contents of consciousness. Moreover, we should not forget that introspective report is not an infallible guide to consciousness (Bayne & Spener, 2010; Dennett, 1991; Schwitzgebel, 2008). Indeed, one reason to think that a subject's introspective reports might be in error is that they are at odds with their intentional behavior.

A very different response to the report problem is to look for *physiological* markers of consciousness. In an interesting study, Naber and colleagues (Naber, Frässle, & Einhäuser, 2011) established that pupil dilation and optokinetic nystagmus (the jerky movements of the eyes when following a moving object) correlate with different aspects of the stimuli presented during rivalry such as contrast and movement (they controlled this with presentation of physically alternating rather than rivaling stimuli too). That is, they found that pupil dilation and optokinetic nystagmus are not blind reflexes to the physical stimuli but reflect the conscious percept. In light of this, one might be tempted to use an agent's pupil dilation or nystagmus as a measure of their state of visual consciousness, even when the agent is not reporting on their experience or using it to carry out an intentional action. In subsequent research, this group conducted a very similar study while, crucially, obtaining functional magnetic resonance imaging data and were thus able to target neural activity that can be presumed to be independent of actually reporting what is seen: they contrasted a rivalry condition that involved perceptual report with a rivalry condition that did not involve perceptual report. Their evidence suggests that frontal activity is tied more to report and introspection than to the selection of content into consciousness (Frässle, Sommer, Jansen, Naber, & Einhäuser, 2014).

Might research of this kind point towards a solution to the report problem? Perhaps not. Firstly, even if participants are not required to either report or act on the contents of their conscious states, it may nonetheless be the case that such contents are *poised* for report and/or the control of intentional agency. In other words, even if the mechanisms implicated in cognitive access are not active those implicated in cognitive access*ability* will be. Thus, to the extent that there are question-marks surrounding the relationship between consciousness and cognitive accessibility then this approach may not be able to resolve them.

Secondly, one might ask whether we actually have evidence that physiological processes such as this can be trusted as *independent* markers of consciousness. What weight – if any – should we give to such factors when they are not correlated with subject's reports or with the presence of intentional behavior? Although optokinetic nystagmus was found to correlate well with button presses for most stimulus parameter settings, there were some stimulus parameter settings for which the nystagmus response indicated very short dominance periods of one or other percept that were not reflected in the subject's button presses. In such situations, should we regard the nystagmus response as a more accurate measure of visual experience than the subject's reports, or should we instead regard the subject's button presses as the more accurate measure of consciousness and take the nystagmus response to be tracking unconscious processing? Arguably, we need evidence in favor of the former alternative if we are to employ a behavioral marker such as optokinetic nystagmus as an independent marker of consciousness.

To sum up, the downstream challenge remains unmet. There are significant methodological hurdles to screening off downstream activity, and there are significant outstanding conceptual questions about how to understand the relation between consciousness and accessibility.

5. The action-dependence challenge

In the previous sections we discussed the challenges posed by screening off the upstream and downstream neural correlates of consciousness. However, the very distinction between upstream and downstream processes is not easily drawn when dealing with a system as dynamic and complex as the conscious brain, for the contents of a person's conscious state are very often modulated by what the subject in question does. In highlighting this issue for consciousness studies, Hurley (1998) noted that when someone with paralyzed eye muscles tries, and fails, to move the eyes sideways, it then looks as if the world jumps sideways. In a more controversial example of this phenomenon, she also argued that some of Levy and Trevarthen's (1976) intriguing split-brain findings can be explained by appeal to the way consciousness depends on the individual's responses. Levy and Trevarthen found that the contents of the split-brain patient's visual experience could apparently be changed by modulating the response that they were required to give to chimeric stimuli. When the patient was asked to produce a verbal report they seemed to be aware of one side of the stimulus, whereas they seemed to be aware of the other side of the stimulus when asked to point with their left hand. Hurley suggested that this phenomenon might be explained by appeal to the action-dependence of consciousness: verbal report involves activation of the left hemisphere which privileges the representation of stimuli in the right half of the visual field, whereas use of the left hand involves activation of the right hemisphere, and thus privileges the representation of stimuli in the left half of the visual field.

The action-dependence of consciousness is also manifest in binocular rivalry. For example, Naber et al. (2011) found that responding to rivalry stimuli with a continuous device (e.g., a joystick) produces different rivalry switch rates than when responding with a discrete response device (e.g., button presses); similarly, the rivalry switch rate decreases when participants are not required to report their conscious states, indicating that responding interferes with the mechanisms for selection into consciousness (see also Frässle et al., 2014). In general, action appears to modulate consciousness by 'looping back' into upstream processes.

How widespread might action-dependence be? Although some kinds of action-dependence – such as those that might be present in split-brain patients – are probably rare, we suspect that other forms of action-dependence are widespread and quite possibly ubiquitous. This is because the action-dependence we have described is triggered by commonly-encountered contexts. The brain is constantly required to both disambiguate and integrate various streams of sensory input, and action plays an important role in both of these tasks as we actively explore the world in order to decrease perceptual uncertainty. In general, sensory input depends in part on the creature's own actions (moving eyes, limbs and body around in the environment), and such action loops are arguably central to sensory processing, which can be viewed as an inferential, Bayesian process that must always conditionalize on action (cf. Hohwy, 2013).

If action-dependence is indeed widespread, then the NCC project must take it into account. A simple response to it would be to view action-dependence as a confound that is best controlled for by screening off upstream and downstream activity as efficiently as possible. Although understandable, this reaction is not entirely unproblematic, for if action-dependence is nearly ubiquitous then identifying the neural correlates of action-*in*dependent conscious states may be of limited interest. It may also mean that the NCC approach is powerless to explain a range of explanatory contrasts that pertain to action dependence (for example, why in certain, action-involving versions of binocular rivalry there are longer periods of conscious experience of one rather than another stimulus). Although identifying the neural correlates of action-independent conscious states would clearly represent a significant advance, it is unclear what implications such progress might have for our understanding of action-dependent states.

6. The vertical challenge

Upstream and downstream correlates are not the only kinds of correlates that need to be screened off from the NCCs. The need for further screening off derives from the fact that there will be various levels of neural activity underlying any conscious state (Figure 3). One level of activity might involve neural systems and effective connectivity between large neural populations, another level might relate to spike trains and modulatory activity of single neurons, and still another might be described in terms of molecular neurobiology and gene expression. In reality, it is of course a rather substantial question what levels of activity there are and how they are organized.

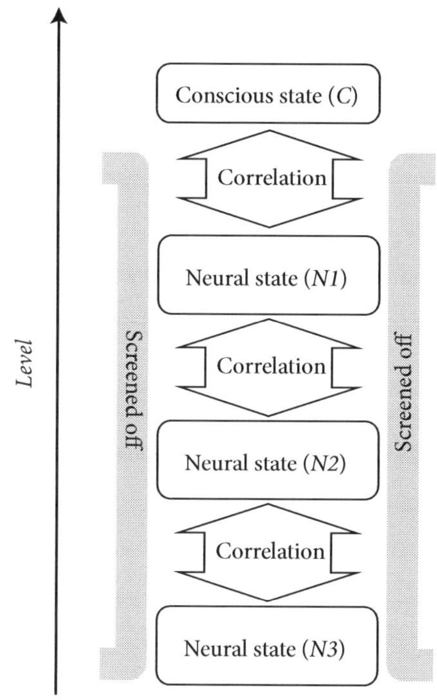

Figure 3. Even when upstream and downstream correlates of *C* have been screened off, further screening off is needed in the 'vertical dimension' – that is, between simultaneous activity at various neurocognitive levels.

In order to see why some levels of underlying neural activity might be better candidates for the NCC label than others we need to first make explicit two assumptions that are widely (albeit not universally) endorsed. The first assumption is that lower levels *realize* higher levels and in so doing necessitate them (cf. Craver, 2007). For example, states at the molecular level of the entire brain fix the states of single cells, which in turn fix the states at a systems level of description, and so on. The second assumption is that of *multiple realizability*: states at one level can be realized by different kinds of states at lower levels, in principle if not in practice. For example, a certain systems level state might be realized by one concatenation of spike trains in one creature and by a different concatenation of spike trains in another creature. So, although lower level states fix higher level states, variation at lower levels can leave higher level states untouched.

What does this imply for the question of which of the various physical states that underpin a conscious state *C* qualify as its NCC? The official characterization of an NCC suggests that *all* of a state's 'vertical correlates' qualify as NCCs. This is because a neural state qualifies as an NCC of *C* in virtue of being minimally sufficient for *C*, and each of the neural states 'below' *C* will be minimally sufficient for it: fixing *N3* fixes *N2*, which in turn fixes *N1*.

However, there is an intuitive case for thinking that not all vertical correlates are of equal relevance to the NCC project, and that certain levels might be more natural candidates for the NCC label than others. For example, one might plausibly think that consciousness is grounded in systems-level properties rather than single cell-level or molecular properties. Suppose that we have three subjects, each of which is in conscious state *C*. And suppose, further, that these three subjects are in high-level neural state of the same kind (*N1*), but that these neural states are realized by different kinds of lower-level neural states in each case (say, *N2*, *N2** and *N2†*). Now, we *could* regard *N2* as the NCC of *C* in subject 1, *N2** as the NCC of *C* in subject 2, and *N2†* as the NCC of *C* in subject 3. After all, each of these states *is* minimally sufficient for the existence of *C*. However, it would be far more elegant to regard *N1* as the *real* NCC of *C*, and to suppose that the other, lower level states suffice for *C* only because they suffice for *N1*. What's driving this thought is a desire for theoretical economy and simplicity: an account that grounds *C* in *N1* alone seems more attractive than an account that grounds *C* in the disjunction of the other three states.

There is a direct connection to the explanatory relevance of NCCs here, which we discussed in Section 2 above. Although one could ensure that the subject was in *C* by ensuring that they were in (say) *N2* (or *N2** or *N2†*), manipulations at the level of *N1* might be more effective with respect to *C* than manipulations of the different *N2*-level states. For suppose that one wanted to ensure that a subject was *not* in *C*. Attempting to prevent the subject from entering state *N2†* might not be the best strategy here, for both *N2** and *N2†* are sufficient for N1. Better, then, to target *N1* directly. So, an interventionist perspective justifies the intuitive thought that it is *N1* rather than the lower levels that deserves to be thought of as the true NCC of the relevant conscious state.

A further strategy for distinguishing a state's NCC from other elements of its underlying neural correlates involves considering how well a given level *integrates* with other NCC findings. On this account one could consider a number of types of conscious states (*C1*, *C2*, *C3*,…) and ask which neural level explains most of the variability in the manifestation of all these conscious states. If it turns out that *N1* activity explains most variability *overall*, then this suggests that activity at this level is a good candidate for the NCC. However, difficulties may arise here. Consider, for example, a situation where *C1* correlates best with *N1*, *C2* with *N2*, and C3 with *N3*. Here there would be an explanatory cost for the strategy of picking any level that overall is the best explainer. In those kinds of cases a multi-level NCC may be a better choice than forcing a single-level solution. In other words, it is possible that some aspects of consciousness have as their NCC neural activity at one level while other aspects of consciousness have as their NCC neural states at another level.

The upshot of these considerations is that although any vertical correlate of *C* will give us some predictive leverage on whether a creature is in *C*, certain levels of description might be more intimately associated with particular kinds of conscious state than are other levels of description. Those levels of description, one might surmise, will then serve better at fulfilling the explanatory ambition that drives the NCC project in the first place. So even if the standard definition of the NCC has it that all vertical correlates are correlates in the proper sense of this notion, there is reason to operate with a notion of the NCC which allows explanatory considerations to distinguish among levels of neural description and to privilege one level of description as capturing *the* neural correlate of the relevant conscious state.

How might one go about screening off the mere vertical nccs from the NCCs proper? We have already provided a partial answer to this question. One method for screening off is to intervene at one level and discover whether or not the conscious state *C* changes as a result. For example, one can in principle isolate a pattern of effective connectivity and intervene on underlying spike trains of a few neurons. If *C* changes as a result of this intervention then that would provide some evidence that spike trains at that level of intervention are part of *C*'s NCC, whereas if *C* does not change then that would be some evidence that it is not part of *C*'s NCC.

7. Conclusion

This chapter has considered a range of conceptual, theoretical and methodological challenges to the search for the neural correlates of consciousness. We began by clarifying the notion of an NCC, and by distinguishing the NCC project from other projects with which it has sometimes been confused. A central aim of our discussion here was to defend the standard characterization of an NCC in terms of minimal sufficiency. We then turned to the question of what exactly the NCC project might hope to achieve, arguing that although the successful realization of this project might tell us less about consciousness than is commonly assumed, a case can be made for locating the search for the NCCs at the heart of consciousness science. Finally, we turned our attention to a series of methodological challenges facing the NCC project, centering our discussion on the challenges posed by screening off 'mere correlates' of consciousness from the NCCs proper (Aru et al., this volume; de Graaf & Sack, this volume; Miller, this volume; Revonsuo, this volume). How might the upstream correlates of consciousness be screened from the NCCs? To what degree might the action-dependent nature of consciousness problematize the task of screening off? And how might screening off proceed with respect to what we have called the vertical NCCs? Our central aim in raising these questions has been to draw attention to a number of important challenges facing the NCC project – challenges that to date have not received the attention that they deserve.

References

Alkire, M. T., & Miller, J. (2005). General anesthesia and the neural correlates of consciousness. *Progress in Brain Research*, 150, 229–244. DOI: 10.1016/S0079-6123(05)50017-7

Aru, J., Bachmann, T., Singer, W., & Melloni, L. (2012). Distilling the neural correlates of consciousness. *Neuroscience & Biobehavioral Reviews*, 36(2), 737–746. DOI: 10.1016/j.neubiorev.2011.12.003

Bayne, T. (2007). Conscious states and conscious creatures: Explanation in the scientific study of consciousness. *Philosophical Perspectives*, 21(1), 1–22. DOI: 10.1111/j.1520-8583.2007.00118.x

Bayne, T. (2013). Agency as a marker of consciousness. In T. Vierkant, J. Kiverstein, & A. Clark (Eds.), *Decomposing the will* (pp. 160–180). Oxford, UK: Oxford University Press. DOI: 10.1093/acprof:oso/9780199746996.003.0009

Bayne, T., & Hohwy, J. (2014). Global disorders of consciousness. *Wiley Interdisciplinary Reviews: Cognitive Science*, 5(2), 129–138. DOI: 10.1002/wcs.1270

Bayne, T., & Hohwy, J. (2015). Modes of consciousness. In W. Sinnott-Armstrong (Ed.), *Consciousness after severe brain damage: Medical, legal, ethical, and philosophical perspectives.* New York, NY: Oxford University Press.

Bayne, T., & Spener, M. (2010). Introspective humility. *Philosophical Issues*, 20(1), 1–22. DOI: 10.1111/j.1533-6077.2010.00176.x

Block, N. (2005). Two neural correlates of consciousness. *Trends in Cognitive Sciences*, 9(2), 46–52. DOI: 10.1016/j.tics.2004.12.006

Block, N. (2007). Consciousness, accessibility, and the mesh between psychology and neuroscience. *Behavioral and Brain Sciences*, 30(5–6), 481–499.

Block, N. J., & Fodor, J. A. (1972). What psychological states are not. *Philosophical Review*, 81(2), 159–181. DOI: 10.2307/2183991

Boly, M., Sanders, R. D., Mashour, G. A., & Laureys, S. (2013). Consciousness and responsiveness: Lessons from anaesthesia and the vegetative state. *Current Opinion in Anesthesiology*, 26(4), 444–449. DOI: 10.1097/ACO.0b013e3283628b5d

Brown, E. N., Lydic, R., & Schiff, N. D. (2010). General anesthesia, sleep, and coma. *New England Journal of Medicine*, 363(27), 2638–2650. DOI: 10.1056/NEJMra0808281

Chalmers, D. J. (1996). *The conscious mind: In search of a fundamental theory*. New York, NY: Oxford University Press.

Chalmers, D. J. (2000). What is a neural correlate of consciousness? In T. Metzinger (Ed.), *Neural correlates of consciousness: Empirical and conceptual issues* (pp. 17–40). Cambridge, MA: MIT Press.

Cohen, M. A., & Dennett, D. C. (2011). Consciousness cannot be separated from function. *Trends in Cognitive Sciences*, 15(8), 358–364. DOI: 10.1016/j.tics.2011.06.008

Craver, C. F. (2007). *Explaining the brain: Mechanisms and the mosaic unity of neuroscience.* Oxford, UK: Oxford University Press. DOI: 10.1093/acprof:oso/9780199299317.001.0001

Crick, F., & Koch, C. (1995a). Are we aware of activity in primary visual cortex? *Nature*, 375(6527), 121–123. DOI: 10.1038/375121a0

Crick, F., & Koch, C. (1995b). Cortical areas in visual awareness – reply. *Nature*, 377(6547), 294–295. DOI: 10.1038/377294a0

Crick, F., & Koch, C. (2001). The zombie within. *Nature*, 411(6840), 893. DOI: 10.1038/35082161

de Graaf, T. A., Hsieh, P.-J., & Sack, A. T. (2012). The 'correlates' in neural correlates of consciousness. *Neuroscience & Biobehavioral Reviews*, 36(1), 191–197. DOI: 10.1016/j.neubiorev.2011.05.012

Dennett, D. C. (1991). *Consciousness explained*. Boston, MA: Little, Brown & Company.

Frässle, S., Sommer, J., Jansen, A., Naber, M., & Einhäuser, W. (2014). Binocular rivalry: Frontal activity relates to introspection and action but not to perception. *Journal of Neuroscience*, 34(5), 1738–1747. DOI: 10.1523/JNEUROSCI.4403-13.2014

Frith, C., Perry, R., & Lumer, E. (1999). The neural correlates of conscious experience: An experimental framework. *Trends in the Cognitive Sciences*, 3(3), 105–114. DOI: 10.1016/S1364-6613(99)01281-4

Giacino, J. T., Fins, J. J., Laureys, S., & Schiff, N. D. (2014). Disorders of consciousness after acquired brain injury: The state of the science. *Nature Reviews Neurology*, 10(2), 99–114. DOI: 10.1038/nrneurol.2013.279

Goldfine, A. M., & Schiff, N. D. (2011). Consciousness: Its neurobiology and the major classes of impairment. *Neurologic Clinics*, 29(4), 723–737. DOI: 10.1016/j.ncl.2011.08.001

Hohwy, J. (2009). The neural correlates of consciousness: New experimental approaches needed? *Consciousness and Cognition*, 18(2), 428–438. DOI: 10.1016/j.concog.2009.02.006

Hohwy, J. (2013). *The Predictive Mind*. Oxford: Oxford University Press.

Hohwy, J., & Frith, C. D. (2004). Can neuroscience explain consciousness? *Journal of Consciousness Studies*, 11(7–8), 180–198.

Hurley, S. L. (1998). *Consciousness in action*. Cambridge, MA: Harvard University Press.

Kanwisher, N. (2001). Neural events and perceptual awareness. *Cognition*, 79(1–2), 89–113. DOI: 10.1016/S0010-0277(00)00125-6

Kim, J. (1972). Phenomenal properties, psychophysical laws, and identity theory. *Monist*, 56(2), 177–192. DOI: 10.5840/monist19725623

Kouider, S., de Gardelle, V., Sackur, J., & Dupoux, E. (2010). How rich is consciousness? The partial awareness hypothesis. *Trends in Cognitive Sciences*, 14(7), 301–307. DOI: 10.1016/j.tics.2010.04.006

Kouider, S., & Dehaene, S. (2007). Levels of processing during non-conscious perception: A critical review of visual masking. *Philosophical Transactions of the Royal Society of London B: Biological Sciences*, 362(1481), 857–875. DOI: 10.1098/rstb.2007.2093

Lau, H. (2008). A higher-order Bayesian decision theory of consciousness. *Progress in Brain Research*, 168, 35–48. DOI: 10.1016/S0079-6123(07)68004-2

Laureys, S. (2005). The neural correlate of (un)awareness: Lessons from the vegetative state. *Trends in Cognitive Sciences*, 9(12), 556–559. DOI: 10.1016/j.tics.2005.10.010

Levine, J. (1983). Materialism and qualia: The explanatory gap. *Pacific Philosophical Quarterly*, 64(4), 354–361.

Levy, J., & Trevarthen, C. (1976). Metacontrol of hemispheric function in human split-brain patients. *Journal of Experimental Psychology: Human Perception and Performance*, 2(3), 299–312. DOI: 10.1037/0096-1523.2.3.299

Lewis, D. (1972). Psychophysical and theoretical identifications. *Australasian Journal of Philosophy*, 50(3), 249–258. DOI: 10.1080/00048407212341301

Lipton, P. (2004). *Inference to the best explanation* (2nd ed.). London, UK: Routledge.

Logothetis, N. K., Leopold, D. A., & Sheinberg, D. L. (2003). Neural mechanisms of perceptual organization. In N. Osaka (Ed.), *Neural basis of consciousness* (pp. 87–103). Advances in Consciousness Research (Vol. 49). Philadelphia, PA: John Benjamins Publishing Company. DOI: 10.1075/aicr.49.09log

Logothetis, N. K., & Schall, J. D. (1989). Neuronal correlates of subjective visual perception. *Science*, 245(4919), 761–763. DOI: 10.1126/science.2772635

Marcel, A. J. (1993). Slippage in the unity of consciousness. In G. R. Bock & J. Marsh (Eds.), *Experimental and theoretical studies of consciousness* (pp. 168–179). Chichester, UK: John Wiley & Sons.

Miller, S. M. (2001). Binocular rivalry and the cerebral hemispheres: With a note on the correlates and constitution of visual consciousness. *Brain and Mind*, 2(1), 119–149. DOI: 10.1023/A:1017981619014

Miller, S. M. (2007). On the correlation/constitution distinction problem (and other hard problems) in the scientific study of consciousness. *Acta Neuropsychiatrica*, 19(3), 159–176. DOI: 10.1111/j.1601-5215.2007.00207.x

Mitchell, W. (1907). *Structure and growth of the mind*. London, UK: Macmillan and Co., Ltd.

Naber, M., Frässle, S., & Einhäuser, W. (2011). Perceptual rivalry: Reflexes reveal the gradual nature of visual awareness. *PLoS One*, 6(6), e20910. DOI: 10.1371/journal.pone.0020910

Naccache, L. (2006). Is she conscious? *Science*, 313(5792), 1395–1396. DOI: 10.1126/science.1132881

Pollen, D. A. (1995). Cortical areas in visual awareness. *Nature*, 377(6547), 293–294. DOI: 10.1038/377293b0

Revonsuo, A. (2000). Prospects for a scientific research program on consciousness. In T. Metzinger (Ed.), *Neural correlates of consciousness: Empirical and conceptual questions* (pp. 57–75). Cambridge, MA: MIT Press.

Revonsuo, A. (2001). Can functional brain imaging discover consciousness in the brain? *Journal of Consciousness Studies*, 8(3), 3–23.

Revonsuo, A. (2006). *Inner presence: Consciousness as a biological phenomenon*. Cambridge, MA: MIT Press.

Schwitzgebel, E. (2008). The unreliability of naïve introspection. *Philosophical Review*, 117(2), 245–273. DOI: 10.1215/00318108-2007-037

Searle, J. R. (2000). Consciousness. *Annual Review of Neuroscience*, 23, 557–578. DOI: 10.1146/annurev.neuro.23.1.557

Shea, N., & Bayne, T. (2010). The vegetative state and the science of consciousness. *British Journal for the Philosophy of Science*, 61(3), 459–484. DOI: 10.1093/bjps/axp046

Sheinberg, D. L., & Logothetis, N. K. (1997). The role of temporal cortical areas in perceptual organization. *Proceedings of the National Academy of Sciences USA*, 94(7), 3408–3413. DOI: 10.1073/pnas.94.7.3408

Shoemaker, S. (1981). Some varieties of functionalism. *Philosophical Topics*, 12(1), 93–119. DOI: 10.5840/philtopics198112145

Smart, J. J. C. (1959). Sensations and brain processes. *Philosophical Review*, 68(2), 141–156. DOI: 10.2307/2182164

On the various neural correlates of consciousness

Are they distinguishable?*

Tom A. de Graaf and Alexander T. Sack
Maastricht University, Maastricht

What sorts of brain processes covary with consciousness? We argue that empirical neural correlates of consciousness (NCCs) include neural substrates (actual conscious experience representation in the brain), neural prerequisites and neural consequences of a conscious experience. In a conventional correlative paradigm, these three NCCs are principally indistinguishable. However a multi-pronged research program might begin to disentangle them. We here integrate our ideas with other recent considerations on the various components of the empirically defined NCC, and propose strategies to address the empirical-epistemological challenges faced by the problem of three NCCs. We conclude that while this problem is important and difficult, it is not destructive. The NCC research program still has much to contribute.

1. Introduction

Over centuries, consciousness has been an obvious truth, a non-topic, unfashionable, the holy grail of scientific endeavor, and at times flat-out denied. Today, though 'consciousness' elicits the occasional grimace in researchers who consider it too vague a concept, it seems acceptable as a research topic. The burgeoning of empirical consciousness research may be related to the advent of new brain research tools. The subfield that aims to understand how consciousness arises from biological processes largely focuses on the brain, looking for the 'neural correlates of consciousness' or 'NCCs'. In short, NCC research tries to relate changes in brain processes to changes in consciousness.

* TAG is supported by NWO, Dutch Organization for Scientific Research, grant number 451-13-024. ATS is supported by the European Research Council under the European Union's Seventh Framework Programme (FP7/2007-2013) / ERC Grant agreement no. [263472].

DOI 10.1075/aicr.92.07gra

Exactly because 'consciousness' is such a vague concept, it is crucial for the future of this research community that terms, topics, and findings are analyzed, operationalized, and schematized as clearly as possible. Therefore, many great minds have turned to this issue (Chalmers, 1996, 2000; Crick, 1994; Edelman & Tononi, 2000; Koch, 2004), contributing to the questions of 'what is consciousness', 'can we find consciousness in the brain', and 'if we empirically find an NCC, what does it mean'? To the latter question, we recently made our own modest contribution by focusing on the question 'what different types of NCC exist?' and suggesting different research paradigms that might dissociate the different NCCs (de Graaf, Hsieh, & Sack, 2012; de Graaf & Sack, 2014). The 'NCCs' that needed dissociating were empirically-defined brain processes which relate to conscious perception in correlation (often neuroimaging) studies using the contrastive method (see below). Such empirically-defined brain processes correlating to conscious experience we henceforth refer to as '*empirical NCCs*'. We will argue that empirical NCCs can reflect three fundamentally different 'roles'.

Independently, different groups (Aru, Bachmann, Singer, & Melloni, 2012; based in part on Bachmann, 2009, and Melloni & Singer, 2010; see also Kanai & Tsuchiya, 2012; Sergent & Naccache, 2012) came to similar distinctions or related ideas. Miller (2001, 2007) moreover provided an extensive analysis on how to interpret an NCC, noting that not every empirically-identified neural correlate of consciousness is necessarily constitutive of that conscious state. He thus made a distinction between the neural correlates of consciousness and the neural constitution of consciousness, which the current volume is addressing from both scientific and philosophic perspectives. Other philosophically inclined contributors have debated how NCCs should be regarded in the grand scheme of understanding consciousness (e.g., Hohwy, 2009; Neisser, 2012; Noë & Thompson, 2004).

Thus, several recent independent discussions of the same relevant question have been published. What they agree on, as we will see below, is that there is indeed a (thus far) often-neglected problem for NCC research, to the extent that such research relies on the contrastive method, which needs confronting. They are not (yet) so agreed on how and whether we can resolve it. Our view of the problem is that empirical NCCs can reflect three different functional roles in the cascade of conscious processing. We here aim to compare and synthesize our previous analysis with aforementioned contributions to provide an updated, empirically-focused analysis. With that goal in mind, we first need to clarify what we mean by 'consciousness' in the current context. We then briefly cover the basic methodology of the NCC research field to be clear on what types of findings we refer to, to set the stage for our central question: what does it mean if brain process B consistently covaries with conscious event C? We will conclude with a discussion of various strategies to confront the central problem of 'multiple functional roles for any given empirical NCC'. As we are not philosophers, our discussion is from an empirical perspective even though the problem is partly conceptual.

2. What is 'consciousness'?

One problem skeptics may have with a true science of consciousness is the very concept of 'consciousness'. Because there is nothing as unfruitful as a debate in which contributors inadvertently speak of different things, 'consciousness' needs to be clearly and unambiguously delineated and defined in any article or discussion considering it. In our view, it is useful to distinguish four notions of 'consciousness'; all valid as types, kinds, or aspects of consciousness, and all worthy of and susceptible to scientific inquiry in their own right, but substantially different from each other conceptually. We call these self-awareness, higher-order awareness, medical awareness (state-consciousness), and consciousness as experience (content-consciousness) (de Graaf, Hsieh, & Sack, 2012). This is not the venue to discuss extensively the relation of these notions to all other published taxonomies, but a brief explanation is important to make clear which 'type' of consciousness is the one on which we focus in the remainder of the chapter. In general, we use 'consciousness' and 'awareness' interchangeably.

Self-awareness, or self-consciousness, refers to all mental and cognitive processes that allow us to identify ourselves as an individual with mind and body, a subject in a world otherwise filled with other individuals and other things. It is the 'you' that you perceive as being at the center of your experiential world, the coordination and continuation of the essence of your personality, the one in control of your body and decisions (e.g., Blanke, 2012). Research about self-consciousness focuses on which brain regions host your 'sense of self' or your personality, how you have a sense of 'agency' when your body moves or performs tasks, or which animals (or humans from which age onward) recognize themselves in a mirror (e.g., see Gusnard, 2005).

Higher-order awareness refers to those mental and cognitive aspects that allow us to reflect and act non-impulsively. It includes many functions that separate us from other animals: the ability to consider things in our minds, such as past, present and future. We feel that discussions about whether consciousness requires language (because otherwise you cannot 'think' as we think) are in this general realm of 'consciousness' as a concept. It is a notion of consciousness similar to for example 'reflective consciousness' (e.g., Edelman & Tononi, 2000), defined in the Oxford English Dictionary as "the recognition by the thinking subject of its own acts or affections". It may be that much of the folk psychology conception of what 'consciousness' ought to refer to lies in this realm.

Medical awareness we have so dubbed because the corner of research that focuses on this type of awareness is often occupied by medical scientists (e.g., Gosseries et al., 2011). The question here is what (in the brain) is necessary for having any 'consciousness' as all? What determines whether we are in a conscious state, and what this state entails? Largely similar to the notion of 'state consciousness' (e.g., Hohwy, 2009), this aspect of consciousness is studied in experiments comparing deep sleep versus wakefulness (Massimini et al., 2005), comatose versus healthy subjects (Owen et al., 2006), and drugged versus sober participants (Ferrarelli et al., 2010). There is some potential overlap here between the study of medical/state consciousness and consciousness as experience/content consciousness, because the state a subject is in (e.g., sober vs. drugged) may affect the phenomenal quality of any conscious experience had. But on the whole, medical awareness – or being in a state of consciousness – is a precondition for the last aspect of consciousness we delineate here: consciousness as experience. You must be conscious (in a conscious state) in order to have any conscious experiences.

Consciousness as experience is the last and here most important type, kind, category or perspective on consciousness. It is at the same time the most difficult and the easiest notion of consciousness. In your mind right now, you experience different things over time. In the sense of 'medical awareness' or 'state-consciousness' you are constantly in a state of consciousness (if you manage to stay awake), but the contents of conscious experience change. Whatever is experienced at any one point in time, in any modality or any intensity, is what is – at that point in time – consciousness as experience. Research questions or paradigms in this category ask 'what (in the brain) defines whether you have this conscious experience or that conscious experience?' or 'what (in the brain) defines whether you do or do not have a particular conscious experience?' This notion of consciousness is the easiest in the sense that everyone continuously has a prime example in their own current experience. It is the most difficult because it entails the 'hard problem' (Chalmers, 1996).

There is some tricky confounding of elements of 'self-consciousness' and 'consciousness as experience'. You may experience, when focusing on it, a 'sense of self', and also a 'sense of control or agency' when doing something. It is important to mention that any such experiences of being 'a self' in this sense belong with 'consciousness as experience'. Also confusing is the idea of a 'pre-reflective self-consciousness' that is always present, facilitating any and all conscious experience as being 'in the eye of the beholder', making it your experience (Gallagher & Zahavi, 2010; Noë & Thompson, 2004). Again, in as far as this constitutes a mental process that is not directly experienced, it would fall in the category of analysis and study we call 'self-consciousness', but as soon as it is part of conscious experience directly it is 'consciousness as experience'.

In our previous article (de Graaf, Hsieh, & Sack, 2012) we were not entirely clear how 'consciousness as experience' relates to notions of phenomenal and access consciousness (Block, 2005). Phenomenal consciousness *is* the experience itself: it is the qualitative aspect of an experience, the 'what it is like' to have that experience, the 'quale' (plural 'qualia'). The hard problem involves the questions: 'how is it possible that such subjective, qualitative experiences arise from a bunch of neurons?' or 'why does an information processing machine like an organism have, or need, any conscious experience if all the same functions could theoretically be performed without the qualia?' or 'why is there this particular neural-phenomenal relationship and not some other?' (Chalmers, 1996). The information processing aspect here – the processes in the brain allowing a piece of information to be experienced consciously, e.g., involving global availability of that item of information to widespread systems across the brain (Dehaene & Changeux, 2011; Dehaene & Naccache, 2001; Tononi, 2004) – is called access consciousness. 'Consciousness as experience' in the current taxonomy, for most intents and purposes, can be said to cover both. In most cases, phenomenal and access consciousness will, after all, coincide. But if a particular empirical study reaches the level of dissociating phenomenal consciousness and access consciousness, 'consciousness as experience' in our framework is intended to refer primarily to phenomenal consciousness.

3. NCC research

3.1 What is an NCC?

A well-known paper in the NCC literature was published by David Chalmers (2000) in a volume about the NCC research field. It included a delineation of what exactly might be meant by an 'NCC':

> An NCC is a minimal neural system N such that there is a mapping from states of N to states of consciousness, where a given state of N is sufficient, under conditions C, for the corresponding state of consciousness. (Chalmers, 2000, p. 31)

This definition is widely accepted, although it does inspire discussion (Neisser, 2012; Noë & Thompson, 2004). This definition can be applied to research about content-consciousness, resting on the contrastive analysis (Aru et al., 2012; Baars, 1988). The "minimal" in the definition above is important in the current context. It acknowledges that several processes (e.g., regional activities, frequency-specific oscillation power modulations, particular connectivities, and so on) in the brain might correlate with a conscious experience in a given paradigm, but that not all of these processes may actually be required for the conscious experience, or even directly involved. This foreshadows the main point of the current article. We appreciate and agree with the definition of 'NCC' quoted above. It corresponds closely to one of the functional roles one might ascribe to (part of) empirical NCCs. So, to re-emphasize, when we discuss 'multiple NCCs' or 'multiple roles of NCCs' below, we are referring to empirically-defined brain processes: 'empirical NCCs' which are neural processes or systems that are found in brain research to correlate with conscious content. As such, these empirical NCCs are in a way 'candidate NCCs' with regards to Chalmers' definition. Not all empirical NCCs will turn out to be NCCs as defined by Chalmers. But these neural processes *did* correlate with consciousness, in a given empirical experiment specifically or in empirical literature more generally, and are therefore – empirically speaking – neural correlates of consciousness. We continue to use 'empirical NCCs' below to refer to these brain processes resulting from NCC research using the contrastive method.

Because brain research and consciousness research have been advancing rapidly, it is becoming more and more important to consider what these empirical NCCs can mean, and what role they can play in the establishment (or subsequent processing) of conscious states. Rather than disagreeing with Chalmers' definition, the current article focuses primarily on how we could move from NCCs as obtained in actual experiments towards NCCs as defined by Chalmers. An alternative to this approach would be to refer strictly to brain processes correlating with conscious experience, leaving empirical findings as they are and avoiding a quagmire of metaphysical issues. But this seems unsatisfactory. Eventually we will want to understand how something works, not just record a collection of correlates without interpretation. But to proceed, we first need to obtain good empirical NCCs.

3.2 How do you find an empirical NCC?

As cognitive neuroscientists, we have several tools at our disposal. These include brain imaging methods (e.g., functional magnetic resonance imaging, fMRI; electroencephalography, EEG; magnetoencephalography, MEG) and brain interference methods (e.g., transcranial magnetic stimulation, TMS; transcranial direct current stimulation, tDCS) for use in human subjects. Brain-imaging methodology revolves around the contrastive method: a subject's brain activity is tracked in an experimental condition that involves the mental function or behavior of interest, and contrasted with the activity in a control condition that mimics the experimental condition in all respects but the process of interest. Motion processing area hMT/V5 is easily identified by presenting moving dots and stationary dots and contrasting activity throughout the brain between these two conditions. But when trying to study the conscious experience of motion, a special problem arises. Moving dots and stationary dots will result in different conscious experiences to be sure, but will also result in various different unconscious processes. Conscious and unconscious brain activity will fully coincide in this experiment. That is why, in NCC research, it is necessary to do one of two things: (1) manipulate the conscious percept without affecting unconscious processes, or (2) manipulate the unconscious processes without affecting the conscious percept. This allows one to separate the neural events in the brain underlying conscious and unconscious processing. In practice, manipulating (or not) the 'unconscious processes' is often approximated by manipulating (or not) the stimuli and stimulation parameters. We have categorized and outlined the various paradigms that implement this strategy.

3.3 Paradigms for the NCC researcher

While probably not exhaustive, and likely not fully original, we have found the following outline of methods useful for maintaining an overview of NCC methodology (see also de Graaf & Sack, 2014). We here delineate three major categories: illusions, multistable perception, and ON-OFF paradigms.

(1) In illusion paradigms, researchers manipulate the conscious percept while changing only minimally, or not changing at all, the stimulation. (1.1) One subclass of illusions involves illusory features. For example, in the Kanisza triangle, three pacman-like shapes can create the illusion of contours forming a triangle. A control condition

involves the same pacman elements, but not illusory contours. A classic study used such a paradigm to find that V2 cells fire already in response to illusory contours (von der Heydt, Peterhans, & Baumgartner, 1984). (1.2) A second subclass of illusions involves hallucinations. For example, schizophrenic patients with auditory hallucinations were found to display activity in primary auditory cortex when hearing voices (conscious percept change) that were not there (no stimulation change) (Dierks et al., 1999). (1.3) Like illusory contours, there are "illusory textures" in the well-known process of filling-in (Weil & Rees, 2011), which can be tracked over time. (1.4) A fourth subclass of illusions involves afterimages. When a stimulus is adapted to and removed, stimulation ceases, but a form of conscious percept remains and fades over time (Zaidi, Ennis, Cao, & Lee, 2012).

(2) Multistable paradigms are something of a staple item in NCC research (see Miller, 2013, and further discussion later in this chapter). Basically, a constant stimulus gives rise to alternating conscious experiences over time (e.g., Blake, 2001; Fox, 1991; Howard & Rogers, 1995; Kim & Blake, 2005; Kleinschmidt, Büchel, Zeki, & Frackowiak, 1998; Levelt, 1965; Wheatstone, 1838). (2.1) In binocular rivalry, one eye is presented with one image (e.g., a face), and the other eye with a second image (e.g., a house). Conscious experience alternates between the two images despite constant visual input, and the subject indicates when a face or house is perceived by pressing two buttons. Important early work examined brain activity related to these switches (Lumer, Friston, & Rees, 1998; Lumer & Rees, 1999) and showed that activity in house- and face-specific regions (Tong, Nakayama, Vaughan, & Kanwisher, 1998) covaried with the conscious percept. (2.2) Monocular rivalry is a variant of this paradigm in which two representations presented to the same eye are 'dominant' alternatively (Breese, 1899), as is (2.3) pattern rivalry, where two images are presented to one eye each, but swapped between eyes in rapid alternation (Logothetis, Leopold, & Sheinberg, 1996). In the latter, the fact that conscious perception changes over time at its own pace (as opposed to strictly following the presentation alternation rates) shows that to some extent the 'higher-order' representations of the images can rival or influence rivalry (Tong, Meng, & Blake, 2006). (2.4) Ambiguous images yield the same conclusion: the Necker cube, Rubin's face-vase, the famous duck-rabbit, can all be perceived in two ways, but never simultaneously. Conscious perception changes while the stimulation remains constant (e.g., Kleinschmidt et al., 1998).

(3) ON-OFF paradigms, as we might call a third collection of paradigms, contrast conditions in which an image is perceived (ON) versus is not perceived (OFF). (3.1) In weak ON-OFF paradigms, this requires a small change in the stimulation parameters. For example in a classic masking study by Dehaene et al. (2001) there was a visible condition (ON) in which a word was flanked by masks but with an intermittent blank period of 71 ms (no masking), and an invisible condition (OFF) in which there was no such blank period (masking). Comparing the ON and OFF conditions revealed, interestingly, that frontoparietal areas displayed significant activity specifically in the ON condition, i.e., an empirical NCC. (3.2) As opposed to weak ON-OFF

paradigms, strong ON-OFF paradigms involve no change in stimulus parameters at all, thus potentially taking even more 'unconscious' processes out of the equation. If the experimental setup requires external control over or certainty regarding the presence or content of a conscious percept (for instance to implement block designs), weak ON-OFF paradigms are best. If, however, this is not required, stimulation parameters may be calibrated such that on some trials, the target stimulus is perceived, but on other times not. Subjects indicate on every trial whether they saw the stimulus or not, and ON and OFF conditions are assigned post-hoc (note that here, the scale need not necessarily be dichotomous, a continuous visibility rating scale is also possible). For examples, see Busch, Dubois, and VanRullen (2009) and Mathewson, Gratton, Fabiani, Beck and Ro (2009).

4. The obtained NCC: What does it mean?

Now that we have obtained our empirical NCC, we are done. Or are we? Philosophically oriented (Hohwy, 2009; Miller, 2007; Neisser, 2012; Noë & Thompson, 2004) and empirically orientated (Aru et al., 2012; Bachmann, 2009; de Graaf, Hsieh, & Sack, 2012; Kanai & Tsuchiya, 2012; Melloni & Singer, 2010; Miller, 2001, 2007; Sergent & Naccache, 2012) contributors have recently taken the next step. Neisser (2012), Hohwy (2009), and Noë and Thompson (2004) have argued that obtaining the NCC will only deliver part of the story. It is not valid to simply conclude that, whatever the NCC is, the conscious experience 'happens there' (Hohwy, 2009). The NCC program is able to provide a piece of the puzzle, but each NCC as resulting from one of the paradigms outlined above should be reinterpreted as one causal link in a complex sequence of actions (e.g., Neisser, 2012; Noë & Thompson, 2004). The background conditions that allow this NCC to make a difference to our conscious perception are not included in any given NCC result, although they significantly affect how much, and what sort of, meaning we should ascribe to the obtained NCC. Certainly, we should continue to look to these contributors for guidance on how to interpret our data and to consider the next empirical steps in sketching the causal chain of events underlying a conscious percept.

Generally, when taking a conventional NCC experiment as our starting point, we are left with a problem. What role, or function, does the empirical NCC we have obtained play? Have we now found the instantiation (or what Miller refers to as the 'constitution') of the conscious experience in the brain? Not really. In our view any empirical NCC, whichever form it takes, in whichever correlative paradigm it was found, can have, at least, one of three different functional roles.

4.1 'Correlates' and 'True correlates'

Various NCC contributors have acknowledged that NCC facts are not so simple. Miller (2007, p. 162) provides a nice overview of this realization in previous work. For example, according to Crick (1994, p. 218): 'it does not follow that these particular neurons are the real seat of awareness. They may by their firing, influence other neurons … that are the true correlates of awareness' (see also Crick & Koch, 1998; Logothetis, 1998; Revonsuo, 2000, 2001, this volume). Miller (2007) points out though, that unequivocal determination of these actual constituents ("true correlates") of consciousness may in the end be impossible. In fact, for this problem "even an impression of a strategic solution is not yet apparent" (Miller, 2007, p. 161). However, that does not imply that substantial scientific progress in this arena cannot be made (Aru et al., 2012; de Graaf, Hsieh, & Sack, 2012; Miller, 2001, 2007, this volume; Revonsuo, 2001, this volume). Although this issue is not always acknowledged, and thus deserves to be brought into the light, throughout the empirical consciousness literature one does find increasing evidence that researchers are aware that an obtained NCC is not the final word. As one example, Beck and colleagues conclude after a brief review of neuroimaging research: "In all these studies, it remains possible that the parietal activity found was a consequence of subjects' awareness and did not play either a necessary or causal role in producing that awareness" (Beck, Muggleton, Walsh, & Lavie, 2006, p. 712). And after using TMS to demonstrate functional relevance of parietal cortex for a change detection task, they state, "It is important to note that we are not arguing that the parietal cortex is the neural locus of consciousness, but rather that the functions associated with parietal cortex, such as attention and VSTM [visual short term memory], may be necessary prerequisites to visual awareness" (Beck et al., 2006, p. 716; also discussed in de Graaf & Sack, 2014). These quotes lead us to the central theme of the current chapter.

5. The three 'correlates' in neural correlates of consciousness

Any empirical NCC can reflect *neural prerequisites* for the conscious experience, may be (part of) the *neural consequences* of the conscious experience, or may be (part of) the *neural substrate* of the conscious experience itself. Again, by 'empirical NCC' we mean any neural event, neural process, chemical concentration, activity change, or whatever else can happen in the brain, that correlates consistently with a conscious experience and thus can come out of the sorts of NCC paradigms and experiments outlined above.

5.1 Neural prerequisites of consciousness

It may be that the obtained empirical NCC was necessary for this conscious experience ('C') to arise, *ceteris paribus*. It is, however, *not* itself the neural substrate of C. Given the state of all other processes in the brain, if this neural event did not occur, C would not have existed (in that form). 'Necessary' is a tricky term in consciousness talk, because it can be taken to suggest that specifically *that* neural event must take place for the conscious experience to arise. We do not claim as much. Perhaps a different neural event could also lead to C (i.e., give rise to the neural event that was the substrate), but it didn't – in this case (insert any real or imaginary correlative NCC experiment) it was the NCC we found that did the job.

Conceptually, neural prerequisites could take several forms. Content-specific prerequisites would be neural events necessary for the establishment of a particular conscious experience. For example, Crick and Koch (1995) have argued that neurons in primary visual cortex (V1) cannot be part of the (true) NCC. Yet, studies have reported a correlation between activity in V1 and conscious experience (Tong, 2003) and abolishment of V1 leads to a complete lack of visual consciousness (Weiskrantz, 1996). So, does consciousness reside in V1 or not? Silvanto (2008) tried to resolve this debate by arguing that processes in V1 might be crucial for consciousness to arise, but that consciousness itself resides elsewhere in the brain. This suggests in our framework that processes in V1 are neural prerequisites, but not substrates, of consciousness, i.e., certainly an empirical NCC, but not the locus of conscious experience. The fact that a particular conscious experience requires a particular constellation of activity in V1 (e.g., a horizontal versus a vertical bar) suggests that V1 activity is a content-specific prerequisite for consciousness. Connectivity between reticular formation and precuneus, for example, may be necessary for any conscious experience to arise (Silva et al., 2010). Such an NCC is then a content-invariant prerequisite. There is a range of possibilities in between content-specific and content-invariant prerequisites for consciousness, for example, there could be such a thing as modality-specific prerequisites.

One last thing to add about neural prerequisites of an experience is that they need not be temporal precursors of that experience, or of the neural substrate of the experience, *per se*. It is certainly logical to think of prerequisites as preceding the 'real' NCC in time, and indeed one of our strategies (de Graaf, Hsieh, & Sack, 2012, and below) focuses on this possibility. But at the moment it still seems possible that, for example, certain functionally relevant neural events in particular regions, particular frequency bands, or with particular neurotransmitters (to name just a few possible empirical NCCs that can be studied), need to *coincide* with the neural substrate of an experience – for that substrate to arise fully and thus yield the conscious experience. Keep in mind: The fact that the neural substrate in and of itself would be sufficient for the experience, makes it the substrate, while the fact that the neural substrate couldn't fully arise without the simultaneous neural prerequisite, makes the latter a prerequisite. In this scenario, which is hypothetical but not necessarily unrealistic, separating the neural prerequisites from the substrates should be rather difficult.

5.2 Neural consequences of consciousness

By neural consequences, we mean that an empirical NCC was a result of the conscious experience. Because the conscious experience was there, this activation arose. It is not itself part of the experience, it is not necessary for the experience, yet it always coincides with the experience. There can be two forms of this scenario (de Graaf & Sack, 2014).

Imagine a binocular rivalry study with two images: a rose and a house. Whenever we consciously experience the visual image of a rose, we are reminded of our deceased grandmother, who grew roses in her garden. We develop a range of (non-visual) emotions and associations, all covarying with the (visual) conscious rose-experience; some conscious and others not. None of these are relevant to the conscious experience of interest. Yet, their neural underpinnings will be an empirical NCC, because they always follow the experience of a rose. This exemplifies the content-specific (or stimulus-specific) form of neural consequences. In this example, the grandmother-association is also participant-specific. Looking at different participants would eliminate for the most part this NCC. But one can imagine content-specific yet participant-invariant neural consequences quite easily. All it requires is for most participants to have a similar association or value-response to the content in question. Such consequences could be countered using different kinds of stimuli.

That will not resolve content-invariant consequences, however. A conscious experience, of any kind, may consistently trigger specific neural events. Think of response preparation, effects on arousal/vigilance, attention capture, or just a general "oh, I just had an experience" effect. Aru et al. (2012) point out that consequences, rather than being useless and epiphenomenal, are a logical consequence of conscious experience, if one assigns any functionality to consciousness. Citing Seth (2009), they note that many theories of consciousness do in fact confer concrete functions to conscious experience, including novel, intentional behavior and enabling long-term memory. So, while troublesome in the context of the NCC program, these neural consequences may actually be highly relevant to the organism.

5.3 Neural substrates

There is a third functional role for any given empirical NCC, and it is the one we are actually most interested in: the NCC may be the neural instantiation, neural constitution (Miller, 2001, 2007), or neural substrate (de Graaf, Hsieh, & Sack, 2012; de Graaf & Sack, 2014), of the experience. The NCC is directly underlying the experience, not a result or a precondition, and is the minimal neural activity that is sufficient for a specific conscious percept, *ceteris paribus* (Chalmers, 2000; Koch, 2004). Considering the definition of Chalmers, this is to an extent the 'real' NCC, or one of the aforementioned 'true' correlates. In identity theory terms: this brain activation *is* the conscious experience, or is at least part of the brain activation that *is* the conscious experience (note that the conceptual distinctions made apply in varying degrees whether identity theory, epiphenomenalism, or even dualism is adopted as the metaphysical starting point). Some NCC studies find certain neural events to correlate with conscious experience, and leave it at that. This is unfortunate, because a deeper reflection on what a given NCC finding can mean, and the role it can play in the greater mechanisms underlying consciousness of emergent or downward causation (Feinberg, 2012; Hohwy, 2009; Neisser, 2012) might improve our understanding of the literature and better inform follow-up work.

5.4 The case of binocular rivalry

Throughout this volume and particularly its companion (Miller, 2013), binocular rivalry has been the basis of discussions of consciousness and NCC research. It is an excellent example for our framework also, considering the wide range of NCCs that have resulted from studies on binocular rivalry. Visual consciousness during binocular rivalry has been correlated with activity at some of the earliest stages of visual processing, from the lateral geniculate nucleus (LGN) (Haynes, Deichmann, & Rees, 2005; Wunderlich, Schneider, & Kastner, 2005) and V1 (Haynes & Rees, 2005; Lee, Blake, & Heeger, 2005; Polonsky, Blake, Braun, & Heeger, 2000; Tong & Engel, 2001), all the way up the hierarchy through extrastriate regions (Lumer et al., 1998; Moutoussis, Keliris, Kourtzi, & Logothetis, 2005; Tong et al., 1998), parietal cortex (Lumer et al., 1998), and finally, even frontal regions (Lumer et al., 1998; Panagiotaropoulos, Deco, Kapoor, & Logothetis, 2012). All of these regions are thus empirical neural correlates of visual consciousness during rivalry, but it seems unlikely to us and others (e.g., Crick & Koch, 1998; Logothetis, 1998; Miller, 2001, 2007, this volume; Revonsuo, 2000, 2001, this volume) that they all play the same role with respect to consciousness. Because of this widespread distribution, it is entirely possible to envision many different scenarios within the constraints of our prerequisites-substrates-consequences framework (see Figure 2 in Miller, this volume). As we discuss in this chapter, V1 has been discounted by some as a candidate region for the actual substrates of consciousness. Thus, perhaps NCCs early in the hierarchy, such as LGN and V1, are prerequisites for conscious experience, while parietal and extrastriate regions are substrates of the experience, and activity in frontal regions reflects various consequences. However, without further evidence, the division of roles could just as easily be completely different. How to proceed in obtaining such extra evidence is what we discuss below.

5.5 Related opinions

Aside from the aforementioned view of Neisser (2012), Hohwy (2009) has pointed out a methodological and interpretational issue with the contrastive (content-consciousness) method: obtained NCCs might not reflect the phenomenality of our conscious experience, but rather the selection of one conscious experience over another (see also Miller, 2001, 2007, on the problem of distinguishing attentional selection and visual consciousness during rivalry, and see further discussion below). Indeed, for any given empirical NCC, this seems possible. Hidden in the totality of observable brain processes during (and immediately preceding) a conscious experience, there must be both the phenomenality (corresponding to our 'substrate') and the selection (a 'prerequisite'). And indeed, it is inherent in our schema that whenever a conscious experience X occurs, the preconditions P and consequences Q, always co-occur.

Miller (2001, 2007) is not very optimistic about this problem. As mentioned above, he makes a distinction between the neural correlates and the neural constitution (or constituents) of consciousness. It is unclear in any given NCC paradigm, whether the results (the correlates) are constituents or not. The constituents are the neural processes/events/etcetera that really are the conscious experience. They seemingly overlap perfectly with what we call substrates. Miller goes to some length explaining why we may never be able to fully parse these constituents from the correlates. It may be, he argues, a fundamental problem, a hard problem, with as yet no foreseeable solution (though see Miller, this volume, for a proposed partial solution). However, as mentioned above, Miller (2001, 2007, this volume) does agree with us (de Graaf, Hsieh, & Sack, 2012) and others (Aru et al., 2012) that significant progress can nonetheless be made using appropriate strategies.

6. Strategies to disentangle the entanglement

We would like to know, of all the NCCs that we are seeing in a particular experiment, which is which: for each activated brain area, modulated frequency spectrum and ERP peak, are we looking at a substrate, prerequisite or consequence? Can we make these distinctions? We previously proposed five strategies for disentangling this entanglement (de Graaf, Hsieh, & Sack, 2012).

6.1 Cross-literature integration

Content-invariant (or modality-specific) neural prerequisites or consequences of consciousness might be retrievable from the literature. We and others before us (e.g., Dehaene & Naccache, 2001; Rees, 2007) have noted, for example, that frontoparietal activations seem to pop up in a wide range of consciousness paradigms, such as multistable paradigms (Lumer et al., 1998; Lumer & Rees, 1999; Schoth, Waberski, Krings, Gobbele, & Buchner, 2007; Sterzer, Kleinschmidt, & Rees, 2009) and ON-OFF paradigms (Dehaene et al., 1998, 2001) (for recent reviews see e.g., Dehaene & Changeux, 2011; Rees, 2007). This suggests that frontoparietal activity is not content-specific, and therefore not (by itself) a neural substrate of any specific conscious experience, but perhaps a prerequisite or consequence. Concretely, frontal and/or parietal cortex activation might reflect the attentional selection of 'consciousness-candidate'-items and thus be a prerequisite, or might activate because the consciously perceived item captures attention or primes a response and thus be a consequence. To search further in the NCC literature for activations or processes that reiterate across NCC studies, stimuli, and paradigms, newly emerging brain activation databases might be used. For instance, BrainMap holds a large number of published positron emission tomography and fMRI studies, enabling meta-analyses and cross-study overviews (Fox & Lancaster, 2002). Related to this, for each candidate NCC, we must take into account basic anatomical knowledge converging with previous research. Because frontoparietal areas seem to play some important role in the establishment of consciousness, it stands to reason that NCCs serving as substrate would be connected to these (see Panagiotaropoulos et al., 2012). V1 is not connected in this way, which could be a reason to doubt V1 as a neural substrate, making it more likely as a prerequisite (Crick & Koch, 1995).

6.2 Brain interference methods

If we have determined that an empirical NCC is unlikely to be a substrate of consciousness, and we hypothesize that it might be a prerequisite or consequence, we need to move forward. How can we distinguish between neural prerequisites and consequences? Again using frontoparietal cortices as an example, one could hypothesize that frontal or parietal regions drive the selection of one or other item for consciousness (e.g., by initiating a re-evaluation of the input; Sterzer et al., 2009; see also Carmel, Walsh, Lavie, & Rees, 2010; Kanai, Bahrami, & Rees, 2010; Zaretskaya, Thielscher, Logothetis, & Bartels, 2010). On the other hand, perhaps frontal and/or parietal cortices are activated as a consequence of a salient new conscious experience (e.g., de Graaf, de Jong, Goebel, van Ee, & Sack, 2011). When the empirical NCC is a regional activation (as opposed to for example a chemical concentration level or interregional coherence), there is now a clear experimental manipulation that can distinguish between regions that are functionally relevant (necessary) for a task or percept, and regions that are not. This is brain interference.

TMS or tDCS allow us to change brain activity in relatively constrained brain regions in healthy, awake, conscious human beings. Thus, the level of activity (or more precisely, cortical excitability) in a region becomes an independent variable (Sack et al., 2002). If frontal cortex activation of a certain level is a neural prerequisite for consciousness, TMS over frontal regions should interfere with conscious perception. TMS over early visual regions has repeatedly been shown to have the ability in principle to affect conscious (and unconscious) perception (Amassian et al., 1989, 1993; Boyer, Harrison, & Ro, 2005; de Graaf, Cornelsen, Jacobs, & Sack, 2011; de Graaf, Goebel, & Sack, 2012; de Graaf, Herring, & Sack, 2011; Jacobs, Goebel, & Sack, 2011; Koivisto, Mäntylä, & Silvanto, 2010; Koivisto, Railo, & Salminen-Vaparanta, 2011; Ro, Shelton, Lee, & Chang, 2004; Silvanto, Lavie, & Walsh, 2005), and it has recently been applied to frontal and parietal regions (Carmel et al., 2010; de Graaf, de Jong, et al., 2011; Kanai et al., 2010; Miller et al., 2000; Zaretskaya et al., 2010) to start evaluating the frontoparietal role in multistable perception and other paradigms (e.g., Amassian et al., 2008). For a recent review on what we have learned from brain stimulation about conscious vision in the brain, in the context of the prerequisites, substrates, consequences scheme, see de Graaf and Sack (2014).

It is clear that there are many possible instantiations of how the brain establishes conscious vision. As Hohwy (2009) and Neisser (2012) recently pointed out, there is likely a complex cascade of causal relations underlying any conscious experience, and the contrastive analysis only yields one piece of the puzzle (and not necessarily always the one we think). For instance, maybe an extrastriate (e.g., face) area needs to connect with a frontal region in order to make a percept globally available and thus conscious. The connectivity itself might be the neural substrate of consciousness, rather than the level of activity in some region or other (e.g., Massimini et al., 2005; Tononi, 2004, 2005). This is certainly possible, and would complicate things. Yet, affecting the excitability of one region might also affect other anatomically or functionally connected areas (Bestmann, Baudewig, Siebner, Rothwell, & Frahm, 2003, 2004; Ruff et al., 2006, 2008; Sack et al., 2007), allowing it to potentially affect networks. Moreover, brain interference methods are becoming increasingly sophisticated, going beyond 'virtual lesions' (Pascual-Leone, Walsh, & Rothwell, 2000), for example, to induce frequency-specific oscillations in brain regions (Romei, Gross, & Thut, 2010; Thut, Schyns, & Gross, 2011; Thut et al., 2011). This is very exciting in our view as TMS might be used to evaluate the causal contribution of empirical NCCs found in EEG/MEG research. Increasing evidence suggests that transcranial alternating current stimulation (tACS), a method related to tDCS in which current direction between electrodes is reversed at a particular frequency, might serve a similar purpose (Helfrich et al., 2014).

Aru et al. (2012) point out that lesion studies can also be meaningful in this context. They draw on an interesting example involving neurons in the medial temporal lobe (MTL). These neurons fire in close correspondence to a subjective percept, and are thus an empirical NCC (Quiroga, Mukamel, Isham, Malach, & Fried, 2008). Yet, lesions to this brain area do not eliminate conscious perception, suggesting that this NCC may be not substrate and not prerequisite. The MTL NCC could instead be a neural consequence (discussed further below).

6.3 Temporal information

At the risk of pointing out the obvious, any empirical NCC that occurs prior to a conscious experience cannot be a substrate or consequence. In this sense, a division of NCCs in the temporal domain, related to the onset or period of a conscious experience, is as useful as it is obvious. For instance, pre-stimulus alpha power determines whether a liminal stimulus will be perceived (van Dijk, Schoffelen, Oostenveld, & Jensen, 2008), and even the phase of alpha waves has a strong influence (Busch et al., 2009; Mathewson et al., 2009). These NCCs must be neural prerequisites of conscious experience. For brain processes occurring after stimulus presentation (e.g., 200 ms ERP negativity increase: Koivisto et al., 2008; Koivisto & Revonsuo, 2009), the question is more difficult. Such processes are not automatically neural consequences of conscious experience, because it is not straightforward at which point in time our phenomenal awareness of a stimulus 'happens' (Breitmeyer & Öğmen, 2006; Koch, 2004; Wilenius & Revonsuo, 2007).

Melloni and colleagues (Melloni, Schwiedrzik, Müller, Rodriguez, & Singer, 2011) recently showed how some neural prerequisites of consciousness – short-latency ERP components occurring early after stimulus presentation and previously thought to be NCC proper (Pins & ffytche, 2003) – could be detected using experimental manipulations (Aru et al., 2012). They compared visibility signatures in conditions with varied levels of expectations. Some components of the visibility ERP signature were invariant to the expectations manipulation (and thus remain NCC-substrate candidates), while others were specific to expectation (thus unlikely to be NCC-substrates). Such examples perhaps cannot unequivocally determine NCC-substrates (see below), but they certainly serve to refine our understanding and constrain our search for the NCCs.

Other methods are increasingly applied that operate in the temporal domain even if temporal resolution is notoriously low. In fMRI, there are blood oxygen level dependent (BOLD) chronometry (Formisano & Goebel, 2003) and connectivity methods (e.g., dynamic causal modeling: Friston, Harrison, & Penny, 2003; Granger causality mapping: Goebel, Roebroeck, Kim, & Formisano, 2003; Roebroeck, Formisano, & Goebel, 2005). While perhaps not perfectly separable in time, neural consequences of consciousness should generally occur after neural substrates of consciousness. If a given network of brain regions in fMRI is an NCC, connectivity methods or BOLD chronometry might determine how information flows within this network, i.e., regions receiving information in later stages of this interactive framework are increasingly likely to be neural consequences.

6.4 Unconscious perception paradigms

By thus tracking down neural prerequisites and neural consequences of consciousness, we can engage in a process of elimination. A network of regions found to correlate with consciousness can be evaluated node by node, using brain interference methods or other methods described in de Graaf, Hsieh and Sack (2012) and Aru et al. (2012). Part of the strategy proposed thus far has been checking which empirical NCCs are content-specific. Neural substrates are likely to be content-specific, but can we say that a content-specific neural event is automatically a substrate? Unfortunately not, as evidenced by the possibility of content-specific prerequisites and consequences discussed above. Nevertheless, we might make advances in this respect by looking for "neural correlates of unconsciousness". Motion area hMT/V5 for example is a content-specific part of an NCC of any conscious motion perception. Some might suggest that the conscious perception of motion thus resides in this motion area (Zeki, 2003, 2007). A key approach then, is to check to what extent such a region is active when motion is presented but not perceived consciously. Thus, unconscious perception paradigms can be used.

Recent studies using various stimuli and paradigms have shown that several modular brain regions in the visual hierarchy can display activity without conscious perception (Dehaene et al., 2001; Fang & He, 2005; Haynes, Driver, & Rees, 2005; Jacobs & Sack, 2012; Luck, Vogel, & Shapiro, 1996; Marois, Yi, & Chun, 2004; Morris, Öhman, & Dolan, 1999; Moutoussis & Zeki, 2002, 2006; Naccache et al., 2005; Pasley, Mayes, & Schultz, 2004; Rees et al., 2000, 2002; Vuilleumier & Driver, 2007). For example, studies showing that the face processing area FFA is active when faces are presented but not perceived (e.g., Moutoussis & Zeki, 2002) suggest that some activity in the face area is not sufficient for a conscious face percept. Regions related to semantic processing may be active when words are presented (Dehaene et al., 2001) but this does not mean that these words make it to consciousness. One might object that the activity level is lower in these studies. But Goebel et al. (2001) showed in a blindsight patient that activity in motion area hMT/V5 could be at a similar level when a motion stimulus was consciously perceived (when presented in the intact hemifield), versus when it was not at all perceived (when presented in the scotoma). Thus, even a 'normal' amount of activity in such a modular region seems insufficient to generate a conscious percept of motion.

Unfortunately, this strategy works only in one direction. That is, null results *(not* replicating an NCC candidate during 'unconscious perception') seem difficult to interpret (see de Graaf & Sack, 2011, concerning null result interpretability). However, lessons from unconscious perception paradigms can surely eliminate content-specific candidates, and in our view have already done so for, for instance, BOLD responses in modular visual regions such as hMT/V5 (see above). The next step seems to be to take into account combinations of different NCCs: is it for example sufficient to have simultaneous hMT/V5 and frontal activity? Or need there be connectivity between the two? Such questions might now be addressed in unconscious perception paradigms.

6.5 Experimental manipulations to partition NCCs

Above, we saw how Melloni et al. (2011) independently manipulated stimulus visibility and stimulus expectation to tease apart NCC prerequisites from substrates and consequences. This relates to a general question whether attention might be confounding the search for NCCs (see van Boxtel & Tsuchiya, this volume). Among others, Koch and Tsuchiya (2007, 2012) believe that attention and consciousness are fundamentally different things. Yet, in NCC research, regions known to be involved in attention (i.e., frontoparietal regions: Corbetta, 1998; Coull, Frith, Frackowiak, & Grasby, 1996; Naghavi & Nyberg, 2005; Nobre, Coull, Frith, & Mesulam, 1999; Pessoa, Kastner, & Ungerleider, 2003) often pop up as correlating with consciousness, for example, in multistable perception paradigms (Inui et al., 2000; Kleinschmidt et al., 1998; Lumer et al., 1998; Schoth et al., 2007; Sterzer, Russ, Preibisch, & Kleinschmidt, 2002). Thus, a debate continues over whether consciousness is nothing more than attention or attentional selection (e.g., Beck & Eccles, 1992; Koch & Tsuchiya, 2007; Mack & Rock, 1998; Merikle & Joordens, 1997; O'Regan & Noë, 2001; Posner, 1994; Velmans, 1996; see also Miller, 2001, 2007). Clearly, attention plays a role in the establishment of consciousness. Classic phenomena, such as the attentional blink (Luck et al., 1996) and inattentional blindness (Mack & Rock, 1998) show that a lapse or (mis)allocation of attention can prevent a particular stimulus from reaching consciousness. But that does not mean attention and consciousness are the same thing. Attention could be an unavoidable prerequisite or consequence of conscious experience, or not even, if it just nearly always comingles with consciousness but is not *per se* an inevitable co-correlate. Attention can be manipulated independently from conscious experience. Orthogonal manipulations of conscious content and attention allocation may therefore possibly tease apart the neural events underlying either/both. In fact, new light was shed on the role of V1 in consciousness, when a recent study employed a 2 × 2 design to orthogonally manipulate stimulus visibility and attention (as already predicted by Koch & Tsuchiya, 2007, 2012): V1 was responsive to attentional changes, but not at all to conscious perception changes (Watanabe et al., 2011).

A second confounder that might affect a wide range of NCC studies is task performance (see van Boxtel & Tsuchiya, this volume). Behavioral performance required by NCC paradigms (some behavioral marker of the conscious experience is necessary in almost all NCC studies) is one form of neural consequence of conscious experience. After all, as Lau (2008) points out, when consciousness differs, performance often differs as well. Ingeniously, Lau and Passingham (2006) used a metacontrast masking paradigm that contained conditions with equal task performance but unequal conscious perception. This was possible because the metacontrast function is a u-curve, and the u-curves for conscious (subjective) perception of stimuli and for correct visual discrimination performance were not in perfect overlap in their study. Having thus controlled for behavioral task performance, Lau and Passingham (2006) noted that only dorsolateral prefrontal cortex showed activity covarying with the conscious percept. Thus, while generally masking paradigms elicited a frontoparietal network, this finding suggests that some of the parietal activations might not have been NCC substrates.

It is promising then, that experimental manipulations, going a little further than classical contrastive methods are able to 'zoom in' on the NCC- substrates, eliminating neural prerequisites and consequences from the candidates obtained previously.

6.6 Can we thus find the NCC substrates?

Miller (2007) claims that the neural constituents, as opposed to correlates, of consciousness may not be found unequivocally by neuroscience – not only now, but by any imaginable methods. He addresses several of the strategies that we have proposed, even enhances their detection power and spatiotemporal resolution for the sake of argument, and then argues why they would still not solve the problem. For example, he imagines a super-version of TMS (and more recently, optogenetics; Miller, this volume), in which particular neurons or neuronal circuits can be stimulated, perhaps even disrupted perfectly. Imagine that such a method would fully be able to shut down at will some NCC candidate. Imagine then that the conscious percept would be absent. Could we conclude that the NCC is the substrate? No, perhaps it is a prerequisite. Imagine then that the conscious percept would be unaffected. Could we conclude that the NCC is a neural consequence? No. To see why, we must go back to the MTL example discussed above. Damage to MTL did not affect conscious perception, so we were inclined to conclude that this particular NCC was a consequence (Aru et al., 2012). But the brain is known to be redundant, able to compensate for disrupted processing in some regions by moving task processing to other regions (e.g., Sack, Camprodon, Pascual-Leone, & Goebel, 2005). Thus, it is possible that in healthy subjects, the MTL neurons *are* a prerequisite, or even a substrate, but that the brain establishes conscious perception in a different way, in different neurons, if the MTL is out of commission. There are two ways to address this: (1) If the MTL, based on previous knowledge, is plausibly involved in another processing task, such as entering items into memory systems when or after they are consciously perceived, this serves as converging evidence for a NCC-consequence. While Miller (2007) may be right that we can never definitively know, we can make an educated guess, which for many empirical researchers might be good enough. (2) The compensation hypothesis can be tested, using reversible virtual lesions (brain interference methods) concurrently with brain imaging. This can further strengthen the case, if no compensating brain events are found when MTL is disrupted, although again the answer would not be definitive (Miller, 2007, this volume).

In short, there is no conceptual way to argue against these arguments, and even against strategies we outlined above that were not directly addressed by Miller (2007), such objections could likely be made. So, we can never be sure. However, even conceding the issue fully, we believe it may become practically irrelevant. This does not mean it should not be considered, accepted, and taken seriously. But at the same time, it should not stop us from following exactly the strategies we have proposed. We may never be entirely sure that the NCC substrate candidate we are left with, after eliminating various candidates that turned out to be (more plausibly) prerequisites or consequences, is actually constitutive. But we will understand a lot better the sequence of neural events underlying consciousness. Converging evidence from multiple strategies will paint a picture that will suggest a cascade of brain events, perhaps in frameworks such as proposed by Neisser (2012), in which some brain events are prerequisites, some substrates, and some consequences. It will be a more refined theoretical model than we have now. We therefore hope that Miller (2007) hit the nail on the head when he said "[F]uture scientific work may shed enough light on the problem that any remaining uncertainties… will appear trivial rather than substantial (p. 165)". Whether the NCC program will turn out like this or not, we will not know until we try.

7. Conclusion

At the very least, a conceptual understanding that empirical NCCs can reflect three 'roles' in the cascade of brain events surrounding a conscious percept is useful. Using new methods and analysis tools, armed with this new understanding we should be able to move forward in a science of consciousness to start disentangling (de Graaf, Hsieh,

& Sack, 2012) or distilling (Aru et al., 2012) the various NCCs into prerequisites, consequences and candidate substrates (constituents). As we progress, reframing the findings in different kinds of causal schemes (Neisser, 2012) may partly address the inherent shortcomings of the contrastive analysis (Hohwy, 2009). While very different, all the contributions made to this topic seem to agree on this much: NCC research is valuable, interesting, and ready to take some steps forward. Even if we may never with certainty distinguish the three NCCs, there is quite some ground to be covered before we reach our epistemological limits.

References

Amassian, V., Mari, Z., Sagliocco, L., Hassan, N., Maccabee, P., Cracco J.B., Cracco, R.Q., & Bodis-Wollner, I. (2008). Perception of phosphenes and flashed alphabetical characters is enhanced by single-pulse transcranial magnetic stimulation of anterior frontal lobe: The thalamic gate hypothesis. *Perception*, 37(3), 375–388. DOI: 10.1068/p5948

Amassian, V.E., Cracco, R.Q., Maccabee, P.J., Cracco, J.B., Rudell, A., & Eberle, L. (1989). Suppression of visual perception by magnetic coil stimulation of human occipital cortex. *Electroencephalography and Clinical Neurophysiology*, 74(6), 458–462. DOI: 10.1016/0168-5597(89)90036-1

Amassian, V.E., Cracco, R.Q., Maccabee, P.J., Cracco, J.B., Rudell, A.P., & Eberle, L. (1993). Unmasking human visual perception with the magnetic coil and its relationship to hemispheric asymmetry. *Brain Research*, 605(2), 312–316. DOI: 10.1016/0006-8993(93)91757-J

Aru, J., Bachmann, T., Singer, W., & Melloni, L. (2012). Distilling the neural correlates of consciousness. *Neuroscience & Biobehavioral Reviews*, 36(2), 737–746. DOI: 10.1016/j.neubiorev.2011.12.003

Baars, B.J. (1988). *A cognitive theory of consciousness*. New York, NY: Cambridge University Press.

Bachmann, T. (2009). Finding ERP-signatures of target awareness: Puzzle persists because of experimental co-variation of the objective and subjective variables. *Consciousness and Cognition*, 18(3), 804–808. DOI: 10.1016/j.concog.2009.02.011

Beck, D.M., Muggleton, N., Walsh, V., & Lavie, N. (2006). Right parietal cortex plays a critical role in change blindness. *Cerebral Cortex*, 16(5), 712–717. DOI: 10.1093/cercor/bhj017

Beck, F., & Eccles, J.C. (1992). Quantum aspects of brain activity and the role of consciousness. *Proceedings of the National Academy of Sciences USA*, 89(23), 11357–11361. DOI: 10.1073/pnas.89.23.11357

Bestmann, S., Baudewig, J., Siebner, H.R., Rothwell, J.C., & Frahm, J. (2003). Subthreshold high-frequency TMS of human primary motor cortex modulates interconnected frontal motor areas as detected by interleaved fMRI-TMS. *Neuroimage*, 20(3), 1685–1696. DOI: 10.1016/j.neuroimage.2003.07.028

Bestmann, S., Baudewig, J., Siebner, H.R., Rothwell, J.C., & Frahm, J. (2004). Functional MRI of the immediate impact of transcranial magnetic stimulation on cortical and subcortical motor circuits. *European Journal of Neuroscience*, 19(7), 1950–1962. DOI: 10.1111/j.1460-9568.2004.03277.x

Blake, R. (2001). A primer on binocular rivalry, including current controversies. *Brain and Mind*, 2(1), 5–38. DOI: 10.1023/A:1017925416289

Blanke, O. (2012). Multisensory brain mechanisms of bodily self-consciousness. *Nature Reviews Neuroscience*, 13(8), 556–571.

Block, N. (2005). Two neural correlates of consciousness. *Trends in Cognitive Sciences*, 9(2), 46–52. DOI: 10.1016/j.tics.2004.12.006

Boyer, J. L., Harrison, S., & Ro, T. (2005). Unconscious processing of orientation and color without primary visual cortex. *Proceedings of the National Academy of Sciences USA*, 102(46), 16875–16879. DOI: 10.1073/pnas.0505332102

Breese, B. B. (1899). On inhibition. *Psychological Monographs*, 3(1), 1–65. DOI: 10.1037/h0092990

Breitmeyer, B., & Öğmen, H. (2006). *Visual masking: Time slices through conscious and unconscious vision*. New York, NY: Oxford University Press.

Busch, N. A., Dubois, J., & VanRullen, R. (2009). The phase of ongoing EEG oscillations predicts visual perception. *Journal of Neuroscience*, 29(24), 7869–7876. DOI: 10.1523/JNEUROSCI.0113-09.2009

Carmel, D., Walsh, V., Lavie, N., & Rees, G. (2010). Right parietal TMS shortens dominance durations in binocular rivalry. *Current Biology*, 20(18), R799–R800. DOI: 10.1016/j.cub.2010.07.036

Chalmers, D. J. (1996). *The conscious mind: In search of a fundamental theory*. New York, NY: Oxford University Press.

Chalmers, D. J. (2000). What is a neural correlate of consciousness? In T. Metzinger (Ed.), *Neural correlates of consciousness: Empirical and conceptual questions* (pp. 17–39). Cambridge, MA: MIT Press.

Corbetta, M. (1998). Frontoparietal cortical networks for directing attention and the eye to visual locations: Identical, independent, or overlapping neural systems? *Proceedings of the National Academy of Sciences USA*, 95(3), 831–838. DOI: 10.1073/pnas.95.3.831

Coull, J. T., Frith, C. D., Frackowiak, R. S. J., & Grasby, P. M. (1996). A fronto-parietal network for rapid visual information processing: A pet study of sustained attention and working memory. *Neuropsychologia*, 34(11), 1085–1095. DOI: 10.1016/0028-3932(96)00029-2

Crick, F. (1994). *The astonishing hypothesis: The scientific search for the soul*. New York, NY: Touchstone.

Crick, F., & Koch, C. (1995). Are we aware of neural activity in primary visual cortex? *Nature*, 375(6527), 121–123. DOI: 10.1038/375121a0

Crick, F., & Koch, C. (1998). Consciousness and neuroscience. *Cerebral Cortex*, 8(2), 97–107. DOI: 10.1093/cercor/8.2.97

de Graaf, T. A., Cornelsen, S., Jacobs, C., & Sack, A. T. (2011). TMS effects on subjective and objective measures of vision: Stimulation intensity and pre- versus post-stimulus masking. *Consciousness and Cognition*, 20(4), 1244–1255. DOI: 10.1016/j.concog.2011.04.012

de Graaf, T. A., de Jong, M. C., Goebel, R., van Ee, R., & Sack, A. T. (2011). On the functional relevance of frontal cortex for passive and voluntarily controlled bistable vision. *Cerebral Cortex*, 21(10), 2322–2331. DOI: 10.1093/cercor/bhr015

de Graaf, T. A., Goebel, R., & Sack, A. T. (2012). Feedforward and quick recurrent processes in early visual cortex revealed by TMS? *Neuroimage*, 61(3), 651–659. DOI: 10.1016/j.neuroimage.2011.10.020

de Graaf, T. A., Herring, J., & Sack, A. T. (2011). A chronometric exploration of high-resolution 'sensitive TMS masking' effects on subjective and objective measures of vision. *Experimental Brain Research*, 209(1), 19–27. DOI: 10.1007/s00221-010-2512-z de Graaf, T.A., Hsieh, P.-J., & Sack, A.T. (2012). The 'correlates' in neural correlates of consciousness. *Neuroscience & Biobehavioral Reviews*, 36(1), 191–197. DOI: 10.1016/j.neubiorev.2011.05.012

de Graaf, T.A., & Sack, A.T. (2011). Null results in TMS: From absence of evidence to evidence of absence. *Neuroscience & Biobehavioral Reviews*, 35(3), 871–877. DOI: 10.1016/j.neubiorev.2010.10.006

de Graaf, T.A., & Sack, A.T. (2014). Using brain stimulation to disentangle neural correlates of conscious vision. *Frontiers in Psychology*, 5, 1019. DOI: 10.3389/fpsyg.2014.01019

Dehaene, S., & Changeux, J.-P. (2011). Experimental and theoretical approaches to conscious processing. *Neuron*, 70(2), 200–227. DOI: 10.1016/j.neuron.2011.03.018

Dehaene, S., & Naccache, L. (2001). Towards a cognitive neuroscience of consciousness: Basic evidence and a workspace framework. *Cognition*, 79(1–2), 1–37. DOI: 10.1016/S0010-0277(00)00123-2

Dehaene, S., Naccache, L., Cohen, L., Bihan, D.L., Mangin, J.-F., Poline, J.-B., & Rivière, D. (2001). Cerebral mechanisms of word masking and unconscious repetition priming. *Nature Neuroscience*, 4(7), 752–758. DOI: 10.1038/89551

Dehaene, S., Naccache, L., Le Clec'H, G., Koechlin, E., Mueller, M., Dehaene-Lambertz, G., van de Moortele, P.F., & Le Bihan, D. (1998). Imaging unconscious semantic priming. *Nature*, 395(6702), 597–600. DOI: 10.1038/26967

Dierks, T., Linden, D.E.J., Jandl, M., Formisano, E., Goebel, R., Lanfermann, H., & Singer, W. (1999). Activation of Heschl's gyrus during auditory hallucinations. *Neuron*, 22(3), 615–621. DOI: 10.1016/S0896-6273(00)80715-1

Edelman, G.M., & Tononi, G. (2000). *Universe of consciousness: How matter becomes imagination*. New York, NY: Basic Books.

Fang, F., & He, S. (2005). Cortical responses to invisible objects in the human dorsal and ventral pathways. *Nature Neuroscience*, 8(10), 1380–1385. DOI: 10.1038/nn1537

Feinberg, T.E. (2012). Neuroontology, neurobiological naturalism, and consciousness: A challenge to scientific reduction and a solution. *Physics of Life Reviews*, 9(1), 13–34. DOI: 10.1016/j.plrev.2011.10.019

Ferrarelli, F., Massimini, M., Sarasso, S., Casali, A., Riedner, B.A., Angelini, G., Tononi, G., & Pearce, R.A. (2010). Breakdown in cortical effective connectivity during midazolam-induced loss of consciousness. *Proceedings of the National Academy of Sciences USA*, 107(6), 2681–2686. DOI: 10.1073/pnas.0913008107

Formisano, E., & Goebel, R. (2003). Tracking cognitive processes with functional MRI mental chronometry. *Current Opinion in Neurobiology*, 13(2), 174–181. DOI: 10.1016/S0959-4388(03)00044-8

Fox, P.T., & Lancaster, J.L. (2002). Mapping context and content: The brainmap model. *Nature Reviews Neuroscience*, 3(4), 319–321. DOI: 10.1038/nrn789

Fox, R. (1991). Binocular rivalry. In D.M. Regan (Ed.), *Binocular vision and psychophysics* (pp. 93–110). London, UK: MacMillan Press.

Friston, K.J., Harrison, L., & Penny, W. (2003). Dynamic causal modelling. *Neuroimage*, 19(4), 1273–1302. DOI: 10.1016/S1053-8119(03)00202-7

Gallagher, S., & Zahavi, D. (2010). Phenomenological approaches to self-consciousness. In E.N. Zalta (Ed.), *The Stanford encyclopedia of philosophy (Winter 2010 edition)*. Retrieved from http://plato.stanford.edu/archives/win2010/entries/self-consciousness-phenomenological/

Goebel, R., Muckli, L., Zanella, F.E., Singer, W., & Stoerig, P. (2001). Sustained extrastriate cortical activation without visual awareness revealed by fMRI studies of hemianopic patients. *Vision Research*, 41(10–11), 1459–1474. DOI: 10.1016/S0042-6989(01)00069-4

Goebel, R., Roebroeck, A., Kim, D.-S., & Formisano, E. (2003). Investigating directed cortical interactions in time-resolved fMRI data using vector autoregressive modeling and granger causality mapping. *Magnetic Resonance Imaging*, 21(10), 1251–1261. DOI: 10.1016/j.mri.2003.08.026

Gosseries, O., Bruno, M.-A., Chatelle, C., Vanhaudenhuyse, A., Schnakers, C., Soddu, A., & Laureys, S. (2011). Disorders of consciousness: What's in a name? *Neurorehabilitation*, 28(1), 3–14.

Gusnard, D. A. (2005). Being a self: Considerations from functional imaging. *Consciousness and Cognition*, 14(4), 679–697. DOI: 10.1016/j.concog.2005.04.004

Haynes, J.-D., Deichmann, R., & Rees, G. (2005). Eye-specific effects of binocular rivalry in the human lateral geniculate nucleus. *Nature*, 438(7067), 496–499. DOI: 10.1038/nature04169

Haynes, J.-D., Driver, J., & Rees, G. (2005). Visibility reflects dynamic changes of effective connectivity between V1 and fusiform cortex. *Neuron*, 46(5), 811–821. DOI: 10.1016/j.neuron.2005.05.012

Haynes, J.-D., & Rees, G. (2005). Predicting the stream of consciousness from activity in human visual cortex. *Current Biology*, 15(14), 1301–1307. DOI: 10.1016/j.cub.2005.06.026

Helfrich, R. F., Schneider, T. R., Rach, S., Trautmann-Lengsfeld, S. A., Engel, A. K., & Herrmann, C. S. (2014). Entrainment of brain oscillations by transcranial alternating current stimulation. *Current Biology*, 24(3), 333–339. DOI: 10.1016/j.cub.2013.12.041

Hohwy, J. (2009). The neural correlates of consciousness: New experimental approaches needed? *Consciousness and Cognition*, 18(2), 428–438. DOI: 10.1016/j.concog.2009.02.006

Howard, I. P., & Rogers, B. J. (1995). *Binocular vision and stereopsis*. New York, NY: Oxford University Press.

Inui, T., Tanaka, S., Okada, T., Nishizawa, S., Katayama, M., & Konishi, J. (2000). Neural substrates for depth perception of the necker cube; a functional magnetic resonance imaging study in human subjects. *Neuroscience Letters*, 282(3), 145–148. DOI: 10.1016/S0304-3940(00)00899-5

Jacobs, C., Goebel, R., & Sack, A. T. (2011). Visual awareness suppression by pre-stimulus brain stimulation; a neural effect. *Neuroimage*, 59(1), 616–624. DOI: 10.1016/j.neuroimage.2011.07.090

Jacobs, C., & Sack, A. T. (2012). Behavior in oblivion: The neurobiology of subliminal priming. *Brain Sciences*, 2(2), 225–241. DOI: 10.3390/brainsci2020225

Kanai, R., Bahrami, B., & Rees, G. (2010). Human parietal cortex structure predicts individual differences in perceptual rivalry. *Current Biology*, 20(18), 1626–1630. DOI: 10.1016/j.cub.2010.07.027

Kanai, R., & Tsuchiya, N. (2012). Qualia. *Current Biology*, 22(10), R392–R396. DOI: 10.1016/j.cub.2012.03.033

Kim, C.-Y., & Blake, R. (2005). Psychophysical magic: Rendering the visible 'invisible'. *Trends in Cognitive Sciences*, 9(8), 381–388. DOI: 10.1016/j.tics.2005.06.012

Kleinschmidt, A., Büchel, C., Zeki, S., & Frackowiak, R. S. J. (1998). Human brain activity during spontaneously reversing perception of ambiguous figures. *Proceedings of the Royal Society of London B: Biological Sciences*, 265(1413), 2427–2433. DOI: 10.1098/rspb.1998.0594

Koch, C. (2004). *The quest for consciousness: A neurobiological approach*. Englewood, CO: Roberts & Company.

Koch, C., & Tsuchiya, N. (2007). Attention and consciousness: Two distinct brain processes. *Trends in Cognitive Sciences*, 11(1), 16–22. DOI: 10.1016/j.tics.2006.10.012

Koch, C., & Tsuchiya, N. (2012). Attention and consciousness: Related yet different. *Trends in Cognitive Sciences*, 16(2), 103–105. DOI: 10.1016/j.tics.2011.11.012

Koivisto, M., Lähteenmäki, M., Sørensen, T. A., Vangkilde, S., Overgaard, M., & Revonsuo, A. (2008). The earliest electrophysiological correlate of visual awareness? *Brain and Cognition*, 66(1), 91–103. DOI: 10.1016/j.bandc.2007.05.010

Koivisto, M., Mäntylä, T., & Silvanto, J. (2010). The role of early visual cortex (V1/V2) in conscious and unconscious visual perception. *Neuroimage*, 51(2), 828–834. DOI: 10.1016/j.neuroimage.2010.02.042

Koivisto, M., Railo, H., & Salminen-Vaparanta, N. (2011). Transcranial magnetic stimulation of early visual cortex interferes with subjective visual awareness and objective forced-choice performance. *Consciousness and Cognition*, 20(2), 288–298. DOI: 10.1016/j.concog.2010.09.001

Koivisto, M., & Revonsuo A. (2009). Event-related brain potential correlates of visual awareness. *Neuroscience & Biobehavioral Reviews*, 34(6), 922–934. DOI: 10.1016/j.neubiorev.2009.12.002

Lau, H. C. (2008). A higher order Bayesian decision theory of consciousness. *Progress in Brain Research*, 168, 35–48. DOI: 10.1016/S0079-6123(07)68004-2

Lau, H. C., & Passingham, R. E. (2006). Relative blindsight in normal observers and the neural correlate of visual consciousness. *Proceedings of the National Academy of Sciences USA*, 103(49), 18763–18768. DOI: 10.1073/pnas.0607716103

Lee, S.-H., Blake, R., & Heeger, D. J. (2005). Traveling waves of activity in primary visual cortex during binocular rivalry. *Nature Neuroscience*, 8(1), 22–23. DOI: 10.1038/nn1365

Levelt, W. J. M. (1965). *On binocular rivalry*. Soesterberg, Netherlands: Institute for Perception R.V.O.-T.N.O.

Logothetis, N. (1998). Object vision and visual awareness. *Current Opinion in Neurobiology*, 8(6), 536–544. DOI: 10.1016/S0959-4388(98)80043-3

Logothetis, N. K., Leopold, D. A., & Sheinberg, D. L. (1996). What is rivalling during binocular rivalry? *Nature*, 380(6575), 621–624. DOI: 10.1038/380621a0

Luck, S. J., Vogel, E. K., & Shapiro, K. L. (1996). Word meanings can be accessed but not reported during the attentional blink. *Nature*, 383(6601), 616–618. DOI: 10.1038/383616a0

Lumer, E. D., Friston, K. J., & Rees, G. (1998). Neural correlates of perceptual rivalry in the human brain. *Science*, 280(5371), 1930–1934. DOI: 10.1126/science.280.5371.1930

Lumer, E. D., & Rees, G. (1999). Covariation of activity in visual and prefrontal cortex associated with subjective visual perception. *Proceedings of the National Academy of Sciences USA*, 96(4), 1669–1673. DOI: 10.1073/pnas.96.4.1669

Mack, A., & Rock, I. (1998). *Inattentional blindness*. Cambridge, MA: MIT Press.

Marois, R., Yi, D.-J., & Chun, M. M. (2004). The neural fate of consciously perceived and missed events in the attentional blink. *Neuron*, 41(3), 465–472. DOI: 10.1016/S0896-6273(04)00012-1

Massimini, M., Ferrarelli, F., Huber, R., Esser, S. K., Singh, H., & Tononi, G. (2005). Breakdown of cortical effective connectivity during sleep. *Science*, 309(5744), 2228–2232. DOI: 10.1126/science.1117256

Mathewson, K. E., Gratton, G., Fabiani, M., Beck, D. M., & Ro, T. (2009). To see or not to see: Prestimulus α phase predicts visual awareness. *Journal of Neuroscience*, 29(9), 2725–2732. DOI: 10.1523/JNEUROSCI.3963-08.2009

Melloni, L., Schwiedrzik, C. M., Müller, N., Rodriguez, E., & Singer, W. (2011). Expectations change the signatures and timing of electrophysiological correlates of perceptual awareness. *Journal of Neuroscience*, 31(4), 1386–1396. DOI: 10.1523/JNEUROSCI.4570-10.2011

Melloni, L., & Singer, W. (2010). Distinct characteristics of conscious experience are met by large-scale neuronal synchronization. In E. K. Perry, D. Collerton, F. E. N. LeBeau, & H.

Ashton (Eds.), *New horizons in the neuroscience of consciousness* (pp. 17–28). Advances in Consciousness Research (Vol. 79). Amsterdam, The Netherlands: John Benjamins Publishing Company. DOI: 10.1075/aicr.79.06mel
Merikle, P. M., & Joordens, S. (1997). Parallels between perception without attention and perception without awareness. *Consciousness and Cognition*, 6(2–3), 219–236. DOI: 10.1006/ccog.1997.0310
Miller, S. M. (2001). Binocular rivalry and the cerebral hemispheres: With a note on the correlates and constitution of visual consciousness. *Brain and Mind*, 2(1), 119–149. DOI: 10.1023/A:1017981619014
Miller, S. M. (2007). On the correlation/constitution distinction problem (and other hard problems) in the scientific study of consciousness. *Acta Neuropsychiatrica*, 19(3), 159–176. DOI: 10.1111/j.1601-5215.2007.00207.x
Miller, S. M. (Ed.). (2013). *The constitution of visual consciousness: Lessons from binocular rivalry*. Advances in Consciousness Research (Vol. 90). Amsterdam, The Netherlands: John Benjamins Publishing Company. DOI: 10.1075/aicr.90
Miller, S. M., Liu, G. B., Ngo, T. T., Hooper, G., Riek, S., Carson, R. G., & Pettigrew, J. D. (2000). Interhemispheric switching mediates perceptual rivalry. *Current Biology*, 10(7), 383–392. DOI: 10.1016/S0960-9822(00)00416-4
Morris, J. S., Öhman, A., & Dolan, R. J. (1999). A subcortical pathway to the right amygdala mediating "unseen" fear. *Proceedings of the National Academy of Sciences USA*, 96(4), 1680–1685. DOI: 10.1073/pnas.96.4.1680
Moutoussis, K., Keliris, G., Kourtzi, Z., & Logothetis, N. (2005). A binocular rivalry study of motion perception in the human brain. *Vision Research*, 45(17), 2231–2243. DOI: 10.1016/j.visres.2005.02.007
Moutoussis, K., & Zeki, S. (2002). The relationship between cortical activation and perception investigated with invisible stimuli. *Proceedings of the National Academy of Sciences USA*, 99(14), 9527–9532. DOI: 10.1073/pnas.142305699
Moutoussis, K., & Zeki, S. (2006). Seeing invisible motion: A human fMRI study. *Current Biology*, 16(6), 574–579. DOI: 10.1016/j.cub.2006.01.062
Naccache, L., Gaillard, R., Adam, C., Hasboun, D., Clémenceau, S., Baulac, M., Dehaene, S., & Cohen, L. (2005). A direct intracranial record of emotions evoked by subliminal words. *Proceedings of the National Academy of Sciences USA*, 102(21), 7713–7717. DOI: 10.1073/pnas.0500542102
Naghavi, H. R., & Nyberg, L. (2005). Common fronto-parietal activity in attention, memory, and consciousness: Shared demands on integration? *Consciousness and Cognition*, 14(2), 390–425. DOI: 10.1016/j.concog.2004.10.003
Neisser, J. (2012). Neural correlates of consciousness reconsidered. *Consciousness and Cognition*, 21(2), 681–690. DOI: 10.1016/j.concog.2011.03.012
Nobre, A. C., Coull, J. T., Frith, C. D., & Mesulam, M. M. (1999). Orbitofrontal cortex is activated during breaches of expectation in tasks of visual attention. *Nature Neuroscience*, 2(1), 11–12. DOI: 10.1038/4513
Noë, A., & Thompson, E. (2004). Are there neural correlates of consciousness? *Journal of Consciousness Studies*, 11(1), 3–28.
O'Regan, J. K., & Noë, A. (2001). A sensorimotor account of vision and visual consciousness. *Behavioral and Brain Sciences*, 24(5), 939–973. DOI: 10.1017/S0140525X01000115
Owen, A. M., Coleman, M. R., Boly, M., Davis, M. H., Laureys, S., & Pickard, J. D. (2006). Detecting awareness in the vegetative state. *Science*, 313(5792), 1402. DOI: 10.1126/science.1130197

Panagiotaropoulos, T. I., Deco, G., Kapoor, V., & Logothetis, N. K. (2012). Neuronal discharges and gamma oscillations explicitly reflect visual consciousness in the lateral prefrontal cortex. *Neuron*, 74(5), 924–935. DOI: 10.1016/j.neuron.2012.04.013

Pascual-Leone, A., Walsh, V., & Rothwell, J. (2000). Transcranial magnetic stimulation in cognitive neuroscience – virtual lesion, chronometry, and functional connectivity. *Current Opinion in Neurobiology*, 10(2), 232–237. DOI: 10.1016/S0959-4388(00)00081-7

Pasley, B. N., Mayes, L. C., & Schultz, R. T. (2004). Subcortical discrimination of unperceived objects during binocular rivalry. *Neuron*, 42(1), 163–172. DOI: 10.1016/S0896-6273(04)00155-2

Pessoa, L., Kastner, S., & Ungerleider, L. G. (2003). Neuroimaging studies of attention: From modulation of sensory processing to top-down control. *Journal of Neuroscience*, 23(10), 3990–3998.

Pins, D., & ffytche, D. (2003). The neural correlates of conscious vision. *Cerebral Cortex*, 13(5), 461–474. DOI: 10.1093/cercor/13.5.461

Polonsky, A., Blake, R., Braun, J., & Heeger, D. J. (2000). Neuronal activity in human primary visual cortex correlates with perception during binocular rivalry. *Nature Neuroscience*, 3(11), 1153–1159. DOI: 10.1038/80676

Posner, M. I. (1994). Attention: The mechanisms of consciousness. *Proceedings of the National Academy of Sciences USA*, 91(16), 7398–7403. DOI: 10.1073/pnas.91.16.7398

Quiroga, R. Q., Mukamel, R., Isham, E. A., Malach, R., & Fried, I. (2008). Human single-neuron responses at the threshold of conscious recognition. *Proceedings of the National Academy of Sciences USA*, 105(9), 3599–3604. DOI: 10.1073/pnas.0707043105

Rees, G. (2007). Neural correlates of the contents of visual awareness in humans. *Philosophical Transactions of the Royal Society of London B: Biological Sciences*, 362(1481), 877–886. DOI: 10.1098/rstb.2007.2094

Rees, G., Wojciulik, E., Clarke, K., Husain, M., Frith, C., & Driver, J. (2000). Unconscious activation of visual cortex in the damaged right hemisphere of a parietal patient with extinction. *Brain*, 123(8), 1624–1633. DOI: 10.1093/brain/123.8.1624

Rees, G., Wojciulik, E., Clarke, K., Husain, M., Frith, C., & Driver, J. (2002). Neural correlates of conscious and unconscious vision in parietal extinction. *Neurocase*, 8(5), 387–393. DOI: 10.1093/neucas/8.5.387

Revonsuo, A. (2000). Prospects for a scientific research program on consciousness. In T. Metzinger (Ed.), *Neural correlates of consciousness: Empirical and conceptual questions* (pp. 57–75). Cambridge, MA: MIT Press.

Revonsuo, A. (2001). Can functional brain imaging discover consciousness in the brain? *Journal of Consciousness Studies*, 8(3), 3–23.

Ro, T., Shelton, D., Lee, O. L., & Chang, E. (2004). Extrageniculate mediation of unconscious vision in transcranial magnetic stimulation-induced blindsight. *Proceedings of the National Academy of Sciences USA*, 101(26), 9933–9935. DOI: 10.1073/pnas.0403061101

Roebroeck, A., Formisano, E., & Goebel, R. (2005). Mapping directed influence over the brain using Granger causality and fMRI. *Neuroimage*, 25(1), 230–242. DOI: 10.1016/j.neuroimage.2004.11.017

Romei, V., Gross, J., & Thut, G. (2010). On the role of prestimulus alpha rhythms over occipito-parietal areas in visual input regulation: Correlation or causation? *Journal of Neuroscience*, 30(25), 8692–8697. DOI: 10.1523/JNEUROSCI.0160-10.2010

Ruff, C. C., Bestmann, S., Blankenburg, F., Bjoertomt, O., Josephs, O., Weiskopf, N., Deichmann, R., & Driver, J. (2008). Distinct causal influences of parietal versus frontal areas on human visual cortex: Evidence from concurrent TMS-fMRI. *Cerebral Cortex*, 18(4), 817–827. DOI: 10.1093/cercor/bhm128

Ruff, C. C., Blankenburg, F., Bjoertomt, O., Bestmann, S., Freeman, E., Haynes, J.-D., Rees, G., Josephs, O., Deichmann, R., & Driver, J. (2006). Concurrent TMS-fMRI and psychophysics reveal frontal influences on human retinotopic visual cortex. *Current Biology*, 16(15), 1479–1488. DOI: 10.1016/j.cub.2006.06.057

Sack, A. T., Camprodon, J. A., Pascual-Leone, A., & Goebel, R. (2005). The dynamics of interhemispheric compensatory processes in mental imagery. *Science*, 308(5722), 702–704. DOI: 10.1126/science.1107784

Sack, A. T., Hubl, D., Prvulovic, D., Formisano, E., Jandl, M., Zanella, F. E., Maurer, K., Goebel, R., Dierks, T., & Linden, D. E. J. (2002). The experimental combination of rTMS and fMRI reveals the functional relevance of parietal cortex for visuospatial functions. *Cognitive Brain Research*, 13(1), 85–93. DOI: 10.1016/S0926-6410(01)00087-8

Sack, A. T., Kohler, A., Bestmann, S., Linden, D. E. J., Dechent, P., Goebel, R., & Baudewig, J. (2007). Imaging the brain activity changes underlying impaired visuospatial judgments: Simultaneous fMRI, TMS, and behavioral studies. *Cerebral Cortex*, 17(12), 2841–2852. DOI: 10.1093/cercor/bhm013

Schoth, F., Waberski, T. D., Krings, T., Gobbele, R., & Buchner, H. (2007). Cerebral processing of spontaneous reversals of the rotating Necker cube. *Neuroreport*, 18(13), 1335–1338. DOI: 10.1097/WNR.0b013e3281668007

Sergent, C., & Naccache, L. (2012). Imaging neural signatures of consciousness: 'What', 'when', 'where' and 'how' does it work? *Archives Italiennes de Biologie*, 150(2–3), 91–106.

Seth, A. K. (2009). Functions of consciousness. In W. P. Banks (Ed.), *Encyclopedia of consciousness*, Vol. 1 (pp. 279–293). Oxford, UK: Academic Press. DOI: 10.1016/B978-012373873-8.00033-5

Silva, S., Alacoque, X., Fourcade, O., Samii, K., Marque, P., Woods, R., Mazziotta, J., Chollet, F., & Loubinoux, I. (2010). Wakefulness and loss of awareness: Brain and brainstem interaction in the vegetative state. *Neurology*, 74(4), 313–320. DOI: 10.1212/WNL.0b013e3181cbcd96

Silvanto, J. (2008). A re-evaluation of blindsight and the role of striate cortex (V1) in visual awareness. *Neuropsychologia*, 46(12), 2869–2871. DOI: 10.1016/j.neuropsychologia.2008.04.014

Silvanto, J., Lavie, N., & Walsh, V. (2005). Double dissociation of V1 and V5/MT activity in visual awareness. *Cerebral Cortex*, 15(11), 1736–1741. DOI: 10.1093/cercor/bhi050

Sterzer, P., Kleinschmidt, A., & Rees, G. (2009). The neural bases of multistable perception. *Trends in Cognitive Sciences*, 13(7), 310–318. DOI: 10.1016/j.tics.2009.04.006

Sterzer, P., Russ, M. O., Preibisch, C., & Kleinschmidt, A. (2002). Neural correlates of spontaneous direction reversals in ambiguous apparent visual motion. *Neuroimage*, 15(4), 908–916. DOI: 10.1006/nimg.2001.1030

Thut, G., Schyns, P. G., & Gross, J. (2011). Entrainment of perceptually relevant brain oscillations by non-invasive rhythmic stimulation of the human brain. *Frontiers in Psychology*, 2, 170. DOI: 10.3389/fpsyg.2011.00170

Thut, G., Veniero, D., Romei, V., Miniussi, C., Schyns, P., & Gross, J. (2011). Rhythmic TMS causes local entrainment of natural oscillatory signatures. *Current Biology*, 21(14), 1176–1185. DOI: 10.1016/j.cub.2011.05.049

Tong, F. (2003). Primary visual cortex and visual awareness. *Nature Reviews Neuroscience*, 4(3), 219–229. DOI: 10.1038/nrn1055

Tong, F., & Engel, S. A. (2001). Interocular rivalry revealed in the human cortical blind-spot representation. *Nature*, 411(6834), 195–199. DOI: 10.1038/35075583

Tong, F., Meng, M., & Blake, R. (2006). Neural bases of binocular rivalry. *Trends in Cognitive Sciences*, 10(11), 502–511. DOI: 10.1016/j.tics.2006.09.003

Tong, F., Nakayama, K., Vaughan, J. T., & Kanwisher, N. (1998). Binocular rivalry and visual awareness in human extrastriate cortex. *Neuron*, 21(4), 753–759. DOI: 10.1016/S0896-6273(00)80592-9

Tononi, G. (2004). An information integration theory of consciousness. *BMC Neuroscience*, 5, 42. DOI: 10.1186/1471-2202-5-42

Tononi, G. (2005). Consciousness, information integration, and the brain. *Progress in Brain Research*, 150, 109–126. DOI: 10.1016/S0079-6123(05)50009-8

van Dijk, H., Schoffelen, J.-M., Oostenveld, R., & Jensen, O. (2008). Prestimulus oscillatory activity in the alpha band predicts visual discrimination ability. *Journal of Neuroscience*, 28(8), 1816–1823. DOI: 10.1523/JNEUROSCI.1853-07.2008

Velmans, M. (Ed.). (1996). *The science of consciousness: Psychological, neuropsychological and clinical reviews*. London, UK: Routledge. DOI: 10.4324/9780203360019

von der Heydt, R., Peterhans, E., & Baumgartner, G. (1984). Illusory contours and cortical neuron responses. *Science*, 224(4654), 1260–1262. DOI: 10.1126/science.6539501

Vuilleumier, P., & Driver, J. (2007). Modulation of visual processing by attention and emotion: Windows on causal interactions between human brain regions. *Philosophical Transactions of the Royal Society of London B: Biological Sciences*, 362(1481), 837–855. DOI: 10.1098/rstb.2007.2092

Watanabe, M., Cheng, K., Murayama, Y., Ueno, K., Asamizuya, T., Tanaka, K., & Logothetis, N. (2011). Attention but not awareness modulates the bold signal in the human V1 during binocular suppression. *Science*, 334(6057), 829–831. DOI: 10.1126/science.1203161

Weil, R. S., & Rees, G. (2011). A new taxonomy for perceptual filling-in. *Brain Research Reviews*, 67(1–2), 40–55. DOI: 10.1016/j.brainresrev.2010.10.004

Weiskrantz, L. (1996). Blindsight revisited. *Current Opinion in Neurobiology*, 6(2), 215–220. DOI: 10.1016/S0959-4388(96)80075-4

Wheatstone, C. (1838). Contributions to the physiology of vision. – Part the first. *On some remarkable, and hitherto unobserved, phenomena of binocular vision. Philosophical Transactions of the Royal Society of London*, 128, 371–394. DOI: 10.1098/rstl.1838.0019

Wilenius, M. E., & Revonsuo, A. T. (2007). Timing of the earliest ERP correlate of visual awareness. *Psychophysiology*, 44(5), 703–710. DOI: 10.1111/j.1469-8986.2007.00546.x

Wunderlich, K., Schneider, K. A., & Kastner, S. (2005). Neural correlates of binocular rivalry in the human lateral geniculate nucleus. *Nature Neuroscience*, 8(11), 1595–1602. DOI: 10.1038/nn1554

Zaidi, Q., Ennis, R., Cao, D., & Lee, B. (2012). Neural locus of color afterimages. *Current Biology*, 22(3), 220–224. DOI: 10.1016/j.cub.2011.12.021

Zaretskaya, N., Thielscher, A., Logothetis, N. K., & Bartels, A. (2010). Disrupting parietal function prolongs dominance durations in binocular rivalry. *Current Biology*, 20(23), 2106–2111. DOI: 10.1016/j.cub.2010.10.046

Zeki, S. (2003). The disunity of consciousness. *Trends in Cognitive Sciences*, 7(5), 214–218. DOI: 10.1016/S1364-6613(03)00081-0

Zeki, S. (2007). The disunity of consciousness. *Progress in Brain Research*, 168, 11–18. DOI: 10.1016/S0079-6123(07)68002-9

On why the unconscious prerequisites and consequences of consciousness might derail us from unraveling the neural correlates of consciousness

Jaan Aru[i,ii], Talis Bachmann[iii], Wolf Singer[i,ii,iv] and Lucia Melloni[i,v,vi]
[i]Max-Planck Institute for Brain Research / [ii]Frankfurt Institute for Advanced Studies, Frankfurt am Main / [iii]University of Tartu, Tallinn / [iv]Ernst Strüngmann Institute in Cooperation with Max Planck Society, Frankfurt am Main / [v]Columbia University Medical Center, New York / [vi]NYU Langone Medical Center, New York

It has been proposed that one key step for solving the mystery of consciousness is to locate the neural correlates of consciousness (NCC). The experimental paradigms for revealing the NCC have commonly applied the contrast between conditions with and without conscious perception. However, such contrast does not exclusively reveal the neural processes directly related to conscious experience of the target but also the prerequisites for and the consequences of conscious perception. Therefore, understanding the neural bases of conscious experience requires the NCC to be experimentally disentangled from these confounding processes. Here we review some recent experimental developments and suggest some new empirical approaches for distilling the neural basis of conscious perception.

1. Introduction

Humans can consciously detect the presentation of a few photons in complete darkness. As expected, such detection performance is not successful on 100% of trials: sometimes the flash is perceived, sometimes it is not. Thus, although objectively the photons are always present, they are not always registered in our awareness. For decades researchers have taken advantage of the fact that while stimulation can be invariant perception does fluctuate, and this approach has crystallized in the so-called contrastive method. The methodology is straightforward: one has to compare

DOI 10.1075/aicr.92.08aru

conditions in which a stimulus is registered into consciousness with situations in which the very same stimulus fails to reach consciousness. By contrasting brain recording data obtained in these two conditions under invariant stimulation conditions it was thought to be possible to unravel the neurobiological processes underlying consciousness. However, in the case of photon detection, it is known that the difference between these two types of trials, where the flash is or is not consciously perceived, partly originates from the very first steps of visual processing at the retina (Field, Sampath, & Rieke, 2005). Namely, spontaneous rhodopsin activation and the threshold-like non-linearity at the rod-to-rod bipolar synapse on the retina have been experimentally found to determine whether the photon is detected or not (Field et al., 2005). Accordingly, one would have concluded that processes at the level of the retina already play a pivotal role on the neural correlate of consciousness. Yet, such conclusion would not be warranted as it is known that one is not directly aware of the retinal activity (e.g., Koch, 2004). For example, one does not perceive the blind spot of our retinas, there is no color loss in the more peripheral parts of our visual field despite the fact that retinal color-sensitivity drops off away from the fovea and eye-movements and blinks blur the activity on the retina but one perceives a coherent and stable world despite them.

It is then clear that merely contrasting neurophysiological data from trials with and without conscious perception will not bring us closer to identifying the neural correlates of consciousness (NCC). In the case of the retinal activity it is clear that it does not correspond to the NCC because one has other arguments to rule that out, for example, it is possible to bypass the retina by using transcranial magnetic stimulation (TMS) over visual cortex, which still leads to conscious percepts (e.g., Kammer, 1999; Pascual-Leone & Walsh, 2001). However, if one moves up the hierarchy using the contrastive method it is not clear how it could be determined whether the activity corresponds to NCC or is just another retina-like prerequisite. As the contrastive method has been the primary methodology in the study of consciousness, it is possible that some of the most heated debates in consciousness research – for instance, whether consciousness arises early, around 200 ms (Bachmann, 2000; Koivisto & Revonsuo, 2010; Pins & ffytche, 2003), or late, after 300 ms (Del Cul, Baillet, & Dehaene, 2007; Lamy, Salti, & Bar-Haim, 2009), or whether it is based on the activity of local sensory cortices (Malach, 2007; Zeki, 2001), or requires (additionally) distributed activity of many higher brain areas (Dehaene & Changeux, 2011; Melloni & Singer, 2010) – partly reflect the lack of specificity in the contrastive method. In fact, it is not unthinkable that previous results reflect processes that do not directly relate to consciousness but instead activity that precedes or follows it, without necessarily contributing directly to consciousness.

The classic contrastive analysis has served consciousness research well (Dehaene & Changeux, 2011; Rees, Kreiman, & Koch, 2002) but science advances by advancing its tools and scrutinizing its methodology. Thus, we should not be afraid to abandon the simple contrastive analysis for methodologically more precise experimental designs.

2. Narrowing the focus on the real NCC

One of the most important research goals since the beginning of the science of consciousness has been to unravel the neural correlates of consciousness (Crick & Koch, 1990). The NCC are defined as the "minimal set of neuronal events jointly sufficient for a specific conscious experience (given the appropriate enabling conditions)" (Koch, 2004, p. 97).

It has been argued that one key reason why identifying the NCC has been particularly elusive is that the experimental methods typically used to investigate them are not specific to unravel the NCC but also unravel *unconscious* processes that precede or follow conscious experience. In other words, contrasting trials with and without conscious perception of a particular target gives us more neural processes than just the desired NCC (Aru, Bachmann, Singer, & Melloni, 2012; Bachmann, 2009; de Graaf, Hsieh, & Sack, 2012; de Graaf & Sack, this volume; Hohwy & Bayne, this volume; Melloni & Singer, 2010; Miller, 2001, 2007, this volume; Revonsuo, this volume).

Miller (2001, 2007) closely scrutinized the problem concluding that although we aim to identify the neural processes that constitute consciousness, our present scientific methods can only unravel neural processes that correlate with consciousness, and the correlates and constituents of consciousness may be distinct. Revonsuo (2000, 2001) also mentioned this problem and argued that our present neural measurements are not necessarily on the level where we would expect to identify the NCC. Miller (2001, 2007) however, held that it is not just technological advancements that are required to address the correlation/constitution distinction problem, but rather entirely new scientific strategies. He discussed brain recording, stimulation and disruption strategies that can be applied to the problem but noted that while these might get science closer to revealing the minimally sufficient NCC, these strategies do not speak to the problem of constitution (see Miller, this volume, for more on the distinction between the minimally sufficient NCC and the constitution of consciousness).

Whatever the case may turn out to be regarding breakthroughs based on technological advancements, and whatever difficulties may or may not ultimately lie in moving from the NCC to the constitution of consciousness, we argue that it is important and possible to devise better and more precise experimental methodologies to identify the NCC. This is because part of the empirical strategy to at least close in on the constitution of consciousness is to first identify tightly-correlated neural activities (Miller, this volume). Furthermore, we argue that in order to advance such understanding, we need a more thorough understanding of the neural processes that might hinder our quest to identify the NCC. For us this has implied that we ought to figure out which other neural processes will be differentially activated when trials with and without conscious perception are compared in the contrastive analysis. Critical to the enterprise of disentangling the NCC is to categorize the neural processes that do not pertain to the NCC. For now, we have explicitly divided these processes into three (Aru, Bachmann, et al., 2012; de Graaf et al., 2012): prerequisites of conscious perception (NCC-pr), NCC, and consequences of conscious perception (NCC-co).

We consider that such explicit categorization is important because it can guide the experimental work towards identifying the NCC. While technological advancements are developed, we already have the tools for doing the first steps in what we call "distilling" the neural correlates of consciousness (Aru, Bachmann, et al., 2012). In particular, we can try to: (1) apprehend which neural processes besides the NCC might be differentially activated in our experiments; (2) figure out ways how to experimentally disentangle these processes from the NCC; (3) assess the previous literature in light of these findings; and (4) get closer to the real NCC (and perhaps the constituents of consciousness). In short, although identifying the processes that constitute consciousness might be a hard problem of consciousness and might be tractable or intractable (Miller, 2007), we argue that one way to proceed here and now is by understanding and untangling neural processes that hinder our quest for identifying the NCC. As Lao Tse said, "Pots are formed from clay, but the empty space within it is the essence of the pot." By precisely showing what neural processes are *not* the NCC, we can get closer to identifying the NCC and in so doing, perhaps get closer to identifying the constituents of consciousness.

3. The prerequisites, the consequences and what they imply

In light of this line of reasoning we proceed by briefly discussing the prerequisites and consequences of conscious perception. We note that the present three-way division needs more scrutiny – the better the understanding of the types and categories of these processes, the higher our chances of disentangling them from the NCC. Thus the present division is not necessarily final.

The example described at the beginning of the chapter corresponds to *prerequisites of consciousness*: those reflect unconscious, neural processes that are different between trials with and without conscious perception, but precede conscious perception (i.e., because for instance they happen at the retina) without directly contributing to it. In turn the *consequences of consciousness* correspond to all those unconscious mental processes that follow consciousness and that are directly enabled by consciousness. Such a process should logically exist if one attributes some function to consciousness in the chain of information processing (Seth, 2009). One clear example is declarative memory. For instance, it is known that neurons in the medial temporal lobe (MTL) follow conscious perception with high fidelity and in an all-or-none fashion (Quiroga, Mukamel, Isham, Malach, & Fried, 2008). In a revealing study, Quiroga and colleagues have shown that whenever a stimulus is consciously perceived, and importantly regardless of the duration of the stimulation (e.g., whether it is presented for 30 or 150 ms), neurons in MTL discharge action potentials, while they are silent if the stimulus is not registered into consciousness. Yet, resecting the MTL has no measurable effect on conscious perception (Postle, 2009). Most famously, the remarkable patient HM could not form any new declarative memories after a bilateral resection of the mesial temporal structures, but could nonetheless and without any problems continue to consciously perceive stimuli. This case clearly shows that MTL is critical for the formation of new declarative memories but not to conscious perception. These two types of processes, the prerequisites and the consequences, hinder our quest to identify the NCC. Furthermore, we claim that this problem exists for most present experimental paradigms regardless of whether they use one transient stimulus (Figure 1a), several transient stimuli (Figure 1b) or longer epochs of stimulation such as in binocular

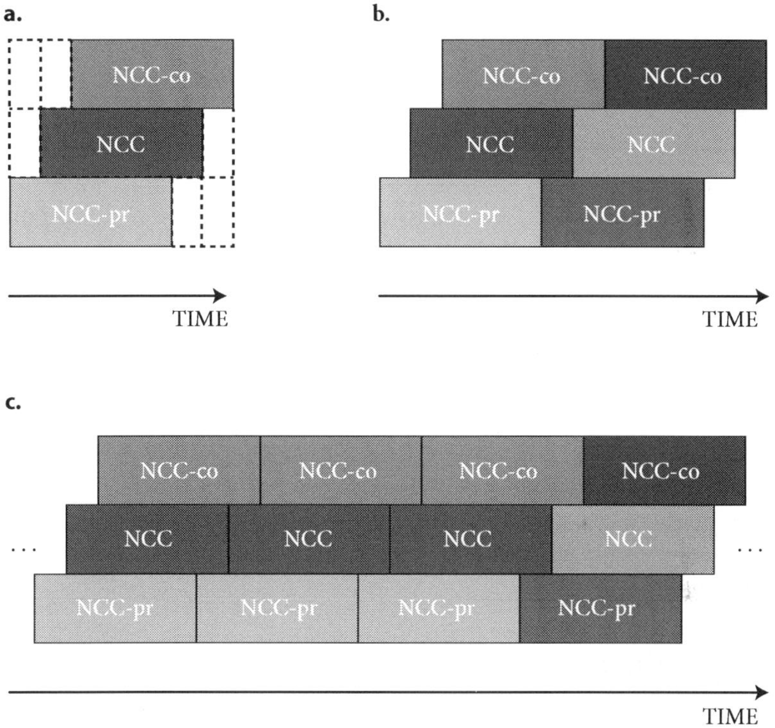

Figure 1. Possible temporal relationships between NCC, NCC-pr and NCC-co in various experimental situations. (**a**) If a single transient stimulus is presented, NCC-pr, NCC and NCC-co are evoked. Empty rectangular boxes indicate that the temporal differences and overlap between the three NCCs is currently unknown. This scenario corresponds to experimental paradigms like threshold stimulation. (**b**) If two (or more) transient stimuli are presented sequentially, the different NCCs of these different stimuli can be overlapping in time. This scenario corresponds to experimental paradigms like masking or attentional blink. (**c**) In experimental situations with longer epochs of perception, each epoch can be understood as a succession of the transient events (as in **a**), where the NCC of time point t can be overlapping with NCC-co from time point t–1 and NCC-pr from time point t+1. This scenario corresponds to experimental paradigms like binocular rivalry or motion-induced blindness. Similar ideas on the temporal overlap of the processes unfolding within pre-conscious and conscious stages of percept formation have been also proposed previously (Brown, 1988).

rivalry (Figure 1c). In general, the NCC might well overlap in time with NCC-pr and/or NCC-co. The onset of NCC might occur while the NCC-pr processes are still active and the consequences of conscious perception might also be elicited while the NCC and the NCC-pr are still expressed. Such temporal coincidence makes it even harder to distill NCC from these other processes because one obviously cannot simply rely on any temporal criteria for separating the NCC from the rest.

It is legitimate to wonder whether it is really necessary to distinguish between the different types of NCC or whether a generic concept of "processes correlating with conscious experience" is sufficient. For example, consequences of conscious perception are processes that are most likely directly related to the functions of consciousness (Seth, 2009). Therefore, studying NCC-co is an important endeavor in understanding the phenomenon of consciousness, as well as how and why it may have evolved. However, if the goal is to uncover which neural mechanisms specifically underlie qualia, constitute consciousness and are the actual NCC, then it is required that our experimental paradigms indeed aim at unraveling this "minimal set" of neural mechanisms. That is, if current experimental paradigms are not specific for the NCC, the quest for the NCC is bound to fail.

As the contrastive method has been the prominent methodology for the study of consciousness in the past decades, one of the major challenges for the future, when acknowledging the lack of specificity of the method to reveal the NCC, is that studies will have to be revisited. Along the same lines, theories will have to be updated and revisited, as it is currently unknown how many of the current findings on which these theories are often based relate to NCC, and how many reflect unconscious processes that either precede or follow conscious perception. The severity of this problem is yet to be determined, as presently we do not have sufficient data to estimate it. Yet, recent studies employing methodologies other than the contrastive method (Aru, Axmacher, et al., 2012; Melloni, Schwiedrzik, Müller, Rodriguez, & Singer, 2011; Pitts, Martínez, & Hillyard, 2012) have already shown that previous results may have tapped into antecedents and/or consequences of conscious perception and not necessarily into the NCC per se. We will review those studies in later sections. Consequently, it is foreseeable that the theoretical landscape will change significantly in the future. It is crucial that researchers acknowledge that the simple contrasts between trials with and without conscious perception of a target are simply not informative for our purposes. It is then imperative to go beyond the simple contrast and consider experimental paradigms, which allow us to disentangle the NCC from these other confounding processes.

4. Moving beyond the contrastive analysis: Recent experimental developments

If the contrastive analysis is not appropriate for bringing the study of consciousness forward, then new experimental paradigms have to be developed. Obviously, there are no simple solutions for this methodological impasse – otherwise those experiments would have already been conducted. Some key experimental ideas to partially solve the problem have been mentioned in the following articles: Aru, Bachmann et al. (2012); de Graaf et al. (2012); de Graaf & Sack (this volume); van Boxtel & Tsuchiya (this volume). Here we will briefly review some more recent experimental advances.

4.1 Distilling NCC-pr from NCC

In principle one would like to experimentally manipulate exclusively the NCC-pr or NCC-co while keeping the NCC untouched; or modulate the NCC while holding the NCC-co and NCC-pr invariant. This selective manipulation might be achieved if we know for instance the different NCC-pr processes leading to a similar NCC. If one assumes that the neural underpinnings of different precursors differ (e.g., attention and top-down predictions appear to affect neural activity in opposing ways; Summerfield & Egner, 2009), then an NCC would correspond to neural processes that invariably appear as the difference between trials with and without conscious perception while different NCC-prs are manipulated. There are a plethora of different NCC-pr processes that could be used to distill NCC-prs from the subsequent processes: one could manipulate sensory evidence, attention, prior knowledge, expectations, or working memory load. On the interventional side, one could even use TMS to enhance or suppress perception (see Aru, Bachmann, et al., 2012, for a longer description and citations). Thus, at least in principle, the NCC-prs could be disentangled from the NCC over the following years. Some informative experiments have already been conducted.

For example, Melloni and colleagues (2011) used either bottom-up sensory information or a combination of bottom-up sensory and top-down expectation-related information (two different types of NCC-pr) to manipulate conscious perception (NCC). They found that, at threshold, both manipulations of NCC-prs modulate the P200 component with more visibility associated with stronger relative negativity. Thus, processes around P200 could reflect the NCC and be different from NCC-pr. In contrast, the early P1 component, which previously has been related to conscious perception (Pins & ffytche, 2003), differed between trials with and without conscious perception only when bottom-up sensory evidence was varied, but not when the combination of bottom-up sensory and top-down expectations were used, demonstrating that the P1 component most likely reflects the NCC-pr. Comparable results were obtained by Pitts and colleagues in an inattentional blindness task (Pitts et al., 2012). Here, the researchers presented diverse visual contour patterns while either diverting attention from the task or asking participants to perform a task on the visual patterns. When subjects were first exposed to the patterns, half of the population failed to notice that different shapes were centrally presented, thus exhibiting inattentional blindness. However, once they were made aware of the presence of the shapes, they easily detected them in a second phase. Importantly, it was found that the initial portion of processing, in this case an event-related potential (ERP) component present around 100 ms (Nd1), was of similar amplitude in all three conditions, i.e., when subjects were unaware of the patterns, when they were aware of the shapes but they were task irrelevant, as well as when shapes were task relevant and subjects were aware of them. The authors conclude that this initial portion of processing reflects unconscious processes indexing contour integration. In contrast, a later component around 200 ms (Nd2) was present only when subjects were aware of the visual shapes, but regardless of whether the shapes were task relevant or irrelevant. Thus, it is likely that this component is indexing neural processes specifically related to conscious perception. By manipulating attention and task relevance in the same type of tasks, researchers could establish which neural processes are likely to reflect unconscious antecedents or consequences, while at the same time shedding light on neural activity that likely reflect the NCC.

The logic could also be turned around: one could measure a potential NCC candidate process and use several NCC-prs to see whether the potential NCC candidate is found despite the different NCC-prs that are tested. This would be expected if the process is an NCC. If, however, the NCC candidate is only modulated by particular NCC-prs, it might be more related to the particular NCC-pr than the NCC. Such a strategy was employed in the experiment of Aru, Axmacher et al. (2012), in which conscious perception was modulated either by sensory evidence or by prior knowledge. In that experiment, it was investigated whether local category specific gamma band response (GBR) constitutes a neural correlate of conscious perception (Fisch et al., 2009). In previous research Fisch and colleagues (2009) observed that when subjects consciously perceived a stimulus (i.e., a face), a strong gamma band response was observed on the intracranial electrodes placed on the cortical areas selective to faces. However, in the framework differentiating NCC-pr, NCC and NCC-co it could be that this activity enhancement in the GBR reflects stronger NCC-pr processes, which leads to conscious perception. Thus, local category specific GBR could be a process preceding conscious perception without reflecting the process that would directly contribute the very mechanism of the currently experienced percept. To directly test this idea, conscious perception was manipulated in two different ways. Either the amount of sensory evidence was changed, which directly modulates local processing, or prior knowledge was provided, which is a factor less dependent on local processing. As both factors enhanced conscious perception to the same extent behaviorally, a clear prediction was that if category-specific GBRs reflect NCC, they should be similarly modulated both by sensory evidence and previous exposure. In contrast, our results showed that local category-specific GBR are only modulated by sensory evidence. Although previous exposure of the pictures also enhanced conscious perception as measured behaviorally, local category-specific GBR were not modulated by previous exposure. The fact that local GBR were only affected by sensory evidence, although conscious perception was enhanced by both factors, leads to the conclusion that local GBR cannot be reflecting the NCC. Most likely the local GBR are related to local sensory processing, which explains why in previous research local GBR was identified as a potential NCC (Fisch et al., 2009): if in a given trial for some reason sensory processing is more effective, the outcome will more likely be consciously perceived. Thus, in a paradigm that relies only on bottom-up information a correlation is established between more effective sensory processing and conscious perception. In such paradigms one cannot know whether the neural process that is different between trials with and without conscious perception of the target is indeed a correlate of consciousness or only a correlate of sensory processing. To rule that out, manipulations similar to that of Aru, Axmacher et al. (2012) or others that orthogonally manipulate the precursors of consciousness need to be used.

In general, the NCC-prs should not be regarded as nuisance processes that hinder us from unraveling the NCC. Rather, acknowledging that some processes are NCC-prs and studying them with this in mind can help us to understand the mechanisms of conscious perception. If there are certain prerequisites for conscious perception to happen, this has direct implications for the mechanisms of consciousness. For example in the neuronal global workspace theory (Dehaene & Changeux, 2011) attention is a critical prerequisite for conscious perception (Dehaene, Changeux, Naccache, Sackur, & Sergent, 2006), as it plays a pivotal role in amplifying the responses in sensory cortex so that those representations get integrated with the global workspace (Dehaene et al., 2006). Apart from attention, several other processes can determine if and how a stimulus is consciously perceived, without, however, being sufficient for generating conscious experience by themselves. In a recent study, Schwiedrzik et al. (2014) found that two such processes are independently active in a paradigm involving intermittent presentation of multistable stimuli. When multistable stimuli such as the Necker cube are presented with brief interruptions, the interpretation that is consciously perceived can either be stabilized (hence, it is perceived again after the interruption), or destabilized (hence, a different interpretation is perceived after the interruption). While the former effect (which is also known as hysteresis) was found to depend on activity in a widespread network of higher visual, parietal, and frontal brain areas, the latter effect (which is known as perceptual adaptation) was due to activity in early visual cortex. In the context of the contrastive method, which interpretation is perceived could then depend on the relative contribution of either of the processes, and even two identical percepts could be brought about by two different mechanisms. However, a contrast between conditions (e.g., a particular interpretation in consciousness vs. not in consciousness) may reveal differential states of stabilization or destabilization instead of the neural processes sufficient for generating conscious experience.

4.2 Distilling NCC from NCC-co

There might also be a variety of NCC-co processes. One example of NCC-co is working memory: items experienced consciously can be passed into working memory. The problem is that for some researchers this step from perception to global broadcasting (e.g., in working memory) *is* access to conscious perception (Baars, 1997; Dehaene & Changeux, 2011). However, the index of this global broadcasting is claimed to be the P300 (Dehaene & Changeux, 2011), which has been shown not to correlate with conscious experience if the working memory representation of that particular target has been previously established (Koivisto & Revonsuo, 2008; Melloni et al., 2011). This particular finding has been taken as an indication that the P300 does not always reflect the NCC but under certain conditions rather the NCC-co (Aru, Bachmann, et al., 2012). This logic also provides the general blueprint for separating NCC from NCC-pr or NCC-co: if a neural process is different between trials with and without conscious perception but can be abolished with some experimental manipulations without a detrimental effect on conscious perception, this neural process is a NCC-pr or NCC-co.

Converging results were obtained by Pitts and colleagues (Pitts, Padwal, Fennely, Martinez, & Hillyard, 2014) when contrasting conditions in which stimuli where either task relevant or irrelevant. Specifically, the authors investigated whether late activity may index NCC or further processing related to the task. Interestingly, they observed that the P300 was present only when the stimuli were relevant for the task. Importantly, subjects were always aware of the stimuli. This led the authors to conclude that late wave of activation may just reflect further processing, relevant for the task at hand, but does not have any bearing on neural processes related to consciousness. The same group of authors recently confirmed these findings in a masking study (Pitts, Metzler, & Hillyard, 2014). Again, P300 was a reliable marker of conscious perception only when the stimuli were task relevant. Altogether, current studies that have manipulated the NCC-co suggest that a late wave of activation may not necessarily index conscious processing. One important caveat is that the neural signatures related to consciousness may not have a fixed latency, but may in turn change depending on how consciousness comes about (Melloni et al., 2011). Thus, a further challenge for future research would be to characterize the timing of the NCC, which in turn would shed light on whether the late wave of activation may reflect an NCC or mostly reflects post-perceptual processing.

5. Moving beyond the contrastive analysis: The general approach

Although we ourselves have successfully implemented some of the new experimental paradigms as explained above, we feel that many more experiments are needed and more stringent criteria are required to isolate the NCC from prerequisites and consequences. In our view, the general approach to distill the NCC should be the following: we should exploit the whole range of the phenomenal experience. In most experiments, conditions are created by separating trials with and without conscious perception. Yet, conscious experience is much richer than this often simplified dichotomy, for instance: (1) across trials, the perceptual quality of a simple stimulus varies gradually (Seth, Dienes, Cleeremans, Overgaard, & Pessoa, 2008); (2) within a given trial, the quality of subjective perception changes over time, a process termed microgenesis

(Bachmann, 2000); (3) if more complex stimuli are used, the perceived contents and their attributes might vary across trials and/or subjects, which also leads to the complex problem of subjective criterion contents in reporting what was perceived by the subject (e.g., Bachmann & Francis, 2014); (4) with learning, conscious perception of stimuli changes over time. We will explain and illustrate some of these points and the respective experimental approaches over the next paragraphs.

One interesting possibility is to exploit the fine-grained information inherent in subjective perception to identify those neural processes whose changes go hand-in-hand with these fine-grained variations of conscious experience. We assume that there exists a tight mapping between nuanced changes of NCC and according nuanced variations in conscious experience (Haynes, 2009). The key idea for distilling the NCC is that while these processes that correspond to NCC should vary according to subjective perception, the confounding prerequisites for and the consequences of conscious experience do not necessarily change in this manner. For example, while conscious experience is a bit clearer when target contrast is increased, the subsequent representation in working memory (NCC-co) might be similar in both cases (Melloni et al., 2011). It is possible that some of the prerequisites and consequences indeed covary with conscious perception even in such experimental paradigms, but it is clear that neural signatures that vary hand-in-hand with nuances in conscious perception are more likely to be related to conscious experience than those that are revealed by comparing trials with and without conscious perception. While this strategy will help to distill out NCC-pr and NCC-co that are only loosely correlated with consciousness (see Miller, this volume), it will be insufficient to disentangle those NCC-pr and NCC-co that go hand-in-hand with the changing NCC. It is still an open question what those tightly correlated NCC-pr and NCC-co will be – in case they exist at all – and whether they should ultimately be considered as a part of the mechanisms underlying consciousness.

5.1 Exploiting the gradual variation of the quality of subjective experience

The gradual variation approach for studying the NCC has been implemented in paradigms with masking and hysteresis (Del Cul et al., 2007; Melloni et al., 2011) where visibility of the item was varied gradually, the subjects gave reports about their subjective perception and the researchers asked which components of the ERPs changed accordingly. In both cases visibility of the items was manipulated objectively either by contrast (Melloni et al., 2011) or by changing the stimulus onset asynchrony (SOA) (Del Cul et al., 2007). Thus, changing neural responses could potentially also have been caused by changes in objective stimulation conditions. The trick used by these research groups was the following: whereas the objective change (contrast or SOA) was linear, the subjective change was sigmoidal (Del Cul et al., 2007; Melloni et al., 2011). This fact allowed the researchers to tease apart those neural responses that varied linearly as a function of objective stimulation from those that varied in sigmoidal fashion as a function of subjective conscious experience. In addition, to directly manipulate visibility, as done in the above mentioned studies, researchers can also take advantage of the known fact that subjective experience varies even under invariant stimulation conditions (Bar et al., 2001; Aru & Bachmann, 2009a, 2009b; Auksztulewicz & Blankenburg, 2013). Furthermore, in the above cited studies the mean neural activity over trials was fitted to the mean visibility ratings over trials. A complementary approach could be to use the inherent variability across trials, observed even under invariant stimulation conditions, to track down the corresponding neural processes underlying this variability on the single trial basis (Rousselet & Pernet, 2011). Also, researchers could use any psychometric function that tracks visibility and correlate those to neurometric functions. For instance, in the study of Melloni et al. (2011) and Del Cul et al. (2007) sigmoidal increases of visibility were used. However, visibility ratings could also take different shapes like the U-shape of typical metacontrast masking (Bachmann, 2000). Thus, any function reflecting subjective visibility could be correlated with changes in neural dynamics (Haynes, Driver, & Rees, 2005).[1] Finally, in the cited studies (Del Cul et al., 2007; Melloni et al., 2011) the ERPs were used as the neural measures, however the general idea of looking for neural processes that track psychological process could well be expanded to analysis of spectral perturbations, phase synchrony, causality and other measures (Gaillard et al., 2009; Melloni et al., 2007) and done with other measurement technologies such as functional magnetic resonance imaging (fMRI) (Christensen, Ramsøy, Lund, Madsen, & Rowe, 2006; Haynes et al., 2005).

Let us have a look at some first results that the above mentioned studies have produced to illustrate some of the issues that arise when such experimental paradigms are used. Del Cul et al. (2007) manipulated the SOA between the target stimulus and the mask stimulus, obtained a sigmoidal function of visibility depending on the SOA and observed that the P300 component of the ERP mimicked the gradual changes of the visibility function. However, in an interesting twist to the story, Melloni and colleagues (2011) demonstrated that the P300 component could reflect a consequence of conscious perception – when the working memory representation of the target was already available, the P300 component did not follow the gradual changes of the visibility function. But if Del Cul and colleagues (2007) observed that P300 changes according to the visibility function while Melloni and colleagues (2011) suggest that P300 represents a consequence of conscious perception, does this imply that the consequences of consciousness are also gradual? This would mean that observing gradual changes of neural measures that follow the changes in subjective perception would not be helpful in disentangling the NCC from their consequences. A closer look explains

1. An important caveat must be mentioned here: metacontrast results as measured objectively or with generalized subjective scales like 'clarity' or 'confidence' may be invariant in the conditions where subjective criterion contents (cf. Kahneman, 1968) still are variable (Jannati & Di Lollo, 2012). Thus, criterion contents become another variable necessary to juxtapose with different NCCs in brain imaging.

Miyawaki, & Kamitani, 2013). In this elegant study, the authors trained a classifier using multivoxel activity patterns of the visual cortex as input to decode different visual stimuli that were presented during wakefulness. Then, while the subjects were asleep the classifier was used to decode and unlock the content of the dreams. Being able to decode subjective contents of conscious experience from the visual cortex suggests that the neural correlates of visual conscious experience could be found in the visual cortex. In general, studying the neural basis of complex conscious experience that is different or independent from the physical stimulation can be a way for closing in on the NCCs.

5.3 Changing conscious perception with learning

Another strategy to probe for the NCC independently of their prerequisites and consequences is to manipulate conscious perception gradually through perceptual learning. It has been demonstrated that blindsight patients can learn to perceive stimuli that were previously unconscious (Sahraie et al., 2006). Moreover, healthy subjects can learn to subjectively see stimuli even when their objective performance was initially at chance (Schwiedrzik et al., 2009). In this experimental paradigm, subjective perception is measured alongside objective performance and one can show that both objective performance and conscious perception of the initially unperceived stimuli improve gradually over days. The NCC should change accordingly, whereas the prerequisites for and the consequences of conscious perception are unlikely to change in the same fashion as subjective perception. In fact, some researchers have argued that one typical confounding factor in the study of consciousness is differences in performance across conditions: seen vs. unseen conditions (Lau, 2008). We have recently exploited such a paradigm to investigate whether performance and subjective visibility arise from the same brain areas. Interestingly, we observed a double dissociation. Across time, both learning effects do not follow the same temporal profile. In particular, only during an early stage of learning did we observe above chance performance on subjectively invisible trials, a form of blindsight-like behavior. However as training progressed, this pattern disappeared and higher performance was always observed for subjectively visible trials. In addition, the brain areas reflecting improvements in subjective visibility and objective performance also differed. While objective performance was mostly localized to early visual areas, subjective visibility appeared to be localized to areas with larger receptive fields as observed in the temporal cortex (Aedo-Jury, Schwiedrzik, Singer, & Melloni, 2010; Schwiedrzik et al., 2011). Thus, in the context of this paradigm we could clearly establish that objective performance and subjective visibility do not track the same phenomena, but instead are implemented by different neural populations. This further emphasizes the need to control for differences in performance when studying the neural correlates of conscious perception (Lau, 2008). In addition, it was observed that while increases in subjective visibility were reflected in early changes in the ERP, increases in performance were reflected by the late ERP, P300 (Schwiedrzik, Jacob,

Singer, & Melloni, 2012). Thus, different learning curves can be used to track those processes that relate closely to subjective visibility, while controlling for confounding processes, such as the consequences, tracked by for instance, changes in performance.

6. Targeting the proposed mechanisms of consciousness

We have argued that the contrast between trials with and without conscious perception has to be refined as in its present format it is not specific for the NCC but may also bring along processes that precede or follow the NCC. As the majority of findings about conscious perception have been obtained with this methodology, many of the previous findings might not reflect the NCC. We have previously suggested that in light of this problem the literature on the correlates of conscious perception has to be re-evaluated. However, a potentially more fruitful approach would be to target the theories and the proposed mechanisms of consciousness that are based on the previous findings rather than all the previous findings themselves.

Many theories of consciousness exist (e.g., Rose, 2006). All the theories that make some claims about the neural basis of consciousness are to some extent based on research on the neural correlates of consciousness. Hence, if the research has flaws such as those mentioned above, some theories might also erroneously claim a mechanism to correspond to conscious perception, although in reality it corresponds rather to the prerequisites for or consequences of conscious perception. The new experimental paradigms designed to distill the NCC should be aimed at these key mechanisms that various theories consider to account for conscious perception. For example, the neuronal global workspace theory (Dehaene & Naccache, 2001) proposes that the mechanism of conscious perception is the late wave of neural activity in the parietal and prefrontal workspace neurons. In particular, in a recent review (Dehaene & Changeux, 2011) the authors list six experimental measures of conscious perception that support their theory: "(1) sudden, all-or-none ignition of fronto-parietal networks; (2) concomitant all-or-none amplification of sensory activation; (3) a late global P3b wave in event-related potentials; (4) late amplification of broad-band power in the gamma range; (5) enhanced long-distance phase synchronization, particularly in the beta range; and (6) enhanced causal relations between distant areas, including a significant top-down component" (p. 219). Interestingly, the first experimental paradigms directly aimed at distilling the NCC have already cast doubt about the relationship between conscious perception and items (3) and (4) on this list (Melloni et al., 2011; Pitts, Metzler, & Hillyard, 2014; and Pitts, Padwal, et al., 2014, about item (3); Aru, Axmacher, et al., 2012, and Pitts, Padwal, et al., 2014, about item (4)). We are looking forward to future experimental paradigms and experiments that target the other items on this list. For instance, item (5) is also tightly related to the idea that long-range synchrony is the key correlate of conscious perception (Melloni & Singer, 2010) and item (6) can be related to the theory that feedback information sent from higher to lower cortical areas is crucial for conscious experience (Lamme, 2006; Klink, Self, Lamme & Roelfsema, this volume). Thus by targeting these mechanisms with new experiments, the landscape of the theories of consciousness can be cropped significantly. In general, we feel that more attention should be given to *mechanisms* of conscious perception rather than to the mere *correlates* of it.

7. Conclusion

For the past two decades the main experimental strategy in consciousness research has been to compare the neural signatures of trials with and without conscious perception. However, it has been acknowledged that this experimental contrast does not only reveal the NCC but also processes that precede them as prerequisites and follow them as consequences, highlighting the need for new experimental approaches aimed at distilling the neural processes that underlie conscious perception.

Here we reviewed some of the first studies that have tried to experimentally disentangle the NCC from their prerequisites and consequences. A fruitful avenue to explore in future studies is to focus more on the fine-grained variations in the visibility or the contents of experimental stimuli, as the neural processes that co-vary with such slight changes in conscious experience will be more closely related to the NCC than any outcome of the traditional contrastive analysis. We have also argued that as the theories of consciousness are based on the comparison between trials with and without conscious perception, these theories have to be re-evaluated. It would be helpful if studies over the next years would try to apply new experimental paradigms to target those mechanisms of conscious perception that have been proposed by various theories. We would not be surprised if several such mechanisms turn out to be associated with the prerequisites for or consequences of conscious perception rather than actual neural mechanisms of conscious experience. These are interesting times for consciousness research!

References

Aedo-Jury, F., Schwiedrzik, C.M., Singer, W., & Melloni, L. (2010, November). *Differential brain activation for increases in objective performance and subjective awareness in perceptual learning*. Paper presented at the *40th Annual Meeting of the Society for Neuroscience (SfN)*, San Diego, USA.

Aru, J., Axmacher, N., Do Lam, A.T.A., Fell, J., Elger, C.E., Singer, W., & Melloni, L. (2012). Local category-specific gamma band responses in the visual cortex do not reflect conscious perception. *Journal of Neuroscience*, 32(43), 14909–14914. DOI: 10.1523/JNEUROSCI.2051-12.2012

Aru, J., & Bachmann, T. (2009a). Boosting up gamma-band oscillations leaves target-stimulus in masking out of awareness: Explaining an apparent paradox. *Neuroscience Letters*, 450(3), 351–355. DOI: 10.1016/j.neulet. 2008.11.063

Aru, J., & Bachmann, T. (2009b). Occipital EEG correlates of conscious awareness when subjective target shine-through and effective visual masking are compared: Bifocal early increase in gamma power and speed-up of P1. *Brain Research*, 1271, 60–73. DOI: 10.1016/j.brainres.2008.12.085

Aru, J., Bachmann, T., Singer, W., & Melloni, L. (2012). Distilling the neural correlates of consciousness. *Neuroscience & Biobehavioral Reviews*, 36(2), 737–746. DOI: 10.1016/j.neubiorev.2011.12.003

Auksztulewicz, R., & Blankenburg, F. (2013). Subjective rating of weak tactile stimuli is parametrically encoded in event-related potentials. *Journal of Neuroscience*, 33(29), 11878–11887. DOI: 10.1523/JNEUROSCI.4243-12.2013

Baars, B. J. (1997). *In the theatre of consciousness: The workspace of the mind*. New York: Oxford University Press. DOI: 10.1093/acprof:oso/9780195102659.001.1

Bachmann, T. (2000). *Microgenetic approach to the conscious mind*. Advances in Consciousness Research (Vol. 25). Amsterdam, The Netherlands: John Benjamins Publishing Company. DOI: 10.1075/aicr.25

Bachmann, T. (2009). Finding ERP-signatures of target awareness: Puzzle persists because of experimental co-variation of the objective and subjective variables. *Consciousness and Cognition*, 18(3), 804–808. DOI: 10.1016/j.concog.2009.02.011

Bachmann, T., Breitmeyer, B. G., & Öğmen, H. (2011). *Experimental phenomena of consciousness: A brief dictionary* (Rev. ed.). New York: Oxford University Press.

Bachmann, T., & Francis, G. (2014). *Visual masking: Studying perception, attention, and consciousness*. Oxford, UK: Academic Press.

Bar, M., Tootell, R. B. H., Schacter, D. L., Greve, D. N., Fischl, B., Mendola, J. D., Rosen, B. R., & Dale, A. M. (2001). Cortical mechanisms specific to explicit visual object recognition. *Neuron*, 29(2), 529–535. DOI: 10.1016/S0896-6273(01)00224-0

Brown, J. W. (1988). *The life of the mind: Selected papers*. Hillsdale, NJ: Lawrence Erlbaum Associates.

Christensen, M. S., Ramsøy, T. Z., Lund, T. E., Madsen, K. H., & Rowe, J. B. (2006). An fMRI study of the neural correlates of graded visual perception. *Neuroimage*, 31(4), 1711–1725. DOI: 10.1016/j.neuroimage.2006.02.023

Crick, F., & Koch, C. (1990). Towards a neurobiological theory of consciousness. *Seminars in the Neurosciences*, 2, 263–275. DOI: 10.1016/B978-0-12-185254-2.50021-8

Davidesco, I., Zion-Golumbic, E., Bickel, S., Harel, M., Groppe, D. M., Keller, C. J., Schevon, C. A., McKhann, G. M., Goodman, R. R., Goelman, G., Schroeder, C. E., Mehta, A. D., & Malach, R. (2014). Exemplar selectivity reflects perceptual similarities in the human fusiform cortex. *Cerebral Cortex*, 24(7), 1879–1893. DOI: 10.1093/cercor/bht038

de Graaf, T. A., Hsieh, P.-J., & Sack, A. T. (2012). The 'correlates' in neural correlates of consciousness. *Neuroscience & Biobehavioral Reviews*, 36(1), 191–197. DOI: 10.1016/j.neubiorev.2011.05.012

Dehaene, S., & Changeux, J.-P. (2011). Experimental and theoretical approaches to conscious processing. *Neuron*, 70(2), 200–227. DOI: 10.1016/j.neuron.2011.03.018

Dehaene, S., Changeux, J.-P., Naccache, L., Sackur, J., & Sergent, C. (2006). Conscious, preconscious, and subliminal processing: A testable taxonomy. *Trends in Cognitive Sciences*, 10(5), 204–211. DOI: 10.1016/j.tics.2006.03.007

Dehaene, S., & Naccache, L. (2001). Towards a cognitive neuroscience of consciousness: Basic evidence and a workspace framework. *Cognition*, 79(1–2), 1–37. DOI: 10.1016/S0010-0277(00)00123-2

Del Cul, A., Baillet, S., & Dehaene, S. (2007). Brain dynamics underlying the nonlinear threshold for access to consciousness. *PLoS Biology*, 5(10), e260. DOI: 10.1371/journal.pbio.0050260

Field, G. D., Sampath, A. P., & Rieke, F. (2005). Retinal processing near absolute threshold: From behavior to mechanism. *Annual Review of Physiology*, 67, 491–514. DOI: 10.1146/annurev.physiol.67.031103.151256

Fisch, L., Privman, E., Ramot, M., Harel, M., Nir, Y., Kipervasser, S., Andelman, F., Neufeld, M. Y., Kramer, U., Fried, I., & Malach, R. (2009). Neural "ignition": Enhanced activation linked to perceptual awareness in human ventral stream visual cortex. *Neuron*, 64(4), 562–574. DOI: 10.1016/j.neuron.2009.11.001

Gaillard, R., Dehaene, S., Adam, C., Clémenceau, S., Hasboun, D., Baulac, M., Cohen, L., & Nacchache, L. (2009). Converging intracranial markers of conscious access. *PLoS Biology*, 7(3), e61. DOI: 10.1371/journal.pbio.1000061

Haushofer, J., Livingstone, M. S., & Kanwisher, N. (2008). Multivariate patterns in object-selective cortex dissociate perceptual and physical shape similarity. *PLoS Biology*, 6(7), e187. DOI: 10.1371/journal.pbio.0060187

Haynes, J.-D. (2009). Decoding visual consciousness from human brain signals. *Trends in Cognitive Sciences*, 13(5), 194–202. DOI: 10.1016/j.tics.2009.02.004

Haynes, J.-D., Driver, J., & Rees, G. (2005). Visibility reflects dynamic changes of effective connectivity between V1 and fusiform cortex. *Neuron*, 46(5), 811–821. DOI: 10.1016/j.neuron.2005.05.012

Horikawa, T., Tamaki, M., Miyawaki, Y., & Kamitani, Y. (2013). Neural decoding of visual imagery during sleep. *Science*, 340(6132), 639–642. DOI: 10.1126/science.1234330

Jannati, A., & Di Lollo, V. (2012). Relative blindsight arises from a criterion confound in metacontrast masking: Implications for theories of consciousness. *Consciousness and Cognition*, 21(1), 307–314. DOI: 10.1016/j.concog.2011.10.003

Kahneman, D. (1968). Method, findings, and theory in studies of visual masking. *Psychological Bulletin*, 70(6), 404–425. DOI: 10.1037/h0026731

Kammer, T. (1999). Phosphenes and transient scotomas induced by magnetic stimulation of the occipital lobe: Their topographic relationship. *Neuropsychologia*, 37(2), 191–198. DOI: 10.1016/S0028-3932(98)00093-1

Koch, C. (2004). *The quest for consciousness: A neurobiological approach*. Englewood, CO: Roberts & Company.

Koivisto, M., & Revonsuo, A. (2008). Comparison of event-related potentials in attentional blink and repetition blindness. *Brain Research*, 1189, 115–126. DOI: 10.1016/j.brainres.2007.10.082

Koivisto, M., & Revonsuo, A. (2010). Event-related brain potential correlates of visual awareness. *Neuroscience & Biobehavioral Reviews*, 34(6), 922–934. DOI: 10.1016/j.neubiorev.2009.12.002

Lamme, V. A. F. (2006). Towards a true neural stance on consciousness. *Trends in Cognitive Sciences*, 10(11), 494–501. DOI: 10.1016/j.tics.2006.09.001

Lamy, D., Salti, M., & Bar-Haim, Y. (2009). Neural correlates of subjective awareness and unconscious processing: An ERP study. *Journal of Cognitive Neuroscience*, 21(7), 1435–1446. DOI: 10.1162/jocn.2009.21064

Lau, H.C. (2008). A higher order Bayesian decision theory of consciousness. *Progress in Brain Research*, 168, 35–48. DOI: 10.1016/S0079-6123(07)68004-2

Malach, R. (2007). The measurement problem in consciousness research. *Behavioral and Brain Sciences*, 30(5–6), 516–517. DOI: 10.1017/S0140525X0700297X

Melloni, L., Molina, C., Pena, M., Torres, D., Singer, W., & Rodriguez, E. (2007). Synchronization of neural activity across cortical areas correlates with conscious perception. *Journal of Neuroscience*, 27(11), 2858–2865. DOI: 10.1523/JNEUROSCI.4623-06.2007

Melloni, L., Schwiedrzik, C.M., Müller, N., Rodriguez, E., & Singer, W. (2011). Expectations change the signatures and timing of electrophysiological correlates of perceptual awareness. *Journal of Neuroscience*, 31(4), 1386–1396. DOI: 10.1523/JNEUROSCI.4570-10.2011

Melloni, L., & Singer, W. (2010). Distinct characteristics of conscious experience are met by large-scale neuronal synchronization. In E.K. Perry, D. Collerton, F.E.N. LeBeau, & H. Ashton (Eds.), *New horizons in the neuroscience of consciousness* (pp. 17–28). Advances in Consciousness Research (Vol. 79). Amsterdam, The Netherlands: John Benjamins Publishing Company. DOI: 10.1075/aicr.79.06mel

Miller, S.M. (2001). Binocular rivalry and the cerebral hemispheres: With a note on the correlates and constitution of visual consciousness. *Brain and Mind*, 2(1), 119–149. DOI: 10.1023/A:1017981619014

Miller, S.M. (2007). On the correlation/constitution distinction problem (and other hard problems) in the scientific study of consciousness. *Acta Neuropsychiatrica*, 19(3), 159–176. DOI: 10.1111/j.1601-5215.2007.00207.x

Mur, M., Meys, M., Bodurka, J., Goebel, R., Bandettini, P.A., & Kriegeskorte, N. (2013). Human object-similarity judgments reflect and transcend the primate-IT object representation. *Frontiers in Psychology*, 4, 128. DOI: 10.3389/fpsyg.2013.00128

Pascual-Leone, A., & Walsh, V. (2001). Fast backprojections from the motion to the primary visual area necessary for visual awareness. *Science*, 292(5516), 510–512. DOI: 10.1126/science.1057099

Pins, D., & ffytche, D. (2003). The neural correlates of conscious vision. *Cerebral Cortex*, 13(5), 461–474. DOI: 10.1093/cercor/13.5.461

Pitts, M.A., Martínez, A., & Hillyard, S.A. (2012). Visual processing of contour patterns under conditions of inattentional blindness. *Journal of Cognitive Neuroscience*, 24(2), 287–303. DOI: 10.1162/jocn_a_00111

Pitts, M.A., Metzler, S., & Hillyard, S. (2014). Isolating neural correlates of conscious perception from neural correlates of reporting one's perception. *Frontiers in Psychology*, 5, 1078. DOI: 10.3389/fpsyg.2014.01078

Pitts, M.A., Padwal, J., Fennelly, D., Martínez, A., & Hillyard, S.A. (2014). Gamma band activity and the P3 reflect post-perceptual processes, not visual awareness. *Neuroimage*, 101, 337–350. DOI: 10.1016/j.neuroimage.2014.07.024

Postle, B.R. (2009). The hippocampus, memory, and consciousness. In S. Laureys & G. Tononi (Eds.), *The neurology of consciousness: Cogntive neuroscience and neuropathology* (pp. 326–338). Oxford, UK: Elsevier Ltd. DOI: 10.1016/B978-0-12-374168-4.00024-1

Quiroga, R.Q., Mukamel, R., Isham, E.A., Malach, R., & Fried, I. (2008). Human single-neuron responses at the threshold of conscious recognition. *Proceedings of the National Academy of Sciences USA*, 105(9), 3599–3604. DOI: 10.1073/pnas.0707043105

Rees, G., Kreiman, G., & Koch, C. (2002). Neural correlates of consciousness in humans. *Nature Reviews Neuroscience*, 3(4), 261–270. DOI: 10.1038/nrn783

Revonsuo, A. (2000). Prospects for a scientific research program on consciousness. In T. Metzinger (Ed.), *Neural correlates of consciousness: Empirical and conceptual questions* (pp. 57–75). Cambridge, MA: MIT Press.

Revonsuo, A. (2001). Can functional brain imaging discover consciousness in the brain? *Journal of Consciousness Studies*, 8(3), 3–23.

Rose, D. (2006). *Consciousness: Philosophical, psychological, and neural theories*. Oxford, UK: Oxford University Press.

Rousselet, G. A., & Pernet, C. R. (2011). Quantifying the time course of visual object processing using ERPs: It's time to up the game. *Frontiers in Psychology*, 2, 107. DOI: 10.3389/fpsyg.2011.00107

Sahraie, A., Trevethan, C. T., MacLeod, M. J., Murray, A. D., Olson, J. A., & Weiskrantz, L. (2006). Increased sensitivity after repeated stimulation of residual spatial channels in blindsight. *Proceedings of the National Academy of Sciences USA*, 103(40), 14971–14976. DOI: 10.1073/pnas.0607073103

Schwiedrzik, C. M., Jacob, P., Singer, W., & Melloni, L. (2012, October). *Perceptual learning effects on sensitivity and subjective awareness rely on different neural systems*. Paper presented at the *42nd Annual Meeting of the Society for Neuroscience (SfN)*, New Orleans, USA.

Schwiedrzik, C. M., Ruff, C. C., Lazar, A., Leitner, F. C., Singer, W., & Melloni, L. (2014). Untangling perceptual memory: Hysteresis and adaptation map into separate cortical networks. *Cerebral Cortex*, 24(5), 1152–1164. DOI: 10.1093/cercor/bhs396

Schwiedrzik, C. M., Singer, W., & Melloni, L. (2009). Sensitivity and perceptual awareness increase with practice in metacontrast masking. *Journal of Vision*, 9(10), 18. DOI: 10.1167/9.10.18

Schwiedrzik, C. M., Singer, W., & Melloni, L. (2011). Subjective and objective learning effects dissociate in space and in time. *Proceedings of the National Academy of Sciences USA*, 108(11), 4506–4511. DOI: 10.1073/pnas.1009147108

Seth, A. K. (2009). Functions of consciousness. In W. P. Banks (Ed.), *Encyclopedia of consciousness*, Vol. 1 (pp. 279–293). Oxford, UK: Academic Press. DOI: 10.1016/B978-012373873-8.00033-5

Seth, A. K., Dienes, Z., Cleeremans, A., Overgaard, M., & Pessoa, L. (2008). Measuring consciousness: Relating behavioural and neurophysiological approaches. *Trends in Cognitive Sciences*, 12(8), 314–321. DOI: 10.1016/j.tics.2008.04.008

Summerfield, C., & Egner, T. (2009). Expectation (and attention) in visual cognition. *Trends in Cognitive Sciences*, 13(9), 403–409. DOI: 10.1016/j.tics.2009.06.003

Zeki, S. (2001). Localization and globalization in conscious vision. *Annual Review of Neuroscience*, 24, 57–86. DOI: 10.1146/annurev.neuro.24.1.57

The neuroevolutionary sources of mind

The ancestral constitution of affective consciousness and the core-SELF

Jaak Panksepp
Washington State University, Pullman

The bipolar affective structures of brain emotional processes – namely negative and positive affects – provide ideal ways to make scientific progress on the "hard problem" of primal consciousness: wherever in subcortical brain regions one applies highly localized electrical deep brain stimulation, and obtains coherent emotional behaviors, animals treat these brain arousals as 'rewards' and 'punishments' using various simple learning tasks. Humans also consistently report experienced affective changes during such artificial brain arousals. Such evidence suggests the first glimmers of consciousness in BrainMind evolution arose in medial brainstem regions. These hedonic effects, of subcortical origin, are here deemed gold standards for the existence of evolved affective qualia in animal and human brains, perhaps the first evolutionary substrates of mind, critical for the emergence of cognitive consciousness.

Introduction

This analysis of primal affective consciousness will be shared in three major parts: The *prelude* will lay out the strategy for understanding the constitution of primal emotional-affective experiences of mammalian brains. The *interlude* will briefly discuss some key terminological issues and why such a straightforward strategy for scientifically studying the evolutionary foundations of mind has not received the attention it deserves by either neuroscientists or psychologists. The *postlude* lays out the affective neuroscience strategy in greater detail, and highlights ways to translate findings from our fellow animals to the human species, and how this continuity of mind among mammals could be empirically strengthened or negated. I conclude with a *denouement* that speculates how cognitive information-based consciousness, exemplified by our experiences of colors, may have grown through higher neural elaborations based on the earlier affective substrates.

DOI 10.1075/aicr.92.09pan

There will be repetition of themes among sections, as in a fugue, or any worthy orchestral score. In a sense, this is how emotions work in the brain, repeated cascades of feelings, self-similar affectively but different cognitively, throughout each lifetime. Thus, like life itself, each section is written amplifying and deepening various themes that have appeared or will appear in other sections, with hopefully some added understanding and appreciation of these radical, but evidence based, arguments. Still, all are written so that they can be independently read, with the same story line converging from different vantages.

I will not dwell at any length on the distinction between the correlates and the constitution of consciousness (well discussed elsewhere; Miller, 2001, 2007, this volume; Revonsuo, 2000, this volume). These important issues are also explored explicitly in other chapters of this volume. Here I explore how the all important constitution issue can be implemented on one of the most neglected, supposedly most difficult problems in the mind sciences – the primal nature of our emotional affective experiences, namely the pleasures and pains of existence, that directly code for survival trajectories. Because of special properties, primary-process emotional feelings may be an ideal target for obtaining provisional answers, and new prediction, for the very hard problem of how qualia are constituted by brain activities. Through the implementation of animal models, which allow us to fully consider critical evolutionary levels of analysis, such issues can be explored in some detail, and thereby fertilize neglected fields of human research.

Prelude – The affective neuroscience strategy for decoding raw emotional experiences

What types of phenomenal experiences (qualia) emerged first in BrainMind evolution?[1] This is a key conceptual question, but also one that can be empirically addressed, especially if one takes a comparative cross-species evolutionary perspective (Panksepp, 2005a, 2007, 2011a; Solms & Panksepp, 2012). Without a reasonable answer to what emerged earliest in the evolution of animals' capacity for raw experiences, presumably linked directly to unconditional survival values, it may be impossible to address the constitution of higher forms of consciousness scientifically. It seems likely that experiential processes that evolved earlier provided scaffolding for those that emerged later. Although it is commonly believed that consciousness is fundamentally based on sensory-perceptual phenomena, which is surely a substantial part of the story, here I explore the counterintuitive idea that primordial raw qualia, such as emotional feelings – states of affective consciousness – were among the earliest types of experiences to

1. The conflated BrainMind usage is premised on the likelihood that mental experiences are fundamental aspects of brain functions, which allow a dual-aspect monism strategy to ferret out the underlying neural nature of various primary-process mental experiences in animals.

have emerged in vertebrate BrainMind evolution. This is because valenced brain states were evolutionarily designed to immediately promote bodily existence. Further, it will be proposed that such intrinsically valuative experiences were substantially based on intrinsic brain-based action schema, specifically the various unconditioned emotional response systems that were obviously essential for bodily survival. Such aspects of experienced brain functions have been overlooked, seemingly actively neglected, in modern consciousness research. This may be because little scientifically incisive progress (deep brain research) can be achieved on such aspects of mind without cross-species brain research. And many, perhaps most, scholars believe one cannot study conscious experiences without syntactic feedback from the experiencers. This bias is shortsighted.

Without the capacity to respond to, perhaps to feel, key survival issues related to aspects of the world, both external and internal, one could not survive. The external stimuli had to be detected by sensory processes, and it would have been "wise" for life-supporting ones to be positively valanced, and life-detracting ones to promote negative feelings. The stimuli that are completely internal to the body may have become automatized – like many actions of the autonomic nervous system – and hence minimally conscious. The exceptions would be internal states like hunger and thirst that required sensory interactions with the world. Thus, here I envision consciousness as an early evolutionary survival facilitator. I am most intrigued by those within-brain emotional functions that are experienced, albeit in global, hard to define ways, because there are good reasons to suspect they may constitute the very core of mental existence, even in humans (Solms & Panksepp, 2012). Based on abundant cross-species affective neuroscience data, the various emotional responses that mandate motoric interactions with the world, and the attending experiences that facilitate survival through primal "anticipation" of survival issues, are likely to be based more on organismic action coordinates than any kind of pure sensory-experiences (Panksepp, 1998a, 1998b, 2005a). This would resituate affective enactment systems to the very core of conscious being: Certain emotional actions actively sample the environment, as with the primal SEEKING system.

That is the intuition I will share here. Raw emotional experiential states, seemingly the spookiest form of phenomenal consciousness, may be ancestral "gifts" – namely within-brain, emotional-affective, action-based feelings systems that were very useful, perhaps critically important, tools for living – yielding states of mind that intrinsically promoted survival in our species, just as in all other mammals (Panksepp, 2005a, 2011b). Indeed, we can claim that this is currently more than an intuition. It is a thesis based on the weight of existing evidence: Raw *emotional feelings* – states of positive and negative valence in all mammals – are closely linked to their evolutionarily ingrained emotional action systems situated among the most ancient body maintenance regions of the brain. *Homeostatic and sensory feelings* – such as hunger and the sting of pain, respectively – may also rely substantially on instinctual action generating infrastructures, but not as much as the basic emotions. Indeed, one empirical reason for focusing on emotions is that the more strictly sensation-based feelings, those not accompanied by clear actions, are much harder to study scientifically in animals than the large-scale emotional feelings that I will focus on here.

There are good conceptual as well as empirical reasons to believe that the most primal phenomenal experiences were in the category that is commonly called *affective* – namely the various "good" and "bad" valenced feelings that signal intrinsic survival issues. The central argument, is that such primordial neuro-mental capacities – perhaps the very foundation of our subjective lives – are integrally linked to neural networks that generate distinct brain emotional action patterns that can be studied objectively, namely neuro-ethologically, in other animals. For instance, if we can demonstrate that such brain systems for emotional actions constitute rewarding and punishing states within the brain, their corresponding behaviors can be used as proxies for feelings in non-neuroscientific ethological studies of animal behaviors – e.g., playful behavior may reflect joyous feelings. Indeed, the gist of existing evidence, not widely recognized even in neuroscience, is as follows: wherever in ancient regions of mammalian brains we can evoke coherent motor/action tendencies (as with localized deep brain stimulation, DBS), various empirical tests for *value* – evaluation of rewarding and punishing properties of the artificially evoked states – indicate that raw affective feelings, valenced emotional experiences, accompany those motoric arousals. Indeed, here I consider that they may be constitutive of those experiences within the brain.

Such evidence allows us to provisionally entertain the possibility that primal emotional feelings, at the very least, are substantially based on the brain's ability to engender primary-process emotional actions that unconditionally supported survival in our evolutionary past. Here I only briefly note evidence that such types of instinctual action related feelings are ones that we still share homologously with other mammals (for fuller coverage, see Panksepp, 1982, 2005a, 2011a, 2011b, 2011c; Panksepp & Biven, 2012). This is not to say that sensory processes do not participate. Of course they do. But sensory inputs (the so-called *unconditioned stimuli*, of behaviorists) could do little in terms of evolutionary survival if they did not have coherent brain action systems (sophisticated *unconditioned responses*), at their beck and call, laid out in motor coordinates within the brain, which constitute the impressive 'presence' of organisms in the world (perhaps a core SELF).

It is regrettable that such integrative action systems have received so little attention in both psychological learning (e.g., classical conditioning) as well as consciousness studies. This is because many believe "responses" are just output channels on which the complexities of sensory experiences impose their "will" – leading to the widespread belief that sensation always precedes action. It is from within the neural networks of this action 'presence' – emanating especially robustly from the SEEKING-foraging system – that I will seek to track down the sources of emotional feelings, as well as the neural foundation of what it means to be mentally alive, to have a motorically dynamic organismic core, full of 'enthusiasm', which may be aptly called the primal SELF (Panksepp, 1998a, 1998b, 2009; Panksepp & Northoff, 2009).

Why did such internal affects evolve? The evolutionary utility – which provisionally answers this "why" or "what for" question (Dennett, 2014) – is that affects, especially emotional ones, allowed organisms to anticipate world events in 'inside-out' ways that dramatically promoted survival and reproduction. The same reasoning applies for unconditioned sensory (e.g., taste and thermal affects) and internal bodily, homeostatic affects (e.g., hunger and thirst) that promote survival. For instance, externally triggered pain informs animals promptly of trajectories that may lead to destruction (indeed all humans with congenital pain detection deficits die young).

Abundant data exists suggesting that raw affects (e.g., pain) are reflexive states of being whose experiential qualities unconditionally promote survival (at least on average). Pain promotes recuperation and thereby avoids bodily destruction, because behaviors that amplify the pain have signaled diminished survival in the past. For instance, when rats are exposed to various nociceptive stimuli that elicit pain reflexes, the animals will seek out environmental locations where they have been given painkillers used in humans (King et al., 2009). When one manipulates brainstem regions locally with general anesthetics or lesions, one can identify medially situated mesencephalic networks that are critical for such engagements with the world (Devor, 2008; Panksepp, 1998a). Thus, animal models provide robust cross-species evidence for the ancestral sources of our own affective feelings, even the higher, socially conditioned, kinds typically studied by psychologists (see Zachar & Ellis, 2012).

The only way we can scientifically conclude animals have affective experiences of certain kinds is that localized DBS that consistently evokes distinct emotional behaviors can equally consistently evoke rewarding and punishing states of mind, reinforced by the fact that humans report homologous feelings during such DBS (Panksepp, 1985). Thus, to the best of our knowledge, the experience of primal emotional feelings and actions both arise from brain activities that function as instincts. Without clear action patterns that are accompanied by valenced affects, which can guide learning, cross species empirical approaches to the study of emotional affective states would be next to impossible. But with the above *lawful* relationship, "self-reports" in a manner of speaking, we can provisionally conclude that emotions derive their core phenomenally experienced "color" through the auspices of the neurodynamics that are isomorphic with certain aroused instinctual action networks within the brain. Thus, one reason I emphasize emotional feelings in my own work so persistently is because they are empirically workable as well as among the most psychiatrically important MindBrain issues for neuroscientists to unravel.[2]

Thus, constrained by available data obtained from studies of ancient brain regions, homologous in all mammals at the primary-process level of analysis, I restrict my coverage largely to *primary-process emotional affects*. These are the strongest, fully internalized, passions of them all – from feelings of intrinsic pre-propositional

2. Again, this is not to deny that various sensory and interoceptive inputs modulate the action circuits, and participate in feelings, but to simply make the claim that the intrinsic action systems do allow us more access to the critical neural infrastructures than any sensory analysis that has yet been achieved. Obviously, at some primary-process level, not yet analyzed, the two have to be fully integrated, but even there, the action coordinates may allow sensory coordinates to be anchored within a robust organismic framework of action coherences (for example in collicular visual systems, see Sparks, 1988).

(primary-process) 'desire' and 'joy' to 'anger' and 'loneliness'. I put these terms in scare quotes because, in using the simple vernacular, it is hard to agree, scientifically, about what we are talking about (Zachar & Ellis, 2012). Thus, for animal research, I typically capitalize primal emotional processes, which can be related to clear neuroanatomical and neurochemical variables. An adequate scientific definition of *primal* emotions must be based on neuroscientific terms – namely, the specification of the underlying neural circuits and dynamics. This level of analysis should not be mixed with higher order secondary (learning and memory) and tertiary (cognitive-thinking) processes, which are probably nested within each other, with more ancient processes being critical for more evolved ones to function (Figure 1). For semantic clarity, we do need to have a special scientific nomenclature to label the primary-process (unconditional) emotional constructs. Accordingly, I will use "strange" yet "familiar" capitalized terms like SEEKING and PLAY, RAGE and PANIC, for the needed emphasis, not unlike the practice of Thomas Hobbes in *Leviathan.* I have long used that terminological convention for primary-process neural networks, to highlight what is fundamental to the emotional/affective nature of mammals.

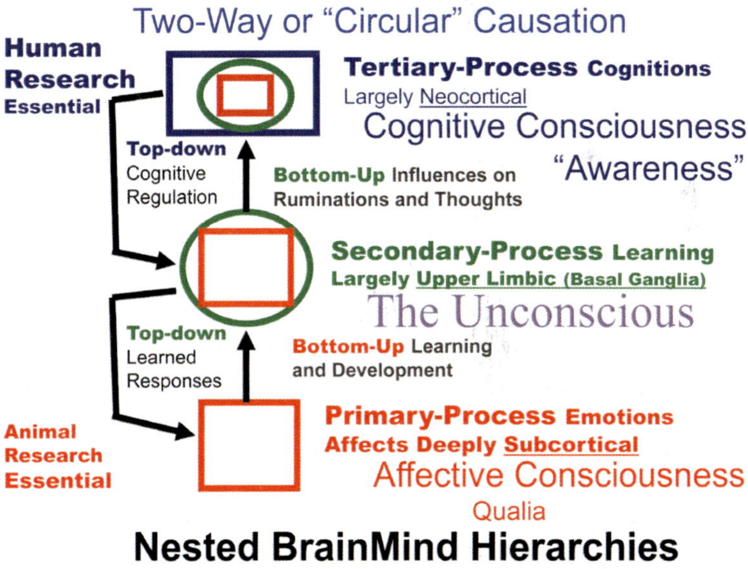

Figure 1. A conceptual summary of hierarchical bottom-up "nested" and top-down (circular) causation that presumably operates in every primal emotional system of the brain. This schematic summarizes the hypothesis that in order for higher MindBrain functions to operate, they have to be integrated with the lower BrainMind functions, with primary-processes being depicted as squares, secondary-processing (learning and memory) as circles, and tertiary processing (higher cognitive functions), at the top, as rectangles (adapted from Northoff, Wiebking, Feinberg, & Panksepp, 2011; Panksepp, 2011c). "Bottom-up" control prevails in early infancy and early childhood development. Top-down control is optimized in adulthood.

At present, we can conclude that diverse instinctual emotional action patterns of animals are routinely accompanied by affective feelings – at least to the degree that "rewarding" and "punishing" brain functions can be used as evidence of subjectively experienced feelings. If such effects are not deemed robust evidence, the present argument would not be valid. However, anyone wishing to advance that skeptical counter-stance would need to explain why evocation of all such complex sensory-motor states, when relevant brain stimulations are applied, are affectively experienced in humans (Panksepp, 1985). They would also need to point out specific "rewards" and "punishments" in humans that are not experienced. It is becoming ever clearer that much of the so-called 'dynamic unconscious' is in fact affectively experienced (Shevrin, Panksepp, Brakel, & Snodgrass, 2012; Solms & Panksepp, 2012).

From this evolutionary perspective, the "ground-of-being" for higher subjective experiences may be constituted of internally-valenced affective states that are largely isomorphic or overlapping, not only with unconditioned sensory processes, but with unconditioned behavioral manifestations that are generally described as emotional – e.g., 'instinctive' behavior patterns reflect, at the very least, (1) 'desire', (2) 'anger', (3) 'fear', (4) 'sexual arousals', (5) 'maternal devotions', (6) the evident 'panicky distress' of young animals separated from caretakers (e.g., lost infants), and (7) the 'joy' of playful social engagements. In primary process terminology, these would be SEEKING, RAGE, FEAR, LUST, CARE, PANIC/GRIEF, and PLAY dispositions, respectively. These scientific terms were chosen to suggest the types of feelings evoked are similar across mammalian species, without any claim of identity in humans and other animals. Obviously evolution creates diversity (e.g., via SNPs: single nucleotide polymorphisms) even in homologous systems of the brain. Thus, the only claim is that there are many evolutionary homologies, at neuroanatomical, neurochemical and neuropsychological levels, across all mammalian species – from mice to men, so to speak.

As noted, the evolutionary "what for" for the emergence of these systems is easy to understand. For instance, all animals that survive on diverse resources in the world have a general-purpose system for SEEKING – foraging for all kinds of stuff needed to promote existence. But as many animals eat other animals, sophisticated creatures must exhibit RAGE to counterattack or FEAR to promote escape and hiding in order to survive. All must reproduce, and LUST facilitates that, and in mammals where offspring are born immature and weak, evolutionary success cannot be had without maternal CARE. And the young must signal their helpless condition when separated from caretakers, so they PANIC with separation calls. It is difficult to build all social rules directly into the brains of complex animals, so the advantage of learning about what one can and cannot do in social encounters is advantaged by a general purposed PLAY system which helps organisms to learn their place in species-typical social structures with mostly positive rather than negative affects.

The underlying systems that generate instinctual actions apparently also engender within-brain mental functions, which are especially important for understanding psychiatric disorders (Panksepp, Wright, Döbrössy, Schlaepfer, & Coenen, 2014). These systems may constitute emotional qualia that not only help facilitate immediate behavioral choices but also learning by yet unstudied "laws of affect" (see Chapter 6 in Panksepp & Biven, 2012). Of course there are various other affects, more strictly linked to externally directed sensory systems (the pleasures and pains of sensation; see Cabanac, 1992) as well as those within the body (homeostatic affects; see Denton, 2006), that are harder to study in animals.

Again, because it is so critical for the present argument, what kind of data allows us to claim that primal emotional brain states are experienced in animals? The gold standard in creatures that cannot talk has to be the formal evaluation of the diverse rewarding or punishing states of the brain, with clear predictions to humans. Indeed, evidence for such valenced feeling effects, using localized DBS, has been observed consistently across species – starting with Olds and Milner (1954) for rewarding effects, and Delgado, Roberts and Miller (1954) for punishing ones. Subsequently affective types of RAGE were found to be punishing, while predatory aggression, a manifestation of the SEEKING system, was rewarding (Panksepp, 1971), as were LUST and CARE (reviewed in Panksepp, 1998a). Many DBS escape studies have been conducted with artificial activation of the FEAR system (summarized in Panksepp, 1981a, 1990a; Panksepp, Sacks, Crepeau, & Abbott, 1991), and then a PANIC type anxiety system was identified in the late 1970s (for first reviews, see Panksepp, 1981b; Panksepp, Bean, Bishop, Vilberg, & Sahley, 1980). The PLAY system came of age in the 1980s (Panksepp, 1993; Panksepp, Siviy, & Normansell, 1984).

But maybe such processes are fundamentally unconscious, one might object. Well, then it is the responsibility of such skeptics to show, in a species whose members can readily talk about their experiences, namely us, that comparable rewards and punishment states, namely internal states that lead to rapid learning, are *not* experienced. No such evidence exists. One might then further object that the human experience actually arises when such primal emotional networks impinge on our uniquely expanded neocortices. Again, there is no evidence in support of such claims. In lieu of evidence, such claim suggests some type of "unique and special higher functions" in well-cerebrated species, reminiscent of creation *stories* of our origins. In any event, it is the responsibility of those willing to make such anti-evolutionary claims, inconsistent with too much existing evidence, to indicate where and how neocortex came to have the capacity to generate affective states in humans, when disconnected from the affective subcortical zones, it cannot sustain any consciousness. No such evidence exists, so it is puzzling that opinion leaders insist that we "will never understand how other animals feel" (LeDoux, 2012), and propose that the dorsolateral working-memory fields of neocortex constitute feelings from unconscious "information" arriving from below (LeDoux, 1996). There is indeed some good evidence for both positive and negative *homeostatic* and *sensory* affects being elaborated by the very ancient insular (Craig, 2003) and orbitofrontal regions (Rolls, 2005) but not emotional affects. The *generators* for *emotional* affects are generally situated in even deeper regions, with periaqueductal gray (PAG) preeminent.

To claim that the above findings from animals apply to humans, we need data confirming that with localized electrical DBS procedures we can also evoke comparable emotional feelings in humans. Although extensive formal studies have not been done matching brain sites precisely, the data that exist are highly supportive of profound homologies within the relevant subcortical regions (Heath, 1996; Panksepp, 1985). Animal research has repeatedly shown that DBS of the dorsal PAG produces intense FEAR and PANIC (Panksepp, 1998a), and correlative associations exist in meta-analyses of human brain imaging of pain and anxiety experiences (Buhle et al., 2013). A remarkable example of the type of feeling evoked in humans is: It feels like "I am about to die!" (Nashold, Wilson, & Slaughter, 1969). It is no wonder that animals do not return to places where they had comparable experiences. A summary of conditioned freezing to DBS arousal of the FEAR system, as it courses through the ventrolateral anterior hypothalamus is depicted in Figure 2. The first report of place avoidance to such DBS was by Roberts and Cox (1987). Stimulation here can promote a depressive phenotype in rats (Wright & Panksepp, 2011).

Admittedly, even in humans, such states of mind are, at times, hard to describe in words. They are better described metaphorically (as above), but best of all in music, song and dance, where the underlying expressive dynamics can be conveyed in varying

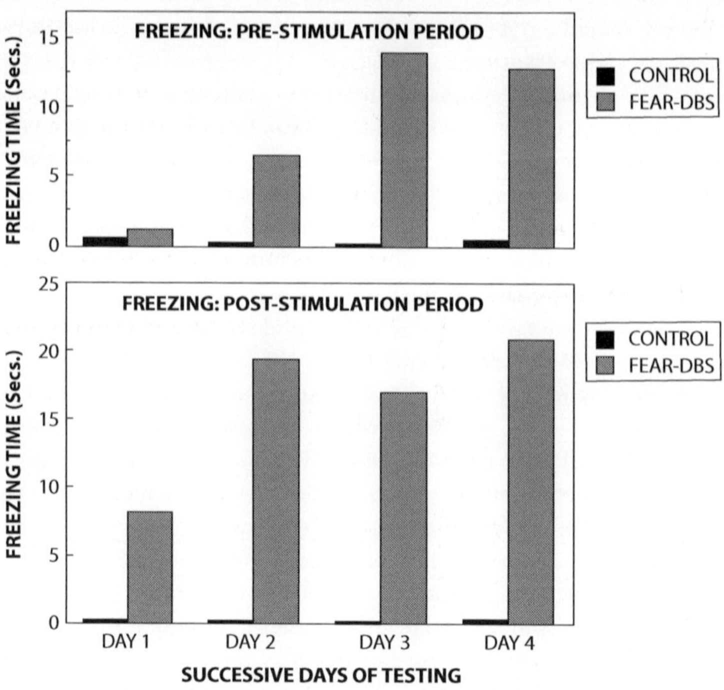

Figure 2. Freezing time in adult male rats during the minute prior to and following deep brain stimulation (DBS) of the hypothalamic trajectory of the FEAR system on four successive days of testing. Adapted from Figure 11.3 of *Affective Neuroscience* (Panksepp, 1998a), with permission of Oxford University Press.

dynamics of sound and movement, which are known to evoke feelings (Clynes, 1988). Indeed, simulation of various full-body action patterns, like laughter and crying, can promote positive and negative moods states respectively, and such effects can even be achieved by motor-imagery based mental simulation of such actions (Panksepp & Gordon, 2003).

Similar effects are evident in our studies of animal PLAY behaviors. When we have studied "rat laughter" induced by tickling, animals consistently find those states to be desirable (Panksepp, 2007). And everywhere in the brain such 'happy' sounds are evoked with DBS, the underlying states are rewarding (Burgdorf, Wood, Kroes, Moskal, & Panksepp, 2007), and such affective states can yield stable affective temperaments through selective breeding (Burgdorf, Panksepp, Brudzynski, Kroes, & Moskal, 2005).

Thereby, visually evident motor arousals of emotional states in all mammals tested may currently be interpreted as veridical markers of underlying affective states. There are no empirically-based exceptions to this rule yet. Unconditioned emotion generators of the brain are experienced, and the qualia are affective – good and bad, rewarding and punishing, in ways that are hard to describe (hence we use capitalizations for these systems). From such a *dual-aspect monism* perspective, it is hypothesized that raw emotional *expressive states* within the brain help constitute primal affective consciousness (Panksepp, 2007). In contrast, although interoceptive sensory participation in the generation of such states is also likely, that is empirically more inferential at present, at least for emotional arousals (but not for hunger). By logical extension, it is important to re-emphasize, such empirical validations of the underlying affective (i.e., rewarding and punishing) properties of the aroused brain emotional networks, provisionally allows us to use externally evident instinctual emotional patterns in animals as read-outs of their internal feelings. Indeed, sensitive observers through the ages, even René Descartes, have long accepted such behavior patterns as *prima facia* indicators of internal affective arousals.

Although some claim Descartes did not subscribe to experiential (primal conscious) states in animals/brutes, no such claim is evident in *The Passions of the Mind.* Descartes apparently simply did not believe animals cognitively reflected on their feelings with a sense of *awareness*, and *self-consciousness*, and hence he did not respect the feelings of animals as much as the related cognitions of humans (Cottingham, 2008). Descartes was clearly an emotionally insensitive fellow, having practiced vivisection on awake animals. Despite this, he believed animals do have emotions (low level passions) comparable to our own. His cruelty (by present day standards) may have been based on his belief that it was the cognitive consciousness of humans that deserved attention, with no clear vision that suffering was directly related to affective consciousness (Panksepp, 2007) which he never adequately conceptualized. His *cogito* got in the way. But that is not an unusual position in modern consciousness studies, where "cognitive imperialism" still rules (see Cromwell & Panksepp, 2011; Panksepp, 1988, for counterpoints).

To reiterate, the affective consciousness perspective is supported by experimental evidence: wherever in the brain one consistently evokes distinct and coherent emotional behavior patterns with localized DBS, with midbrain and upper brainstem (hypothalamic) levels being best studied, with some sites further up in basal ganglia (e.g., amygdala), the evoked internal states can serve as rewards and punishments in learning tasks. This is so in all animals where such circuitry exists. To reiterate: accordingly, we provisionally employ the presence of those types of behavior patterns, without any imposition of DBS, as potentially veridical read-out of distinct categories of internal affective states. How far down in evolution this goes is an open question (Huber, Panksepp, Nathaniel, Alcaro, & Panksepp, 2011).

Such a *dual-aspect monism* perspective on neuromental emotional action processes (Panksepp, 2005b), if true, could advance empirical inquiries and judicious theoretical advances into the neuro-evolutionary sources of consciousness (Panksepp, 1998a; Solms & Panksepp, 2012; Solms & Turnbull, 2002). So far, the evidence for such a strategy is substantial and pragmatically useful, including the identification of new anti-depressant pathways in preclinical models by taking the primary-process emotional feelings (raw qualia) of animals seriously (Burgdorf, Panksepp, & Moskal, 2011; Panksepp, 2012; Panksepp et al., 2014).

In my estimation, affective states are currently our best options – the lowest common denominators – for qualia generating foundations for higher mental processes. So a few more reflections about evolutionary levels of control in the BrainMind are needed to clarify key issues: any clear discussion of the massive homologies across mammals in subcortical emotional regions of the brain requires us to recognize specialized *primary-process* emotions and their affects as foundational for higher mental abilities (see Figure 1). In this *nested-hierarchy* perspective, the intermediate, *secondary-process*, levels of external information processing promote learning whereby primal affects guide linkages of external events to predictable arousals of affective states; the resulting learning and memory algorithms, in the absence of countervailing evidence, need to be recognized as deeply unconscious, simply parsing affective reactions in animals ever more effectively in the time and space relations in their *Umwelt*. This function is concentrated in "limbic" brain regions that are collectively called "basal ganglia" (e.g., amygdala, bed nucleus of stria terminalis, nucleus accumbens, extending into adjacent septal, preoptic and ventral pallidal regions.) On top of this, we have *tertiary processes,* which deploy the lower brain functions and their memorial products, partly via hippocampal gateways, into various higher brain functions ranging from temporal-spatial planning and decision-making to intrapsychic processes, such as explicitly experienced thoughts and ruminations. Our inability to access explicit thoughts in animals should not paralyze our much greater ability to clearly discuss and understand their emotional feelings.

Regrettably, many opportunities to illuminate the affective underpinnings of human consciousness have not been grasped by neuroscientists because of long-standing historical dilemmas and diverse linguistic problems. Such avoidances have recently been reinforced by the assumption that "We can never know what other animals feel" (LeDoux, 2012). Of course we can, at least in a general way, namely whether the animal is having positive or negative feelings, and even whether certain negative feelings are different (discriminable) from each other, and likewise for positive feelings (Stutz, Rossi, Hastings, & Brunner, 1974). This does not mean that any scientists would claim that the feelings are identical between human and other animals, simply that homologies exist if similar brain manipulations produce comparable response tendencies accompanied by rewarding and punishing effects (further elaborated below, and also see footnote 22 in Miller, 2007). As Miller (2007) notes, the absence of certainty about these subtle scientific issues should not lead us away from the most promising approach, from getting as far as we can get toward scientifically-grounded inferences about *phenomenal* consciousness in animals. As we all know, science does not have absolute knowledge (proof) of anything, but just the weight-of-evidence for interpretive positions.

Interlude: A synopsis of the reasons emotional feelings of other animals remain hardly recognized among behavioral scientists and the need for new nomenclatures as we pursue cross-species conversations and experimental strategies toward understanding core consciousness

A reasoned cross-species evolutionary approach has not been widely embraced for guiding research into the neural infrastructure of emotional feeling. Partly this is due to long-standing biases against speaking about potential internal affective feelings in the animals we study (for summary, see Panksepp, 2011a, 2011b, and for resistances see LeDoux, 2012). In fact, this bias cannot be coherently linked to the philosophical tradition of Cartesian dualism. René Descartes never claimed that animals do not feel their passions, only that they do not think about them. In the modern era, the bias against any talk about subjective experiences was established by American behaviorists long before neuroscience had matured, which of course, had to be a critical ingredient in making empirical progress on such a difficult topic. The behaviorists' biases have come down to the present day, at least among Anglo-American behaviorally-oriented researchers, only because of dogmatic pronouncements that stifled open discussion. As Skinner (1953) famously claimed: "The 'emotions' are excellent examples of the fictional causes to which we commonly attribute behavior" (p. 160). Such a claim was also advanced by eminent ethologists: For instance, concurrently Nobel-heralded ethologist Nico Tinbergen (1951), asserted in his influential *Study of Instinct* that as "subjective phenomena cannot be observed objectively in animals, it is idle to claim or deny their existence" (p. 4). This bias has remained relatively intact to the present day (for overviews, see Panksepp, 2011a, 2011c). Although an increasing number of prominent animal lovers, with scientific credentials, are advancing the minority position (Balcombe, 2006; Bekoff, 2007; Grandin & Johnson, 2005), their voices have had little influence in promoting the needed conversations among behavioral and cognitive neuroscientists. Perhaps they would be more successful had they had conducted relevant neuroscientific studies. But that is unlikely, as my own efforts, guided by strict empiricism, have been rejected *ad hominem* by prominent colleagues to the present day: I only need direct readers to LeDoux's (2012) remarks at the end of that recent review.

Still, there are good reasons to suspect that many ethologists, like Konrad Lorenz, did not accept the 'never-mind' ideology of behaviorists, but most did not make their voices heard, perhaps because they simply did not have relevant data, which simply had to be neuroscientific. And they were surely also reticent because of the tedium of arguments with American behaviorists about the proper way to study animal behavior (e.g., Lehrman, 1953). There are reasons to believe that many ethologists, as exemplified by van Holst, thought emotions could eventually be studied, but there was little sign of that among behaviorists. With such a sense of assurance, passed down through generations of Anglo-American behaviorists, about what might truly remain fictitious as opposed to realistic, the conversation about animal emotional feelings remained muted throughout the 20th century (see Panksepp, 1990b, for an extensive one-sided conversation with Skinner).

The 'never-mind' agnostic position has remained the standard *pro forma* attitude that is at least outwardly supported by most emotion investigators in ethology and comparative psychology to this day (e.g., Dawkins, 2001; de Waal, 2011; Mendl, Burman, & Paul, 2010 – for critique, see Panksepp, 2011a). That skeptical attitude is sustained despite the massive evidence against the traditional agnostic position (see author's many citations herein). An equally powerful force that implicitly prevented the emergence of more realistic visions of mammalian affective minds was the power of the "Cognitive Revolution", which caught full steam in the 1970s, leading to two unsympathetic consequences: (1) a computational theory of mind, where animal research was widely deemed irrelevant, and (2) the concurrent mass movement of behaviorists into neuroscience, because of shifting funding- and job-opportunity policies favoring the emerging "Neuroscience Revolution" of the early 1970s. Behaviorists, accustomed to high reinforcement contingencies, knew how to follow the money, which led to the conversion of "physiological psychology" to "behavioral neuroscience" which favored the study of secondary processes rather than primary ones. Philosophers, too, primarily devoted their intellectual energies to the higher, namely tertiary-process level of analysis.

Thus, ever since Descartes' *cogito*, the mind sciences have been captivated by the vision that consciousness is a uniquely human ability, endowed by our higher cerebral capacities – a result of our massively expanded neocortex. Although this anti-evolutionary bias has declined somewhat in recent years, in my reading of the literature, this change toward evolutionary psychobiology has had little impact on investigators who are best positioned to ferret out the constitution of consciousness through neurophysiological research on other animals (e.g., LeDoux, 2012). And a meaningful wide-scale conversation will not emerge until scholars steeped in the behavioristic and cognitive traditions consider abundant evidence that affective brain functions do exist in humans and other animals which are critically linked to subcortical functions that are dramatically homologous across vertebrate species.

It has not helped that prominent investigators of animal behaviors have argued that propositional thought and/or language, so well developed in our own species, is necessary for consciousness to emerge (e.g., LeDoux, 1996; Macphail, 1998; Rolls,

1999). Of course, they are correct when it comes to the highest cognitive powers of human minds – aspects of consciousness that allow for complex decision-making that we obtained by massive encephalization and our unparalleled capacity to learn, and to reflect upon our nature and the world. However, for these skeptics, "consciousness" seems to be synonymous with self "awareness" rather than raw phenomenal experiences (qualia). Thus, many disagreements may arise from differences in semantic conceptualizations rather than from any disciplined differences in how the available data should be critically evaluated. Because of the semantic ambiguities in the field, one can have little confidence that there are currently any disciplined differences in views of how experiential aspects of mind evolved through the emergence of certain neural dynamics. Indeed, few "constitutional" proposals for the sources of phenomenal experiences have been advanced (Miller, 2007, this volume). In any event, in the area of emotional affects, the lack of progress may arise as much from active neglect, during the past century, rather than the lack of relevant evidence.

Thus, the focus here is on primal phenomenal, affectively valenced experiences that are of great importance for every mammalian life, and surely many other avian and reptilian species, and potentially even lower creatures (Huber et al., 2011). Thus, we currently can characterize the affectively experienced life that can be evoked in various animals through DBS. This level of analysis, I would submit, has enormous implications for understanding the constitutive nature of affective mind functions, with abundant implications for novel approaches to human psychiatric systematics (Panksepp, 2004, 2006), therapeutics (Coenen, Schlaepfer, Maedler, & Panksepp, 2011; Coenen, Panksepp, Hurwitz, Urbach, & Mädler, 2012; Schlaepfer et al., 2008) and the emergence of personality dimensions (Davis & Panksepp, 2011).

The ongoing cultural dilemma, in science, that promotes 'never-mind' agonisticism on such primal issues is simply that most practitioners of behavioral neuroscience remain loathe to consider or talk about the experiences of the animals they study, for well understood historical reasons (for synopsis, see Panksepp's 2010 Foreword to the *Encyclopedia of Behavioral Neuroscience*). However, as I noted there, it now seems likely "that we will not make progress on some of the most momentous questions about the brain if we continue to avoid the language of experience" (p. xxviii) in our studies of other animals.

I will repeat, like a mantra, the simple fact that practically everywhere investigators can evoke clear emotional behavior patterns with localized DBS, they can utilize such pulses of DBS to reward and punish simple behavior patterns. A variety of distinct emotional behavior patterns can be evoked, but a great dilemma has been: How shall we label these affectively tinged primal states? As we all appreciate human cognitive complexities, we do not want to misuse our vernacular linguistic terms, which grew out of and support human communicative convenience, and hence are intrinsically confusing and not well suited for scientific inquiries.

Any clear discussion of the *primary* neuroaffective processes of the mind will require development of artificial but understandable terminologies. The convention I chose (again reminiscent of language usages by Hobbes in his *Leviathan*) – was to use vernacular terms capitalized, with the specification that these were reasonable labels for primal brain networks that concurrently elaborated behavioral, autonomic, and affective characteristics. By this criterion, as noted, we have identified at least seven primary-process (evolutionarily engraved, but experientially refined), unconditional, emotional-affective systems in the brain: SEEKING, RAGE, FEAR, LUST, CARE, PANIC, and PLAY, with many overlapping controls and functions (Panksepp, 1998a). The capitalizations highlight a new nomenclature – one premised on the existence of brain networks that govern class-similar emotional behaviors and emotional-affective experiences in all mammals. The other levels (Figure 1) need different terms, and vernacular may be fine for the tertiary-process level where most of our skills are socially constructed. The primal nomenclature could be used for sensory pleasures and pains, and homeostatic affects as well (e.g., DISGUST, HUNGER and THIRST). But those mind functions are harder to study because their affects are not as clearly expressed in distinct action patterns that can be evoked with DBS. But progress can be made there also, as it has with DISGUST evoked from stimulation of the insula (Caruana, Jezzini, Sbriscia-Fioretti, Rizzolatti, & Gallese, 2011).

To the best of our knowledge, all seven systems are concentrated in overlapping brain areas shared homologously by all mammals. They may be the foundations of many higher mental processes: when these systems are destroyed so is our capacity for higher mental life. Due to evolutionary diversification, as noted above, we will probably never be able to determine the precise nature of such feelings in either other humans or other animals, but we can have some confidence of class similarities. This is because humans consistently report not only arousal of emotional feelings during such forms of DBS (e.g., Heath, 1996; Panksepp, 1985), but they are consistent with the behavioral displays and positive and negative valences that have been demonstrated in animals. This same line of argumentation applies for many neurochemical/neuropharmacological manipulations across species (Koob, Le Moal, & Thompson, 2010; Panksepp, 1986, 1991, 1998a, 1998b).

Of course, one could argue that the feelings only arise when unconscious subcortical "information" impinges on neocortical regions that are endowed with the capacity to generate reflective awareness. That, of course, would resemble James-Lange type visions of emotional arousal, which placed the originating signals in the peripheral body as opposed to the subcortical brain, a view initially also advanced in *Descartes' Error* by Damasio (1994) but fully corrected by 2010, in his *The Self Comes to Mind*. A critical point against a restrictive cortical read-out view is that subcortical reward and punishment functions survive radical destruction of higher brain regions in animals (e.g., Huston & Borbely, 1973, 1974; Valenstein, 1966). This does not eliminate some contribution from peripheral feedbacks, but the mass of data is consistent with the view that subcortical circuits can sustain various primal affective experiences on their own (Panksepp, 1998a; Velmans, 2009), a view that is supported by human data (Merker, 2007; Shewmon, Holmse, & Byrne, 1999). Perhaps the dynamic unconscious of Freudian theory is, in fact, experienced in terms of the mental experiences of diverse valences and arousals (Shevrin et al., 2012; Solms & Panksepp, 2012; Zachar & Ellis, 2012).

In sum, abundant evidence suggests that "emotional" feelings arise largely from complex networks that reside completely within our brains, but which move our bodies intensely in various distinct ways. One reason we have focused on emotional feelings is because they are most important for understanding psychiatric disorders (Panksepp, 2004, 2006; Panksepp & Biven, 2012) and discovery of new treatments (e.g., Panksepp et al., 2014). Thus, we now have a great deal of knowledge about which brain systems contribute substantially to various basic emotional feelings (Panksepp, 1998) – experiences like desire (SEEKING), anger (RAGE), anxiety (FEAR), sexual desire (LUST), motherly love (CARE), loneliness and grief (PANIC also now called GRIEF, to facilitate understanding) and joyful social interactions especially prominent in youth (PLAY). To reiterate, because it seems so poorly understood, the capitalizations are used instead of the vernacular "tertiary-process" terms included above, because it is a specialized nomenclature, useful for clear scientific discourse, for labeling the primary-process affective networks of the brain, which arise from those lowest layers of brain integration where raw emotional behaviors intertwine with associated feelings (see Figure 1). Distinct nomenclatures are also needed for secondary and tertiary levels of analysis.

Despite the above historical constraints, it has long been clear that animal models can be used to estimate the fundamental nature of the raw emotional feelings of human beings. Such projects are important for understanding psychiatric disorders in humans, because they provide access to the affective circuits that can become imbalanced in all mammalian brains (Panksepp, 2004, 2006, 2012). To repeat, because this principle is not widely understood, such translational knowledge relies on one robust and consistent observation: artificial activation of distinct subcortical brain systems, especially those that generate clear emotional behavioral reactions, consistently serve as "rewards" and "punishments" in simple approach/anticipation and escape/avoidance various learning tasks. Such rigorous models provide remarkable advantages for empirically decoding the neural constitution of phenomenal-affective consciousness, namely the raw experiences of various emotional qualia. The epistemology is as follows:

1. Identification of brain sites across diverse species of mammals that evoke such hedonic effects;
2. Identification of the major additional brain regions that are most strongly impacted by such brain arousals (e.g., via c-fos histochemistry);
3. Harvesting various fluctuating neurodynamic correlates from these brain regions (as with quantitative electroencephalography [EEG], etc.) as a function of intensity and duration parameters of relevant brain stimulations and behavioral changes;
4. Identification of key chemistries that modify – i.e., attenuate and intensify – these effects in animals as well as humans (to the extent possible, in elective (informed-consent) neuro-psychosurgery to implant cerebral pacemakers (e.g., see Schlaepfer et al., 2008; Schlaepfer, Bewernick, Kayser, Mädler, & Coenen, 2013);
5. And finally, providing additional testable predictions, especially for humans, from the above cross-species findings (Panksepp, 1985).

This program of research constitutes the underlying strategy of a cross-species affective neuroscience approach to understanding primal affective consciousness – research which can now be pursued rigorously even in humans, as with DBS and diverse pharmacological agents (Koob et al., 2010), even in creatures as evolutionarily primitive as crayfish (Huber et al., 2011). This can be optimized because of the already existing objective behavioral indices of the bipolarity – positive and affective valences – of various affective neural circuits in so many other mammals (summarized in Panksepp, 1998a, 2005a, 2005b; Panksepp & Biven, 2012). Evidence for the utility of this sparsely used strategy is the limited but consistent work in humans indicating the efficacy of the above scenario, especially the fifth item above: there is abundant "historical" data that humans commonly report experiences during subcortical stimulations yielding emotional effects resembling those found in other animals (Heath, 1996; Panksepp, 1985). Our knowledge of these basic emotional systems in animals has also now been extended to new psychiatric therapeutics in humans (e.g., Coenen et al., 2011, 2012; Mayberg, 2009; Schlaepfer et al., 2008, 2013).

Once we understand the brain chemistries that control the primary-process emotional feelings in animals, we will better understand our own emotional feelings, and hopefully have critical evidence to develop better mind medicines for human emotional problems (Burgdorf et al., 2011; Moskal Burgdorf, Kroes, Brudzynski, & Panksepp, 2011; Panksepp & Harro, 2004; Panksepp et al., 2014). As we come to understand the neuroanatomies and neurodynamics of the underlying neural networks ever more precisely, we can aspire to a constitutive understanding of raw emotional experiences.

Postlude: Fleshing out the ancestral subcortical sources of affective consciousness and potential linkages to cognitive awareness

To summarize, although it often seems impossible to fathom the origins of the evolved qualia of human mental life, it is increasingly clear that the deep subcortical terrain that has traditionally been seen to be the source of a dynamic "unconscious" now needs to be envisioned as the source of primal phenomenal experiences (Merker, 2007; Panksepp, 1998a, 1998b, 2005a, 2005b; Solms & Panksepp, 2012). This allows us to deploy animal research to provide a neurobiological understanding of a foundational affective phenomenal consciousness that at least all mammals share because of homologous brain systems. This remains a radical idea, especially because the guiding view of the western intellectual tradition has long been that consciousness emerges primarily from neocortical brain dynamics that may be uniquely human, because of our capacity for language and syntactic thought. The fact that we are the only species that can speak about their experiences perennially reinforces that bias (e.g., Rolls, 2005). Hence consensual agreement is bound to take considerable time to emerge.

However the ontological underpinning of the affective neuroscience views summarized here are based on a pragmatic *dual-aspect monism* view of how the mind is related to brain functions (Panksepp, 2005a, 2005b; Solms & Turnbull, 2002). Although dual-aspect approaches to consciousness have commonly had panpsychic ("mind dust") orientations, with religious overtones, where mind and matter were unified manifestations of a universal God (Spinoza), a more modern variant of dual-process theory has been *neutral monism* which posits a fundamental stuff that is neither mental nor physical, upon which both depend (Seager, 2009), perhaps at the sub-quantum level.

I deploy the *dual-aspect monism* concept in a more mundane way – perhaps it should be called *dual-perspectival monism* (as suggested by a friend philosopher Paul Davies, 2011) – with no need to consider the ultimate nature of the universe or any creation stories other than natural selection and the evolution of survival traits, both behavioral and psychological. It simply recognizes that certain global physical properties of neural-dynamics, especially the extensive within-brain electrodynamic fields, are concurrently sufficient to generate visually evident emotional behavior patterns to instantiate the affective mind as an emergent property of the underlying neural network complexities.

Perhaps a critical ingredient here is a primal representation of the organism's body, especially an intimate coordination of visceral and somatic parts, deep within the brainstem, constituting a neural matrix for a core-SELF within the brain (Panksepp, 1998b). It is the large-scale changes in this neurosymbolic-matrix for core consciousness, as reflected most objectively in peripheral bodily changes (emotional expression with accompanying autonomic changes), that are here seen to constitute primary-process emotional affects (Panksepp, 2007, 2009). Here *dual-perspectival* means that the more easily observed bodily dynamics of emotions and the corresponding harder to monitor psychoneural dynamics subsist hand-in-glove. Thus, the best we can hypothesize right now is that the within-brain neurodynamics that engender emotional actions are also critical for generating the feelings (with abundant bodily feedbacks to support and sustain such activities, no doubt). Thereby, the most conservative *dual-perspectival* interpretation is that the raw emotional within-brain instincts, that engender distinct emotional behaviors, do actually constitute raw emotional feelings.

This then, is a practical dual-aspect vision that fully respects the emergent properties that can arise from certain large-scale electrophysiological patterns of the brain that can be studied systematically in the laboratory. And this view is empirically useful because it makes explicit predictions. If the same neural systems that generate internal emotional feelings are those that lead to observable intense emotional behaviors in animals and humans – especially young creatures that cannot yet cortically regulate (inhibit/repress) their outward actions – we may have a better handle on psychiatric disorders than the various Diagnostic and Statistical Manuals of Mental Disorders provide. A primal emotional feeling *is* a property of the neurodynamics that engender the corresponding instinctual behaviors. During human development, with the accretion of emotional wisdom, higher cortical processes gradually develop the capacity to regulate both the outward expressions and, with Aristotelian *phronesis,* even the inward intensity of emotions. Thus, the current vision, based on emergent properties of complex neural interactions, can be an antidote to ruthless physical reductionism. Of course higher language/conceptual capacities help make sense of our feelings through our capacity to think, reflect, and ruminate through our higher cognitive abilities (Figure 1), which, with emotional development and education, also provides top-down control of emotionality. Internal visual imagery may serve similar functions in other animals (Grandin & Johnson, 2009), but currently that is hard to evaluate empirically.

Although we know a great deal about the neuroanatomies and neurochemistries of emotions, how might we proceed to an even deeper understanding of the actual neurodynamics that constitute each of the affective feelings? It is surely no understatement to note that we know very little about the details of how the underlying neural dynamics relate to emotional feelings, but as a first approximation we might want to focus on the external motor dynamics of primal emotional arousals (Panksepp & Gordon, 2003), and perhaps seek similar three dimensional dynamics within the subcortical emotional networks, as analysis of cortical networks may not suffice (Panksepp, 2000).

These global dynamics would be very hard to monitor, not only because of problems with situating recording electrodes "correctly" in massively overlapping emotional systems, but also because of the horrible motor artifacts that commonly accompany electrophysiological recordings when organisms are emotionally aroused. As humans can inhibit their emotional actions, we have tried to pursue this question with human surface EEG recordings (*vide infra*). In the rest of this and the next section I will consider how such issues may be further clarified and also suggest several hypothetical ways affective neural influences from below may control information processing in higher cognitive forms of consciousness.

In sum, the position advanced here is that phenomenal emotional experiences first emerged via ancient subcortical neural dynamics, arising perhaps initially from simple bivalent forms of negative and positive experiences, although this is highly debatable (for rich debates, see Zachar & Ellis, 2012). Because of the neuroscience revolution, we currently have solid ways to probe those ancient evolved BrainMind mechanisms of affective experiences. Those antecedents of higher human mental abilities can be studied, perhaps optimally, in the brains of non-speaking animals. To the best of our knowledge, all vertebrate creatures that still exist share the evolutionary imprints of those primordial neural functions in their brains. To reiterate, the most ancient regions still remain situated in the more caudal and medial regions within all of our brainstems. The more recent brain developments emerged more rostrally and laterally in the brain. This is true without any need to claim that there were *no* additional genetic readjustments in these brainstem survival circuits.

From such an affective foundation for psychological life, primal affective networks probably promote rapid memory integrations of associated sensory inputs from the *Umwelt* into learned behavior patterns, namely unconscious habits. As abundant evidence has now indicated, much of this occurs in higher (e.g., basal ganglia) regions of the brain – e.g., neuronal networks in amygdala, ventral striatum (i.e., nucleus accumbens) and related regions yielding exquisite learning and memory mechanisms, guided, I would propose, by unconditioned affective arousals that are not in themselves unconscious, although the resulting behavioral habits may be. For instance, it is clear that in "The Brain Reward System" concentrated in the medial forebrain bundle (MFB) which is the major substrate of SEEKING, a psychoneural substrate for vigorous foraging, with "enthusiasm" (for human and animal neuroanatomy, see Coenen et al., 2012, and Wright & Panksepp, 2012, respectively), the more medial electrode sites among dopamine neuron fields (i.e., the ventral tegmental area (VTA) which ascends to the ventral striatal/nucleus accumbens regions and project further onward to medial frontal cortex) are more rewarding than those more laterally situated, in substantia nigra, that project to the more recently evolved dorsal striatum, where habit structures are formed. As VTA dopamine neurons are probably more ancient than the lateral nigral ones, one can see how the more affective medial systems participate in immediate behavioral control while the lateral ones are more devoted to the gradual laying down of habitual behavior patterns.

Such functional levels of horizontal (medial-lateral) control make good evolutionary sense (for a fuller discussion, see Wright & Panksepp, 2012). And such functional distinctions reflect evolutionary levels of control in the brain, and again support the contention that raw affects are very ancient brain controls. From such a vantage, primordial organisms may have experienced themselves affectively earlier in neural evolution before they came to have any fine-tuning of behavior via learning (secondary processes) and surely neither well-resolved decision-making capacities nor thoughts (tertiary-processes) about the outside world. Further, in contrast to the evidence we have for affective brain networks, our ability to appreciate the sensory-perceptual experiences of other animals must remain more conjectural. In contrast to the difficulty of "seeing into" their cognitive minds, our ability to study their affective experiences seems rock solid, simply because it can be based on the rich and abundant cross-species evidence that emotional network arousals can mediate rewarding and punishing states of the brain, effects that are also clearly evident in humans. Obviously such conclusions in no way diminish the fact that gradual encephalization added much to the overall equation – the breadth and depth – of consciousness (Figure 1). Before such encephalization, animals were neither cognitive nor confused. Their actions, affects and memories were fully integrated, sufficing for simple learning.

This evolutionary view also raises the possibility that cognitive developments in consciousness, critically linked to secondary-level learning and memory capacities, is somehow promoted by the unconditional feelings of the lower brain regions. Three lines of neural evidence have long suggested these conclusions: (1) forebrain waking is critically dependent on midbrain regions initially labeled the "ascending reticular activating system" about which much is known (Moruzzi & Magoun, 1949; Pfaff, 2006; Watt & Pincus, 2004). (2) As we have already discussed, stimulations along this trajectory can promote general arousal, along with many emotional attitudes. (3) Most recently, localized facilitation of GABA in this circuitry, mediating neural inhibition, can produce unconsciousness (Sukhotinsky et al., 2007). Overall, this perspective is also concordant with the well-established neuropsychological fact that cognitive consciousness is fundamentally dependent on very ancient subcortical systems of the brain (Merker, 2007; Panksepp, 1998b, 2007; Parvizi & Damasio, 2001; Solms & Panksepp, 2012).

This, of course is not to claim that there have been no species typical genetic adjustments of subcortical circuit strengths and sensitivities. Obviously there were abundant evolutionary fine-tunings (and experiential/epigenetic ones as well) that are reflected in the strengths and patterns of the various instinctual emotional systems across species. Within such constraints, the key argument here is that many brainstem areas that have long been considered simply "permissive" for cognitive consciousness, including thalamic intralaminar nuclei that help sharpen external sensations and perceptions (for review see Watt & Pincus, 2004), work side by side with those that monitor internal survival issues engendering global states of affective core consciousness (Damasio, 2010; Panksepp, 1998a, 1998b, 2007, 2009). At present, it is within these evolutionarily ancient emotional-affective networks, that the very make-up of phenomenal constitution – the warp and weft of the neural mechanisms that generate experiences – first emerged from neural activities.

Denoument: The affective constitution of cognitive consciousness – A speculative argument

Of course, we are at the very beginning of utilizing such epistemologies effectively. And we also barely know how the lower affective substrates of mind actually permit higher cognitive functions to emerge. This is currently a rich area for theorizing, hopefully in ways that lead to empirical predictions. For instance, cognitive consciousness may have piggybacked on the electrochemical coding of incoming sensory processes, allowing resolved images of the external world. Alternatively, it may have been more dependent on pre-existing forms of affective consciousness. I prefer the latter option, for that has the potential to solve perennial problems of neuroscience, such as how did the internal experiences of color – e.g., blue, green and red – evolve as subjective experiences in organisms where color vision is typically triggered by retinal detectors for distinct bands of electromagnetic radiation during waking (but which can be free-running during dreaming)? Clearly colors and sounds are not properties of the outside world. They reflect the way our minds were constructed in evolution, with survival issues being foremost in the underlying natural selection processes.

Thus there must have been some survival advantage in seeing apples as red, and grass as green. At a strictly cognitive information-computational level of analysis, it is hard to imagine how such phenomenal aspects of the world evolved. It is easier, at least for me, to envision that there may exist deep relationships between pre-existing subcortical emotional dynamics and the overlying resonant electrochemical frequencies in cortex that code for the affective value of incoming visual stimuli. Blood red may help signal strong passions such as RAGE and LUST, not to mention our deep desire for food. Green may signal life supportive environments that attract and reflect SEEKING dynamics. Blue may reflect a peaceful CAREing attitude. YELLOW may have emerged as a response to signals of warmth, and BLACK stark coldness. But this conjecture cannot be empirically evaluated… yet. The point is, ancestral emotional and other affective dynamics were probably guiding "forces" (pre-adaptations or exapdations) in diverse later BrainMind developments. Just like the evolution of feathers for warmth eventually permitted flight, affective consciousness may have been a critical ingredient for the eventual emergence of cognitive activities.

The idea that natural affective dynamics of the brain can be re-represented as cognitive forms of external information processing through resonant neurodynamics has some evolutionary allure: What came first should provide a dynamic foundation for what came later. Such a vision helps make sense of how important emotional intonations and *motherese* are for early language acquisition (Panksepp, 2008). It may make sense of the emotional dynamics of music (Clynes, 1977, 1988), and the emotional linkage seems self-evident in many other arts, from dance to theater. It may help explain why our cognitive mind is so easily exhilarated and devastated by our emotional feelings, and why such effects are more evident in children. To make any empirical sense out of such potential relationships, we surely need to know much more about global affective neurodynamics within the brain.

Further, there are currently abundant reasons to worry if there currently exists any credible evidence for genetically provided modularity of cognitive processes within neocortical regions of the brain (Panksepp & Panksepp, 2000, 2001). The repetitive expansions of neocortical columns were so rapid in human encephalization, indirectly permitted perhaps by the cultural discovery of cooking, that it seems unlikely that language has any more of an evolved "instinctual" foundation than does our ability to make rich emotional sounds with our inheritance of a highly flexible and resonant vocal apparatus. This is a capability that differs little from that of any other animal. In essence, our vast mental abilities – from language, to reading, to writing, and composition of music – have obviously been largely matters of cultural learning.

The neocortex truly resembles *tabula rasa,* like random-access memory of brand new computers. It is gradually programmed by experiences in the world. This is true even for vision (Sur & Rubinstein, 2005). In contrast the subcortical realm is full of evolved instinctual urges, homologous in all mammals. At such lower levels of mind, the study of animals has told us much more than has the study of humans, at least about the affective fundamentals of our primary-process emotional lives, along with abundant knowledge of the unconscious secondary-mechanisms of learning and memory (Panksepp, 1998; Solms & Panksepp, 2012). Human research continues to illuminate how the higher reaches of our minds get programmed. But so much upstairs in the brain may have been programmed by, as it now remains guided by, the affective issues that transpired in downstairs brain regions during both early neural evolution in mammalian species as well as the ontogenetic development of each individual, which can be devastated by emotional vicissitudes (Narvaez, 2014).

Regrettably the affective network neurodynamics that characterize these emotion-cognition progressions remain poorly characterized, except in the case of certain psychopathologies, for instance depression (e.g., Alcaro, Panksepp, Witczak, Hayes, & Northoff, 2010). So here we can just consider possibilities arising from some relevant animal research: It is clear that one of the key neurodynamics of the SEEKING system is theta rhythms, engendered by the MFB coursing from ventromedial midbrain regions through the lateral hypothalamus to hippocampus and diverse forebrain regions, especially medial frontal ones (Coenen et al., 2012). When they are exploring and foraging, animals typically exhibit characteristic theta rhythms in SEEKING relevant brain regions, not only during their explicit explorations of the world, but also during the implicit dopamine driven emotional urges manifested during rapid eye-movement sleep (Panksepp, 1998a; Solms, 2000).

Theta rhythm is most especially well studied and evident during the sniffing-investigatory-foraging (i.e., SEEKING) behavior of rats (Panksepp, 1998a; Vanderwolf, 1988). Indeed, the sniffing response correlates strictly with the threshold of DBS reward from the MFB (Ikemoto & Panksepp, 1994; Rossi & Panksepp, 1992), and it conditions spontaneously in an anticipatory way when rewards are given freely at fixed intervals (Panksepp, 1981a, 1998a; see Figure 3). Another indicator of this all-important and most tonically active of emotional systems in action, can be indexed by 50 kHz ultrasonic vocalizations. The study of this excellent indicator of positive affect, especially social feelings, has allowed us to identify neurochemical pathways for new antidepressant medication development (Burgdorf et al., 2007, 2011).

In the late 1980s we surmised that one way to translate such findings to human emotional experiences, and related higher brain functions might be to characterize how the human cortex is aroused by various emotional stimuli. The results were chaotic (Bekkedal, Rossi, & Panksepp, 2011; Panksepp, 2000). Gradually we narrowed our analysis to discrete emotional sounds in dimensional affective space favored by many psychologists (for extensive coverage, see Zachar & Ellis, 2012): we deployed anger sounds for negativistic, high-arousal simulation; joy sounds for positive high-arousal; and sounds of pleasure and disgust for positive and negative low arousal feelings, respectively. Although we devoted considerable effort to studying such neocortical effects, it was next to impossible to identify clear emotion-specific EEG signatures in human brains from topographic event-related recordings (especially power-shifts within the resting alpha range, which were often dramatically large but highly variable from person to person: for the author's own brain analyses, see depictions of his EEG fluctuations archived at his WSU web site http://www.vetmed.wsu.edu/research_vcapp/Panksepp/ – by clicking "EEGs" right above "Research Interests"). However, in re-analysis of such data, it became clear that the next lower energy band – theta range – was more systematically sensitive to discrete emotional inputs, namely primal emotional sounds (for a summary, see Figure 2 in Bekkedal et al., 2011).

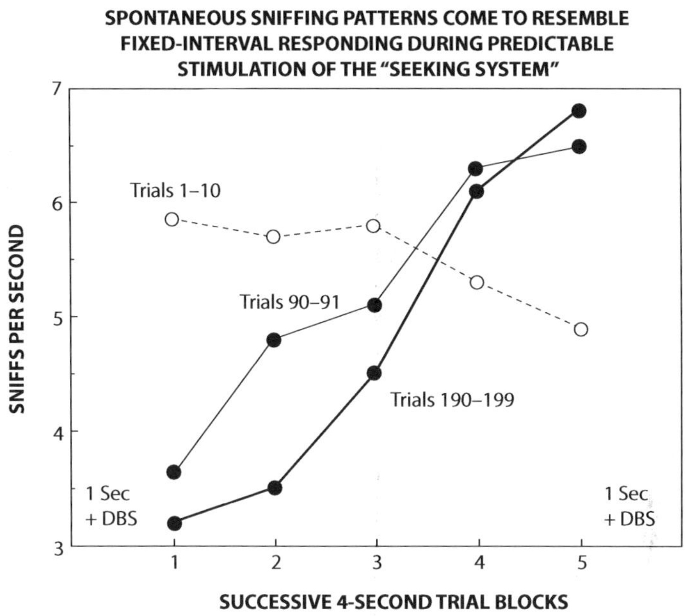

Figure 3. Elaboration of sniffing in adult male rats during free fixed-interval 20-second administration of rewarding medial forebrain bundle/lateral hypothalamic deep brain stimulation (DBS) given freely for 200 successive trials (i.e., no operant response was required). During the beginning of training (first 10 trials), animals exhibited only generalized overall energization of sniffing throughout the interstimulation interval. During middle trials, a spontaneous anticipatory trend had emerged. By the end of training (trials 190–199), animals were exhibiting a scalloped pattern, which is reminiscent of animals working for conventional rewards on a fixed-interval schedule. An important point to note is that all of these stimulations were free, and the animals did not have to change their behavior patterns in any way to obtain all "rewards." However, the SEEKING system spontaneously developed an instrumental-type pattern of behavioral output. In a sense, a rat's brain begins to anticipate its own pure desires/enthusiasms (Panksepp & Moskal, 2008). This can help explain how anticipatory patterns of behavior emerge on operant schedules of reinforcement that have long been described in the behavioral literature. Adapted from Figure 8.4 of *Affective Neuroscience* (Panksepp, 1998a), with permission of Oxford University Press.

Considering that theta is the frequency most commonly associated with appetitive arousal, and that it is critically linked to the SEEKING urges of the MFB, we can begin to consider whether the representations of such primal rhythms carry related affective information into neocortical fields that mediate cognitive processing. Although this remains a poorly developed field of inquiry, I will at least consider one possibility of how affective urges arising from lower brain regions may have promoted higher cognitive modes of external information processing, especially during neocortical encephalization, using concepts introduced in Solms and Panksepp (2012).

Let us consider that the slower EEG rhythms tend to reflect what has been considered to be "free energy" in the nervous system: namely many neural ensembles working together to produce high voltage patterns characteristic of the lower EEG frequencies (e.g., delta, theta, as well as low frequency alpha). During waking, certain of these rhythms, such as theta, may be parsed into higher resonant frequencies resembling vocal formants – namely the resonant overtones created by the structures of the vocal apparatus. These higher and weaker frequencies can be considered to be more "bound" in the sense their energy levels are lower voltage, but higher frequency, formant derivatives of the lower theta frequencies. Could it be that such high frequency, low power, brain waves, so abundant in the awake neocortex – evident as high frequency beta and especially gamma rhythms – are parsing lower survival related information, into more fine-grained and discrete forms of "bound energy" that are better able to resolve the surrounding world into detailed exteroceptive perceptions, thereby providing discrete information for higher thought processes (intrapsychic ruminations)? Alternatively, perhaps the fine-grain of perceptions arises completely through the sensory processing channels, with the higher cognitive processes binding these inputs into thought patterns through powerful affective energies from below. Although these are just hypotheses and thought-experiments at the present time, they at least offer a way to envision how the nested-hierarchies of the MindBrain (Figure 1) send upward cascades of neural patterns that also reflect ancient affective survival-indicative signals from the lower affective brain networks into higher brain regions, and thereby promote and coordinate affectively guided thinking patterns within cognitive mental functions. From this perspective, it may have been wiser for us to pursue our EEG studies in animals first in order to examine how emotion-evoking DBS of lower brain regions influenced dynamic patterns in the neocortex. But we failed to make that choice (Panksepp, 2000).

In any event, a great deal of empirical progress has already been achieved in decoding how mammalian brains generate primal forms of affective consciousness using DBS and related neurochemical manipulations (Panksepp, 1998a; Panksepp & Biven, 2012). The utility of the present speculative exercise is to merely show how potential neuro-empirical bridges to higher cognitive processes can be theoretically envisioned, at least in rough outline. The key point is: perhaps only through disciplined neuroscientific hypotheses of how the lower affective reaches of the mind help mold diverse higher brain functions, can we envision how we came to be self-aware of our place in the world – first in our local communities and environments, and then within the solar system, initially with Galileo's spy-glass, and now the much vaster universe with magnificent tools such as the Hubble. With similar intellectual progressions, we may gradually come to understand the evolution of the unique aspects of the human mind, recently privileged by vast associative and memory storage potentials of our neocortical expansions. Perhaps these passages were promoted by ancestral neurodynamics and affective mental abilities we still share with the other animals. In order to understand our mental origins, we may need to envision what happened in hierarchical brain organization (Figure 1), and rostro-lateral encephalization, during vast passages of time.

The notion that the very foundation of mind may be affective is novel, but strongly suggested by existing data (Panksepp, 1998a; Solms & Panksepp, 2012). Such an understanding may eventually turn much of consciousness studies on its head, as we come to terms with the long course of evolution of the human BrainMind, with higher functions being built not only *upon*, but *from*, lower functions. Most of these passages are incapable of being studied directly because they transpired when our ancestors were animals not much different from shrew-like primates that existed some hundred million years ago. From a slightly different vantage, the suggestion here is that in order to understand our higher self-awareness, we must first come to terms with *anoetic* forms of consciousness such as raw affective and perceptual experiences. That knowledge may set the stage for progressing from *noetic* (knowledge-based) toward complex *autonoetic* (thought-based) forms of consciousness (Tulving, 2005; Vandekerckhove & Panksepp, 2009, 2011).

If so, a fruitful inquiry from the neural correlates of perceptual consciousness, as is popular these days, to the constitution of consciousness in general, may need to be supplemented with affective neuroscience strategies: to understand how those correlates derive their power to generate phenomenal perceptual experiences, short of positing several higher-order evolutionary paths to consciousness, we may need to consider that the neural underpinnings of perceptual and other cognitive experiences arise from (and retain) affective foundations. Thereby understanding the neural constitution of consciousness may require us to fathom the aboriginal types of affective experiences that first arose from brain dynamics, yielding various positive and negative states of mind – various feelings of "goodness" and "badness" reflecting direct survival issues of the body operating in the world. The major alternative is to posit separate evolutionary progressions for perceptual-cognitive consciousness, which for me, is intellectually unsatisfying and, at present, neuroscientifically unsupported. In any event, as already repeatedly noted, our ancestral neuroaffective experiences can be studied, by various behavioral *approach* and *escape* measures, in "lower" animals. Thus, from my affective neuroscience vantage, our constitutive understanding of "higher" forms of consciousness currently lags behind our understanding of emotional affects.

Let us recall the two major evolutionary questions we have to answer at all levels of the BrainMind: As Dan Dennett (2014) usefully parsed it, the blind evolutionary 'teleology' of organismic functional capacities are conceptual "what for" questions (why did something emerge; what adaptation did it serve), which need to be related empirically to "how come" questions (experimentally ferreting out the underlying natural constitution of the functional processes). The "what for" evolutionary line of reasoning advanced here is premised on the recognition that affects are very useful *anticipatory* mechanisms for survival (e.g., Figure 3), especially when mere unconscious behavioral responses do not suffice. The Rubicon toward the first glimmers of consciousness was presumably crossed when ancient organismic abilities emerged allowing animals to find, defend and anticipate external resources and also to defend themselves, based upon experiential issues, as opposed to affectively "blind" behavioral strategies alone.

As soon as one makes this transformation in theoretical perspective, along with the recognition of the mass of relevant evidence that already exists, deepened by ever advancing superlative tools of modern neuroscience, one has immediate opportunities to study the more mechanistic "how come" constitutive questions in ever greater detail in diverse animal models. Perhaps good experimental progress on the most primal affective-mental functions will provide a foundation for understanding further evolutionary developments in cognitive realms. Regrettably, emotional feelings are still viewed by many as higher cerebral skills possessed only by humans (e.g., as neocortical functions, perhaps based on language – e.g., see Rolls, 1999, 2005). I have argued that a study of the primal emotional foundations of certain affective experiences in other animals can explicitly model the constitution of human *anoetic* affective consciousness – primal forms of phenomenal valenced experience, which may have set the stage for the emergence of higher mental faculties. In so doing, it is worth re-emphasizing that such ancestral states of mind may not deserve either the ambiguous label of "awareness" or the more precise descriptor "self-awareness". Affective consciousness does not imply that organisms cognitively *know* what they are experiencing. It is merely an assertion about the evolutionary nature of certain types of qualia and the affective nature of our core-selves (Damasio, 2010; Panksepp, 1998a, 1998b), shared by all mammals, perhaps even other creatures, in kind, if not precise form and detail.

References

Alcaro, A., Panksepp, J., Witczak, J., Hayes, D. J., & Northoff, G. (2010). Is subcortical–cortical midline activity in depression mediated by glutamate and GABA? A cross-species translational approach. *Neuroscience & Biobehavioral Reviews*, 34(4), 592–605. DOI: 10.1016/j.neubiorev.2009.11.023

Balcombe, J. (2006). *Pleasurable kingdom: Animals and the nature of feeling good*. London, UK: MacMillan.

Bekkedal, M. Y. V., Rossi, J., III, & Panksepp, J. (2011). Human brain EEG indices of emotions: Delineating responses to affective vocalizations by measuring frontal theta event-related synchronization. *Neuroscience & Biobehavioral Reviews*, 35(9), 1959–1970. DOI: 10.1016/j.neubiorev.2011.05.001

Bekoff, M. (2007). *The emotional lives of animals*. Novato, CA: New World Library.

Buhle, J. T., Kober, H., Ochsner, K. N., Mende-Siedlecki. P., Weber, J., Hughes, B. L., Kross, E., Atlas, L. Y., McRae, K., & Wager, T. D. (2013). Common representation of pain and negative emotion in the midbrain periaqueductal gray. *Social Cognitive & Affective Neuroscience*, 8(6), 609–616. DOI: 10.1093/scan/nss038

Burgdorf, J., Panksepp, J., Brudzynski, S. M., Kroes, R., & Moskal, J. R. (2005). Breeding for 50-kHz positive affective vocalization in rats. *Behavior Genetics*, 35(1), 67–72. DOI: 10.1007/s10519-004-0856-5

Burgdorf, J., Panksepp, J., & Moskal, J. R. (2011). Frequency-modulated 50kHz ultrasonic vocalizations: A tool for uncovering the molecular substrates of positive affect. *Neuroscience & Biobehavioral Reviews*, 35(9), 1831–1836. DOI: 10.1016/j.neubiorev.2010.11.011

Burgdorf, J., Wood, P. L., Kroes, R. A., Moskal, J. R., & Panksepp, J. (2007). Neurobiology of 50-kHz ultrasonic vocalizations in rats: Electrode mapping, lesion, and pharmacology studies. *Behavioural Brain Research*, 182(2), 274–283. DOI: 10.1016/j.bbr.2007.03.010

Cabanac, M. (1992). Pleasure: The common currency. *Journal of Theoretical Biology*, 155(2), 173–200. DOI: 10.1016/S0022-5193(05)80594-6

Caruana, F., Jezzini, A., Sbriscia-Fioretti, B., Rizzolatti, G. & Gallese, V. (2011). Emotional and social behaviors elicited by electrical stimulation of the insula in the macaque monkey. *Current Biology*, 21(3), 195–199. DOI: 10.1016/j.cub.2010.12.042

Clynes, M. (1977). *Sentics: The touch of emotions*. New York, NY: Doubleday & Company.

Clynes, M. (1988). Generalised emotion: How it may be produced, and sentic cycle therapy. In M. Clynes & J. Panksepp (Eds.), *Emotions and psychopathology* (pp. 107–170). New York, NY: Plenum Press. DOI: 10.1007/978-1-4757-1987-1_6

Coenen, V. A., Panksepp, J., Hurwitz, T. A., Urbach, H., & Mädler, B. (2012). Human medial forebrain bundle (MFB) and anterior thalamic radiation (ATR): Imaging of two major subcortical pathways and the dynamic balance of opposite effects in understanding depression. *Journal of Neuropsychiatry and Clinical Neurosciences*, 24(2), 223–236. DOI: 10.1176/appi.neuropsych.11080180

Coenen, V. A., Schlaepfer, T. E., Maedler, B., & Panksepp, J. (2011). Cross-species affective functions of the medial forebrain bundle – Implications for the treatment of affective pain and depression in humans. *Neuroscience & Biobehavioral Reviews*, 35(9), 1971–1981. DOI: 10.1016/j.neubiorev.2010.12.009

Cottingham, J. (2008). *Cartesian reflections: Essays on Descartes's philosophy*. New York, NY: Oxford University Press.

Craig, A. D. (2003). Interoception: The sense of the physiological condition of the body. *Current Opinion in Neurobiology*, 13(4), 500–505. DOI: 10.1016/S0959-4388(03)00090-4

Cromwell, H. C., & Panksepp, J. (2011). Rethinking the cognitive revolution from a neural perspective: How overuse/misuse of the term 'cognition' and the neglect of affective controls in behavioral neuroscience could be delaying progress in understanding the BrainMind. *Neuroscience & Biobehavioral Reviews*, 35(9), 2026–2035. DOI: 10.1016/j.neubiorev.2011.02.008

Damasio, A. (2010). *Self comes to mind: Constructing the conscious brain*. New York, NY: Pantheon.

Damasio, A. R. (1994). *Descartes' error: Emotion, reason, and the human brain*. New York, NY: Avon Books.

Davies, P. S. (2011). Ancestral voices in the mammalian mind: Philosophical implications of Jaak Panksepp's affective neuroscience. *Neuroscience & Biobehavioral Reviews*, 35(9), 2036–2044. DOI: 10.1016/j.neubiorev.2010.10.010

Davis, K. L., & Panksepp, J. (2011). The brain's emotional foundations of human personality and the Affective Neuroscience Personality Scales. *Neuroscience & Biobehavioral Reviews*, 35(9), 1946–1958. DOI: 10.1016/j.neubiorev.2011.04.004

Dawkins, M. S. (2001). Who needs consciousness? *Animal Welfare*, 10(Suppl. 1), 19–29.

Delgado, J. M. R., Roberts, W. W., & Miller, N. E. (1954). Learning motivated by electrical stimulation of the brain. *American Journal of Physiology*, 179(3), 587–593.

Dennett, D. (2014). The evolution of reasons. In B. Bashour & H. D. Muller (Eds.), *Contemporary philosophical naturalism and its implications* (pp. 47–62). New York, NY: Routledge.

Denton, D. (2006). *The primordial emotions: The dawning of consciousness*. New York, NY: Oxford University Press. DOI: 10.1093/acprof:oso/9780199203147.001.0001

Devor, M. (2008). Consciousness and pain. In A. I. Basbaum & M. C. Bushnell (Eds.), *The senses: A comprehensive reference, Volume 5: Pain* (pp. 961–967). San Diego, CA: Academic Press. DOI: 10.1016/B978-012370880-9.00207-3

de Waal, F. B. M. (2011). What is an animal emotion? *Annals of the New York Academy of Sciences*, 1224, 191–206. DOI: 10.1111/j.1749-6632.2010.05912.x

Grandin, T., & Johnson, C. (2005). *Animals in translation: Using the mysteries of autism to decode animal behavior*. New York, NY: Scribner.

Grandin, T., & Johnson, C. (2009). *Animals make us human: Creating the best life for animals*. Orlando, FL: Houghton Mifflin Harcourt Publishing Company.

Heath, R. G. (1996). *Exploring the mind-body relationship*. Baton Rouge, LA: Moran Printing, Inc.

Huber, R., Panksepp, J. B., Nathaniel, T., Alcaro, A., & Panksepp, J. (2011). Drug-sensitive reward in crayfish: An invertebrate model system for the study of SEEKING, reward, addiction, and withdrawal. *Neuroscience & Biobehavioral Reviews*, 35(9), 1847–1853. DOI: 10.1016/j.neubiorev.2010.12.008

Huston, J. P., & Borbély, A. A. (1973). Operant conditioning in forebrain ablated rats by use of rewarding hypothalamic stimulation. *Brain Research*, 50(2), 467–472. DOI: 10.1016/0006-8993(73)90753-1

Huston, J. P., & Borbély, A. A. (1974). The thalamic rat: General behavior, operant learning with rewarding hypothalamic stimulation, and effects of amphetamine. *Physiology & Behavior*, 12(3), 433–448. DOI: 10.1016/0031-9384(74)90121-8

Ikemoto, S., & Panksepp, J. (1994). The relationship between self-stimulation and sniffing in rats: Does a common brain system mediate these behaviors? *Behavioural Brain Research*, 61(2), 143–162. DOI: 10.1016/0166-4328(94)90155-4

King, T., Vera-Portocarrero, L., Gutierrez, T, Vanderah, T. W., Dussor, G., Lai, J., Fields, H. L., & Porreca, F. (2009). Unmasking the tonic-aversive state in neuropathic pain. *Nature Neuroscience*, 12(11), 1364–1366. DOI: 10.1038/nn.2407

Koob, G. F., Le Moal, M., & Thompson, R. F. (Eds.). (2010). *Encyclopedia of behavioral neuroscience*. New York, NY: Elsevier.

LeDoux, J. E. (1996). *The emotional brain: The mysterious underpinnings of emotional life*. New York, NY: Simon & Schuster.

LeDoux, J. E. (2012). Evolution of human emotion: A view through fear. *Progress in Brain Research*, 195, 431–442. DOI: 10.1016/B978-0-444-53860-4.00021-0

Lehrman, D. S. (1953). A critique of Konrad Lorenz's theory of instinctive behavior. *Quarterly Review of Biology*, 28(4), 337–363. DOI: 10.1086/399858

Macphail, E. M. (1998). *The evolution of consciousness*. Oxford, UK: Oxford University Press. DOI: 10.1093/acprof:oso/9780198503248.001.0001

Mayberg, H. S. (2009). Targeted electrode-based modulation of neural circuits for depression. *Journal of Clinical Investigation*, 119(4), 717–725. DOI: 10.1172/JCI38454

Mendl, M., Burman, O. H. P., & Paul, E. S. (2010). An integrative and functional framework for the study of animal emotions and mood. *Proceedings of the Royal Society of London B: Biological Sciences*, 277(1696), 2895–2904. DOI: 10.1098/rspb.2010.0303

Merker, B. (2007). Consciousness without a cerebral cortex: A challenge for neuroscience and medicine. *Behavioral and Brain Sciences*, 30(1), 63–81.

Miller, S. M. (2001). Binocular rivalry and the cerebral hemispheres: With a note on the correlates and constitution of visual consciousness. *Brain and Mind*, 2(1), 119–149. DOI: 10.1023/A:1017981619014

Miller, S. M. (2007). On the correlation/constitution distinction problem (and other hard problems) in the scientific study of consciousness. *Acta Neuropsychiatrica*, 19(3), 159–176. DOI: 10.1111/j.1601-5215.2007.00207.x

Moruzzi, G., & Magoun, H. W. (1949). Brain stem reticular formation and activation of the EEG. *Electroencephalography and Clinical Neurophysiology*, 1(1–4), 455–473. DOI: 10.1016/0013-4694(49)90219-9

Moskal, J. R., Burgdorf, J., Kroes, R. A., Brudzynski, S. M., & Panksepp, J. (2011). A novel NMDA receptor glycine-site partial agonist, GLYX-13, has therapeutic potential for the treatment of autism. *Neuroscience & Biobehavioral Reviews*, 35(9), 1982–1988. DOI: 10.1016/j.neubiorev.2011.06.006

Narvaez, D. (2014). *Neurobiology and the development of human morality: Evolution, culture, and wisdom*. New York, NY: W. W. Norton & Company, Inc.

Nashold, B. S., Jr, Wilson, W. P., & Slaughter, D. G. (1969). Sensations evoked by stimulation of the midbrain of man. *Journal of Neurosurgery*, 30(1), 14–24. DOI: 10.3171/jns.1969.30.1.0014

Northoff, G., Wiebking, C., Feinberg, T., & Panksepp, J. (2011). The 'resting-state hypothesis' of major depressive disorder – A translational subcortical–cortical framework for a system disorder. *Neuroscience & Biobehavioral Reviews*, 35(9), 1929–1945. DOI: 10.1016/j.neubiorev.2010.12.007

Olds, J., & Milner, P. (1954). Positive reinforcement produced by electrical stimulation of the septal area and other regions of rat brain. *Journal of Comparative and Physiological Psychology*, 47(6), 419–427. DOI: 10.1037/h0058775

Panksepp, J. (1971). Aggression elicited by electrical stimulation of the hypothalamus in albino rats. *Physiology & Behavior*, 6(4), 321–329. DOI: 10.1016/0031-9384(71)90163-6

Panksepp, J. (1981a). Hypothalamic integration of behavior: Rewards, punishments, and related psychobiological process. In P. J. Morgane & J. Panksepp (Eds.), *Handbook of the hypothalamus, Vol. 3, Part A. Behavioral studies of the hypothalamus* (pp. 289–487). New York, NY: Marcel Dekker.

Panksepp, J. (1981b). Brain opioids: A neurochemical substrate for narcotic and social dependence. In S. Cooper (Ed.), *Progress in theory in psychopharmacology* (pp. 149–175). London, UK: Academic Press.

Panksepp, J. (1982). Toward a general psychobiological theory of emotions. *Behavioral and Brain Sciences*, 5(3), 407–422. DOI: 10.1017/S0140525X00012759

Panksepp, J. (1985). Mood changes. In P. Vinken, G. Bruyn, & H. Klawans (Eds.), *Handbook of clinical neurology: Clinical neuropsychology*, Vol. 45 (pp. 271–285). Amsterdam, The Netherlands: Elsevier Science.

Panksepp, J. (1986). The neurochemistry of behavior. *Annual Review of Psychology*, 37, 77–107. DOI: 10.1146/annurev.ps.37.020186.000453

Panksepp, J. (1988). Brain emotional circuits and psychopathologies. In M. Clynes & J. Panksepp (Eds.), *Emotions and psychopathology* (pp. 37–76). New York, NY: Plenum Press. DOI: 10.1007/978-1-4757-1987-1_3

Panksepp, J. (1990a). The psychoneurology of fear: Evolutionary perspectives and the role of animal models in understanding human anxiety. In G. D. Burrows, M. Roth, & R. J. Noyes (Eds.), *Handbook of anxiety, Vol. 3: The neurobiology of anxiety* (pp. 3–58). Amsterdam, The Netherlands: Elsevier/North-Holland Biomedical Press.

Panksepp, J. (1990b). Can "mind" and behavior be understood without understanding the brain?: A response to Bunge. *New Ideas in Psychology*, 8(2), 139–149. DOI: 10.1016/0732-118X(90)90003-K

Panksepp, J. (1991). Affective neuroscience: A conceptual framework for the neurobiological study of emotions. In K. T. Strongman (Ed.), *International review of studies on emotions* (pp. 59–99). Chichester, England: Wiley.

Panksepp, J. (1993). Rough-and-tumble play: A fundamental brain process. In K. B. MacDonald (Ed.), *Parent-child play: Descriptions and implications* (pp. 147–184). Albany, NY: SUNY Press.

Panksepp, J. (1998a). *Affective neuroscience: The foundations of human and animal emotions*. New York, NY: Oxford University Press.

Panksepp, J. (1998b). The periconscious substrates of consciousness: Affective states and the evolutionary origins of the self. *Journal of Consciousness Studies*, 5(5–6), 566–582.

Panksepp, J. (2000). The neurodynamics of emotions: An evolutionary-neurodevelopmental view. In M. D. Lewis & I. Granic (Eds.), *Emotion, development, and self-organization: Dynamic systems approaches to emotional development* (pp. 236–264). New York, NY: Cambridge University Press. DOI: 10.1017/CBO9780511527883.011

Panksepp, J. (Ed.). (2004). *Textbook of biological psychiatry*. Hoboken, NJ: Wiley.

Panksepp, J. (2005a). Affective consciousness: Core emotional feelings in animals and humans. *Consciousness and Cognition*, 14(1), 30–80. DOI: 10.1016/j.concog.2004.10.004

Panksepp, J. (2005b). On the embodied neural nature of core emotional affects. *Journal of Consciousness Studies*, 12(8–10), 158–184.

Panksepp, J. (2006). Emotional endophenotypes in evolutionary psychiatry. *Progress in Neuro-psychopharmacology and Biological Psychiatry*, 30(5), 774–784. DOI: 10.1016/j.pnpbp.2006.01.004

Panksepp, J. (2007). Affective consciousness. In M. Velmans & S. Schneider (Eds.), *The Blackwell companion to consciousness* (pp. 114–129). Malden, MA: Blackwell Publishing, Ltd. DOI: 10.1002/9780470751466.ch9

Panksepp, J. (2008). The power of the word may reside in the power of affect. *Integrative Physiological & Behavioral Science*, 42(1), 47–55. DOI: 10.1007/s12124-007-9036-5

Panksepp, J. (2009). Core consciousness. In T. Bayne, A. Cleeremans, & P. Wilken (Eds.), *The Oxford companion to consciousness* (pp. 198–200). Oxford, UK: Oxford University Press.

Panksepp, J. (2010). Foreword: Perspectives on passages toward an affective neurobiology of mind? In G. Koob, M. Le Moal, & R. F. Thompson (Eds.), *Encyclopedia of behavioral neuroscience* (pp. xxii–xxix). New York, NY: Elsevier. DOI: 10.1016/B978-0-08-045396-5.09006-0

Panksepp, J. (2011a). Toward a cross-species neuroscientific understanding of the affective mind: Do animals have emotional feelings? *American Journal of Primatology*, 73(6), 545–561. DOI: 10.1002/ajp.20929

Panksepp, J. (2011b). The basic emotional circuits of mammalian brains: Do animals have affective lives? *Neuroscience & Biobehavioral Reviews*, 35(9), 1791–1804. DOI: 10.1016/j.neubiorev.2011.08.003

Panksepp, J. (2011c). Cross-species affective neuroscience decoding of the primal affective experiences of humans and related animals. *PLoS One*, 6(9), e21236. DOI: 10.1371/journal.pone.0021236

Panksepp, J. (2012). The vicissitudes of preclinical psychiatric research: Justified abandonment by big pharma? *Future Neurology*, 7(2), 113–115. DOI: 10.2217/fnl.12.1

Panksepp, J., Bean, N. J., Bishop, P., Vilberg, T., & Sahley, T. L. (1980). Opioid blockade and social comfort in chicks. *Pharmacology Biochemistry and Behavior*, 13(5), 673–683. DOI: 10.1016/0091-3057(80)90011-8

Panksepp, J., & Biven, L. (2012). *The archaeology of mind: Neuroevolutionary origins of human emotion*. New York, NY: W. W. Norton & Company, Inc.

Panksepp, J., & Gordon, N. (2003). The instinctual basis of human affect: Affective imaging of laughter and crying. *Consciousness & Emotion*, 4(2), 197–205. DOI: 10.1075/ce.4.2.04pan

Panksepp, J., & Harro, J. (2004). Future of neuropeptides in biological psychiatry and emotional psychopharmacology: Goals and strategies. In J. Panksepp (Ed.), *Textbook of biological psychiatry* (pp. 627–659). Hoboken, NJ: Wiley.

Panksepp, J., & Moskal, J. (2008). Dopamine and SEEKING: Subcortical "reward" systems and appetitive urges. In A. J. Elliot (Ed.), *Handbook of approach and avoidance motivation* (pp. 67–87). New York, NY: Taylor & Francis Group, LLC.

Panksepp, J., & Northoff, G. (2009). The trans-species core SELF: The emergence of active cultural and neuro-ecological agents through self-related processing within subcortical-cortical midline networks. *Consciousness and Cognition*, 18(1), 193–215. DOI: 10.1016/j.concog.2008.03.002

Panksepp, J., & Panksepp, J. B. (2000). The seven sins of evolutionary psychology. *Evolution & Cognition*, 6(2), 108–131.

Panksepp, J., & Panksepp, J. B. (2001). A continuing critique of evolutionary psychology: Seven sins for seven sinners, plus or minus two. *Evolution & Cognition*, 7(1), 56–80.

Panksepp, J., Sacks, D. S., Crepeau, L. J., & Abbott, B. B. (1991). The psycho- and neurobiology of fear systems in the brain. In M. R. Denny (Ed.), *Fear, avoidance and phobias: A fundamental analysis* (pp. 7–59). Hillsdale, NJ: Lawrence Erlbaum Associates, Inc.

Panksepp, J., Siviy, S., & Normansell, L. (1984). The psychobiology of play: Theoretical and methodological perspectives. *Neuroscience & Biobehavioral Reviews*, 8(4), 465–492. DOI: 10.1016/0149-7634(84)90005-8

Panksepp, J., Wright, J. S., Döbrössy, M. D., Schlaepfer, T. E., & Coenen, V. A. (2014). Affective neuroscience strategies for understanding and treating depression: From preclinical models to three novel therapeutics. *Clinical Psychological Science*, 2(4), 472–494. DOI: 10.1177/2167702614535913

Parvizi, J., & Damasio, A. (2001). Consciousness and the brainstem. *Cognition*, 79(1–2), 135–160. DOI: 10.1016/S0010-0277(00)00127-X

Pfaff, D. (2006). *Brain arousal and information theory: Neural and genetic mechanisms*. Cambridge, MA: Harvard University Press.

Revonsuo, A. (2000). Prospects for a scientific research program on consciousness. In T. Metzinger (Ed.), *Neural correlates of consciousness: Empirical and conceptual questions* (pp. 57–75). Cambridge, MA: MIT Press.

Roberts, V. J., & Cox, V. C. (1987). Active avoidance conditioning with dorsal central gray stimulation in a place preference paradigm. *Psychobiology*, 15(2), 167–170.

Rolls, E. T. (1999). *The brain and emotion*. Oxford, UK: Oxford University Press.

Rolls, E. T. (2005). *Emotion explained*. Oxford, UK: Oxford University Press. DOI: 10.1093/acprof:oso/9780198570035.001.0001

Rossi, J., III, & Panksepp, J. (1992). Analysis of the relationships between self-stimulation sniffing and brain-stimulation sniffing. *Physiology & Behavior*, 51(4), 805–813. DOI: 10.1016/0031-9384(92)90119-M

Schlaepfer, T. E., Bewernick, B. H., Kayser, S., Mädler, B., & Coenen, V. A. (2013). Rapid effects of deep brain stimulation for treatment resistant depression. *Biological Psychiatry*, 73(12), 1204–1212. DOI: 10.1016/j.biopsych.2013.01.034

Schlaepfer, T. E., Cohen, M. X., Frick, C., Kosel, M., Brodesser, D., Axmacher, N., Joe, A. Y., Kreft, M., Lenartz, D., & Sturm, V. (2008). Deep brain stimulation to reward circuitry alleviates anhedonia in refractory major depression. *Neuropsychopharmacology*, 33(2), 368–377. DOI: 10.1038/sj.npp.1301408

Seager, W. (2009). Dual aspect theories. In T. Bayne, A. Cleeremans, & P. Wilken (Eds.), *The Oxford companion to consciousness* (pp. 243–244). Oxford, UK: Oxford University Press.

Shevrin, H., Panksepp, J., Brakel, L. A. W., & Snodgrass, M. (2012). Subliminal affect valence words change conscious mood potency but not valence: Is this evidence for unconscious valence affect? *Brain Sciences*, 2(4), 504–522. DOI: 10.3390/brainsci2040504

Shewmon, D. A., Holmse, D. A., & Byrne, P. A. (1999). Consciousness in congenitally decorticate children: Developmental vegetative state as self-fulfilling prophecy. *Developmental Medicine & Child Neurology*, 41(6), 364–374. DOI: 10.1017/S0012162299000821

Skinner, B. F. (1953). *Science and human behavior*. New York, NY: Macmillan.

Solms, M. (2000). Dreaming and REM sleep are controlled by different brain mechanisms. *Behavioral and Brain Sciences*, 23(6), 843–850. DOI: 10.1017/S0140525X00003988

Solms, M., & Panksepp, J. (2012). The "Id" knows more than the "Ego" admits: Neuropsychoanalytic and primal consciousness perspectives on the interface between affective and cognitive neuroscience. *Brain Sciences*, 2(2), 147–175. DOI: 10.3390/brainsci2020147

Solms, M., & Turnbull, O. (2002). *The brain and the inner world: An introduction to the neuroscience of subjective experience*. New York, NY: Other Press.

Sparks, D. L. (1988). Neural cartography: Sensory and motor maps in the superior colliculus. *Brain, Behavior and Evolution*, 31(1), 49–56. DOI: 10.1159/000116575

Stutz, R. M., Rossi, R. R., Hastings, L., & Brunner, R. L. (1974). Discriminability of intracranial stimuli: The role of anatomical connectedness. *Physiology & Behavior*, 12(1), 69–73. DOI: 10.1016/0031-9384(74)90069-9

Sukhotinsky, I., Zalkind, V., Lu, J., Hopkins, D. A., Saper, C. B., & Devor, M. (2007). Neural pathways associated with loss of consciousness caused by intracerebral microinjection of GABAA-active anesthetics. *European Journal of Neuroscience*, 25(5), 1417–1436. DOI: 10.1111/j.1460-9568.2007.05399.x

Sur, M., & Rubinstein, J. L. R. (2005). Patterning and plasticity of the cerebral cortex. *Science*, 310(5749), 805–810. DOI: 10.1126/science.1112070

Tinbergen, N. (1951). *The study of instinct*. Oxford, UK: Clarendon Press.

Tulving, E. (2005). Episodic memory and autonoesis: Uniquely human? In H. S. Terrace & J. Metcalfe (Eds.), *The missing link in cognition: Origins of self-reflective consciousness* (pp. 3–56). New York, NY: Oxford University Press. DOI: 10.1093/acprof:oso/9780195161564.003.0001

Valenstein, E. S. (1966). The anatomical locus of reinforcement. In E. Stellar & J. M. Sprague (Eds.), *Progress in physiological psychology*, Vol. 1 (pp. 149–190). New York, NY: Academic Press.

Vandekerckhove, M., & Panksepp, J. (2009). The flow of anoetic to noetic and autonoetic consciousness: A vision of unknowing (anoetic) and knowing (noetic) consciousness in the remembrance of things past and imagined futures. *Consciousness and Cognition*, 18(4), 1018–1028. DOI: 10.1016/j.concog.2009.08.002

Vandekerckhove, M., & Panksepp, J. (2011). A neurocognitive theory of higher mental emergence: From anoetic affective experiences to noetic knowledge and autonoetic awareness. *Neuroscience & Biobehavioral Reviews*, 35(9), 2017–2025. DOI: 10.1016/j.neubiorev.2011.04.001

Vanderwolf, C. H. (1988). Cerebral activity and behavior: Control by central cholinergic and serotonergic systems. *International Review of Neurobiology*, 30, 225–340. DOI: 10.1016/S0074-7742(08)60050-1

Velmans, M. (2009). *Understanding consciousness* (2nd ed.). New York, NY: Routledge.

Watt, D. F., & Pincus, D. I. (2004). Neural substrates of consciousness: Implications for clinical psychiatry. In J. Panksepp (Ed.), *Textbook of biological psychiatry* (pp. 75–110). Hoboken, NJ: Wiley.

Wright, J. S., & Panksepp, J. (2011). Toward affective circuit-based preclinical models of depression: Sensitizing dorsal PAG arousal leads to sustained suppression of positive affect in rats. *Neuroscience & Biobehavioral Reviews*, 35(9), 1902–1915. DOI: 10.1016/j.neubiorev.2011.08.00

Wright, J. S., & Panksepp, J. (2012). An evolutionary framework to understand foraging, wanting, and desire: The neuropsychology of the SEEKING System. *Neuropsychoanalysis*, 14(1), 5–39. DOI: 10.1080/15294145.2012.10773683

Zachar, P., & Ellis, R. D. (2012). *Categorical versus dimensional models of affect: A seminar on the theories of Panksepp and Russell*. Consciousness & Emotion (Vol. 7). Amsterdam, The Netherlands: John Benjamins Publishing Company. DOI: 10.1075/ceb.7

The future of consciousness science

From empirical correlations to theoretical explanation*

Antti Revonsuo
University of Turku, Turku, and University of Skövde, Skövde

In this paper I overview my previous work concerning a multilevel framework for consciousness science. Constitutive, etiological and contextual dimensions of explanation are described. The multilevel framework is then applied to current issues within consciousness science including understanding the convergence of top-down and bottom-up constraints, the level of measurement problem and sorting out t he correlates, causes and constituents of consciousness. Drawing on the dreaming brain as a model system, I also briefly describe my group's research using electrophysiology and transcranial magnetic stimulation. I conclude that consciousness science will gradually adopt a unified multilevel model with a systematic description of phenomenology, the phenomenal level in the brain and their relation with the causal networks of the physical world.

1. Introduction

The one sacred mantra that every psychology undergraduate is supposed to learn about research methodology is this: *Correlation* does not necessarily entail *causation*. A similar-sounding statement has recently been repeatedly uttered in consciousness science: When it comes to discovering the neural basis of consciousness, finding the mere neural *correlates* of consciousness does not entail finding the neural *causes* or the neural *constituents* of consciousness. Another way of putting this has led to a distinction between just finding some unspecific neural correlates of consciousness versus identifying the *true* or the *direct* neural correlates of consciousness.

While all these distinctions make intuitive sense, it appears that the empirical neuroscientists are driving at something important that they are not quite capable of

* This research is supported by the Academy of Finland, research program HUMAN MIND, project number 266434.

DOI 10.1075/aicr.92.10rev

formulating explicitly. By here mixing in some insights from the philosophy of science, the crucial underlying principle underlying these intuitions could be stated as follows: Empirical observations of the simple co-occurrence of phenomena, or patterns of correlation and covariance between variables in empirical data, are not as such theoretical explanations describing the underlying causal-mechanical structure of the world. There is a crucial difference between *empirical patterns of data*, and *theoretical, explanatory models of phenomena*. A correlation observed in the empirical data does not automatically translate into some specific causal-mechanical relationships within a theoretical model that tries to describe and explain the phenomena in question.

Obviously, the ultimate aim of science is not observation or collection of piles of data, but explanation. Thus, the science of consciousness ultimately aims to *explain* consciousness. So, how do we get from correlations in data to explanations in theories? For starters, we need a clear understanding of what "explanation" consists of in the sciences whose task it is to account for consciousness. Broadly, the burden of explaining consciousness falls on the cognitive neurosciences, the biology of the mind. This is the branch of science whose explicit goal it is to integrate the cognitive and psychological sciences with the biological sciences. In this endeavor, cognitive neuroscience includes the explanation of consciousness. These days, any undergraduate textbook of cognitive neuroscience includes a chapter on consciousness, thus showing that this phenomenon should be studied and explained within the context of cognitive neuroscience.

Thus, a general framework is needed of what "explanation" means in cognitive neuroscience. Once this explanatory framework is spelled out, we can place consciousness into that context and see more clearly what it means to have an "explanation" of consciousness, and what, if anything, do the "neural correlates of consciousness" contribute to it.

In this paper I will briefly outline such an explanatory framework and then place consciousness into it. I will also take up questions relating to the distinction between empirical measurements or data, and theoretical models and explanations of phenomena, in the context of the science of consciousness. Most of what I will say here I have said before at greater length and in more detail, especially in Revonsuo (2006; see also Revonsuo, 2010). Many other chapters in the present volume, most notably that by Opie and O'Brien, develop similar ideas.

2. The multilevel framework of explanation

As both Revonsuo (2006) and Opie and O'Brien (this volume; see also chapters by Hohwy & Bayne, this volume; Mahner, this volume; and Miller, this volume) point out (following Craver, 2007; and Bechtel, 2008), explanation in neuroscience is different from explanation in the basic physical sciences and does not follow the deductive-nomological model. Instead, the biological sciences in general, and neuroscience in particular, apply mechanistic explanations. Neuroscientists construct multilevel mechanistic models of phenomena to describe and explain them. A mechanistic model describes the phenomenon of interest itself (explanandum), its internal composition and dynamic organization, as well as the causal structure of the world surrounding and interacting with the phenomenon.

A multilevel explanatory model involves several different dimensions of explanation that track the different dimensions of the causal-mechanical network in touch with the explanandum. These different sub-explanations correspond to different "directions" of causal-mechanical pathways surrounding the phenomenon. The explanandum has been explained and made intelligible when the phenomenon and the causal reticulum surrounding it has been described in detail in a multilevel model, without any substantial gaps anywhere.

3. The explanandum: Description of the phenomenon to be explained

The explanation of all biological phenomena starts out with the characterization or systematic description of the explanandum. The internal organization of the phenomenon, its temporal dynamics and holistic features must first be systematically described before it will be possible to start relating the explanandum to higher or lower levels of organization or to the temporally preceding events. In the case of consciousness, a general description of the structure, temporal dynamics, and qualities of subjective experience should be given. This description of the phenomenology of consciousness should be based on all the different sources of empirical science that inform us about aspects and features of phenomenal experience.

I have argued that the dreaming brain is a model system to describe and explain consciousness (Revonsuo, 2006). Dreaming as a conscious experience at a generic level can be defined as an immersive spatiotemporal hallucination that simulates a sensory-perceptual world (Revonsuo, 2006; Windt, 2010). Dreams are world-simulations experienced from the first-person's point of view. A more specific description of the contents of dreaming would have to include more specific descriptive statistics from dream research. Such data shows that within this world-simulation, visual percepts, places, objects, people, animals, social interactions, and dangerous situations, for example, very typically and universally occur when dream experiences are generated in the brain.

Note that the pure description of consciousness does not try to relate experiential features of consciousness to anything outside the simultaneous experiences themselves. Once we have a sufficiently detailed description of the explanandum on its own terms, we can start to track the different explanatory pathways that anchor the explanandum to the surrounding causal-mechanical network. Typically, this network has the following dimensions: (1) a downward-looking or constitutive explanation; (2) a backward-looking or an etiological explanation; and (3) an upward-looking or contextual explanation.

4. The downward-looking, constitutive explanation of consciousness

Constitutive explanation moves downwards, to a smaller spatiotemporal scale than where the explanandum as a whole resides. It describes the lower levels of organization (the constitutive mechanisms) that themselves lack the holistic properties of the explanandum (in this case consciousness). Nonetheless, the lower-level mechanisms can be seen to non-magically constitute the higher level of organization where the explanandum itself resides.

In consciousness research the issue of constitutive explanation has been implicitly identified with the search for the "neural correlates" of consciousness. However, there is a crucial difference between the correlates of consciousness and the constitutive mechanisms of consciousness (Miller, 2001, 2007, this volume; Revonsuo, 2000, 2001, 2006): correlation is a non-explanatory relationship. Almost any phenomenon in the brain could conceivably correlate with consciousness, but only a very restricted class of phenomena could count as the constitutive basis of consciousness.

The task of the downward-looking explanation in the mechanistic model of consciousness is to specify the lower-level phenomena whose holistic properties realize the organization and dynamics of subjective experience at the higher phenomenal level. Thus, the relationship in the model between the higher phenomenal level and the lower level of constitutive mechanisms must be an intelligible structural (Opie & O'Brien, this volume) or part-whole relation, not a mere inexplicable correlation or a mere observed co-variance in some sets of empirical data between the occurrence of a neural activity and the occurrence of a conscious mental phenomenon.

The downward-looking, constitutive explanation stays within the spatial and temporal confines of the phenomenon, but zooms in on the lower-level or underlying mechanisms from which the higher-level phenomenon emerges. In the case of consciousness, this dimension of explanation is the very one that faces the explanatory gap: How do we get from lower-level neural mechanisms to higher level phenomenal experiences, so that the latter necessarily follow from the former and thus manage to explain them?

Consciousness is typically divided into the general *state* of being conscious vs. unconscious, and the *specific contents* of consciousness. To be in the conscious as opposed to being in the unconscious state means to have the phenomenal level of organization in the brain enabled as opposed to not enabled. Once it is enabled, any kinds of contents of consciousness can appear within it.

A minimal contrast between being in the conscious vs. unconscious state is the contrast between dreamless sleep and vivid dreaming. In dreamless sleep, we experience nothing, and if woken up, cannot remember any dreams. In dream sleep, we can have any type and quality of subjective experience, and if woken up directly from it, we will, at least for a moment, remember that experience clearly.

The constitutive explanation of the state of being conscious should tell us what happens when, from the lower-level non-conscious brain processes comes out the capacity to experience a spatiotemporal world that is being present for us. This miracle also must happen during dreaming, as dreaming simulates the experience of being within a spatiotemporal world. Some sort of higher-level neurophysiological activities constituting consciousness must become engaged as the unconscious state of dreamless sleep suddenly turns to the opposite state of vivid dreaming with rich phenomenological contents. The case of dreaming vs. dreamless sleep is particularly informative, because it shows that the constitutive explanation of consciousness is a purely internalistic explanation: all the empirical differences between the total presence and the total absence of consciousness are differences in some processes and activities inside the brain. Nothing external is necessarily required to turn consciousness on and off.

Conversely, any explanation of consciousness that takes external stimuli or behavioral embodied interaction with the external world as constitutive of consciousness, can be discarded. They confuse the constitution of consciousness (the downward-looking explanation) with the other explanatory dimensions (the backward-looking and the upward/forward looking explanations) that have to do with the prior causes and the functional roles and causal consequences of consciousness.

The constitutive explanation(s) of specific contents of consciousness are, of course, specific to each particular type of content. In the literature, "NCC" is often defined as being *only* about the NCC of contents of consciousness (rather than the state of being conscious). For example, Koch (2004) defines the NCC as the minimal set of neuronal events and mechanisms jointly sufficient for a specific conscious percept. Koch's definition also does not make a clear distinction between causes, constituents, and consequences of the contents of consciousness.

Again, we might take specific dream images as examples of how to construct constitutive explanations of conscious percepts, because when we deal with dream images, we will at least not confuse the internal conscious percept with any external physical stimuli or behavioral interactions with them (as embodied approaches regularly do).

Let us assume that, as the dreamless sleep turns to vivid dreaming, the visuo-spatial opening scene in the dream is a view to a room with some objects of furniture and a familiar person walking in the room towards the dream self. Now, even this simple scene contains many separate visual objects. Each visual object is first bound together from basic visual features such as contour, shape, color, and motion (I call the result of this phenomenal binding of features a "gestalt window"; Revonsuo, 2006). Then the visual object is recognized and semantically categorized as a certain type of object (e.g., table) and familiar persons are identified as who they are (I call this the opening of a "semantic window" for each coherent visuo-spatial object within the perceptual space of consciousness; Revonsuo, 2006).

Thus, the simulated objects within dream consciousness consist of two types of information: the concrete surface pattern of phenomenal features (the gestalt window) and conscious access to a large body of semantic and episodic memory information that turns the gestalt window into a familiar meaningful object. Correspondingly, the lower-level constituents of these phenomenal contents will thus have to map into several different neural mechanisms that create a coherent set of qualia, spatial structure and conscious access to abstract information and pull them together into the conscious percept that is a content of consciousness. The constituent mechanisms of particular contents of consciousness are thus likely to be different from the constituent mechanisms of the state of consciousness, but the former always only can work in the context created by the latter: there can be no contents without the state first being enabled.

5. The etiological explanation of consciousness

In this type of explanation, the preceding causal chains that led to the occurrence of the explanandum should be specified: etiological explanation looks backwards in the temporal dimension to describe the causal pathways that preceded the current state of the explanandum and causally modulated it.

Three different etiological explanations can be distinguished on the basis of how far backwards in time these explanations look: first, the short or immediate causal pathway describes how a particular phenomenal content in consciousness was brought about by the immediately preceding external physical stimulus events that caused changes in sensory organs and sensory input pathways which led to the modulation of the phenomenal level. The sequence of neurophysiological events immediately preceding the emergence of the phenomenal content in consciousness is probably not a simple linear causal chain, but involves complex neural interactions and feedback loops between top-down and bottom-up influences. The description of the immediate causal pathway ignores the more distant past and takes for granted that at present the organism has the kind of consciousness, brain and sensory systems it does, and describes the changes in these systems caused by different types of external and internal events, resulting in changes of the state or content of consciousness at the phenomenal level. By contrast, the developmental and the evolutionary pathways look much further back in time and describe how the adult individual originally ended up having the kind of consciousness, brain and sensory systems it does.

Second, the developmental (ontogenetic) pathway describes how the nervous system during ontogeny was originally wired up to eventually give rise to the phenomenal level. This story will be enormously complex, involving accounts of genetic expression in the brain and the modulatory influences of internal and external stimulation to the brain in the fetus and the neonate.

Third, the evolutionary or ultimate explanation looks even further backwards in time and describes how, at some point during evolutionary history, the emergence of brains that included the phenomenal level solved a greater number of adaptive problems than non-conscious zombie-brains lacking the phenomenal level were able to. Furthermore, it describes how the organization of the phenomenal level gradually became a finely tuned species-specific adaptation in the different species of mammals.

6. The contextual explanation of consciousness

This dimension of explanation zooms *upwards*, away from the level of organization where the explanandum itself lies, to higher levels of organization at coarser spatial and temporal scales. Thus, it describes how the phenomenon relates to and interacts with other phenomena at the higher levels to produce effects that require interaction between several different phenomena. The phenomenon at the higher level of organization has causal powers different from its parts at lower levels. In the case of consciousness, contextual explanation describes the special role that the phenomenal level plays, in interaction with several non-conscious sensory, cognitive, and motor systems, first inside the brain and then consequently at the behavioral level of organism-environment interaction. Although the phenomenal level of consciousness alone cannot realize sensory perception or externally observable behavior, but needs to interact with many non-conscious mechanisms for the organism to perceive or to realize behavioral acts, the contribution of the phenomenal level to the higher level of organism-environment is absolutely necessary. Without that critical contribution the organism cannot find or realize adaptive behavioral trajectories in its environment.

7. The multilevel framework at work

The full explanation of consciousness is, for a biological research program on consciousness, the task of constructing a multilevel mechanistic model with a detailed phenomenal-level description, and a detailed causal-mechanical network surrounding this phenomenon and making explicit its relationships to the lower and higher levels as well as to the temporally preceding events and the causally consequent events.

The framework outlined above (and described in detail in Revonsuo, 2006) has the potential to clarify many empirical and theoretical confusions in the study of consciousness. It might also lead towards a more unified research program on consciousness, because it outlines what a successful explanation of consciousness ultimately is: it is a multilevel mechanistic model that shows the place of consciousness within the causal-mechanical networks of the brain and the rest of the physical world. Some issues that the multilevel framework could potentially clarify include the following.

7.1 Convergence of top-down and bottom-up constraints

Any biological phenomenon that spans over multiple levels of organization is best captured by combining two converging approaches: a bottom-up strategy and a top-down strategy of research. When it comes to consciousness science, the top-down strategy takes into account all the information we have about the phenomenal level itself: its internal organization, its temporal dynamics, its unity, and so on. Next, we try to figure out what must be required from the directly underlying constitutive mechanisms in order to support such a higher level of organization. That is, we use *top-down constraints* to guide us from the phenomenology of consciousness to the underlying neural sources of consciousness. In the bottom-up strategy, we analyze the higher levels of neural organization, already established in neuroscience. We try to figure out whether some of them could support the phenomenal level. Thus, we use *bottom-up constraints* to lead us *upwards from neurons to consciousness*. At some levels, the top-down path and the bottom-up path should meet. Somewhere there lie the direct neural constituents of consciousness (Revonsuo, 2006).

Top-down constraints take the features of subjective experience as the starting point, and try to descend from them to the features of the constitutive mechanisms. Bottom-up constraints look at neural systems that could realize large-scale coherent states and thus be plausible candidates for mechanisms of consciousness. So far as we can tell, based on the present evidence in cognitive neuroscience, the top-down strategy suggests that the phenomenal level is internally integrated, continuously and rapidly reorganizing itself, has a center-surround structure in an egocentric frame of reference, and an immense combinatorial capacity. The bottom-up strategy suggests that the phenomenal level is based on the coherent and rapidly changing activity of large-scale recurrent neural networks. They are anatomically distributed within the brain but they create physiologically integrated loops of bioelectrical activity (Revonsuo, 2006).

7.2 Neuroimaging consciousness

From the multilevel framework it follows that consciousness and its immediately underlying neural mechanisms reside at some particular levels of complexity and organization in the brain, and not in others. The question for the empirical measurement or imaging of consciousness can thus be formulated in the following way: do we have any research instruments available in current cognitive neuroscience that capture signals from the levels of organization where the constituents of consciousness reside and where consciousness itself resides?

I have argued elsewhere (Revonsuo, 2001, 2006) that currently no methods exist for directly imaging (or otherwise capturing empirically) the levels of electrophysiological organization in the brain that would allow the reconstruction of the contents of a person's consciousness. The brain data we have available do not allow outlining a multilevel model of the phenomenal level and its relation to other biological levels of organization in the brain. Thus, for the time being, empirically discovering consciousness and its immediate constituents in the brain is not feasible. The biological signals detected by our current research instruments in neuroscience do not allow the reconstruction of the phenomenal level in the brain. Cognitive neuroscience is still very far from having a neuroimaging method whose data would directly mirror the contents, organization, and dynamics of the phenomenal level of conscious experience. However, almost in the same breath, I have also argued that it is possible to invent such methods in the future, and when they will be available, cognitive neuroscience will be able to present a full multilevel model of consciousness and, consequently, the hard problem will disappear (Revonsuo, 2006).

7.3 Sorting out the correlates, the causes and the constituents of consciousness

Finally, we come back to the separation of the mere *correlates* and mere *preceding causes* of consciousness from the *underlying constituents* or the *direct neural mechanisms* of consciousness. This separation can and it should be used in the empirical search for the neural basis of consciousness. Here, I will mention how, in my own group's research on the neural basis of visual consciousness, we have attempted to make this distinction.

I will briefly mention three methods by which we have approached the NCC of visual consciousness. First, we have measured the event-related potentials to seen and unseen visual stimuli, and explored the electrophysiological differences between those two conditions. To make a long story short (for reviews, see Koivisto & Revonsuo, 2010; Railo, Koivisto, & Revonsuo, 2011), the differences appear in two separate time windows, the first one around 150–250 ms as a negative enhancement, called visual awareness negativity (VAN), and the second one around 300–400 ms, called late positivity (LP). Both of these electroencephalography (EEG) phenomena are *correlates* of consciousness, in the sense that they tend to co-occur with reports of seeing the presented stimulus, but interpretations differ as to which one, VAN or LP, is the direct correlate.

According to our own interpretation, VAN reflects visual phenomenal consciousness generated primarily within the visual cortex, whereas LP reflects post-perceptual access and reflective consciousness in fronto-parietal areas (Railo et al., 2011). According to a competing interpretation, VAN is pre-conscious (thus only reflecting some preceding causes of visual consciousness), whereas only the LP is the genuine direct correlate of perceptual consciousness emerging in the global workspace. Thus, this purely correlative evidence is not capable of telling which of these two opposing interpretations is correct, because we do not have any independent way of ascertaining in which time window visual consciousness first appears, and which time windows then are pre-conscious and which post-perceptual in relation to that critical time-window in which visual consciousness of a stimulus emerges.

To go beyond merely correlative evidence, we have employed transcranial magnetic stimulation of specific areas in the visual cortex. These studies have shown that stimulation of the visual cortical area V2 causally interferes with visual consciousness of a stimulus only when the transcranial magnetic stimulation is applied in an early time window around 80 ms from stimulus onset (Salminen-Vaparanta, Koivisto, Noreika, Vanni, & Revonsuo, 2012). We have interpreted this causal data as showing that V2 activity at 80 ms reflects a pre-conscious stage of processing which is necessary for the stimulus to reach consciousness at a later stage of processing upstream in the visual processing hierarchy. Further evidence from stimulating later areas of visual cortex (not yet published) has shown that activity in higher visual areas in the same time windows when VAN appears in the event-related potentials (ERPs), is probably a direct correlate of visual consciousness. It reflects the activation of cortical mechanisms that somehow *enable* the visual percept or some feature of it to emerge into subjective consciousness at the same time as the neural activities occur.

But is it possible in any way to rule out the competing view according to which visual consciousness appears later than VAN and is reflected by the LP? One potential way to do this would be to empirically separate the neural mechanism of consciousness from the behavioral consequences of consciousness. What is the earliest time window at which a behavioral response triggered by a conscious visual experience can occur? If the fastest and earliest consciousness-triggered responses occur before the LP appears in the EEG data, then the LP occurs too late to be the direct neural mechanism of visual consciousness. Instead, in that case the LP must be reflecting some post-perceptual processes.

Thus, by measuring the earliest timing of behavioral responses to conscious perception, it is possible to draw a definite timeline before which the NCC of a visual stimulus must have occurred for it to be a causal antecedent of the response. Our data (not yet published) from experiments that relate the timing of earliest behavioral responses to consciousness of visual stimuli with the ERPs to visual consciousness indeed suggest that the fastest behavioral responses typically occur before the LP, and therefore, whatever processes the LP reflects, visual consciousness itself happened already in an earlier time window and was generated by mechanisms different from the LP response to conscious visual perception.

By thus combining data from electrophysiological correlates of consciousness, cortical stimulation studies, and timing of behavioral responses to visually conscious stimuli, we can get converging evidence about the time and the space in which visual consciousness emerges in the brain and thus about the spatiotemporal localization of the constituent mechanisms of visual consciousness.

8. Conclusion

All this growing empirical evidence will help us to gradually add missing pieces to the multilevel model of consciousness, and to place the different parts and different dimensions of the explanation in their rightful places. Correlates, preceding causes, and consequences of consciousness all fit into the explanatory picture, but they should be kept separate from the actual constitutive mechanisms of consciousness. When we are clear about these distinctions, every new piece of evidence will contribute something of value to the multilevel model of consciousness. Thus the science of consciousness will gradually move towards a unified theory: the full multilevel model of consciousness, with a systematic phenomenological description of the subjective states and contents of consciousness at the phenomenal level and how they fit together with the causal networks of the physical world surrounding the phenomenal level in time and space.

References

Bechtel, W. (2008). *Mental mechanisms: Philosophical perspectives on cognitive neuroscience*. London, UK: Routledge.

Craver, C. F. (2007). *Explaining the brain: Mechanisms and the mosaic unity of neuroscience*. Oxford, UK: Oxford University Press. DOI: 10.1093/acprof:oso/9780199299317.001.0001

Koch, C. (2004). *The quest for consciousness: A neurobiological approach*. Englewood, CO: Roberts & Company.

Koivisto, M., & Revonsuo, A. (2010). Event-related brain potential correlates of visual awareness. *Neuroscience & Biobehavioral Reviews*, 34(6), 922–934. DOI: 10.1016/j.neubiorev.2009.12.002

Miller, S. M. (2001). Binocular rivalry and the cerebral hemispheres: With a note on the correlates and constitution of visual consciousness. *Brain and Mind*, 2(1), 119–149. DOI: 10.1023/A:1017981619014

Miller, S. M. (2007). On the correlation/constitution distinction problem (and other hard problems) in the scientific study of consciousness. *Acta Neuropsychiatrica*, 19(3), 159–176. DOI: 10.1111/j.1601-5215.2007.00207.x

Railo, H., Koivisto, M., & Revonsuo, A. (2011). Tracking the processes behind conscious perception: A review of event-related potential correlates of visual consciousness. *Consciousness and Cognition*, 20(3), 972–983. DOI: 10.1016/j.concog.2011.03.019

Revonsuo, A. (2000). Prospects for a scientific research program on consciousness. In T. Metzinger (Ed.), *Neural correlates of consciousness: Empirical and conceptual questions* (pp. 57–75). Cambridge, MA: MIT Press.

Revonsuo, A. (2001). Can functional brain imaging discover consciousness in the brain? *Journal of Consciousness Studies*, 8(3), 3–23.

Revonsuo, A. (2006). *Inner presence: Consciousness as a biological phenomenon*. Cambridge, MA: MIT Press.

Revonsuo, A. (2010). *Consciousness: The science of subjectivity*. Hove, UK: Psychology Press.

Salminen-Vaparanta, N., Koivisto, M., Noreika, V., Vanni, S., & Revonsuo, A. (2012). Neuronavigated transcranial magnetic stimulation suggests that area V2 is necessary for visual awareness. *Neuropsychologia*, 50(7), 1621–1627. DOI: 10.1016/j.neuropsychologia.2012.03.015

Windt, J. M. (2010). The immersive spatiotemporal hallucination model of dreaming. *Phenomenology and the Cognitive Sciences*, 9(2), 295–316. DOI: 10.1007/s11097-010-9163-1

SECTION II

Philosophy of mind

The philosophy of phenomenal consciousness
An introduction

Zoe Drayson
University of Stirling, Stirling

The scientific study of consciousness is constantly making new discoveries, but one particular aspect of consciousness remains problematic to explain. This is the fact that conscious experiences present themselves to us in a first-person way: there is something it feels like to be the subject of a conscious experience. This 'phenomenal' aspect of consciousness seems to be subjective, private, and knowable in a special way, making it difficult to reconcile with the scientific focus on objective, third-person data. This introduction provides an overview of phenomenal consciousness, explores philosophical arguments about its nature, and considers whether or not we should expect to find an explanation for the properties of phenomenal consciousness.

1. Introduction

Human consciousness remains largely mysterious to scientists and philosophers alike. Part of the problem comes down to technological and experimental constraints, and we can be confident that advances in brain-imaging and new experimental techniques will continue to yield more data. But another part of the problem seems to lie in the phenomenon to be explained, and how we understand it. For instance, the term 'consciousness' is used in a multitude of ways. First, creatures can be considered conscious or not conscious: we generally assume that humans are conscious creatures while bacteria are not. But conscious creatures can be in unconscious states, as when asleep or in a coma, for example. And even when a conscious creature is in a conscious state, they might not be *conscious of* a particular stimulus: 'being conscious' can be used both transitively and intransitively. These are, of course, terminological issues, and easily settled by clarifying our terms. But even once the terminology is settled, providing explanations of consciousness seems to face challenges that do not arise for other scientific problems. Conscious experiences have *phenomenal* properties: they present themselves to us in a first-person way, quite unlike the third-person data that are familiar to science.

DOI 10.1075/aicr.92.11dra

In this introduction to phenomenal consciousness, I'll begin by distinguishing the phenomenal aspect of consciousness from related notions, and showing how scientific advances have left it unexplained. In Section 3, I'll analyse the notion of phenomenal consciousness in more detail, considering its subjectivity, its privacy, and the special knowledge we seem to have of our phenomenally conscious states. Some philosophers think that any states possessing such properties can't be *physical* states, and therefore can't be scientifically explained. In Section 4, I introduce the physicalist and non-physicalist views of consciousness, looking at the varieties of physicalism and the two main arguments for non-physicalism. Section 5 explores philosophical approaches to theories of consciousness that attempt to explain what consciousness is and how it arises. In Section 6, I focus on the very idea of providing explanations of consciousness, and on different responses to the claim that there is an 'explanatory gap' between our best explanations of consciousness and what we're actually trying to explain.

2. The conscious brain

In order to understand the ways in which consciousness remains problematic for philosophers, it helps to first consider the ways in which consciousness has become *less* mysterious in recent decades. Not long ago, our only knowledge of the human brain came from experiments on animal brains or from dissected human brains at autopsies; now, we can harmlessly scan the brains of living human subjects to get information about both the structure of the brain and its functioning. These advances have been accompanied by more precise and ingenious ways of measuring non-neural behavior (such as eye movements, reaction times, and verbal reports), cleverly-designed experiments, and enhanced data-analysis techniques. As a result, there are new discoveries being made about our mental mechanisms on a daily basis.

Consider, for example, how the eyes and brain build up our conscious visual experience of the world. When we visually experience the world, we can overtly focus our attention on different aspects of the visual scene. But our experience is also shaped by very fast 'saccadic' eye movements between foveal fixation points. (See Liversedge & Findlay, 2000, for more on saccadic eye movements and their relation to cognition.) Cutting-edge technology in the form of eye-tracking equipment can measure the location and duration of fixation, and monitor the direction of the saccades. Using these measurements of attention-switching and scan-paths, psychologists can demonstrate how our visual system builds up the information made available to us in conscious experience. (For a more detailed account of visual system anatomy and physiology, see chapter by Price, 2013, in the companion volume.)

Scientific developments have also been made in the study of pain, a paradigm state of conscious experience. We now understand the role of neurotransmitters, the chemicals that relay messages across the brain's synapses, in the pain of migraine headaches. During a migraine, levels of the neurotransmitter serotonin drop significantly, which causes blood vessels to dilate, resulting in extreme pain. (Data on serotonin and migraine are reviewed in Panconesi, 2008.) With this knowledge of how the pain is produced, doctors can intervene to change it: migraine sufferers can be treated with drugs that optimize serotonin levels in the brain.

In addition to conscious sensations, human beings possess consciousness of themselves in the form of self-awareness. While we don't expect other animals to share our extensive capacity for reflective self-aware thought, behavioral psychologists have devised an experiment to show that some creatures have a basic form of self-consciousness. Experimenters mark an animal with an odorless dye on the front of their body, and then observe the creature in front of a mirror. Some animals, such as chimpanzees, poke at the marking or move to get a better view of the marking in the mirror, suggesting that they recognize the reflection as themselves. (Some of the most recent mirror-test experiments have been done on rhesus monkeys: see Rajala, Reininger, Lancaster, & Populin, 2010.)

Given these scientific advances in our understanding of conscious states, it is tempting to think that we're well on the way to a complete science of consciousness. But there is an aspect of consciousness that none of the above results touch upon: the way that our conscious states appear to us 'from the inside'. Work on eye movements, for example, tells us how our visual experience of a scene is built up by the way we attend to it; but none of this tells us what it feels like to be looking at an optical illusion and suddenly experience a change – for example, when looking at the duck-rabbit ambiguous image and switching from seeing it as a duck to seeing it as a rabbit, or when switching between two binocularly rivaling images. And work on the role of neurotransmitters in migraine pain can enable interventions to ease or even prevent the pain, but it doesn't tell us what it's like to experience a migraine headache, or how that feeling differs from other kinds of pains associated with different ailments. Finally, experiments like the mirror-test help us to understand the cognitive abilities of non-human animals, but they don't seem to explain why, when I look in the mirror and recognize myself, my realization that the reflection is *me* is accompanied by a sensation of recognition.

What's going on here is that our conscious experiences tend to have two sets of properties: a set of causal or functional properties, and a set of 'phenomenal' properties. The causal or functional properties of conscious states are exhibited in the interactions into which they enter. Notice, for example, that conscious states like perception, pain, and self-awareness seem able to guide our behavior (including our speech and our thought) in a way that unconscious states don't. We can verbally report our pains, for example, we can use our perceptions of the world to update our beliefs, and we can reflect on our self-awareness. Our non-conscious states, on the other hand, play isolated causal roles and don't enter into our everyday mental lives: they are not available for explicit decision-making and memory-formation processes, for example, and they can't control a wide range of behavior or become the objects of our introspection. The functional properties of conscious states, however, do not exhaust our everyday concept of consciousness. The causal interactions outlined above are normally accompanied by certain *experiential* qualities: conscious states, in addition to their functional roles, 'feel' like something when we undergo them.

Non-conscious states, on the other hand, aren't accompanied by any sort of feeling, sensation, or experiential quality.

The scientific work on consciousness outlined above focuses on the functional aspects of conscious states: their "cognitive accessibility" (Block, 2007) or their "availability for global control" (Chalmers, 1997). This leads to greater understanding of what conscious states do and how they do it, but doesn't seem to add to our understanding of the phenomenal properties of consciousness. (See Block, 1995, for further discussion of the distinction between these two aspects of consciousness.) What should we conclude from this? Perhaps these particular scientific experiments weren't trying to explain phenomenal consciousness, and other experiments could do a better job. Perhaps there aren't any good explanations of phenomenal consciousness now, but they will follow advances in science and technology. Or perhaps, as some philosophers think, there's something about the very *nature* of phenomenal consciousness that evades scientific explanation. In order to understand such a claim, it is necessary to first say more about the phenomenal properties of conscious experience.

3. Phenomenal consciousness

When one hears the piercing shriek of the alarm clock, smells freshly-brewed coffee, endures the pain of a piece of grit in one's eye, or enjoys the sense of relaxation at the end of a busy day, there is something it *feels* like to have each experience. Furthermore, the 'something' that it feels like is peculiar to the kind of experience one is having – the visual experience of seeing a rainbow, for example, has a different kind of feeling from the auditory experience of hearing fingernails scrape down a chalkboard. It is this aspect of consciousness that has proved particularly fascinating to philosophers: the phenomenal character of conscious experience. (Philosophers also often use the term 'qualia' to refer to the qualities that make up the phenomenal character of the experience.) Phenomenal consciousness has a number of interesting features: it is *subjective*, it is seemingly *private*, and we have some form of *special access* to our phenomenally conscious states. This section covers each of these features in turn.

One way to understand what we mean by the subjectivity of conscious experience is through terminology introduced by Nagel (1974), who suggests that when you are undergoing a conscious experience, there is *something it is like* to be you:

> [F]undamentally an organism has conscious mental states if and only if there is something that it is like to *be* that organism – something it is like *for* the organism. We may call this the subjective character of experience.
>
> (Nagel, 1974, p. 436, italics in original)

There is something it is like for me to see the color red, and there is something it is like for me to hear the sound of a bell (and *what* it is like differs across the two experiences.) There is presumably nothing it is like to be a rock or a piece of furniture. What about non-human animals? We tend to assume that other mammals, at least, experience a world of sights and sounds. But not all mammals have visual and auditory systems like our own: consider the bat, which uses echolocation instead of vision to build up information about the world:

> [B]at sonar, though clearly a form of perception, is not similar in its operation to any sense that we possess, and there is no reason to suppose that it is subjectively like anything we can experience or imagine. (Nagel, 1974, p. 438)

Nagel asks us to think about *what it is like* to be a bat: what sort of feeling or sensory quality accompanies the echolocation process? Nagel's point is that no matter how much we study the bat's physiology, we don't get close to understanding what the bat's subjective experiences are like. This poses a problem for the attempt to provide a science of consciousness:

> If we acknowledge that a physical theory of mind must account for the subjective character of experience, we must admit that no presently available conception gives us a clue how this could be done. (Nagel, 1974, p. 445)

Part of the problem doubtless lies in the limits of our current technology, and the restrictions governing ethical experimentation. Functional neuroimaging technology, for example, does not allow us direct access to people's thoughts. Instead, it measures the amount of oxygen in the blood across different regions of the brain, which can be used as evidence of cognitive activity only after interpretation. There are more direct ways of measuring the brain's relation to conscious experience, but these involve invasive experiments on living brains, such as single-cell recordings, which are usually only carried out on non-human animals. The neural data from such experiments are more precise than in neuroimaging, but how can we establish with which conscious experiences they are correlated? These experiments are restricted to non-human animals which cannot verbally describe their experiences as humans can.

Technological advances, however, are being made. Human and animal behavioral, electrophysiological and brain-imaging studies of visual consciousness during binocular rivalry are summarized by Miller (this volume), and described in detail in the companion volume (Miller, 2013). But even if still further technological and experimental advances occur, will we be able to identify and measure conscious experiences? There remains the problem that phenomenal consciousness seems markedly different from the other sorts of data that scientists study: not only is it subjective, it is also seemingly *private*. You might easily be able to imagine the experiences of other human beings (in the way you can't imagine what it's like to be a bat) but verification is a different matter. Were you and I to experience a sunset together, you would have no way of knowing whether my color experiences – what it was like for me – were the same as your own. We can use the same words to describe our experiences, but this doesn't guarantee that the experiences themselves have the same sort of subjective quality for each of us. Science deals in data that are public in the sense of being shareable and measurable by others; the privacy of conscious experiences seems to prevent them fulfilling these criteria.

Of course, there is a wealth of public data *associated* with our conscious states: psychological data such as our verbal reports of our conscious states, and our behavioral discriminations between different kinds of stimulus; and neurological data such as those from electroencephalography and neuroimaging. Our ability to discriminate between different colors can be measured, for example, as in color-blindness tests. And when someone is undergoing a migraine headache, the chemical composition of their neurotransmitters can be measured. But measuring a person's ability to discriminate colors doesn't establish *what it is like* for them to experience those colors, and measuring the bodily activity that correlates with the pain is not the same as measuring the feeling of the pain itself for the person undergoing it. The privacy of conscious experience makes it markedly different from standard scientific data.

Given that psychology and neuroscience *can* measure the neural and behavioral markers associated with phenomenal consciousness, it might seem tempting to simply treat the conscious experience as nothing more than its measurable markers. For example, if a person's experience of pain is reliably correlated with a particular pattern of blood-oxygenation in the brain, then we might feel tempted to say that to record that particular pattern of neural activity just *is* to record the experience of pain. This would be to 'operationalize' the concept of phenomenal consciousness, and identify the experience with the markers of that experience. While this would make phenomenal consciousness a less mysterious subject of scientific study, there are good reasons to resist this move. To see why it's important to retain the distinction between the experience itself and the experience-related behavior, consider the asymmetry between our knowledge of our own conscious states and those of others. When I'm in pain, a doctor can know I'm in pain on the evidence of my pain-related behavior: she infers that I'm in pain from my verbal reports, my bodily injuries, my neural activity. All of these count as evidence for the doctor that I am in pain. But notice that I don't need any of these pieces of evidence to know that *I* am in pain. The existence of my pain isn't something I infer from anything else: when I know that I'm in pain, I know it directly, in a way that doesn't seem accessible to anyone else. It doesn't even seem to make sense to ask me what my evidence is. I am simply directly aware of my pain. There is an asymmetry, then, between the (non-inferential, direct) way I know my own conscious states and the (inferential, evidence-based) way that others know my conscious states.

This asymmetry only applies to our *conscious* states, and not our other internal states: when it comes to the results of a blood test, for example, the doctor and I both base our knowledge on the same evidential data. If I disagree with the doctor about the results, our disagreement will ultimately be settled by further public data; I don't have any special access to the properties of my blood that the doctor lacks. But such an appeal to the evidence wouldn't settle the issue if I was disagreeing with a doctor about whether I'm in pain, because my first-person knowledge of my conscious experience is a different sort of knowledge from that provided by third-person scientific evidence. Furthermore, it's hard to see how the third-person scientific evidence could 'trump' my first person knowledge of my experience: what sort of evidence could a doctor use to persuade you that you're in pain, when you are awake and conscious but not consciously experiencing pain?

The 'special access' that we have to our conscious states goes along with their subjectivity and privacy to create a problem for our scientific understanding of consciousness. Science deals with data that is objective, measurable, and knowable to different people via the same evidence; phenomenal consciousness seems not to meet these requirements. If we want to have a scientific understanding of consciousness, it looks like we need an explanation of the first-person nature of conscious experience in third-person terms. But to expect a scientific explanation of consciousness is already to assume that consciousness is part of the physical world that scientists study – and this assumption is a matter of philosophical debate, as the following section will discuss.

4. Is consciousness physical?

Scientific research helps us achieve an understanding of the physical world of particles, charges, enzymes, cells, organisms, and so on. We can only have a scientific understanding of consciousness, therefore, if conscious experiences are part of the physical world. And there is good reason to think that consciousness is closely connected to the physical brain: we know that changes to the brain, such as those caused by head injury or by toxins in the bloodstream, can result in changes to conscious experiences; and brain scans performed on meditating subjects show their altered conscious states correlating with differences in their neural activity. Such systematic and reproducible effects persuade many of the truth of *physicalism*, the view that consciousness is part of the physical world. But there are reasons to doubt physicalism. If conscious experiences are just brain states, then why have they proved so elusive to scientific explanation? And how could a physical thing like a brain state have a 'phenomenal feel'?

If we had a complete description of our world in physical terms, physicalism and non-physicalism would disagree about what follows from this description. According to physicalism, once the physical facts are fixed then the facts about conscious experience are also fixed: from a complete physical description of the world, facts about consciousness would follow. Non-physicalism claims that even once the full physical description of the world is fixed, facts about conscious experience are further facts which are not directly entailed by the physical facts. This section will examine both views.

4.1 Physicalism

The claim that consciousness is part of the physical world can be understood in different ways. One obvious way is to claim that each type of conscious experience is *identical* with a certain type of brain event: to experience the smell of fresh coffee, for example, is just to have a particular pattern of neural firing in a certain brain area. Proponents of this so-called 'type-physicalism' include Smart (1959) and more recently Polger (2004). Notice that *identifying* a type of conscious experience with a type of neural event entails that anyone lacking that type of neural event also lacks the relevant type of conscious experience. Imagine we come to identify the sensation of pain with a certain kind of neural firing, and then discover a creature – human or otherwise – that lacks the appropriate kind of neural firing. According to type-physicalism, that creature cannot be in pain, no matter what behavioral evidence we have to the contrary. And consider the case of creatures, such as octopuses, that have very different nervous systems from humans; if there aren't any kinds of neural event that humans and octopuses share, we'd have to deny that octopuses could ever be in pain. Notice that the opposite also holds: if we find a creature that has the appropriate pattern of neural activity, we'd have to conclude it was in pain, even if it demonstrated none of the behavioral signs.

A common way to avoid these problems is to adopt 'token-physicalism' about consciousness. While type-physicalism claims that each *type* of conscious experience is identical with a *type* of neural event, token-physicalism claims merely that each instance (or 'token') of a particular conscious experience is identical with some neural event or another. Token-physicalism allows that my pain experience is identical with a neural firing (and therefore physical), and that another creature's pain experience is identical with a neural firing (and therefore physical), without those neural firings being of the same type. This picture allows for the 'multiple realizability' of conscious mental states: the idea that one kind of conscious experience can be physically realized in multiple ways (Putnam, 1967).

While token-physicalism allows us to retain the claim that conscious experiences are physical things, it lacks the scientific usefulness of type-physicalism. Type-physicalism, if true, would allow us to make predictions and generalizations: if a type of experience is identical with a type of neural event, we know that other creatures with that kind of neural event have the same kind of experience, and vice versa. Token-physicalism, however, leaves us seeking explanations. In virtue of what, for example, do two distinct kinds of neural event realize the same kind of experience? Philosophers have tried to remedy this situation by finding generalizations at a more abstract level, for instance by claiming that two types of neural event realize the same type of conscious experience in virtue of playing the same *functional role*.

According to this 'functionalist' approach, the neural event identical with my pain and the neural event identical with another creature's pain are playing the same functional role: each is caused by physical injury, and leads one to believe that one is in pain, and to the desire to be pain-free, for example. Although the neural events themselves are of different neural types, they are both realizers of the same functional type: pain. Functionalism works reasonably well as a theory of mental states like beliefs and desires, but is less convincing when it comes to capturing the qualitative character of conscious experiences. To see why, notice that the functionalist claims that any system with the same functional organization as you will have all the same mental states as you. And then consider what would happen if we took the functional organization of your one-billion neurons and implemented the functional roles in something other than your brain:

> Suppose we convert the government of China to functionalism, and we convince its officials to realize a human mind for an hour. We provide each of the billion people in China (I chose China because it has a billion inhabitants) with a specially designed two-way radio that connects them in the appropriate way to other persons and to [an] artificial body [...] It is not at all obvious that the China-body system is physically impossible. It could be functionally equivalent to you for a short time, say an hour. (Block, 1978, p. 279)

An intuitive response to Block's thought-experiment is to deny that the nation of China has any mental states at all, suggesting that functional role is an insufficient characterization of mentality. In particular, it is hard to see how the China-body system could have the phenomenal properties of conscious experience:

> there is prima facie doubt whether it has any mental states at all – especially whether it has what philosophers have variously called "qualitative states," "raw feels," or "immediate phenomenological qualities." [...] In Nagel's terms (1974), there is a prima facie doubt whether there is anything which it is like to be the [China-body] system. (Block, 1978, p. 281)

These problems for both type- and token-physicalism need not deter the physicalist, as the most minimal form of physicalism requires neither. Minimal physicalism about consciousness requires only that conscious experience *supervenes* on the physical world. To understand the concept of supervenience, consider David Lewis's (1986) example of a dot-matrix image:

> A dot-matrix picture has global properties – it is symmetrical, it is cluttered, and whatnot – and yet all there is to the picture is dots and non-dots at each point of the matrix. The global properties are nothing but patterns in the dots. They supervene: no two pictures could differ in their global properties without differing, somewhere, in whether there is or there isn't a dot. (Lewis, 1986, p. 14)

The point Lewis is making is that there is nothing more to the picture than the dots: any identical arrangement of dots will yield the same patterns, because the patterns supervene on the dots. By analogy, if consciousness supervenes on the physical, then there is nothing more to it than the underlying physical arrangement of the world: no two identical physical worlds could differ with regard to consciousness. (For a more detailed discussion of the varieties of supervenience, see Kozuch & Kriegel, this volume.)

Approaching consciousness in terms of supervenience gives us a minimal form of physicalism, but one which is without explanatory power. To say the dot-matrix patterns supervene on the dots does not tell us why those particular patterns exist, or how we should get clearer on the relationship between the dots and the patterns.

Similarly, supervenience physicalism doesn't tell us *how* consciousness arises from the physical world: it merely states that there is a co-variation between the world's physical properties and its conscious properties. Despite its minimalist nature, however, supervenience physicalism is still open to objections from the non-physicalist.

4.2 Non-physicalism

The non-physicalist does not have to deny that the physical world plays an important role in generating our mental states. They merely have to deny the supervenience physicalist's claim that physical facts about neural activity, for example, fix the existence and nature of conscious experience. Non-physicalists have developed several thought experiments to persuade us of the falsity of physicalism, the most famous of which are Jackson's (1982) 'knowledge argument' and Chalmers' (1996) 'zombie argument'.

Frank Jackson's knowledge argument introduces the character of Mary. Jackson asks us to imagine that Mary has been brought up from birth in an entirely black-and-white room. Mary has grown up reading black-and-white books and watching black-and-white television, and has developed a vast scientific knowledge as a result. In particular, she has learned how color vision works in humans: she knows everything that science can tell her about light wavelengths, for example, and visual circuitry in the brain. Suppose that after many years of study in her black-and-white room, Mary has come to know all the physical facts about human color vision. What will happen when Mary leaves the black-and-white room and enters the world of color for the first time? When Mary sees something colored red for the first time, for example, will she learn something new?

> It seems just obvious that she will learn something about the world and our visual experience of it. But then it is inescapable that her previous knowledge was incomplete. But she had *all* the physical information. *Ergo* there is more to have than that, and Physicalism is false. (Jackson, 1982, p. 130, italics in original)

Most people share the intuition that Mary will learn something new: she will learn what it's like to experience the color red. But because the thought experiment stipulates that Mary had already learned all the *physical* facts about color in her black-and-white room, Mary must be learning something *non-physical* when she learns what it is like to see red. The strength of the knowledge argument, as Jackson realizes, is that cases like Mary's compel us to think that "one can have all the physical information without having all the information there is to have" (Jackson, 1982, p. 130).

The knowledge argument has created a great deal of literature, most of it attempting to defend physicalism by challenging the thought experiment. Some philosophers claim that Mary could not have all the physical facts in the first place (Alter, 1998), while others argue that Mary's new knowledge is made true by physical facts she already knew (Lycan, 1996). Another physicalist tactic involves denying that Mary acquires new factual knowledge at all: instead she has perhaps gained a set of abilities

(Lewis, 1983) or 'become acquainted' with color experience (Conee, 1994). (For a more detailed discussion of these options, see Brogaard, this volume.)

David Chalmers' zombie argument asks you to imagine an organism that is physically identical to you, but which lacks the phenomenal experiences that you have: call this a 'zombie'. Zombies behave just like human beings. When a zombie cuts itself, for example, it bleeds, it emits sounds of pain, and certain areas of its brain are activated (and these are the same areas that are activated in your own brain when you cut yourself). The only difference is that there is not "something it is like" to be a zombie: the zombie does not experience any painful sensations. Chalmers argues that the very fact we can imagine zombies fitting this description entails that physicalism is false. To see why, remember that physicalism takes the facts about conscious experience to be determined by the physical facts. If physicalism is true, therefore, it would be *impossible* for a world physically identical to ours to differ in terms of phenomenal consciousness. This means that in order to prove physicalism false, it is enough to show the *possibility* of a world physically identical to ours that differs in its phenomenally conscious properties. A world containing zombies would be such a world: if zombies are possible, physicalism is false. But does *imagining* zombies show that they are *possible*? Chalmers thinks that zombies are conceivable, where conceivability amounts to "ideal conceivability, or conceivability on ideal rational reflection" (Chalmers, 1999, p. 47): there is no contradiction, he claims, in the idea of zombies. While some physicalists respond by denying that zombies are actually conceivable (e.g., Dennett, 1995), the more common physicalist response to the zombie argument is to deny that the conceivability of zombies entails their possibility (see e.g., Hill & McLaughlin, 1999; Loar, 1990; Yablo, 1993). Chalmers (1996, 1999) responds to the physicalist by characterizing the notions of conceivability and possibility in the formal framework of two-dimensional semantics, and arguing that claims about conceivability entail claims about possibility when we isolate the relevant meanings of 'conceivable' and 'possible'. (The 'zombie' argument is discussed at greater length by Brogaard, this volume.)

One of the most famous historical arguments against physicalism by Descartes also makes claims about what is possible on the basis of claims about what we can conceive. In his Sixth Meditation, Descartes suggests that he can conceive of his mind existing without his body, therefore it is not possible for his mind to be dependent upon his body:

> although I certainly do possess a body with which I am very closely conjoined; nevertheless, because, on the one hand, I have a clear and distinct idea of myself, in as far as I am only a thinking and unextended thing, and as, on the other hand, I possess a distinct idea of body, in as far as it is only an extended and unthinking thing, it is certain that I, [that is, my mind, by which I am what I am], is entirely and truly distinct from my body, and may exist without it.
>
> (Descartes, 1641/1996, p. 107)

This leads Descartes to conclude that the mind is an entirely distinct substance from the body. His view, that the physical world of measurable and locatable objects is supplemented by a distinct realm of mental substance, has become known as 'substance dualism'. It is important to notice that not all arguments against physicalism lead to substance dualism. While substance dualism is committed to the idea that the mind could exist without the physical body, the knowledge argument and the zombie argument, for example, are intended only to establish that the physical facts don't fix the facts about phenomenal consciousness. As a result, the knowledge argument and the zombie argument can only be used to establish that there are non-physical *properties*, not (without amendment) that there are non-physical *substances*. The resulting 'property dualism', unlike substance dualism, is committed to the claim that all substance is physical. However, property dualists (e.g., Kim, 2005) suggest that at least some things have non-physical properties in addition to their physical properties. In the case of human brains, for example, the property dualist might think that neural matter can have non-physical properties (e.g., subjective feel) in addition to physical properties (e.g., firing rate). Property dualism is consistent with some forms of physicalism. If, for example, we interpret 'token-physicalism' as the claim that every conscious state has physical properties, then it looks like one can be a token-physicalist *and* a property dualist: having physical properties is consistent with also having non-physical properties. However, the relationship between property dualism and physicalism is a complex one, and Schneider (2012) has argued that property dualists must reject physicalism altogether. Property dualism, she argues, "does not lend itself to any physicalism worth having" (Schneider, 2012, p. 62).

Both substance and property dualism face problems when it comes to accounting for causal interactions between the mind and the rest of the world. Our conscious states seem to be causally integrated with aspects of the physical world: my feeling of embarrassment (conscious state) causes me to blush (physical state); my low levels of blood-sugar (physical state) cause me to feel dizzy (conscious state). If substance dualism is correct, then these events require physical and non-physical substances to interact with each other. Our knowledge of causes and effects, however, comes from observing interactions between wholly physical objects, and it's difficult to understand how a non-physical substance could participate in causal transactions. Property dualism doesn't face the same problem, as it denies the existence of non-physical substances. The property dualist can claim that conscious states are physical states, and thus there is no mystery about how they can cause physical events. But there is still a residual problem here for the property dualist: in virtue of which of its properties does the conscious state play that causal role? If it is in virtue of its non-physical properties, we are back to a version of the problem for substance dualism: it seems utterly mysterious how non-physical properties can interact with physical properties. But if the conscious state plays its causal role in virtue of its physical properties, then it looks like the (non-physical) conscious feeling of embarrassment is not what is causing the blushing. Without physical properties, any causal interactions seem mysterious; but as soon as we have physical properties doing the causal work, the non-physical properties seem to be irrelevant. This is problem of 'causal exclusion' (Kim, 1989). Options for solving the problem include allowing events to have both a physical and non-physical cause ('overdetermination') or denying that conscious properties are causal at all ('epiphenomenalism'). (See Bennett, 2007, for discussion of the various problems surrounding mental causation.)

5. Theories of consciousness

To take a stance in the debate over physicalism versus non-physicalism is to take a stance on the metaphysical nature of consciousness. It is not yet to provide a *theory* of consciousness: to say that consciousness is physical is not to commit to any particular view of what consciousness is, how it arises, or why it exists.

The main strategy of philosophers attempting to explain the phenomenal properties of conscious states has been to analyse consciousness in terms of *representation*. The notion of representation already features in the literature on mental states more generally, as philosophers use representation to make sense of how beliefs, desires, and other thoughts can be *about* certain things or states of affairs. To believe that Paris is in France or to desire that the rain stays off is to be in a representational state with a certain content: the content *that Paris is in France* or *that the rain stays off*. Philosophers have used this concept of representation in two different ways to account for phenomenal consciousness. The first way involves understanding phenomenal properties as straightforward 'first-order' representational properties, while the second way involves understanding phenomenal properties as 'higher-order' representational properties: representations of representations.

The first way to understand phenomenal properties in terms of representations is simply to think that the phenomenal properties of a conscious state are just its representational properties. Experiences, like beliefs and desires, can have representational contents. When I see a red balloon or hear a trumpet, I am having a perceptual experience with a representational content. The 'representationalist' about consciousness (e.g., Dretske, 1995; Tye, 1994) wants to say that the qualitative properties of the experience (what it is like to see red, to hear the trumpet) are just properties of the representation. They acknowledge that I can have a *belief* about a red balloon or a desire to hear the trumpet without any accompanying qualitative features, but when this same representational content appears in a perceptual state, we *experience* some of those representational properties.

One problem faced by the representationalist approach to consciousness is that, while it works well for visual experiences, it is more difficult to see how it applies to other perceptual modalities. How should we characterize the representational contents of smells and tastes, for example? The problem becomes more obvious when we consider non-perceptual conscious states, like pains and moods: it seems to make sense to think of a perceptual experience representing the world in a certain way, but it is less clear how pains and moods can be understood as representing anything.

The second approach to understanding phenomenal consciousness in terms of representations focuses on 'higher-order' representations. Higher-order theories of consciousness start from the assumption that we have lots of representational mental states, not all of them conscious. They claim that phenomenally conscious mental states are those representational mental states that are (or are disposed to be) the object of a further representational state: a higher-order representation. An unconscious mental state becomes a conscious mental state, according to higher-order theories, when we reflect or focus on it. The exact nature of this 'reflecting' or 'focusing' depends on whether we think of the higher-order mental state as a kind of perception, or as a kind of belief. On the former view (e.g., Lycan, 1996), mental states are consciously experienced when they are perceived or sensed in the right way; while on the latter view (e.g., Rosenthal, 1986), mental states are consciously experienced when they become the object of a belief-like thought.

One problem for higher-order theories of consciousness is that they posit fairly extensive cognitive mechanisms and capacities. This is a problem for all versions of the view, but particularly for those who focus on higher-order *thought* rather than perception. To represent one's own mental representations, and particularly to think about one's own thoughts, puts high demands on the cognitive architecture possessed by a creature that has conscious states. One might think that many non-human animals possess basic phenomenally conscious states, without possessing the capacity for thought at all, let alone higher-level thought. Higher-order views of consciousness seem to link the ability for basic conscious experience too tightly to complicated cognitive capacities.

Some theories of consciousness also attempt to explain *why* consciousness exists: what is it *for*? Given that our brains can perform all sorts of complex processes unconsciously, why do we consciously experience some of it? Going back to the functional properties of consciousness discussed in section two, recall that our conscious states interact in a certain way with other mental states: our conscious states can be verbally reported, stored in memory, introspected, used to guide action, and so on. One might think that the function of consciousness is to make certain information 'cognitively accessible' or 'globally available' to other parts of the cognitive system. The interactions between conscious states seem to enable the integration of lots of information from different areas of the cognitive system: sensory information, linguistic data, motivational concerns, and so on. This leads some theorists (e.g., Baars, 1988) to propose that the function of consciousness is to 'broadcast' information, by providing a 'global workspace' for sharing information.

All of the approaches to consciousness discussed thus far are 'top-down', in the sense that they start from our concept of consciousness and attempt to analyze it in terms of other notions such as representation, information, and function. They are all compatible with physicalism, but they are framed at a higher level of abstraction than the neural level: these theories show how a physicalist theory of consciousness might work without mentioning biochemical features of the brain. But once the theoretical details are in place, we can look for the neural events that implement these abstract roles. Representationalist theories of consciousness, for example, can look to work in computational psychology and neuroscience that invoke semantically-interpreted and physically-implemented functional states. (For a neuroanatomical interpretation of representationalism, see Mehta & Mashour, 2013.) Higher-order theories of consciousness seem to require a 'metacognitive' monitoring process, and such processes are associated with the prefrontal cortex of the brain, so evidence for the neural implementation of higher-order theories might best be sought in prefrontal neural processing (Lau & Rosenthal, 2011). And the global workspace theory of consciousness has also been developed as a global *neuronal* workspace theory, using computer modeling of neural networks to simulate brain activity (Dehaene, 2001).

The motivation behind all of these top-down approaches to consciousness is the idea that consciousness arises in the human brain in virtue of its organization and structure: while we may seek the implementation of consciousness in neurons, the molecular properties of the brain are less important than its higher-level functioning. The alternative to top-down approaches involves starting from basic brain activity, and using neural features such as firing activity, chemical composition, or location to shed light on consciousness. These 'bottom-up' approaches to consciousness variously suggest that conscious experience might be the result of neural activity in a particular area of the cortex, for example, or the speed at which neurons fire, or the complex interaction of such features. Bottom-up approaches can differ with regard to the level of neural activity they focus on: some propose that consciousness might be the product of individual neurons, or of populations of neurons, or of whole brains. In the case of individual neurons, this might mean that a conscious experience of a certain feature is the product of a receptive-field neuron that responds to a particular sensory property, such as a particular frequency in the auditory field, or a particular direction of motion in the visual field. Alternatively, conscious experience might be the product of neural networks: conscious experience of a certain sort might depend on the outcome of a competition between neural coalitions, or on the synchrony of neural populations oscillating at a particular frequency. A further suggestion is that the source of consciousness is not single neurons or groups of neurons, but the brain as a whole: according to this view, we should be looking at global patterns of brain activity such as the resonance of an electromagnetic field, or quantum effects occurring in subcellular structures. (For examples of each of these approaches, see Kouider, 2009.)

Notice that one doesn't need to commit to physicalism about consciousness in order to be interested in the neurobiological research associated with consciousness. A non-physicalist can accept that there are correlations between neural features and conscious experiences, as long as they deny that these neural correlates of consciousness are sufficient to fix the facts about conscious experience.

6. Explaining consciousness

It's not always clear whether a theory of consciousness is attempting to explain everything about consciousness, or merely some aspect of conscious states. Some theories of consciousness focus solely on visual consciousness and say nothing about other sensory modalities, while others concentrate on the varieties of conscious experience associated with imagination or proprioception. Even those theories attempting to account for consciousness more generally tend to focus on explaining certain properties of conscious experience: functional properties like its integrational or introspectable properties, or structural properties like its unity or its temporal dynamics. What's less clear, however, is whether any theory of consciousness explains the *phenomenal* properties of conscious experience: *what it is like* to be having a conscious experience. Whenever a theory presents us with an analysis of consciousness, we always seem to be able to ask "But why does it *feel* like this?" There seems to be what Levine (1983) calls an "explanatory gap" between what explanations of consciousness actually tell us, and what we want them to tell us.

To understand this explanatory gap, consider a standard scientific explanation of heat as the motion of molecules. We understand why heat has the properties it does by identifying it as a certain kind of molecule, and we don't feel that something crucial has been left unexplained:

> It ["Heat is the motion of molecules"] is explanatory in the sense that our knowledge of chemistry and physics makes intelligible how it is that something like the motion of molecules could play the causal role we associate with heat. [...] Once we understand how this causal role is carried out, there is nothing more we need to understand.
> (Levine, 1983, p. 357)

By contrast, notice what happens if we were to identify a certain kind of conscious experience with a certain physical state – seeing red as a pattern of activity in area V4 of the visual cortex, for example, or Levine's own example of pain as C-fibers firing. As in the heat case, the claim that "pain is the firing of C-fibers" is explanatory insofar as it explains why the firing of C-fibers results in avoidance effects or verbal responses: it tells us that the causal role of pain is being played by C-fibers. But explaining the causal role seems insufficient, as Levine (1983) points out:

> However, there is more to our concept of pain than its causal role, there is its qualitative character, how it feels; and what is left unexplained by the discovery of C-fiber firing is *why pain should feel the way it does!* [...] the identification of the qualitative side of pain with C-fiber firing (or some property of C-fiber firing) leaves the connection between it and what we identify with it completely mysterious.
> (Levine, 1983, p. 357, italics in original)

The problem is that by identifying consciousness with a physical state (or a functional state), we're left with an incomplete explanation. The explanation fails to make it intelligible to us why conscious states feel the way they do, or indeed why they feel like anything at all.

The claim that there is an explanatory gap in our explanations of phenomenal consciousness is an epistemological claim: a claim about how we understand (or fail to understand) the world, rather than a metaphysical claim about how the world is independently of our understanding. But for a physicalist, the explanatory gap poses a particular challenge. If phenomenal consciousness is part of the physical world, as the physicalist claims, why do we fail to capture it with our explanations? One physicalist response is to simply deny the existence of an explanatory gap, or claim that it is only an *apparent* explanatory gap. The fact that we can imagine a sensation other than pain, or no sensation at all, accompanying the firing of C-fibers doesn't necessarily mean that C-fibers are not an adequate explanation of pain. To think that there is something missing from the explanation is to be misguided, according to deniers of the explanatory gap. A second physicalist response is to accept that there is currently an explanatory gap between what we know about the brain and the phenomenal properties of consciousness we want to explain, but claim that this is due to the limits of current scientific knowledge. On this view, the explanatory gap will be closed when we make further progress on brain science. A third way for the physicalist to respond is to suggest that the explanatory gap is due not to the limitations of current science, but to the way we understand consciousness. Perhaps our *concept* of consciousness leads to the explanatory gap: consciousness itself is a physical phenomenon, but the way we think about consciousness leads us to find our physical explanations unsatisfactory. These three responses to the explanatory gap all constitute attempts to save physicalism: they claim that if there is a gap, it's a gap in our knowledge or understanding. The alternative view, proposed by the non-physicalist, is that the explanatory gap exists because there really is a 'gap' in the world. In other words, there is a gap between physical descriptions of the world and phenomenal consciousness because phenomenal consciousness cannot be captured by any physical description of the world. We cannot give an adequate physical explanation of consciousness, according to this position, precisely because consciousness is not part of the physical world. Sometimes this argument is put forward as an inference to the best explanation for the explanatory gap, but there is a stronger argument available: Chalmers and Jackson (2001) argue that the existence of a genuine explanatory gap would be proof that consciousness is not physical; they claim that if consciousness were physical, then we would be able to explain it.

Sometimes when we have trouble explaining a certain phenomenon, it's because we are mistaken about the nature of the phenomenon we are trying to explain. In pre-Copernican times, for example, people tried to explain the movement of the sun around the earth and ended up with inadequate explanations. It turned out that what they actually wanted to explain was the movement of the earth around the sun, which was responsible for the apparent movement of the sun around the earth. Examples like these suggest that perhaps we find an explanatory gap between our physical explanations and phenomenal consciousness because we're wrong about the nature of phenomenal consciousness. But it's not clear that we can be wrong about phenomenal consciousness in the way that people were wrong about the sun's movement around the earth. In the latter case, aspects of the world turned out to be different from how people experienced them. In the case of phenomenal consciousness, however, we'd be committed to saying that aspects of our experience are not how we experience them to be. Can we even make sense of this notion? It seems to require saying that we could be *wrong* about what it is like to see colors or hear sounds, and that we could be *wrong* about our own pain sensations. The very concept of phenomenal consciousness, as we saw earlier, seems to involve a kind of subjectivity and special access that make it difficult to understand how we could be wrong.

Many of the phenomena studied by scientists and philosophers are highly technical and seem far-removed from everyday life. Consider a physicist exploring the behavior of fundamental particles, for example, or a metaphysician pondering the relation between facts and propositions. But the topic of *consciousness* seems to be different, in the sense that we're already familiar with consciousness through our everyday experiences without requiring special training or expertise. Long before we're capable of learning from textbooks, we know what it is like to experience sights and sounds, and pains and pleasures. And the way we know about our conscious experiences is 'from the inside', in a way that is difficult to share or to measure. These peculiarities of phenomenal consciousness pose problems for both scientists and philosophers in their attempts to reconcile our everyday view of conscious experience with our scientific knowledge of the brain.

7. Conclusion

Scientific research on consciousness has made, and continues to make, significant breakthroughs. Some aspects of conscious experience, however, render it more difficult to approach scientifically: our experiences seem to have subjective and qualitative features that elude scientific techniques of experimentation and explanation. This prompts philosophical questions regarding the nature of conscious experience itself, and its place in the physical world. Such concerns, however, should not hinder progress in the science of consciousness: science can provide information about the neural activity that correlates with conscious experience, without making claims about the kind of dependency relations (identity, supervenience, etc.) that ground these correlations (see Hohwy & Bayne, this volume). But any theory of consciousness faces the question of how to account for the phenomenal properties of consciousness: how to bridge the 'explanatory gap' between the physical world and the features of experience. It is this task that Chalmers (1995) has labelled the 'hard problem' of consciousness:

> It is widely agreed that experience arises from a physical basis, but we have no good explanation of why and how it so arises. Why should physical processing give rise to a rich inner life at all? It seems objectively unreasonable that it should, and yet it does. If any problem qualifies as *the* problem of consciousness, it is this one. (Chalmers, 1995, p. 201, italics in original)

References

Alter, T. (1998). A limited defense of the knowledge argument. *Philosophical Studies*, 90(1), 35–56. DOI: 10.1023/A:1004290020847

Baars, B. J. (1988). *A cognitive theory of consciousness*. Cambridge, MA: Cambridge University Press.

Bennett, K. (2007). Mental causation. *Philosophy Compass*, 2(2), 316–337. DOI: 10.1111/j.1747-9991.2007.00063.x

Block, N. (1978). Troubles with functionalism. In C. W. Savage (Ed.), *Minnesota studies in the philosophy of science*, Vol. 9, Perception and cognition: Issues in the foundations of psychology (pp. 261–325). Minneapolis, MN: University of Minnesota Press.

Block, N. (1995). On a confusion about a function of consciousness. *Behavioral and Brain and Sciences*, 18(2), 227–247. DOI: 10.1017/S0140525X00038188

Block, N. (2007). Consciousness, accessibility, and the mesh between psychology and neuroscience. *Behavioral and Brain Sciences*, 30(5–6), 481–499.

Chalmers, D. J. (1995). Facing up to the problem of consciousness. *Journal of Consciousness Studies*, 2(3), 200–219.

Chalmers, D. J. (1996). *The conscious mind: In search of a fundamental theory*. Oxford, UK: Oxford University Press.

Chalmers, D. J. (1997). Availability: The cognitive basis of experience? In N. Block, O. Flanagan, & G. Güzeldere (Eds.), *The nature of consciousness: Philosophical debates* (pp. 421–424). Cambridge, MA: MIT Press.

Chalmers, D. J. (1999). Materialism and the metaphysics of modality. *Philosophy and Phenomenological Research*, 59(2), 473–496. DOI: 10.2307/2653685

Chalmers, D. J., & Jackson, F. (2001). Conceptual analysis and reductive explanation. *Philosophical Review*, 110(3), 315–361. DOI: 10.1215/00318108-110-3-315

Conee, E. (1994). Phenomenal knowledge. *Australasian Journal of Philosophy*, 72(2), 136–150. DOI: 10.1080/00048409412345971

Dehaene, S. (2001). *The cognitive neuroscience of consciousness*. Cambridge, MA: MIT Press.

Dennett, D. C. (1995). The unimagined preposterousness of zombies. *Journal of Consciousness Studies*, 2(4), 322–326.

Descartes, R. (1641/1996). *Meditations on first philosophy. With selections from the objections and replies* (J. Cottingham, Trans., Rev. ed.). Cambridge, UK: Cambridge University Press.

Dretske, F. (1995). *Naturalizing the mind*. Cambridge, MA: MIT Press.

Hill, C. S., & McLaughlin, B. P. (1999). There are fewer things in reality than are dreamt of in Chalmers's philosophy. *Philosophy and Phenomenological Research*, 59(2), 445–454. DOI: 10.2307/2653682

Jackson, F. (1982). Epiphenomenal qualia. *Philosophical Quarterly*, 32(127), 127–136. DOI: 10.2307/2960077

Kim, J. (1989). The myth of non-reductive materialism. *Proceedings and Addresses of the American Philosophical Association*, 63(3), 31–47. DOI: 10.2307/3130081

Kim, J. (2005). *Physicalism, or something near enough*. Princeton, NJ: Princeton University Press.

Kouider, S. (2009) Neurobiological theories of consciousness. In W. P. Banks (Ed.), *Encyclopedia of consciousness*, Vol. 2 (pp. 87–100). Oxford, UK: Elsevier. DOI: 10.1016/B978-012373873-8.00055-4

Lau, H.C., & Rosenthal, D. (2011). Empirical support for higher-order theories of conscious awareness. *Trends in Cognitive Sciences*, 15(8), 365–373. DOI: 10.1016/j.tics.2011.05.009

Levine, J. (1983). Materialism and qualia: The explanatory gap. *Pacific Philosophical Quarterly*, 64(4), 354–361.

Lewis, D. (Ed.). (1983). Postscript to "Mad pain and martian pain". In *Philosophical Papers*, Vol. 1 (pp. 130–132). Oxford, UK: Oxford University Press.

Lewis, D.K. (1986). *On the plurality of worlds*. Oxford, UK: Blackwell Publishers.

Liversedge, S.P., & Findlay, J.M. (2000). Saccadic eye movements and cognition. *Trends in Cognitive Sciences*, 4(1), 6–14. DOI: 10.1016/S1364-6613(99)01418-7

Loar, B. (1990). Phenomenal states. *Philosophical Perspectives*, 4, 81–108. DOI: 10.2307/2214188

Lycan, W.G. (1996). *Consciousness and experience*. Cambridge, MA: MIT Press.

Mehta, N., & Mashour, G.A. (2013). General and specific consciousness: A first-order representationalist approach. *Frontiers in Psychology*, 4, 407. DOI: 10.3389/fpsyg.2013.00407

Miller, S.M. (Ed.). (2013). *The constitution of visual consciousness: Lessons from binocular rivalry*. Advances in Consciousness Research (Vol. 90). Amsterdam, The Netherlands: John Benjamins Publishing Company. DOI: 10.1075/aicr.90

Nagel, T. (1974). What is it like to be a bat? *Philosophical Review*, 83(4), 435–450. DOI: 10.2307/2183914

Panconesi, A. (2008). Serotonin and migraine: A reconsideration of the central theory. *Journal of Headache and Pain*, 9(5), 267–276. DOI: 10.1007/s10194-008-0058-2

Polger, T.W. (2004). *Natural minds*. Cambridge, MA: MIT Press.

Price, N.S.C. (2013). Overview of visual system structure and function. In S.M. Miller (Ed.), *The constitution of visual consciousness: Lessons from binocular rivalry* (pp. 37–76). Advances in Consciousness Research (Vol. 90). Amsterdam, The Netherlands: John Benjamins Publishing Company. DOI: 10.1075/aicr.90.03pri

Putnam, H. (1967). Psychological predicates. In W.H. Capitan & D.D. Merrill (Eds.), *Art, mind, and religion* (pp. 37–48). Pittsburgh, PA: Pittsburgh University Press.

Rajala, A.Z., Reininger, K.R., Lancaster, K.M., & Populin, L.C. (2010). Rhesus monkeys (*Macaca mulatta*) do recognize themselves in the mirror: Implications for the evolution of self-recognition. *PLoS ONE*, 5(9), e12865. DOI: 10.1371/journal.pone.0012865

Rosenthal, D.M. (1986). Two concepts of consciousness. *Philosophical Studies*, 49(3), 329–359. DOI: 10.1007/BF00355521

Schneider, S. (2012). Why property dualists must reject substance physicalism. *Philosophical Studies*, 157(1), 61–76. DOI: 10.1007/s11098-010-9618-9

Smart, J.J.C. (1959). Sensations and brain processes. *Philosophical Review*, 68(2), 141–156. DOI: 10.2307/2182164

Tye, M. (1994). Qualia, content, and the inverted spectrum. *Noûs*, 28(2), 159–183. DOI: 10.2307/2216047

Yablo, S. (1993). Is conceivability a guide to possibility? *Philosophy and Phenomenological Research*, 53(1), 1–42. DOI: 10.2307/2108052

The philosophy of mind needs a better metaphysics

Martin Mahner
Center for Inquiry – Europe, Rossdorf

The philosophy of mind employs plenty of metaphysical concepts such as "(mental) property", "state", "event", "identity", "causation", or "supervenience". However, it has no fully fledged metaphysical theory, let alone a generally accepted one. This flaw slows down the progress of the field in that the same old problems keep being discussed over and over without much hope of resolution. Examples are the (in)famous zombie argument against materialism, and the functionalist claim that machines could develop consciousness. This paper expounds the materialist ontological theory of Mario Bunge and explores its problem-solving power.

1. Introduction

In examining the relationship between brain and mind, the philosophy of mind refers to mental properties, mental states, mental events, etc. It also uses concepts such as "identity", "causation", "supervenience" or "emergence". Thus the philosophy of mind is full of metaphysics, but it has no fully fledged metaphysical theory, let alone a generally accepted one. In addition, the metaphysical notions used in the philosophy of mind are often based on ordinary language concepts rather than scientific ones. This is unfortunate, because in my view this slows down the progress of the field in that the same old problems, if not pseudo-problems, keep being discussed over and over without much hope of resolution. For example, both the (in)famous zombie argument against materialism, and the functionalist claim that computers or other machines could develop consciousness, simply dissolve in certain ontologies.

It should be interesting, therefore, to introduce a promising metaphysical theory, and to see why these examples are non-problems in the light of such a metaphysics. As analytic metaphysics has been a thriving philosophical field for quite some time, there

DOI 10.1075/aicr.92.12mah

are lots of approaches from which to choose.[1] The in my opinion most promising ontology does not exactly belong to the philosophical mainstream, which is why it is worthwhile to examine its power here: the ontology developed by Mario Bunge (1977, 1979), who applied his approach to the mind-body problem early on (Bunge, 1979, 1980; Bunge & Ardila, 1987), without, however, exploring all its possible ramifications and consequences. As I have applied Bunge's ontology to the philosophy of biology before (Mahner & Bunge, 1997), and as I have summarized his metaphysics in a German book (Bunge & Mahner, 2004), I shall borrow from these works whenever convenient.

2. The materialist metaphysics of Mario Bunge

2.1 Things and properties

Figure 1 illustrates the logical structure of Bunge's ontology – a structure which I shall follow in this section.

Bunge's ontology is a so-called substance metaphysics, which considers the notion of a material thing as the most fundamental concept. (By contrast, process metaphysics regard processes as more fundamental than things.) In the style of Aristotelian metaphysics, the notion of a (material) thing is developed from the concepts of property and substance. A substance or bare individual is that which "bears" or "carries" properties. Note that neither properties nor substances are real in the sense of having autonomous existence: there are neither self-existing properties nor self-existing substances; there are only propertied substances, that is, things. Thus properties and substances precede things only analytically, not factually.

We may distinguish several types of properties. The first distinction is between intrinsic and relational properties. An *intrinsic* property is one that a thing possesses independently of any other thing, even if acquired under the influence of other things. Examples: composition, electric charge, mass, consciousness. *Relational* properties, by contrast, are of course properties that a thing has only in relation to some other thing(s). Examples: speed, weight, descent. A special type of relational property is the so-called secondary or phenomenal property. The prime example is of course color. Whereas reflected wave length (or, more precisely, the distribution of spectral reflectances) of some thing is a primary property, color is a secondary property, that is, wave length (or, more precisely, spectral reflectance distribution) as represented by some organism

1. Note that in this paper I use "metaphysics" and "ontology", as well as the corresponding adjectives, synonymously. This is in tune with the philosophical tradition that introduced the term "ontology" as a name for a de-theologized metaphysics. In my view it is regrettable that nowadays "ontology" is often just used in the sense of the union of the reference classes of scientific theories, that is, as that which tells us "what there is".

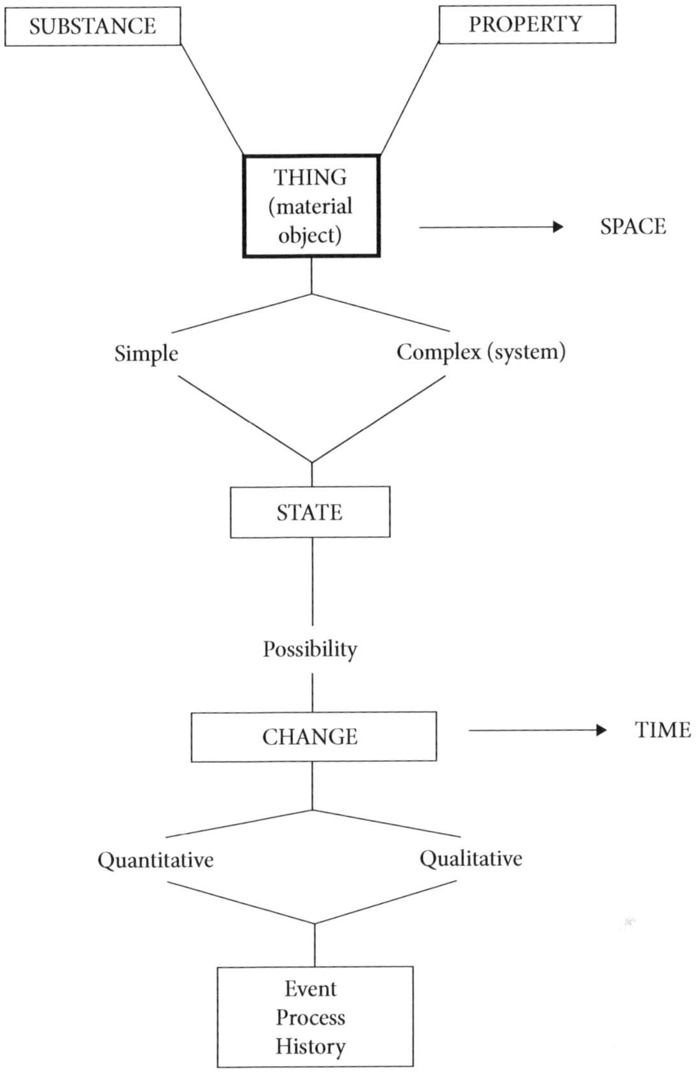

Figure 1. The basic structure of Mario Bunge's ontology (modified from Bunge & Mahner, 2004). The figure is to be read from top to bottom, and the nodes are to be understood in the sense of a logical or definitional precedence, that is, a given concept at a certain level is defined with the help of the preceding concept(s). For example, the concept of property is logically prior to the concept of a state, which in turn is prior to that of an event. The arrows towards the concepts of space and time indicate that they are not basic, but derived from the concepts of thing and change. That is, being a material or concrete thing is not defined in terms of spatiotemporality.

equipped with suitable sensory organs and a sufficiently complex nervous system. In this construal secondary properties are relational in that they are possessed by the subject/object system rather than by either the subject or the object alone. The object has only primary properties, and if a subject has a phenomenal experience without actually perceiving (representing) an outer object, it is either dreaming or hallucinating.

Another distinction (also going back to Aristotle) is the one between essential and accidental properties. Essential (constitutive) properties are those that determine the nature or essence of a thing. They are those that we need to describe of what kind a thing is. For example, the difference between my brain and a rock is given by the essential properties of both. An accidental property, by contrast, makes no difference to what a thing is. For instance, whether a quartz crystal is located in Australia or in Africa makes no difference to its being a quartz crystal. These examples indicate that essential properties come in clusters: they are *lawfully* related. This implies an ontological construal of laws, not an epistemological one in the sense of law statements. Laws or, more precisely, lawfully related properties are what law statements refer to, if true. Ontic laws in this sense are *inherent* in the things which possess them. They are neither contingent nor imposed from without. Laws belong to the nature of things. Not even God could change the lawful behavior of things without changing their nature.

Thus, Bunge is a representative of what in the philosophy of nature is called the "new essentialism" (Ellis, 2002), which may better be called *scientific* or *nomological essentialism*.[2] This essentialist view of laws as properties of things is very important, because a thing's lawfully related properties determine what is *actually* possible for a thing, as opposed to what is just *logically* possible.

Furthermore, there are qualitative and quantitative properties, as well as manifest and dispositional ones, where dispositions can be either causal (e.g., the disposition of a glass to break) or stochastic (e.g., the propensity of an atom to decay).

Finally, we have a type of property that is most relevant to the philosophy of mind: systemic (or emergent or supervenient) properties as opposed to merely resultant ones. Most things are complex, that is, they are composed of parts, which may in turn be composed of further parts: they are systems. A property that only a system as a whole possesses, yet none of its parts in isolation, is a *systemic* property; otherwise, a property is *resultant*. If I assemble a computer in a factory, its parts have a mass, and so has the final product. The mass of the whole is just the (additive) result of the

2. As is well known, essentialism is not exactly going strong these days, in particular in the philosophy of biology, which has become rather anti-essentialist. For example, due to the enormous variation of organisms, many philosophers of biology believe that there are no laws (= law statements) in biology. But this does not entail that organisms do not behave lawfully: it is just that it often makes not much sense to try to find general, let alone universal, law statements because their reference class is rather small, holding only for some subspecies, variety or even smaller units, for example; that is, only for those organisms sharing the same lawful properties. In other words, biological kinds often have only a small number of specimens (more on laws in biology in Mahner & Bunge, 1997, and Ellis, 2002). Consequently, anti-essentialism in biology and its philosophy is just as misleading as it is everywhere else, such as in the philosophy of mind.

(quantitative) mass property of its parts. By contrast, the various properties that only the correctly assembled computer as a whole displays – most conspicuously its specific functions – are its systemic properties. We may as well call these systemic properties "supervenient properties" or "emergent properties". Bunge prefers the term "emergent", which he defines in purely ontological terms: as a property of a whole that is not present in its parts. "Emergent" is often defined in epistemological terms, namely as a property of a whole that cannot be explained or predicted from the knowledge of its parts. Yet whether or not a systemic property can be explained (or predicted) by reference to the parts of a system is immaterial for its being a (new) property of a whole. Nonetheless, the systemic properties of a whole do lawfully depend on the (essential) properties of its parts (the so-called base properties). This is why, contrary to the belief of the functionalists, your green cheese is never going to think or have feelings: its parts lack the relevant base properties.

To illustrate the importance of lawfully related essential properties and emergence, let us take a look at an example (Figure 2). A thing *x* has two properties P and Q, which are lawfully related, or in other words, related by the law L_{PQ}. A more complex thing *y* may consist of some things of the same kind as *x*, but possesses in addition a new (emergent) property R. If R is an essential property, it must be lawfully related with either P or Q or both. That is, *y* must possess at least one new law L_{PR} or L_{QR}, or perhaps even both. As a consequence, if *y* fails to have one or even both of the base properties P and Q, there will be no lawful emergent property R. Replace Q by a different property S (which means you replace the part *x* with a different part *z*), and you will obviously get neither R nor L_{RQ} but at most some different property T and perhaps a new law L_{ST}.

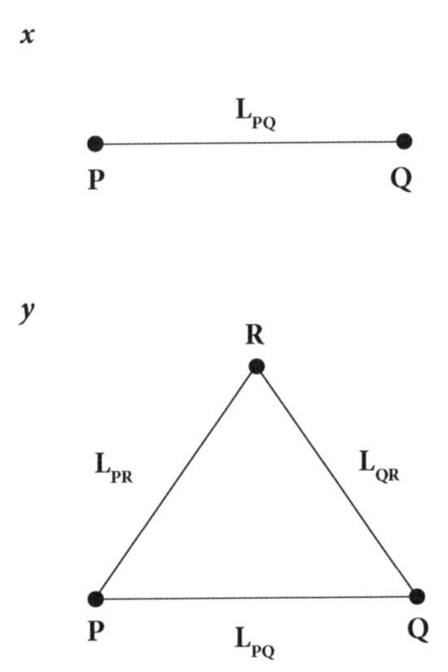

Figure 2. The lawful relationship between essential properties in thing *x*, and the emergence of new laws in the new thing *y*. Explanation in the text (modified from Bunge & Mahner, 2004).

A thing is individuated (or identified) by the set of its properties at a given time. These properties are individual properties in the sense that only the given thing possesses them. No other thing can possess *my* mass or *my* age, although many other things also have a certain mass or age. We can thus distinguish general (or universal) properties from individual ones.[3] If things share a number of general properties, they are of the same type or kind, but each token of a given type is an individual which is individuated by its particular properties.

Finally, we should emphasize the difference between properties and predicates. Properties are always properties of concrete things, whereas predicates are conceptual representations of properties. Thus, whereas real things possess properties, only the model things in our mind have predicates. Evidently, some of our representations may be wrong in that some predicates do not represent real properties. We sometimes hypothesize that a certain thing has a certain property only to find out later that our hypothesis is false. Moreover, there are two kinds of predicates that never represent real properties. These are negative and disjunctive predicates. The absence of a property is not a property of a thing, even though it is often convenient for us to describe some things by the absence of some property. For example, as a mammal, I do not possess wings, but this does not imply that the absence of wings is a property of mine. Rather, the relevant property is that I possess forearms of a certain structure that allow me to grasp, touch, etc. Negation is *de dicto,* not *de re*. The same holds for disjunctive predicates. For example, "heavy or transparent" is not a property of any thing, which can only have the property of being heavy, of being transparent, or of being both heavy and transparent.[4]

2.2 States

In ordinary language a state is something like a uniform phase or stage of some process. For example, one says that an object is in a state of motion, or that a person is in a state of confusion. In Bunge's ontology, however, a state is something static, and this static concept is used to define the (dynamic) concepts of event and process.

As we saw above, every thing has a number of properties. The totality of properties of a thing at a certain time determines the state of the thing at the given time. Because every property can be formalized as a mathematical function, the list of n such functions is called a state function of things of the kind concerned. That is, if we have *n*

3. Individual properties are often called "tropes" in analytic ontology.

4. A consequence of Bunge's theory of properties is that Boolean algebra cannot be used to formalize ontological concepts like "property" or "supervenience". All such attempts are doomed from the start. Real properties have the formal structure of an inf-semilattice, which is a much poorer structure than Boolean algebra. For a criticism of Kim's (1978) early analysis of the concept of supervenience in terms of Boolean algebra, see Mahner and Bunge (1997, p. 32f.).

functions F_i, the state function F of the given thing is the list or n-tuple $F = < F_1, F_2,\ldots, F_n>$. The value of F at time t, i.e., $F(t) = <F_1(t), F_2(t),\ldots, F_n(t)>$, represents the state of the thing at time t.

The set of possible states of a thing can be represented in a state space or possibility space for the thing. This is the abstract space spanned by the corresponding state function $F = <F_1, F_2,\ldots, F_n>$. If, for the sake of simplicity, we consider only two properties, the corresponding state space is a region of the plane determined by the axes F_1 and F_2 – see Figure 3. A state space for a thing with n properties is n-dimensional.

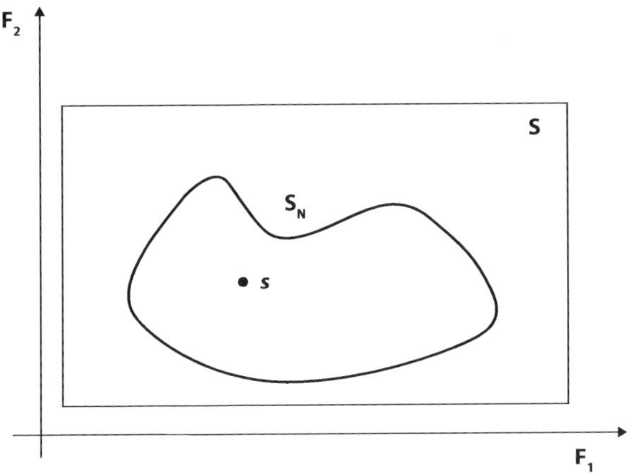

Figure 3. Two properties F_1 and F_2 span a two-dimensional state space S. Any state s of the given thing is represented by a point. The laws of a material thing of a given kind restrict the logically possible state space S to a proper subset: its nomological state space S_N (modified from Bunge & Mahner, 2004).

Because essential properties are lawfully related, a material thing cannot be in all its logically possible states: its really possible states are restricted by the laws that define its kind. The subset of really possible states of the logically possible state space of the given thing is called its *lawful* or *nomological* state space S_N – see again Figure 3.

According to this construal, the set of conscious states of a brain (or of some neuronal subsystem) is a proper subset of its nomological state space. Anyway, it should be possible in principle, though perhaps not in practice, to map out the conscious state space of a brain.

Obviously, if a thing acquires a new (in particular systemic) property, we must add a new axis to its state space representation, and if it loses one, we must remove the corresponding axis. In this way, emergence can be represented by the addition of new axes to a thing's state space. The converse process, that is, the loss of properties in the course of system formation or dissolution, may be called *submergence*, and it is represented by the removal of axes.

2.3 Events and processes

Things hardly stay in the same state. In fact they change all the time. By "change" we understand a change of state and thereby a change of the properties of a thing. Change can be illustrated by a line in a state space (Figure 4). Whereas a point in a state space represents a state, a line represents a sequence of states. An event can be represented as an ordered pair of states <initial state, final state> or $<s, s'>$. As with the logically possible states of a thing, we can collect all the logically possible events in (or changes of state of) a thing to form the conceivable event space of the thing in question. And as every thing can only be in nomologically possible states, it can only undergo nomologically possible changes of state, i.e., events. Thus, the set of really possible events is restricted to the nomological event space of the changing thing(s) in question.

Just as things don't stay in the same state, they usually don't just undergo singular events but sequences of such. A sequence of states or, alternatively, a sequence of two or more events of a thing is a *process* (or complex event). Thus, processes can be represented by a curve in a state space. This is important because not any old set of events is a process: only a sequence of states of one thing, however complex, qualifies as a process. Needless to say, two or more things may interact and thus form a system, whose states and changes of state can be represented in a state space of its own.

Some special types of processes are called *mechanisms*. Mechanisms are *specific* processes (characteristic functions), that is, they occur only in things of a certain kind. More in Section 3.

Finally, the *history* of a thing is the total set of its changes of state, from its very beginning s_0 to its end, if any.[5] See Figure 4.

2.4 Causes

What Bunge calls simply 'process' is often called a 'causal process'. However, in Bunge's ontology a state of a thing is not the cause of a later state of the same thing. Youth is not the cause of old age, and the caterpillar is not the cause of the butterfly. Bunge speaks of an (external) cause only if a change of state of, i.e., an event in, a given thing generates a change of state, i.e., an event, in some other thing; or if an event in one part of a thing generates an event in another part. Thus the causal relation only holds among events.

The concept of causation can be elucidated in terms of the state space approach. Consider two different things, or parts of a thing, of some kind(s). Call them x and y, and call $\mathrm{H}(x)$ and $\mathrm{H}(y)$ their respective histories over a certain time interval. Further, call $\mathrm{H}(y|x)$ the history of y when x acts on y. Then we say that x acts on y if, and only if, $\mathrm{H}(y) \neq \mathrm{H}(y|x)$, that is, if x induces changes in the states of y. The corresponding event e in x that brought about the event e' in y is the cause, while e' is the effect.

5. Bunge's ontology is therefore a specimen of what is called *endurantism*.

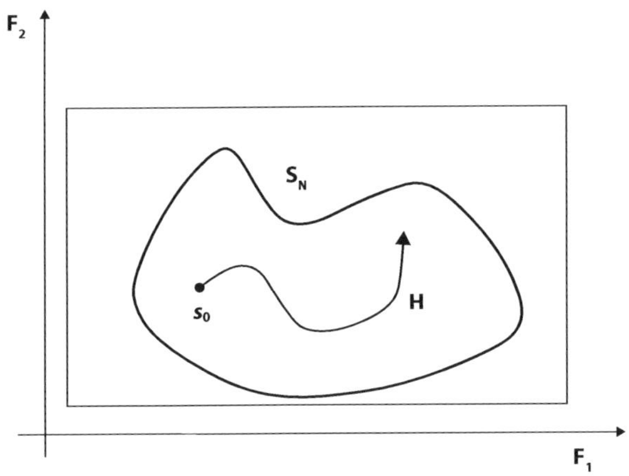

Figure 4. Processes may be represented by a line in the given nomological state space S_N of a thing, starting with some original state s_0. The line H is the history of the given thing between some original and some later or even final state (modified from Bunge & Mahner, 2004).

Just as the concept of law, the notion of causation here is ontological, not epistemological. It can be analyzed as a form of energy transfer between two things or two parts of a complex thing. It goes without saying that especially in the biological sciences many causes are hard to detect, and they require elaborate experimental and statistical methods.

If only events as defined here are causes, strictly speaking neither things nor properties are causes. In the context of the debate about mental causation (see, e.g., Robb & Heil, 2008, for an overview), it is often claimed that if mental properties are real, they need to have "causal powers". But if mental properties are simply systemic properties of certain neuronal systems, they do not cause anything. (Indeed, we may consider this as a form of property epiphenomenalism.) At most the whole changing neuronal system can cause something; in other words, a neuronal system with (emergent) mental properties may behave differently than one without such properties; or, to be more precise, an organism with neuronal systems possessing emergent mental properties should behave differently than one without such properties.

There can be no mental causation without mental events, and there can be no mental events without mental things. And because, according to Bunge's emergentist materialism, there are no mental things (that is, immaterial minds in themselves), there are no mental events and hence no mental causation. While the talk of mental states and events may be a convenient shorthand in the daily business of the neurosciences, the use of metaphysically ill-conceived terms may be seriously misleading in the philosophy of mind.

3. Systems and mechanisms

Most things are not simple but complex: they are composed of other things. If a complex thing is just an aggregate of other things, such as a pile of sand, it is a heap rather than a system. Systems, by contrast, are cohesive: they have a specific structure formed by strong bonds. Except for microphysical entities, such as quarks and electrons, which are not known to be composed of further parts, virtually all things studied by science, from atoms through societies, are systems (Bunge, 1979).

In the analysis of any system three aspects are important: its composition, its environment, and its structure. Bunge calls this the *CES-analysis* of systems. The *composition* of a system is of course the set of its (natural and material) parts.[6]

The environment of a system is the complement of its composition, that is, the set of all things other than the given system. However, for a scientific model of a concrete system *s* we do not need to take the rest of the universe into account. We can restrict our analysis to those things that may act upon *s*, or which *s* may act upon. What is relevant, then, is this *immediate* (or *causally proximate*) *environment* of *s*.

Finally, the structure of a system *s* is the set of relations among its components. Of particular relevance here are those relations that make for the cohesiveness of *s*. These are the *bonding* or *causal* relations. In tune with the state space approach introduced above, we can say that a relation between a thing *x* and a thing *y* is a *bonding* relation iff the states of *y* alter when the relation to *x* holds. Consequently, the nomological state space of a system is not the union (or mereological sum) of the nomological state spaces of its components, but it must be construed anew taking into account in particular the emergent (lawful) properties of the given system.

The *internal structure* (or *endostructure*) of a system *s*, then, is the set of bonding and nonbonding relations among the components of *s*. Often we are interested only in the bonding endostructure of *s*, for example, when we want to know how neurons are connected into complex systems. As systems, or some of their parts, also interact with some external things, they do have an *exostructure* as well. Just as its endostructure, a system's exostructure is the union of the bonding and nonbonding relations among the system (or of some of its parts) and the items in its environment. Again, we are usually interested only in the bonding exostructure of a system.

---

6. In ordinary language as well as in mereology the set of parts of a thing may include arbitrary parts which do not exist really but are the result of artificially (or conceptually) slicing up a thing into as many parts as we wish. An example are relational parts, such as the upper, middle, and lower part of a tower, whereas the natural parts of a tower are the stones, steel beams, tiles, windows, or whatever the tower is made of, as well as the further natural parts these parts consist of. The qualification "natural" excludes such arbitrary parts, focusing on parts that belong to natural kinds. Finally, the qualification "material" excludes so-called temporal parts, which occur in perdurantist ontologies.

The notion of a bonding exostructure makes it obvious that many systems are structured hierarchically: they consist of subsystems and they are part of some supersystem(s). A scientific study of systems will therefore have to focus on some specific level of organization, that is, it will consider a system's subsystems and some of the supersystems it is part of. For example, a study of neuronal systems and their functioning needs to look not only at their molecular and cellular components but also at the whole brain, and, in the case of consciousness, at the social input of the given person. In other words, what is of interest for a scientific explanation is not the entire composition, environment, and structure of a system but only the composition, environment, and structure of some of the adjacent levels. The CES-analysis of systems is thus usually restricted to a $C_LE_LS_L$-anaylsis, where L refers to the relevant sub- or super-system levels of the given system. In any case, what is quite irrelevant in the explanation of the mental in its emergentist conception is any reference to the microphysical level, because it disregards all the emergent properties of the higher-level systems in between.

As it is quite common to say that the special sciences deal with different levels of systems, such as the physical, chemical, biological, and social levels, the question arises whether there is also a mental level (see e.g., Revonsuo, this volume). In Bunge's metaphysics there is no mental level because the mental is conceived of as an emergent property of certain neuronal systems. There would be a mental level only if there were mental things above and beyond neuronal systems. So if the brain produced a self-existing mind or mental thing, such as a gland secreting some hormone, there would be a mental level. If the mental is just an emergent property existing only and whenever certain neuronal systems undergo certain processes, then there is no mental thing and hence no mental level, unless we wish to stipulate that such a mental level is just the set of all neuronal systems capable of exhibiting mental properties.[7]

The CES-analysis of systems is static. To get closer to real-life situations we need to take into account the changes of systems. For example, as consciousness is most likely a certain activity or activity pattern of highly complex neuronal systems, it cannot be fully understood by a merely static analysis of neuronal systems. As we saw in Section 2.3, every thing has its own nomological event space, that is, the set of nomically possible changes it is able to undergo. What is nomically possible is determined by the lawful properties of the given system, including its emergent properties. A subset of all the possible processes of a system *s* is the set of kind-specific processes of *s*. For example, many cells share a similar basic physiology, but only some cells are able to gain energy through photosynthesis including the corresponding physiological

7. Thus, the question of the "constitution of consciousness" (Miller, 2007; see Miller, this volume) must be understood in the sense of the (compositional, structural, environmental, and mechanismic) constitution of neuronal systems *with* mental properties in contrast to those *without* mental properties. Needless to say, it remains a most formidable task for neuroscience to distinguish these neuronal systems.

processes. These specific processes or functions may be called the *mechanisms* of the given system. A mechanism is thus a process function, not a structured thing.[8]

Note that "function" is often understood not in the sense of "process function" or "functioning" (or *modus operandi*) but in the sense of "role function". A role function, however, is something a system does with respect to some higher-level system it is part of (Mahner & Bunge, 1997, 2001). For example, the role function of the heart is to pump blood. But this role function can be achieved by at least two different mechanisms or process functions: the muscular contractions of a normal biotic heart (including of course all the relevant lower-level processes) or the electric mechanics of an artificial pump replacing the heart of patients with heart failure. It seems therefore that role functions are multiply realizable, whereas process functions are not. If consciousness is a process function of certain neuronal systems, then systems of a different kind won't be able to be conscious (more on this in Section 5).

In sum, taking into account the characteristic changes of systems of a given kind – its mechanisms – we may add a fourth coordinate M to the CES triple, obtaining a CESM-quadruple. Analyzing systems in terms of CESM is essentially what scientific and mechanismic explanations do.[9]

4. Why many metaphysical approaches are unsatisfactory

Of course there are many alternative ontological approaches. But I submit that they are more or less unsatisfactory. To see why, let's take a look at some of the metaphysical considerations of Jaegwon Kim, because he is one of the major players in the philosophy of mind, and he has also dealt with the concepts of event, substance, state etc.

8. In the literature on mechanismic explanation both a structured thing and its processes are called mechanisms (see, e.g., Glennan, 2002; Machamer, Darden, & Craver, 2000; Opie & O'Brien, this volume). It is of course correct that we talk about the mechanism of a watch, for example, but this belongs to the description of the composition and structure of a watch. It is only the specific processes that this composition and structure allows for that we call mechanisms here. Note that Bunge prefers the new adjective "mechanismic" over "mechanistic", so as to avoid misunderstandings in terms of physical mechanics or machine metaphors. A social mechanism, for instance, is as far from mechanics as it gets.

9. Although mechanismic explanation (as opposed to the classical, merely subsumptive deductive-nomological explanation) has become increasingly popular over the past two decades, in the philosophy of science it was proposed already back in 1967 by Bunge (1967, p. 25ff.). Unluckily, he had called it "interpretive explanation", and, unfortunately, his work was largely ignored by the philosophical community. So was his elaboration on mechanismic explanation from 1983 (Bunge, 1983). Thus, it was left to others to reinvent and popularize the concept. Nowadays Peter Railton is (wrongly) credited for having invented the idea of a mechanism in 1978 (Glennan, 2002, p. 343).

Kim (1993) characterizes an event thus:

> We think of an event as a concrete object (or n-tuple of objects) exemplifying a property (or n-adic relation) at a time. In this sense of 'event' events include states, conditions, and the like, and not only events narrowly conceived as involving changes. (p. 8; similarly, p. 33ff.)

We further learn that "[b]y 'substance' I mean things like tables, chairs, atoms, living creatures, bits of stuff like water or bronze, and the like..." (p. 33), and "[a] change in a substance occurs when that substance acquires a property it did not previously have, or loses a property it previously had." (p. 33). All this is the so-called "property exemplification account of events" (p. 34).

Why is this approach unsatisfactory? (1) It strikes me as odd and confusing to not regard the aspect of change as essential for the meaning of "event". A thing possessing a property at some time is a fact, but it is not an event. Not all facts are events. (2) An n-tuple of concrete objects is not itself a concrete object, but a mathematical representation and hence a conceptual object. Of course there are complex concrete objects, composed of many parts, but these are systems or complexes of things, forming a higher-level entity. The composition of these systems may be formally *represented* by n-tuples, but n-tuples are not out there. (3) Talk of the exemplification of properties is certainly common, but to a materialist it has a ring of Platonism to it. It sounds as if properties hovered in an immaterial realm of ideas, and once in a blue moon concrete objects instantiated or exemplified these properties. I therefore avoid any such talk. (4) Traditionally, a substance is not a concrete object, but the "bearer of properties". But as there are no such bare individuals without properties, a substance is at best an ontological concept, not a real thing. (5) Acquiring or losing a property is a qualitative change. Yet more frequently concrete objects change only quantitatively. For example, growing or getting older does not entail the acquisition or loss of a property, but only a change of the respective property value. Indeed, in science quantitative properties are represented as real-valued functions, so that the change of a property can be graphically illustrated as a curve in some coordinate system. A misconception of quantitative changes like these may be the reason why Kim adopts the property exemplification approach: if we consider only one general property, such as age, it seems that a concrete ageing object exemplifies the property of ageing. But this is not so: it has the general property of age, but the individual values of this property change. So we do have a change of state in this case, not just the possession of a property.

The defects of Kim's ontology provide an example for how wide-ranging the import of an ontological theory is and how important it is to base the philosophy of mind on the best available ontology, that is, an ontology that is more in tune with scientific practice and which has greater analytic power.

5. Zombies and thinking machines

It is rather trivial to point out that philosophical views and arguments (unless they are purely formal perhaps) have explicit or tacit metaphysical presuppositions. If we accept some argument as convincing, we must then also accept its metaphysical presuppositions. Conversely, if we have no reason to accept these presuppositions, we have no reason to accept the corresponding argument. I shall argue here that in the light of the metaphysics sketched in the preceding, we have no reason to accept two well-known ideas occurring in the philosophy of mind: functionalism and the zombie problem. Functionalism is mistaken, and the zombie problem is a non-problem.

Functionalism and the associated notion of multiple realizability presuppose that matter doesn't matter because structure is all there is to mental life, so that it could occur in many different things than brains, even in artificial ones such as computers. One of the hypothetical arguments of this approach is what is called "neuron replacement". Imagine that we replace one neuron of a human brain with a functionally equivalent artificial electronic neuron. (The adjective "electronic" is important here, because we are not concerned with artificially synthesized biological neurons as they would be materially equivalent with the original natural neurons.) Do the patient's brain functions and hence his mental life change after that? Probably not. Now let's continue with this neuron replacement until the entire brain consists of artificial neurons. According to the functionalists, this artificial brain would work just as well as the original one and hence display consciousness, for all that matters is the functional organization of input/output behavior, not the matter of which brains are made.

According to emergentist materialism *cum* nomological essentialism, consciousness or, more precisely, *being conscious* is an emergent property of certain complex neuronal systems undergoing certain coordinated activities. Which systemic properties are nomically possible is determined by the essential base properties of the given system's parts. This is why you cannot obtain a given systemic property out of any base properties, that is, out of parts of different kinds. What holds for the components of the system, also holds for the processes it can undergo. Being conscious is not a property of a static system, but an emergent property of a complex changing system: it involves process functions, not just some input/output role functions. But process functions are changes of state of the given system with a given composition and structure, so they cannot occur in systems that have completely different nomological state and event spaces. (It may be possible, however, to replace some role functions, such as those providing sensory input to some neuronal system capable of phenomenal consciousness, with artificial devices.)

This is why, according to our view here, multiple realizability of the mental is restricted to a variety of neuronal systems of the same kind. For example, your and my brain are most likely wired somewhat differently, so that your thinking of "$2+2=4$" may involve somewhat different neuronal systems and processes than my thinking of the same proposition. But this is just a variation within the same kind of matter, namely neuronal systems. Such variation in "realizability" is not multiple in the sense that it applies to *different kinds* (or even all kinds) of systems. This view is sometimes derided as neuro-chauvinism but it is a natural companion of nomological essentialism. (So is carbo-chauvinism in the case of life.) For these (and many other) reasons, functionalism, such as in strong Artificial Life and Artificial Intelligence, turns out to be untenable in the light of this metaphysics (Kary & Mahner, 2002; Mahner & Bunge, 1997).

Let us turn to the alleged zombie problem. This problem rests on the view that logical possibility is all there is to possibility. If something is conceivable it is logically possible, and whatever is logically possible is also really possible. This approach often comes together with possible worlds semantics, possible worlds metaphysics, modal logics, etc.[10]

Thus, we get arguments telling us, for example, that as it is not logically necessary that water is H_2O, it could be composed of different molecules in other (logically) possible worlds.[11] And here we go: because it is conceivable or, in other words, as it is not logically necessary that (normal) human brains have consciousness, it is logically possible that there are zombies in the sense of humans that function just as we do, but who fail to have any "mental life" at all (Chalmers, 1996). So there is no necessary or lawful connection between neuronal systems and phenomenal conscious or other mental "states", and the existence of mental properties becomes a mystery. Supposedly, the explanatory and metaphysical gap is so wide that materialism is incapable of closing it.

Now logical possibility is the only possibility that applies in logics and mathematics, but in science the relevant possibility is *nomic* or *real* possibility. (Sometimes real possibility is also called "metaphysical possibility", but just as often it is unclear what exactly a metaphysical possibility is supposed to be.) Of course the logically impossible is not really possible, but not everything that is logically possible is actually possible. As we have seen in Sections 2.2 and 2.3, the nomologically possible state and event spaces of material things are proper subsets of their logically possible state and event spaces, respectively. And what is really possible is determined by the lawful essential properties of the things in question. A given system composed of parts of certain kinds necessarily comes with all its systemic properties, where the necessity in question is *real* or *nomic*, not logical. So if consciousness or the mental in general is a systemic property of neuronal systems of a certain kind (or, if preferred, of whole brains), these systems will always and necessarily come with their systemic properties – under the given conditions. Accordingly, it makes no sense to ask why there is consciousness as though a certain system of a certain kind had a choice to not come with all its lawful properties. The existence of systemic properties is first of all a (ubiquitous) fact of nature, and an explanation of consciousness can only consist in the correct description

10. You do not make friends in mainstream analytic philosophy if you claim that possible worlds semantics and metaphysics as well as modal logics are rather useless tools for a science-oriented philosophy.

11. This is of course Putnam's example. The Kripkeans would disagree.

of the special states or changes of state (mechanisms) of the brain that consist in being conscious. Asking for an explanation for why our brains come with consciousness at all rather than being zombie brains is like asking why there is something rather than nothing: it is a pseudo-question. For all these reasons, the zombie argument dissolves in the light of Bunge's ontology or in the light of nomological essentialism, respectively (see, e.g., Garrett, 2009, for a more detailed criticism).

Of course, one could argue that mental properties are different from other emergent properties because they are subjective, that is, one needs to be that neuronal system in a brain in a body in a certain state to "detect" or "access" (or rather have) mental properties. However, considering the ubiquity of systemic properties and of lawfulness throughout the entire world, we have good reasons to assume that mental properties are no different from other systemic properties. While it is true that mental properties are not physical properties (in the sense of physics), they are still material properties of material things. But then Bunge's metaphysics combines substance monism with property pluralism: there are physical, chemical, biotic, social, and mental properties. However, the latter are not separated by an ontological gap from the rest of the world, as Chalmers seems to assume in his conception of property dualism: they just are yet another example of qualitative novelty in this world. This, at least, should in my view be the metaphysical working assumption of a (neuro)scientific approach to the mental.

It goes without saying that the implications of Bunge's metaphysics for the philosophy of mind deserve a much more extensive study than what I could do in this short overview here. So it must suffice to point out in concluding that by adopting a science-oriented and materialist metaphysics such as Bunge's, the philosophy of mind could avoid many fruitless debates and thus focus on important problems rather than self-inflicted pseudo-problems based on fragmentary metaphysics.

References

Bunge, M. (1967). *Scientific research II: The search for truth*. Berlin: Springer-Verlag. DOI: 10.1007/978-3-642-48138-3

Bunge, M. (1977). *Treatise on basic philosophy. Ontology I: The furniture of the world*. Dordrecht: Reidel. DOI: 10.1007/978-94-010-9924-0

Bunge, M. (1979). *Treatise on basic philosophy. Ontology II: A world of systems*. Dordrecht: Reidel. DOI: 10.1007/978-94-009-9392-1

Bunge, M. (1980). *The mind-body problem*. Oxford, UK: Pergamon Press.

Bunge, M. (1983). *Treatise on basic philosophy, Vol. 6, Epistemology & methodology II: Understanding the world*. Dordrecht: Reidel. DOI: 10.1007/978-94-015-6921-7

Bunge, M., & Ardila, R. (1987). *Philosophy of psychology*. New York, NY: Springer-Verlag. DOI: 10.1007/978-1-4612-4696-1

Bunge, M., & Mahner, M. (2004). *Über die Natur der Dinge. Materialismus und Wissenschaft*. Stuttgart: Hirzel-Verlag.

Chalmers, D. J. (1996). *The conscious mind: In search of a fundamental theory*. Oxford, UK: Oxford University Press.

Ellis, B. (2002). *The philosophy of nature: A guide to the new essentialism*. Chesham, UK: Acumen Publishing.
Garrett, B.J. (2009). Causal essentialism versus the zombie worlds. *Canadian Journal of Philosophy*, 39(1), 93–112. DOI: 10.1353/cjp.0.0042
Glennan, S. (2002). Rethinking mechanistic explanation. *Philosophy of Science*, 69(S3), S342–S353. DOI: 10.1086/341857
Kary, M., & Mahner, M. (2002). How would you know if you synthesized a thinking thing? *Minds and Machines*, 12(1), 61–86. DOI: 10.1023/A:1013738831686
Kim, J. (1978). Supervenience and nomological incommensurables. *American Philosophical Quarterly*, 15(2), 149–156.
Kim, J. (1993). *Supervenience and mind*. Cambridge, UK: Cambridge University Press. DOI: 10.1017/CBO9780511625220
Machamer, P., Darden, L., & Craver, C.F. (2000). Thinking about mechanisms. *Philosophy of Science*, 67(1), 1–25. DOI: 10.1086/392759
Mahner, M., & Bunge, M. (1997). *Foundations of biophilosophy*. Berlin: Springer-Verlag. DOI: 10.1007/978-3-662-03368-5
Mahner, M., & Bunge, M. (2001). Function and functionalism: A synthetic perspective. *Philosophy of Science*, 68(1), 75–94. DOI: 10.1086/392867
Miller, S.M. (2007). On the correlation/constitution distinction problem (and other hard problems) in the scientific study of consciousness. *Acta Neuropsychiatrica*, 19(3), 159–176. DOI: 10.1111/j.1601-5215.2007.00207.x
Robb, D., & Heil, J. (2008). Mental causation. In E.N. Zalta (Ed.), *The Stanford encyclopedia of philosophy (Summer 2009 edition)*. Retrieved from http://plato.stanford.edu/archives/sum2009/entries/mental-causation/

The scientific evidence for materialism about pains*

Andrew Melnyk
University of Missouri, Columbia

This paper argues in unprecedented empirical and philosophical detail that, given only what science has discovered about pain, we should prefer the materialist hypothesis that pains are purely material over the dualist hypothesis that they are immaterial. The empirical findings cited provide strong evidence for the thesis of empirical supervenience: that to every sort of introspectible change over time in pains, or variation among pains at a time, there corresponds in fact a certain sort of simultaneous neural change over time, or variation at a time. The empirical supervenience of pain on the neural is shown in turn to favor the hypothesis that pains are, in a sense that is made precise, purely material.

Introduction

Philosophical discussions of the mind-body problem have often taken pain as their leading example of a phenomenally conscious mental state (see, e.g., Kripke, 1980). In this paper, I discuss the implications for the mind-body problem of what science has to say about pain – and I aspire to do so in a way that is accessible to interested non-philosophers.

Science has clearly taught us much about the *etiology* of pain. It has taught us that there are several different types of specialized nociceptive neurons, distinct from tactile sensors and proprioceptors, that are sensitive to noxious stimuli of different kinds, e.g., to thermal, mechanical, or chemical stimuli (Price, 1999, pp. 76–79). It has taught us that bundles of these neurons run first to the spine, where they synapse with neurons that then run, along several distinct pathways, to various regions of the brain, some of which project further neurons to the cortex (Price, 1999, pp. 98–107). It has taught us that the presentation of a noxious stimulus reliably activates various distinct cortical areas – primary somatosensory cortex (S1), secondary somatosensory cortex

* I am much indebted to an anonymous reader for very helpful comments that led to significant revisions of an earlier draft of this paper.

DOI 10.1075/aicr.92.13mel

(S2) and its vicinity in the parietal operculum, insular cortex, anterior cingulate cortex, and prefrontal cortex (see, e.g., McMahon & Koltzenburg, 2006, p. 128).

Less clear but still – I claim – true is that the science of pain bears on the *nature* of pain, i.e., on the question whether pain sensations are – in some sense that needs to be made precise – immaterial rather than purely material states. My main conclusion in this paper is that what science has discovered about pain favors the hypothesis that pains are purely material over the rival hypothesis that they are immaterial; that is, given *only* the evidence that science has discovered, we should prefer the materialist hypothesis over the dualist (i.e., immaterialist) one.[1]

This conclusion is a modest one. It is consistent with the claim that, given *all* relevant rational considerations, we should *not* prefer the materialist hypothesis over the dualist one. For it may be that what science has discovered about pain does not exhaust the relevant rational considerations. It may be, as many philosophers think, that materialism can be refuted a priori, or by appeal to what is conceivable, or by appeal to what introspection tells us about the nature of pain. And it may be that such non-scientific considerations support dualism about pain strongly enough to outweigh the evidence against it provided by scientific discoveries. I strongly doubt that in fact they do, but it is beyond the scope of this paper to explain why.[2]

Does anyone actually *deny* that what science has discovered about pain favors the materialist hypothesis about pains over the dualist one? Some dualists may deny it. At any rate, I do not recall ever having read a dualist acknowledge that science at least makes it *appear* that pain is purely material; and some dualists resort rather readily to sociological explanation of the popularity of materialism among philosophers and scientists, as if the existence of apparent evidence for materialism could not explain it. Some pain scientists do not deny but still hesitate to affirm the main conclusion of this paper. For they characterize the relationship between pains and neural states in strikingly imprecise and non-committal terms, as if reluctant to assert definite materialist theses. Consider, for a representative example, a recent journal article that speaks of "brain areas *involved in* pain processing", and "the neural *basis of* pain processing" (Schweinhardt & Bushnell, 2010, p. 3788, italics added); the article makes no attempt to sharpen the meanings of the italicized expressions. The main conclusion of this paper will presumably meet no resistance from materialist philosophers, but the way I reach it is controversial. The materialist philosophers Christopher Hill and Brian McLaughlin have argued for a conclusion similar to mine about sensations of all kinds (Hill, 1991; McLaughlin, 2010). But the way in which scientific findings favor materialism over dualism is not the same on their account as on mine – and my way has a few advantages, as we shall see.

1. I do not argue against idealism in this paper, though it is, of course, an alternative to both materialism and dualism.

2. Criticism of arguments for dualism may be found in Hill (1991, pp. 19–43; 2009, pp. 100–127), Papineau (2002, pp. 47–95), and Melnyk (2001).

It will throw the key issue raised by this paper into sharp relief to consider at length the epistemic position of *Aliens*. Aliens are non-human cognitive neuroscientists who want to know what sensations of (human) pain are, and who have access to everything that (human) science has discovered about pain, as well as to the testimony of pain-feeling humans who report on their own pains and what they are like. What distinguishes Aliens from human scientists is that they are so different from humans physiologically and phylogenetically (let's say they evolved from a distinct origin of life) that they hold – rightly – that nothing they know about their *own* mental lives through introspection (assuming they know anything at all about their own mental lives through introspection) has any evidential bearing on the nature of the internal states that the English-speaking objects of their inquiry call "pains". Consequently, anything that Aliens come to think about what (human) pain sensations are must be evidenced *solely* by what (human) science has discovered about pain, including what humans report about the occurrence and nature of their own pains.

Give these restrictions, what should Aliens conclude about the nature of human pains? Perhaps nothing; perhaps the science of pain has merely discovered information about the causal chain that typically begins with a noxious stimulus and ends with a sensation of pain, while leaving it open what the final link in this chain – pain – actually is, e.g., whether it is a neural state of some kind or some sort of immaterial state. I claim, however, that Aliens should conclude that pains are purely material (in a sense to be explained) rather than immaterial. First I argue that the science of pain has discovered evidence favoring the hypothesis that pains are purely material over the rival hypothesis that they are immaterial. Then I argue that the science of pain has discovered no evidence favoring the dualist hypothesis over the materialist hypothesis. Hence the totality of evidence available to Aliens favors the materialist hypothesis. The first argument occupies Section 2 and most of Section 3; the second occupies the balance of Section 3. Section 4 infers from the conclusion about Aliens some morals about human inquirers. Section 1 is devoted to an essential preliminary.

Section 1

We need to be more precise about what materialism and dualism amount to.[3] For present purposes, materialism is best understood as the view that every mental state that a human can be in is *purely material* in the sense that it meets one of the following two conditions:

1. It is identical with – one and the same thing as – some or other uncontroversially material state that a human can be in (e.g., a neural state);

3. Most of what I say in this section about the formulation of materialism and dualism is a simplified version of the position I defend at length elsewhere (Melnyk, 2003, pp. 1–70). The position is, of course, controversial.

2. It is identical with – one and the same thing as – some or other *higher-order* state that a human can be in, *and* every actual case of a particular human's being in that higher-order state is *realized* by the human's being in some or other uncontroversially material state (e.g., a neural state).[4]

The expressions "higher-order" and "realized" that appear in 2 are philosophical terms of art. I understand them as follows. A *higher-order* state of a thing is a special sort of state that a thing can be in – a state such that the thing's being in that state just is the thing's being in any (lower-order) state that meets a certain condition, e.g., that plays a particular causal or functional role in relation to other (lower-order) states.[5] And a thing's being in a particular higher-order state is *realized* by the thing's being in a particular (lower-order) state iff the (lower-order) state is one of those that meet the relevant condition for the higher-order state in question. If there is more than one (lower-order) state that can meet the relevant condition, the higher-order state in question is said to be *multiply realizable.*

Why is meeting condition 2 logically sufficient for materialism? If a thing happens to be in one of the (lower-order) material states that meet the relevant condition for a certain higher-order state, then the thing absolutely must be in that higher-order state.[6] And if the high-order state is identical with – one and the same thing as – a certain mental state, then the thing absolutely must be in that mental state. It follows that, if the thing is in the (lower-order) material state in question, it absolutely must be in the mental state in question – which is a way of saying that there is no more to the thing's being in the mental state (on this occasion) than its being in that (lower-order) material state. Or, more colorfully, if God put you into the material state, he wouldn't need to do anything else to bring it about that you were in the mental state.

A simple illustration of these very abstract ideas is provided by the state (that a gun can be in) of being *loaded.* A gun's being loaded is plausibly regarded as a higher-order state of the gun, specifically, as being one and the same as the gun's being in some or other state such that, if the gun's trigger is pulled, the gun rapidly emits a projectile.

4. In claiming that a mental state is purely material if and only if it meets one of these two conditions, I set the bar for pain's being purely material higher than do Kenneth Sufka and Michael Lynch, who claim that pain is purely material if it "naturally supervenes on a distinct neural subsystem" (Sufka & Lynch, 2000, p. 311).

5. Two notes on terminology. (1) What I here call a "higher-order" state is usually called a "functional" state in the philosophical literature. (2) In this section, when I speak of a "mental state", I mean something that multiple persons, or a single person at multiple times, can be *in*, i.e., what the literature calls a "mental state-type". But there is also a usage of "mental states" in which a person's mental states are not the states (i.e., state-types) that she is in, but rather those particular states of affairs each of which consists of her being in some or other mental state (i.e., state-type); such particular states of affairs are called " mental state-tokens" in the literature.

6. That is, must be in that higher-order state, given the actual laws of nature. I shall take this qualification as read from now on.

A particular gun's being loaded on a particular occasion is realized by its having a certain complex constitution and construction. But because different guns are made of different materials, and constructed on different principles, being loaded is a multiply realizable higher-order state. In consequence, being loaded is not identical with – one and the same thing as – any kind of (first-order) material state. But materialism about guns is still true, because every particular gun's being loaded is in fact realized by some particular material state of the gun.

In exactly the same way, pain is purely material if it turns out to be identical with a specific neural state, e.g., with the state of undergoing such-and-such activity in so-and-so parts of the pain-feeler's primary somatosensory cortex. But it's *also* purely material if, even though it isn't identical with a particular neural state, it turns out to be one and the same as a specific higher-order state, *and* every pain-feeler's being in that higher-order state turns out to be realized by the pain-feeler's being in some or other material state. The material state might be a human neural state, or a neural state but one that's different from any *human* neural state that realizes pain, or an electronic state of some microprocessor in a pain-feeling robot, or something else again. What might the higher-order state be? A natural – though imprecise – hypothesis would be this: to be an organism that is in pain = to be a system containing a subsystem which (1) has the function of detecting imminent or actual damage to the system and of getting the system to respond appropriately, where appropriate response includes preventing the damage from occurring or making it stop and letting the system recover, and which (2) is activated in such-and-such ways. But I only mention this hypothesis for the sake of giving a relatively concrete illustration.[7]

Two final points about the formulation of materialism. First, there is a difference between: (1) saying that every mental state is identical with some or other material state, or materially-realized higher-order state; and (2) actually specifying, for each mental state, *which* material state, or materially-realized higher-order state, that mental state is. The formulation of materialism given above does the former, but it does not aspire to do the latter. The second point is epistemological. That a certain mental state turns out to be identical with a certain material state, or materially-realizable higher-order state, is not something that we should expect to be discoverable by any a priori means, e.g., by reflecting on the meanings of the words (concepts) we use to talk about (think about) mental states. Rather, such identity claims must be discovered empirically, as was the identity of water with H_2O or of genes with segments of the DNA molecule: hypotheses that this kind of thing is one and the same as that kind of thing must be proposed and then tested against the evidence. A corollary is that materialism itself – which asserts the holding of an identity claim for every mental state – has the status of an empirical hypothesis, albeit one of great generality. It is analogous to the uncontroversially scientific hypothesis that every kind of atom is identical with

7. Colin Klein has proposed an interestingly detailed and more plausible hypothesis (Klein, 2007).

some or other kind of microphysical structure composed of protons, electrons, and (in nearly all cases) neutrons.

Dualism can now be formulated as the view that every mental state – or perhaps every mental state of a certain sort – is *im*material in the sense that it meets *neither* of the two conditions above: it is neither identical (1) with any uncontroversially material state nor (2) with any higher-order state every particular instance of which is realized by some or other uncontroversially material state.

Section 2

The science of pain has discovered certain remarkable correspondences between: (1) changes in pains over time (or variation among pains at a time), as revealed by the introspective reports of experimental subjects; and (2) changes over time (or variations at a time) in the subjects' simultaneous neural states, as revealed by various imaging techniques. In this section, I describe five such correspondences in some detail and then argue that they support quite a strong claim to the effect that pain depends on the neural. Part of the reason for going into detail is to show that the evidence I allege for materialism results from genuine empirical discovery, and not just the influence of materialist presuppositions; part is to show, by means of extensive quotation, that I am not interpreting the science tendentiously; and part is to show how surprisingly fine-grained the neural dependence of pain is.

First, however, a brief preliminary. Pain researchers Price, Barrell, and Rainville (2002) report that:

> Psychophysical observers [i.e., the subjects in pain experiments] can be trained to detect very small differences in sensory qualities and intensities and to differentially judge magnitudes of different dimensions or qualities of their experience…
> (p. 600)

One such difference that observers can be trained to detect is – perhaps surprisingly – between the *intensity* and the *unpleasantness* of the pains they are undergoing. Anecdotal evidence for this distinction is the case of a man, reported by Ploner, Freund, and Schnitzler (1999), who had a cortical lesion that altered his capacity to feel pain in the left hand when it was subjected to noxious thermal stimuli:

> For left hand, up to an intensity of 600 mJ, no pain sensation could be elicited. However, at intensities of 350 mJ and more, the patient spontaneously described a 'clearly unpleasant' intensity dependent feeling emerging from an ill-localized and extended area 'somewhere between fingertips and shoulder', that he wanted to avoid. The fully cooperative and eloquent patient was completely unable to further describe quality, localization and intensity of the perceived stimulus. Suggestions from a given word list containing 'warm', 'hot', 'cold', 'touch', 'burning', 'pinprick-like', 'slight pain', 'moderate pain' and 'intense pain' were denied…
> (p. 213)

The subject of the experiment is apparently reporting a sensation with some of the *affective* features of pain but without its usual *sensory* features. More systematic evidence is provided by two studies (Hofbauer, Rainville, Duncan, & Bushnell, 2001; Rainville, Duncan, Price, Carrier, & Bushnell, 1997) in which hypnotic suggestion was used to alter the reported *unpleasantness* of experimental subjects' pains without at the same time altering the pains' reported *intensity* – and conversely to alter the reported *intensity* of the pains without at the same time altering their reported *unpleasantness*.

Now for the first correspondence. Bushnell et al. (1999) report finding "that S1 activation is modulated by cognitive manipulations that alter perceived pain intensity" (p. 7709). Similarly, Hofbauer et al. (2001) report that:

> [a]s shown in previous brain imaging studies, noxious thermal stimuli presented during the alert and hypnosis-control conditions reliably activated contralateral structures, including primary somatosensory cortex (S1), secondary somatosensory cortex (S2), anterior cingulate cortex, and insular cortex. *Hypnotic modulation of the intensity of the pain sensation led to significant changes in pain-evoked activity within S1...* (p. 402, italics added)

Corresponding to differences in the *felt intensity* of *different pains*, then, are differences in the simultaneous level of pain-evoked activity in S1.

A second correspondence concerns change in the felt intensity of a *single* pain over time. Porro et al. (Porro, Cettolo, Francescato, & Baraldi, 1998) provide the following abstract of their study of "the time course of perceived pain intensity and the activity of discrete cortical populations during noxious somatic stimulation lasting several minutes" (p. 3316):

> We used a high-resolution functional magnetic resonance imaging (fMRI) technique in healthy right-handed volunteers to *demonstrate cortical areas displaying changes of activity significantly related to the time profile of the perceived intensity of experimental somatic pain over the course of several minutes*. Twenty-four subjects (ascorbic acid group) received a subcutaneous injection of a dilute ascorbic acid solution into the dorsum of one foot, inducing prolonged burning pain (peak pain intensity on a 0–100 scale: 48 ± 3, mean ± SE; duration: 11.9 ± 0.8 min). fMRI data sets were continuously acquired for ~20 min, beginning 5 min before and lasting 15 min after the onset of stimulation, from two sagittal planes on the medial hemispheric wall contralateral to the stimulated site, including the cingulate cortex and the putative foot representation area of the primary somatosensory cortex (SI). *Neural clusters whose fMRI signal time courses were positively or negatively correlated ($P < 0.0005$) with the individual pain intensity curve were identified by cross-correlation statistics in all 24 volunteers. The spatial extent of the identified clusters was linearly related ($P < 0.0001$) to peak pain intensity.* Regional analyses showed that positively correlated clusters were present in the majority of subjects in SI, cingulate, motor, and premotor cortex. Negative correlations were found predominantly in medial parietal, perigenual cingulate, and medial prefrontal

> regions. To test whether these neural changes were due to aspecific arousal or emotional reactions, related either to anticipation or presence of pain, fMRI experiments were performed with the same protocol in two additional groups of volunteers, subjected either to subcutaneous saline injection (saline: $n = 16$), inducing mild short-lasting pain (peak pain intensity 23 ± 4; duration 2.8 ± 0.6 min) or to nonnoxious mechanical stimulation of the skin (controls: $n = 16$) at the same body site. Subjects did not know in advance which stimulus would occur. The spatial extent of neural clusters whose signal time courses were positively or negatively correlated with the mean pain intensity curve of subjects injected with ascorbic acid was significantly larger ($P < 0.001$) in the ascorbic acid group than both saline and controls, suggesting that the observed responses were specifically related to pain intensity and duration. These findings reveal distributed cortical systems, including parietal areas as well as cingulate and frontal regions, involved in dynamic encoding of pain intensity over time, a process of great biological and clinical relevance. (p. 3312, italics added)

Corresponding to changes in the felt intensity over time of a single pain, then, are simultaneous changes in the intensity of neural activity in certain regions (S1, cingulate, motor, and premotor cortex) of a pain-feeler's brain.

A third correspondence concerns the introspectible difference between the intensity and the unpleasantness of a single pain at a given time. As we saw, in two studies hypnotic suggestion was used to alter the reported unpleasantness of experimental subjects' pains without at the same time altering their reported intensity – and vice versa. Even more fascinating is what was revealed by these studies to happen in the subjects' brains as the reported unpleasantness and the reported intensity of their pains were modified independently of one another (Hofbauer et al., 2001; Rainville et al., 1997). In the first study, changes in the reported *unpleasantness* of pain (with no change in the reported *intensity* of pain) were correlated with changes in the level of activation in the anterior cingulate cortex, though there was no change in the level of activation in S1. In the second study, changes in the reported *intensity* of pain (with no change in the reported *unpleasantness* of pain) were correlated with changes in the level of activation in S1, though there was no change in the level of activation in the anterior cingulate cortex activation. As Hofbauer et al. (2001) put it:

> This double dissociation of cortical modulation indicates a relative specialization of the sensory and the classical limbic cortical areas in the processing of the sensory and affective dimensions of pain. (p. 402)

So, corresponding to changes in the introspectible sensory and affective dimensions of a single pain are, respectively, simultaneous changes in neural activity in two distinct regions of the brain, with changes in the affective dimension of a pain apparently varying with levels of activation in "the classical limbic cortical areas".

A fourth correspondence concerns the phenomenon known as *first pain* and *second pain*, which can be characterized as follows (Ploner, Gross, Timmermann, & Schnitzler, 2002):

> … single painful stimuli yield two successive and qualitatively distinct sensations referred to as first and second pain sensation [citation omitted]. First pain is brief, pricking, and well localized, whereas second pain is longer-lasting, burning, and less well localized. (p. 12444)

A single painful stimulus yields two successive sensations because of the different arrival times of impulses from two different kinds of nociceptive nerve fibers – Aδ fibers and C fibers – which differ in their myelination and hence conductance. But what happens when the impulses arrive at the cortex? Ploner et al. (2002) report as follows:

> We… used magnetoencephalography to record and directly compare first and second pain-related cortical responses to cutaneous laser stimuli in humans. […] Cortical activity was located in primary (S1) and secondary (S2) somatosensory cortices and anterior cingulate cortex. Time courses of activations disclosed that *first pain was particularly related to activation of S1 whereas second pain was closely related to anterior cingulate cortex activation.* Both sensations were associated with S2 activation. (p. 12444, italics added)
>
> In the early time window, the time courses of activations show significant activation of S1, bilateral S2, and ACC reflecting Aδ fiber-mediated and first pain-related activation of these areas. In the late time window bilateral S2 and ACC show strong activations, whereas no significant activation is seen in S1 indicating C fiber-mediated and second pain-related activation of bilateral S2 and ACC but not of S1. (p. 12446)

Corresponding to the introspectible differences between first pain and second pain, then, is a difference in the locations of simultaneous cortical activity.

A fifth correspondence concerns the *felt locations* that pains typically have. Various studies (e.g., Andersson et al., 1997; Bingel et al., 2004) have shown that S1 exhibits somatotopic organization: roughly, neighboring neurons in S1 can be traced back, via synaptic connections, to neighboring nociceptive neurons in the body. But although these studies aimed to reveal a correspondence between the *actual* locations of noxious stimuli and activity in specific regions of S1, rather than between the *felt* locations of the pains caused by the stimuli and activity in specific regions of S1, they nonetheless support the existence of the latter correspondence. For in both studies the subjects did in fact report on their pains, and had the felt locations they reported not coincided with the actual locations of the noxious stimuli, the researchers would surely have noted the fact, which they did not do. I conclude that corresponding to the different felt locations of pains is simultaneous neural activity in different regions of S1.

Each of these five correspondences is an instance in which corresponding to a certain sort of introspectible change over time in pains, or variation among pains at a time, there is a certain sort of simultaneous neural change over time, or neural variation at a time. Moreover, despite extensive studies of the kinds cited above, no sort of introspectible change over time in pains, or variation among pains at a time, has been discovered to which there *fails* to correspond some sort of simultaneous change in, or variation among, neural states, even though discovering such failures of correspondence is readily conceivable and lies within our current observational abilities. But observed positive instances of a universal generalization (with no observed negative instances) provide inductive evidence that the universal generalization is true.[8] Therefore, the five correspondences noted above provide inductive evidence for the conclusion that to *every* sort of introspectible change over time in pains, or variation among pains at a time, there corresponds a certain sort of simultaneous neural change over time, or variation at a time. Let us call this conclusion the *empirical supervenience claim*, because it says that *in fact* no sort of introspectible change or variation in pains occurs without a certain sort of simultaneous change or variation in neural state.

The empirical supervenience claim belongs to a family of empirical claims to the effect that the mental depends on the neural. It is worth comparing the strength of the empirical supervenience claim with that of other members of the family. It is obviously much stronger than the claim that, if one is ever in pain, then one has a properly functioning brain, for the same is true of a properly functioning circulatory system. It is stronger too than the claim that, if one is in pain (no matter of what sort), then one is in so-and-so neural state, for the latter claim leaves open the possibility that pains with *different* introspectible characters do *not* require being in *different* kinds of neural state. The empirical supervenience claim excludes this possibility, because it says that change or variation in the introspectible character of pain *never* occurs without a certain sort of neural change or variation.

On the other hand, the empirical supervenience claim is weaker than at least one of its kin. Christopher Hill's and Brian McLaughlin's argument for materialism about sensations rests on a certain empirical claim that they call the "correlation thesis" (Hill, 1991; McLaughlin, 2010). McLaughlin (2010) formulates the thesis as follows:

> For any type of state of phenomenal consciousness C there is a type of physical state P such that it is true and counterfactual supporting that a being is in C if and only if the being is in P. (p. 267)

Even if the scope of the correlation thesis is limited to conscious states involved in pain, it goes well beyond what the empirical supervenience claim affirms, because it claims that for each such state there is a physical state that is not just necessary but also sufficient for the conscious state. The empirical supervenience claim affirms only that a certain sort of simultaneous neural change (or variation) is necessary for each sort of change (or variation) in pain. A corollary of this difference in logical strength is that it is much easier to come up with evidence for the empirical supervenience claim than for the Hill-McLaughlin correlation thesis. Indeed, evidencing the correlation thesis would seem to require discovering the so-called "neural correlates" of at least some

8. This inductive principle fails in certain well-known pathological cases that give rise to paradoxes of confirmation such as Nelson Goodman's "grue" paradox and Hempel's paradox of the ravens. But there is no reason to think that the present case is pathological.

conscious mental states. That doing so has proved to be problematic is presumably why neither Hill nor McLaughlin actually asserts the correlation thesis; they present their argument for materialism as *conditional* on our discovering in the future that the correlation thesis is true.

Section 3

What, then, is the evidential significance for Aliens of the empirical supervenience claim? The first point to note is that materialism – as formulated in Section 1 – is consistent with and indeed predicts the empirical supervenience claim. It is worth spelling out why. If materialism is true, then there are just two sensible possibilities regarding pain:

1. Pain is one and the same as a certain complex neural state. The different kinds of pain (e.g., pain in the right foot, intensely unpleasant pain in the right foot, intensely unpleasant pain in the right foot of duration 18 seconds) are one and the same as certain more specific neural states.
2. Pain is one and the same as a certain higher-order state, such that every particular pain-feeler's being in that higher-order state is realized by the pain-feeler's being in some or other neural state. The different kinds of pain are one and the same as certain more specific kinds of higher-order state, such that every particular pain-feeler's being in a higher-order state of any of these more specific kinds is realized by the pain-feeler's being in some or other more specific neural state.

Suppose that the first possibility is actual, and that kinds of pain just *are* kinds of neural state. Then obviously there must be a certain sort of neural change or variation corresponding to, and simultaneous with, each sort of change over time in pains (or variation at a time among pains). Nothing at all can possibly change or vary without itself changing or varying.

Suppose now that the second possibility is actual. The empirical supervenience claim must be true in this case too, though seeing why is harder. Consider Jan, whom we may safely assume to be a biologically normal human whose extra-cranial neuronal wiring doesn't spontaneously change in any significant way over the short term; the data we're trying to accommodate concern precisely such humans.[9] Suppose that Jan is in pain of kind P at time t, and her being in pain of kind P at t is *realized* by her being in complex neural state N at t. By the definition of "realized" in Section 1, P must be identical with a certain higher-order state H, and N must meet the relevant condition

9. The assumption means that we can disregard the possibility that Jan's state of pain can change simply because of a change in circumstances *external* to her brain; such a possibility exists if pain turns out to be an essentially *representational* state whose content is determined in part by circumstances external to the subject's brain.

for H; that is, N must meet condition C, where to be in H = to be in one of the states that meet C. Because Jan is in N, and because N meets C, Jan must be in H. Further, as H = P, she must be in P. So, as Jan is in N, she *must* be in P. But now imagine that Jan *ceases* to be in P; perhaps she enters a pain state of a different kind, or perhaps she stops being in pain of any kind. How can this happen? The physico-chemical laws governing neural states cannot change, and H cannot cease to be identical with P, as that would require that H cease to be identical with itself. So the only way in which Jan can cease to be in P is for her to undergo a change of neural state, i.e., to cease to be in N. The upshot, then, is that, if Jan ceases to be in P, then she undergoes some simultaneous change of neural state. And this upshot may be generalized: given possibility 2, *every* sort of introspectible diachronic change in pains is accompanied by a certain sort of simultaneous diachronic neural change. Finally, analogous reasoning shows that possibility 2 also entails that the other half of the empirical supervenience claim is true, i.e., that every sort of introspectible variation among pains *at* a time is accompanied by a certain sort of simultaneous neural variation. The key point is that, if Jen's twin brother, Jon, were also in N, then he would have to be in P too; so if he is not also in P, he cannot be in N.

What about dualism? Consider, first, a version of dualism that regards pain as a state of the immaterial mind, that treats the immaterial mind as receiving sensory input from the brain and emitting motor instructions for the brain to execute, but that treats the brain as unnecessary for mentality *except* insofar as it is needed to send sensory input to the mind and to execute the mind's motor instructions. On this version of dualism, sensory states, including pain, can change without there being any corresponding simultaneous neural changes. Such a view is falsified by the empirical supervenience claim.

But there are, of course, dualist views which allow and indeed predict the empirical supervenience claim. One such dualist view regards pain as a state of the immaterial mind, but a state that the mind is *caused* to enter by a certain *simultaneous* neural state of the subject. Another such dualist view treats pain as an *immaterial* state that the subject's *brain* is caused to enter by a certain simultaneous *neural* state; it therefore assumes that the brain can instantiate immaterial properties.[10] A third and a fourth dualist view can be formed by replacing the appeal to simultaneous neural-to-mental *causation* in the two preceding views with an appeal to non-causal neural-to-mental *laws of association*.

Because there are versions of dualism that, like materialism, entail and are consistent with the empirical supervenience claim, it is tempting to conclude that the empirical supervenience claim cannot possibly favor materialism over the relevant versions of dualism. And this conclusion is correct if a naïve Popperian falsificationism is true according to which the *only* regulative role for evidence is to contradict hypotheses; for the empirical supervenience claim does *not* contradict the relevant versions of dualism. Indeed, I conjecture that the widespread endorsement of naïve Popperian

10. It seems to be David Chalmers' positive view (Chalmers, 1996).

falsificationism by scientists is what explains why, as noted in the introduction, pain scientists are reluctant to treat their findings as favoring materialism over dualism.[11] The conclusion that the empirical supervenience claim cannot possibly favor materialism over the relevant versions of dualism is *also* correct if an extreme form of empiricism is true according to which the empirical accuracy of competing hypotheses is the *only* feature relevant to their relative evidential status; for materialism and the relevant versions of dualism are *equally* accurate empirically. And I conjecture that the possibly tacit assumption of this form of empiricism is what explains why, as noted in the introduction, few dualists seem willing to acknowledge that science at least makes it appear that pain is purely material.

But naïve Popperian falsificationism and the extreme form of empiricism in question are both open to serious objections (Laudan, 1995; Newton-Smith, 1981, Chapter 3). One especially important objection is that both views lead to an unacceptable skepticism. The crux is that, for pretty much *any* hypothesis that we presently favor, and *any* evidence that the hypothesis entails and is consistent with, we can concoct a *rival* hypothesis that entails and is consistent with the very same evidence. So, for example, the hypothesis that the universe is only ten minutes old can be formulated to be consistent with all the evidence usually taken to support the conventional view; likewise, of course, for creationism. And if either naïve Popperian falsificationism or the extreme form of empiricism in question is true, it follows that we have no evidential grounds for preferring the original hypothesis over the concocted one. For, by assumption, the concocted hypothesis is not contradicted by any of the evidence, and it is just as accurate empirically as the original hypothesis.

To avoid such skepticism, we need to allow that factors other than empirical accuracy can be relevant to the comparative evidential merits of competing hypotheses, such factors as parsimony and fit with background knowledge (these factors are often called "super-empirical criteria"). We can do so in a way adequate for present purposes by adopting the following principle of evidence:

Evidence E favors hypothesis H1 over hypothesis H2 if

- each of H1 and H2 entails and is consistent with E;
- H1 fares better than H2 on at least one super-empirical criterion; and
- H2 does not fare better than H1 on *any* super-empirical criterion.

This principle plausibly implies that the standard evidence favors the conventional view of the age of the universe over the ten-minute hypothesis, because the latter is so spectacularly unparsimonious, and fits so poorly with background knowledge, in comparison with the former. The principle could be embedded in different overall accounts of evidence and theory-choice, e.g., in a Bayesian account in which the initial prior probability of a hypothesis is assessed by reference to super-empirical criteria, or

11. One need only read the first chapter of half a dozen college textbooks to see the pervasive influence of naïve Popperian falsificationism in science.

in Philip Kitcher's eliminativist account in which that hypothesis is preferred which is consistent with all the evidence and which achieves this consistency at the lowest cost in terms of the super-empirical criteria (Kitcher, 1993, p. 237ff.).

I will, of course, use the principle to argue that the empirical supervenience claim favors materialism about pains over the relevant versions of dualism about pains. Arguing in this way enables me to sidestep an objection that Jaegwon Kim has made to the Hill-McLaughlin argument for materialism about sensations (Kim, 2005, Chapter 5). The Hill-McLaughlin argument uses the principle of inference to the best explanation, whereby the *explanatory power* of a hypothesis counts in favor of its truth: they argue that their correlation thesis (see above) is better explained on the hypothesis that sensations are purely material than on any rival hypothesis saying that they are immaterial. Kim's (2005) objection is that the materialist hypothesis is an *identity* claim (which, as we saw in Section 1, it is), and that identity claims never have genuine explanatory power. Using the principle above, however, I need not assume that identity claims have explanatory power.

Here is why the empirical supervenience claim favors materialism about pains over the relevant versions of dualism about pains. Both materialism and the relevant versions of dualism entail and are logically consistent with the empirical supervenience claim, as we have seen. But materialism fares better than the relevant versions of dualism on the super-empirical criteria of (1) parsimony and (2) fit with background knowledge, while the relevant versions of dualism do not fare better than materialism on any such criterion.[12] With regard to parsimony, it's true that both materialism and these versions of dualism are committed to the neural states corresponding to the various kinds of pain *and* to the various kinds of pain themselves; but what this commitment comes to is not the same in each case. According to any dualist view, even after God has created Jen in neural state N, and instituted the right physico-chemical laws, he has to do further work to put Jen into the state of pain P to which N corresponds; P is no ontological free lunch. According to materialism, however, once God has created Jen in neural state N and instituted the right physico-chemical laws, he has nothing further to do, for whether it turns out that P = N or that P = H, if Jen is in N and the physico-chemical laws hold, she must be in P. So the versions of dualism in question are less parsimonious than materialism, because they treat mental states as fundamental, non-neural states, rather than as real states that are, however, nothing over and above neural states.

The versions of dualism in question are less parsimonious than materialism in a second way too. As we have just seen, materialism can reductively explain the empirical supervenience thesis *without* taking it to reflect the holding of a myriad

12. And perhaps also on the criterion of *explanatory power*. The versions of dualism in question certainly *entail* the empirical supervenience claim, but to entail something is not necessarily to *explain* it. Perhaps an empirical generalization is not explained, or explained only poorly, by saying merely that it holds as a matter of law.

of irreducible neural-to-mental laws over and above the standard physico-chemical laws that ultimately govern neural states. However, the versions of dualism in question take mental states to be immaterial states, and so, as no physico-chemical laws govern immaterial states, they cannot reductively explain the empirical supervenience thesis, and therefore *must* take it to reflect the holding of a myriad of irreducible neural-to-mental laws. Like materialism, therefore, the versions of dualism in question are committed to the holding of the standard physico-chemical laws that ultimately govern neural states; but, unlike materialism, they are *also* committed to the myriad of irreducible neural-to-mental laws. That is what makes them less parsimonious than materialism.

Turning to fit with background knowledge (of Aliens), consider the thesis that all states *other* than mental states are ultimately realized by physical states, i.e., states describable in the proprietary vocabulary of physics.[13] Such a claim is a commonplace among scientists, and in fact accepted by nearly all contemporary dualists – unsurprisingly, in light of the strong evidence for it.[14] Now materialism about the mind coheres well with this thesis, because, if mental states are identical with, or realized by, neural states, then mental states turn out to be just like all other kinds of state in being ultimately realized by physical states. By contrast, however, all forms of dualism cohere poorly with the thesis, because, if mental states were immaterial, then they could not turn out to be ultimately realized by physical states; mental states would be the sole exceptions to an otherwise exceptionless generalization.

Let us now ask whether the relevant versions of dualism fare better than materialism on any of the super-empirical criteria. Apparently they do not. There is no reason to think it is part of the background knowledge of Aliens that all or most sensations *other* than pain are immaterial. And Aliens are so different from humans that they hold – rightly – that everything they know through introspection about their *own* mental lives is irrelevant to the nature of human mental states.

My argument that the empirical supervenience claim favors materialism about pains over the relevant versions of dualism about pains has assumed the legitimacy of appealing to super-empirical criteria in assessing the comparative evidential merits of rival hypotheses. And for some readers, despite my earlier remarks, this assumption will be unacceptable. I ask them to reconsider. As the assumption raises fundamental issues about the justification of induction, I cannot adequately defend it here; but I should add two brief remarks.[15] First, the appeal to super-empirical criteria to discriminate between empirically equivalent hypotheses is pervasive in both science and everyday life. So we face a trilemma. We must do one of the following:

---

13. To mental states should be added any sociological states partially constituted by mental states.

14. See Melnyk (2003, Chapter 6) for some of this evidence.

15. For a fuller defense, see Melnyk (2003, pp. 244–251).

1. Accept the appeal as legitimate;
2. Candidly acknowledge that we aren't really warranted in thinking that, for example, the universe is more than ten minutes old; or
3. Provide an alternative account of empirical evidence that vindicates our rejection of the ten-minute hypothesis but without appealing to super-empirical criteria.

I say that option 1 looks pretty good when compared to options 2 and 3; 2 is preposterous, and no one knows how to do 3.

Second, it is true that the appeal to, say, parsimony can be part of a reliable mode of inductive inference only if the world itself is parsimonious to some degree, i.e., correctly describable by theories that are parsimonious. It is true too that there is no a priori deductive guarantee that the world is parsimonious, and that any attempted inductive proof that it is would be circular. But so what? The points I have just conceded precisely mimic Hume's argument for skepticism about enumerative induction; the role played here by the parsimony of the world is played in Hume's argument by the resemblance of the future to the past. But although philosophers disagree as to *where* precisely Hume's argument for skepticism about enumerative induction goes wrong, they nearly all agree that it must go wrong somewhere, and they do *not* recommend the abandonment of enumerative induction.[16] I suggest that by parity of reasoning we should take exactly the same attitude as this toward skepticism about appeals to parsimony. Skeptics about appeals to parsimony almost invariably assume that such appeals are problematic in a way in which enumerative induction is not; but I see no basis for that assumption.

My conclusion thus far, then, is that, for Aliens, the empirical supervenience claim favors materialism about pains over dualism about pains. Let us now ask whether science has discovered anything about pains that points the other way, i.e., that favors dualism over materialism. The answer is that it has not. There are two kinds of evidence that, if discovered, would favor dualism over materialism, but neither kind – to the best of my knowledge – has actually been discovered. First, the discovery of changes over time in pains, or variations among pains at a time, that do *not* correspond to simultaneous changes in, or variations among, neural states would be irresistible evidence for dualism; but, as we noted in Section 2, no such changes or variations have been discovered. Second, a pain that is, or is realized by, a neural state must owe all its causal powers to that neural state. So there would be irresistible evidence for dualism if some of the known behavioral or neural effects of pains were found to be such that the neural states that were the best candidates for being identical with, or for realizing, pains were incapable in principle of causing the effects. The discovery of such effects would show that the physical was not *causally closed*, i.e., that there were physical effects for which there did not exist a sufficient physical cause. But I am unaware of any claims that such effects of pain have been discovered empirically.

---

16. I endorse James Van Cleve's line on Hume's inductive skepticism (Van Cleve, 1984).

Section 4

The conclusion of Sections 2 and 3 is that, for Aliens, what science has discovered about pain favors materialism over dualism about pains. And this entails that, *for us*, what science has discovered about pain favors materialism over dualism about pains. For we are neither inferior nor superior to Aliens in our ability to appreciate the evidential force of what science has discovered about pain. It may be true that introspection can provide us humans (but not Aliens) with reason to think that pains are immaterial; I take no stand on the matter here. But even if it is true, and introspective considerations favor dualism over materialism, it does not contradict the claim that what science has discovered about pain favors materialism over dualism. Indeed, there is no contradiction even if introspective considerations favor dualism over materialism so strongly that, all things considered, we ought to prefer dualism. As noted in the introduction, the main conclusion of this paper is a modest one.

It might be objected that, if introspective considerations could favor dualism over materialism in the sense of raising the probability of dualism about pains to *one*, then a scientific discovery could not lower dualism's probability at all, and so presumably could not favor materialism over dualism.[17] I reply that introspection could never generate such considerations, because any case for dualism based directly or indirectly on introspection, even if it raised the probability of dualism very high, could never raise it to one; in the real world of non-ideal reasoners, there is always the possibility that any such case might be defective in some hitherto unrecognized way. Proper defense of this fallibilist view would take us deep into epistemology, so I will say no more. But if it is correct, then the conclusion of Sections 2 and 3 does indeed entail that, for us, what science has discovered about pain favors materialism over dualism about pains.

The conclusion of this paper is modest in a second way too. As we saw in Section 1, there are, at the highest level of abstraction, just two ways in which pain could turn out to be purely material: it could turn out to be a certain kind of complex neural state or it could turn out to be a certain kind of neurally-realized higher-order state. But the conclusion of this paper is neutral between the two options; arguing for it has not required choosing between them. This is noteworthy, because, though choosing between them has traditionally been a major issue in the philosophy of mind, we may well be unable to do so on the basis of empirical evidence. Crucial evidence for the second option over the first would be the discovery that pain is multiply realized. But if pain is uniformly (i.e., non-multiply) realized in humans, which seems plausible, evidence of multiple realization would have to come from non-human animals: it would

17. If the probability of dualism on introspective considerations is one, then the new prior probability of dualism, formed by conditionalization on this posterior probability, is also one; and, according to the Bayesian account of evidence, no evidence can lower the probability of a hypothesis whose prior probability is one.

have to be evidence that certain animals (1) are in pain, but (2) are not in any (human-type) neural state plausibly identifiable with pain. But what evidence could show that they are in pain? They obviously cannot tell us, and any behavior analogous to human pain-behavior might well be deemed inconclusive. That they were in a (human-type) neural state plausibly identifiable with pain would certainly be evidence that they are in pain, but would defeat the attempt to demonstrate multiple realization. That they were in a *higher-order* state plausibly identifiable with pain would also be evidence that they are in pain, but the plausibility of the identification would be challenged as question-begging by the advocates of the neural-state identity theory.

The conclusion of this paper is modest, finally, in that it carries no commitment to any particular specification, for each state of pain, of *which* neural state, or neurally-realized higher-order state, that state of pain is. One might have assumed the opposite, i.e., that, by the reasoning described in Section 3, features of pain are (or are realized by) the neural states which correspond to them, e.g., that pain intensity = activity in such-and-such regions of S1, S2, anterior cingulate cortex, and insular cortex. But this assumption would be incorrect. Suppose that a certain sort of change over time in pains corresponds to a certain sort of simultaneous neural change over time. To account for this correspondence by hypothesizing that pains are purely material states entails that the changing feature of pain in question is, or is realized by, some neural state that *overlaps* the simultaneous neural state; but no stronger claim is entailed.

It is noteworthy that one can provide evidence that pains are purely material without being committed to specific hypotheses as to which kinds of pain or features of pain are (or are realized by) which neural states.[18] At least one other argument that pains are purely material does not have this feature. If the Hill-McLaughlin argument were applied to the particular case of pain, it would draw an inference to the best explanation from the fact that people are in pain when, and only when, they are in so-and-so neural state. The conclusion inferred would be the specific hypothesis that pain = so-and-so neural state.

It is a good thing, at least for materialists, that one can provide evidence that pains are purely material without being committed to specific hypotheses as to which kinds of pain or features of pain are (or are realized by) which neural states. For even if we knew necessary and sufficient neural conditions for every aspect of our state of mind when in pain, and even if we accepted that pains are purely material, it would still not be clear which neural states to treat as identical with (or as realizing) pain. The reason is that, when we are in pain, we are typically in a variety of distinguishable mental states, and it's not clear which of these mental states are parts, and which just concomitants, of being in pain. For example, when experiencing the pain caused by a sharp object's penetrating the skin, is the pressure one may feel at the point of contact a part of the pain? What about the sudden anxiety that one might feel? There is no

18. If I understand them correctly, a similar claim is made (on different grounds) by Thomas Polger and Kenneth Sufka (Polger & Sufka, 2005, p. 344).

reason to think – and every reason to doubt – that either the everyday term "pain" or the ordinary concept of pain is precise enough to yield definite answers to all questions of this sort. But there is no threat to the thesis that pains are purely material so long as the thesis turns out to be true on every precisification of "pain".

References

Andersson, J. L. R., Lilja, A., Hartvig, P., Långström, B., Gordh, T., Handwerker, H., & Torebjörk, E. (1997). Somatotopic organization along the central sulcus, for pain localization in humans, as revealed by positron emission tomography. *Experimental Brain Research*, 117(2), 192–199. DOI: 10.1007/s002210050215

Bingel, U., Lorenz, J., Glauche, V., Knab, R., Gläscher, J., Weiller, C., & Büchel, C. (2004). Somatotopic organization of human somatosensory cortices for pain: A single trial fMRI study. *Neuroimage*, 23(1), 224–232. DOI: 10.1016/j.neuroimage.2004.05.021

Bushnell, M. C., Duncan, G. H., Hofbauer, R. K., Ha, B., Chen, J.-I., & Carrier, B. (1999). Pain perception: Is there a role for primary somatosensory cortex? *Proceedings of the National Academy of Sciences USA*, 96(14), 7705–7709. DOI: 10.1073/pnas.96.14.7705

Chalmers, D. J. (1996). *The conscious mind: In search of a fundamental theory*. New York, NY: Oxford University Press.

Hill, C. S. (1991). *Sensations: A defense of type materialism*. New York, NY: Cambridge University Press. DOI: 10.1017/CBO9781139173827

Hill, C. S. (2009). *Consciousness*. New York, NY: Cambridge University Press. DOI: 10.1017/CBO9780511804274

Hofbauer, R. K., Rainville, P., Duncan, G. H., & Bushnell, M. C. (2001). Cortical representation of the sensory dimension of pain. *Journal of Neurophysiology*, 86(1), 402–411.

Kim, J. (2005). *Physicalism, or something near enough*. Princeton, NJ: Princeton University Press.

Kitcher, P. (1993). *The advancement of science: Science without legend, objectivity without illusions*. New York, NY: Oxford University Press.

Klein, C. (2007). An imperative theory of pain. *Journal of Philosophy*, 104(10), 517–532.

Kripke, S. (1980). *Naming and necessity*. Oxford, UK: Blackwell Publishing.

Laudan, L. (1995). Damn the consequences! *Proceedings and addresses of the American Philosophical Association*, 69(2), 27–34. DOI: 10.2307/3130494

McLaughlin, B. P. (2010). Consciousness, type physicalism, and inference to the best explanation. *Philosophical Issues*, 20(1), 266–304. DOI: 10.1111/j.1533-6077.2010.00192.x

McMahon, S., & Koltzenburg, M. (Eds.). (2006). *Wall and Melzack's textbook of pain* (5th ed.). Philadelphia, PA: Elsevier/Churchill Livingstone.

Melnyk, A. (2001). Physicalism unfalsified: Chalmers' inconclusive conceivability argument. In C. Gillett & B. Loewer (Eds.), *Physicalism and its discontents* (pp. 331–349). New York, NY: Cambridge University Press. DOI: 10.1017/CBO9780511570797.018

Melnyk, A. (2003). *A physicalist manifesto: Thoroughly modern materialism*. New York, NY: Cambridge University Press. DOI: 10.1017/CBO9780511498817

Newton-Smith, W. H. (1981). *The rationality of science*. London, UK: Routledge. DOI: 10.4324/9780203317211

Papineau, D. (2002). *Thinking about consciousness*. Oxford, UK: Clarendon Press. DOI: 10.1093/0199243824.001.0001

Ploner, M., Freund, H.-J., & Schnitzler, A. (1999). Pain affect without pain sensation in a patient with a postcentral lesion. *Pain*, 81(1–2), 211–214. DOI: 10.1016/S0304-3959(99)00012-3

Ploner, M., Gross, G., Timmermann, L., & Schnitzler, A. (2002). Cortical representation of first and second pain sensation in humans. *Proceedings of the National Academy of Sciences USA*, 99(19), 12444–12448. DOI: 10.1073/pnas.182272899

Polger, T. W., & Sufka, K. J. (2005). Closing the gap on pain: Mechanism, theory, and fit. In M. Aydede (Ed.), *Pain: New essays on its nature and the methodology of its study* (pp. 325–350). Cambridge, MA: MIT Press.

Porro, C. A., Cettolo, V., Francescato, M. P., & Baraldi, P. (1998). Temporal and intensity coding of pain in human cortex. *Journal of Neurophysiology*, 80(6), 3312–3320.

Price, D. D. (1999). *Psychological mechanisms of pain and analgesia*. Progress in Pain Research and Management (Vol. 15). Seattle, WA: IASP Press.

Price, D. D., Barrell, J. J., & Rainville, P. (2002). Integrating experiential–phenomenological methods and neuroscience to study neural mechanisms of pain and consciousness. *Consciousness and Cognition*, 11(4), 593–608. DOI: 10.1016/S1053-8100(02)00018-1

Rainville, P., Duncan, G. H., Price, D. D., Carrier, B., & Bushnell, M. C. (1997). Pain affect encoded in human anterior cingulate but not somatosensory cortex. *Science*, 277(5328), 968–971. DOI: 10.1126/science.277.5328.968

Schweinhardt, P., & Bushnell, M. C. (2010). Pain imaging in health and disease – how far have we come? *Journal of Clinical Investigation*, 120(11), 3788–3797. DOI: 10.1172/JCI43498

Sufka, K. J., & Lynch, M. P. (2000). Sensations and pain processes. *Philosophical Psychology*, 13(3), 299–311. DOI: 10.1080/09515080050128132

Van Cleve, J. (1984). Reliability, justification, and the problem of induction. *Midwest Studies in Philosophy*, 9(1), 555–567. DOI: 10.1111/j.1475-4975.1984.tb00077.x

The status of consciousness in nature*

Berit Brogaard
University of Miami, Miami

The most central metaphysical question about phenomenal consciousness is that of what constitutes phenomenal consciousness, whereas the most central epistemic question about consciousness is that of whether science can eventually provide an explanation of the phenomenon. Many philosophers have argued that science doesn't have the means to answer the question of what consciousness is (the explanatory gap) but that consciousness nonetheless is fully determined by the physical facts underlying it (no ontological gap). Others have argued that the explanatory gap in the sciences entails an ontological gap. This position is also known as 'property dualism'. Here I examine a fourth position, according to which there an ontological gap but no explanatory gap.

1. The hard problem of consciousness

One of the most puzzling features of consciousness is the problem David Chalmers has named 'the hard problem'. In "Facing up to the problem of consciousness", Chalmers (1995, cf. 1996) describes the hard problem as follows:

> The really hard problem of consciousness is the problem of *experience*. When we think and perceive, there is a whir of information-processing, but there is also a subjective aspect. As Nagel (1974) has put it, there is *something it is like* to be a conscious organism. This subjective aspect is experience. When we see, for example, we *experience* visual sensations: the felt quality of redness, the experience of dark and light, the quality of depth in a visual field. Other experiences go along with perception in different modalities: the sound of a clarinet, the smell of mothballs. Then there are bodily sensations, from pains to orgasms; mental images that are conjured up internally; the felt quality of emotion, and the experience of a stream of conscious thought. What unites all of these states is that there is something it is like to be in them. All of them are states of experience.

* I am grateful to an anonymous reviewer and an audience at Union College for helpful comments on an earlier version of the paper.

DOI 10.1075/aicr.92.14bro

> It is undeniable that some organisms are subjects of experience. But the question of how it is that these systems are subjects of experience is perplexing. Why is it that when our cognitive systems engage in visual and auditory information-processing, we have visual or auditory experience: the quality of deep blue, the sensation of middle C? How can we explain why there is something it is like to entertain a mental image, or to experience an emotion? It is widely agreed that experience arises from a physical basis, but we have no good explanation of why and how it so arises. Why should physical processing give rise to a rich inner life at all? It seems objectively unreasonable that it should, and yet it does.
> (p. 201, italics in original)

The hard problem of consciousness is not to specify the neural correlates of consciousness but to explain 'why and how' phenomenal consciousness arises. Even though we know a lot about the brain, we don't yet know how neural or other physical states lead to the rich inner life that we are all familiar with. The causal chain from neural or other physical states to conscious states remains a mystery.

Physicalists hold that physical reality is all there is. Some physicalists think that physical theory ultimately will be able to explain the process by which physical states lead to conscious states. Others propose that there is no way that physics or any other field of study could ever provide an explanation of how conscious states arise but that the physical still determines the mental. Conscious states somehow supervene on physical states in a non-causal but constitutive fashion. Dualists like Chalmers himself think that we cannot provide an explanation of consciousness in purely physical terms. He furthermore holds that the physical isn't constitutive of consciousness. Rather, consciousness is an extra property of brain states that emerges from physical processes.[1]

I agree with Chalmers that consciousness probably isn't purely physical, and that it therefore isn't possible to explain consciousness in terms of purely physical states. But recognizing as much does not rule out that science can explain consciousness. Here I look at how scientific theories might help close the explanatory gap in the future at the fundamental level of reality.

2. A priori physicalism

There is an explanatory gap between the mental and the physical just in case we cannot rule out on a priori grounds alone that they can come apart. The ontological gap, on the other hand, is a state of the universe in which the physical does not fully determine the mental. If there is an ontological gap, it is possible for there to be two physically and behaviorally identical systems such that the first system is conscious, whereas the other is not.

1. Chalmers is sympathetic to a number of different forms of dualism as well as panpsychism.

A priori physicalism, or what Chalmers calls 'type A materialism', is the view that if you knew all the physical facts, you would need no further information in order to infer all the mental facts. This is also sometimes known as 'reductive physicalism'. Most a priori physicalists think that there is currently an explanatory gap but that it will eventually close (Levine, 1983). A priori physicalism contrasts with a posteriori physicalism, or what Chalmers calls 'type B materialism'. On this view, you cannot infer the mental facts, even if you are given all the physical facts. This is because there is a lasting, explanatory gap between mental and physical facts but the physical facts nonetheless fully determine the mental facts. This is also sometimes known as 'non-reductive physicalism'.

One motivation for a posteriori physicalism is that it provides a good way to explain the intuitive pull of cases like Frank Jackson's knowledge argument. The knowledge argument runs as follows (Jackson, 1982, 1986). Mary is an excellent neuroscientist confined to a black-and-white room with black-and-white television screens hooked up to external cameras and access to everything that has ever been written about colors and color perception. After years of studying in her cell Mary comes to know every physical fact about colors and color perception. Yet when Mary finally leaves the black-and-white room and sees the colored world for the first time, she learns something new: what it is like to perceive in colors.

The story about Mary was originally meant to undermine physicalism of any kind. If Mary knows every physical fact about colors and color perception but is still able to learn something new about phenomenal properties upon her release, then phenomenal truths are not physical.[2] So, physicalism is false.

As it stands, there is an obvious worry about the argument. If Mary already knows every physical fact about the colors and color perception prior to her release, and facts about phenomenal properties are physical, then she already knows every fact about phenomenal properties. So, for it to be true that Mary learns something new upon her release, it must be implicitly assumed that phenomenal properties are not physical. But this begs the question against the physicalist. To avoid begging the question it is better to say that, prior to her release, Mary knows all the lower-level physical truths (e.g., the truths of ideal physics, chemistry, and biology) (Chalmers, 2004b, 2006).

Even if modified in this way, however, the knowledge argument does not threaten to undermine just any kind of physicalism. It is open to argue that Mary cannot come to know all phenomenal truths in her black-and-white cell because the phenomenal truths are not a priori necessitated by the lower-level physical truths and therefore are not deducible from the lower-level physical truths. The knowledge argument is thus best construed as an argument against a priori physicalism, the position that the higher-level phenomenal truths are a priori necessitated by the lower-level physical truths. To refute a posteriori physicalism, the position that phenomenal truths are

2. Following Chalmers (2004a) I take phenomenal properties ("what it's like") to be properties of a mental state, a brain state or an individual.

necessitated but not a priori necessitated by the lower-level physical truths, additional premises are needed.

The success of the knowledge argument stands and falls with the learning claim, the claim that upon her release Mary learns a new fact about color perception, a fact which she would have known prior to her release had a priori physicalism been true. To refute the knowledge argument a priori physicalists must explain away the appeal of the learning claim.

One way to do this is to argue that while Mary acquires new knowledge of what it's like to perceive in colors upon her release, the knowledge that she acquires is not propositional but either a form of knowledge-how or a form of direct epistemic access sometimes known as 'acquaintance'. Knowledge-how is the kind of knowledge we possess when we know how to swim, how to play the piano or how to multiply two-digit numbers. On a classical account of knowledge-how, knowledge-how is not propositional knowledge but an ability (Ryle, 1945–1946, 1949 [Chapter 2]). So, when you acquire knowledge-how, you do not come to possess a new fact, rather you simply acquire an ability. Likewise, if you become acquainted with something, then you do not come to possess any new information, you merely change your cognitive access to information you already had. Several thinkers have treated the intuition that Mary learns something new by appealing to knowledge-how or acquaintance. Lawrence Nemirow (1980, 1990), David Lewis (1983, 1988), and others have argued that to acquire new knowledge of what it's like to perceive in colors just is to acquire new abilities to imagine, recognize and memorize color experiences, and Terry Horgan (1984), John Bigelow and Robert Pargetter (1990), and Earl Conee (1985, 1994) have argued that knowledge of what it's like to perceive in colors reduces to direct acquaintance with phenomenal color properties.

The ability and acquaintance replies, as originally formulated, must be distinguished from closely related replies to the effect that pre-release Mary already knows what it's like to perceive in colors yet acquires new knowledge or new skills nonetheless, knowledge or skills that are distinct from knowledge of what it's like to perceive in colors. Whereas the first kind of reply attempts to reduce knowledge of what it's like to perceive in colors to non-propositional knowledge, the latter kind of reply merely attempts to explain away the intuition that Mary comes to know what it's like to perceive in colors by appealing to other kinds of knowledge, skills or concepts which Mary acquires upon her release. I shall deal with the latter reply in the next section.

The first sort of reply is considerably easier to refute than the latter. If 'knowing what it's like' ascriptions attribute propositional knowledge, then it is simply false that Mary both learns what it's like to perceive in colors and fails to gain propositional knowledge. It may be that our intuitions about what Mary learns upon her release are unreliable and that Mary doesn't really learn what we think she learns. But if 'knowledge what it's like' ascriptions attribute propositional knowledge, and Mary comes to know what it's like to perceive in colors upon her release, then Mary gains knowledge of a new fact, a fact which it would seem she should already have known if a priori physicalism had been true.

Do 'knowledge what it's like' ascriptions attribute propositional knowledge? On a common analysis of knowledge-*wh*, Mary knows what it is like for her to see blue at t if and only if there is an x such that Mary knows that x is what it is like for her to see blue at t (Brogaard, 2009, 2011). 'What it's like for Mary to see blue at t' is equivalent to 'what seeing blue is like for Mary at t'. This, in turn, is equivalent to the predicate nominal 'the x: seeing blue is like x for Mary at t', where 'is like x' plays the same semantic role as 'has the property x'. When embedded in attitude contexts, predicate nominals denote properties. So, 'what it's like for Mary to see blue at t' denotes a property.

The learning intuition as formulated above was expressed in the form of a knowledge-*wh* claim. But one can also express it in the form of a know-how claim, viz. the claim that upon her release Mary comes to know how it feels to see blue. This version of Jackson's (1982, 1986) original knowledge argument is, in my view, much more forceful than the original. While it is somewhat plausible that pre-release Mary already knows what it's like to see blue, it is highly implausible that pre-release Mary already knows how it feels to see blue. So, by formulating the argument in terms of knowing how it feels to have color experiences, we can make the reply that pre-release Mary already had the relevant knowledge less tempting. But, now, there are several good reasons to think that knowledge-how just is a species of knowledge-*that* (Bengson & Moffett, 2007; Brogaard, 2009, 2011; Stanley & Williamson, 2001). So, if Mary comes to know how it feels to see blue at t, then there is a phenomenal property or state Q such that Mary knows that Q is how it feels to see blue at t. So, Mary gains new propositional knowledge.

There are various sophisticated ways of explaining away the intuition that post-release Mary comes to know what it's like or how it feels to see blue. These ways involve denying the legitimacy of the learning intuition, viz. the intuition that Mary comes to know what it's like or how it feels to see blue. For example, even if 'knowledge of what it's like' and 'knowledge of how it feels' ascriptions attribute propositional knowledge, it is still open to argue that pre-release Mary already knows what it's like or how it feels to perceive in colors and that post-release Mary simply acquires new abilities without thereby gaining new propositional knowledge.

The ability reply, however, is unsuccessful. As I have argued elsewhere, if a person acquires new abilities, she also acquires new propositional knowledge (Brogaard, 2011). Abilities are states that are constituted by bodily capacities and procedures that have been internalized by the agent and that are therefore essentially mind-involving. The new knowledge you acquire when you acquire a new ability is a kind of implicit knowledge. An ability to ride a bike involves the skills it takes to ride a bike but also an implicit strategy for achieving the results in the right sort of environment. An ability to recognize colors requires an internalized categorization system and a strategy for correctly classifying new stimuli. Though there may be other possible ways to explain away the learning intuition, explaining it away is not child's play. It is obvious that some new mental event takes place when Mary first sees a red flower.

Regardless of the nature of the new event, it is unexplainable by third-person physical fact. To see this, consider the following version of the knowledge argument.

Suppose dualism is true, and that Mary learns everything that one can learn in a black-and-white room about the lower-order physical and mental facts. Mary still learns something new the first time she sees a red flower. She learns what experiencing red is like from her first-person perspective. What the knowledge argument shows is that because of the special first-person acquaintance that it takes for someone to be conscious, third-person scientific theory cannot fully explain consciousness. Let us call this the first-person explanatory gap. Owing to the subjective character of conscious experience, I doubt that there is a way to close the 'first-person explanatory gap' and that physics will ever have anything relevant to say about it. There is, however, a further potential explanatory gap about which the knowledge argument does not have anything to say. This explanatory gap arises if not all third-person mental facts follow a priori from physical facts. Let us call this explanatory gap 'the third-person explanatory gap'.

3. A posteriori physicalism

A posteriori physicalism does not posit that the mental facts follow a priori from the lower-level physical facts. So exponents of a posteriori physicalism can take the learning intuition in Jackson's (1982, 1986) argument at face value. They can admit that Mary learns something new upon her release. Even though Mary couldn't figure out everything in her black and white room, these physicalists will say, the lower-level physical facts fully determine all mental facts.

This position strikes some people as odd. If the lower-level physical facts fully determine the mental facts, then why do the mental facts not follow a priori from the physical facts? It may be thought that it turns on incompleteness of information: 'Allen Stewart Konigsberg directed Annie Hall' does not follow a priori from 'Woody Allen directed Annie Hall'. But because Allen Stewart Konigsberg is Woody Allen, the last statement necessitates the first. In this case we cannot infer on a priori grounds that Allen Stewart Konigsberg directed Annie Hall, because the premises are incomplete. If we were told that Woody Allen is identical to Allen Stewart Konigsberg, then we would have been able to make the inference on a priori grounds.

A posteriori physicalism, however, holds that we could have a complete collection of lower-level physical facts that necessitate all the mental facts but nonetheless does not a priori imply them. How is that possible? One suggestion is that the information we need to get from the physical facts to the mental facts is not strictly about the physical world. So, knowing all the lower-level physical facts will not put us in a position to infer all the mental facts because making this inference would require information about how the physical is connected to the mental. Let us call the extra information we need to infer the mental from the physical on a priori grounds 'bridge laws'. This way of understanding a posteriori physicalism, however, does not seem to help. Even if Mary learns all lower-level physical facts *and* the bridge laws in the black and white room, and she has great deductive powers, it is quite plausible that she still learns something new when she is released from her captivity and is first exposed to colors. So we are back where we started.

One strategy that has been adopted by a posteriori physicalists to deal with the knowledge argument is the phenomenal concepts strategy (Carruthers, 2000, 2005; Chalmers, 2006; Stoljar, 2005; Tye, 2000). Phenomenal concepts are concepts that refer to our experiences. They are unlike all other concepts and cannot be explained by or reduced to other concepts. They are conceptually isolated and to acquire them, a particular kind of acquaintance with how the experience in question feels is required. What Mary learns upon her release from captivity is a phenomenal concept, a new way to refer to color experience. The explanatory gap arises, the proponents say, because a physical explanation of phenomenal concepts would require using only theoretical concepts, which would not capture what is special about phenomenal concepts. However, defenders of the phenomenal concept strategy hold that the explanatory gap does not entail an ontological gap because they think all mental facts supervene on the physical. Mary's possession of the phenomenal concept, for example, supervenes on physical facts.

The type of explanatory gap that the proponents of the phenomenal concepts strategy think the strategy can explain is what I called 'the first-person explanatory gap' above. Whether the phenomenal concepts strategy can also explain the potential existence of a third-person explanatory gap is far from obvious. I return to this question at the end of the next section.

4. The zombie argument

There are other options for those unconvinced by the physicalist strategies for accommodating our feeling that physical and mental properties are distinct. One option is to take the appearance at face value. This view is also known as 'property dualism'. Chalmers is famous for having advanced the so-called conceivability argument (a.k.a., zombie argument) in favor of some kind of property dualism. The first premise of the argument concerns conceivability, or what is consistent with what we know on a priori grounds. The premise says that we cannot rule out on a priori grounds, or by reflection alone, that there are creatures that are physically and functionally identical to us but that don't have phenomenal consciousness. Chalmers calls these creatures 'zombies'. If the first premise of the argument is true, then there is a third-person explanatory gap: Even if we set aside that our special first-person relationship to our conscious experiences cannot be inferred from the third-person data of physics, we cannot a priori infer all facts about consciousness on the basis of physical facts. The second premise of the conceivability argument states that if we cannot rule out on a priori grounds that there are philosophical zombies, then it is possible that there are zombies. It follows that there are creatures physically and functionally identical to us but without phenomenal consciousness. But this conclusion is inconsistent with a priori and a posteriori physicalism, which hold that the physical *necessitates* the mental. Or to put it differently: A priori and a posteriori physicalism hold that it is necessary that our physically and functionally identical twins are conscious.

Though some thinkers have denied that zombies are conceivable, the most frequently challenged premise in the zombie argument is the second, which says that if it is conceivable that there are zombies, then it is possible that there are zombies. Chalmers' main argument for this premise is that conceivability and possibility come apart only for a posteriori necessities. A posteriori necessities are necessities the truth of which can only be established via empirical discovery. For example, as 'Hesperus' and 'Phosphorus' both refer to Venus, and it is necessary that Venus is self-identical, it is necessary that Hesperus is identical to Phosphorus. But the truth that both names refer to Venus is an empirical discovery, not something we can discover through reflection alone. So we cannot rule out on a priori grounds, or by reflection alone, that Hesperus is not identical to Phosphorus. So a scenario in which Hesperus is not identical to Phosphorus is conceivable, despite being impossible. This could be a scenario in which Hesperus, the brightest object in the evening star, is Mars, and Phosphorus, the brightest object in the morning sky, is Jupiter. Here is another case: it is necessary that chemically pure water is H_2O, but we were unable to determine this on the basis of reflection; it took empirical investigations to determine water's molecular structure. It is consistent with what we know on a priori grounds that chemically pure water is XYZ, a chemical compound distinct from H_2O. But as 'water' refers to H_2O, and H_2O is self-identical, it is not possible that chemically pure water is not H_2O. So, these truths are a posteriori necessities.

There are both necessary and contingent truths with an a priori status. Good examples of necessary a priori truths are mathematical, logical and analytic truths. We don't need empirical discovery to figure out that $2+2=4$, that modus ponens is valid or that no bachelor is married. When we introduce names by description, we create various a priori contingent truths. For example, when the police introduced the name Jack the Ripper as a name of the murderer of the London prostitutes, it became a priori true that Jack the Ripper murdered prostitutes. But the man we call 'Jack the Ripper' could have failed to murder prostitutes. So 'Jack the Ripper murdered prostitutes' is not a necessary truth, even though we can figure out by reflection alone that it is true.

A posteriori necessary truths contain proper names and common nouns, such as 'Hesperus' and 'water'. This class of expressions are rigid designators, that is, they refer to the object they actually refer to in every possible world in which that object exists. Returning to the zombie scenario, this scenario can be described in terms that do not include any rigid designators. As only descriptions that contain rigid designators can block the route from conceivability to possibility, the conceivability of the zombie scenario entails the possibility of the scenario. But the possibility of the zombie scenario is squarely at odds with a priori and a posteriori physicalism, which imply that the physical necessitates the mental. If sound, Chalmers' argument shows that it is not necessary that the physical determines the mental. So the physical and the mental are ontologically distinct, which is to say that there is an ontological gap between the physical and the mental.

Proponents of the phenomenal concept strategy have argued that this strategy can also be used to refute the zombie argument (Balog, 2012; Tye, 2000). Let us consider a simple scenario. red-Zombie is physically and functionally identical to me, she even has most of the mental states that I have. But she has no awareness of the color red. The phenomenal concept strategy in the case of red-Zombie would be to say that when we conceive of red-Zombie, what we really conceive of is someone who lacks a phenomenal concept of red. But defenders of phenomenal concepts will say that a phenomenal concept of red is needed for awareness of red; so, we cannot infer from the conceivability of this scenario that physicalism is false.

There is a strong objection to this strategy for blocking the zombie argument.[3] The strategy assumes that it is conceivable that my zombie twin doesn't possess phenomenal concepts and hence that phenomenal concepts cannot be explicated in physical terms. But the zombie scenario can be described in a neutral language that doesn't contain types of words that can generate a posteriori necessities, such as nouns and names. As conceivability and metaphysical possibility can come apart only in a non-neutral language, it is metaphysically possible that my zombie twin doesn't possess phenomenal concepts. So the physical facts don't fully determine whether someone possesses phenomenal concepts. It follows that there is an ontological gap between the physical facts and phenomenal concepts. So, physicalism is false.

If phenomenal concepts can be explicated in physical terms, then the microphysical facts describing my zombie twin a priori imply that she has phenomenal concepts. So, my zombie twin is not conceivable. As defenders of the phenomenal concepts strategy grant that zombies are conceivable, this makes the phenomenal concepts strategy unsuitable for blocking the zombie argument. It may be argued that zombies are conceivable, because phenomenal concepts pick out qualia if they exist and physical states if qualia do not exist. This would enable the physicalist to say that when phenomenal concepts pick out physical states, then phenomenal concepts can be explicated in physical terms. So, zombies that have phenomenal concepts are conceivable. But this move is unlikely to help, as we can run the above arguments again by substituting 'phenomenal concept that refers to qualia' for 'phenomenal concept'. That is, it's conceivable and hence metaphysically possible that there are zombies that do not possess any phenomenal concepts that refer to qualia. But then there is an ontological gap between the physical facts and phenomenal concepts that refer to qualia.

Bob Stalnaker (2002), John Hawthorne (2002) and David Braddon-Mitchell (2003) have defended a conditional analysis of conceivability. It is not conceivable that there are zombies, they say. Rather, it is conceivable that it is possible that there are zombies. According to them, it is a priori that if the microphysical facts are the way they actually are, then there are (perhaps physically reducible) qualia. But if this conditional is a priori, then it can be ruled out on a priori grounds that there are creatures which are physically and functionally constituted the way we are but who

3. A variant of this argument can be found in Chalmers (2006).

lack phenomenal consciousness. Torin Alter (2007) denies that the conditional 'if the microphysical facts are the way they actually are, then there are qualia' is a priori. He claims that we can come to know that we are phenomenally conscious only on the basis of experience. So the conditional 'if the microphysical facts are the way they actually are, then there are qualia' is a posteriori.

I think this is incorrect. Consider a case of locked-in syndrome (see Charland-Verville, Vanhaudenhuyse, Laureys, & Gosseries, this volume), a case like the one depicted in the *The Diving Bell and the Butterfly*. Jean-Dominique Bauby, the editor-in-chief of *Elle*, suffered a stroke that left him nearly unable to communicate with the external world. Bauby (1997) had visual experiences and some very limited muscle control, which ultimately allowed him to communicate with the external world by blinking an eye. But someone could plausibly be born without any outer experience at all and yet be able to form conscious thoughts or images. This suggests that our knowledge of the fact that we are conscious may ultimately be based on inner conscious states rather than outer experience. But if this is so, then it may be a priori that I have phenomenal consciousness.[4] If it is a priori that I have phenomenal consciousness, then it follows that it is a priori that if the microphysical facts are the way they actually are, then there are qualia. So defenders of the conditional analysis are right that this conditional is a priori. But this sort of move does not block the zombie argument. Even if I can establish on a priori grounds that I am phenomenally conscious, I cannot establish on a priori grounds whether other people are phenomenally conscious or live in inner darkness. Because it is not a priori that other people have phenomenal consciousness, it is not a priori that if the microphysical facts are the way they actually are, other people have phenomenal consciousness. So the conditional analysis does not entail that the zombie scenario is inconceivable.

The zombie argument, if sound, refutes physicalism.[5] What to put in its place? Chalmers (1996) does not propose a single candidate view to replace physicalism. But he makes several suggestions. One is that the mental emerges from the physical in a strong sense of 'emergence'. In this strong sense, the physical doesn't determine the mental but nonetheless gives rise to it on a certain level of organization or complexity (Strawson, 2006). I have offered some reasons against strong emergence as a theory of consciousness elsewhere (Brogaard, forthcoming). Another suggestion is that consciousness is a fundamental feature of the universe. I will look at some implications of this proposal in the next section.

---

4. If it is not a priori that I exist, then it is a priori that if I exist, then I have phenomenal consciousness but I will leave aside this complication here.

5. Chalmers (2009) adds that the zombie argument does not undermine a position known as 'Russellian monism'. Russellian monism (see Pereboom, this volume) holds that elementary particles have an intrinsic nature that can vary between this world and the zombie scenario, even if my zombie twin and I share all (relational) physical and functional properties.

5. The beginning of a solution

We have looked at three positions regarding consciousness. A priori physicalists hold that there is neither an explanatory gap nor an ontological gap. A posteriori physicalists hold that there is an explanatory gap but deny that that entails an ontological gap. Property dualists, as we have seen, can hold that there is an explanatory gap and that this entails an ontological gap. But what about the fourth possibility? Could there be an ontological gap but no explanatory gap? I think the answer depends on what we mean by 'explanatory gap'. As I mentioned earlier, there are two kinds of explanatory gap. One is between physical facts and first-person conscious experience. Jackson's Mary-thought experiment illustrates this kind of gap. The other is between physical facts and third-person conscious experience. The zombie scenario illustrates this type of gap. It's unlikely that the first-person character of consciousness can be accounted for by physics, which is explicitly concerned with third-person data. So, I don't think there is a way to close the first-person explanatory gap. However, I believe there can be an ontological gap without a third-person explanatory gap. This sort of scenario could happen if the fundamental theory of the universe posited at least two fundamental properties, which together could explain how macroscopic conscious experiences arise.

There are several ways that such a theory might go. On the older theory known as 'panpsychism', everything around us, whether animate or inanimate, is conscious or proto-conscious. As we will see, this type of theory is bound to lead to what is sometimes called the 'combination problem'. A different version of this theory that avoids the combination problem takes the micro-phenomenal to be a fundamental force alongside the elementary forces and the elementary particles posited by the standard model in physics (Brogaard, forthcoming). The fundamental forces posited by the standard model include electromagnetism, gravity and the weak and the strong forces. On a variant of panpsychism, the micro-phenomenal would be an elementary force that can explain the existence of macroscopic conscious experiences. Given this suggestion, there is no third-person explanatory gap. Science can in principle give a full third-person explanation of how macroscopic conscious experiences arise from elementary forces and particles. But consciousness and physical phenomena, such as gravity, arise from different types of fundamental entities that do not reduce to one another. As physical and phenomenal elementary entities are ontologically distinct, the theory does not close the ontological gap.

Given this theory, it is plausible that there's something it is like to be conscious, in some very primitive sense of 'what it is like', for some entities with elementary consciousness. So, the theory on offer does not imply that the subjective features of consciousness are strongly emergent properties; they are merely weakly emergent. However, it is unlikely that there will be a way of accessing the most primitive first-person data, as they presumably will not be instantiated in systems that can convey these data to us. Perhaps we can envisage building automata that are behaviorally sophisticated but only minimally conscious, and perhaps such systems will be able to give us some insight into the first-person aspect of elementary consciousness. But it is unlikely that we will ever be able to fully understand the nature of the first-person aspect of conscious experience. So, the prediction made here is that we cannot close the first-person explanatory gap but that we might be able to close the third-person explanatory gap.

Because the proposed theory predicts that there is no third-person explanatory gap in principle, it also predicts the inconceivability of the zombie scenario. It's not conceivable that there are replicas of us that replicate all the elementary particles and forces that constitute us and the exact relationships among them yet fail to be conscious. That is not to say that we could not generate a Mary-scenario in which a person cannot infer all aspects of consciousness, including first-person data, from third-person data. But given this theory, a genuine zombie scenario is inconceivable. A scenario that is similar in spirit to the original zombie scenario and that *is* conceivable is one that replicates all the elementary particles and forces except consciousness. But the conceivability of this scenario cannot be used to generate a conceivability argument against the theory on offer.

Simply saying that conscious experience is partially constituted by a special elementary force does not solve the hard problem of consciousness. The theory on offer defers the third-person aspect of the hard problem of consciousness to physics. Doing so, of course, presupposes that it's even plausible to think that micro-phenomenal properties can combine to form macroscopic subjective experiences. William James is famous for thinking that this is not plausible. As he puts it:

> Take a sentence of a dozen words, and take twelve men and tell to each one word. Then stand the men in a row or jam them in a bunch, and let each think of his word as intently as he will; nowhere will there be a consciousness of the whole sentence…. Where the elemental units are supposed to be feelings, the case is in no way altered. Take a hundred of them, shuffle them and pack them as close together as you can (whatever that might mean); still each remains the same feeling it always was, shut in its own skin, windowless, ignorant of what the other feelings are and mean. There would be a hundred-and-first feeling there, if, when a group or series of such feeling were set up, a consciousness *belonging to the group as such* should emerge. And this 101st feeling would be a totally new fact; the 100 original feelings might, by a curious physical law, be a signal for its *creation*, when they came together; but they would have no substantial identity with it, nor it with them, and one could never deduce the one from the others, or (in any intelligible sense) say that they *evolved* it. (James, 1890/1950, p. 160, italics in original)

The problem outlined here is also known as the 'combination problem'. It challenges theories that posit micro-experiences or micro-subjects as fundamental to explain how these micro-experiences or micro-subjects could add up to macroscopic subjective experiences. As far as James is concerned, it is ridiculous to suppose that once we pile up enough microscopic experiences, it all adds up to the familiar macroscopic experience.

Chalmers (forthcoming) has argued that the combination problem is not a single problem but a number of distinct problems. The problem most true to James' original concern is the subject combination problem, which Chalmers (forthcoming) formulates in terms of the following Subject Combination Argument:

1. If panpsychism is true, the existence of a number of micro-subjects with certain experiences necessitates the existence of a distinct macro-subject.
2. It is never the case that the existence of a number of subjects with certain experiences necessitates the existence of a macro-subject.
3. Panpsychism is false.

Chalmers (forthcoming) provides a conceivability argument for the second premise. It seems true that *micro-subject* S_1 *through* S_n *exist* does not a priori entail that *micro-subject* S_1 *through* S_n *compose a macro-subject*. But as long as this claim is purely descriptive, it entails that *micro-subject* S_1 *through* S_n *exist* does not necessitate *micro-subject* S_1 *through* S_n *compose a macro-subject*. However, as I have argued elsewhere (Brogaard, forthcoming), the position that the existence of a number of micro-subjects necessitates the existence of a distinct macro-subject is implausible. In our scenario, this would amount to saying that fundamental micro-phenomenal qualities necessitate our macroscopic conscious experiences. However, our macroscopic conscious experiences are not simply made up of consciousness-stuff. Arguably, our conscious experiences also have properties of representing how the world is. For example, if I am looking at a red flower, then my conscious experience represents a red flower. One lesson of the zombie scenarios is that there can be representational properties, such as the property of representing a red flower, that are not phenomenal properties. Thus, our conscious experiences must partly supervene on micro-physical properties. But if this is so, then fundamental micro-phenomenal properties do not necessitate our macroscopic conscious experiences. Rather, microphysical and micro-phenomenal properties together necessitate our conscious experiences. So, on a plausible version of the theory that consciousness can be found at the fundamental level of reality, the subject combination problem does not arise.

Chalmers (forthcoming) formulates another version of the combination problem in terms of what he calls the 'palette argument':[6]

1. If panpsychism is correct, macrophenomenal qualities are constituted by micro-phenomenal qualities.
2. If panpsychism is correct, there is only a single micro-phenomenal quality.
3. Macrophenomenal qualities are too diverse to be constituted by a single micro-phenomenal quality.
4. Panpsychism is false.

6. I have substituted 'a single' for 'a few'. I also do not draw a distinction between constitutive panpsychism and other versions, as the version proposed here is constitutive.

The reply to the subject combination problem can be turned into an argument against either premise 1 or premise 3. Macro-phenomenal qualities are indeed too diverse to be constituted by a single micro-phenomenal quality. Their diversity stems from their different representational character. What is constituted by the micro-phenomenal quality is the aspect of conscious experience that all conscious experiences have in common. But their diversity shows that there normally is more to macroscopic conscious experience than the conscious aspect of experience. What conscious experiences represent also contributes to their nature. On a reading of premise 1 that is plausible, it says that a micro-phenomenal quality constitutes the conscious character of macrophenomenal qualities. But premise 3, then, turns out to be false, as the diverse macrophenomenal qualities are not constituted only by micro-phenomenal qualities.

There is much more to be said about the combination problem and theories that posit micro-phenomenal qualities at the fundamental level of reality. However, the combination problem, as James envisaged it, is most obviously a problem for certain classical theories that take consciousness to be present in all aspects of reality. It doesn't threaten theories that take micro-phenomenal qualities to be one among many fundamental properties.

6. Concluding remarks: Nonreductive neuroscience

The story told so far about consciousness may appear to suggest that our search for neural correlates of consciousness is futile, as it will be unable to shed light on the nature of consciousness. There is, however, plenty of work left for neuroscience to do, even if it cannot provide us with the essence of consciousness. Before looking at some examples of substantial questions that neuroscience can contribute to, let us first take a closer look at the definition of 'neural correlate of consciousness'. Though we often think of a neural correlate as something that is required for consciousness, we cannot take a neural correlate of awareness of a particular feature to be whatever is required for awareness of that feature.[7] Lots of neurons in areas buried deep inside the brain's subcortical matter, in the thalamus and the brain stem are no doubt required for consciousness of any feature whatsoever. Aware of these kinds of problems, Chalmers (2000) has proposed the following definition of a neural correlate of consciousness (or NCC):

> An NCC is a minimal neural system N such that there is a mapping from states of N to states of consciousness, where a given state of N is [nomically] sufficient, under conditions C, for the corresponding state of consciousness. (p. 31)

7. Miller (2007) distinguishes between (nomic) constitution and correlation. Constitution is also what some thinkers call the 'true correlate of consciousness'. It is the notion of constitution or true correlate that I am referring to here.

Conditions C are to be understood as conditions involving 'normal brain functioning, allowing unusual inputs and limited brain stimulation, but not lesions or other changes in architecture' (p. 31). It is important that 'sufficient' is understood as "nomically sufficient'. A is nomically sufficient for B just in case, in any situation that obeys our laws of nature, B is present whenever A is. There could be a single neuron that always fires when you see me, a freak coincidence. This is certainly not unthinkable. If 'neural state N is sufficient for state of consciousness S' were to be understood as a material conditional in which the given state of N is the antecedent and the state of consciousness is the consequent, then this kind of neuron would count as a neural correlate of your visual perception of me. However, the neuron wouldn't be nomically sufficient for the state of consciousness.

Chalmers' (2000) definition does not suggest that all states of consciousness must have a neural basis or that there can't be neural systems not associated with consciousness. If consciousness is a fundamental feature of reality, elementary consciousness presumably can combine with other elementary particles and forces and yield macroscopic conscious experiences in non-neural systems (e.g., silicon). Likewise, there are neural correlates in which elementary consciousness does not combine in the right way with other forces and particles to yield macroscopic conscious experience.

If, however, neural correlates are neither necessary nor sufficient for consciousness, the question may arise why we should be interested in searching for neural correlates of consciousness. I think that there are many reasons why our continued search is a worthwhile enterprise. Identifying the neural areas that manifest consciousness in our world, just like studying evolutionary patterns that could have been very different, is of fundamental interest. In their paper "Is the brain a quantum computer?", Litt et al. (Litt, Eliasmith, Kroon, Weinstein, & Thagarda, 2006) argue that 'explaining brain function by appeal to quantum mechanics is akin to explaining bird flight by appeal to atomic bonding characteristics' (p. 593). Their criticism is not meant to be a criticism of appeals to quantum processes in explaining consciousness per se. Rather, it is meant to be a criticism of appeals to microscopic events as an explanation of macroscopic phenomena. Though what counts as a satisfying explanation is context-dependent, macroscopic phenomena often are not adequately explained by appeal to microscopic phenomena. If I tell you my house burned down, and you ask how the fire occurred, it would normally suffice to reply with 'there was a short circuit'. I don't need to provide a story about microphysical events. In fact, it would normally be highly inappropriate if I did.

Neuroscience can serve the purpose of providing adequate explanations of many of our questions about consciousness. It will not give us an explanation of what consciousness is, nor will it solve the hard problem. But it can nonetheless provide answers to interesting questions, such as 'Why do my visual experiences alternate in binocular rivalry?', 'Why don't blindsighters have conscious visual experience?' or 'Why don't human beings have conscious experiences of ultraviolet?'

Our search for neural correlates may also be of interest from the point of view of intervention. If we know which neurons manifest different kinds of consciousness, we may be able to generate altered states of consciousness in controlled ways. In fact, we already do generate altered states of consciousness using techniques such as transcranial magnetic stimulation (TMS). Using TMS we are in a position to alter visual consciousness by suppressing it or enhancing it, but we are in a position to do this only insofar as we have identified a particular region as the neural correlate of visual consciousness or at least a neural region that transmits to a neural correlate of consciousness.

So, even though neuroscience will not be able to answer the questions of how and why consciousness arises, there are many important questions about consciousness for the field to tackle. These questions concern the correlations between consciousness and neural systems, and presuppose that there is such a thing as consciousness as a qualitative and subjective phenomenon. In this sense neuroscience is nonreductive.

References

Alter, T. (2007). On the conditional analysis of phenomenal concepts. *Philosophical Studies*, 134(2), 235–253. DOI: 10.1007/s11098-005-1485-4

Balog, K. (2012). In defense of the phenomenal concept strategy. *Philosophy and Phenomenological Research*, 84(1), 1–23. DOI: 10.1111/j.1933-1592.2011.00541.x

Bauby, J.-D. (1997). *The diving bell and the butterfly: A memoir of life in death*. New York, NY: Vintage Books.

Bengson, J., & Moffett, M. A. (2007). Know-how and concept-possession. *Philosophical Studies*, 136(1), 31–57. DOI: 10.1007/s11098-007-9146-4

Bigelow, J., & Pargetter, R. (1990). Acquaintance with qualia. *Theoria*, 56(3), 129–147. DOI: 10.1111/j.1755-2567.1990.tb00179.x

Braddon-Mitchell, D. (2003). Qualia and analytic conditionals. *Journal of Philosophy*, 100(3), 111–135.

Brogaard, B. (2009). What Mary did yesterday: Reflections on knowledge-*wh*. *Philosophy and Phenomenological Research*, 78(2), 439–467. DOI: 10.1111/j.1933-1592.2009.00250.x

Brogaard, B. (2011). Knowledge-how: A unified approach. In J. Bengson & M. A. Moffett (Eds.), *Knowing how: Essays on knowledge, mind, and action* (pp. 136–160). Oxford, UK: Oxford University Press.

Brogaard, B. (forthcoming). In search of mentons: Panpsychism, physicalism and the missing link. In G. Brüntrup & L. Jaskolla (Eds.), *Panpsychism*. New York, NY: Oxford University Press.

Carruthers, P. (2000). *Phenomenal consciousness: A naturalistic theory*. Cambridge, UK: Cambridge University Press. DOI: 10.1017/CBO9780511487491

Carruthers, P. (2005). *Consciousness: Essays from a higher-order perspective*. New York, NY: Oxford University Press.

Chalmers, D. J. (1995). Facing up to the problem of consciousness. *Journal of Consciousness Studies*, 2(3), 200–219.

Chalmers, D. J. (1996). *The conscious mind: In search of a fundamental theory*. New York, NY: Oxford University Press.

Chalmers, D. J. (2000). What is a neural correlate of consciousness? In T. Metzinger (Ed.), *Neural correlates of consciousness: Empirical and conceptual questions* (pp. 17–39). Cambridge, MA: MIT Press.

Chalmers, D. J. (2004a). The representational character of experience. In B. Leiter (Ed.), *The future for philosophy* (pp. 153–181). Oxford, UK: Oxford University Press.

Chalmers, D. J. (2004b). Phenomenal concepts and the knowledge argument. In P. Ludlow, D. Stoljar, & Y. Nagasawa (Eds.), *There's something about Mary: Essays on phenomenal consciousness and Frank Jackson's knowledge argument* (pp. 269–298). Cambridge, MA: MIT Press.

Chalmers, D. J. (2006). Phenomenal concepts and the explanatory gap. In T. Alter & S. Walter (Eds.), *Phenomenal concepts and phenomenal knowledge: New essays on consciousness and physicalism* (pp. 167–194). New York, NY: Oxford University Press.

Chalmers, D. J. (2009). The two-dimensional argument against materialism. In B. P. McLaughlin, A. Beckermann, & S. Walter (Eds.), *The Oxford handbook of philosophy of mind* (pp. 313–335). Oxford, UK: Oxford University Press.

Chalmers, D. J. (forthcoming). The combination problem for panpsychism. In G. Brüntrup & L. Jaskolla (Eds.), *Panpsychism*. New York, NY: Oxford University Press.

Conee, E. (1985). Physicalism and phenomenal properties. *Philosophical Quarterly*, 35(140), 296–302. DOI: 10.2307/2218909

Conee, E. (1994). Phenomenal knowledge. *Australasian Journal of Philosophy*, 72(2), 136–150. DOI: 10.1080/00048409412345971

Hawthorne, J. (2002). Advice for physicalists. *Philosophical Studies*, 109(1), 17–52. DOI: 10.1023/A:1015731311853

Horgan, T. (1984). Jackson on physical information and qualia. *Philosophical Quarterly*, 34(135), 147–152. DOI: 10.2307/2219508

Jackson, F. (1982). Epiphenomenal qualia. *Philosophical Quarterly*, 32(127), 127–136. DOI: 10.2307/2960077

Jackson, F. (1986). What Mary didn't know. *Journal of Philosophy*, 83(5), 291–295. DOI: 10.2307/2026143

James, W. (1890/1950). *The principles of psychology* (Vol. 2). New York, NY: Henry Holt and Company.

Levine, J. (1983). Materialism and qualia: The explanatory gap. *Pacific Philosophical Quarterly*, 64(4), 354–361.

Lewis, D. (Ed.). (1983). Postscript to "Mad pain and martian pain". In *Philosophical papers*, Vol. 1 (pp. 130–132). Oxford, UK: Oxford University Press.

Lewis, D. (1988). What experience teaches. *Proceedings of the Russellian Society*, 13, 29–57.

Litt, A., Eliasmith, C., Kroon, F. W., Weinstein, S., & Thagarda, P. (2006). Is the brain a quantum computer? *Cognitive Science*, 30(3), 593–603. DOI: 10.1207/s15516709cog0000_59

Miller, S. M. (2007). On the correlation/constitution distinction problem (and other hard problems) in the scientific study of consciousness. *Acta Neuropsychiatrica*, 19(3), 159–176. DOI: 10.1111/j.1601-5215.2007.00207.x

Nemirow, L. (1980). [Review of the book *Mortal questions*, by Thomas Nagel]. *Philosophical Review*, 89(3), 473–477. DOI: 10.2307/2184400

Nemirow, L. (1990). Physicalism and the cognitive role of acquaintance. In W. G. Lycan (Ed.), *Mind and cognition: A reader* (pp. 490–499). Oxford, UK: Blackwell.
Ryle, G. (1945–1946). Knowing how and knowing that: The presidential address. *Proceedings of the Aristotelian Society*, 46, 1–16.
Ryle, G. (1949). *The concept of mind.* New York, NY: Barnes and Noble, Inc.
Stalnaker, R. (2002). What is it like to be a zombie? In T. S. Gendler & J. Hawthorne (Eds.), *Conceivability and possibility* (pp. 385–400). Oxford, UK: Oxford University Press.
Stanley, J., & Williamson, T. (2001). Knowing how. *Journal of Philosophy*, 98(8), 411–444. DOI: 10.2307/2678403
Stoljar, D. (2005). Physicalism and phenomenal concepts. *Mind and Language*, 20(5), 469–494. DOI: 10.1111/j.0268-1064.2005.00296.x
Strawson, G. (2006). Realistic monism: Why physicalism entails panpsychism. *Journal of Consciousness Studies*, 13(10–11), 3–31.
Tye, M. (2000). *Consciousness, color, and content*. Cambridge, MA: MIT Press.

Identity over time, constitution and the problem of personal identity

Benjamin L. Curtis and Harold W. Noonan
Nottingham Trent University / University of Nottingham

What am I? And what is my relationship to the thing I call 'my body'? Thus each of us can pose for himself the philosophical problems of the nature of the self and the relationship between a person and his body. One answer to the question about the relationship between a person and the thing he calls 'his body' is that they are two things composed of the same matter at the same time (like a clay statue and the piece of clay which presently constitutes it). This is the 'constitution view'. In this paper we give a novel overview of the literature on personal identity, the constitution view, and surrounding topics.

1. Introduction

What am I? And what is my relationship to the thing I call 'my body'? Thus each of us can pose for himself the philosophical problems of the nature of the self and the relationship between a person and his body. The nature of personal identity over time and the link, if any, between personal identity and bodily identity, are aspects of these problems, and it is this, of course, which accounts for the immense philosophical interest in the concept of personal identity.

The problem of giving an account of the conditions of personal identity over time is a special case of the general problem of providing an account of the diachronic identity conditions of a kind of persisting thing. It is a philosophical platitude, going back to Locke, that conditions of identity over time are kind-dependent. That is, they vary with the kind in question: "It being one thing to be the same *Substance*, another the same *Man*, and a third the same *Person*, if *Person*, *Man* and *Substance*, are three Names standing for three different *Ideas*" (Locke, 1700/1975, Book II, Chapter xxvii, §7; italics in original). Thus, in the following section we provide an account of what one is asking when one asks, about a specific kind of thing K, what the conditions of identity over time of things of kind K are. Our answer is that to ask this question is equivalent to asking for the specification of certain necessary conditions of being a K, those which constitute the constraints on the history of anything of kind K and

DOI 10.1075/aicr.92.15cur

hence determine the line between the changes which are possible for a K and those which are not.

One answer to the question about the relationship between a person and the thing he calls 'his body' is that they are two things composed of the same matter at the same time (like a clay statue and the piece of clay which presently constitutes it). This is a common view, called by Olson (2001) the 'constitution view'. (Strictly, as Olson defines it, the constitution view is that a human person and the human being through whose eyes he currently views the world are two things composed of the same matter at the same time, but by a 'human being' Olson means an entity with purely biological persistence conditions, which is the same as what philosophers discussing the relation between a person and his body mean by 'a body'; see Williams, 1973.) The generic contention that non-identical things can stand in the relation of being composed of the same matter at the same time is called by Olson, 'constitutionalism'. If generic constitutionalism (GC) is false and things simultaneously composed of the same matter must be identical the constraints on the histories of materially coincident things must be the same. Thus neither can undergo any change the other cannot. Consequently, questions about identity over time interweave with questions about the constitution relation. These are the topics of Sections 3 to 5 following. At first sight it seems obvious that the piece of clay is not identical with the statue it temporarily constitutes, but on reflection some philosophers find themselves perplexed. How can there be two wholly material things of wholly identical constitution in exactly the same place at exactly the same time? If there are two such things, differing in their histories, how can they differ in their histories? If, for example, the statue is rolled into a ball it is destroyed, but the piece of clay is not, so they differ in their histories after the reshaping. Hence, even before the reshaping they must differ in their capacities, for before the reshaping the piece of clay has the capacity to survive it, but the statue does not. How can this be because before the reshaping they are materially identical and in no way differ down to the smallest particle?

In response to these perplexities several positions have been adopted. Nihilism: there are no statues or pieces of clay. Extreme monism: the temporarily coincident statue and piece of clay are identical, i.e., even temporary coincidence is identity. Four-dimensional (perdurantist) moderate monism: the temporarily coincident statue and piece of clay both exist and are distinct because they have temporal parts as well as spatial parts; constitution is part-sharing and they differ in past and future temporal parts. Three-dimensional (endurantist) moderate monism: the temporarily coincident statue and piece of clay both exist and are distinct, though they have only spatial parts, because they differ in their histories, their past and future properties. Pluralism: the statue and the piece of clay are distinct and would have been so even if they had been materially coincident throughout their histories, because even so they could have had different histories.

In Section 6 we return to the specific question about personal identity over time to ask whether it differs in any significant way from the question about the identity over time of the statue, or other familiar kinds of material object discussed in the literature.

Four differences are noted and explored. First, the concept of a person is indexical, it is the concept of an object of first-person reference, a self. Secondly, the option of saying that it is indeterminate or vague in a particular case whether personal identity obtains is less attractive than saying, in the case of a statue or tree, that it is vague whether it still exists because it is difficult for any person to conceive of a future as one in which it is indeterminate whether he himself still exists (Swinburne, 1984; Williams, 1970). Thirdly, 'best candidate' accounts of personal identity over time (Nozick, 1981; Shoemaker, 1984) are less plausible in the case of persons than in the case of artefacts (such as the Ship of Theseus discussed in Section 5, for example) because, although logically consistent, the idea that what happens elsewhere, and does not causally affect what happens here, can nonetheless logically determine the number of people here, is less plausible than the idea that what happens elsewhere may logically determine the number of ships here. Fourthly, the problem of the 'thinking animal' or 'too many thinkers' makes the constitution view of persons more problematic than GC and poses epistemological and semantic problems that do not arise merely if one maintains that the temporarily coincident statue and clay are distinct things sharing various material properties.

Much of the discussion in this chapter covers ground that is well-trodden in the literature on material constitution, and consequently this chapter can be viewed as an overview of that literature. But we do more than give a mere overview. The way in which we set the issues out is novel. The account of persistence conditions given in Section 2 is our own. This informs the rest of the chapter and the way in which we formulate the various positions that are available, and the arguments for them. In particular, the argument given in Section 3 in favor of GC is formulated in a way that is not only original, but that is also more persuasive than any formulation that has hitherto been given.

2. Identity over time

David Lewis (1986) famously denied that there are problems about identity: "We do state… genuine problems in terms of identity. But we needn't state them so. Therefore, they are not problems about identity" (p. 193). If so the traditional problem of personal identity over time should be capable of reformulation in a way that shows that it is not a question about identity, and in general, what is at issue when questions about identity over time are asked should be capable of formulation without the language of identity. In this section we provide an account, conforming to Lewis's dictum, of what one is asking when one asks, about a specific kind of thing, K, what the conditions of identity over time of things of kind K are.

Let us recall the case of the statue and the piece of clay which constitutes it, which according to GC is one in which there are two non-identical things composed at the same time of the same matter. The argument that there are two things is that each can survive changes the other cannot. For pieces of clay can survive changes statues cannot and vice versa. Hence a statue (Goliath) and the piece of clay from which it is made (Lumpl) may be *actually* at all-times-coincident but *possibly* divergent. Our concept of a statue plausibly implies that *no statue can survive radical reshaping.* Our concept of a piece of clay plausibly implies that *any piece of clay must survive radical reshaping in which all its matter is preserved in one coherent whole.* These propositions specify persistence conditions for statues and pieces of clay and, as they illustrate, these persistence conditions are of two types.

The proposition that no statue can undergo radical reshaping can be expressed as:

> Necessarily, if x is a statue then if the matter that constitutes x at t is radically reshaped at t, then x ceases to exist.
> – this specifies a 'passing away' condition for statues (this terminology comes from Penelope Mackie, personal communication).

The proposition that any piece of clay must survive radical reshaping in which all its matter is preserved in one coherent whole can be expressed as:

> Necessarily, if x is a piece of clay then if the matter that constitutes x at t is radically reshaped at t but preserved in one coherent mass, x survives.
> – this specifies a 'preservation' condition for pieces of clay.

Sortal concepts for persisting things (i.e., concepts associated with identity conditions under which persisting things fall) are governed by such conditions because they constrain the histories of the things they apply to, and such constraints can always be expressed in the form:

> Necessarily, if x is a K then if x exists at t and t^* then $Rxtt^*$

or in the form:

> Necessarily, if x is a K then if $Rxtt^*$ x exists at t and t^*.

Here 'R' expresses a three-place relation, e.g., x has the same shape at t and t^*. The 'passing-away' condition for statues is entailed by a principle of the first form (stating that a statue cannot have radically different shapes at different times) and the 'preservation condition' for pieces of clay is entailed by a principle of the second form (stating that if the matter composing a piece of clay at one time is in one coherent mass at that time and at another, whatever shape it is in, the piece of clay exists at both times). (In the sequel we will use 'passing away' and 'preservation condition' more liberally, to refer to what principles of these forms state as well as to what is stated by the propositions they entail.)

Principles of these forms state necessary conditions for being a thing of sortal kind K. A principle of the first form rules out certain changes in the history of a K. A principle of the second form rules out something's being a K if its history is not extensive enough; it tells us that if something is a K and there occur appropriately related events, one of which is in its history, the other must be in its history also. What distinguishes sortal concepts under which persisting things fall from non-sortal concepts under which persisting things fall (even ones that necessarily apply to a thing at any time it exists, like *permanent bachelor*) is that they are governed by such modal principles.

Questions about personal identity over time can thus be rephrased as questions about necessary conditions of membership of the sortal kind *person*. One question we can ask, without mention of identity, is

> Q1. What conditions R satisfy the following schema: (P1) Necessarily, if x is a person then if x exists at t and t^*, Rxtt^*?

Another is:

> Q2. What conditions R satisfy the following schema: (P2) Necessarily, if x is a person then if Rxtt^* x exists at t and t^*?

Solutions to the problem of diachronic personal identity will take the form:

> 'all and only the following conditions satisfy (P1):… and all and only the following conditions satisfy (P2):…'

Of course, in answering these questions we only specify *some* of the necessary conditions of personhood. One other type of necessary condition can be thought of as a synchronic constraint, capturable in the form:

> Necessarily, if x is a person then if x exists at t, Fxt

where 'F' represents an expression for a non-historical property, i.e., one entailing nothing about the past or future.

In addition, the general problem of the criterion of identity for persons, asked without reference to time, can be formulated by asking for a specification of the relation R satisfying the condition:

> (1) Necessarily, if x is a person and y is a person then ($x = y$ iff Rxy).

> (1) is equivalent to the conjunction of:
> (1a) Necessarily, if x is a person then Rxx
> and
> (1b) Necessarily, if x is a person then if y is a person and Rxy then ($x = y$).

Together these imply that necessarily any person is (identical with) *the* person R-related to it. They thus give a sufficient condition for identity with any person by giving a necessary condition of personhood (to say that any person is the person R-related to it is to say something of the form 'any person is…' which is the form of a statement of a necessary condition).

Thus all intelligible questions about personal identity are equivalent to questions about the necessary conditions for being a person. And, in general, all intelligible questions about the identity of things of sortal kind K are equivalent to questions about the necessary conditions for being a thing of kind K (though, of course, intelligible questions about necessary conditions for being a K are not all equivalent to questions about the identity conditions of things of kind K). In particular, all intelligible questions about personal identity over time are equivalent to questions of the forms Q1 and Q2, about the constraints on the history of a person and all intelligible questions about the identity over time of things of sortal kind K are equivalent to questions of the form of Q1 and Q2 in which 'K' replaces 'person'. Answers to these questions are what one is seeking when one enquires about the conditions of K-identity over time. The puzzles about constitution to be discussed in the next section are puzzles precisely because they challenge what otherwise seem plausible answers to these questions, when asked about familiar kinds of persisting things, including persons.

3. The arguments for and against generic constitutionalism

As we have said, GC is the view that non-identical things can stand in the relation of being composed of the same matter at the same time. *Composition* is a strict mereological relation that holds between the proper parts of an object and the object itself. To say that two non-identical things, such as the statue and the clay, stand in the relation of being composed of the same matter at some time t is to say that they share all their *proper material parts* at t. Thus, we can define GC more precisely as:

> GC: Possibly, for some material things x and y such that x≠y and for some time t, any z is a proper part of x at t iff z is a proper part of y at t.

In this section we will first make a few remarks about the relationship between GC and some more specific constitution views, before going on to outline in detail the argument for GC and the arguments against it. In Section 4 we then turn to positions adopted by those who reject GC on the basis of the arguments against it. The temporal parts view, which offers a novel way of maintaining GC, is also briefly discussed. We conclude our remarks on constitution itself in Section 5 by briefly considering two further problems that relate to material constitution: (1) The problem of permanent part-sharing; and (2) The same kind coincidence problem.

We focus throughout this paper almost exclusively on the puzzle case that has already been introduced, viz.:

> *The statue and the clay*
> A lump of clay sits on the artist's table throughout 2009 in an unfashioned ball-shape. In 2010 the artist sculpts the clay into the shape of Goliath to produce a statue. In 2011, dissatisfied with her work, the artist squashes the clay back into a ball-shape.

But it should be noted that there are a variety of other standard puzzle cases that have been discussed in the literature. Most are strictly analogous to the statue and the clay (e.g., Wiggins's 1968 example of an aggregate of cellulose molecules constituting a tree; see p. 91) and what we say about the statue and the clay applies *mutatis mutandis* to them. However, one standard puzzle case, the ship of Theseus, has features that are different from the statue/clay case in important respects, and we will also consider this case later.

What, then, is the relationship between GC and other less generic constitutionalist views? GC is the view that is held by *anyone* who rightly calls herself a constitutionalist. So, there being two non-identical things composed of the same parts at the same time is a *necessary* condition for the occurrence of constitution, i.e.,:

> Nec: If x constitutes y at t, then x≠y, and z is a proper part of x at t iff z is a proper part of y at t.

Most constitutionalists agree with Nec as stated, but some only agree with it with the notion of 'part' restricted to *microphysical* parts. This is the view held by Fred Doepke (1982) and Lynne Rudder Baker (2000), for example, who both hold that non-identical coinciding objects differ with regard to their macroscopic parts. Baker, for example, writes:

> Pretheoretically, I would have thought that [the statue] had a nose as a part but that [the clay] did not. Part of [the clay] is (i.e. constitutes) [the statue's] nose; but [the clay] itself does not have a nose. (Baker, 2000, p. 81)

Furthermore, most constitutionalists do not regard the sharing of parts as being a *sufficient* condition for the occurrence of constitution, i.e., they reject

> Suf: If z is a proper part of x iff z is a proper part of y and x≠y, then x constitutes y,

and so wish to add further necessary conditions for the occurrence of constitution. To see why consider that Suf entails that the constitution relation is symmetrical. Some are happy to accept this (Rea, 2000, for example, explicitly does so; see p. 173 and footnote 6). But most are not (influenced, perhaps, by the everyday use of the verb 'constitutes'). Here is Lynne Rudder Baker again:

> Pretheoretically, I take the constitution relation to be an asymmetrical relation. [The clay] constitutes [the statue]; [The statue] does not constitute [the clay]. This asymmetry induces a kind of ontological hierarchy… The object (y) that is constituted by something (x) but that constitutes nothing else is ontologically more significant than the thing (x) that constitutes it. (Baker, 2000, p. 33)

Constitutionalists who think that the relation is asymmetrical take on the substantial commitment of explaining precisely what this asymmetry consists in. Various suggestions have been made, and criticisms made. However, for current purposes, this can be put to one side, for the problems of material constitution can be generated by a commitment to GC alone.

Turning now to the details of the argument for GC, first consider the Indiscernibility of Identicals, the principle that if something x possesses a property that is not possessed by y, then x and y are non-identical (strictly speaking this is the contrapositive of the principle). The standard way of arguing that GC is true is by appealing to this principle and pointing to differences in the properties possessed by the statue and the clay when they coincide in 2010. Such arguments often appeal to differences in *de re* temporal or modal properties. It is said, for example, that the clay possesses but the statue lacks (in 2010) both the *de re* temporal property of *having been composed of parts p1, p2... pn in 2009* and the *de re* modal property of *being possibly ball-shaped.* Whilst there is nothing wrong with these arguments, so far as they go, they muddy the water by relying upon mention of *de re* modal and temporal properties about which there is much controversy. But no mention of any such properties is needed. Objects have their *de re* modal and temporal properties *in virtue of* being the kinds that they are. The clay and statue have the *de re* temporal and modal properties that they have precisely because they fall under different sortals that are associated with different passing away and preservation conditions. Questions about the *de re* modal and temporal properties of objects reduce to questions about the passing away and preservation conditions of the sortals they fall under. The argument for the non-identity of the statue and the clay can thus be framed directly in these terms.

Start with the following undeniable principle:

> *The Distinctness of the Temporally Separated (DTS):* If x exists at a time t, and y does not, then x≠y.

Next, note that the concept of a *statue* and the concept of a *piece of clay* are both genuine sortal concepts, i.e. both have associated with them passing away and preservation conditions. Consider again the following suggestions:

> Passing away condition for statues: Necessarily, if x is a statue then if x exists at t and t*, x has (roughly) the same shape at t and t*.
>
> Preservation condition for pieces of clay: Necessarily, if x is a piece of clay then if the matter x is composed of at t exists at t* and is in a coherent mass at both times, x exists at t and t*.

Now, note that both of the following propositions certainly seem to be true:

1. In 2009 there is something composed of parts p1, p2... pn that is a piece of clay.
2. In 2010 there is something composed of parts p1, p2... pn that is a statue.

1 tells us that in 2009 there is something composed of p1, p2... pn that is a piece of clay. The preservation condition for pieces of clay tells us that that thing is composed of p1, p2... pn and also exists in 2010. 2 tells us that there is something that is composed of p1, p2... pn in 2010 that is a statue. The passing away condition for statues tells us that that thing does not exist in 2009. Thus we have that there is something x that is composed of p1, p2... pn in 2010 and that exists in 2009 (i.e., the lump of clay), and something y that is composed of p1, p2... pn in 2010 that does not exist in 2009 (i.e., the statue). So, by DTS we have that x ≠ y. Thus, there is something x and something y that are composed of the same parts in 2010, but x ≠ y. So, GC is true.

DTS is undeniable, so the above argument shows that anyone who denies GC is committed either to (a) denying either proposition 1 or 2, or (b) denying that statues or pieces of clay have the passing away and preservation conditions that we ordinarily think they do. We will shortly describe positions that take each of these options. But first let us turn to the question of *why* anyone would want to deny GC in the first place.

There are a number of standard arguments against GC. Some are generally considered to fail. The *mass argument* is one such argument: the statue has mass M, so the argument goes, and so does the clay. So how can it be that their combined mass is M too, rather than 2M? The reply is simply that, because the statue and the clay share the same parts, they also share the same mass. (Indeed, quite generally, the statue and the clay share all their intrinsic material properties whilst they coincide.) Other arguments are generally thought to have some weight against GC, but to be by no means decisive. The *mereology argument* is one such argument: there are some theorems of standard formal systems of mereology, so the argument goes, that appear to contradict GC, so the defender of GC must reject standard mereology, which is a substantial price to pay. In a little more detail, the assumption is standardly made within formal mereology that the parthood relation is reflexive and antisymmetrical. From this one can derive the principle of Extensionality: x is identical to y iff x and y share all of their parts. Some do reject Extensionality (and so standard mereology) outright. Others argue that, because parthood is a time-relative notion, Extensionality needs reformulating as follows: x is identical to y iff *for all times t*, if x and y exist at t, then x and y share all of their parts (see Thomson, 1983, for details). Reformulated in this way, Extensionality poses no problem for the defender of GC.

The objection to GC that is generally thought to be the strongest (and is taken by many to be conclusive) is the *grounding objection*. The objection is sometimes made by asking how it can be that objects share their parts at a time and yet differ in their *de re* modal or temporal properties. But, as we have seen, such questions reduce to questions about the passing away and preservation conditions of kinds. So, the basic objection is more properly made directly in terms of kinds themselves. Here is how Eric Olson puts it:

> By definition, materially coinciding objects are made up entirely of exactly similar particles, related in precisely the same way, in identical surroundings… That would seem to make the objects so similar that not even God could tell them apart. How then could they have the qualitative differences that constitutionalists say they have? By virtue of what, for instance, could they belong to different kinds? What could give them different identity-conditions? (Olson, 2001, p. 339)

This objection has been fleshed out in a number of ways (see Rea, 1997, p. 367), but one simple way of doing so is by reference to the following principle, expounded by Mark Johnston:

> The Paradigm F Principle: If y is a paradigm F and x is intrinsically exactly like y then y is an F. (Johnston, 1992, p. 98)

Those who object to GC find this principle compelling. How can it be, they ask, that something intrinsically like a piece of clay (in our case a statue) is not itself a piece of clay?

The responses to the grounding objection have also been many and varied, but the one that seems to us to be most convincing is the following: the grounding objection assumes that the only properties relevant in determining whether some object is an F at a time are those properties the object has *at that time*. But this is to commit what Jonathan Lowe (2002) has called 'the cinematographic fallacy'. We have stressed throughout that for an object to fall under a genuine sortal is for it to meet certain passing away and preservation conditions. These conditions make reference to multiple times, thus an object's being of a kind K entails that it has a certain history, and thus properties had by the object at times other than t are relevant in determining whether or not it is a K at t. To put the point another way, consider that the Paradigm F Principle has two alternative readings:

> Reading A: If y is a paradigm F and x is intrinsically exactly like y *at some time t* then y is an F.
>
> Reading B: If y is a paradigm F and x is intrinsically exactly like y *at all times t* then y is an F.

A is false for the reasons given, and B causes no problem for the defender of GC because in the statue and the clay case (which was used to establish GC), the statue and the clay are *not* intrinsically exactly alike at all times. (Note that we will discuss a case in which the statue and the clay *are* intrinsically exactly alike at all times shortly.)

Despite the fact that we find the above response to the grounding objection convincing, many do not, and have developed positions that deny GC, to which we now turn.

4. Positions developed in response to the perceived problems with generic constitutionalism

To reiterate, those who deny GC must deny either (a) that there is a piece of clay present in 2009 or that there is a statue present in 2010, or (b) that statues or pieces of clay have the passing away and preservation conditions that we ordinarily think that they do. The first position we consider here (nihilism) takes option (a). The second (the dominant kind view) takes option (b) and is a version of extreme monism.

The nihilist claims that there are no composite objects – no chairs, tables, cats or curries (the most well known defence of this position is by Unger, 1980). She thus rejects *both* that there is a piece of clay present in 2009 and that there is a statue present in 2010. The claim that there are no composite objects appears to be crazy, but the nihilist mitigates this appearance by arguing that it is only in *a strict and literal sense* that there are no such things. She maintains that in *a loose and popular sense* there are composite objects, and offers us a translation scheme so that everything we say about composite objects when speaking loosely comes out as true once translated into strict nihilist terms. There are no tables, but there are *parts arranged tablewise*. There are no chairs, but there are *parts arranged chairwise*... There are no Ks, but there are *parts arranged K-wise*. Why do we need tables/chairs/Ks in our ontology, the nihilist asks, when we can get by just as well with parts arranged table-/chair-/K-wise? Giving up composite objects is a price worth paying, according to the nihilist, because everything that we want to say can be said without them, and in doing so we avoid a commitment to GC.

The main objection to nihilism is that it is hostage to empirical fortune, as no metaphysical theory should be. The nihilist requires that there is some bed-rock of fundamental parts to be arranged K-wise. But, so the argument goes, it is epistemically possible that the world is *gunky*, i.e., that everything is infinitely divisible – that there are parts *all the way down*. If this turns out to be true, then *every* object turns out to be composite (because every object, no matter how small, has parts). But then there are no fundamental parts to be arranged K-wise and the nihilist is forced to say that *there are no objects at all*, which is absurd. Perhaps some nihilists have absolute faith that the world is *not* gunky, but this, it seems, can offer them no real refuge. Gunk is certainly a metaphysical possibility – i.e., there is a possible world out there made of gunk. So in that world, at least, nihilism must be false. But metaphysical theses are supposed to be either necessarily true or necessarily false, so if it is false in that world it must be false in the actual world too. Considerations of these sorts lead many to reject nihilism.

The dominant kinds position has been defended most thoroughly by Michael Burke (1994) and Michael Rea (2000). The leading idea is that whenever we have an object x that falls under some sortal F sharing all of its parts with an object y that falls under some distinct sortal G, then one of the sortals *dominates* the other such that the object that falls under the dominated sortal has the persistence conditions associated with the dominating sortal (and so has the same *de re* modal and temporal properties too).[1] This obliterates any differences between x and y, and so removes any reason for thinking that x and y are distinct. In the statue and the clay case, for example, Burke and Rea both argue that the sortal *statue* dominates the sortal *piece of clay* so that in 2010, when the statue and the clay coincide, the thing referred to by the phrase 'the piece of clay' picks out an object that satisfies the passing away and preservation conditions of a statue – or, in other words, it picks out a statue. Burke and Rea do not deny, however, that there is a piece of clay present in 2010. Rather, they argue that there are two ways in which an object can satisfy a sortal – it can satisfy it in a *classificatory* way or a *nominal* way. If an object satisfies a sortal in a classificatory way, then it has the persistence conditions associated with that sortal, but if an object satisfies a sortal in a nominal way it only has the qualitative features of things that satisfy the sortal in a classificatory way. Thus, there is a single object present in 2010 that satisfies the sortal

1. It should be noted that for ease of presentation we have conflated some aspects of Burke and Rea's accounts. Rea, for example, prefers to present the basic idea in terms of kind-membership rather than in terms of falling under a sortal. The conflation does not affect our presentation of their accounts.

piece of clay in a nominal way and the sortal *statue* in a classificatory way, but it is still true that there is a statue present in 2010 and a piece of clay present in 2010. What is clear is that both Burke and Rea deny that two objects can ever even temporarily coincide and so their position is an extreme monist position.

In giving the above account Burke and Rea commit themselves to denying that statues have the preservation conditions that we ordinarily think they do. For note that in 2009 there is an object that satisfies the sortal *piece of clay* in a classificatory way (for in 2009 the kind *piece of clay* is not dominated). On their account, however, this object cannot survive being moulded into a statue, for if it did then there *would* be two distinct objects present in 2010 (i.e., one that satisfies the sortal *statue* in a classificatory way and that consequently came into existence in 2010 and one, the original piece of clay, that did not come into existence in 2010), which they deny. Consequently, pieces of clay cannot survive being moulded into statues, and so it cannot be that the suggested preservation condition for pieces of clay given above is correct.

Aside from the implausibility of denying that pieces of clay have the persistence conditions that we think they have, the major problem for the dominance approach is with the notion of dominance itself. It is one thing for Burke and Rea to say that the sortal *statue* dominates the sortal *piece of clay*, but we need some principled reason for thinking this is the case. Both Burke and Rea offer a criterion for when one sortal dominates another, but Rea's is considered to be the most serviceable (here put in terms of kinds):

> (KD) For any *x*, K is *x*'s dominant kind just in case (i) *x* is essentially a K, and (ii) for any kind K′ such that *x* is essentially a K′, *x*'s being a K entails *x*'s being a K′. (Rea, 2000, p. 187)

The problem that faces Rea's criterion is that it relies upon our having an independent grasp of when an object is *essentially* a K. Rea offers no criterion for this, but apparently thinks that no criterion will be forthcoming, as he is perfectly happy to rely upon our having intuitions about such matters. But for those of us who do not have such clear intuitions as Rea, and who find the notion of being essentially a K obscure, the dominant kinds account is still, at best, a promissory account.

We now turn to the temporal parts view, associated most closely with David Lewis (1976), which offers a novel account of how GC can be true. According to the temporal parts theorist objects are composed not only of spatial parts, but temporal parts too. So, according to this view, persisting objects do not exist wholly and completely at each moment of time at which they exist, but are stretched out in time and have distinct parts at each moment of time that they exist. Consequently the clay is an object that exists from 2009 until 2011. It has ball-shaped temporal parts in 2009, statue shaped temporal parts in 2010, and ball-shaped temporal parts in 2011. The statue, on the other hand, exists only in 2010 and has statue-shaped temporal parts throughout its existence. During 2010 the statue and the clay coincide and share all of their spatial parts during that time – but this is utterly unproblematic for the temporal parts theorist because for two objects to share their spatial parts at a time is simply for them to share their temporal parts at that time. And just as two objects can unproblematically overlap by sharing spatial parts, two objects can unproblematically overlap by sharing temporal parts too. Consider your body and your head. Your head is a part of your body because all of its (spatial) parts are parts of your body. But this gives us no reason to think that your body and your head are identical because your body has (spatial) parts that your head does not. Similarly, according to the temporal parts theorist, the statue is a part of the clay because all of its (temporal) parts are parts of the clay. But this gives us no reason to think that the clay and the statue are identical because the clay has (temporal) parts that the statue does not.

Whether one should accept the temporal parts view is not something that we can assess here. There is a whole literature on the temporal parts view containing many independent arguments for and against it that we cannot possibly hope to do justice to here. Instead we point the reader to Hawley (2010), which contains an excellent summary of that literature, and content ourselves by noting that the temporal parts view is an attractive position, and that if one does accept it, then GC is trivially true.[2]

5. Further constitution problems

Let us now turn to two problems that are related to the ones discussed above and the issue of constitution. Consider first the following example:

> *The statue and the clay 2*
> Two lumps of clay are fashioned in 2008 by our artist into pieces that resemble two halves of Goliath. The two pieces are then brought together in 2009 to simultaneously form both a new lump of clay and a statue of Goliath. In 2011, dissatisfied with her work, the artist incinerates the statue simultaneously destroying it and the piece of clay.

This illustrates the problem of permanent part-sharing. In this example the piece of clay and the lump do not just temporarily coincide; they permanently coincide. Thus, they share their parts at *all* times. It is tempting to say that there is no *real* difference between this case and the previous one. Before we had two objects, a piece of clay

2. In fact, this is not quite true. There is a non-standard version of four-dimensionalism according to which ordinary objects do not *have* temporal parts, but are in fact identical to temporal parts (calling them temporal *parts* is thus something of a misnomer on this view). This is the "stage-view" of Ted Sider (1996). On this view, strictly speaking, ordinary objects exist only for an instant (or for however long temporal parts last for) but truths about their past and future are made true by their bearing relations of certain sorts to past and future (non-identical) temporal parts. On this view GC is certainly not trivially true, but false. The statue and the clay, when they coincide, are one and the same thing because they are one and the same instantaneous temporal part. Because no objects ever strictly speaking persist on this view, no objects ever temporally overlap either, so any case of supposed temporal overlap is actually a case of identity. The stage-view is thus a version of *extreme monism*.

and a statue, which shared all of their parts at a time, and here we have a case where two objects, a piece of clay and a statue share all of their parts at *all* times. That is, it is tempting to accept in addition to GC the stronger principle GC*:

> GC*: Possibly, there are material objects x and y such that x ≠ y and *for all times t*, any z is a proper part of x at t iff z is a proper part of y at t.

Indeed, this *pluralist* view is the mainstream view which is implicitly held by the majority of metaphysicians (and is explicitly defended by some, e.g., Fine, 2008; Mackie, 2008). But matters are not as simple here as they were in the case of temporary coincidence.

Note first that the argument we gave for GC depended upon there being a time at which the clay existed and the statue did not, but as this is not the case here, we cannot run a parallel argument for GC*. We *can* run an argument, utilising the Indiscernibility of Identicals, that attempts to distinguish between the statue and the lump directly in terms of their falling under different sortals. This type of argument is precisely the type favored by Mackie (2008), for example. But note second that the grounding objection has considerably more force in this case. To see why note that in response to the grounding objection we gave two readings of the Paradigm F Principle thus:

> The Paradigm F Principle A: If y is a paradigm F and x is intrinsically exactly like y *at some time t* then y is an F.

> The Paradigm F Principle B: If y is a paradigm F and x is intrinsically exactly like y *at all times t* then y is an F.

We said that A is false and that B causes no problems for the defender of GC. For the defender of GC*, however, B does cause problems, and nothing that we have said has suggested that B is false. Mackie's (2008, p. 170) solution is to maintain that sortal properties are intrinsic properties such that the statue and the clay are not intrinsically alike precisely because they differ in their sortal properties. We do not have space here to offer a full response to Mackie (2008), but we note that (even if it is granted that sortal properties are intrinsic) we find this response unconvincing because we find the appeal to sortal properties to be inappropriate in the current context. The sortal properties that an object possesses, we think, are grounded in its possession of non-sortal properties. So, if a difference is to be found between some paradigm F and an object that permanently coincides with it, that difference must be a non-sortal intrinsic difference. Thus, the Paradigm F Principle B is better stated as:

> The Paradigm F Principle B*: If y is a paradigm F and x is exactly like y in its non-sortal intrinsic properties at all times t then y is an F.[3]

3. We have adapted this principle from Mackie (2008, p. 171) herself. Mackie is perfectly aware that this move can be made by the defender of moderate monism, but finds the new principle *ad hoc* and offers an argument against it. Again, we do not have the space here to adequately address Mackie's concern, but we do note that we think that there are principled reasons for adopting this principle and that is not *ad hoc*.

Fine (2008) offers a different solution to this problem. He maintains that objects are not mere fusions of matter, but rather fusions of matter and a particular form. This allows him to say that the statue is, in fact, a fusion of the matter it is made from and also the particular shape that it is, and that although the lump of clay shares its matter with the statue, it does not have the same form as part of it. Thus, according to Fine, there are non-sortal intrinsic differences between the statue and lump of clay. Again, we do not have space to fully respond to this suggestion here, but we again find it unconvincing because of its use of non-standard mereology and its hypostatization of forms.

Note thirdly that the mereology objection also has more force in the case of permanent coincidence than in temporary coincidence. In response to the objection applied to temporary coincidence we suggested that the defender of GC needed to adopt a temporally relativized version of Extensionality, i.e. something like the following: x is identical to y iff *for all times t*, if x and y exist at t, then x and y share all of their parts. But this temporally relativized version entails that in the case of permanent coincidence the statue and clay are identical. For similar reasons even the temporal parts theorist has problems with permanent coincidence. They can no longer distinguish between the statue and the clay by maintaining that one has temporal parts that the other does not.

What the above points towards is that it is much harder to defend the non-identity of permanently coinciding objects than it is to defend the temporary coincidence of objects. This has led many to conclude that in the case of permanent coincidence, unlike in temporary coincidence, the objects that coincide really *are* identical. It is this view that is sometimes called (somewhat confusingly) the view that *constitution is identity*. Here we have instead called it *moderate monism*. It is perhaps more often held by those who believe that objects have temporal parts, i.e., by perdurantists but it can also be upheld by those who deny this, i.e., by endurantists (see Noonan, 1993).

There is one loose end to tie up regarding the above view. Remember that some argue using the indiscernibility of identicals that in the original case the statue and the clay are non-identical because they differ in their *de re* modal properties. This difference still seems to apply here. It seems that even if the statue and the clay permanently coincide it is still true that the clay has and the statue lacks the *de re* modal property of *being possibly ball-shaped*. How do those who hold that permanent coincidence is identity deal with this? The answer is that they deny that *being possibly ball shaped* determinately stands for a genuine *de re* modal property. They cash this out by giving a non-standard account of *de re* modal predication according to which the references of modal predicates such as '… might have been ball-shaped' alter depending upon the sense of the singular term to which they are attached. Thus, the modal predicate when attached to the term 'the statue' stands for the property *might have been a ball-shaped statue* but when attached to the term 'the clay' stands for the property *might have been a ball-shaped piece of clay*. These are genuine modal properties, but both the statue and the clay lack the first and possess the second, so there is no difference between them, and the Indiscernibility of Identicals cannot be applied (see Noonan, 1993).

For the final issue in the section we consider the same kind coincidence problem, which is illustrated by the following example:

> *The Ship of Theseus*
> In the year 1250 B.C. a ship is built out of 100 planks of wood. Call this ship 'A'. In 1249 B.C. a single plank is removed from the ship by a plank hoarder, stored away, and replaced by a new one. In 1248 B.C. another single plank is removed by the hoarder, stored away, and replaced... These replacements continue until 1150 B.C. The resultant ship in 1150 (call it 'B') is spatiotemporally continuous with the original ship in 1250 but shares none of its parts. But now, in 1150, the planks that have been removed and stored away by the hoarder are reassembled to make another ship that is an exact replica of the original ship. Call this ship 'C'.
> (This scenario was first described by Thomas Hobbes.)

There is a sense in which this example gives us nothing new: exactly the same things can be said about the relationship between the collection of planks and the ship is as can be said about the relationship between the statue and the clay. But there is an extra problem here. To see this suppose that 'A' designates a single ship in 1250 B.C., as seems to be the case. Further suppose that 'B' and 'C' designate single ships in 1150 B.C., as also seems to be the case. Plausibly ships can both survive a gradual replacement of their parts and being taken apart and put back together again (i.e. these are both plausible preservation conditions for ships). But if both of these are preservation conditions for ships then both B and C are identical to A. But B and C can't *both* be identical to A, because the identity relation is symmetrical and transitive, so from A = B and A = C is follows that B = C, and this is plainly false. So what do we say here? There are five possible responses.

Response 1: maintain that there are actually *two* ships present in 1250 A.D. that share all of their parts, one of which is identical to B and one of which is identical to C (so 'A' is indeterminate in reference). In one sense this is just another case of two objects sharing their parts, but in the statue and the clay case the objects were of different kinds, whereas here they are of the *same* kind. Some find this difference unproblematic. The temporal parts theorist, for example, will maintain that this is just another case of temporal part-sharing. But others do find this difference problematic, and so will reject this response. Wiggins, for example, who defends GC (using an argument similar to the one we gave above), nevertheless thinks that the following principle is a *conceptual truth*:

> S*: No two things *of the same kind* can occupy exactly the same volume at the same time. (Wiggins, 1968, p. 93)

Response 2: deny that there are any ships at all. This is the nihilist response and is entirely analogous to the response given above. Accordingly, however, the same concerns as were voiced above about this strategy apply here, so many will reject this response too.

Response 3: deny outright that ships survive replacements of parts, or deny outright that they survive being taken apart and put back together again. This response denies that ships have the preservation conditions that we think that they have. One way of maintaining this thesis is to deny that objects ever persist over time at all. This is to take a mereological essentialist line, which has been defended most thoroughly by Roderick Chisholm (1973). According to it, all objects have the parts that they have essentially so that no object ever survives a change in parts. This view appears to be crazy in a similar way that the nihilist view appears to be, but the mereological essentialist attempts to mitigate this appearance using a similar tactic to the nihilist. She argues that it is only in a strict and literal sense that objects cannot survive a change in parts and that in a loose and popular sense they can. In this case, however, a translation scheme that preserves the truth of our ordinary utterances is harder to find than in the case of nihilism. In addition, as Alvin Plantinga (1975) has forcefully argued, we are paradigm examples of things that persist over time, but if mereological essentialism is true none of us ever survive (for example) having our hair cut. This is absurd, so at the very least mereological essentialism cannot be universally true, reducing its appeal. Another way of maintaining this is to deny that ships survive one type of change but hold that they survive the other, such that A is identical to either B or C, but not both. This is particularly implausible because unless one candidate preservation condition is significantly more *natural* in some way than the other, then there seems to be no grounds for thinking one to be correct and the other incorrect.

Response 4: the fourth response is similar to the third in that it locates the problem with the preservation conditions associated with the sortal *ship*. But unlike in the third case it does not deny *outright* that either preservation condition is associated with the sortal *ship*. Rather, according to this response, our concept *ship* is vague in such a way that it is indeterminate which preservation condition is correctly associated with it. We can thus say that there is a single ship A present in 1250 B.C., two ships B and C present in 1150 B.C., but that it is indeterminate whether the original ship A is identical to B or identical to C. The position is that whether A survives as B or C is a matter of semantic indecision. We have two candidate preservation conditions associated with the term 'ship', but it is indeterminate which one is correct.

Response 5: the best-candidate account. According to this proposal, most thoroughly defended by Robert Nozick (1981), ships do not always survive being taken apart and put back together again. Whether they do depends on things that happen elsewhere, which need have no causal effect on the processes of disassembly and reconstruction. It does seem plausible to say that B (and not C) is in fact identical to A, in virtue of B being a better candidate than C for being identical to A. But it also seems plausible to say that C would have been identical to A if B had not existed. To insist that a ship reconstructed from the parts of a dismantled ship is not identical to that ship even when no other candidate exists seems absurd – for ships can certainly undergo dismantling and reconstruction. But to accept this description of the situation we must acknowledge that C – that very ship – would not have existed if B had not existed.

Again, we must say that the assembly of the stored planks into a ship, which in fact constitutes the origin of C in the situation described above, would not have constituted the origin of C, or any ship, in the absence of the continuously repaired ship. Hence that: events which constitute the origin of a ship in one situation may not constitute the origin of that or any ship in a second situation, even though all the events constituting the history of the ship in the first situation remain present in the second. Again, if we accept a 'best candidate' account of the ship of Theseus we must say that two events may be parts of the history of a single ship in one situation, but fail to be parts of the history of that, or any single ship, in a second situation in which both they, and all the events which are parts of the history of the ship in the first situation, remain present.

In our view the fifth response, the best-candidate account, is the most tempting response to the problem as it best captures our intuitions that the spatiotemporally continuous ship is identical to the original whilst allowing that the later reconstructed ship would have been identical to the original ship in the absence of the spatiotemporally continuous one.

6. Personal identity

We ourselves are persons and paradigms of persisting things. But 'person' is neither a paradigm sortal concept, nor uncontroversially a sortal concept at all. It is undeniable that I am a person in the sense relevant to the philosophical debate about personal identity over time because 'person', in this debate, just means 'the object of the first-person reference', the self. Thus it is analytic that all and only persons are objects of first-person reference. In this sense the term 'person' is an indexical term, unlike the familiar sortal terms discussed in the last section: it means 'the kind of thing which can be the denotation of the indexical "I"'. But then it is a substantial claim that there is a sortal kind which 'person' denotes – perhaps there are different kinds of person, with different passing-away and preservation conditions, perhaps some are immaterial, others material, some organic, others inorganic. One might attempt to resist this conclusion by proposing that the relevant concept is not the concept of an object of first-person reference, but rather the concept Locke defines: an intelligent, thinking thing with reason and reflection. But this is pointless. The concept Locke defines is not a sortal concept, but a functional concept, the concept of a possessor of capacities which can be gained or lost (like 'genius' or 'prophet'). The first thing that is special about the problem of personal identity, therefore, is that it is controversial that its subject matter exists. We exist and are persons and we persist over time. But there may be no account to be given of the persistence conditions of persons as such. We may have to settle for the view that there are different criteria of identity for different kinds of person.

A second difference is that indeterminacy in personal identity is less easily accepted than indeterminacy in the identity of other kinds of persisting thing; for it is difficult for anyone to conceive of his own identity as indeterminate. We are inclined to think, as Parfit (1971) puts it, that questions of personal identity must have answers even in cases in which, though we know the answer to every other question, we have no idea how to answer the question of personal identity.

At first sight it is tempting to say that in the puzzle cases in the literature on personal identity it is an open question whether the original person is identical with the candidate for identity with him that the case presents. It is uncontroversial that it is possible to construct puzzle cases concerning the identity of other things about which this is the correct thing to say. Events can be imagined which, to use a phrase of Williams (1970), cast conceptual shadows over the identity of things. Shoemaker (1963) gives the example of a bridge destroyed and rebuilt from partly new stone. Parfit (1984, p. 213) gives the example of a club disbanded and then reconstituted, perhaps with partly new rules and members.

Clearly in these cases to insist on an answer to the question of identity would be absurd. But can we similarly imagine cases in which a conceptual shadow is cast over our own identity? Williams (1970) insists that we cannot. Suppose I am told that someone will be tortured tomorrow who will be so related to me to make it conceptually undecidable whether he is me. I cannot regard the indeterminacy as something that will be eliminated when tomorrow comes; so I cannot think of any future situation in which I am definitely present as one I might live through. But then what I have been told cannot serve as the basis of any hopes, fears or imaginings; it seems, as Williams puts it, that what I have been told has "no comprehensible representation in my expectations and the emotions that go with them" (1970, p. 175).

Williams's (1970) point is restated by Swinburne (1973–1974). Suppose A is the person who is told that a person with whom his identity will be conceptually shadowed will be tortured tomorrow:

> Has he cause to fear? Presumably less than if the person to be tortured were fully himself, and more than if he were not at all himself. But how can an intermediate reaction be justified? Each subsequent person will either be tortured or not; no half tortures will be laid on. An intermediate reaction would be justified if A did not know who would be tortured… But A has been told who will be tortured, i.e. someone who is equally well described as A and not A. How can any suffering affect A unless he suffers it all or suffers part of it? – And neither of these alternatives is being suggested here. (Swinburne, 1973–1974, pp. 237–238)

The people existing at any future time divide into two groups: those being tortured then and those not been tortured then. And so the people in existence now can be similarly divided into two groups: those being tortured at the future time and the rest (comprising those not alive then and those alive but not being tortured then). Any presently existent person must fall into one of these latter two groups, it seems, and so how can it be, as supposed, that A is in neither? This is the basic perplexity Williams (1970) and Swinburne (1973–1974) point to. The most straightforward response from a defender of the possibility of vague personal identity is to question the presupposition in Swinburne's argument that 'A' is a term determinately denoting a single individual and the presupposition of Williams's argument that 'I' in the mouth of the person faced with the prospect he envisages determinately denotes.

The analogous response to indeterminacy in identity in cases of things other than persons is familiar. The indeterminacy results from semantic indecision. In Parfit's example of the club, 'the earlier club' and 'the later club' are terms without determinate denotation. Because our concept of a club is imprecise there are two candidates for the denotation of 'the earlier club' (mutatis mutandis, for 'the later club'), each of which is a club on a precisification of the term. One ceases to exist when the original members cease to have regular meetings. The other continues to exist and still exists when the new members begin to meet. Because of this indeterminacy in the denotation of the terms the identity statement 'the earlier club is the later club' is indeterminate in truth-value. To say the same about personal identity we must say that in a case where a conceptual shadow is cast over the identity of a person, 'I' as uttered beforehand by the original person is indeterminate in denotation. That is to say, it is definitely true that there is just one person uttering 'I' (because that will be true under all precisifications of 'person'), but there is no one of whom it is definitely true that he is the denotation of the 'I'-utterance in question. Rather there are two candidates, with different futures, one of whom definitely ought to fear future torture, and one of whom definitely need not. But neither candidate can think anything the other cannot.

Of course, this conclusion goes against deeply ingrained convictions. For all I know this might be my situation; the brain transplant or whatever might be future, not merely science-fictional and if so my present utterances of 'I' must be without determinate denotation, for although it is definitely true that I am just one person there is no one person whom I definitely am.

Thus, it is the fact that questions about personal identity are ultimately first person questions, together with our deeply ingrained conviction that we are guaranteed to denote when we use the first person pronoun, that explains the deep implausibility of the idea that personal identity can be indeterminate.

A third difference between the problem of personal identity and problems about the identity over time of other things is that an account of the structure of sortal concepts which is tempting in the case of other things is less tempting in the case of persons. This is the 'best candidate' account, which is the most tempting response to the problem of the ship of Theseus. Corresponding to the puzzle of the ship of Theseus in the discussions of personal identity are cases of fission, which may be equal (no candidate is better) or unequal, in which, for example, a person's brain hemispheres are divided and transplanted into different bodies with consequent, equal or unequal, transference of psychological traits. Best candidate accounts of such cases are possible too. But it seems absurd that we should be able to say of one of the fission products, who is distinct from the original owner of the two hemispheres, what the best candidate account requires to be true: 'You should consider yourself lucky the transplant of the other hemisphere went so well, otherwise you wouldn't have existed'. However it may be with artefacts, we do not think our own existence logically dependent on such causally inefficacious events.

The fourth difference between the problem of personal identity and other familiar problems of identity is that what Olson (2001) calls the constitution view of persons (which is the view one must adopt if one regards persons as a distinctive sort of thing with distinctive persistence conditions) is more problematic than GC. As argued previously GC is very plausible; the argument for it requires only the apparently undeniable principle DTS and empirical propositions that seem certainly true. And the thought that a temporarily coincident statue and piece of clay, though distinct, temporarily share many properties, such as weight, size, shape and color, seems unproblematic. But the constitution view of persons is that in everyday life each person is composed at any time of the same matter as a body, or human being – an entity with purely biological persistence conditions distinct from those of the person – with which he is non-identical, but shares many properties, including psychological properties. The most recently discussed objection to this view is the 'too many thinkers' argument, which is briefly as follows.

It seems indisputable that human animals, i.e., human beings, or at least, all normal healthy adult human beings, are thinkers. But so, by definition, are persons. However, according to the constitution view of persons, persons are not human beings (they differ in their persistence conditions). So the constitution view entails the existence of too many thinkers. Moreover, it creates an irresoluble epistemic problem: how do I know that I am the person sitting here thinking truly that he is a person and not the coincident human animal thinking falsely that he is a person? Finally, if human animals, in addition to persons, are thinkers, they must be persons after all, because their thoughts have whatever complexity and sophistication any ordinary definition of 'person' could require – they have just the same thoughts, after all, as the persons with whom, on constitution view, they 'cohabit', so the position of the defender of the constitution view that there are distinctive persistence conditions for persons collapses into incoherence as he has to acknowledge different kinds of person with different persistence conditions – as it were person-persons and animal-persons.

One response to this argument is to deny that the animal is a thinker (Shoemaker, 2007). According to this response a property like thinking that it is about to rain is one only an entity with certain persistence conditions can possess, so despite the present and maybe extremely long-lasting coincidence of the animal and the person, they do not share their thoughts because the animal lacks the persistence conditions required of a thinker.

A second response is that of the philosopher whom Olson (2001) calls the first-person pronoun revisionist (this would have to be, in particular, the response of any four-dimensionalist). This philosopher says that the temporarily coincident person and animal are indeed two thinkers – the multiplicity is accepted – but that only the person thinks of himself in the first-person way. The animal has and expresses first-person thoughts, but these thoughts are not about him, but about the person with whom he coincides. Hence there is no epistemic worry because the question whether I am a person or an animal answers itself, and there is no worry that we must say that there are two persons present, as there is a difference between the person and the animal which justifies denying that the animal is a person, namely that it is not an object of first-person reference, a self.

The concern many have had is that this proposal creates a mystery. Given that the person and the animal are both thinkers and thinkers at the same level of sophisticated thought, how can it be that the animal is not thinking of itself in the first-person way if the person is? And how can it be that the animal is thinking of something other than itself in the first-person way if the person is not? How can two thinkers that are so alike differ in this way in their cognitive capacities?

The first-person pronoun revisionist's answer to this must be that the person and the animal do not differ in their cognitive capacities, they are we may say, cognitively identical. Each is thinking of exactly the things of which the other is thinking, in exactly the same way. So each is thinking of the person in the first-person way, and neither is thinking of the animal in the first-person way. It is because this is so that the animal is not, though the person is, thinking of himself in the first-person way. To the question 'Why is the animal not thinking of itself in the first-person way given that the coincident person is?' the answer is that this must be so given that that they are the same in this respect: namely, that each is thinking of the person in the first-person way and neither is thinking of the animal in the first-person way. So the question for the first-person pronoun revisionist is not how the animal and person can differ in their cognitive capacities, given their coincidence, but why, given their numerical distinctness, they are cognitively identical. But the answer to this is twofold. First, numerically distinct things can have many (almost all) things in common. Secondly, from the materialist viewpoint shared by the animalist and the defender of the constitution view of persons it is incomprehensible that things like the coincident person and animal, which are microphysically indistinguishable throughout the relevant period (differing only in irrelevant far off past or future respects), could be cognitively distinct, could be thinking about different things or thinking of them in different ways; the mystery would be if they did.

Whether either of these responses to the too-many-thinkers-objection to the constitution view is acceptable is hotly debated. It is at any rate obvious that the constitution view of persons is more problematic than GC, and is so in large part because persons are subjects of first-person thoughts.

7. Conclusion

We started this chapter with the following questions that each of us can pose to ourselves: What am I? And what is my relationship to the thing I call 'my body'? We have now surveyed the main answers that have been given to these questions in the philosophical literature. We noted that the answers one gives depends upon one's general account of personal and bodily identity over time, and gave a novel way of formulating such accounts in Section 2 that does not involve the language of identity. In Section 3 we then turned to the view that one material object can constitute a distinct but coincident material object, and discussed the arguments for and against this view. In Section 4 we outlined a number of positions that have been developed in light of perceived problems with this view, before considering, in Section 5, two further related problems that arise from the constitution literature, *viz.* the problem of permanent part sharing and the same kind coincidence problem. We rounded off the survey in Section 6 by returning explicitly to the problem of personal identity over time, noting four key differences between persons and other types of persisting things that suggest that the identity of persons over time cannot be treated in the same way as ordinary material objects. We have only been able to cover each of these topics briefly in this survey, and encourage interested readers to follow up on them by consulting the references given in the text and the bibliography below.

References

Baker, L. R. (2000). *Persons and bodies: A constitution view.* Cambridge, UK: Cambridge University Press. DOI: 10.1017/CBO9781139173124

Burke, M. B. (1994). Preserving the principle of one object to a place: A novel account of the relations among objects, sorts, sortals, and persistence conditions. *Philosophy and Phenomenological Research*, 54(3), 591–624. DOI: 10.2307/2108583

Chisholm, R. M. (1973). Parts as essential to their wholes. *Review of Metaphysics*, 26(4), 581–603.

Doepke, F. C. (1982). Spatially coinciding objects. *Ratio*, 24(1), 45–60.

Fine, K. (2008). Coincidence and form. *Proceedings of the Aristotelian Society Supplementary Volume*, 82(1), 101–118. DOI: 10.1111/j.1467-8349.2008.00164.x

Hawley, K. (2010). Temporal parts. In E. N. Zalta (Ed.), *The Stanford encyclopedia of philosophy (Winter 2010 Edition).* Retrieved from http://plato.stanford.edu/archives/win2010/entries/temporal-parts/

Johnston, M. (1992). Constitution is not identity. *Mind*, 101(401), 89–105. DOI: 10.1093/mind/101.401.89

Lewis, D. (1976). Survival and identity. In A. O. Rorty (Ed.), *The identities of persons* (pp. 17–40). Berkeley, CA: University of California Press.

Lewis, D. (1986). *On the plurality of worlds.* Oxford, UK: Blackwell Publishers.

Locke, J. (1700/1975). An essay concerning human understanding. In P. H. Nidditch (Ed.), *The Clarendon edition of the works of John Locke. An essay concerning human understanding.* Oxford, UK: Clarendon Press.

Lowe, E. J. (2002). Material coincidence and the cinematographic fallacy: A response to Olson. *Philosophical Quarterly*, 52(208), 369–372. DOI: 10.1111/1467-9213.00274

Mackie, P. (2008). Coincidence and identity. *Royal Institute of Philosophy Supplement*, 62, 151–176. DOI: 10.1017/S1358246108000623

Noonan, H. W. (1993). Constitution is identity. *Mind*, 102(405), 133–146. DOI: 10.1093/mind/102.405.133

Nozick, R. (1981). *Philosophical explanations.* Cambridge, MA: Harvard University Press.

Olson, E. T. (2001). Material coincidence and the indiscernibility problem. *Philosophical Quarterly*, 51(204), 337–355. DOI: 10.1111/1467-9213.00233

Parfit, D. (1971). Personal identity. *Philosophical Review*, 80(1), 3–27. DOI: 10.2307/2184309

Parfit, D. (1984). *Reasons and persons*. Oxford, UK: Oxford University Press.

Plantinga, A. (1975). On mereological essentialism. *Review of Metaphysics*, 28(3), 468–476.

Rea, M.C. (1997). Supervenience and co-location. *American Philosophical Quarterly*, 34(3), 367–375.

Rea, M.C. (2000). Constitution and kind membership. *Philosophical Studies*, 97(2), 169–193. DOI: 10.1023/A:1018311406047

Shoemaker, S. (1963). *Self-knowledge and self-identity*. Ithaca, NY: Cornell University Press.

Shoemaker, S. (1984). Personal identity: A materialist's account. In S. Shoemaker & R. Swinburne (Eds.), *Personal identity* (pp. 67–132). Oxford, UK: Blackwell.

Shoemaker, S. (2007). *Physical realization*. Oxford, UK: Oxford University Press. DOI: 10.1093/acprof:oso/9780199214396.001.0001

Sider, T. (1996). All the world's a stage. *Australasian Journal of Philosophy*, 74(3), 433–453. DOI: 10.1080/00048409612347421

Swinburne, R. (1984). Personal identity: The dualist theory. In S. Shoemaker & R. Swinburne (Eds.), *Personal identity* (pp. 3–66). Oxford, UK: Blackwell.

Swinburne, R.G. (1973–1974). Personal identity. *Proceedings of the Aristotelian Society*, 74, 231–247.

Thomson, J.J. (1983). Parthood and identity across time. *Journal of Philosophy*, 80(4), 201–220. DOI: 10.2307/2026004

Unger, P. (1980). The problem of the many. *Midwest Studies in Philosophy*, 5(1), 411–468. DOI: 10.1111/j.1475-4975.1980.tb00416.x

Wiggins, D. (1968). On being in the same place at the same time (with one remark about categories and materialism). *Philosophical Review*, 77(1), 90–95. DOI: 10.2307/2183184

Williams, B. (1970). The self and the future. *Philosophical Review*, 79(2), 161–180. DOI: 10.2307/2183946

Williams, B. (1973). *Problems of the self*. Cambridge, UK: Cambridge University Press. DOI: 10.1017/CBO9780511621253

Constitution, realization and identity

Empirical implications for three theories of the metaphysics of consciousness

Douglas Keaton
Flagler College, St Augustine

In this paper I will discuss the kinds of dependence relation that philosophers have suggested may obtain between neural events and conscious events; between Ns and Cs. The three candidate relations that I will spend the most time discussing are *constitution*, *realization*, and *identity*. There are other candidates for the mind/body relation, but these will serve as the major options. Indeed, these are already more than three options, because philosophers do not agree on the best way to understand constitution; still less to understand realization.

Introduction

I have two goals for the paper that follows. My first goal is to provide an introduction to some ideas in contemporary metaphysics of mind. I introduce the reader to some of the sorts of relationship that contemporary philosophers have suggested may obtain between brain and consciousness. Of particular interest is the way philosophers have shown that the expression "conscious states are brain states" under-specifies the relationship between conscious states and brain states. There is more than one way for one thing to "be" another thing. (There are, for example, the three ways listed in the title of this paper.) Thus people may agree in affirming that conscious states are brain states yet disagree, perhaps unknowingly, about which relationship is being affirmed. My second goal is to offer a way of understanding the metaphysical options that makes them particularly useful for the scientific study of consciousness. This second goal will involve some original philosophical work on my part – work with which other philosophers may disagree. But my work towards the first goal should be uncontroversial and merely expository.

I will proceed as follows. In Section 1 I will offer a brief introduction to the mind/body problem. In Section 2 I will introduce the general idea of "naturalistic" metaphysics – metaphysics that tries to take its cue from the sciences. I will also introduce

DOI 10.1075/aicr.92.16kea

the idea of an "explanatory necessitation relation", species of which are candidates for being the mind/body relation. Then in Section 3 I will provide a bestiary of explanatory necessitation relations; five in all. I will offer a brief description of each of the five, and then contrast them as a group with one further relation that I will call "brute necessitation". After that, I will devote the next three sections, 4–6, to discussing three of these explanatory necessitation relations in more detail: constitution, realization, and identity. I will explain how each of these relations works and why each is currently considered to be a good candidate for being the mind/body relation.

Then in Section 7 I will shift ground and offer some remarks that philosophers themselves might find useful, concerning recent scientific work on the search for "neural correlates of consciousness" or NCCs. I will discuss a quandary that has recently been recognized by neuroscientists regarding the empirical search for NCCs.

So far, everything has been introductory, though I will sprinkle some thoughts in Sections 4–6 that will be foreshadowings of original ideas concerning constitution, realization, and identity that I will present in Section 8. Finally, in Section 8, I will offer some original work. I will suggest a new way to think about the difference between the constitution, realization, and identity relations – a way that provides a framework for thinking about the scientific quandary presented in Section 7.

It is sometimes said that philosophical theories, especially theories in metaphysics, have no practical, scientific import. I don't personally believe that a metaphysical theory *must* have scientific import in order to be important and valuable; nonetheless I do think that current metaphysical accounts of the mind/body relation have more scientific import than even their own advocates sometimes claim.

Section 1

The mind/body problem may be put as a question, like so: *what is the relationship between minds and bodies?* This question, or puzzle, or mystery, has been around at least since Descartes. But the question has changed in subtle ways over the centuries. In the last few decades in particular, it is fair to say that the character of the mind/body question has changed considerably. Due to recent work by scientists and philosophers we have become better – we think – at asking the question; and we have narrowed down the range of plausible answers.

When philosophers and neuroscientists ask about the relation between minds and bodies, the question is no longer usually intended, as Descartes intended it, to be about two wholly distinct entities – two wholly distinct, shall we say, *objects* – a material body and an immaterial mind. Rather, the question is much more likely to be intended as a question about the relationship between two different aspects of the same object – the brain. On the one hand there are states or processes of the brain of the sort studied by the neurosciences; and on the other hand there are *states of consciousness* that are also states of the brain, though states of a sort that seem to be wholly different than the sort studied by the neurosciences, at least at first glance. The contemporary form of the mind/body question asks, "What is the relationship between these apparently distinct aspects of the brain?"

Another difference: the old-fashioned, Cartesian version of the question concerns the relationship between two sorts of entities (minds, bodies) both of which *would have existed anyway*, even in the absence of a relation between them. The mental "substance" that is the Cartesian mind is not produced or created by the material "substance" that is the Cartesian body.[1] The Cartesian mind could (and after death possibly does) exist without the body. In contrast to this, the contemporary version of the mind/body problem assumes that neurological states of the brain *result in* the brain's states of consciousness. It is assumed that the states of consciousness enjoyed by the brain depend for their existence on the neurological states of the brain in a way that is not symmetric: the neurological states of the brain do not depend on the brain's states of consciousness for their existence.[2]

Thus, the contemporary version of the mind/body problem is not a whole lot like the Cartesian version, and so it is not obvious that we are stuck in "the terms in which Descartes set the debate" (Searle, 1992, p. 54) as philosophers occasionally say. There may be a deep sense in which we are stuck, but then again there seems to be a deep sense in which we are not.

What we are after, then, is the right kind of *explanatory necessitation relation* – a relationship that *explains* the fact that elements on one side of the relation (neural states or processes) *necessitate the existence of* elements on the other side of the relation (conscious states or processes). Constitution, realization, and identity are each species of explanatory necessitation relation. I will proceed from here by first discussing the idea of explanatory necessitation relations as part of a more general discussion of philosophical metaphysics; from there I will move on to a discussion of particular types.

Section 2

It is famously difficult to say exactly what "metaphysics" is. Aristotle did not use the word, but dubbed the same general subject as the one that we now call "metaphysics", "first philosophy". A standard definition of metaphysics is "the study of being as such". Jaegwon Kim and Ernst Sosa open a recent anthology of readings in metaphysics like this: "Metaphysics is a philosophical inquiry into the most basic and general features of reality and our place in it" (Kim & Sosa, 1999, p. ix). Kim and Sosa's definition will do nicely for our purposes.

1. Indeed, the traditional definition of "substance" is "entity which depends on no other entity for its existence."

2. One qualification: *identity* is a symmetric dependence relation; so if it turns out that conscious states are strictly identical to neural states, then each will equivalently depend on the other. Still, there is a useful sense in which the neural description of such states might be explanatorily prior to (more explanatorily important than) the conscious description of such states.

The idea of *generality* is important, here. When we try to conduct metaphysical inquiry in a way that is in line with scientific inquiry – when we try, in other words, to do "naturalistic" metaphysics – we are thinking of metaphysics simply as the most general possible study of the categories of entity that the sciences employ in their investigations.[3] Thus if the sciences study "events" of now a biological, now a chemical, now a physical sort, then a metaphysician will ask, in the most general possible way, what an *event* is. If a sociologist or biologist says that had the population distribution in a given environment been different, then birth rates would have been different, a metaphysician will ask, in the most general sense, what a *non-actual but possible state-of-affairs* is. What are the identity conditions of events, of states-of-affairs? What are things that could have been but aren't? What are the constituents of each of these things? If the sciences study the properties of objects of various sorts (neurology: axons; geology: tectonic plates) a metaphysician will ask what "objects" are, and what, "properties".

Thus, if an image is wanted, we may think of the sciences as forming a ladder with the most general science, physics, at the bottom. On the rung just above physics is chemistry, and then above that biology, followed by neurology and finally, perhaps, psychology and then sociology. (Obviously this image is not perfect – is meteorology above or below geology, on this sort of ladder? – but the image will serve our current expository purpose.) We can think of the phenomena studied by a science on a given rung as forming a special class of the phenomena studied by the science on the next rung down. Neurological phenomena are a special class of biological phenomena, which are in turn a special class of chemical phenomena. All phenomena in the natural world are ultimately physical phenomena.[4]

The idea would then be that metaphysics is on the lowest rung of all, studying the most general phenomena of all, or studying phenomena in the most general way.

Now, one of the general types of thing that metaphysicians concern themselves with is *relationships*. If the sciences say, or if common sense says, that sometimes smaller things *compose* bigger things, then what is the relation of composition? Under what circumstances does it obtain? If sometimes we find out through inquiry that two apparently different things (the Morning Star, the Evening Star) are in reality the same thing (Venus), then what can we say about this relationship of identity, of *being the same thing as*?

One thing that we can say of these sorts of relationship is that once we discover that they obtain between things in the world, we have learned something new about the world, something we didn't know before. And further, this knowledge adds some explanatory structure to our picture of the world. Identity has a different structure than composition. These relations are different in their explanatory import in part because they are structurally distinct.

3. For good introductions to naturalism in philosophy see Maddy (2001) and Kitcher (1992).

4. Of course, this image suggests a very reductive view of the subject matter of each of the non-physical sciences. I am not sure that such a reductive view is correct, but for the purposes of the image I suppose it is fine.

In the next section, I will introduce the bestiary of relations that I mentioned in the Introduction: five sorts of explanatory necessitation relation that metaphysicians have investigated over the years. We will see that three of the five have seemed to philosophers to be especially good candidates for being the relationship between minds and bodies.

Section 3

Here is a baseball. And here, in the same place, is collection of quite a lot of atoms of such and such a sort, arranged just so. If a friend asks us "Why is it the case that whenever there is collection of quite a lot of atoms of such and such a sort, arranged just so, there is also, in the same place, a baseball?" We answer, "Because the atoms, arranged just so, *compose* the baseball."[5]

Composition is an example of an explanatory necessitation relation. Given that this collection of atoms, arranged just so, is present, it is *necessary* that this (or, perhaps, *a*) baseball be present. There is just no way to have the atoms here, arranged like this, and *not* have a baseball.[6] Thus, once we invoke the composition relation, there is no mystery left as to why baseballs occur wherever collections of atoms of this sort occur. Composition is *explanatory* not (only) in the psychological sense that invoking it produces an "aha" moment for our friend, but (also) in the sense that the presence of the composition relation genuinely accounts for the necessitation of the baseball by the atoms.[7]

We should note several things about the composition relation. First, in order for parts to compose a whole in this strict sense of "composition" it is necessary that the parts remain objects in their own right. It is not the case that eggs can "compose" or be "parts of" a cake in the relevant sense of "composition" because the eggs are destroyed in the process of making the cake. Second, composition is paradigmatically

5. In this section I follow Bennett's (2011) catalog of relations though with modifications. Bennett catalogs what she calls "building relations." I am interested in "necessitation relations," a broader category since it includes the relation of identity.

6. Note that I waffled between saying, on the one hand, that whenever we have these specific atoms arranged just so we get *this* baseball, and saying, on the other hand, that whenever we have these specific atoms arranged just so we get *a* baseball, not necessarily the same one. Metaphysicians worry about cases such as the following: if we take apart the baseball and then resemble the parts, perhaps years later, is the result the same baseball as the original? This may seem a medieval, monkish worry, but it is tied to more interesting questions of what it means to *be the same thing as* and thus, nearby: what it means for a thing to exist, at all.

7. I am here skipping lightly past an entire subfield of philosophy that studies the nature of explanation, especially scientific explanation. For a good first read on the general topic I recommend Salmon (1989).

a relationship between *objects*, and not between, say, properties or events. Certainly, one may speak of events as having parts: the Battle of the Bulge was part of WWI. And metaphysicians do speak of events, properties and processes as admitting of composition (Varzi, 2011). Nonetheless this sort of thing gets messy in a hurry; and it is not clear just when it is appropriate to say that an event or property is even a candidate for composition. (How many parts did your dream have last night? And, importantly, which came first, the dream or its parts? If the dream is "prior to" its parts then the parts do not compose the dream.) Thus it is common to restrict the discussion of composition to objects.

Recall from Section 1 that although Descartes thought of the mind/body relation as a relation between objects, a brain and a mind, contemporary theorists take the mind/body relation to be a relation between, on the one hand, neurological states or processes of the brain and, on the other hand, states of consciousness or conscious events (such as dreams). Because composition is hard to apply to things like states and events, there is no currently popular theory of the mind/body relation according to which the mind/body relation is composition – so far as I know, no current metaphysicians of mind thinks that an experience of, say, *itch* is literally composed of parts of the brain. (Unless, that is, the experience of itch is *identical to* some brain structure that is in turn composed of parts of the brain; but in that case the key mind/body relation is identity, not composition.) Now we move on to the next relation: determination.

Determination. This is an explanatory necessitation relation that may obtain between two properties of the same object. Determination holds when one of an object's properties is a *determinate* of the other. For example, given that this cube is crimson, it is *necessary* that this cube be red. The cube's crimsonness necessitates its redness. "Red" names a determinable property, and "crimson" names one of red's determinates. Further, given that this cube is red, it is *necessary* that this cube be colored. "Colored" names a determinable property, and "red" names one of its determinates. (Thus we see that "determinate" and "determinable" are relative terms. A property may be a determinate with respect to one property and a determinable with respect to another.) The determination relation (or at least the word we now use for it) was introduced in 1921 by the Cambridge logician W. E. Johnson.

It is possible to hold that the mind/body relation is the determination relation. Stephen Yablo (1992) has famously argued that mental properties are determinables that have neurological properties as determinates. The idea would be something like this: *red* is to *crimson* and *triangular* is to *isosceles* just as *having the experience of a face* is to *having activity in the fusiform gyrus*. One very nice feature of this line of thought is that it allows for different neural (or even completely alien) brain states to necessitate the same conscious state, just as different shades of red necessitate the presence of red. But Eric Funkhouser has recently argued, pretty convincingly, that neural and phenomenal properties just aren't good candidates for being relata of the determination relation (Funkhouser, 2006).

Identity. Identity is the relationship that everything bears to itself and to nothing else. This brief definition of "identity" is not rigorous as it presupposes the notion of identity that it purports to define ("itself"). Nonetheless it gets the intuitive idea across. The Morning Star is identical to the Evening Star. Samuel Clemens is identical to Mark Twain. Lighting is identical to electrical discharges in the atmosphere. Some philosophers think that sensations and other mental states are identical to brain processes.[8] This view has been, perhaps surprisingly, out of fashion since its initial popularity in the 1950s. But in recent years the Identity Theory (as it's called) has made something of a comeback (Jackson, 2012; McLaughlin, 2010; Polger, 2004). In Section 4 I will discuss the identity relation as a solution to the mind/body problem. Here I will briefly describe philosophical views concerning the relation of identity itself.

Leibniz's Law tells us that when two objects are identical they have exactly the same properties. (This raises a puzzle about co-located objects such as statues and hunks of granite, to which the constitution relation is supposed to be a solution; see below.) More controversial than Leibniz's law is the converse of Leibniz's Law: the claim that if two objects have all the same properties then the objects must be identical. At first this sounds wrong: surely two electrons are exactly alike, but are not the same thing. However, if we allow that an electron's *location* is one of its properties, and insist that no two electrons can be in the same place, then the converse of Liebniz's Law is more plausible. The question is whether we should allow features such as "location" to count as properties of objects.

Some philosophers believe in "relative identity". Philosophers who believe in relative identity are moved by the idea that it is possible to have two objects x and y such that they are "the same thing" in some ways but not others. Thus two different locomotives and their passenger cars can "be the same train" if they take the same route on different days. Some philosophers think that no rigorous sense can be made of the idea of relative identity.[9]

Some philosophers think that identity is contingent, some think it is necessary. Philosophers who think that identity is necessary think, for example, that when it turns out to be true that water is identical to H_2O then it also turns out to be true that water *could not have been* anything else. Some philosophers disagree. (This gets more interesting when the issue is consciousness. If scientists (somehow) discover that the experience of *itch* is identical to (not merely correlated with) a specific sort of neural activity, will they thereby have discovered that the experience of *itch* could not have been anything else?)

Sticking with the water/H_2O example, the issue is partly how we are to understand the term "water". Does the term "water" refer to the actual chemical stuff in our lakes and streams, whether we actually know what that stuff is, or not; or does the term refer to "the watery stuff in our lakes and streams" full stop – i.e., *no matter what that* turns out to be? On the latter option, note, water does not have to be H_2O. If the watery stuff

8. The key paper is Smart (1959).

9. For a primer on relative identity, see Deutsch (2008).

on an alien planet is XYZ rather than H_2O, then on that alien planet "water" refers to XYZ and not H_2O (Putnam, 1973). On the former understanding, there is nothing on the alien planet to which "water" refers – the stuff on the alien planet is simply not water. This has obvious implications for the meaning of terms such as "consciousness" and claims such as "consciousness is brain activity".[10]

For the purposes of this paper all we need is the easiest, most intuitive idea of identity. Everything is identical to itself and to nothing else. Identity may obtain between properties, objects, events, and states.

Constitution. Constitution is the relationship between, for example, a *hunk of granite* on a pedestal in a museum and the *statue* on that same pedestal. The hunk of granite *constitutes* the statue. Like composition, constitution is paradigmatically a relationship between *objects*, though one may speak of the constitution of one event by another and of one property by another.

When it comes to objects, the primary research problem for metaphysicians who work on the relation of constitution is this: when one object constitutes another object, are the two objects the same, or not? For example when a lump of clay constitutes a statue is the statue the same thing as the lump of clay? Most philosophers who work on this problem would say that they are not the same thing; in such a situation the lump and the statue are "coincident objects". They are two distinct objects that occupy the same physical space at the same time (Baker, 1997; Bennett, 2004; Fine, 2008). Philosophers tend to adopt this initially counter-intuitive view because they are convinced by a pretty straightforward argument: the lump of clay and the statue have different properties, and so by Leibnitz's Law they can't be the same thing. The easiest properties to point to in which the lump and the statue differ are *modal properties*, properties that ground counterfactual facts about the two objects.

To wit: if we were to squash this statue-shaped lump of clay, the lump of clay would survive, but the statue would be destroyed. The lump and the statue thus differ in certain characteristics (they differ in *persistence conditions*) and so they can't be the same thing.

A currently standard treatment of constitution is provided by Lynn Rudder Baker. We will look more closely at her view in Section 6, but for now we can say this: on Baker's account, whether one object constitutes another depends crucially on facts about the surrounding environment. For example, in order for a lump of clay to constitute a statue there must be a surrounding art community that regards the lump of clay *as* a statue. So we have two key ideas when it comes to constitution: the idea of modal properties such as persistence conditions, and the idea of features of the surrounding environment. Given that both of these are working properly, there will be a sense of "is" in which the lump of clay "is" a statue, even though it is not necessarily the case

10. For the classic argument that consciousness cannot be identical to brain processes for reasons having to do with the metaphysics of reference, see Kripke (1980). For a classic rejoinder see Levine (1983).

that the lump of clay is identical to the statue. We call the "is" that obtains between them "the 'is' of constitution".[11]

Realization. "Realization is… well, it's hard to say exactly what realization is", writes Karen Bennett in the midst of providing a catalog of relations similar to the one that I am providing here (Bennett, 2011, p. 82). I agree with Bennett that realization is hard to pin down, and I add that the lack of agreement about realization goes a long way towards explaining why current philosophy of mind is "a mess" (Polger, 2004, p. 71). Because the most popular current solution to the mind/body problem is to say that mental states are *realized* by neural states, and as there is so little agreement about what, exactly, *that* means, we are left with a puzzling and somewhat embarrassing quandary: what is the most popular current philosophers' solution to the mind/body problem supposed to be, again?

On the usual understanding, realization is a relationship between two properties of the same system or object. (In this respect realization is similar to determination.) The most common version of realization is called the "causal role-playing" version of realization. According to it, to say that property x of some system "realizes" a property y of that system is to say property x "plays the causal role" that is definitive of instances of property y. We will see more about what this means in Section 5.

One thing that we can say about the realization relation up front is that it is the *newest* of the explanatory necessitation relations. Realization was invented (or, if you prefer, discovered) by Hilary Putnam at Harvard in the 1960s.[12] We can also say what Putnam thought that realization was. Putnam thought of realization as, roughly, the relation that holds between a computer that is running a computer program and the program that the computer is running. So, originally, realization was something like *implementation*. Putnam held that certain kinds of objects (computers and brains, for example) implement the states of specifiable *machine tables* – abstract programs that describe the operations of Turing Machines.

To put it simply, Putnam's idea was that the states of a brain, or a computer – considered in abstraction from physical details – could be described as carrying out, step-wise, the state transitions described by a computer program. Thus the brain or computer implements or *realizes* the program. If the program that a brain implements is the program that describes the patterns of rational thought (at the time Putnam assumed that there could be such a program), then the brain that implements the machine table realizes rational thought (Putnam, 1967a, 1967b).

11. For a statement of the view that constitution is not identity, see Baker (1997). For a rundown of reasons to think that constitution is identity (that is: arguments against the idea of coincident objects), see Wasserman (2014).

12. At least that is the usual thing to say. One can find earlier references to "realization" as a key relation in naturalistic metaphysics, for example in Nagel (1954). This still makes realization the most recent of these relations, though.

Putnam's specific version of realization, "machine table functionalism", didn't last very long; and it is not clear that many people ever actually held it.[13] Machine table functionalism serves very well, though, as a way of introducing the general idea of the realization of mental states because machine table functionalism clearly relates one of the initially attractive ideas about functionalism. Functionalism provides a metaphysical framework for mental states that allows computers to be genuinely intelligent, perhaps even conscious. Thus functionalism is the metaphysical framework that undergirds enthusiasm for the possibility of genuine artificial intelligence.[14]

Additionally, realization and functionalism provide a way of saying that consciousness can be "multiply realized" – that is, realized in alien biology as well as our own. (This is another way that realization is similar to determination.) All that is needed is that the different biological systems be "doing the same thing" at an appropriately abstract level. Philosophers who find plausible the idea that we could meet alien creatures with similar minds to our own but quite dissimilar brains thus often find the realizationist solution to the mind/body problem attractive.

Finally, as functionalism provides a justification for the study of mind in abstraction from the brain, functionalism is used as a metaphysical justification for some projects in cognitive science.[15]

The general idea of realization survived the waning of Putnam's specific version of it. In the 1980s Ned Block showed how a version of functionalism could be formulated that did not use Putnam's machine tables but instead used David Lewis's separately-arrived-at principles for defining theoretical terms (Block, 1980; Lewis, 1983, 1999). We will see how this works in more detail in Section 5, but the basic idea is that Lewis showed how to use *patterns of causal interactions* to define theoretical terms (basically, the terms of a theory that refer to unobservables), and to define all of these theoretical terms at the same time.[16] Once this was done, a physical system that satisfied the conditions of a theory could be said to have states that were referred to by the terms of that theory – in such a case the physical system was said to *realize* the theory. Lewis's account of scientific theories morphed into the more metaphysical

13. Machine table functionalism was criticized effectively early on by Block and Fodor (1972).

14. At least this is how philosophers who were fond of functionalism conceived things for a long time. But according to recent historical work by Gualtiero Piccinini (2004, 2010) those philosophers were conflating two distinct ideas, (i) the functionalist thesis that mental states are functional states, and (ii) the thesis that the laws of psychology are computational in nature. While these theses can be held simultaneously, they need not be.

15. An excellent example of functionalist philosophers offering succor to cognitive scientists who think that the details of neuroscience are not critical to cognition is Ross and Spurrett (2004).

16. For the sake of exactness I should state that Lewis denied that theoretical terms referred to unobservables, necessarily. By "theoretical term" he simply meant a term that appears in a theory and that receives its definition from the theory itself.

idea that the theoretically posited states of a system were themselves *realized* by the physical states of the system. Thus states of consciousness could be realized by the causally interacting states of a brain that, in sum, satisfied the appropriate theory – say, a psychological theory.

Is it fair to say that realized psychological states *just are* the neural states that realize them? In the case of consciousness, is it fair to say that states of phenomenal consciousness *just are* the states of neural systems that realize them? The answer to this question depends upon one's view of the metaphysics of the realization relation. Currently, most philosophers who study realization would say that the realizer and realized states are not quite the same thing, thus providing a "non-reductive" account of mental states (cf. Antony & Levine, 1997; Fodor, 1997). However, there are some philosophers who hold a "reductive" view of realization – holding that realized states are strictly identical to their realizers (Jackson, 2012; Kim, 1998).

Before wrapping up this first look at realization, it should be noted that completely other versions of realization are currently on offer. According to one, due to Sydney Shoemaker, to say that property x of a system "realizes" property y of that system is to say that the causal potential that a system has due to its possession of y is a subset of the causal potential that it has due to its possession of x (Shoemaker, 2001). According to another take on realization, due to Carl Gillett (2002), the properties of the *parts* of a system may realize properties of the system as a whole. These versions of realization are important, but I will not consider them further, here.

Brute Necessitation. Finally, taking in all of the relations that we have looked at so far, allow me to contrast them as a group with "Brute Necessitation". Doing this will help us to see what it means to say that the previous five relations are "explanatory". If one object, state, event, property, or process x *brutely necessitates* another, y, then it is simply a *brute fact about reality* that whenever an object, etc., of the x-type occurs, then an object, etc., of the y-type occurs. There is nothing further to be said about *why it is* that the xs create or generate or result in the ys. They just do.

Composition, determination, identity, constitution, and realization are each perfectly good answers to the question "*Why* does that x, or those xs necessitate that y?" Thus they are explanatory, not brute, necessitation relations.

Now that I have given this bestiary of metaphysical relations a first pass, let us take up the three contenders for the mind/body relation again, a bit more slowly. In Section 4 we will look at the Identity Theory, which holds that states of phenomenal consciousness are identical to the brain processes with which they correlate. Then, in Section 5, we will look at functionalism, which holds that states of phenomenal consciousness are realized by their neural correlates. Finally in Section 6 we will look at the view that states of phenomenal consciousness are constituted by their neural correlates.

Section 4

The metaphysical thesis that episodes of phenomenal consciousness are strictly identical to occurrences of neural processes gained prominence in the 1950s, due to papers by U.T. Place (1956), J.J.C. Smart (1959), and Herbert Feigl (1958).

A couple of things should be noted about the Identity Theory at once. First, however it fared in the remainder of the twentieth century, the Identity Theory was undeniably central to the renewal of the idea that philosophers had to take consciousness seriously. In the decades just prior to the advent of the Identity Theory, philosophers did not take consciousness seriously; they were much more likely to want to analyze ordinary talk of "consciousness" as not being talk about a real thing in the world at all, but rather as talk concerning dispositions to behave, or as sophisticated interjections (to say "I feel pain" is not to refer to an interior experience but just to *yelp* in a complicated way – to replace primitive pain behavior with a complex verbal expression). These behaviorist/emotivist views were motivated in part by a desire to tell a story about the world using only scientifically respectable elements – a stricture which ruled out, it was thought, consciousness, especially phenomenal consciousness.[17] But for the identity theorists of the 1950s this rejection of consciousness would not quite do. J.J.C. Smart wrote in his 1959 "Sensations and brain processes":

> Though… I am very receptive to the above "expressive" account of sensation statements, I do not feel that it will quite do the trick. Maybe this is because I have not thought it out sufficiently, but it does seem to me as though, when a person says "I have an after-image," he *is* making a genuine report, and that when he says "I have a pain," he *is* doing more than "replace pain behavior," and that "this more" is not just to say that he is in distress. I am not so sure, however, that to admit this is to admit that there are nonphysical correlates of brain processes.
>
> (Smart, 2002, pp. 61–62, italics in original)

Thus the identity theorists thought that it was philosophically inadequate to dismiss consciousness. Consciousness, they thought, is a real thing; so a place must be found for it in the natural world. The most likely solution, if we wish to avoid adding spooky non-material stuff to our picture of the world, was to identify conscious episodes – paradigmatically, sensations – with brain processes. Sensations, in order to exist, need not be "nonphysical correlates of brain processes", they could, instead, be the brain processes themselves. To repeat, whatever happened to this idea over the course of the second half of the twentieth century, it was a very welcome return to seriousness about consciousness.

17. "Phenomenal consciousness" refers to the experiential aspects of consciousness. The subjective sound of a clarinet, the taste of wine, the experience of color one gets when looking at the stars in a Van Gogh painting, are each examples of phenomenal consciousness.

The second thing that I want to note about The Identity Theory up front is that the Identity Theory as put forward by Smart, Place, and Feigl was (what is called) a "type identity" theory. To explain what this means, consider an episode of phenomenal consciousness. For example, consider the conscious experience you might have upon seeing a (specific) friend's face in good light, straight on, from a distance of ten feet. Now consider this experience as of a *type* that may recur at different times (you see your friend now in the coffee shop, now in the park). The idea is that this experience *type* is identical to a single *type* of neurological event (or property or process).

So the idea fronted by the Identity Theory is not *merely* that each time you have a conscious experience of your friend's face that the experience is identical to some simultaneously occurring brain process or other (on Tuesday one sort of brain process, on Thursday of another sort of brain process). The idea is rather that there is a single type of brain process (and it's the same for all humans) that always and only occurs when the friend-face experience occurs. Thus there could not be a given sensation type, particular instances of which are identical to more than one type of neural episode. Nor could there be a given type of neural episode, particular instances of which are identical to different types of conscious experience. This turned out to be the Achilles Heel of the Identity Theory, once Putnam (1967b) argued that it had the implausible consequence that creatures with very different kinds of brain structures than we could not have the same kind of conscious experience as we.

Now that we have an idea of what the Identity Theory says, we should observe how its originators regarded it. Place (1956) regarded the Identity Theory as an empirical hypothesis; Smart (1959) did not. Smart thought of the Identity Theory as a purely philosophical theory with no empirical significance. In each case, what is of interest are the theories that each philosopher *contrasted* with the Identity Theory.

Smart, who did not think that the Identity Theory had empirical import, contrasted the Identity Theory (which he sometimes simply called "materialism") with a competing philosophical thesis called "epiphenomenalism". Epiphenomenalism is the thesis that sensations are immaterial entities produced (somehow) by the brain, but which, having been produced, have no influence on the goings-on of the brain. According to epiphenomenalism, then, consciousness is real, immaterial, and causally impotent. Smart's idea was that no empirical test could rule out epiphenomenalism.

In the following passage, Smart writes about the lack of empirical import of Identity Theory. He contrasts his view with Place's:

> U.T. Place seems to hold that [the Identity Theory] is a straight-out scientific hypothesis. If so, he is partly right and partly wrong. If the issue is between (say) a brain process thesis and a heart thesis, or a liver thesis, or a kidney thesis, then the issue is a purely empirical one, and the verdict is overwhelmingly in favor of the brain… On the other hand, if the issue is between a brain-or-heart-or-kidney theses (that is, some form of materialism) on the one hand and epiphenomenalism on the other hand, then the issue is not an empirical one. For there is no conceivable experiment which could decide between materialism and epiphenomenalism. (Smart, 2002, pp. 66–67)

Thus, Smart accepts the Identity Theory on grounds of ontological simplicity, and *not* for empirical reasons. The Identity Theory simply populates the world with fewer entities than does epiphenomenalism.

As a rejoinder, Place (1960) wrote that the Identity Theory is indeed a falsifiable empirical hypothesis. The hypothesis is that neural events could be found, the description of which would *logically entail* that sensations would be enjoyed by the subject. If no neural events could be found which satisfy this requirement, then the Identity Theory would be falsified. Thus Place thought that the Identity Theory had a very strong requirement: that the correct description of the relevant neural structures would simply *imply* the presence of consciousness. If a creature lacks structures the correct description of which implies consciousness, then the creature lacks consciousness. This certainly seems to be an empirical bet: the bet is that humans, who are undeniably conscious, will turn out to have brain structures with descriptions that imply consciousness. Place would lose the bet if, for example, Cartesian dualism were true.

The disagreement between Place and Smart about the nature of the Identity Theory is of great interest. For now the key point, though, is the *agreement* between them. Smart and Place thought of the Identity Theory as contrasting with dualist theories of one sort or another – that is, with theories of mind that deny that "sensations are brain processes". But this is not the way we would set up the contrast classes today.

Today we would say that the Identity Theory contrasts with *other materialistic theories*, including the theory that conscious episodes stand in the realization relation to their neural correlates and the theory that conscious episodes stand in the constitution relation to their neural correlates.[18] None of these views are examples of either epiphenomenalism or Cartesian dualism and for each materialist approach it is fair enough (or very nearly fair enough) for its advocates to say "sensations are brain processes". Thus the Identity Theory is currently in competition with other theories of mind all of which claim the right to say that "sensations 'are' (perhaps 'more or less are') brain processes".

It is interesting to note how this shift in contrast classes has affected what philosophers think is distinctive and important about the Identity Theory itself. Back in the 1950s it would not have been necessary to emphasize the "type" aspect of the Identity Theory in order to contrast the Identity Theory with its opponents. And indeed Smart and Place did not seem much concerned to emphasize the type claim in their early papers. It was enough for an identity theorist to say that each conscious episode is (1) a real thing and (2) identical to a brain process. The identity theorist did not need to add that the *type* of conscious experience to which a specific conscious experience belongs is strictly identical to a *type* of neural episode, so that species of creature incapable of a given type of neural episode simply could not have a given type of conscious

18. Thus in a recent retrospective on the anniversary of the publication of Smart's (1959) paper, Polger (2011), a current-day identity theorist, contrasts the Identity Theory with functionalism, in addition to the older-fashioned views that Smart and Place mentioned.

experience. *That* would be a claim considerably stronger than needed, just to get away from dualism and behaviorism.

On the other hand, in order to contrast the Identity Theory with current-day ideas, especially functionalism, the identity theorist *does* need to emphasize the "type" aspect of the Identity Theory. This is because certain versions of the functionalist theory affirm that specific conscious episodes are identical to specific neural events, even as they deny that any *type* of conscious episode could be identified with a *type* of neural event.

This, note, makes the choice between the Identity Theory and functionalism (between the relations of identity and realization) empirically testable. If we found that subjects had the same type of conscious experiences when different types of neural events occurred, the Identity Theory as currently construed would be falsified. This much is well-known.

But the suggested test would not decide between realization and constitution. In Section 8 I will argue that there is another way to empirically contrast the Identity Theory with functionalism, and both with the constitution thesis. But for now let us examine functionalism more closely, the view that episodes of phenomenal consciousness stand in the realization relation to their neural correlates.

Section 5

Suppose we operationalize the notion of "pain" like this:

> *Pain* is the property P such that whenever any entity that is awake suffers tissue damage the entity acquires P; the entity's having of P tends to cause the entity both to wince and to form the belief that it has property P. If the entity has three beliefs: (1) the belief that it has P, (2) the belief that aspirin will cause it to cease having P, and (3) the belief that aspirin is in the medicine cabinet, these three factors will cause the entity to go to the medicine cabinet.

Of course, this is not a good operationalization of the notion of pain because it's incomplete, to put it mildly. Also, it gets at one unobservable, *pain*, via other unobservables, such as *the belief that one is in pain*. But we get the general idea: "pain" is to be defined in terms of causes and effects. In philosophy this is called a "functional" definition of "pain".

In order to completely fill in the functional picture, here, we would need to provide functional definitions for each of the mental terms used in the functional definition of "pain". Then if those definitions appealed to other mental terms, those tertiary mental terms would need to be given functional definitions. This would continue until we had a complete functional psychological story that used only terms that referred to observables – inputs and outputs for the whole psychological system. The full story would *define* every psychological term at once via those inputs and outputs. Functionalism defines psychological states "from the outside in" as it were.

Let us suppose that we have done all of this and provided a complete functional account of human psychology. The idea, then, would be to have a look at the human brain and see which neural states of the brain actually satisfy the account. In the case of the term "pain", we would look for the state or process in the brain that has the causes and effects that pain has in the functional psychological story. Let us call the neural state that satisfies this description, "*N*".

A few things should be noted about *N* and pain. First of all, "pain" is being defined entirely in terms of causes and effects; another way to say this is that "pain" is being given a functional definition or a "causal role definition". What *N* does is "play the causal role of pain" or "play the pain-role".

An analogy with baseball positions will help us get a grip on what is going on, here. Suppose Jorge Posada is on the New York Yankees baseball team. And suppose Posada satisfies this causal description: when the "pitcher" throws the ball towards home plate, and the "batter" fails to hit it, Posada catches the ball. If there is a "baserunner" on first base and Posada sees the "baserunner" start to go towards second base, this will cause Posada to throw the ball to the "second baseman". And so on.

Provided Posada plays this causally defined role then he is "playing the catcher role". But notice: *it is impossible successfully to occupy the catcher role unless other athletes are occupying the roles named by the terms in quotes in the above paragraph.* It is not just that the terms "second baseman", "baserunner", "pitcher" and so on are defined against each other; the roles being thus defined cannot be occupied unless they are all occupied. The overall "theory of baseball" must be satisfied in order for any part of it to be satisfied. In the case of the term "baserunner", of course there does not need at all times to be a baserunner on a base in order for Posada successfully to be playing the catcher role, but there must be potential baserunners – actual specifiable athletes who *would* occupy the baserunner role under appropriate conditions. You're not really playing catcher unless there is an opposing team.

Let's say that the baseball theory is satisfied, and that Posada successfully plays the catcher role. Is it is fair to say that Posada is identical to the catcher? Perhaps not quite; because strict identity is absolute, whereas Posada is identical to the catcher only *given that these facilitating role-theoretic conditions are in place.* Now, replace "Jorge Posada" with "*N*", "catcher" with "pain", and we get (with a little fudging, this is not a perfect analogy but it gets the main things right) a metaphysical story about the brain/mind relation. What functionalist philosophers say about the relationship between *N* and pain is this: *N* "realizes" pain. A functionalist philosopher of a certain reductive bent would say that *N* is identical to pain but would add that this identity is contingent *on the holding of facilitating facts about the rest of the brain.* Just as you can't really be the catcher on a baseball team unless someone is the left-fielder, so too a neural state or process can't really be pain in a human being unless some other neural state or process is, say, thirst. That doesn't mean that you can't be in pain unless you're thirsty. All that is needed is that there be some specifiable neural state or process that *would* occupy the thirst role should the appropriate causal conditions arise. Given that this (and a whole lot else) is true of the brain, then *N* when it occurs can be said to occupy the pain role and so to be pain.

At this point it is fair to ask how serious the functionalist philosopher is being. We have seen the claim that *N* is pain provided that a very big set of facilitating facts about the rest of the brain obtains. Some of these facts can be very distant from the *N*-facts, indeed – just as there can be baseball positions that have nothing much to do with the catcher but that nonetheless need to be filled in order for Posada to "be" the catcher. All that is needed in order for a brain-fact to count as a pain-facilitating fact is that it figure somewhere in the satisfaction of the complete psychological story or theory, which is no doubt enormous. But, again, how serious is the functionalist philosopher being? Is the claim that when a subject undergoes neural state *N* the subject *will only feel pain if the rest of the facilitating facts obtain*?

Well, yes. But some qualifications are in order. The issue is slightly tricky because functionalist philosophers do not use the idea of feeling, of phenomenal consciousness, to define "pain" in the first place. They use relational causal roles to define mental states, not intrinsic "feels". What functionalist philosophers are likely to say is that the feeling of pain itself can be exhaustively explained via a relational story involving the causal roles.

In Section 8 I will say something about what I think this means for the study of NCCs. For now I want to get to the third of the main candidates for the mind/body relation: constitution.

Section 6

Leaving questions about the mind aside for a moment, the relation of *constitution* was originally posited to resolve certain paradoxes, some as old as the debtor's paradox recounted by the ancient playwright Epicharmus. A lender asks a debtor for repayment, but the debtor claims he is not the man to whom the lender lent the money. After all, the matter that makes up a person is constantly changing, and because the debtor is not the same collection of matter as the collection of matter to which the lender lent the money, the debtor is therefore not the same man, and so it is inappropriate for the lender to ask for repayment from *him*. The lender then assaults the debtor and the debtor complains. But the lender says that he, the lender, cannot be blamed, because he is not the same man he was moments ago.

So the puzzle is this: how can two distinct aggregates of matter literally "be" the same person? Solution: two distinct aggregates may *constitute* the same person.

But under what conditions does one entity constitute another? Here I will adopt Baker's account wholesale. Baker uses the idea of a "primary kind property". We may think of these primary kind properties as properties that things essentially have as the kind of things that they are. Thus, Socrates' property *being a human* is his primary kind property – *human* is what Socrates most essentially is. A rock's primary kind property is, presumably, *being a rock*. And so on. Objects with certain sorts of primary kind properties are appropriate to constitute certain other objects with certain other primary kind properties. Thus objects that have the primary kind property *being a lump of clay* are of the right sort to constitute objects that have the primary kind property *being a statue*… but objects that have the primary kind property *being a bumble bee* presumably are not fit to constitute objects that have the primary kind property *being a statue*. Further, certain primary kind properties are such that objects with those primary kind properties *can only exist by being constituted*. Statues can only exist by being constituted, while lumps of clay exist because they are *composed*; they are not and cannot be *constituted* at all. With this notion of a primary kind property in hand, we may quote Baker:

> An informal idea of material constitution is this: Where *being an F* and *being a G* are distinct primary-kind properties, it is possible that an F exists without there being any spatially coincident G. However, if an F exists in G-favorable circumstances, then there is a new entity, a G, that is spatially coincident with the F but not identical to it. (Baker, 2000, p. 42, italics in original)

Let us return to the topic of consciousness. Suppose we want to say that a given brain system's activity constitutes an episode of phenomenal consciousness. The primary-kind property of the brain system and its activity would be a kind that is described in the language of the neurosciences – perhaps the combination of V1, the extrastriate cortex, and the fusiform gyrus form a system. The activity of this system has a primary kind property – let us call this property "*F*". Now let us suppose that coincident with this activity, the system is also the location of an episode of consciousness – the perception of a familiar face. This episode has the primary kind property of G. Perhaps F constitutes a G.

Notice what Baker (2000) says. She says if Fs constitute Gs then Fs *may* occur without Gs. If activity in the described system constitutes an episode of consciousness than it is possible for that activity to occur in the absence of any episode of consciousness. Part of the reason that the activity *in fact does* constitute an episode of consciousness has to do with the "G-favorable circumstances" in which the activity occurs. This idea of "favorable circumstances" is obviously similar to the idea of "facilitating facts" that I said earlier were essential to functionalism and the realization relation.

I'm going to argue that the difference between facilitating facts and favorable circumstances is the most important difference between realization and constitution. Indeed, the hypothesis that conscious states are realized can be empirically distinguished from the hypothesis that conscious states are constituted in just this way. If core correlates of consciousness require facilitating facts in order to "be conscious" then functionalism is true. If core correlates of consciousness require "favorable circumstances" in order to be conscious, then constitutionalism is true. If core correlates of consciousness don't require anything further at all in order to be conscious, then the identity theory is true. But I will say more about this in Section 8.

Section 7

In this section I want to leave metaphysical talk for a bit and introduce some ideas from recent work by neuroscientists who are engaged in the scientific study of consciousness. Then, in Section 8, I will show how I believe this recent scientific work may be aided by the philosophical ideas I have outlined in this paper.

Since the early 1990s there has been a resurgence in neuroscience in "the scientific study of consciousness", the attempt to locate the seat of consciousness in the brain. This resurgence was largely due to papers by Francis Crick and Christof Koch, in which they argued that the difficult metaphysical questions which seem to make the mind/body problem scientifically intractable could be, in fact, set aside in favor of more obviously empirical questions (Crick & Koch, 1990, 1995, 1998). The primary or at any rate initial *empirical* question, they said, was this: what exactly are the neural activities that correlate with episodes of phenomenal consciousness? Once we pin down these NCCs, we will be in much better shape to move forward in the scientific study of consciousness.

However, even this seemingly purely empirical question was in need of conceptual clarification. For suppose we have identified a sort of brain activity that always and only occurs in tandem with a specific sort of conscious episode. The neural activity would then be an NCC for the conscious episode, to be sure. But this neural activity may be *wide-ranging* and it may not be obvious just which of its aspects are really the aspects that "comprise" or "constitute" the episode of consciousness. (Here I use "constitute" in a non-metaphysically-loaded way, merely to gesture to the part in the NCC where "the rubber hits the road", where the consciousness actually happens.)

As an example of this kind of problem at work in the neuroscientific literature, let us have a quick look at the study of binocular rivalry. Binocular rivalry is a phenomenon in which a subject is presented with differing visual stimulation in each eye. For example, eyesight may be partitioned in such a way that a photograph of the face is presented to the left eye while a photograph of a house is presented to the right eye. In such a situation, the subject will not have a conscious visual experience that is some merging of the two images, face and house; rather, the subject's conscious experience will switch back and forth between being now of the house, now of the face, each switch lasting a few seconds (Miller, 2013; Rees, Kreiman, & Koch, 2002, p. 267).

When such studies are done it is found that in the initial areas of visual processing in the brain there is not much activity-switching that correlates with the switching between the conscious experiences. As one moves further "downstream" in the brain's visual processing, however, one finds that more and more neural activity becomes correlated with the switching of the conscious percepts. More specifically, not much correlation occurs in V1, while more correlation occurs in extrastriate areas and the most occurs at the highest levels of visual processing. This, however, creates a problem. There is after all *some* correlation in the early V1 area. Is the activity in V1 a *part* of where "the rubber hits the road" – a constitutive part of conscious experience itself – or is the V1 activity merely preparatory for genuinely constitutive activity further downstream?

This concern regarding which correlated neural activity truly constitutes (as opposed to merely covaries with) the visual states during binocular rivalry originates with Steven Miller (2001). For a sample of the complexity of the issues involved, consider this recent discussion by neuroscientist Frank Tong:

> The powerful effects of binocular rivalry found in V1 demonstrate that neurons can reflect visual awareness at a much earlier level of the visual pathway than previously thought (Crick and Koch, 1995). These results have one of two implications. One possibility is that some aspects of conscious vision begin to emerge at the earliest stage of cortical processing among monocular V1 neurons. Alternatively, these findings may suggest a new role for V1 as the "gatekeeper" of consciousness, a primary cortical region that can select which visual signals gain access to awareness. In either case, primary visual cortex appears to have an important role in binocular rivalry, and perhaps also in conscious vision.
>
> These findings contribute to an ongoing debate regarding the role of V1 in visual awareness (Tong, 2003). According to hierarchical models, V1 provides the necessary input to higher extrastriate areas that are crucial for awareness, but does not directly contribute to awareness per se (Crick and Koch, 1995; Rees, Kreiman, and Koch, 2002). By contrast, interactive models propose that V1 forms dynamic recurrent connections with high-level extrastriate areas, and these integrative loops are necessary for maintaining a representation in awareness (Lamme and Roelfsema, 2000; Pollen, 1999). There is evidence to support both views, although some recent studies suggest that disruption of V1 activity can impair awareness even when considerable extrastriate activity remains present (Goebel et al., 2001; Pascual-Leone and Walsh, 2001). The fMRI rivalry data further indicate that in the intact network, V1 activity can be tightly linked with visual awareness. Taken together, these findings raise the intriguing possibility that primary visual cortex may have an important and perhaps necessary (though not sufficient) role in conscious vision. (Tong, 2005, pp. 77–78)

Tong (2005) lays out two options: either (1) the activity in V1 "provides necessary input" to brain areas that are "crucial for awareness" though V1 does not "directly contribute to awareness per se" or (2) activity in V1 is "necessary (though not sufficient)" for conscious experience.

Tong seems to mean that the two options are these: (1) V1 activity is not partially or wholly constitutive of awareness but is nonetheless a necessary causal precursor to the downstream activity that does constitute awareness; or (2) V1 activity is actually occurrently "contributing" to conscious awareness – i.e., V1 activity is not upstream of the consciousness but rather is constitutive of consciousness. In (2) the V1 activity is not sufficient, to be sure, for a conscious percept, but it is *synchronically necessary* for such a percept.

Tong offers a useful distinction. However, so described, Tong's two options do not exhaust the possibilities. Tong writes that on the second option the V1 activity is "necessary for maintaining a representation in awareness". But this could mean two different things. It could mean that V1 activity is actually partially constitutive of consciousness or it could mean that V1 activity is a necessary real-time "companion" to the activity that actually is constitutive of consciousness.

I'm arguing that there are three, not two, possibilities here. Let's be sure we understand what they are. Suppose that a subject has a conscious experience at time *t*1. Suppose that N1 comprises all of the neural activity at time *t*1 that is necessary for this experience. But suppose that only some of the neural activity that makes up N1 is actually *constitutive* of the experience at *t*1. Call this constitutive activity "NC1" for "core" or "constitutive" neural activity at *t*1. And suppose that there is some necessary preparatory work done at time *t*0 (some arbitrary time before the conscious experience) by neural activity N0. Then the options for how to regard the activity in V1 are these:

Option 1 The V1 activity is part of N0.
Option 2 The V1 activity is part of N1 but not NC1.
Option 3 The V1 activity is part of NC1.

Let's be sure we understand one further thing. *All* of the N1 activity is necessary for the conscious experience. If the core activity, NC1, occurred at time *t*1 without the *remaining* N1 activity occurring at *t*1, there would be no conscious experience at *t*1 – at least no conscious experience of the same sort. This is true even though when all of N1 occurs it is only the part of N1 that we are calling "NC1" that is really constitutive of consciousness.

I take it that deciding between, on the one hand, Option 1, and on the other hand, Option 2 or Option 3, is a more obviously empirically tractable task then deciding between Option 2 or Option 3. And I take it that the more tractable task is what neuroscientist Daniel Pollen is discussing when he writes in a recent paper:

> There is currently an insurmountable gap between identifying the neural representations that correlate with perceptual experience and for accounting for such experience itself. If we want to narrow that gap, we may attempt to identify the minimal necessary requirements for perceptual experience because then we will have identified the minimal gap that needs to be closed. (Pollen, 2011, p. 1)

Once we can locate *and discard* the N0 activity we will have located the "minimal necessary requirements" and so we will have done much to locate the seat of consciousness. But a "minimal gap" will remain. This "minimal gap" will only be closed when we learn how to distinguish brain activity that is in N1 but not NC1 from activity that is actually in NC1. That is, the gap will only be closed once we learn how to locate the part of the minimally necessary NCC that is actually constitutive of consciousness. And this final puzzle, I take it, is what Miller considers the correlation/constitution distinction problem:

> A major concern for the scientific study of consciousness arises when considering the distinction between the neural *correlates* and the neural *constitution* of consciousness (10). This distinction presents a challenge for which, I argue, even an impression of a strategic solution is not apparent.
>
> (Miller, 2007, p. 161, italics in original)

In the final section of this paper I will take a stab at offering an impression of a strategic solution, one that uses a novel way of distinguishing between identity, realization, and constitution.

Section 8

For the final section of this paper it will be useful to have a diagram (and some new names) for elements of brain activity of the sort that I labeled in the previous section "N0", "N1", and "NC1".

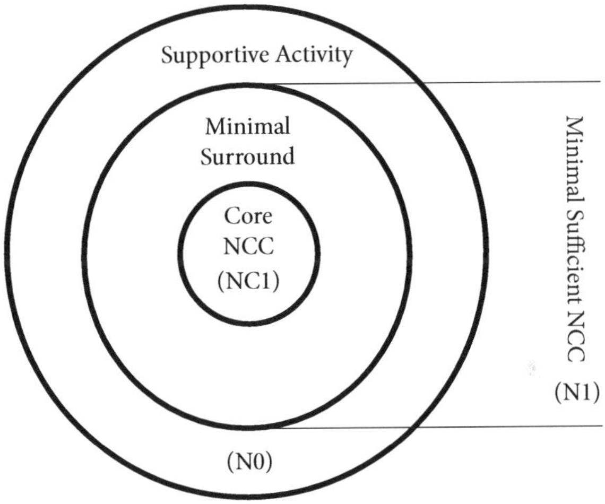

Figure 1. Core NCC, Minimal Sufficient NCC, and Supportive Activity. The Core NCC and the Minimal Surround combine to form the Minimal Sufficient NCC. The Minimal Surround is more than a mere biological support system for the Core. (Thus it is distinct from the Supporting Activity in the outer ring above.) Rather, the Minimal Surround is structurally (i.e., "metaphysically") necessary for the Core to constitute consciousness. Thus if any Minimal Surround exists then the Core is not strictly identical to the conscious episode that it alone constitutes. This makes the nature of the Minimal Surround – if there is such a thing – theoretically intriguing.

In this diagram the brain activity that is actually constitutive of consciousness is dubbed the "Core NCC". The brain activity (or brain facts more generally) that must hold in tandem with the activity of the Core NCC in order for the Core NCC to be conscious I call the "minimal surround".[19] The core NCC and the minimal surround together comprise what I call the "minimal sufficient NCC". As long as any entity anywhere has a minimal sufficient NCC for a conscious episode of type C, the entity will have a conscious episode of type C. It may be that the minimal sufficient NCC requires some external supportive activity in order (biologically, say) to persist. This external supportive activity I have labeled "supportive activity" in the diagram. I include it in the diagram just to set it aside: this external supportive activity is not metaphysically relevant to consciousness.

With Figure 1 in hand, I want to suggest that *a relevant difference between identity, realization, and constitution has to do with what each requires to be in the minimal surround.* Therefore, the three hypotheses that derive from positing each of these relations as the mind/body relation will make different predictions about what kinds of brain activity (or brain facts more generally) must be in the surround; must synchronically obtain *alongside the occurrence of the core activity* in order for the core activity to be conscious. The predictions that each theory makes drop out of our discussion of each relation itself, earlier in the paper. Let us go through each in turn, starting with realization, then constitution, and finally identity.

The hypothesis that *the realization relation* is the relationship between a core NCC and its correlated episode of conscious experience entails the prediction that *the minimal surround will include the obtaining of certain counterfactual facts about the brain.*[20] For example, suppose that a subject has a core NCC for the experience of hunger at time *t*1. The realization hypothesis entails that the subject will only have a conscious experience of hunger at *t*1 if it is true at *t*1 that *had the subject had* appropriate causes of, rather, anger at *t*1, the subject *would have had* a propensity for a specifiable NCC for anger at *t*1. *Had the subject undergone* some appropriate cause for a visual percept at *t*1 then the subject *would have had* a core NCC for the visual percept at *t*1. And so on, for (figuratively?) uncountably many non-actual but potential conscious experiences.

This requirement follows from the standard causal-role account of realization. On this account what is realized – hunger, a mental state – is itself defined in terms of a causal role. And the causal role only exists as embedded in a holistic theory. Just as a person on a baseball field cannot "be the catcher" unless a whole lot of actual and counterfactual information is true of at least 17 other human beings (one's teammates plus the other team), so a core NCC in the brain cannot be "an experience of hunger"

19. I adopt the terms "core" and "surround" from work on the nature of realization by Sydney Shoemaker (2003, 2007).

20. On this account, the hypothesis that the mind/body relation is realization would fit with Integrated Information Theory as discussed by Miller (this volume), whereby *inactive* neural elements are considered just as relevant to consciousness as active neural constituents.

unless a whole lot of actual and counterfactual information is true of other brain systems and patterns of activity.

Note that this entails that a core NCC can fail to *realize* a conscious experience if some theoretically very distant region of the brain is not working properly at the time the core NCC occurs. The malfunctioning brain area need not be an area that normally "lights up" in accompaniment with the core NCC in question; it just has to be an area that normally *would have lit up* in response to some stimulus that did not occur, but now, due to damage, *would not have* lit up even if the appropriate stimulus had occurred. Because of this counterfactual failure the correctly functioning core fails to realize a conscious experience.

One thing that this means is that if the realization hypothesis is correct it would be very problematic to test for a core NCC in a subject that has a lesion *anywhere* in the brain – at least, in any area that is implicated in any potential conscious experience whatever.[21]

The hypothesis that *the constitution relation* is the relationship between a core NCC and its correlated episode of conscious experience entails the prediction that *the minimal surround will include the obtaining of certain facts about the brain, but not counterfactual facts.* Just as a lump of clay cannot constitute a statue at time *t*1 unless there is a surrounding art community at time *t*1, so too a core NCC cannot constitute an episode of phenomenal consciousness at time *t*1 unless there is a surrounding neural system of the appropriate sort at time *t*1. This requirement, I believe, falls out of the discussion of the constitution relation in Section 6. If the constitution hypothesis is correct, then core NCC will have as a "primary kind property" a property that makes it a candidate core NCC for some sort of conscious experience. (The nature of this neural primary kind property would be described in the language of the neurosciences.) Then, provided that the core NCC occurs in "favorable circumstances" the core NCC will constitute a conscious experience of the relevant sort. Those "favorable circumstances" would comprise brain activity in what I am calling the minimal surround. I take it that it would be a matter of scientific investigation to determine what those "favorable circumstances" are, and how much variation they may tolerate.

Now, the constitution hypothesis *could* morph into the realization hypothesis. All that would be needed is for the "favorable circumstances" mentioned in the constitution hypothesis to look more and more like the theory satisfaction condition required by the realization hypothesis. In practice, I suggest, what the morph would require is for the favorable circumstances to include not just brain activity, but also specifiable potential but non-occurrent brain activity.

21. I believe that this is the reason Chalmers (2000) casts such a dim eye on the utility of lesion studies in the search for neural correlates of consciousness. Chalmers assumes the correctness of some sort of functionalist metaphysics (hence his appeal to "core" and "total" NCCs, borrowing functionalist terminology (p. 26). The disutility of lesion studies follows from the adoption of functionalism or quasi-functionalism.

Finally, the hypothesis that *the identity relation* is the relationship between a core NCC and its correlated episode of conscious experience entails the prediction that *the minimal surround will include nothing*. To put that another way, if the identity hypothesis is correct, then the core NCC for a given type of conscious experience is the same thing as the minimal sufficient NCC for that type of conscious experience.

There are two reasons to hold that the Identity Theory entails this claim. First, the Identity Theory seems to be committed to this claim inasmuch as it is a *type identity* theory. On the type identity theory, a given type of conscious episode, say of smelling an orange, just is *identical to* – is the same thing as – having an NCC of a certain type. To experience a specific orangey smell *just is* to have a neural state of such and such a type – and that type is singular, for all creatures everywhere in the universe. This universal NCC is the core NCC of the conscious experience… and this universal NCC is also entirely sufficient for the conscious experience – after all, it *is* the conscious experience, and the conscious experience *is it*. There is nothing for any facilitating activity to do; nothing for any surround to do.

Second, even if we don't want to hit the "type" requirement too hard, we should still say that the Identity Theory predicts that the minimal surround will contain nothing because this is the cleanest way to distinguish the identity hypothesis from the realization hypothesis and the constitution hypothesis. What we want are three distinguishable, plausible candidates that seem potentially open to empirical investigation. This way of running things provides that.

So far I have characterized the differences between these three hypotheses in terms of the minimal surround. But it may also be that the realization, constitution, and identity hypotheses make different predictions about the core NCCs themselves. Most obviously, the Identity Theory predicts that there will be no variation in core NCCs for a given type of conscious experience, at least as such variation is described at the appropriate "grain" of neurology. The realization and constitution hypotheses, on the other hand, may well allow for variation in the core NCCs for a given type of conscious experience… provided in each case that the candidate core has an appropriate facilitating minimal surround. Thus there may be human surrounds for human cores, arachnid surrounds for arachnid cores, robot surrounds for robot cores, and so on. This may be true in either the realization or the constitution case. (Though perhaps greater variation is more likely to be allowed by the realization hypothesis than the constitution hypothesis, because the intrinsic nature of the core itself seems to be more important to the constitution hypothesis than the realization hypothesis.)

As I say, it may be that the realization, constitution, and identity hypotheses may make different predictions about the core NCCs themselves. But it seems to me that the different accounts of the minimal surround may be enough to provide a "wedge" into empirical significance for these metaphysical ideas. The different accounts of the minimal surround that these three hypotheses provide may create an initial framework for empirical investigations into the mind/body relation.

In this paper my goal has been to describe metaphysical accounts of the mind/body relation that are employed by current-day "naturalistic" philosophers – philosophers who wish to ground their work in the sciences. Three such relations have been discussed: strict identity, constitution, and realization. We have seen that each of these is a subtle variation on the claim that conscious states are neural states. The key to the subtle theoretical differences lies in attending to the circumstances under which, and only under which, a given NCC theoretically constitutes, realizes, or "just is" a conscious state.

References

Antony, L. M., & Levine, J. (1997). Reduction with autonomy. *Noûs*, 31(Suppl. 11), 83–105. DOI: 10.1111/0029-4624.31.s11.4

Baker, L. R. (1997). Why constitution is not identity. *Journal of Philosophy*, 94(12), 599–621. DOI: 10.2307/2564596

Baker, L. R. (2000). *Persons and bodies: A constitution view*. Cambridge, UK: Cambridge University Press. DOI: 10.1017/CBO9781139173124

Bennett, K. (2004). Spatio-temporal coincidence and the grounding problem. *Philosophical Studies*, 118(3), 339–371. DOI: 10.1023/B:PHIL.0000026471.20355.54

Bennett, K. (2011). Construction area (no hard hat required). *Philosophical Studies*, 154(1), 79–104. DOI: 10.1007/s11098-011-9703-8

Block, N. (1980). Introduction: What is functionalism? In N. Block (Ed.), *Readings in Philosophy of Psychology*, Vol. 1 (pp. 171–184). Cambridge, MA: Harvard University Press.

Block, N. J., & Fodor, J. A. (1972). What psychological states are not. *Philosophical Review*, 81(2), 159–181. DOI: 10.2307/2183991

Chalmers, D. J. (2000). What is a neural correlate of consciousness? In T. Metzinger (Ed.), *Neural correlates of consciousness: Empirical and conceptual questions* (pp. 17–39). Cambridge, MA: MIT Press.

Crick, F., & Koch, C. (1990). Toward a neurobiological theory of consciousness. *Seminars in the Neurosciences*, 2, 263–275. DOI: 10.1016/B978-0-12-185254-2.50021-8

Crick, F., & Koch, C. (1995). Are we aware of neural activity in primary visual cortex? *Nature*, 375(6527), 121–123. DOI: 10.1038/375121a0

Crick, F., & Koch, C. (1998). Consciousness and neuroscience. *Cerebral Cortex*, 8(2), 97–107. DOI: 10.1093/cercor/8.2.97

Deutsch, H. (2008). Relative identity. In E. N. Zalta (Ed.), *The Stanford encyclopedia of philosophy (Winter 2008 edition)*. Retrieved from http://plato.stanford.edu/archives/win2008/entries/identity-relative/

Feigl, H. (1958). The "mental" and the "physical." In H. Feigl, M. Scriven, & G. Maxwell (Eds.), *Minnesota Studies in the Philosophy of Science, Vol. 2: Concepts, theories, and the mind-body problem* (pp. 370–497). Minneapolis, MN: University of Minnesota Press.

Fine, K. (2008). Coincidence and form. *Aristotelian Society Supplementary Volume*, 82(1), 101–118. DOI: 10.1111/j.1467-8349.2008.00164.x

Fodor, J. A. (1997). Special sciences: Still autonomous after all these years. *Noûs*, 31(Suppl. 11), 149–163. DOI: 10.1111/0029-4624.31.s11.7

Funkhouser, E. (2006). The determinable-determinate relation. *Noûs*, 40(3), 548–569. DOI: 10.1111/j.1468-0068.2006.00623.x

Gillett, C. (2002). The dimensions of realization: A critique of the standard view. *Analysis*, 62(4), 316–323. DOI: 10.1093/analys/62.4.316

Jackson, F. (2012). In defense of the identity theory mark I. In S. Gozzano & C.S. Hill (Eds.), *New perspectives on type identity* (pp. 150–166). Cambridge, UK: Cambridge University Press. DOI: 10.1017/CBO9780511687068.008

Kim, J. (1998). *Mind in a physical world: An essay on the mind-body problem and mental causation*. Cambridge, MA: MIT Press.

Kim, J., & Sosa, E. (1999). Preface. In J. Kim & E. Sosa (Eds.), *Metaphysics: An anthology* (pp. ix–x). Malden, MA: Blackwell.

Kitcher, P. (1992). The naturalists return. *Philosophical Review*, 101(1), 53–114. DOI: 10.2307/2185044

Kripke, S.A. (1980). *Naming and necessity*. Cambridge, MA: Harvard University Press.

Levine, J. (1983). Materialism and qualia: The explanatory gap. *Pacific Philosophical Quarterly*, 64(4), 354–361.

Lewis, D. (Ed.). (1983). How to define theoretical terms. In *Philosophical Papers*, Vol. 1 (pp. 78–96). Oxford, UK: Oxford University Press.

Lewis, D. (1999). Reduction of mind. In *Papers in Metaphysics and Epistemology*, Vol. 2 (pp. 291–324). Cambridge, UK: Cambridge University Press. DOI: 10.1017/CBO9780511625343.019

Maddy, P. (2001). Naturalism: Friends and foes. *Noûs*, 35(Suppl. 15), 37–67. DOI: 10.1111/0029-4624.35.s15.3

McLaughlin, B.P. (2010). Consciousness, type physicalism, and inference to the best explanation. *Philosophical Issues*, 20(1), 266–304. DOI: 10.1111/j.1533-6077.2010.00192.x

Miller, S.M. (2001). Binocular rivalry and the cerebral hemispheres: With a note on the correlates and constitution of visual consciousness. *Brain and Mind*, 2(1), 119–149. DOI: 10.1023/A:1017981619014

Miller, S.M. (2007). On the correlation/constitution distinction problem (and other hard problems) in the scientific study of consciousness. *Acta Neuropsychiatrica*, 19(3), 159–176. DOI: 10.1111/j.1601-5215.2007.00207.x

Miller, S.M. (Ed.). (2013). *The constitution of visual consciousness: Lessons from binocular rivalry*. Advances in Consciousness Research (Vol. 90). Amsterdam, The Netherlands: John Benjamins Publishing Company. DOI: 10.1075/aicr.90

Nagel, E. (1954). Naturalism reconsidered. *Proceedings and Addresses of the American Philosophical Association*, 28, 5–17. DOI: 10.2307/3129209

Piccinini, G. (2004). Functionalism, computationalism, & mental states. *Studies in the History and Philosophy of Science Part A*, 35(4), 811–833. DOI: 10.1016/j.shpsa.2004.02.003

Piccinini, G. (2010). The mind as neural software? Understanding functionalism, computationalism, and computational functionalism. *Philosophy and Phenomenological Research*, 81(2), 269–311. DOI: 10.1111/j.1933-1592.2010.00356.x

Place, U.T. (1956). Is consciousness a brain process? *British Journal of Psychology*, 47(1), 44–50. DOI: 10.1111/j.2044-8295.1956.tb00560.x

Place, U.T. (1960). Materialism as a scientific hypothesis. *Philosophical Review*, 69(1), 101–104. DOI: 10.2307/2182270

Polger, T.W. (2004). *Natural minds*. Cambridge, MA: MIT Press.

Polger, T.W. (2011). Are sensations still brain processes? *Philosophical Psychology*, 24(1), 1–21. DOI: 10.1080/09515089.2010.533263

Pollen, D.A. (2011). On the emergence of primary visual perception. *Cerebral Cortex*, 21(9), 1941–1953. DOI: 10.1093/cercor/bhq285

Putnam, H. (1967a). The mental life of some machines. In H.-N. Castaneda (Ed.), *Intentionality, minds and perception*. Detroit, MI: Wayne State University Press.
Putnam, H. (1967b). Psychological predicates. In W. H. Capitan & D. D. Merrill (Eds.), *Art, mind, and religion* (pp. 37–48). Pittsburgh, PA: Pittsburgh University Press.
Putnam, H. (1973). Meaning and reference. *The Journal of Philosophy*, 70 (19), 699–711.
Rees, G., Kreiman, G., & Koch, C. (2002). Neural correlates of consciousness in Humans. *Nature Reviews Neuroscience*, 3(4), 261–270. DOI: 10.1038/nrn783
Ross, D., & Spurrett, D. (2004). What to say to a skeptical metaphysician? A defense manual for cognitive and behavioral scientists. *Behavioral and Brain Sciences*, 27(5), 603–627.
Salmon, W. C. (1989). *Four decades of scientific explanation* (1st ed.). Minneapolis, MN: University of Minnesota Press.
Searle, J. R. (1992). *The rediscovery of the mind*. Cambridge, MA: MIT Press.
Shoemaker, S. (2001). Realization and mental causation. In C. Gillett & B. Loewer (Eds.), *Physicalism and its discontents* (pp. 74–98). Cambridge, UK: Cambridge University Press. DOI: 10.1017/CBO9780511570797.005
Shoemaker, S. (2003). Realization, micro-realization, and coincidence. *Philosophy and Phenomenological Research*, 67(1), 1–23. DOI: 10.1111/j.1933-1592.2003.tb00023.x
Shoemaker, S. (2007). *Physical realization*. Oxford, UK: Oxford University Press. DOI: 10.1093/acprof:oso/9780199214396.001.0001
Smart, J. J. C. (1959). Sensations and brain processes. *Philosophical Review*, 68(2), 141–156. DOI: 10.2307/2182164
Smart, J. J. C. (2002). Sensations and brain processes. In D. J. Chalmers (Ed.), *Philosophy of mind: Classical and contemporary readings* (pp. 60–68). Oxford, UK: Oxford University Press.
Tong, F. (2005). Investigations of the neural basis of binocular rivalry. In D. Alais & R. Blake (Eds.), *Binocular rivalry* (pp. 63–80). Cambridge, MA: MIT Press.
Varzi, A. (2011). Mereology. In E. N. Zalta (Ed.), *The Stanford encyclopedia of philosophy (Spring 2011 edition)*. Retrieved from http://plato.stanford.edu/archives/spr2011/entries/mereology
Wasserman, R. (2014). Material constitution. In E. N. Zalta (Ed.), *The Stanford encyclopedia of philosophy (Summer 2014 edition)*. Retrieved from http://plato.stanford.edu/archives/sum2014/entries/material-constitution/
Yablo, S. (1992). Mental causation. *Philosophical Review*, 101(2), 245–280. DOI: 10.2307/2185535

Correlation, causation, constitution

On the interplay between the science and philosophy of consciousness*

Benjamin P. Kozuch and Uriah Kriegel
University of Arizona, Tucson

Why is there need for a philosophy of consciousness, in addition to the science of consciousness? For two reasons: first, as a young science operating as yet under no guiding paradigm, the science of consciousness has been subject to considerable confusion regarding its methodological, conceptual, and philosophical foundations, and it is philosophy's mandate to address such confusion in an attempt to regiment scientific practice; second, the identification of a neural feature that correlated perfectly with consciousness would still leave open a certain metaphysical question, namely, whether that correlation is indicative of a deeper, more intimate relation between the two. In this paper, we offer an opinionated overview of the philosophy of consciousness as it addresses these two dimensions of consciousness research.

1. Introduction

Consciousness is a natural phenomenon, the object of a flourishing area of research in the natural sciences, research whose primary goal is to identity the "neural correlates" of consciousness. This raises the question: why is there need for a philosophy of consciousness? As we see things, the need for a philosophy of consciousness to supplement the science of consciousness arises for two main reasons.

First, as a young and energetic science operating as yet under no guiding paradigm, the science of consciousness has been subject to somewhat uncontrolled proliferation of approaches and presuppositions regarding the methodological, conceptual, and philosophical foundations of the search for the neural correlates of consciousness. It is philosophy's mandate to address such methodological confusion in an attempt to

* For useful comments on a previous draft of this chapter, we would like to thank Steven Miller and an anonymous referee.

DOI 10.1075/aicr.92.17koz

regiment scientific practice, and many philosophers have indeed weighed in on these foundational issues for consciousness science.

Secondly, the identification of a neural feature that correlated perfectly with consciousness would still leave open a certain metaphysical question: is the relation between consciousness and the relevant neural feature merely correlation, or is that correlation indicative of a deeper, more intimate relation between the two? Work addressing this further question can be thought of as attempting a philosophical *interpretation* of scientific theories, somewhat on a par, say, with philosophical interpretations of quantum mechanics: in both cases, philosophy has to take over where science proper ends in order to articulate an intelligible conception of how the world must be given what the science suggests.

Thus a philosophy of consciousness appears necessary both to firm up the foundations of the science of consciousness and to take over where the science proper leaves off. In what follows, we offer an opinionated overview of the philosophy of consciousness as it addresses these two dimensions of consciousness research: Section 2 discusses conceptual issues regarding the notion of neural correlates of consciousness and methodological approaches to the search for these neural correlates; Section 3 discusses the variety of metaphysical relationships neural correlation might suggest.

2. From philosophy to science: Neural correlates of consciousness and the content-matching paradigm

It has sometimes been claimed that consciousness is now "largely a scientific problem", one that might proceed in isolation from philosophy (Crick, 1996). This looks implausible on the face of it, given the vexing metaphysical issues attending the study of consciousness (see Section 3). But philosophy appears to have a role in the scientific study of consciousness itself, by way of clarifying its conceptual and methodological foundations. Our aim in this section is to survey and (briefly) extend some of this work.

Scientific research into consciousness has had two research foci: the neural correlates of consciousness (NCC) and the function of consciousness. Here we discuss exclusively the NCC, indeed what is sometimes referred to as the content NCC, as opposed to the background NCC (Chalmers, 2000; Crick & Koch, 2003; Frith, Perry, & Lumer, 1999; Rees, Kreiman, & Koch, 2002).[1] Although there has been important research on the background NCC, the better-known work concerns the content NCC.

1. The content of a conscious experience is given by whatever one is conscious of. (In an experience as of a blue expanse, for example, the blueness is the content of one's experience.) Whatever neural systems correlate with the content of experience are the *content* NCC. The *background* NCC are whatever neural systems correlate with general modes of consciousness, such as dreaming, being wide awake, or being disoriented.

We begin with a look at the standard explication and regimentation of the concept of an NCC, as this suggests an initially plausible methodology for (content) NCC research. (Henceforth, by "NCC" we will mean specifically content NCC.)

The regimentation we have in mind is due to Chalmers (2000, p. 31), who defines an NCC as follows: "An NCC (for content) is a *minimal* neural representational system N such that representation of a content in N is sufficient… for representation of that content in consciousness." Three central features of this definition should be noted.

First, the definition requires neural representation of a content to be only sufficient, not necessary, for conscious representation of that content (contra Teller & Pugh, 1983; Kanwisher, 2001). This leaves open the possibility of there being more than one neural system able to represent some content in consciousness.

Secondly, and relatedly, Chalmers' definition also states that the NCC will be the minimal neural representational system sufficient for representation of the content in consciousness. This delimits the NCC so that they contain "only the core processes that suffice for the conscious state in question" (Chalmers, 2000, p. 9). Suppose N is a neural system that represents content C and is sufficient for some conscious experience E to represent C. Typically there will be some other, vaster neural system N*, such that N is a proper part of N*. It will then be trivial both that N* contains a representation of C and that N*'s representation of C is sufficient for E's representing C. Yet it seems that the parts of N* that do not have to do with N are in some sense irrelevant to the NCC. It is to rule out of the NCC these parts that the definition appeals to a *minimal* sufficient condition. This feature of the definition shows sensitivity to the idea that the search for the NCC is a search for the *basis* of consciousness. (Thus a distinction is sometimes made between the notions of a neural "correlate" and a neural "basis," with the thought that the neuroscience of consciousness should seek the latter.[2] The sensibility behind this thought is partially spoken to by the minimality condition, whether it is considered a condition on a neural "correlate," as in Chalmers' definition, or only on a neural "basis." Below, we use the two terms interchangeably.)

---

2. Among authors who make this distinction, or ones very like it, are Kanwisher (2001), Crick and Koch (2003), Block (2007), Revonsuo (2000, 2001, this volume) and Miller (2001, 2007, this volume). While not all these commentators use the term "neural basis", it is clear that they have something along these lines in mind. Crick and Koch (2003), for example, speak of looking for "the minimal set of neuronal events that gives rise to a specific aspect of a conscious experience" (p. 119). Kanwisher (2001) argues that one should seek those "patterns of neural activity [that] are necessary and/or sufficient for perceptual awareness" (p. 98). Block (2007) claims that "at a minimum, one wants the neural underpinnings of a match of content between the mental and neural state[s]" (p. 481). Revonsuo (2000) asks, "What is the relation between the neural *correlates* of consciousness and the actual neural *constituents* of consciousness?" (p. 60, italics in original). And Miller (2007) writes, "not every neural correlate of a conscious state is necessarily constitutive of that state" (p. 161).

Finally, Chalmers' (2000) definition requires an NCC for some experience E to match E in content. This requirement seems driven by a certain metaphysical assumption regarding the neural basis of the content of an experience: that as a matter of natural necessity, any neural system forming the basis of E must have the same representational content as E.[3] Noë and Thompson (2004) have dubbed this the "isomorphism constraint". To see the rationale for the isomorphism constraint, suppose some neural system N represented a horizontal line and an experience E was as of a vertical line. To think that N could be E's neural basis would be "to suppose that there was no intelligible connection (beyond brute correlation) between the experience and the neural locus in question" (Noë & Thompson, 2004, p. 5).[4]

The isomorphism constraint suggests conditions under which one would be justified in thinking that one had found an NCC. Noë and Thompson (2004, p. 7) write:

> Suppose one discovered a neural representational system *N* such that (i) *N* represents that *p*, and (ii) *N*'s activity is correlated with the occurrence of a perceptual experience with the content that *p*. If one discovered such a neural representational system, it might seem reasonable to think… one had discovered the place in the brain where the conscious experience happens.

This suggests a certain methodology for identifying the NCC, to which Noë and Thompson (2004, p. 4) refer as the content-matching paradigm: "The first task of the neuroscience of consciousness is to uncover the neural representation systems whose contents systematically match the contents of consciousness."[5]

In the remainder of this section, we take a critical look at the content-matching paradigm, arguing that it cannot justify conclusions concerning the location of the NCC. Content matches cannot provide strong justification for thinking some neural system is an NCC, because a neural system can match an experience in content and yet fail to be the neural basis of that experience; namely, in case there is some other neural system whose content also matches the experience and which is actually operative in yielding the experience.[6] We will suggest that a paradigm emphasizing content *mismatches* has more to recommend it, as a content mismatch decisively shows a neural system to be *not* the neural basis of an experience.

---

3. By "natural necessity," we mean necessity dictated by the laws of nature. This is what philosophers often refer to as "nomological necessity".

4. Beyond the matter of intelligibility, or perhaps partly in light of it, the isomorphism constraint seems to be a ground-floor metaphysical assumption for any materialist theory of consciousness, as well as the kind of naturalistic dualism propounded by Chalmers (1996).

5. It should be noted that Noë and Thompson themselves do not advocate this view (see their 2004 paper for their critique), but do ascribe it to most NCC researchers.

6. Here we intend the term "yield" to be neutral as between causal and constitutive readings; more on this below.

Some prominent NCC research appears in the mold of a content-matching paradigm. Consider the following study by Tong, Nakayama, Vaughan and Kanwisher (1998). If a subject is given a different stimulus to each eye, this can result in so-called binocular rivalry: Instead of experiencing a single image that fuses the stimuli, the subject's experience oscillates between the two. In the Tong et al. study, subjects were fed an image of a face to one eye and of a house to the other, inducing binocular rivalry. The experimenters employed functional magnetic resonance imaging, with special attention to two temporal areas: the fusiform face area (FFA), thought to specialize in the processing of faces, and the parahippocampal place area (PPA), thought to specialize in the processing of locales (such as houses). Tong et al. found increased activity in the FFA when the subject experienced the face and in the PPA when the subject experienced the house. Such results seem to indicate a content match, in that activity in the FFA (which represents faces) increased when and only when the subject saw the face, while activity in the PPA (which represents house, *inter alia*) increased when and only when the subject saw the house. Likely, it is this apparent content match that brought Tong et al. (1998, p. 75) to claim that this experiment "support[s] the notion that multiple extrastriate regions [i.e., the FFA and PPA]... participate in our awareness of... the visual world."[7]

Let us assume that this experiment presents an instance of a content match between the FFA and face experience. We maintain that this match in content, on its own, provides little justification for thinking that the FFA is the neural basis of face experience. To be well-justified in thinking this, one would need reason for thinking that there is no other neural system(s) also matching the face experience in content. For if some other neural system also matches the face experience in content, then it is possible that this other neural system (and *not* the FFA) is actually the neural basis of face experience. And so it seems that, even if Tong et al.'s experiment demonstrates a content match, on its own it provides but limited support to the hypothesis that the FFA is an NCC.

To clarify, we are not denying that content matches should play an important role in NCC research. In the Tong et al. study, the content match provides reason to further pursue the hypothesis that the FFA is the neural basis of face experience. We are also not denying that the FFA might in fact *be* the neural basis of face experience (we take no stand on that), for there may be good reasons to think that no other neural system besides the FFA matches the experience in content. But it is the absence of other content matches, and not the presence of this content match, that we believe central for supporting the hypothesis that the FFA is the neural basis of face experience. Thus we think that strong justification for believing the FFA to be an NCC is gained in the process of *ruling out* other potential content-matchers. And so, while the content match in the Tong et al. study is significant (insofar as it suggests a direction for future

7. For more on the relation between binocular rivalry research and the NCC, see Rees et al. (2002), Miller (2001, 2007, this volume), and chapters in Miller (2013).

research), it can play but a subsidiary role in actually justifying the hypothesis that the FFA is the neural basis of face experience. This is because (to repeat) a content match between the FFA and face experience is consistent with the FFA not being the neural basis of that experience.

This observation applies, of course, to all content matches: any content match between some neural system N and experience E does little to support the idea that N is the neural basis of E, because the content match (on its own) does nothing to rule out there being some other neural system N* that also matches E in content and is the real neural basis of E.

Perhaps this should not be surprising, given a content match is a *confirmation* of the hypothesis that N is the neural basis of E, and confirmations of a hypothesis are always consistent with its being false (Popper, 1959). In any case, it seems the content-matching paradigm – which recommends looking for the NCC by looking for content matches – is founded on a mistaken assumption; namely, that content matches can (on their own) provide strong justification for thinking that a neural system is the basis of some experience. We suspect, rather, that strong justification comes when the relevant content *mismatches* have been established.

To see why, consider again the inspiration for the content-matching paradigm, the isomorphism constraint (a neural system N is the basis of an experience E only if N matches E in content). Assuming the isomorphism constraint, if some neural system N and particular experience E mismatch in content, N can definitely not be the neural basis of E. Content mismatches appear of much higher evidential value than content matches. This suggests that, when looking for the neural basis of some experience E, if one could use content mismatches to rule out all but one of the relevant[8] candidates for being the neural basis of E, one would have much stronger evidence for the hypothesis that some particular neural system is the neural basis of E. (More on this when we discuss the potential for an "eliminative inference" below.)

To get a better idea of what this would look like, consider a study by Zeki (1983; see also Zeki, 1982). Zeki (1983) took single-cell recordings from monkeys' V1 (primary visual cortex) while they viewed a Mondrian (an arrangement of contiguous rectangles of various colors, resembling the work of painter Piet Mondrian). The stimulus was presented in either standard lighting conditions (bathed in "white" light) or aberrant lighting conditions (bathed in, e.g., red light). Because of the primate visual system's ability to maintain color constancy (Land, 1974), the aberrant lighting brings about no significant difference in the appearance of the colors of the Mondrian, even though it greatly changes the composition of light reflected from it. A tan area on the Mondrian, for example, continues to look tan, rather than taking on a red hue because

8. What exactly is to be considered a "relevant" candidate is an important issue that we lack the space to adequately address here. It seems clear to us, however, that at least certain kinds of candidate (e.g., neural systems that process something other than visual information) are easily excluded.

of the lighting.[9] Zeki (1983) found, however, that activity of cells in V1 was affected by the aberrant lighting conditions. A cell that had a preference for red light, for example, showed increased spiking even though its receptive field fell on a tan area.[10] As the monkey experienced that part of the Mondrian as being tan, but V1 represented it as being red, there is a content mismatch between V1 and the experience of the monkey. This rules out V1 as a neural basis of the monkey's color experience, because (according to the isomorphism constraint) the neural basis of an experience must match that experience in content.

One could debate, of course, whether this experiment successfully reveals a content mismatch.[11] But if, after careful consideration, one found that there was strong reason for thinking that the Zeki experiment successfully presents a content mismatch, one would also have strong reason for thinking that V1 is not the neural basis of color experience, as the mismatch would constitute a *falsification* (Popper, 1959) of the hypothesis that V1 is the neural basis of color experience.[12] Compare this to a content match: even if, after careful consideration, one accepted that the aforementioned Tong et al. (1998) experiment presents a content match, this would provide but weak reason for thinking the FFA is the neural basis of face experience, as it leaves open the possibility of there being another neural system matching the face experience in content.[13]

---

9. Clearly, this is not known on the basis of the monkey's verbal report; rather, it is inferred from how a normal human observer experiences the colors of the Mondrian (under aberrant lighting), along with great similarities between the monkey and human visual systems.

10. The term "receptive field" refers to the part of the visual field to which a cell is responsive. The receptive fields of cells in earlier parts of the cortical visual system (like V1) are rather small, with them becoming gradually larger as one ascends to higher parts.

11. As Zeki (1982) himself points out, these results do not necessarily "imply that there are not other wavelength selective cells in monkey striate cortex whose responses do correlate with colours as perceived by us" (p. 58).

12. It would falsify this hypothesis because, if V1 was the neural basis of color experience, this along with the isomorphism constraint entails that V1 matches color experience in its content. Put another way, the isomorphism constraint constitutes a *psychophysical law*, one that is violated if V1 both is the neural basis of color experience, and mismatches the content of color experience.

13. In the background of this discussion lurks the issue of under what precise circumstances one should think a content match or mismatch has been found. While we lack space to treat this issue here, it is important to point out that many experiments will not *demonstrate* a content match or mismatch, but rather just provide weaker or stronger reason to think that one has found a match or mismatch (though, or course, some experiments will fail to do either). Nonetheless, the asymmetry between content matches and mismatches is still present in any of these scenarios. We believe, for example, that an experiment giving one weak reason for

There appears, then, a stark asymmetry in the kind of justification that content matches and mismatches can provide. To us, this suggests it is content mismatches, and not content matches, that undergird strong conclusions about the NCC. Particularly promising would be a paradigm in which content mismatches are used to support a method of "eliminative inference" (Earman, 1992; Kitcher, 1993; Mill, 1843/2002; Platt, 1964). In eliminative inference, support for some theory T is gained by falsifying competitors of T: through a process of elimination, one shows that theory T must be true. In the present context, the idea would be that content mismatches (perhaps along with lesion studies) could be used to eliminate hypotheses concerning the neural basis of a type of conscious experience (e.g., color, shape, motion) until only one potential neural basis remains viable. Whenever one is able to do this, it seems one would have much stronger justification for thinking that one had found an NCC than could be provided by content matches.

This content-mismatch paradigm might offer some remedy to a persistent problem in NCC research, that of separating what merely correlates with an experience from what actually forms its neural basis (Miller, 2001, 2007, this volume; Revonsuo, 2000, 2001, this volume; see several other chapters in this volume): while the occurrence of any type of experience E probably entails concomitant activation of multiple neural systems, it is likely that not all of them will match E in their content.[14] The isomorphism constraint provides the leverage with which such neural systems might be weeded out from being the neural basis of E. Wherever one eliminates all neural systems but one from being the neural basis of E, it seems one will have found the neural basis, rather than *mere* correlate, of (the content of) E.

Naturally, what we have presented here is a mere outline of a paradigm for finding the NCC (for more on this, see Kozuch, 2013). Nonetheless, we think that the content-match paradigm is most likely off-track. We agree that the most important task facing a neuroscience of consciousness is finding those neural systems that match experiences in content. But we contend that it is not content matches, but rather content mismatches, that strongly justify conclusions concerning the neural bases of consciousness.

---

thinking that one has found a content *mismatch* between neural system N and experience E will ultimately have more evidential value (when it comes to trying to locate the neural basis of E) than an experiment giving one weak reason for believing that one has found a content *match* between N and E.

14. The content-mismatch paradigm can help, of course, only with the problem as it affects the content NCC. It may survive for the background NCC.

3. From science to philosophy: Neural correlates and the metaphysics of consciousness

Assume that we are at the end of neuroscientific inquiry, and the NCC has been fully and accurately identified. It would seem that certain questions remain regarding the exact relationship between consciousness and the relevant neural structure. Thus it is natural to take the correlation between the two to be indicative of a more intimate connection between them. Perhaps the most sanguine view in this area is that consciousness is in fact identical to the relevant neural structure – indeed, that every phenomenal property is identical to some neural property it correlates with. This identity thesis is sometimes recommended on the grounds that it is the best explanation of the correlation, being the most parsimonious (Smart, 1959). One may formulate the thesis as follows:

> (I) Phenomenal properties are identical to neural properties.

Just as the correlation between Mark Twain and Samuel Clemens is no coincidence, but rather due to the fact that the man is one, so the correlation between some phenomenal property P and some neural property N is most straightforwardly explained by the hypothesis that P = N. This kind of identity thesis is the hallmark of reductive materialism about consciousness.

As elegant as the identity thesis is, many philosophers have taken it to be disproved by the apparent fact that one and the same phenomenal property can be multiply realized by two different neural properties (Putnam, 1967). This fact is taken to falsify reductive materialism, but not materialism as such. For it does not threaten the notion that the phenomenal facts are *fully fixed* by the neural facts. This fixing relation is sometimes captured by the notion of metaphysical supervenience, the idea that variation in phenomenal properties must involve variation in neural properties as well. Call this the thesis of metaphysical supervenience:

> (MS) Phenomenal properties merely metaphysically supervene upon neural properties.

Such metaphysical supervenience is the hallmark of non-reductive materialism about consciousness.[15]

---

15. Two qualifications are in order. First, arguably metaphysical supervenience is not sufficient for materialism. At the very least, one needs to add that the particulars that have phenomenal and neural properties are all material. For a view according to which mind and matter are two separate substances, each having its own distinctive properties but in such a way that mind's properties supervene metaphysically upon matter's properties, would not be a materialist view (Papineau, 1993). Secondly, as Horgan (1993) has argued, quite convincingly, taking the metaphysical supervenience of phenomenal on neural properties to be primitive and inexplicable seems offensive to the spirit of materialism. A true materialist position would have not only to posit such metaphysical supervenience, but also explain it. Horgan calls the relations

The qualifier "merely" is needed because, at least on the standard conception of supervenience, metaphysical supervenience of A on B does not preclude the identity of A and B; any such precluding would have to be explicit. On this conception, supervenience strictly so-called is a purely logical relation, mandating the sufficiency in all metaphysically possible worlds of B for A. This is to be contrasted with a more robust implicature of the term "supervenience", whereby the supervenience of A on B guarantees the ontological priority of B to A. This implicature casts supervenience as an anti-symmetrical relation: if A supervenes on B, then B does not supervene on A.[16] Strictly speaking, however, supervenience is only an asymmetric relation, in the sense that the supervenience of A on B entails neither the presence nor the absence of supervenience of B on A. It therefore does not preclude identity. In fact, one may plausibly see the identity relation as nothing but, or at least as underlying, two-way metaphysical supervenience: A = B just in case A metaphysically supervenes on B and B metaphysically supervenes on A.

To repeat, what motivates the move from identity, or two-way metaphysical supervenience, to one-way metaphysical supervenience is the apparent fact that a single phenomenal property can be realized by multiple neural properties. It is worth distinguishing two scenarios here. One is where a phenomenal property has a different neural realizer in the actual world, the other where it has a different realizer only in some counterfactual world. Call the former multiple realization and the latter multiple realizability. Putnam's (1967) case against reductive materialism asserted multiple realization (humans and octopi were claimed to have different realizers for pain). However, Putnam's claim has been challenged on empirical and methodological grounds, and many philosophers have maintained that mental properties probably have unique realizers in the actual world, though may well have other realizers in counterfactual worlds.[17]

In any case, as is well-known, the metaphysical supervenience of consciousness on neural properties is also controversial. Wielding a variety of (mostly epistemic) arguments, assorted dualists have claimed that phenomenal properties cannot ultimately metaphysically supervene on neural properties (see, e.g., Chalmers, 1996). Nonetheless, they insist that it is possible to explain the correlation between phenomenal and neural properties, namely, as due to certain primitive laws of nature that

---

of 'explained supervenience' superdupervenience. His claim is thus that materialism requires metaphysical superdupervenience of phenomenal on neural properties.

16. This implicature does preclude identity, which is symmetrical. This kind of anti-symmetrical supervenience-cum-priority relations is closely associated with what is sometimes called a "grounding relation" (see, e.g., Fine, 2001).

17. Such multiple realizability would suffice to undermine the identity of phenomenal and neural properties, given that identity is in all likelihood a necessary relation (if it holds at all, it holds necessarily). If it turns out some identity is contingent (Gibbard, 1975), however, then multiple realizability may cohabit with the identity thesis.

dictate the co-instantiation of neural and phenomenal properties. The existence of such laws of nature guarantees that even though phenomenal properties do not metaphysically supervene on neural properties, they nonetheless nomologically supervene on them. Call this the thesis of nomological supervenience:

> (NS) Phenomenal properties merely nomologically supervene upon neural properties.

Such nomological supervenience is the hallmark of what Chalmers (1996) calls naturalistic dualism.[18] It is plausible to construe the relevant laws of nature as causal laws, laws of the form "under conditions C, neural feature N causes phenomenal property P."[19] In this causal variety, naturalistic dualism attempts to explain correlation by causation: the thought is that the best explanation of neural-phenomenal correlation is neural-phenomenal causation.

It is interesting to note here that, although philosophers take the obtaining of mere nomological supervenience to demonstrate the truth of dualism, scientists typically regard it as underwriting materialism. The scientists' guiding idea seems to be that any phenomenon which could be shown to be causally integrated in an ordinary way into the web of natural laws connecting natural phenomena should be regarded as a physical phenomenon. Thus insofar as consciousness can be embedded into the causal web of the material world, it ceases to present a challenge to a materialist conception of the world. This kind of "inclusive materialism" (Kriegel, 2007) is closer to dualism than to reductive materialism in some respects but closer to reductive materialism in others. Thus, unlike dualism both inclusive and reductive materialism deny that anything is non-physical; on the other hand, unlike reductive materialism both inclusive materialism and dualism deny that consciousness is nothing but some already familiar physical property.

We have surveyed a number of explanations of neural correlation, in a decreasing order of metaphysical exaction: reductive materialism appeals to identity, non-reductive materialism to mere metaphysical supervenience, and naturalistic dualism to mere nomological supervenience. A final view worth stating explicitly is non-naturalistic dualism, according to which any supervenience of the phenomenal on the neural is merely contingent: no two systems in the world differ phenomenally but not physically, yet not grounded in any natural laws, this fact is purely accidental. Call this the thesis of contingent supervenience:

---

18. As before, the "merely" is needed because the obtaining of a nomological supervenience relation between two properties does not preclude the obtaining of a stronger supervenience relation. Also, here too the view would qualify as genuinely naturalistic only if the particulars that have the phenomenal and neural properties are all material particulars.

19. This version of naturalistic dualism is reminiscent of some emergentist views of consciousness, according to which phenomenal property instantiations causally emerge from neural property instantiation.

(CS) Phenomenal properties merely contingently supervene upon neural properties.

Although conceding that neural properties happen to be contingently sufficient for phenomenal properties, this view (in virtue of the "merely") deems this sufficiency positively inexplicable. It is in this sense that the view is non-naturalistic.[20]

Given the various options surveyed in this section, the metaphysical question left over once the science of consciousness has identified the NCC can be posed succinctly as follows: what is the best metaphysical explanation of the empirical correlation between phenomenal and neural properties? Non-naturalistic dualism offers no explanation of this, of course, but reductive materialism, non-reductive materialism, and naturalistic dualism do. According to reductive materialism, what explains the correlation is the identity of phenomenal and neural properties. For non-reductive materialism and naturalistic dualism, the explanation is in terms of metaphysical and nomological supervenience, respectively.[21]

One problem here, however, is that, as logical relations, it is hard to see in what sense metaphysical or nomological supervenience of the phenomenal on the neural can be said to *explain* the correlation between them. Metaphysical and nomological supervenience may entail, or at least *suggest*, correlation, but even entailment is not yet explanation. To address this issue, non-reductive materialism and naturalistic dualism could identify a specific relation that would underlie metaphysical/nomological supervenience and would be the reason why the supervenience holds. For naturalistic dualism, the relation of causation seems to be of the right kind: the reason phenomenal properties nomologically supervene on neural properties is that they are caused by them. For non-reductive materialism, it is natural to appeal to a relation of constitution as underlying metaphysical supervenience: phenomenal properties supervene on neural ones because they are constituted by those neural properties.

The relation of constitution, which is supposed to be stronger (more intimate) than causation but weaker (less intimate) than identity, is also more prima facie mysterious

20. Interestingly, non-naturalistic dualism not only fails to explain neural correlation, in a sense it fails to describe it as well. For correlation between A and B implies more than the contingent sufficiency of A for B – it involves the contingent sufficiency of B for A as well. That is, correlation is a symmetric relation. For just as identity can be seen as (underlying) two-way metaphysical supervenience, correlation is naturally understood as two-way contingent supervenience. (This is so, of course, only so long as supervenience is not construed as involving priority relations.)

21. However, if one does construe correlation as two-way contingent supervenience, as per the previous note, it becomes a problem that metaphysical and nomological supervenience are one-way supervenience, whereas correlation is two-way supervenience. To address this issue, both non-reductive materialism and naturalistic dualism would have to add to MS and NS a claim of contingent supervenience going the other way – essentially, making the neural properties that are metaphysically or nomologically sufficient for phenomenal properties also contingently necessary for them.

than identity and causation, because less familiar from other contexts of inquiry.[22] Nonetheless, pending a full analysis of the nature of this relation, the philosopher can maintain that something like it must be posited to capture the possibility of mere metaphysical supervenience – something stronger than nomological supervenience but weaker than two-way metaphysical supervenience (i.e., identity). Short of providing a full analysis of the relevant notion of constitution, one can enhance its intelligibility through certain examples and analogies (e.g., to material constitution of a statue by a lump of clay; see Curtis & Noonan, this volume; Keaton, this volume; and Pereboom, this volume). One may also hold that in its intrinsic opacity constitution is forsooth on a par with causation: just as the causal "secret connexion" is a sort of metaphysical je ne sais qua that underlies constant conjunction, so the constitutive connection is a sort of metaphysical je ne sais qua that underlies metaphysical supervenience.

With these considerations in place, we now have three competing "metaphysical hypotheses" to explain the fact that phenomenal properties correlate with neural properties:

(H1) Phenomenal properties are identical to neural properties.
(H2) Phenomenal properties are constituted by neural properties.
(H3) Phenomenal properties are caused by neural properties.

The three hypotheses may well turn out to be empirically equivalent: it is quite plausible that they will ultimately make the same predictions (and retrodictions) regarding what phenomenal properties would be instantiated in what neural conditions.[23] If so, what will distinguish them is how they "score" on the so-called "super-empirical virtues": parsimony, modesty, conservatism, unity, simplicity, and so on (see also Melnyk, this volume).[24]

22. Indeed, this is part of the *raison d'ëtre* of the present volume.

23. According to some views in the philosophy of science – most notably, logical positivism – when two theories are empirically equivalent in this way, their disagreement cannot be substantive. If this is right, then there is no place for a metaphysics of consciousness in addition to the science of consciousness, and in general logical positivists thought metaphysics was nonsense (Carnap, 1932). This view is often regarded as untenable, for reasons we cannot go into here. A gentler kind of deflationary attitude can be found in van Fraassen (1980), according to whom empirically equivalent scientific theories are such that one may choose to *accept* one over the other for non-cognitive reasons, but one has no reason to *believe* one more than the other. This would deflate the metaphysical issue under consideration without quite dismissing it as non-substantive. This line of thought is much more plausible than logical positivism (Kriegel, 2011), though of course it is highly controversial. More on that below.

24. For a fuller development of an approach to the metaphysics of consciousness that emphasizes comparisons of theoretical virtues in this way, see Biggs (2011). Biggs also offers some explicit statements of the nature of some of these virtues. For a classic discussion of the nature of these virtues, see Quine and Ullian (1970).

This is not the place to conduct a wide-ranging assessment of the overall comparative strengths and weaknesses of H1–H3 along these various dimensions. We will restrict ourselves to preliminary remarks, indicating where our own preferences lie.

As far as parsimony is concerned, it is fairly clear that H1 fares best and H3 worst. The status of H2 is harder to assess. On the one hand, constitution does not amount to identity, so when A constitutes B, A and B are numerically distinct, and one has here as many entities as when A causes B. On the other hand, on a natural understanding of the notion of constitution, when A constitutes B one is justified in saying that B is "nothing but" A, which may suggest that B is an "ontological free lunch".[25] It may well be that the notion of parsimony itself would have to be disambiguated, such that H2 is as parsimonious as H1 on some disambiguations but as H3 on others.

The situation with modesty appears to be the converse of that with parsimony: as identity is the strongest, most demanding of the three relations, and causation the weakest, it would seem that H3 is the most modest of the three hypotheses and H1 the least modest, with H2 lying somewhere in-between. Note well: this does not imply that parsimony and modesty cancel each other out, as one may weigh more in a final "tally" of comparative virtues.

How the hypotheses rank in terms of conservatism, and thus in terms of continuity with reigning belief, depends on what one designates as the reigning belief in the relevant sense. As far as folk belief is concerned, there is good reason to think it generally dualist (Bloom, 2004), even though it is not committed to the machinery of nomological supervenience, causal laws, etc. Folk belief is thus most closely aligned with H3, and farthest removed from H1. It is not entirely clear, however, that folk belief should function here as the kind of belief the hypotheses should attempt to depart least from other things being equal. One might wish to designate the dominant *philosophical* conviction as the belief it would be virtuous to conserve. From this perspective, it would seem that H2 is the most conservative, as non-reductive materialism has approached the status of philosophical orthodoxy since the late sixties.[26] In any event, conservatism does not seem to be of central importance (great weight) in the present context, as philosophical theorization does not always exhibit the pattern of continuity and directedness that, say, the history of physics does.

25. Some potentially imperfect analogies here might be the idea that the table is constituted by its legs, its top, and their spatial arrangement, and is therefore nothing but all that, or that the table's redness is constituted by its vermillion-ness, and is therefore nothing but it.

26. Relatedly, in a recent survey of 3226 philosophers, 56.4% of respondents said they were physicalists, and 27% that they were "non-physicalists" (which presumably covers not only dualists, but also neutral monists and the like). Among philosophers of mind specifically, the proportion was even more acute: 61.2% physicalists and 21.9% non-physicalists (see http://philpapers.org/surveys/results.pl).

A theoretical virtue that is clearly of great importance is unity: the more unified an overall theory of the world, the more virtuous it is.[27] Here it is clear that, as all other non-microphysical properties are thought to be identical to or constituted by microphysical properties, any theory of the world that denies this of phenomenal properties would be less unified than one that does not. Likewise, the current overall image of the world seems to cast properties from the manifest image of the world as generally nothing but some properties from the scientific image of the world (Stoljar, 2006); excepting phenomenal properties diminishes the unity of one's overall image of the world. Thus H3 scores much lower on unity than H1 and H2. Which of H1 and H2 scores higher depends on whether one takes the general rule to involve identity or constitution. Is water, for example, strictly identical to H_2O or merely constituted thereby? Most philosophers go for identity here, though there are very good arguments for mere constitution (see especially Johnston, 1997). Furthermore, if (as is plausible) multiple realizability applies not only to phenomenal properties but to all special-science properties (Fodor, 1974), then a constitution-based theory of the world is more unified than an identity-based one, making H2 score higher than H1 on unity.

The foregoing discussion has treated the super-empirical virtues as recommending belief in the truth of the theories that exhibit them: the more virtuous a theory or hypothesis, the higher one's credence in it should be. It should be pointed out, however, that some philosophers deny this. In van Fraassen's (1980) constructive empiricism, for instance, the super-empirical virtues are taken to provide pragmatic or instrumental reasons for adopting theories, but not epistemic reasons for believing them. While this is quite a radical view, its fundamental attraction is straightforward: for no super-empirical virtue is it particularly clear how it is supposed to be truth-conducive; if it is not truth-conducive, the fact that a theory exemplifies it does not make it more likely that the world is the way the theory says it is; and if it does not make it more likely that the world is the way the theory says it is, then it is unclear why one should believe the theory. We have considerable sympathy toward this line of reasoning and hope to explore it more fully in future work. Its upshot would be that there may be no way to choose among H1–H3: as they are empirically equivalent, and the super-empirical virtues are not truth-conducive, there is no epistemic reason to believe one more than the others.

In any case, this is not the place to produce a final verdict on the matter. The main purpose of this section has been to point out one way a philosophy of consciousness is required to go beyond the science of consciousness; namely, by producing metaphysical hypotheses about the ultimate relationship between consciousness and neural activity that would explain the correlation between them.

27. There is a legitimate question of why this is so, which we will not take up here, except to note that according to Kitcher (1981), unity enhances explanatoriness; that the Humean principle of the 'unity of nature' recommends a unified theory of nature; and that insofar as one is willing to grant esthetic virtues of a theory, such as unity, simplicity, and symmetry, a role in theory construction, unity would certainly enhance esthetics.

4. Conclusion

In this paper, we have discussed two ways in which the philosophy of consciousness is relevant to the science of consciousness. The first concerns the precise analysis of the notion of a neural correlate of consciousness (understood as a neural basis for it) and the proper methodology for studying it; this was the subject of Section 2. The second concerns potential inferences to the best explanation from phenomenal-neural correlation to various more intimate phenomenal-neural relations; this was the topic of Section 3. Our main claims have been two: that a methodology for NCC research that focuses on content mismatches may be more epistemically sound than one relying on content matches, and that the choice between dualist and materialist theories of consciousness can be profitably cast as a choice between different potential explanations of the correlation between consciousness and its NCC, whatever it turns out to be.

References

Biggs, S. (2011). Abduction and modality. *Philosophy and Phenomenological Research*, 83(2), 283–326. DOI: 10.1111/j.1933-1592.2010.00412.x

Block, N. (2007). Consciousness, accessibility, and the mesh between psychology and neuroscience. *Behavioral and Brain Sciences*, 30(5–6), 481–499.

Bloom, P. (2004). *Descartes' baby: How the science of child development explains what makes us human*. New York, NY: Basic Books.

Carnap, R. (1932/1959). The elimination of metaphysics through logical analysis of language. (A. Pap, Trans.). In A. J. Ayer (Ed.), *Logical positivism* (pp. 60–81). New York, NY: The Free Press.

Chalmers, D. J. (1996). *The conscious mind: In search of a fundamental theory*. Oxford, UK: Oxford University Press.

Chalmers, D. J. (2000). What is a neural correlate of consciousness? In T. Metzinger (Ed.), *Neural correlates of consciousness: Empirical and conceptual questions* (pp. 17–39). Cambridge, MA: MIT Press.

Crick, F. (1996). Visual perception: rivalry and consciousness. *Nature*, 379(6565), 485–486. DOI: 10.1038/379485a0

Crick, F., & Koch, C. (2003). A framework for consciousness. *Nature Neuroscience*, 6(2), 119–125. DOI: 10.1038/nn0203-119

Fodor, J. A. (1974). Special sciences (or: The disunity of science as a working hypothesis). *Synthese*, 28(2), 97–115. DOI: 10.1007/BF00485230

Earman, J. (1992). *Bayes or bust? A critical examination of Bayesian confirmation theory*. Cambridge, MA: MIT Press.

Fine, K. (2001). The question of realism. *Philosophers' Imprint*, 1(2), 1–30. Retrieved from http://hdl.handle.net/2027/spo.3521354.0001.002

Frith, C., Perry, R., & Lumer, E. (1999). The neural correlates of conscious experience: An experimental framework. *Trends in Cognitive Sciences*, 3(3), 105–114. DOI: 10.1016/S1364-6613(99)01281-4

Gibbard, A. (1975). Contingent identity. *Journal of Philosophical Logic*, 4(2), 187–221. DOI: 10.1007/BF00693273
Horgan, T. (1993). From supervenience to superdupervenience: Meeting the demands of a material world. *Mind*, 102(408), 555–586. DOI: 10.1093/mind/102.408.555
Johnston, M. (1997). Manifest kinds. *Journal of Philosophy*, 94(11), 564–583. DOI: 10.2307/2564589
Kanwisher, N. (2001). Neural events and perceptual awareness. *Cognition*, 79(1–2), 89–113. DOI: 10.1016/S0010-0277(00)00125-6
Kitcher, P. (1981). Explanatory unification. *Philosophy of Science*, 48(4), 507–531. DOI: 10.1086/289019
Kitcher, P. (1993). *The advancement of science: Science without legend, objectivity without illusions*. New York, NY: Oxford University Press.
Kozuch, B. P. (2013). *Merging the philosophical and scientific studies of consciousness*. (Doctoral Dissertation, 2013, University of Arizona). Retrieved from http://arizona.openrepository.com/arizona/bitstream/10150/293397/1/azu_etd_12640_sip1_m.pdf
Kriegel, U. (2007). Functionalism, intentionalism, and the search for NCC in Jeffrey Gray's work. *Journal of Consciousness Studies*, 14(4), 96–116.
Kriegel, U. (2011). Two defenses of common-sense ontology. *Dialectica*, 65(2), 117–204. DOI: 10.1111/j.1746-8361.2011.01262.x
Land, E. H. (1974). The retinex theory of colour vision. *Proceedings of the Royal Institution Great Britain*, 47, 23–57.
Mill, J. S. (1843/2002). *A system of logic*. Honolulu, HI: University Press of the Pacific.
Miller, S. M. (2001). Binocular rivalry and the cerebral hemispheres: With a note on the correlates and constitution of visual consciousness. *Brain and Mind*, 2(1), 119–149. DOI: 10.1023/A:1017981619014
Miller, S. M. (2007). On the correlation/constitution distinction problem (and other hard problems) in the scientific study of consciousness. *Acta Neuropsychiatrica*, 19(3), 159–176. DOI: 10.1111/j.1601-5215.2007.00207.x
Miller, S. M. (Ed.). (2013). *The constitution of visual consciousness: Lessons from binocular rivalry*. Advances in Consciousness Research (Vol. 90). Amsterdam, The Netherlands: John Benjamins Publishing Company. DOI: 10.1075/aicr.90
Noë, A., & Thompson, E. (2004). Are there neural correlates of consciousness? *Journal of Consciousness Studies*, 11(1), 3–28.
Papineau, D. (1993). *Philosophical naturalism*. Oxford, UK: Blackwell Publishers.
Platt, J. R. (1964). Strong inference. *Science*, 146(3642), 347–353. DOI: 10.1126/science.146.3642.347
Popper, K. R. (1959). *The logic of scientific discovery*. New York, NY: Basic Books.
Putnam, H. (1967). Psychological predicates. In W. H. Capitan & D. D. Merrill (Eds.), *Art, mind, and religion* (pp. 37–48). Pittsburgh, PA: University of Pittsburgh Press.
Quine, W. V., & Ullian, J. S. (1970). *The web of belief*. New York, NY: Random House.
Rees, G., Kreiman, G., & Koch, C. (2002). Neural correlates of consciousness in humans. *Nature Reviews Neuroscience*, 3(4), 261–270. DOI: 10.1038/nrn783
Revonsuo, A. (2000). Prospects for a scientific research program on consciousness. In T. Metzinger (Ed.), *Neural correlates of consciousness: Empirical and conceptual questions* (pp. 57–75). Cambridge, MA: MIT Press.

Revonsuo, A. (2001). Can functional brain imaging discover consciousness in the brain? *Journal of Consciousness Studies*, 8(3), 3–23.

Smart, J. J. C. (1959). Sensations and brain processes. *Philosophical Review*, 68(2), 141–156. DOI: 10.2307/2182164

Stoljar, D. (2006). *Ignorance and imagination: The epistemic origin of the problem of consciousness*. New York, NY: Oxford University Press. DOI: 10.1093/0195306589.001.0001

Teller, D. Y., & Pugh, E. N. (1983). Linking propositions in colour vision. In J. D. Mollon & L. T. Sharpe (Eds.), *Colour vision: Physiology and psychophysics* (pp. 576–589). London, UK: Academic Press.

Tong, F., Nakayama, K., Vaughan, J. T., & Kanwisher, N. (1998). Binocular rivalry and visual awareness in human extrastriate cortex. *Neuron*, 21(4), 753–759. DOI: 10.1016/S0896-6273(00)80592-9

van Fraassen, B. C. (1980). *The scientific image*. New York, NY: Oxford University Press. DOI: 10.1093/0198244274.001.0001

Zeki, S. (1982). Do wavelength selective cells in monkey striate cortex respond to colours? *Journal of Physiology*, 330(Suppl.), 57P–58P.

Zeki, S. (1983). Colour coding in the cerebral cortex: The reaction of cells in monkey visual cortex to wavelengths and colours. *Neuroscience*, 9(4), 741–765. DOI: 10.1016/0306-4522(83)90265-8

The material constitution of phenomenal consciousness

Derk Pereboom
Cornell University, Ithaca

In this article I set out in concise form the physicalist account of the mental I develop in *Consciousness and the Prospects of Physicalism* (Pereboom, 2011). I first set out a response to the knowledge and conceivability arguments against physicalism, one that features the open possibility that introspection represents phenomenal states as having qualitative features they actually lack. I then propose an alternative Russellian Monist answer to these arguments, according to which currently unknown absolutely intrinsic physical properties provide categorical bases for known microphysical properties and also yield an account of phenomenal consciousness. Lastly, I defend a nonreductive physicalist account of the mental, in which the fundamental relation between the mental and the microphysical is material constitution and not identity.

Consciousness and qualitative inaccuracy

Frank Jackson's knowledge argument features super-scientist and ideal reasoner Mary, who has lived her entire life in a room that displays only various shades of black, white, and gray (Jackson, 1982, 1986; cf. Nagel, 1974; Nida-Rümelin, 2010). She acquires information about the microphysical bases of things in the world, including human beings and their various capacities, by means of a black-and-white television monitor. By watching television programs, Mary eventually comes to have knowledge of all of the microphysical information there is about the nature of the human being and, we might imagine, all of the microphysical information there is about the actual world. She also comes to have all of the knowledge that is derivable from this microphysical information, which includes, for example, complete biological knowledge of various human body parts. But even if she has all of this knowledge, the argument continues, there is much she does not thereby know and cannot thereby come to know about human experience. When Mary leaves the room and sees a red tomato, she will come to know for the first time – she will *learn* – what it is like to see red. She will come to have knowledge for the first time of a particular phenomenal property or of a mental

DOI 10.1075/aicr.92.18per

state that has this property – a phenomenal state. The conclusion is that there are facts about phenomenal states that are not physical facts, and thus phenomenal states are not completely physical. (The argument, formulated in this way, assumes that Mary, the ideal reasoner that she is, could derive every true physical statement from her microphysical knowledge. This is an assumption that Chalmers and Jackson (2001) accept. My challenge to the argument won't focus on this assumption.)

The core concern about physicalism expressed in the knowledge argument begins with the observation that phenomenal states have phenomenal properties, and that it seems plausible that:

(1) Introspective modes of presentation represent a phenomenal property as having a specific qualitative nature, and the qualitative nature that an introspective mode of presentation represents a phenomenal property as having is not among the features that any physical mode of presentation would represent it as having.

Moreover, it is also seems plausible that:

(2) The introspective mode of presentation *accurately represents* the qualitative nature of the phenomenal property. That is, the introspective mode of presentation represents the phenomenal property as having a specific qualitative nature, and the attribution of this nature to the phenomenal property is correct.

One way to characterize the qualitative natures that introspective modes of presentation represent phenomenal properties as having is by way of resemblance to modes of presentation (cf. Locke, 1689/1975): Mary's introspective representation of her phenomenal-red sensation presents that sensation in a characteristic way, and it is plausible that a qualitative nature that resembles this mode of presentation is accurately attributed to the sensation's phenomenal property. Alternatively specified, this qualitative nature is just as the introspective mode of presentation represents it to be.

Given these claims about what at least initially seems plausible, the proponent of the knowledge argument can account for its force in the following way. Mary, upon leaving her black-and-white room and seeing the tomato comes to have the belief:

(A) Seeing red has R,

where 'R' is the phenomenal concept that directly refers to phenomenal redness, that is, to phenomenal property R. The qualitative nature of phenomenal redness is accurately represented introspectively by Mary's introspective phenomenal mode of presentation. The argument can usefully be interpreted to assume that if physicalism is true, then every truth about the qualitative nature that an introspective mode of presentation accurately represents a phenomenal property as having will be derivable from a proposition detailing only features that physical modes of presentation represent the world as having (an assumption I don't challenge). However, (A) is not derivable from this proposition. Consequently, not every truth about the qualitative nature that introspective modes of presentation accurately represent phenomenal properties as having is so derivable. Therefore physicalism about phenomenal properties is false.

This version of the knowledge argument can be challenged by calling into question one or both of the claims about what is intuitive just listed. I take issue with (2), the claim about the accuracy of introspective phenomenal representation. The idea that motivates the objection is that given the supposition of (1), it is an open possibility that introspective representation is inaccurate in the sense that it represents phenomenal properties as having qualitative natures they in fact lack; that is, it is an open possibility that the *qualitative inaccuracy hypothesis* is true. For example, upon seeing the red tomato, Mary introspectively represents the qualitative nature of phenomenal redness in the characteristic way, but it is an open possibility that she is representing phenomenal redness as having a qualitative nature that it actually does not have (Pereboom, 1994).

The seriousness of this open possibility can be supported by an analogy with our visual representation of colors (Pereboom, 1994). Our visual system represents colors as having certain specific qualitative natures, and it is an open possibility, widely regarded as actual, that colors actually lack these qualitative natures. It's open that phenomenal property introspection features representational systems relevantly similar to those involved in visual color perception, and this would explain how the qualitative inaccuracy hypothesis about phenomenal properties might be true. It's plausible that part of what explains qualitative inaccuracy about color representation is that it's causal, and this allows for a discrepancy between the real nature of colors and how we represent their qualitative natures. It might well be that introspective representation of phenomenal color is also causal, and that this gives rise to a similar discrepancy.

Supposing that this open possibility is in fact realized, how should we formulate what happens when Mary leaves the room and sees the red tomato? She now comes to have a belief of the form:

(A) Seeing red has R.

First consider the proposal that the concept 'R' in this belief refers to a property with the qualitative nature accurately represented by the characteristic introspective mode of presentation. Supposing our open possibility is actual, phenomenal redness lacks this qualitative nature, and as a result belief (A) will be false. Then coming to believe (A) wouldn't amount to Mary's learning something about the qualitative nature of phenomenal redness, that is, to acquiring a new true belief about it. Alternatively, consider the proposal that phenomenal property R is introspectively misrepresented and lacks such a qualitative nature, and is uncontroversially entirely physical. We can suppose that this belief is then true, but under this supposition Mary already had this belief when in her room, or was able to derive it from the true beliefs she then already had, and then she also does not acquire a new true belief. Consequently, either Mary's belief (A) about phenomenal redness would then not be true, or wouldn't be new.

It might be objected that this account merely shifts the problem for a physicalist explanation from accounting for phenomenal properties to accounting for their introspective phenomenal modes of presentation. Given the qualitative inaccuracy hypothesis, Mary's phenomenal state lacks the qualitative nature that is accurately represented by her introspective phenomenal mode of presentation – call it MPR. Consequently, Mary cannot learn that the sensation has a property of this particular sort. However, she nevertheless appears to learn something about how MPR presents this sensation. Because MPR presents the sensation phenomenally, Mary would seem to learn something about a feature of MPR – in particular, something about its essential property of presenting red sensations in a characteristic phenomenal way. And it's at least initially plausible that Mary cannot derive the corresponding truth about MPR from her microphysical base. This is a general concern for old-fact/new guise responses to the knowledge argument (Alter, 1995; Chalmers, 1996; Churchland, 1985; Pereboom, 1994).

But in response, if the qualitative inaccuracy hypothesis applies to introspective representations of phenomenal states, it stands to reason that it also applies to introspective representations of phenomenal modes of presentation. It would also be an open possibility that Mary introspectively represents MPR's essential phenomenal property as having a qualitative nature it really lacks. Then, despite how MPR is introspectively represented, she might be able derive every truth about its real nature from her microphysical base even back in her black and white room. The same type of point can be made for any further iteration of introspective representations of introspective phenomenal modes of presentation (Pereboom, 1994, 2011).

At this point we might ask: how plausible must the qualitative inaccuracy hypothesis be for it to provide a successful reply to the knowledge argument? One might concede that it's open that it's true, but perhaps that's not enough (Adams, 2013; Stoljar, 2013). The original dialectical context was this: the knowledge argument requires that the qualitative inaccuracy hypothesis be ruled out. If it's instead open that introspective phenomenal representation is qualitatively inaccurate, the soundness of this argument is in question. However, at this point one might shift away from this original dialectical context, and ask instead whether physicalism, given the total evidence, is more plausible than its falsity. In this new context, one might ask: how credible must a physicalistic account of phenomenal properties be for physicalism to be more plausible than not? One might conjecture, for instance, that a physicalistic account of phenomenal properties itself would then need to be more plausible than not.

But even in this new context such a physicalistic account of phenomenal properties, considered independently of other reasons to accept physicalism, does not need to be more plausible than not. When we restrict the evidence to introspective experience of phenomenal properties and leave out evidence, or example, from the history of success of physical explanations in science, the credibility of the physicalistic account need only be modestly high, and in particular it need not be more plausible than not. It would only be together with such broader evidence that physicalism would be more credible than its falsity.

An example from Alvin Plantinga's (1996) discussion of the problem of evil yields an instructive analogy to this epistemic situation. Imagine that I know that Feike is a

Frisian, and the only evidence I have relevant to his being able to swim is my awareness of the statistical fact that only one in ten Frisians can swim. My rational credence that Feike can swim is arguably just 1/10. However, suppose that I swim with him every morning. Now it's a near certainty for me that Feike can swim. In this example, we can say that my experience of Feike swimming carries the main burden of raising my credence to a high level. This burden cannot be shouldered by my statistical evidence. By analogy, if consideration of evidence restricted to introspection supports only a modest rational credence in a proposed physical account of the phenomenal, the broader evidence may still raise the rational credence in that account to a much higher level. My sense of the prospects for physicalism is that if the evidence is restricted to introspection, only a very modest rational credence in a physicalistic account of the phenomenal can be expected, and that the burden of raising that credence to a significantly high level will need to fall on broader evidence from the history of science. This picture, at least as one of how things currently stand, accords with the sensibilities of most physicalists. Their confidence that physicalism is true is due mainly to the history of success of physical explanations in science, and not to a high credence in a physicalist account of phenomenal consciousness considered independently of these wider considerations.

The qualitative inaccuracy hypothesis also provides a challenge to the conceivability argument. I will focus on David Chalmers's (2002) version, the formulation of which involves the following toolkit. First, a set of statements: 'P' is a statement that details the entire microphysical truth about the actual world; 'T' is a "that's all" claim, so that 'PT' specifies all the physical truths about the actual world together with the provision that there are no additional truths (i.e., other than those entailed by those physical truths); and 'Q' is some phenomenal truth. Second, a catalogue of notions of conceivability and possibility: Statement S is ideally conceivable when it is conceivable on ideal rational reflection; S is positively conceivable when we can form a mental picture of a scenario in which S is true. Primary and secondary conceivability are less familiar notions. They are crucial for understanding the argument, and so I will set them out in some detail.

In Chalmers's view, one way to think about a possible world is as a kind of epistemic possibility, that is, as the way the world might actually turn out to be, given what we can know a priori. When we do this, we consider that possible world as actual. Thus S is possible in this sense just in case S is true in a world considered as actual. For example, when one considers as actual a world in which all the 'water' samples are not H_2O but XYZ instead, then 'water = XYZ' is true in that world, and consequently 'water $\neq H_2O$' is primarily possible. The term 'considering as actual' is linked to Chalmers's idea that to determine whether a statement S is primarily possible, one can evaluate indicative conditionals of the form 'If possible world W *is* actual, then S'. In the case of our XYZ world, the indicative conditional 'if the XYZ world is actual, then water $\neq H_2O$' is true, and thus the 'water $\neq H_2O$' is primarily possible. One might by contrast consider a world W as counterfactual. One then holds the nature of the actual world fixed and thinks of W as a way things might have been. If one considers the XYZ world in this way, then at the XYZ world 'water = XYZ' and 'water ≠ H_2O' turn out to be false. In Chalmers's framework, S is secondarily possible just in case S is true in some world considered as counterfactual. Hence, 'water ≠ H_2O' is primarily possible, but not secondarily possible. Secondary possibility is what is more commonly known as metaphysical possibility. The term 'considering as counterfactual' derives from Chalmers's proposal that to determine whether a statement S is possible in this sense, one can evaluate subjunctive conditionals of the form 'if possible world W *were* actual, then S'. Accordingly, S is primarily conceivable just in case S can be conceived as true in some world considered as actual, and S is secondarily conceivable just in case S can be conceived as true in some world considered as counterfactual.

Finally, Russellian Monism provides a way of escaping the force of the argument. Here is a way to think about this position. There's a fairly widespread consensus that consciousness is not a fundamental phenomenon, and that there are thus more fundamental features of reality that underlie and explain it. Contemporary physics encourages the hypothesis that the fundamental features of reality are physical; candidates include particles, forces, and quantum fields. However, there are serious considerations such as the conceivability argument that count against anything physical of the sort we currently understand accounting for consciousness. This predicament gives rise to the idea that the account of consciousness must consist at least in part in presently unknown fundamental features of reality. Add to this that the history of philosophy has witnessed a strong predilection for ontological monism, that is, for thinking that the world has fundamental features only of a single sort – physicalism and idealism are cases in point. These motivations suggest a proposal in which both consciousness and the properties encountered in current physical theories are grounded in presently unknown fundamental features of a single kind. This type of position is known as Russellian Monism, named for one of its proponents, Bertrand Russell (1927). A physicalist version of this view claims that these features are not phenomenal, but instead *protophenomenal* (Chalmers, 2002), and similar enough to paradigmatic physical properties to count as physical themselves.

With these elements in place, here is the argument:

(1) 'PT and ~ Q' is ideally, positively, primarily conceivable.
(2) If 'PT and ~ Q' is ideally, positively, primarily conceivable, then 'PT and ~ Q' is primarily possible.
(3) If 'PT and ~ Q' is primarily possible, then 'PT and ~ Q' is secondarily possible or Russellian Monism is true.
(4) If 'PT and ~ Q' is secondarily possible, physicalism is false.
(5) Physicalism is false or Russellian Monism is true.

The qualitative inaccuracy hypothesis motivates a challenge to Premise (1). In Chalmers's way of seeing it, rejecting that premise commits one to the claim that an ideal reasoner could derive a priori the phenomenal truth 'Q' from 'PT', with the provision that she possesses the minimal information required to facilitate adequate possession of the phenomenal concepts involved in representing 'Q'. Chalmers contends that it is strongly intuitive that this claim is false. By contrast, an ideal reasoner could derive truth like 'water exists' a priori from 'PT', and consequently 'PT and there is no water' will not be ideally, positively, primarily conceivable. However, Premise (1) can be challenged as follows. Partly because the qualitative inaccuracy hypothesis is an open possibility, the analysis of phenomenal concepts reveals a conjunction of conditionals of the following kind:

(P1+) If a world is actual in which experiences are qualitatively exactly as we introspectively represent them to be, then:

> the concept 'phenomenal red' correctly applies to phenomenal redness as it is introspectively represented, and

(P2+) If a world is actual in which no experiences instantiate phenomenal redness as it is introspectively represented, but there is a unitary property that is the normal cause of their introspectively appearing phenomenally red, then:

> the concept 'phenomenal red' correctly applies to the property that is the normal cause of the introspective appearance of phenomenal redness (where 'the normal cause of introspective representations of phenomenal redness' functions merely as a reference-fixer), and

(P3+) If a world is actual in which no experiences instantiate phenomenal redness as it is introspectively represented, but there are many different sorts of causes of their introspectively appearing phenomenally red, and there are no salient similarities among the intrinsic properties of these causes, then:

> the concept 'phenomenal red' correctly applies to whatever properties cause (or could cause) instances of the introspective appearance of phenomenal redness.

This conjunction of conditionals allows us to see that in a scenario microphysically just like the actual one (and in which 'T' holds) but without instantiated phenomenal properties whose qualitative natures are accurately represented by introspective modes of presentation, phenomenal properties might well nevertheless be instantiated. And if a scenario of this sort were actually realized, there would be no less reason to believe that 'PT and ~ Q' would be ruled out by ideal a priori reasoning than to believe that 'PT and no physical objects are red' or that 'PT and there is no water' would be so ruled out. As a result, the status of the ideal, positive, primary conceivability of 'PT and ~ Q' will not differ from that of 'PT and there is no water' and 'PT and no physical objects are red.' Thus, because the qualitative inaccuracy hypothesis is an open possibility, Premise (1) is insecure.

Russellian Monism

The advocate of the knowledge and conceivability arguments might at this point argue that introspective consciousness provides a kind of privileged epistemic access to phenomenal states, so that we can be sure that our introspective representations of their qualitative natures are generally accurate, and that therefore the qualitative inaccuracy hypothesis is false (Chalmers, 2003; Goff, forthcoming). To my mind the best response is one that Daniel Dennett (1992; and in conversation) develops – it's more plausible that such representations of phenomenal states are not privileged in this way, but are instead subject to empirical-theoretic confirmation. If this is accepted, the advocate of accuracy can still contend that her view is nevertheless more credible, in particular given the degree of illusionism about introspective representations of phenomenal states taken on board. Russellian Monism offers hope to an advocate of qualitative accuracy who nevertheless wants to defend physicalism. More broadly, my sense is that if phenomenal consciousness is wholly physical, then either phenomenal consciousness isn't what it seems, or else the physical is different from what current theories indicate. The qualitative inaccuracy hypothesis reflects the first alternative, Russellian Monism the second.

One specific Russellian Monist proposal favors the notions of dispositional and categorical properties. Dispositional properties are essentially tendencies to produce certain effects, and although categorical properties may include tendencies to produce effects, their natures do not consist only in such tendencies. Many find it intuitive that categorical properties are needed to explain dispositional properties. For example, a ball's disposition to roll requires an explanation, and it is plausibly provided by its categorical properties of spherical shape and rigidity. Accordingly, the more specific Russellian Monist proposal is this: the most fundamental properties current physics invokes are exclusively dispositional, and it leaves us ignorant of the categorical properties required to explain them, and these currently unknown categorical properties account for consciousness. The negative charge of an electron, for example, might be one of those basic physical properties, and it is a disposition to repel other particles with negative charge and to attract particles with positive charge. This dispositional property must have a categorical basis, and it, the Russellian Monist hypothesizes, is the sort of property that can also explain consciousness. Russellian Monists have proposed a range of such more fundamental but yet undiscovered properties – from conscious properties of microphysical entities, to properties of such entities similar enough to paradigmatic physical properties to qualify as physical themselves but yet different enough to explain consciousness, to properties different from any we're now familiar with, but capable of accounting for consciousness.

The specific sort of Russellian Monism that I set out is one on which the currently unknown properties that explain consciousness are of the second sort, similar enough in kind to our paradigmatic physical properties to qualify as physical. What distinguishes my version of Russellian Monism from others is that in mine the currently unknown properties are not only categorical but also intrinsic – that is, non-relational – in a particularly demanding sense. The idea of this kind of intrinsic property derives from Leibniz's critical discussion of the Cartesian proposal on which matter consists just in extension in three spatial dimensions. Leibniz argues that this view is unsatisfactory for the reason that extension is in a sense an extrinsic property, and that any real thing cannot have only properties that are extrinsic in this way, but must possess fundamentally intrinsic properties as well: "there is no denomination so extrinsic that it does not have an intrinsic denomination at its basis. This is itself one of my important doctrines" (Leibniz to de Volder, April 1702; in Leibniz, 1969, pp. 526–527).

Leibniz's formulation of this claim indicates that he thinks properties can be more and less extrinsic. Note first that it's plausible that extrinsic properties can have intrinsic components. For example, *being wise* is an extrinsic property of Sophie because it involves a relation to a comparison class: she is wiser than Ann, Fred, and so on. But *being wise* also features an intrinsic component – having a certain type and level of intelligence. Hence *being wise* is a complex property that has at least one extrinsic and one intrinsic component. It is thus not a *purely* extrinsic property, which can be characterized in this way:

> P is a *purely extrinsic property* of X just in case P is an extrinsic property of X and P has no intrinsic components.

Being one among many is a plausible example of a purely extrinsic property – of a point in space, for instance.

To Leibniz's charge against Descartes it might be countered that properties such as *having such-and-such an extension* and *being spherical* are clearly intrinsic properties of the things that have them. However, Leibniz's claim is that a sphere's extension is not intrinsic to it in a more demanding sense. He contends that there is a respect in which the extension of a thing is after all extrinsic:

> Nor do I think that extension can be conceived in itself, but I consider it an analyzable and relative concept, for it can be resolved into plurality, continuity, and coexistence or the existence of parts at one and the same time.
>
> (Leibniz to de Volder, April 1699; in Leibniz, 1969, pp. 169–170)

The extension of the sphere can be analyzed as, or reduces to, the plurality, continuity, and coexistence of parts of the sphere. Properties of each of these three sorts are purely extrinsic properties of these parts. Thus it may be that P is an intrinsic property of X, while P is not in a sense fundamentally intrinsic to X, or, as James van Cleve specifies, in Kant's terminology, *absolutely* intrinsic to X (Kant, 1791/1787/1998; van Cleve, 1988). This is so when X's having P can be analyzed as, or reduces to, X's parts having properties Q, R, S…, and these properties will be purely extrinsic properties of these parts. When P *can* be analyzed as or reduces to purely extrinsic properties of these parts, P is instead, in Kant's terminology, a merely comparatively or relatively intrinsic property.

However, it's best to avoid the notions of analysis and reduction in characterizing these kinds of intrinsic properties. Even if for general reasons supporting anti-reductionism, properties of the whole fail to be analyzable in terms of or to reduce to properties of the parts, an intrinsic property of the whole could still be merely comparatively intrinsic. We can instead appeal to the notion of constitution without identity (my version of material constitution is spelled out below; this account can be modified to accommodate property constitution):

> P is an *absolutely intrinsic* property of X just in case P is an intrinsic property of X, and P is not even partly constituted by purely extrinsic properties of parts of X.
> (Pereboom, 2013a, p. 722, italics in original)

By contrast,

> P is a *comparatively intrinsic* property of X just in case P is an intrinsic property of X, and P is wholly constituted (at some level) by purely extrinsic properties of parts of X. (Pereboom, 2013a, p. 723, italics in original)

Leibniz then argues, in effect, that every substantial entity has at least one absolutely intrinsic property, and so, contrary to the Cartesian proposal, extension all by itself cannot be constitutive of material substance (cf. Ney, 2007). One component of Russellian Monism can be explained along these same lines: the properties that current physics invokes are all extrinsic or only comparatively intrinsic, and so there must be unknown absolutely intrinsic properties that underlie them.

Chalmers's Russellian Monist hypothesis is that one can ideally, positively, primarily conceive 'PT and ~ Q' (that is, conceive it as true in some world considered as actual) only because one is conceiving only extrinsic/dispositional properties on the physical side. We can now suggest that if 'P' were replaced with an embellished 'P*' that includes concepts that facilitate direct representation of the natures of the unknown absolutely intrinsic properties, the resulting 'P*T and ~ Q' would no longer be ideally, positively, primarily conceivable (Chalmers, 2002). Although 'Q' – let's suppose, 'Mary senses red at time t' – is not a priori derivable from 'PT', this truth about Mary's phenomenal experience would be a priori derivable from 'P*T'. The Russellian Monism that results has variants in which the natures of the absolutely intrinsic properties are phenomenal, as in Galen Strawson's micropsychism, or protophenomenal, as Chalmers advocates. On the version of protophenomenalism I set out, these properties are absolutely intrinsic and are similar enough to paradigmatic physical properties to count as physical themselves. It would be advantageous if these absolutely intrinsic properties provided explanations for both phenomenal properties and the properties invoked by current microphysics. I contend that it's an open possibility that a protophenomenalist version of Russellian Monism is equipped for these two explanatory roles.

Nonreductive physicalism and the constitution relation

On either the qualitative inaccuracy or the Russellian Monist response to the challenge to physicalism from phenomenal consciousness, it's an open question whether the relation between the underlying microphysical states and properties and the mental states and properties is reductive or nonreductive. In my view, the main reason for accepting the nonreductive option is not methodological but metaphysical. Mental natural kinds are not identical to natural kinds in physics because mental causal powers are not identical to microphysical causal powers. The fact that mental kinds are multiply realizable at the level of microphysical kinds provides an important clue as to why this is so. The nonreductivist view I propose departs from others insofar as it rejects the token identity of mental and microphysical entities of any kind – including causal powers. The deepest relation between the mental and the microphysical is material constitution, where this relation is not to be explicated by the notion of identity.

On this view, material constitution is a grounding relation between concrete physical entities, whether they are states, events, property instances, or causal powers. Let me set out a formal characterization of this relation. Suppose that x and y are concrete physical entities. The *made up of* relation is asymmetric, irreflexive, and directed, so that the less fundamental is made up of the more fundamental, while its core is primitive. The *made up of* relation is asymmetric and irreflexive: the lattice is not made up of the diamond, and the diamond is not made up of itself. It has a particular directedness: the less fundamental made up of the more fundamental. Entities x and y are materially coincident just in case they, at some level, are made out of the same parts. Then,

(C1) x materially constitutes y at t if and only if
  (a) y is made up of and materially coincident with x at t;
  (b) necessarily, if x exists at t, then y exists at t and is made up of and materially coincident with x at t; and
  (c) possibly, y exists at t and it is not the case that y is made up of and materially coincident with x at t.

The last clause (c) precludes the identity of x and y (on the assumption of the necessity of identity), as does clause (a), because the *made up of* relation is irreflexive.

Lynne Baker's discussion of constitution features a number of counterexamples that would pose a threat to clause (b) of this characterization, the necessitation of the constituted entity by its constitutor (Baker, 2007, pp. 11–13, 106–110). The existence of the dollar bill in my pocket is not necessitated by its cellulose molecule and ink constitutor, for its existence also requires the U.S. Federal Reserve Bank and the laws governing it. For a psychological example, on an externalist view about mental content of the kind developed by Tyler Burge (1979), the existence of a token belief with some specific content will not be necessitated by the existence of its neural or microphysical constitutor, for the reason that in an alternative physical and social environment, this same neural or microphysical constitutor would not yield a belief with that content. Phenomena of these kinds can be accommodated by a characterization very similar to (C1), but in which, on the recommendation of Baker's account, (b) is revised to specify that the existence of y is necessitated by the existence of x in an appropriate relational context, and (c) is similarly altered. Suppose 'D' designates the y-favorable circumstances – the relational context required for something to constitute y. Then:

(C2) x materially constitutes y at t if and only if
 (a) y is made up of and materially coincident with x at t;
 (b) necessarily, if x exists and is in D at t, then y exists at t and is made up of and materially coincident with x at t; and
 (c) possibly, y exists at t and it is not the case that y is made up of and materially coincident with x in D at t.

Baker (2013) provides a further reason to prefer (C2) to (C1): it's desirable that the constitutor and the constituted be the same type of entity. In her view, an object can be constituted of an object, but an object can't be constituted by a state of affairs. The object head-and-hammer – let's call it 'HH' – which can exist even if its head-part and the hammer-part are detached, would be a candidate for constituting the hammer, but *HH arranged hammer-wise* would not be, for the reason that *HH arranged hammer-wise* is a state of affairs and not an object. However, if this is granted, it seems that constitutions may not necessitate the constituted thing, for the obtaining of HH alone will not necessitate the existence of the hammer. An attractive response is to specify that the hammer is indeed constituted just by HH, but only when it has a hammer-wise arrangement. And this result can be secured by adopting (C2), and allowing the y-favorable circumstances for which 'D' stands range over circumstances of part-arrangement, and not only over external sorts of relational contexts (Pereboom, 2013b).

Finally, I prefer a model of the mental that is not functional in the standard external-relations sense, that is, one in which the essences of mental kinds do not consist in their causal relations to entities external to them – sensory inputs, behavioral outputs, and other mental states. Rather, mental properties are identical to physical compositional properties, i.e., properties things have solely by virtue of intrinsic features of their parts, either proper or improper, and relations these parts have to one another. This model would secure the causal efficacy of the mental in a way that external-relations functionalism arguably cannot – intuitively, purely relational properties alone cannot be causally efficacious. It is also consistent with nonreductivism, for the reason that multiple realizability arguments indicate that mental compositional properties would not be essentially neural or microphysical. Given the identities that it affirms, the position espoused amounts to a compromise with the type-type reductionist views of U. T. Place (1956) and J. J. C. Smart (1959).

The scientific realist model inherited from other domains is plausibly interpreted as explaining the temporally forward-looking causal relata of kinds not simply by external functional relations, but rather in central cases by properties intrinsic to those kinds – that is, by properties intrinsic to every possible instance of the kind – and in particular by intrinsic properties at the same level as the kinds themselves (Boyd,

1999). The forward-looking causal relata of chemical compounds are explained partly by their compositional properties, chemical properties intrinsic to those kinds of compounds, which each molecule of the compound possesses by virtue of the intrinsic properties of its component parts and the relations these parts have to each other. Polio symptoms are explained in part by an intrinsic biological property of that type of disease, being a particular viral infection. Analogously, in this model properties intrinsic to types of mental states that explain their forward-looking causal relata.

This model might be embellished with the analogy of artifacts of internally complex types, for instance, a ball piston engine, a recent version of the rotary internal combustion engine (Pereboom, 2002). Characteristic of this engine is having parts with particular shapes and rigidities, arranged in a particular way. These features make up a compositional property intrinsic to such an engine. Significantly, this compositional property is multiply realizable – the parts of the engine can be made of materials of different sorts, as long as these materials can play the right roles. Similarly, it might be that the different physical realizations of a dog's and a human's belief *that this fire is dangerous* feature a compositional property of a single kind that is intrinsic to this kind of mental state. This property would be more abstract than any specific sort of neural compositional property in the sense that it can be realized in different kinds of neural systems. In addition, it may be that this same compositional property can also be realized in a silicon-based electronic system, and such a system could then have the belief about danger. Suppose that engineers built a silicon-based system that reproduced the capacities of and interconnections among neurons in a human brain as exactly as possible, and then ran it to replicate what occurs when someone has such a belief about danger. It's entirely possible that the resulting silicon-based state would realize that very belief and have an internal structure sufficiently similar to the internal structure of the human neural system for each to instantiate the same compositional property.

Final words

I've proposed that if consciousness is physical, then either phenomenal properties are different from how they seem and we introspectively represent them as having features that they don't in fact possess, or else the physical is different from what our current theories reveal it to be and there are currently unknown absolutely intrinsic physical properties that explain consciousness. In the account of the physical constitution of consciousness and of the mental more generally that I subsequently set out, the mental is grounded in the physical in two distinct ways: first, by constitution in the microphysical and intervening levels, and second by identity with compositional properties that are sufficiently abstract to preclude classification at any level more basic than the mental.

References

Adams, R. M. (2013). Consciousness, physicalism, and panpsychism. *Philosophy and Phenomenological Research*, 86(3), 728–735. DOI: 10.1111/phpr.12028

Alter, T. (1995). Mary's new perspective. *Australasian Journal of Philosophy*, 73(4), 582–584. DOI: 10.1080/00048409512346931

Baker, L. R. (2007). *The metaphysics of everyday life: An essay in practical realism*. Cambridge, UK: Cambridge University Press. DOI: 10.1017/CBO9780511487545

Baker, L. R. (2013). Pereboom's robust nonreductive physicalism. *Philosophy and Phenomenological Research*, 86(3), 736–744. DOI: 10.1111/phpr.12029

Boyd, R. (1999). Kinds, complexity, and multiple realization: Comments on Millikan's "Historical kinds and the special sciences". *Philosophical Studies*, 95(1–2), 67–98. DOI: 10.1023/A:1004511407133

Burge, T. (1979). Individualism and the mental. *Midwest Studies in Philosophy*, 4(1), 73–121. DOI: 10.1111/j.1475-4975.1979.tb00374.x

Chalmers, D. J. (1996). *The conscious mind: In search of a fundamental theory*. Oxford, UK: Oxford University Press.

Chalmers, D. J. (2002). Does conceivability entail possibility? In T. S. Gendler & J. Hawthorne (Eds.), *Conceivability and possibility* (pp. 145–200). Oxford, UK: Oxford University Press.

Chalmers, D. J. (2003). The content and epistemology of phenomenal belief. In Q. Smith & A. Jokic (Eds.), *Consciousness: New philosophical perspectives* (pp. 220–272). Oxford, UK: Oxford University Press.

Chalmers, D. J., & Jackson, F. (2001). Conceptual analysis and reductive explanation. *Philosophical Review*, 110(3), 315–360. DOI: 10.1215/00318108-110-3-315

Churchland, P. M. (1985). Reduction, qualia and the direct introspection of brain states. *Journal of Philosophy*, 82(1), 8–28. DOI: 10.2307/2026509

Dennett, D. (1992). Quining qualia. In A. J. Marcel & E. Bisiach (Eds.), *Consciousness in contemporary science* (pp. 42–77). New York, NY: Oxford University Press. DOI: 10.1093/acprof:oso/9780198522379.003.0003

Goff, P. (forthcoming). Real acquaintance and physicalism. In P. Coates & S. Coleman (Eds.), *Phenomenal qualities: Sense, perception, and consciousness*. Oxford, UK: Oxford University Press.

Jackson, F. (1982). Epiphenomenal qualia. *Philosophical Quarterly*, 32(127), 127–136. DOI: 10.2307/2960077

Jackson, F. (1986). What Mary didn't know. *Journal of Philosophy*, 83(5), 291–295. DOI: 10.2307/2026143

Kant, I. (1781/1787/1998). *Critique of pure reason* (P. Guyer & A. W. Wood, Eds. and Trans.). Cambridge, UK: Cambridge University Press.

Leibniz, G. W. (1969). *Philosophical papers and letters* (2nd ed.), (L. E. Loemker, Ed. & Trans.). Dordrecht, The Netherlands: D. Reidel Publishing Co.

Locke, J. (1689/1975). An essay concerning human understanding. In P. H. Nidditch (Ed.), *The Clarendon edition of the works of John Locke. An essay concerning human understanding*. Oxford, UK: Oxford University Press.

Nagel, T. (1974). What is it like to be a bat? *Philosophical Review*, 83(4), 435–450. DOI: 10.2307/2183914

Ney, A. (2007). Physicalism and our knowledge of intrinsic properties. *Australasian Journal of Philosophy*, 85(1), 41–60. DOI: 10.1080/00048400601154376

Nida-Rümelin, M. (2010). Qualia: The knowledge argument. In E. N. Zalta (Ed.), *The Stanford encyclopedia of philosophy (Summer 2010 edition)*. Retrieved from http://plato.stanford.edu/archives/sum2010/entries/qualia-knowledge

Pereboom, D. (1994). Bats, brain scientists, and the limitations of introspection. *Philosophy and Phenomenological Research*, 54(2), 315–329. DOI: 10.2307/2108491

Pereboom, D. (2002). Robust nonreductive materialism. *Journal of Philosophy*, 99(10), 499–531. DOI: 10.2307/3655563

Pereboom, D. (2011). *Consciousness and the prospects of physicalism*. New York, NY: Oxford University Press. DOI: 10.1093/acprof:oso/9780199764037.001.0001

Pereboom, D. (2013a). Précis of *Consciousness and the Prospects of Physicalism*. *Philosophy and Phenomenological Research*, 86(3), 715–727. DOI: 10.1111/phpr.12027

Pereboom, D. (2013b). Replies to Daniel Stoljar, Robert Adams, and Lynne Baker. *Philosophy and Phenomenological Research*, 86(3), 753–764. DOI: 10.1111/phpr.12031

Place, U. T. (1956). Is consciousness a brain process? *British Journal of Psychology*, 47(1), 44–50. DOI: 10.1111/j.2044-8295.1956.tb00560.x

Plantinga, A. (1996). Epistemic probability and evil. In D. Howard-Snyder (Ed.), *The evidential argument from evil* (pp. 69–96). Bloomington, IN: Indiana University Press.

Russell, B. (1927). *The analysis of matter*. London, UK: Kegan Paul, Trench, Trubner.

Smart, J. J. C. (1959). Sensations and brain processes. *Philosophical Review*, 68(2), 141–156. DOI: 10.2307/2182164

Stoljar, D. (2013). Qualitative inaccuracy and unconceived alternatives. *Philosophy and Phenomenological Research*, 86(3), 745–752. DOI: 10.1111/phpr.12030

van Cleve, J. (1988). Inner states and outer relations: Kant and the case for monadism. In P. H. Hare (Ed.), *Doing philosophy historically* (pp. 231–247). Buffalo, NY: Prometheus Books.

Material constitution, the neuroscience of consciousness, and the temporality of experience

Benjamin L. Curtis
Nottingham Trent University, Nottingham

Drawing upon material from my earlier chapter (with Noonan), in this paper I argue that if a completed neuroscience of consciousness is to be attained, we must give the synchronic and diachronic application conditions for brain states and phenomenal states. I argue that, due to the temporal nature of our experiences, such states must be viewed as being temporally extended events, and illustrate how to give such application conditions using examples of other temporally extended events. However, I also raise some difficulties for the project of giving application conditions for brain states and phenomenal states and suggest these as challenges for further philosophical work.

1. Introduction

Earlier in this volume Harold Noonan and I outlined in some detail the issues from the philosophical literature that surround the puzzles of material constitution and how different solutions proffered to those puzzles interact with problems about identity over time and personal identity. In that chapter, however, we did not explicitly consider how those issues relate to issues in the neuroscience of consciousness literature. The purpose of this chapter is to do just that. My aim is somewhat modest. I aim merely to raise some questions that will need to be addressed if we are to attain a completed neuroscience of consciousness. By drawing upon material from the earlier chapter I will argue that if a *complete* neuroscience of consciousness is to be achieved, much preparatory conceptual-cum-metaphysical work is in need of being done. In particular, I will argue that because phenomenal states are temporally extended affairs, work needs to be done in laying down both the synchronic *and* diachronic application conditions of both brain states (B-states) and phenomenal states (P-states). I raise some difficulties that I see for carrying through such a project, and they are difficulties that I hope can be overcome.

DOI 10.1075/aicr.92.19cur

The argument I present runs as follows: in Section 2 I make a few preliminary remarks on the terms 'correlation' and 'constitution' as they are used in the neural correlates of consciousness (NCC) literature and introduce the notion that P-states must be thought of as temporally extended events, and therefore so must B-states, and that as such, synchronic and diachronic application conditions must be laid down for each. In Section 3 I draw upon the material from my earlier chapter (with Noonan) to illustrate what it means to give synchronic and diachronic application conditions for temporally extended events. Then in Section 4 I raise some questions that give rise to difficulties for laying down such conditions for B-states and P-states.

2. Preliminary remarks on correlation and constitution

In the NCC literature it is said that certain B-states *constitute* certain P-states.[1] (As the term 'constitution' is used in a different sense elsewhere in the philosophical literature, from hereon I will capitalize the 'c' in 'constitution' when using the term in the NCC sense.) It is clear that whatever relation the term is supposed to pick out, it must be supposed to be an especially intimate one, *viz.* a metaphysical dependency relation. This is because the Constitution relation is supposed to be one that contrasts with the relation of (mere) correlation. Without attempting to explicate the two notions in any detail just yet, in order to make the requisite point it is enough to note that whereas correlation is supposed by many to be a metaphysically innocent relation, Constitution is not. The claim that a B-state *Constitutes* a P-state commits one to the view that there is a metaphysical connection between the B-state and P-state in question, whereas the claim that a B-state is *correlated* with a P-state does not. If a B-state Constitutes a P-state it is supposed to entail that the B-state in question is 'the true seat' of that P-state, whereas if the B-state is merely correlated with the P-state, it does not entail this.

What is a metaphysical dependency relation? I know of no way to explicate the concept in any more basic terms, and think it must be taken as fundamental.[2] But I know what kinds of relations are metaphysical dependency relations. One example is the composition relation, i.e., the relation that holds between a whole and its parts. Another is the material constitution relation itself.[3] My claim, then, is that the term 'Constitution', if it is to play the role it is supposed to, must pick out a relation like these.

1. In fact, the term 'Constitutes' is used predominantly by Steven Miller. But others use terminology that has an equivalent sense. See, e.g., Miller (2007, this volume) for an overview of such usage.

2. I don't think it helps to say that it is one that is such that if it holds in a world then it holds in all metaphysically possible worlds too, for I think the notion of a metaphysically possible world is even more elusive, and suspect that it is best defined in terms of metaphysical dependency rather than the other way round.

3. See mine and Noonan's previous chapter in this volume for explanations of these positions.

Metaphysical dependency relations, like all other relations, have entities as relata. The material constitution relation, for example, has material objects as relata. But what are the relata of the Constitution relation? In fact, they are events or processes (i.e., series of events). To see this consider that the search for the neural correlates of consciousness (NCCs) is the attempt to correlate B-states with P-states in a systematic way. Specifically, it is the attempt to establish nomological correlations between them. But the very concept of a *correlation* demands that B-states and P-states are events. Consider the example from studies on binocular rivalry according to which a certain type of process located in the inferior temporal cortex (i.e., the firing of certain neurons located in that region of the brain) is correlated with changes in a certain type of visual experience in subjects (i.e., the change from a visual experience of parallel lines to horizontal lines).[4] There *are* objects involved in this correlation (*viz. neurons* in IT, and *subjects* of phenomenal properties) and there *are* properties involved in this correlation (*viz.* the properties possessed by the neurons when they fire, and phenomenal properties possessed by the subjects). But it is the neurological event of *the firing of the neurons in IT* that is correlated with the phenomenological event of *the having of visual phenomenal properties by subjects* that are strictly speaking correlated and not these objects or properties themselves. This is because it simply makes no sense to suppose that objects or properties are themselves correlated, except in a derivative sense in which they are correlated because the events they are constituents of are correlated. We may say, that is, that the neurons in IT *when they fire* are correlated with *the occurrence in a subject* of certain phenomenological properties, but this is to say that an event or process involving neurons and their physical properties are correlated with an event or process involving subjects and their phenomenological properties. At any rate, because correlations hold between neurological and phenomenal events, and because the Constitution relation is supposed to contrast with the correlation relation, we must take the Constitution relation to hold between neurological and phenomenal events too.

We now come to an important point, for my purposes in this paper. In the philosophical NCC literature, P-states are often conceived of as being finely grained, i.e., as being individuated by their precise contents. As Chalmers puts it:

> Such states might include the experience of a particular visual image, of a particular sound pattern, of a detailed stream of conscious thought, and so on. A detailed visual experience, for example, might include the experience of certain shapes and colors in one's environment, of specific arrangements of objects, of various relative distances and depths, and so on. (Chalmers, 2000, p. 19)

4. This is somewhat simplified, and Logothetis and colleagues have used a number of other stimuli that produce different experiences in their primary subjects (*viz.* monkeys). But the details are not relevant here. For details see e.g., Leopold and Logothetis (1996), Logothetis (1998a, 1998b), and several chapters in Miller (2013).

Chalmers here can be seen as giving voice to the way in which P-states are to be conceived of in a completed neuroscience of consciousness in which we have discovered, for all specific P-states, which specific B-states give rise to them. An analogy perhaps makes this point clear. If we did not already have an understanding of how computers give rise to the images that appear on their screens, we might wish to discover this by looking for correlations between internal states of the computer and representations on the screen. At the limit of this enquiry we would want to know which precise internal states, specified as explicitly as can be, correlate with which precise images on the screen, specified as precisely as can be. A precise specification of such internal states in the computer would be one in which the arrangement of every component of the computer, no matter how small, is detailed. A precise specification of an image on the screen would be a pixel-by-pixel description of it. As such, at its limit, we would have knowledge of how, at least in principle, to bring about any possible pixel-by-pixel image on the computer screen by bringing about a specific arrangement of the computer's internal components. By analogy, at the end of enquiry in the neuroscience of consciousness, at least as Chalmers and others in the philosophical literature conceive of it, we will want to know which internal states of a person's brain, specified as precisely as can be, correlate with which phenomenal states in a person, specified as precisely as can be. It is such precisely specified B-states and P-states that I refer to as 'fine-grained' B-states and P-states. In such a completed neuroscience of consciousness, it would be in principle possible to bring about a fine-grained phenomenal experience in a subject (e.g., the experience of a fiery sunset with birds chirping in the background, or the experience of a monkey on a bicycle singing God Save the Queen) via the direct manipulation of their brains to produce a fine-grained B-state. Needless to say, such a completed neuroscience of consciousness is currently beyond our abilities. However, if this is the eventual aim of our endeavors, it is pertinent to ask what limitations such a completed science would have, and what obstacles stand in the way to our achieving it?

There may be a number of limitations and obstacles, but the obstacle that I will focus on here is that of clearly individuating fine-grained P-states and B-states.[5] Before we can hope to establish correlations between them, and to obtain any evidence that one Constitutes the other, we need to know precisely which entities we are talking about. And here a disanalogy between images on a computer screen and phenomenal states becomes pertinent. Whilst images on a computer screen are momentary affairs, phenomenal states are temporally extended affairs, and their contents have a temporal aspect to them. This is simply because our P-states are not momentary events, but events that take place over time, as even a cursory glance at the literature on the

5. One putative limitation is that even if we manage to discover precisely which fine-grained B-states correlate with which fine-grained P-states, we will never be able to know whether those fine-grained B-states Constitute the fine-grained P-states they correlate with. This is the Cr/Cn distinction problem. For an overview of the problem and a detailed treatment of it see Miller (2001, 2007, this volume).

experience of temporal passage indicates. There are many passages from the literature that could be used to illustrate this, and for an excellent overview of the issue see Ismael (2011), but the following classic passage from William James' *The Principles of Psychology* serves well to make the point:

> The unit of composition of our perceptions of time is a duration, with a bow and a stern, as it were – a rearward – and a forward-looking end... It is only as parts of this duration-block that the relation of succession of one end to the other is perceived. We do not first feel one end and then feel the other after it, and from the perception of the succession infer an interval of time between, but we seem to feel the interval of time as a whole, with its two ends embedded in it. The experience is from the outset a synthetic datum, not a simple one. (James, 1890, p. 610)

No neuroscience of consciousness can ignore the temporal aspects of our experience, and so must attempt to correlate B-states with P-states that are temporally extended. But, if P-states are to be viewed as being temporally extended, then we must have a clear idea of their diachronic application conditions as well as their synchronic ones. And this is where the issues from the material constitution literature are of great relevance.

3. Correlation, constitution, and material constitution

Harold Noonan and I explained in detail earlier in this volume how material objects fall under sortal kinds that have associated with them synchronic application conditions (i.e., conditions that any thing of a kind K must meet at each individual time at which it exists), passing away conditions, and preservation conditions (these latter two conditions I here lump together under the term 'diachronic application conditions'). I do not repeat the details here, but note simply that every material object falls under some sortal kind K that determines the object's synchronic and diachronic extent. So, every object *o* falls under some kind K that determines the answer to the following questions:

(1) What is the spatial extent of *o* at any time at which it exists?
(2) When does *o* come into existence and when does *o* go out of existence?

It is not required that the sortal kind that *o* falls under determines *fully precise* answers to these questions; that there is a certain level of indeterminacy present is acceptable. For example, the term 'human being' is a sortal kind term, for we can answer these questions about human beings to a certain level of precision. We know, for example, that my synchronic extent includes this molecule in my heart, but not this molecule in the cup I am holding. And we know that human beings come into existence *in utero*, and go out of existence when their vital signs cease. But it is not clear *precisely* where the spatial boundaries of human beings are. Is the bit of skin hanging from my thumb part of my body? And it is not clear *precisely* when human beings come into existence and go out of existence. Does a human being come into existence at syngamy? Or when the primitive streak appears? Or at some later point during the growth of the embryo or foetus? Despite this indeterminacy, however, *human being* is a perfectly good sortal kind, and human beings are perfectly respectable objects. As another example consider a more mundane sortal kind term, say, 'table'. We know pretty well where the spatial boundaries of tables are and we know when they come into and go out of existence, so tables are respectable objects. But there is nonetheless some indeterminacy in their synchronic and diachronic extents. Is the fleck of paint peeling off the table leg part of the table? And if we burn the table is there some *exact* moment when it ceases to exist?[6]

When one claims that the material constitution relation holds, under what conditions are one's claims intelligible? One necessary condition is that the entities you say material constitution holds between must be understood to have relatively clear synchronic and diachronic application conditions, otherwise one's claim has no truth-conditions. Suppose, for example, that Smith claims that one putative object *a* materially constitutes another *b* at t. Of course, in order for this claim to be *true*, *a* and *b* must be non-identical and have the same spatial extent at t. But more fundamental than this is the following: in order for the claim to be *intelligible* we must have some grasp of what the spatial extents of *a* and *b* are, otherwise we simply cannot know which objects Smith is referring to. Suppose we ask Smith: "What are *a* and *b*?" He should reply by supplying us with a sortal kind. Suppose he replies that *a* is a lump of clay and *b* is a statue. Then his claim is intelligible. *Lump of* clay and *statue* are both sortal kinds and supply us with synchronic and diachronic application conditions. We now know which objects Smith is referring to and can also determine whether the claim is true. But suppose instead that Smith tells us that *a* is a lump of clay and *b* is a *snark*. And suppose we further press Smith to tell us what a snark is. If he cannot supply us with, for example, the synchronic application conditions for snarks then his claim must be rejected as being simply unintelligible. Not only can we not determine its truth, but we have no idea how to do so because we have no grasp of what object '*b*' refers to. Similar points apply regarding diachronic application conditions. Suppose Smith claims that *a* materially constitutes *b* throughout their existences. Again we ask: what are *a* and *b*? If Smith replies that *a* is a lump of clay and *b* is a statue then again his claim is intelligible. The respective sortal kinds supply us with diachronic application conditions and so allow us to grasp which objects Smith is referring to and evaluate

6. The presence of a sortal kind is even compatible with indeterminacy of a more radical nature than has so far been described. Consider the sortal kind *restaurant* and consider Luigi's, the Italian restaurant that closed down last week on the high street, and Luigi's (the Italian restaurant with the same name and same owners) that opened by the train station this week. Is the old Luigi's the same restaurant as the new Luigi's, i.e., has the restaurant merely re-located? Or is the new Luigi's a new restaurant, albeit one with the same name and owners as the old Luigi's? Questions such as these simply have no determinate answer. Nonetheless, because in ordinary cases we can give determinate answers to such questions, *restaurant* is a perfectly good sortal kind.

the truth of this claim. But if Smith replies instead that *a* is a lump of clay and *b* is a *tove* then we must again press him: what is a tove? Even if Smith can supply us with synchronic application conditions for toves, if he does not supply us with diachronic application conditions then his claim must once more be rejected as unintelligible. Again, we have no idea how to evaluate the truth of the claim because we have no idea which object 'b' refers to.

'Snark' and 'tove' are not genuine English noun-phrases and it is for this reason that they have no synchronic or diachronic application conditions associated with them. But I could easily have used genuine English noun-phrases. Suppose, for example, that Smith tells us that *a* is a *wind* and *b* is a *storm*. *Storm* is perhaps a borderline sortal kind term, but *wind* is certainly not such a term. We simply have no idea how to answer questions about whether a wind at one moment in one place is the same wind or a different wind as a wind at another moment in another place. So again, Smith's claim is unintelligible.

Return now to correlation and Constitution. As I have said, these relations hold not between objects, but between events. Events do not persist over time as objects do, and events do not strictly speaking have material parts. Nevertheless, given what was said above about the temporality of our experiences, P-states at least are events that have diachronic as well as synchronic extents, and so if a claim that one such event *e1* stands in a relation to another *e2* is to be intelligible, we must have some grasp of which events are being referred to by 'e1' and 'e2'. In other words, any putative temporally extended event *e* must also fall under some event sortal kind that determines the answer to the following questions:

1*. What is the synchronic extent of *e* at any time at which it is occurring t?
2*. When does *e* start and when does *e* finish?

To illustrate this consider the event sortal kind *battle*. Battles too are not momentary events, but events with temporal extents. They are, roughly, planned offensives (or a coherent series of such offensives) that are defended against by an opposing force. Being physical events they have more-or-less determinate *spatial* extents. They also begin at more-or-less determinate times (when the first planned offensive begins) and finish at more-or-less determinate times (when combat ceases or one side surrenders). Of course, it is not required that there are fully precise answers to these questions: just as some indeterminacy is acceptable with object sortal kinds, so it is acceptable with event sortal kinds. Consider a particular battle, say, the Battle of the Somme. This event began at around 7.30 a.m. on the 1st July 1916 when thirteen British and eleven French infantry divisions began their advance across the river Somme. It ended at around 3.15 p.m. on 21st November 1916 when 45 survivors of the Highland Light Infantry battalion surrendered to the German forces. Other contemporaneous events are 'proper parts' of the Battle of the Somme, whilst others are not. The fighting of Bazentin Ridge, that took place from 14th–22nd July that year, was part of the Battle of the Somme. So was the attempt by the Anzacs to capture the Mouquet Farm on the 12th August. So were the many firings of bullets that occurred on Bazentin Ridge between the 14th–16th July. By contrast, the Ninth Battle of the Isonzo, the Italian offensive against the Austro-Hungarians between 1st–4th November 1916, was not part of the Battle of the Somme. And nor was Pavel Milyukov's famous "stupidity or treason" speech that took place on 1st of November 1916 in the Russian State Duma. And nor was the birth of the poet Shakeel Badayuni in India on 3rd August 1916. All of the above facts are determined by the event sortal kind *battle*.

There is an analog of material coincidence for events. Two events coincide at a time if the two events have the same synchronic extent. Consider a particular event *e1* and *e2*. Suppose *e1* is a performance of Donizetti's *L'Elisir d'Amore* that occurs in a particular place *p* across a particular timeframe (say, from *t1* to *t100*), and suppose *e2* is a particular piece of improvised singing that takes place in *p* during the piece's tenor aria cadenza *Una furtiva lagrima* (say, from *t12* to *t14*). These two events plausibly fall under distinct event sortal kinds (i.e., something like *performance* and *act of singing*) and the second plausibly constitutes the first from *t12* to *t14* in an analogous way to which an object materially constitutes another that it coincides with at a time. Call this analogous sense of constitution 'occurral constitution'. In addition, two events coincide over time if they not only have the same synchronic extent at all times at which they exist, but also the same diachronic extent, i.e., if they start and finish at the same time. Consider, for example, *the placing of the Great Seal by King John* onto a particular piece of paper on 15th June 1215 and *the ratification of Magna Carta*. These two short events plausibly fall under distinct sortals (i.e., something like *placing of a seal* and *ratifying of a treaty*) and plausibly have the same synchronic and diachronic extents, so the first plausibly occurrally constitutes the second in an analogous way to which one object is said to constitute another that it permanently coincides with.

Let us now return to B-states and P-states once more. So far we have established that if B-states are to correlate with or Constitute P-states it must be possible to answer questions 1* and 2* with regard to them. That is to say, B-states and P-states must fall under some event sortal kind that determines their synchronic and diachronic extents. We have not established precisely what the Constitution relation is, but one natural thought is that it just *is* the occurral constitution relation described above. However, it should be noted that there is a difficulty that stands in the way of maintaining this with regards to B-states and P-states: B-states and P-states apparently have different kinds of synchronic extents. B-states are physical events so their synchronic extents will be spatial, whereas P-states are mental events, so their synchronic extents will be in some sense mental. So, it is difficult to make sense of how they can synchronically coincide. That said, because the relation between B-states and P-states is plausibly not one of *material* constitution, perhaps the synchronic problem does not need to be solved. It seems at least plausible to suggest that so long as B-states and the P-states they correlate with (or Constitute) occur at the same time, and the P-states are reported to be present by the individuals in the B-states in question, then we need not worry too much about whether they can be said to have the same synchronic extent.

Whether or not B-states that correlate with P-states must be said to coincide synchronically, it is clear that they certainly must coincide *diachronically*. That is, if a B-state is to correlate with (or Constitute) a P-state it must begin and end at the same time. So, even without being able to give a full analysis of the correlation relation, by putting together everything that has so far been said we can lay down the following necessary conditions for correlation:

A B-state *b* correlates with a P-state *p* only if:
(1) *b* and *p* fall under distinct event sortal kinds that determine their diachronic extents.
(2) *b* and *p* begin and end at the same time.

4. Difficulties with solving the diachronic extent problem

In this final section I raise some difficulties for the task of specifying the diachronic application conditions for B-states and P-states, and less importantly, raise some issues with specifying their synchronic application conditions too. B-states are supposed to be neuronal events – i.e., occurrences of certain behavior by, and the instantiation of properties in, collections of neurons. Consider the following representative list:

- 40 Hz oscillations in the cerebral cortex
- Intralaminar nuclei in the thalamus
- Re-entrant loops in thalamocortical systems
- 40 Hz rhythmic activity in thalamocortical systems
- Extended reticular-thalamic activation system
- Neural assemblies bound by NMDA
- Certain neurochemical levels of activation
- Certain neurons in inferior temporal cortex
- Neurons in extrastriate visual cortex projecting to prefrontal areas
- Visual processing within the ventral stream

My lack of neuroscientific knowledge makes it difficult for me to evaluate whether these events fall under event sortal kinds or not. Certainly many of them seem to be spatially well prescribed. The occurrence of a 40 Hz oscillation in the cerebral cortex, for example, seems to be quite determinately extended through the cerebral cortex and not present elsewhere. The question of whether the events are temporally well prescribed is harder for me to call. Suppose the 40 Hz oscillation reduces to a 39 Hz oscillation, or a 39.9 Hz oscillation (if such things are possible). Is one and the same event still occurring? Or is this the end of the 40 Hz oscillation event and the start of a new event? One might be tempted to reply here that *of course* this is a case in which one event ends and a new one begins, because the first is a *40 Hz* oscillation and the second a *39.9 Hz* oscillation. However, this reply is too quick. What we *call* events is not relevant to whether the events are the same events or distinct events. To see this consider an analogous case for material objects. Consider a red table that is painted blue at time t, and ask: At t does one material object continue to exist into the future? Or is this a case in which one material object goes out of existence and another comes into existence? A reply analogous to the one above is possible here. One might say *of course* this is a case in which one object ceases to exist and another comes into existence, because the first is a *red* table and the second a *blue* table. However, it is quite clear that in this case this reply would be incorrect. Red tables do not cease to exist when they are painted blue (even though they can no longer be called '*red* tables' any more). The key point is that we are able to answer the question regarding tables precisely because we have the sortal kind *table* that determines when tables come into existence and cease to exist. So, likewise in the oscillation case above, in order to answer the question we need to have some event sortal kind that determines an answer to the question. The general term 'neuronal event' doesn't seem to be a genuine event sortal kind as it doesn't seem to supply diachronic application conditions. But perhaps there are genuine event sortal kinds here that neuroscientists work with, and so perhaps there are perfectly good answers to the question above and to similar ones regarding other neuronal events. I simply don't have the expertise to judge whether or not this is so. However, one thing that is clear is this: if neuroscientists do not already work with genuine sortal kinds, if we are to achieve a completed neuroscience of consciousness, genuine sortal kinds must be laid down that give answers to questions about the diachronic extent of B-states.

The same is true of P-states. However, they are more problematic than B-states. P-states are mental events and do not seem to have spatial extents at all, but we *can* make sense of the idea that they have some kind of synchronic extent. Consider a particular occurrence of a putative mental event at a time t, say an experience of a red blob in the center of the visual field. One might say that some red patch in the center of the blob is determinately within the synchronic extent of the event at t, whilst some blue patch at the edge of the visual field at t is not. Perhaps there are always more-or-less determinate answers to questions about the synchronic extent of P-states (although I doubt it is so). At any rate, as has already been said, perhaps this issue is of lesser importance than the issue of determining the diachronic extents of P-states. But here real trouble sets in too, and the trouble can be illustrated with some simple questions. Suppose the experience of a red blob is followed by an experience of a slightly larger red blob – i.e., the blob seems to "grow". Is this a case in which one P-state continues, or does one P-state end and another begin? Or suppose I close my eyes for a second and then reopen them and am confronted with an exactly similar red blotch experience as before. Again, is one and the same P-state occurring? Or is this a new P-state? And consider more complicated cases. How many P-states make up my experience of a lighting strike? Is the experience of the whole strike a single event, or is it composed of smaller sub-events? Is the afterimage that I experience part of it? And how about the transient image of it that remains in my imagination for a few seconds following it? Now consider one's experiences of a busy market place and try to start cutting it up into distinct temporally extended phenomenal events. It is not obvious how to answer questions like the ones raised, but answers must be given if a completed neuroscience of consciousness is to be attained. The difficulty is that our experiences seems to run continuously one into the next, which makes it very difficult to see how to effect a division between one P-state and the next. I finish with another quote from James that again illustrates the point well:

> Consciousness, then, does not appear to itself chopped up in bits. Such words as 'chain' or 'train' do not describe it fitly as it presents itself in the first instant. It is nothing jointed: it flows. A 'river' or a 'stream' are the metaphors by which it is most naturally described. In talking of it hereafter, let us call it the stream of thought, of consciousness, or of subjective life. (James, 1890, p. 233)

5. Conclusion

I have argued that any completed neuroscience of consciousness must at some point tackle the question of what the synchronic *and* diachronic extents of B-states and P-states are. This is because our experiences, and thus our P-states, have a temporal element to them that no neuroscience of consciousness can ignore. I have suggested that the way to tackle this question is to lay down the synchronic and diachronic application conditions for B-states and P-states, conceived of as temporally extended events. However, I have also raised some questions that point to difficulties for laying down such conditions. My hope is that others will either show that my arguments here are misguided, or be able to see how to answer these questions.

References

Chalmers, D. J. (2000). What is a neural correlate of consciousness? In T. Metzinger (Ed.), *Neural correlates of consciousness: Empirical and conceptual questions* (pp. 17–39). Cambridge, MA: MIT Press.

Ismael, J. (2011). Temporal experience. In C. Callender (Ed.), *Oxford handbook of philosophy of time* (pp. 460–482). Oxford, UK: Oxford University Press.

James, W. (1890). *Principles of psychology*. London, UK: Macmillan. DOI: 10.1037/11059-000

Leopold, D. A., & Logothetis, N. K. (1996). Activity changes in early visual cortex reflect monkeys' percepts during binocular rivalry. *Nature*, 379(6565), 549–553. DOI: 10.1038/379549a0

Logothetis, N. (1998a). Object vision and visual awareness. *Current Opinion in Neurobiology*, 8(6), 536–544. DOI: 10.1016/S0959-4388(98)80043-3

Logothetis, N. K. (1998b). Single units and conscious vision. *Philosophical Transactions of the Royal Society of London B: Biological Sciences*, 353(1377), 1801–1818. DOI: 10.1098/rstb.1998.0333

Miller, S. M. (2001). Binocular rivalry and the cerebral hemispheres: With a note on the correlates and constitution of visual consciousness. *Brain and Mind*, 2(1), 119–149. DOI: 10.1023/A:1017981619014

Miller, S. M. (2007). On the correlation/constitution distinction problem (and other hard problems) in the scientific study of consciousness. *Acta Neuropsychiatrica*, 19(3), 159–176. DOI: 10.1111/j.1601-5215.2007.00207.x

Miller, S. M. (Ed.). (2013). *The constitution of visual consciousness: Lessons from binocular rivalry*. Advances in Consciousness Research (Vol. 90). Amsterdam, The Netherlands: John Benjamins Publishing Company. DOI: 10.1075/aicr.90

The structure of phenomenal consciousness

Jonathan P. Opie and Gerard J. O'Brien
University of Adelaide, Adelaide

Philosophers have largely abandoned the claim that the special sciences will ultimately reduce to microphysics in favour of the view that the special sciences trade in *functional* explanations. However, a careful examination of scientific practice reveals that the explanatory strategy of the special sciences is neither reductionist *nor* functionalist, but *mechanistic*. Mechanistic explanations appeal to active material entities organized so as to produce the target phenomena. We claim that phenomenal consciousness will also succumb to mechanistic explanation: it will turn out to be the activity of specific neural mechanisms in the brain. In this chapter we explore the implications of this perspective for the ontology of consciousness, arguing that it has a complex *structural* essence.

1. Introduction

Among all the mysteries of the modern era, the nature of phenomenal consciousness is one of the most profound. Many philosophers regard the problem as uniquely difficult: either an ultimate mystery (McGinn, 1991), or requiring explanatory principles not yet provided by the sciences (Chalmers, 1996; Nagel, 1974). We think this gloomy prognosis is a mistake; the result of taking a too narrow view of the nature and power of scientific explanation. Our aim here is to reflect on recent progress in cognitive neuroscience and the philosophy of science, and show how these disciplines jointly promise to illuminate the deep nature of consciousness.

The question before us – what kind of thing is phenomenal consciousness? – is an ontological question. Ontology is the study of what there is. Although sometimes regarded as an arcane pursuit suited only to philosophers, there is a very real and intimate connection between scientific explanation and ontology. To begin with, the form of our explanations is influenced by the nature of the things we seek to understand. Very different mathematical and conceptual resources are required to explain, say, fundamental *physical* processes (such as quantum tunneling), and *biological* processes (such as mitosis). Secondly, and more importantly for our purposes, we look to our best scientific explanations for guidance as to the essential nature of things.

DOI 10.1075/aicr.92.200pi

Philosophers of science generally acknowledge just two kinds of material essence[1]: the *microphysical* and the *functional*. A focus on microphysics issues from the view that the special sciences have a common grounding in subatomic physics. Explanation is here conceived as an iterated series of reductions that will ultimately permit us to comprehend the behavior of any system, be it chemical, neural, social etc., in terms of processes occurring at the subatomic level. From this point of view, the essence of any material system is its *composition*, that is, its analysis as a collection of subatomic constituents. A focus on functional analysis issues from the multiple realizability arguments that dominated discussions in the philosophy of science during the 1970s and 1980s.[2] These arguments led many philosophers to conclude that the special sciences are not reducible to microphysics, because the natural kinds of the special sciences are not (type) identifiable with their subatomic constituents – they have *functional*, rather than microphysical essences.

However, philosophers have recently been paying closer attention to the practice of the special sciences and to the nature of the explanations they generate. What is apparent is that the explanatory strategy of the special sciences is neither functionalist nor strongly reductionist. It is *mechanistic*. Rather than seeking to understand phenomena by way of decomposition into their subatomic parts, the special sciences investigate the manner in which the behavior of material systems is constituted by relationships among their components. The focus here is on *organization* rather than (microphysical) composition. Nor does this mechanistic strategy appeal to functional essences, because the types of organization at issue are not limited to the causal analyses associated with functional explanation.

Philosophy of science has yet to fully appreciate the ontological significance of this mechanistic strategy. We will argue that the success of mechanistic explanation requires the introduction of a new ontological category. Phenomena produced by mechanisms are best understood as possessing *structural* essences. This result has important implications for our understanding of phenomenal consciousness. Conscious experiences, like many other natural kinds, are not identifiable with their microphysical parts. But neither can they be properly characterized in a way that ignores the material properties of their realising mechanisms. Conscious experiences are emergent phenomena that are metaphysically dependent on their material components, without being identical to them.

---

1. The "essence" or essential nature of something is that which makes it the kind of thing it is. So, for example, the essence of combustion is that it involves a sequence of exothermic chemical reactions between a fuel and an oxidant. By "material essence" we mean to distinguish our target from, e.g., logical and conceptual systems, whose essence is arguably non-material. The viability of essentialism is a matter of some controversy among philosophers (see, e.g., Robertson, 2008), but we will take it for granted that it provides a useful way to think about ontology.

2. A property or kind is "multiply realizable" if its different instances need not have a common set of building blocks. For example, a wing can be composed of bone, sinew and feathers, balsa and canvas, or aluminium and steel.

Our task in this chapter will be to defend this set of claims. We begin by offering a brief history of the philosophy of science responsible for generating the dichotomy between microphysical and functionalist metaphysics. We then consider at greater length the mechanistic model of explanation. This much is merely descriptive. The chapter turns polemical when we consider the metaphysical implications of this model of explanation, and their application to the case of consciousness. Our conclusion is that conscious experiences, from an ontological perspective, are emergent structures.

2. Microphysicalism versus functionalism

Throughout the better part of the twentieth century the orthodox account of scientific explanation was one that focused on the "laws of nature". To explain a phenomenon was to derive it from statements describing laws and boundary conditions. This view, most clearly expounded in the work of Hempel (1966), is known as the Deductive Nomological (DN) model, because it treats explanation as the logical derivation of explananda from laws (Greek: nomoi). For example, to explain why the pressure on the walls of a gas-filled piston doubles when its volume is halved, we invoke Boyle's law. This law states that the product of pressure and volume for an ideal gas at a fixed temperature is constant ($PV = c$, where P is pressure and V is volume). The measured change in pressure can be derived using this law, with the change in volume and the other criteria operating as boundary conditions.

What distinguishes one scientific discipline from another, on the DN model, is the theoretical vocabulary, ontology, and proprietary laws that apply to their respective domains. The various gas laws thus serve to pick out the discipline of thermodynamics, which (among other things) deals with gases conceived as fluids with a characteristic set of macroscopic properties. Kinetic theory, by contrast, deals with the behavior of the microscopic constituents of matter, treated either as classical particles governed by the Newtonian laws of motion, or quantum systems governed by the laws of quantum mechanics. Laws themselves stand in need of explanation, but this is typically achieved using the resources of a more fundamental discipline. To explain Boyle's gas law, for example, we invoke mechanical and statistical principles which do not belong to classical thermodynamics, and which are arguably more wide-ranging. If we can derive the laws of one discipline from those of another, without remainder, then the former is said to *reduce to* the latter.

With this view of explanation and reduction in mind, Oppenheim and Putnam (1958) developed an influential scheme for organizing natural objects. They divide nature into the following six levels, where each level comprises a set of entities with a characteristic scale, and subject to the laws of an attendant discipline: Elementary Particles (Particle Physics), Atoms (Atomic Physics), Molecules (Chemistry), Cells (Cell Biology), Organisms (Biology), Society (Social Science). A principal motivation for this scheme is to provide a basis for the putative unity of science, a unity constituted by reductive relationships among levels. The idea is that social science will eventually reduce to biology (presumably via such intermediate special sciences as psychology and neuroscience), biology to cell biology, cell biology to chemistry, and so on. DN reduction is transitive in this scheme: if cell biology reduces to chemistry, and chemistry to atomic physics, then cell biology also reduces to atomic physics because the derivation of cell biology piggy-backs on the derivation of chemistry, allowing one to explain cellular phenomena in atomic terms. Were this sequence of reductions to be completed, all of science would be unified by its grounding in subatomic physics, which would provide a common starting point for the derivation of phenomena at all levels.

So the DN model of explanation goes hand in hand with *strong reductionism*: the view that the special sciences will eventually be replaced by explanations couched in the terminology of subatomic physics. This view results from privileging the ontology of microphysics over all others. We might agree that all phenomena in the universe ultimately depend on the elementary parts of matter, in the sense that were the latter to spontaneously disappear, so would the former. But strong reductionism suggests a further, more radical claim, namely, that the universe and all the systems it contains is *nothing but* a vast congeries of elementary particles. From this perspective, conscious experience, like every other material phenomenon, is nothing more than a (mind-numbingly) complex conjunction of sub-atomic particles behaving in accordance with the fundamental laws of physics.

During the 1970s and 1980s, this reductionist conception of the unity of science started to come unstuck, in large part because of so-called *multiple realizability* arguments. In an important early paper, Fodor (1974) argued that the special sciences don't reduce to (micro)physics, because the properties over which their laws are defined don't have unique decompositions into the properties of elementary particles. While individual cells, tectonic plates, airfoils, galaxies, and so on, are no doubt composed of fundamental particles, the property of being a cell, a tectonic plate, an airfoil, or a galaxy is realized by such a heterogeneous and unsystematic set of microphysical properties that, in principle as well as in practice, no reduction of the laws of the special sciences is possible. This analysis precipitated an avalanche of further reflections on the significance of multiple realizability, and resulted in widespread abandonment of the reductionist program.

The ontological consequences of the demise of strong reductionism were immediate and profound. Most theorists embraced the view that the phenomena of the special sciences have *functional*, rather than microphysical, essences. This is the basis of the *functionalist metaphysics* that dominates contemporary philosophy, just as microphysicalism did during the first half of the twentieth century. According to functionalism, special science kinds belong to the abstract domain of *causal organization*. This view appears to follow immediately from the existence of multiple realizability. If there is nothing materially in common to the entities targeted by some special science, what *could* unite them apart from causal organization? Airfoils, for example, are certainly composed of subatomic particles. However, when it comes to aerodynamics, it is not the composition of an airfoil that matters, but rather the pattern of causal relations into which it enters, or so a functionalist would argue.

Functionalism has a number of significant implications for the relationship between the sciences. Most significantly, it licenses the *autonomy* of the special sciences. Because each science operates with its own proprietary level of causal organization, even cognate disciplines will have little to say to one another about the fundamental nature of their respective kinds. It was functionalist metaphysics that motivated strong claims about the independence of cognitive science from neuroscience late in the twentieth century. Although neuroscience undoubtedly has something interesting to say about the substrate of our own cognitive processes, the essential nature of cognition is not illuminated by analysing the material properties of the brain.

Although multiple realizability arguments have been almost universally thought to undermine strong reductionism, a number of their proponents, including Fodor, did not take them to undermine the DN model of explanation. However, at more or less the same time as these arguments were proving destructive of reductionism, other philosophers were applying pressure more directly on the DN model. In an influential paper, Salmon (1978) argued that scientists generally seek to discover the *causes* of some range of phenomena, rather than subsume them under laws. To explain variations in the pressure on the walls of a piston one describes: (1) the system involved – a fixed quantity of gas made up of a huge number of fast-moving particles, a closed but expandable container with rigid walls; and (2) the way the parts of the system produce the phenomenon – pressure variations are caused by changes in the mean rate of particle-wall impacts as a result of changes in the size of the container. In other words, one describes the *mechanism* that produces the explanandum phenomenon.

3. The mechanistic model of explanation

The mechanistic model of explanation has a venerable history, dating back to Democritus and the Greek atomists. During the early modern era it was championed by the likes of Galileo Galilei, René Descartes, and Robert Boyle (Bechtel, 2006, pp. 20–22). Recent work in this tradition has focused on providing a general account of the nature of mechanisms and their role in scientific explanation (Bechtel, 2006, 2008; Bunge, 1997; Craver, 2001, 2007; Glennan, 2002; Machamer, Darden, & Craver, 2000; Woodward, 1989).

Our everyday conceptions of mechanism, which are informed by experience with relatively simple devices such as clocks and corkscrews, are potentially at odds with scientific usage. Such artefacts certainly embody mechanisms, but they are poor models for the kinds of processes scientists typically invoke to explain natural phenomena. Natural mechanisms – such as thermal conduction, protein synthesis, bacterial conjugation, perspiration, sexual selection, gravitation, and so on – need not have rigid parts, nor must they be linear, denumerable, or easily understood. Indeed, many natural phenomena result from complex, non-linear processes that defy our best attempts at analysis.

In the broadest terms, a mechanism is a process in a material system that produces (or prevents) some change or brings something into being.[3] Material systems themselves are sometimes referred to as "mechanisms" but it is more consistent with scientific usage to identify mechanisms with productive processes. Bechtel (2006) stipulates that "[a] mechanism is a structure performing a function in virtue of its component parts, its component operations, and their organization" (p. 26). Likewise, Craver (2007) regards a mechanism as "a set of entities and activities organized such that they exhibit the phenomenon to be explained" (p. 5). The emphasis here is on the way operations or activities are organized to produce a specific outcome. To specify a mechanism one must identify: (1) the relevant parts of the system, (2) the activities of those parts, and (3) how the organization of those parts and their activities gives rise to the phenomenon of interest. For example, the pumping of the heart depends on certain of its parts (ventricles, atria, valves), their activities (contraction and relaxation, opening and closing), and their spatial, temporal and causal relations (valves connect chambers and vessels, atria and ventricles contract and valves open in a specific sequence).

According to the mechanistic account of explanation, to explain some behavior or capacity Φ of a material system S is to identify and describe a process M in S that produces Φ. If S is an open system, M will be subject to outside influences, so fully specifying Φ will involve specifying the environmental conditions that bear on M. For example, blood is part of the heart's environment, and the condition of the blood has an impact on the heart's activity. If we aim to explain the pumping of the heart, we must first establish how variation in the properties of the blood (pH, $pO2$, viscosity, etc.) affects this behavior. Thus, mechanistic explanation almost always encompasses at least two distinct levels: (1) the level of the system S and its environment, including any relevant containing systems; and (2) the level of the active parts of S (Bechtel, 2008, p. 148). As mechanistic explanation iterates, deeper explanations will reveal further levels of organization in the structure of the parts of S.

Bechtel (2008) and Craver (2007) argue that material organization is the basis of this level hierarchy. As remarked, every mechanistic explanation involves at least two levels of organization, and mechanistic explanations typically also refer to the organization of one or more subsystems of the primary system. What belong at each level are the active entities whose organization produces the explanandum phenomenon at the next level. Thus, atria, ventricles and valves are at one level, because their organized activity constitutes the pumping of the heart; the heart, blood and vessels a next higher level, because they collectively act to circulate nutrients, hormones and gases around the body. A mechanism at one level is *composed of* entities at the next lowest level of organization. Those entities are themselves composed of entities at a yet lower level,

3. This formulation is adapted from Bunge (1997). A material system is a bundle of real things that behave in some respects as a unit by virtue of their interactions or bonding. Atoms, crystals, synapses, transistors, cells, organisms, families, firms and galaxies are material systems, which are to be contrasted with conceptual systems, such as theories and classifications. (ibid, p. 415)

and so on. Composition implies spatial and temporal containment, that is, the parts and activities of a mechanism cannot exceed the size and duration of the whole process. However, it is important to recognize that a mechanism is no mere bag of parts. A mechanism is a *physical gestalt* (Köhler, 1920); a material whole that is constituted by the organization of its parts and their activities.

There are a number of significant respects in which this mechanistic approach to levels differs from Oppenheim and Putnam's scheme. First, mechanistic levels are always local (Craver, 2007, pp. 192–193). They do not comprise a single, global hierarchy, because they are always defined relative to the current explanatory target. Second, the order associated with mechanistic levels is partial, not total (Bechtel, 2008, p. 147; Craver, 2007, p. 191). Some things are related by level membership, others are not. Even though the heart is composed of cells, osteocytes (bone cells) do not appear at a lower level than the heart in the mechanism of circulation. Third, entities of a given kind can appear at more than one level in the same mechanism. For example, some sensory neurons detect acidity via proton-gated ion channels, which open a pore in the cell membrane, thereby inducing a sensory signal (Waldmann, Chamigny, Bassilana, Heurteaux, & Lazdunski, 1997). Free protons are at the same level as ion channels in this context, because the two must interact for acid-sensing to occur. However, as protons are a basic building block of matter, protons are also constituents of the ion channels themselves. Thus protons appear on at least two organizational levels in this mechanism.[4]

The mechanistic approach to levels is at odds with some very entrenched intuitions. It is by now second-nature to associate levels with well-defined types, each having a fixed place in a monolithic, global hierarchy. The simplicity of this picture is one of its chief attractions, but also its principal flaw, because it fails to reflect the complexities of scientific practice. Most disciplines pay little attention to boundaries defined by scale or type, seeking out whichever entities, activities and forms of organization illuminate their explanatory targets. Indeed, it is reasonable to ask why anyone would expect a global level hierarchy to make sense of the very different explanatory demands of, say, cell biology and plasma physics. Both disciplines investigate processes whose ultimate constituents are protons, neutrons and electrons, but organized in such vastly different ways that the two domains essentially have no structures in common at any scale.[5]

There is both reduction and emergence here. Mechanisms emerge from the organized activity of lower-level entities, and have effects that their constituents in isolation lack. The existence of this kind of novelty is not miraculous, although it can be difficult to understand, especially when the organization involved is complex or nonlinear. Mechanistic explanation is reductive in the sense that it reveals the connection

4. See Bechtel (2008, p. 147) for a similar example.

5. A plasma is a high-temperature gas of unbound protons, neutrons and electrons, which do not combine to form atoms because of their high kinetic energy.

between phenomena and the lower level entities that produce them. Yet it doesn't thereby eliminate high-level phenomena, which depend not only on the constituents of their mechanisms, but also on the way those constituents are organized. Nor does mechanistic explanation eliminate disciplines, in the sense of making them redundant. Disciplines span levels, and must cooperate to discover the multi-level mechanisms of complex phenomena. The unity of science, such as it is, does not depend on reductive relationships among disciplines, but on the shared ambition to reveal the hidden structure of nature.

4. The metaphysics of mechanistic explanation

The outline of a mechanistic approach to explanation has been well delineated by a number of philosophers. What of its ontological entailments? Given its rejection of a hierarchical conception of the unity of science, and of strong reductionism, the mechanistic model clearly doesn't comport well with microphysicalism. This, we think, has prompted most philosophers to assume that it leads inevitably to functionalism. But this assumption sits awkwardly with several aspects of the mechanistic story.

One thing that distinguishes mechanistic explanation from abstract functional analysis (Cummins, 1975) is a focus on the material basis of systemic behaviors. A functional analysis decomposes an overall system capacity into a set of sub-capacities, but is typically silent on how those sub-capacities are realized. By contrast, a mechanistic explanation reveals how some phenomenon depends on the constitution and organization of particular material entities. Organization has spatial, temporal, and hierarchical dimensions. The parts of a mechanism have characteristic structures, positions and arrangements. Their activities occur with specific timings, rates and durations, and in sequences or cycles which may incorporate feedback and other kinds of orchestration. Organization also has a hierarchical dimension because mechanisms typically contribute to the behavior of superordinate systems, and are composed of subordinate systems with structure of their own (Bechtel, 2008, pp. 10–17; Craver, 2001).

This emphasis on material structure suggests that the mechanistic model of explanation does not entail a functionalist metaphysics. But how can this disconnect between mechanism and functionalism be made consistent with multiple realizability? Let us consider one of Fodor's (1989, pp. 61–62) favourite examples: the humble airfoil. It is certainly true, as Fodor avers, that airfoils can be constructed from a variety of materials – wood, sheet metal, fiberglass, even sheets of canvas – and hence that they need have nothing in common with respect to their composition. It is also true that all airfoils, regardless of composition, have a common causal role: they all bring about lift by causing air to flow more rapidly across one surface than another. What is not true is that this functional property is the *only* thing airfoils have in common. An airfoil generates lift when it moves through the air because its upper surface has *greater curvature* than its lower surface. Airfoils are thus distinguished from other kinds of things not merely by their causal role, but also by their *shape*.[6] And that property is multiply realizable: an airfoil can be constructed from any material rigid enough to maintain the differential curvature of upper and lower surfaces. If we think more generally about shape, it is clear that an object's shape is not fixed by its subatomic composition. But neither is it determined by its causal role or causal organization (even if the causal relations into which an object enters are sometimes determined by its shape). Metaphysically speaking, shape lies somewhere between these two extremes. Like causal or functional role, shape abstracts away from the microphysical composition of an object. But unlike causal role or causal organization, shape is an *intrinsic material* property.

We need a general term to describe such abstract material properties. We will call them *structural* properties. The functional properties of an airfoil are clearly multiply realizable, but so are its structural properties. The question that arises, of course, is whether airfoils are better classified as possessing a functional or a structural essence. Is it structure or function that determines membership of this kind? In answer, we note that the class of objects that can generate lift is much larger than the class of airfoils – think of jet engines, for example. What distinguishes airfoils from other lift-generating mechanisms is their characteristic curvature. Furthermore, it is this structural property which explains the functional characteristics of an airfoil, not the converse. This suggests that structural properties are more fundamental than functional ones, and that any classification into kinds should privilege structure over function.

On the basis of this tripartite distinction between microphysical, structural, and functional properties, we would argue that the special sciences are founded principally on the metaphysical emergence of structural kinds. Many of the examples philosophers use to illustrate multiple realizability turn out on closer inspection to highlight the significance of structure for natural kinds. Cells, for example, as the nexus of a host of biological processes, and the product of a long and complex causal history, are often treated as the quintessential functional kind. But there are many respects in which a cell is fundamentally reliant on structure: a cell is an entity whose very existence depends on the presence of a semi-permeable boundary, the cell wall, which marks the distinction between the cell's internal components and the environment in which it makes a living. This boundary ensures that the internal milieu of a cell is maintained in its highly organized, far-from-equilibrium condition, in the face of enormous variability in the cell's surroundings. And it hardly needs saying that a cell wall is a (highly specialized) material structure. So in this case, function again follows form, and structure appears to be essential to the identity of the kind in question.

Perhaps even more importantly, many special science kinds which have not been considered multiply realizable are best understood as possessing structural rather than microphysical essences. Ever since the discovery of isomerism by Liebig and Wöhler

6. The lift generated by an airfoil, such as a wing, doesn't just depend on its shape, but also on its surface area and angle of attack. Nonetheless, the term "airfoil" is usually reserved for objects with differential curvature of their two principal surfaces.

in the 1820s it has been known that chemical compounds cannot be identified with their atomic constituents. The mercury salts of cyanate and fulminate, for example, are composed of mercury, carbon, nitrogen and oxygen atoms in identical proportions, yet these two compounds have very different chemical properties. Mercury fulminate is a highly unstable substance that explodes under light impacts, friction or heating. It was used extensively during the industrial revolution as a detonator (Kurzer, 2000). Mercury cyanate, by contrast, is thermally and mechanically stable. Why do these two substances behave so differently, despite their common atomic basis? It turns out that materials with identical atomic constituents can have distinct molecular structures. The structure of the cyanate ion is O-C≡N whereas in the fulminate ion the nitrogen and carbon atoms change positions: O-N≡C. What distinguishes the two mercury salts is thus not a matter of the nature or proportion of their constituents, but differences in their bonding patterns.

Here we have the converse of multiple realizability: rather than a single higher level kind with different realizers, we have distinct special science kinds constructed from the *same* constituents. Let's call this a case of *multiple composability*. A property or kind is multiply realizable if its instances don't share a common set of building blocks. A set of parts are multiply composable if they can be combined and organized so as to produce numerous distinct higher-level kinds.

Multiple realizability undermines microphysicalism, you will recall, because special science kinds are typically realized by such a heterogeneous set of microphysical properties. Multiple composability leads to the same conclusion via a different route. To make sense of the very different physical and chemical properties of the cyanate and fulminate ions it does not suffice to identify their constituents. The mechanism that explains the explosive properties of mercury fulminate, for example, depends not only on its lower-level atomic components, but also on the manner in which they are combined, in particular, the triple-bond on the carbon atom causes it to be negatively charged and thereby renders the ion thermodynamically unstable.[7] Furthermore, because an explosion is a macroscopic phenomenon involving vast numbers of ions (or molecules), a full account of the detonation of mercury fulminate will describe chemical and mechanical processes occurring at the level of its crystalline structure (see, e.g., Brown & Swallowe, 1981; Faust, 1989). Microphysicalism is inadequate to this kind of explanation, because it downplays or ignores the ontic significance of emergent structure: the various levels of organization that occur in any real-world system. By the same token, a functionalist metaphysics fails to grapple with the consequences of multiple composability, because the kinds it envisages are so abstract as to render invisible the very processes that distinguish, say, fulminates from cyanates.

7. Fulminate is actually a resonance hybrid of two principal Lewis structures, O-N≡C and O=N=C, both of which result in a negative formal charge on carbon and a positive formal charge on nitrogen. It is this energetically unfavourable electron configuration that makes fulminate so unstable.

Multiple composability is ubiquitous in the sciences. Just as one set of atomic constituents can compose distinct chemical compounds, the same cell types can compose different biological organisms, the same neural cells different neural architectures, the same neural networks different cognitive mechanisms, and so on. Composition alone is not of the essence for the kinds of the special sciences, nor, it seems, is causal organization. Material structure trumps function in mechanistic explanation, hence special science kinds, whenever they feature in such explanations, are best conceived as having structural essences.

So much for the philosophy of science. It is now time to apply the mechanistic approach to the explanation of phenomenal consciousness.

5. The ontology of consciousness

In the foregoing we sought to tease out the general metaphysical implications of mechanistic explanation in the special sciences. Our next task is to apply the lessons learned there to the specific case of consciousness. We saw earlier that according to the mechanistic model, to explain some phenomenon Φ in a material system S one must identify: (1) the relevant parts of S; (2) the activities of those parts; and (3) how those parts and their activities are organized so as to produce Φ. As other contributions to this volume demonstrate, contemporary neuroscience has made some progress in identifying the parts and activities of the brain involved in producing consciousness. What remains to be achieved is some consensus on how the organization of the brain gives rise to this phenomenon.[8] In this section we will provide a brief overview of the account of consciousness that is emerging from neuroscience, and consider what it implies about the ontology of consciousness.

Although there are some dissenters, the neuroscience community is converging on the view that consciousness is produced by a neural system that incorporates the cerebral cortex and thalamus, together with their dense bidirectional connections. Rather than a single, anatomically discrete consciousness-making center in the brain, consciousness seems to depend on activity in both cortical and subcortical structures. The evidence for this hypothesis comes from a variety of sources, but especially from an examination of the neural activity associated with sleep, anesthesia, coma and epileptic seizures (Revonsuo, 2010, pp. 159–164). There is a significant amount of activity in this system even during non-rapid eye movement eye sleep, anesthesia, and

8. Admittedly, it remains a tough problem to discern which of the brain's activities constitute consciousness, as opposed to being merely correlated with it (Miller, this volume; Revonsuo, this volume). To fully address this problem we need a detailed mathematical account of the structure of consciousness, and a far more sophisticated understanding of the dynamics of neural activity than we currently possess. These, we believe, will ultimately provide the basis for an exhaustive neurophenomenology, which will solve the constitution problem and also ease the minds of those troubled by Chalmers' (1996) "hard problem".

generalized epileptic seizures, when consciousness is largely absent. So it is reasonable to conclude that "some additional dynamic feature of neural activity must be present to generate conscious content" (Tononi & Koch, 2008, p. 248).

Lamme (2000, 2004; see Klink, Self, Lamme, & Roelfsema, this volume) argues that conscious experience is the result of *recurrent* neural activity. The processing of visual information in the cortex is marked by two distinct phases: a rapid feedforward sweep that reaches V1 about 40ms after stimulus onset, and recurrent processes that involve feedback between early and late visual areas. The feedforward sweep influences activity in all extra-striate visual areas by around 80ms, but recurrent interaction doesn't arise until 100ms after stimulus onset. Lamme contends that the feedforward sweep, despite its ability to influence activity throughout the brain, is not sufficient for visual experience. Instead, visual consciousness is the result of recurrent interactions between early and late visual areas.[9] Recurrent activity depends on both horizontal intra-area connections, and feedback-feedforward circuits between areas, so there is a tight coupling in Lamme's account between the anatomical and physiological forms of organization that are required for (visual) consciousness.

Not every neuroscientific account of consciousness addresses the mechanism of consciousness head-on. Tononi (2004, 2008), for example, argues that what renders a cognitive system conscious is its capacity to integrate information. This capacity is not an all-or-nothing affair, but depends on the size and complexity of the system, its current level of activity, and the nature of the input it receives. Stated in such general terms this might not sound like a hypothesis with any implications for the mechanism of consciousness. However, as the brain's capacity to integrate information depends on the ability of neural networks to influence each other, either directly or indirectly, Tononi's hypothesis suggests that this mechanism involves high levels of reciprocal connectivity and physiological processes that enhance inter-areal communication, e.g., synchronized neural firing (Singer, 1999).

Llinás et al. (Llinás, Ribary, Contreras, & Pedroarena, 1998), Newman (1995) and Revonsuo (2006) argue for the importance of thalamocortical interaction in the production of conscious states. These interactions are supported by both *specific* and *non-specific* thalamocortical loops. Specific thalamic nuclei, such as the lateral geniculate nucleus (LGN), are reciprocally connected to specialized cortical areas (V1 in the case of the LGN), whereas non-specific nuclei, such as the pulvinar, connect to multiple cortical areas, relaying information between first-order and higher-order cortical areas. There is increasing evidence that these two systems are involved in synchronizing cortical activity, binding anatomically distinct regions into transient neuronal assemblies (Singer, 2007; Varela, Lachaux, Rodriguez, & Martinerie, 2001). Llinás et al. (1998) suggest that both systems are necessary for consciousness, the former binding

9. There are many pieces of evidence for this claim. For example, feedforward activation of neurons can be recorded in anesthetized animals with receptive field properties that hardly differ from those in the awake state, whereas recurrent processing is largely suppressed or absent.

specific sensory and motor processes into locally synchronous patches of gamma-band (20–50 Hz) activity, the latter providing a global, unifying context by coincidence detection right across the cortex.[10] On this picture, conscious experience is a globally unified pattern of recurrent bioelectrical activity operating with a characteristic temporal dynamics.

A number of issues remain open here. It is unclear whether thalamocortical synchrony is sufficient to generate conscious experiences, or if other features of neural activity, such as a *recurrence* (Lamme, 2004) or *stability* (O'Brien & Opie, 1999; Tononi & Koch, 2008, pp. 248–250) might also be essential. There is also disagreement about the amount of cortical tissue required to generate a conscious state. Zeki and Bartels (1999) argue that consciousness-making in the brain is highly localized and modular, such that, for example, each distinct processing module in the visual cortex generates an element of visual experience – a "microconsciousness". Whether or not one believes that conscious states can occur at this scale, the extent to which global consciousness is dissociable into independent phenomenal parts remains an open question (O'Brien & Opie, 1998, 2000).

Despite these points of difference, recent neuroscientific accounts of consciousness have two important features in common: (1) they are all mechanistic theories; and (2) they all equate conscious experiences with specific kinds of activity in the neural networks of the thalamocortical system. Our focus here is the metaphysical implications of this consensus. Neuroscientists sometimes claim that their work only reveals the *neural correlates* of consciousness. Such caution is commendable on empirical grounds. It is a significant methodological challenge to demonstrate that some emergent phenomenon is constituted by the activity of systems at a lower level of organization.[11] But whether they realize it or not, theorists who explore the mechanisms of consciousness are going beyond mere correlation (Revonsuo, 2006, pp. 293–303). Each of the hypotheses surveyed above is an *identity claim* – an assertion to the effect that conscious experience (or a particular class of conscious experiences) is *none other than* a particular kind of activity in the thalamocortical system of the brain. At one blow these proposals dispense with dualism and offer us a variety of mechanisms whereby the brain might generate conscious experiences.[12]

10. When a neural network is locked into gamma-band oscillations, this doesn't imply that its constituent neurons are all firing at the same rate, but rather that the network as a whole is dominated by activity in this frequency range. Gamma-band activity is an emergent statistical feature of a neural population. Fries, Nikolić and Singer (2007) have suggested that sensory and motor information might be encoded in the temporal offset of spikes relative to the gamma-band "metronome".

11. See Craver (2007) for a detailed discussion of this point.

12. Dualism is the view that phenomenal consciousness depends on laws, principles or properties that are not within the scope of the sciences as we currently conceive them.

An identity claim equates one thing with another. The classic philosophical example is the identification of lightning with electrical discharges. Prior to the experiments of Thomas-François D'Alibard and Benjamin Franklin in 1752, the nature of lightning was still a matter of conjecture. Franklin found that lightning could be communicated along the string of a kite or a metal rod during a storm, giving rise to discharges which behave in every respect like discharges of terrestrial origin (Priestley, 1775, pp. 216–218). He thereby provided the first evidence that these two seemingly distinct phenomena have the same essential nature: lightning just is an (atmospheric) electrical discharge. This is identity "in the strict sense" (Smart, 1959, p. 145), in which a single kind of thing is known under two descriptions. Likewise, when a neuroscientist proposes a mechanism for consciousness, this is an attempt to identify conscious experiences with particular processes in the brain, processes that are subject to both first-person and third-person descriptions, but which nonetheless constitute a unitary phenomenon.

Existing attempts to identify conscious experiences with a particular class of neural mechanisms already tell us a great deal about the metaphysics of consciousness. To begin with, they rule out microphysicalism, which identifies consciousness with the activity of the subatomic constituents of the brain. We have already rejected this form of reductionism on the grounds that it recognizes neither the multiple realizability of special science kinds, nor the multiple composability of their parts. A less extreme view might be that consciousness will ultimately be understood in terms of the *neural* composition of the brain. But again, this approach fails to grapple with multiple composability, and specifically, the discovery that neural systems can give rise to both conscious and unconscious processes.

So we return to the view that consciousness is a phenomenon which depends in some way on the organization of the brain. Most philosophers take this to settle the matter in favour of functionalism. On this view, what neuroscientists are pointing to when they identify particular kinds of neural activity with conscious experience are objects or events that play a particular role in the causal organization of the brain. And it is that causal role, that specific set of causal connections with other processes and events, which is the essence of consciousness. In other words, what makes a pattern of neural activity a conscious experience has nothing (directly) to do with its intrinsic material properties, and everything to do with its causal role.

Although it appears unobjectionable when stated in such abstract terms, this position has the unpalatable consequence of rendering conscious experience causally inert. Functionalism is committed to the view that consciousness is a mere by-product of brain activity with no impact on the subsequent behavior of the system, rather like the static produced by an AM radio. This result is perhaps unexpected, given functionalism's focus on the causal organization of the brain, but it follows directly from the fact that functionalism identifies consciousness with a causal *role*. A causal role has *no effect on anything*, rather, it is the material state or process that fills that role which is causally efficacious. Functionalism explicitly separates role from realizer, and identifies consciousness with the former, not the latter. In slightly different language, functionalism identifies consciousness with the *doing*, not the *doer*.

But of course, we are not stuck with functionalism. Our discussion in the previous section suggests an alternative metaphysics, one which, like functionalism, focuses on the organization of the brain, but which better reflects the mechanistic style of explanation employed by neuroscientists. To describe a consciousness-making mechanism is to identify conscious experience with the activity of a particular kind of material system, and show how it emerges from the organization of that system. It would be tempting to suggest, as does Revonsuo (2006), that consciousness is in fact a level of organization in the brain. But this isn't quite right, at least not if one adopts the definition of mechanistic level we gave in Section 3. What belong at each level in a mechanistic hierarchy are the entities whose organization produces the phenomena at the next level, the level at which those parts and their activities constitute an organized whole of some kind. The heart, vessels, blood, and valves of the circulatory system are a level of organization in the mechanism that delivers oxygen and nutrients to the body. But picked out in this way, these entities are merely a collection of parts, not a working mechanism. To produce their characteristic activity, those parts must be organized in the right way. Likewise, a collection of neural systems do not amount to a conscious experience, rather, consciousness is constituted jointly by those systems, their activities, and the manner in which they are organized (Miller, 2007). In other words, consciousness is a certain kind of *material structure*, and the metaphysics appropriate to a mechanistic account of consciousness is *structuralism*.[13]

What does consciousness look like from this perspective? According to structuralism, it is in virtue of possessing certain structural properties that a pattern of neural activity constitutes a conscious experience. Structural properties, like functional properties, are *abstract* in the sense that they may be realized by a variety of substrates. But unlike functional properties, structural properties are characterized by specific types of material organization. An airfoil must have a particular shape; a cell wall, the right topology; a detonator, the right bonding structure, and so on. Two kinds of organization are germane to our understanding of consciousness: (1) those that distinguish conscious from unconscious brain activity; and (2) those that distinguish one species of conscious experience from another, e.g., a visual experience from an auditory experience. Most of the proposals described above address the former issue. To finish, we will briefly explore an idea about the kind of material organization that might distinguish one species of experience from another.

It turns out there is a branch of cognitive science that has already been investigating the structure of patterns of neural activity, albeit in a very simplified form: the neurocomputational approach to cognition known as *connectionism*. Connectionist networks are idealized models of real neural networks, which, although unrealistic in certain respects, capture many of the salient features of mammalian cognition (see, e.g., Bechtel & Abrahamsen, 2002). A connectionist network consists of a set of interconnected processing units, each of which has an activity level that is communicated

13. Notice that the structure of consciousness is dynamic, like the organization of the homeostatic processes in a cell, rather than static, like the macroscopic structure of an airfoil.

to other units via modifiable, weighted connections. Each unit sums the weighted activity it receives, and generates a response that is some threshold function of its current activity and that input. Via this process, a network transforms patterns of activity across its input layer into patterns of output activity. Altering the network's connection weights alters the nature of the mapping between input and output layers. Consequently, a network can be taught to generate a range of target patterns in response to a range of inputs.

For our purposes, one of the most interesting results of connectionist research is that networks with an identical architecture, but with distinct initial (random) assignments of connection weights, can learn to perform the same input-output mapping. Each network does this by way of a unique final configuration of weights. Some theorists see this as a vindication of functionalism: the only thing that such "microphysically" distinct networks appear to have in common is the input-output mapping they perform, that is, a particular set of causal relations between inputs and target outputs.[14] But closer inspection reveals a deeper kind of similarity.

Consider Cottrell's face-recognition network (Churchland, 1995, pp. 38–55). This network has a three-layer feed-forward architecture: a 64×64 input array, fully connected to a hidden layer of 80 units, which in turn is fully connected to an output layer comprising 8 units. Each unit in the input layer can take on one of 256 distinct activation values, so it is ideal for encoding discretized grey-scale images of faces and other objects. After squashing through the hidden layer these input patterns trigger three units in the output layer that code for face/non-face status and gender of subject, and five which encode arbitrary 5-bit names for each of 11 different individuals. Different realizations of this network architecture, trained on the same data set, have distinct weight values. However, cluster analysis reveals that they have something significant in common: their hidden layer activity is organized in the same way.

This similarity can be visualized in terms of an *activation space*, in which the activity of each hidden unit is represented using a distinct coordinate axis. A pattern of hidden-layer activation corresponds to a point in this space, and physically similar patterns are represented by nearby points (as measured using the standard Cartesian metric). Post-training analysis reveals that each face-recognition network partitions its hidden unit activation space in the same way: into face and non-face regions, male and female sub-regions, and still smaller regions corresponding to the cluster of patterns associated with each subject (see Figure 1). Each network captures the relations among faces that underlie our judgments of gender, identity, etc., in the distance relations among the points in its hidden unit activation space. Faces that are similar are coded by nearby points, dissimilar faces are coded by points that are further apart.

14. In this context, a "microphysical" difference is a difference in connection weights, *not* a difference at the atomic or subatomic scale. Two networks can share a network architecture, i.e., have the same number of units at each layer and an identical set of connections between layers, yet be microphysically distinct in this sense.

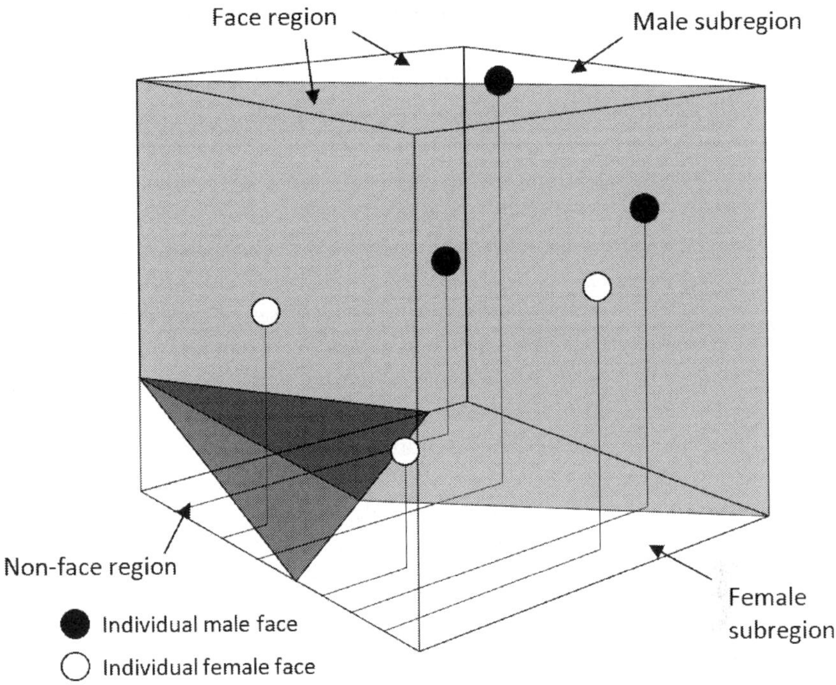

Figure 1. The hierarchy of learned partitions across the hidden unit activation space of Cottrell's face recognition network (after Churchland, 1995, p. 49).

So, although it is certainly true that microphysically distinct face-recognition networks have a common causal profile, this functional similarity is grounded in something else: a common partitioning of hidden unit activation space. A partitioning is an abstract yet intrinsic material feature of a network. As activation patterns are themselves physical objects, the distance relations in the activation space of a network codify *physical* similarities and dissimilarities between those patterns. And when such distance relations are preserved across networks, it marks the fact that despite differences in their connection weights, these networks embody a common *set* of similarity and dissimilarity relations. This is a shared, but abstract property. And it is an abstract property that is grounded in the intrinsic material organization of each individual network. Consequently, when networks partition their hidden unit activation spaces in the same way, what they have in common is a *structural* property, a property, moreover, that underpins and explains their functional similarity.

Despite the idealized nature of the connectionist analysis of neural activity, it may well have something to teach us about the ontology of consciousness. It provides a framework for understanding how patterns of neural activity can possess common structure, in the face of microphysical differences, and how these abstract properties underlie the capacity of distinct networks to enter into similar causal relations.

Furthermore, the identification of such structural properties allows for both multiple realizability and multiple composability. On the one hand, it is quite possible that microphysically different networks (across different brains, for example, or even in radically different kinds of physical materials) are capable of realizing a set of vehicles that are subject to the same set of distance relations. On the other, we see how it is possible for the same material mechanism to generate a vast range of structurally distinct vehicles.

This last fact about neural activation patterns is critical when thinking about one of the major puzzles about consciousness. The neural correlates of very different conscious experiences, at least at one level of description, can look very much the same – at the base level each of these experiences is correlated with a pattern of neural activity. The puzzle is how this one substrate is capable of generating such a diverse range of conscious experiences. But the framework we have just been exploring offers us a way of resolving this puzzle. This one neural substrate is capable of generating very different kinds of conscious experiences because it is capable of generating a vast range of structurally distinct activation patterns.[15]

6. Concluding remarks

Applying a structuralist ontology to consciousness has a number of appealing features. It enables us to unify the science of consciousness with the other special sciences. On this story, conscious experiences are emergent structures just like molecules, airfoils, and cells. It also allows us to escape the pitfalls of both microphysicalism and functionalism. The existence of emergent structures is consistent with both multiple realizability and multiple composability. And because such structures are intrinsic to their realizing vehicles, they make sense of the causal relations into which these vehicles enter. This middle-ground alternative to both microphysicalism and functionalism would seem to get things just right.

References

Bechtel, W. (2006). *Discovering cell mechanisms: The creation of modern cell biology*. New York, NY: Cambridge University Press.

Bechtel, W. (2008). *Mental mechanisms: Philosophical perspectives on cognitive neuroscience*. New York, NY: Lawrence Erlbaum Associates.

Bechtel, W., & Abrahamsen, A. (2002). *Connectionism and the mind: Parallel processing, dynamics, and evolution in networks* (2nd ed.). Oxford, UK: Basil Blackwell.

15. See O'Brien and Opie (1999) for further discussion of this point.

Brown, M. E., & Swallowe, G. E. (1981). The thermal decomposition of the silver (I) and mercury (II) salts of 5-nitrotetrazole and of mercury (II) fulminate. *Thermochimica Acta*, 49(2–3), 333–349. DOI: 10.1016/0040-6031(81)80185-2
Bunge, M. (1997). Mechanism and explanation. *Philosophy of the Social Sciences*, 27(4), 410–416. DOI: 10.1177/004839319702700402
Chalmers, D. J. (1996). *The conscious mind: In search of a fundamental theory*. New York, NY: Oxford University Press.
Churchland, P. M. (1995). *The engine of reason, the seat of the soul*. Cambridge, MA: MIT Press.
Craver, C. F. (2001). Role functions, mechanisms, and hierarchy. *Philosophy of Science*, 68(1), 53–74. DOI: 10.1086/392866
Craver, C. F. (2007). *Explaining the brain: Mechanisms and the mosaic unity of neuroscience*. New York, NY: Oxford University Press. DOI: 10.1093/acprof:oso/9780199299317.001.0001
Cummins, R. (1975). Functional analysis. *Journal of Philosophy*, 72(20), 741–765. DOI: 10.2307/2024640
Faust, W. L. (1989). Explosive molecular ionic crystals. *Science*, 245(4913), 37–42. DOI: 10.1126/science.245.4913.37
Fodor, J. A. (1974). Special sciences (or: The disunity of science as a working hypothesis). *Synthese*, 28(2), 97–115. DOI: 10.1007/BF00485230
Fodor, J. A. (1989). Making mind matter more. *Philosophical Topics*, 17(1), 59–79. DOI: 10.5840/philtopics198917112
Fries, P., Nikolić, D., & Singer, W. (2007). The gamma cycle. *Trends in Neurosciences*, 30(7), 309–116. DOI: 10.1016/j.tins.2007.05.005
Glennan, S. (2002). Rethinking mechanistic explanation. *Philosophy of Science*, 69(S3), S342–S353. DOI: 10.1086/341857
Hempel, C. G. (1966). *Philosophy of natural science*. Englewood Cliffs, NJ: Prentice-Hall, Inc.
Köhler, W. (1920). *Die physischen Gestalten in Ruhe und im stationären Zustand*. Braunschweig: Vieweg und Sohn. DOI: 10.1007/978-3-663-02204-6
Kurzer, F. (2000). Fulminic acid in the history of organic chemistry. *Journal of Chemical Education*, 77(7), 851–857. DOI: 10.1021/ed077p851
Lamme, V. A. F. (2000). Neural mechanisms of visual awareness: A linking proposition. *Brain and Mind*, 1(3), 385–406. DOI: 10.1023/A:1011569019782
Lamme, V. A. F. (2004). Separate neural definitions of visual consciousness and visual attention; A case for phenomenal awareness. *Neural Networks*, 17(5–6), 861–872. DOI: 10.1016/j.neunet. 2004.02.005
Llinás, R., Ribary, U., Contreras, D., & Pedroarena, C. (1998). The neuronal basis for consciousness. *Philosophical Transactions of the Royal Society of London B: Biological Sciences*, 353(1377), 1841–1849. DOI: 10.1098/rstb.1998.0336
Machamer, P., Darden, L., & Craver, C. F. (2000). Thinking about mechanisms. *Philosophy of Science*, 67(1), 1–25. DOI: 10.1086/392759
McGinn, C. (1991). *The problem of consciousness: Essays toward a resolution*. Oxford, UK: Basil Blackwell.
Miller, S. M. (2007). On the correlation/constitution distinction problem (and other hard problems) in the scientific study of consciousness. *Acta Neuropsychiatrica*, 19(3), 159–76. DOI: 10.1111/j.1601-5215.2007.00207.x
Nagel, T. (1974). What is it like to be a bat? *Philosophical Review*, 83(4), 435–450. DOI: 10.2307/2183914

Newman, J. (1995). Thalamic contributions to attention and consciousness. *Consciousness and Cognition*, 4(2), 172–193. DOI: 10.1006/ccog.1995.1024

O'Brien, G., & Opie, J. (1998). The disunity of consciousness. *Australasian Journal of Philosophy*, 76(3), 378–395. DOI: 10.1080/00048409812348511

O'Brien, G., & Opie, J. (1999). A connectionist theory of phenomenal experience. *Behavioral and Brain Sciences*, 22(1), 127–148. DOI: 10.1017/S0140525X9900179X

O'Brien, G., & Opie, J. (2000). Disunity defended: A reply to Bayne. *Australasian Journal of Philosophy*, 78(2), 255–263. DOI: 10.1080/00048400012349541

Oppenheim, P., & Putnam, H. (1958). Unity of science as a working hypothesis. In H. Feigl, M. Scriven, & G. Maxwell (Eds.), *Minnesota studies in the philosophy of science*, Vol. 2, Concepts, theories, and the mind-body problem (pp. 3–36). Minneapolis, MN: University of Minneapolis Press.

Priestley, J. (1775). *The history and present status of electricity, with original experiments*, Vol. 1 (3rd ed.). London, UK: C. Bathurst & T. Lowndes, et al.

Revonsuo, A. (2006). *Inner presence: Consciousness as a biological phenomenon*. Cambridge, MA: MIT Press.

Revonsuo, A. (2010). *Consciousness: The science of subjectivity*. Hove, UK: Psychology Press.

Robertson, T. (2008). Essential vs. accidental properties. In E. N. Zalta (Ed.), *The Stanford encyclopedia of philosophy (Fall 2008 edition)*. Retrieved from http://plato.stanford.edu/archives/fall2008/entries/essential-accidental

Salmon, W. C. (1978). Why ask, "Why?"? An inquiry concerning scientific explanation. *Proceedings and Addresses of the American Philosophical Association*, 51(6), 683–705. DOI: 10.2307/3129654

Singer, W. (1999). Neuronal synchrony: A versatile code for the definition of relations? *Neuron*, 24(1), 49–65. DOI: 10.1016/S0896-6273(00)80821-1

Singer, W. (2007). Binding by synchrony. *Scholarpedia*, 2(12), 1657. DOI: 10.4249/scholarpedia.1657

Smart, J. J. C. (1959). Sensations and brain processes. *Philosophical Review*, 68(2), 141–156. DOI: 10.2307/2182164

Tononi, G. (2004). An information integration theory of consciousness. *BMC Neuroscience*, 5, 42. DOI: 10.1186/1471-2202-5-42

Tononi, G. (2008). Consciousness as integrated information: A provisional manifesto. *Biological Bulletin*, 215(3), 216–242. DOI: 10.2307/25470707

Tononi, G., & Koch, C. (2008). The neural correlates of consciousness: An update. *Annals of the New York Academy of Sciences*, 1124, 239–261. DOI: 10.1196/annals.1440.004

Varela, F., Lachaux, J.-P., Rodriguez, E., & Martinerie, J. (2001). The brainweb: Phase synchronization and large-scale integration. *Nature Reviews Neuroscience*, 2(4), 229–239. DOI: 10.1038/35067550

Waldmann, R., Chamigny, G., Bassilana, F., Heurteaux, C., & Lazdunski, M. (1997). A proton-gated cation channel involved in acid-sensing. *Nature*, 386(6621), 173–177. DOI: 10.1038/386173a0

Woodward, J. (1989). The causal mechanical model of explanation. In P. Kitcher & W. C. Salmon (Eds.), *Minnesota studies in the philosophy of science*, Vol. 13, Scientific explanation (pp. 357–383). Minneapolis, MN: University of Minneapolis Press.

Zeki, S., & Bartels, A. (1999). Toward a theory of visual consciousness. *Consciousness and Cognition*, 8(2), 225–259. DOI: 10.1006/ccog.1999.0390

Index

D

E